A New
New Testament

BOOKS BY HAL TAUSSIG

Sophia: The Future of Spirituality
(with Susan Cady and Marian Ronan)

Many Tables: The Eucharist in the New Testament and Liturgy Today
(with Dennis Smith)

Re-Imagining Christian Origins
(editor, with Elizabeth A. Castelli)

Wisdom's Feast: Sophia in Study and Celebration
(with Susan Cole and Marian Ronan)

Jesus Before God: The Prayer Life of Historical Jesus

Re-Imagining Life Together in America: A New Gospel of Community
(with Catherine Nerney)

A New Spiritual Home: Progressive Christianity at the Grass Roots

In the Beginning Was the Meal:
Social Experimentation and Early Christian Identity

The Thunder: Perfect Mind
(with Jared Calaway, Maia Kotrosits, and Celene Lillie)

Meals in the Early Christian World
(editor, with Dennis Smith)

Meals and Religious Identity in Early Christianity/Mahl und
religioes Identitaet im fruehen Christentum
(editor, with Matthias Klinghardt)

Marking Loss: Re-Reading a Gospel in the Midst of Pain and Trauma
(with Maia Kotrosits)

A New New Testament

A New New Testament

A BIBLE FOR THE TWENTY-FIRST CENTURY

Combining Traditional and Newly Discovered Texts

EDITED WITH COMMENTARY BY HAL TAUSSIG

With a Foreword by John Dominic Crossan

HarperOne

An Imprint of HarperCollins*Publishers*

BOSTON   NEW YORK

www.harpercollins.com

Library of Congress Cataloging-in-Publication Data
A new New Testament : a reinvented Bible for the twenty-first century combining
traditional and newly discovered texts / edited with commentary by Hal Taussig ;
with a foreword by John Dominic Crossan.
pages cm
Includes index.
ISBN 978-0-547-79210-1 (hardcover)
ISBN 978-0-544-57010-8 (pbk.)
1. Bible. N.T. — Criticism, interpretation, etc. 2. Christian literature, Early —
History and criticism. I. Taussig, Hal, editor of compilation.
BS2361.3.N467 2013
225.5'208 — dc23   2012046359

Book design by Melissa Lotfy

Printed in the United States of America
24 25 26 27 28 LBC 13 12 11 10 9

Photograph of Papyrus P52 courtesy of John Rylands University Library of Manchester.
Translation of the traditional New Testament (except for the Letter to the Colossians) from the
    Open English Bible, with permitted revisions by Hal Taussig. Courtesy of Russell Allen, holder
    of copyright, and under Creative Commons Zero license, http://creativecommons.org
    /publicdomain/zero/1.0.
Translation of the Acts of Paul and Thecla, the Gospel of Mary, the Gospel of Truth, the Letter
    of Paul to the Colossians, the Letter of Peter to Philip, the Prayer of the Apostle Paul, and the
    Prayer of Thanksgiving by Celene Lillie. Permission granted to HarperCollins Publishers.
    All rights reserved.
Translation of the Odes of Solomon by Elizabeth Ridout Miraglia. Permission granted to HarperCollins
    Publishers. All rights reserved.
Translation of the Gospel of Thomas by Justin Lasser. Permission granted to HarperCollins
    Publishers. All rights reserved.
Translation of The Thunder: Perfect Mind by Hal Taussig, Jared Calaway, Maia Kotrosits, Celene
    Lillie, and Justin Lasser. Permission granted to HarperCollins Publishers by Hal Taussig.
Translation of the Secret Revelation of John by Karen King. Reprinted by permission of the pub-
    lisher from *The Secret Revelation of John* by Karen L. King, pp. 28–81, Cambridge, Mass.: Har-
    vard University Press, Copyright © 2006 by the President and Fellows of Harvard College.
Introduction to the Secret Revelation of John by Karen L. King. Permission granted to HarperCollins
    Publishers. All rights reserved.

Contents

The Books of
A New New Testament

AN ANCIENT PRAYER FROM THE EARLY CHRIST MOVEMENTS

GOSPELS FEATURING JESUS'S TEACHINGS

GOSPELS, POEMS, AND SONGS BETWEEN HEAVEN AND EARTH

THE WRITINGS OF PAUL AND AN INTRODUCTORY PRAYER

LITERATURE IN THE TRADITION OF PAUL, WITH A SET OF INTRODUCTORY PRAYERS

DIVERSE LETTERS, WITH A SET OF INTRODUCTORY PRAYERS

LITERATURE IN THE TRADITION OF JOHN, WITH AN INTRODUCTORY SET OF PRAYERS

A Companion to
A New New Testament

BASIC HISTORICAL BACKGROUND
FOR THIS NEW BOOK OF BOOKS

Foreword

THE TRADITIONAL NEW TESTAMENT was already established by the end of the fourth century. The pressing question, then, is why suggest *A New New Testament* — even with *A*, not *The* — after a millennium and a half have passed?

It is not — emphatically not — that all or most of what is *inside* that traditional New Testament is bad or deficient while most or all of what is *outside* it is perfect and preferable. But why, then, entitle this book *A New New Testament* rather than, say, *Other Early Christian Texts*?

For myself, I see two reasons why this particular book and this precise title are necessary and needed. I put them to you as challenges, maybe even as principles, and in aphoristic format to facilitate memory and thought.

My first reason is a rather simple redundancy with regard to the traditional New Testament: *to know what is outside it, you must know what is outside it*. In other words, it is a matter of adult education because education affirms options while indoctrination denies them. Since that is probably obvious, I offer only one example.

You open your standard New Testament and find four versions — four "according to"s — of the gospel. Stay *inside* that volume and you could easily conclude that all existing versions had been gathered and presented. Go *outside* to *A New New Testament* and you realize immediately that many other versions — and indeed types, modes, and styles — of gospel were available — and avoided.

What you do with that knowledge, and how you judge between texts in or out, is a separate issue. But you should know that *all* gospel versions were not taken, that a selection was made, that some were accepted and others rejected. And that knowledge is, to repeat, an education, and education is about knowing options.

My second reason for *A New New Testament* is that, with regard to the traditional New Testament, *to know what is inside it, you must know what is outside it*. I offer you two examples of that principle, two cases to illustrate that, even if you are exclusively focused on the traditional New Testament, you cannot do so. You must know what was rejected to understand what was accepted. And why, and when, and where. Both of my examples involve *images* to remind us that we do not live in a world made only of words — be they old words or new words.

A first example. High on the northern slopes of the Bülbül Daği, off the mid-Aegean coast of Turkey, is a small flat clearing on the hillside with a stone frontal for a small doorway. This opens into a cave carved in antiquity to an eight-by-eight-by-fifty-foot passageway shrine called the Grotto of St. Paul by excavators from the Austrian Archaeological Institute in the 1990s. Beneath later plaster they found frescoes from around the year 500 CE.

On entrance, to your immediate left, is a scene almost completely obliterated but still residually recognizable. A standing man holds aloft a large knife above a much smaller kneeling figure whose tiny feet are about all that has been left by time the destroyer. It is, of course, the story of Abraham and Isaac from Genesis 22.

You turn next to the fresco on the wall at entrance right. It is much better preserved, with the upper half almost totally untouched by decay. But it is not a scene you recognize from either the Hebrew Bible or the Christian New Testament. Of its three figures, the central one is definitely "Paulos" — bald-headed, double-goateed, named, but not haloed. He is seated and reading from an open book on his lap (*A New New Testament,* maybe?). His right hand is raised in the teaching-and-blessing gesture of Byzantine iconography — fingers separated into two and three, for the two natures in Christ and the three persons in the Trinity.

To viewer right of Paul is a standing woman named "Theoklia," coiffed as a matron by the veil around her hair. She is slightly taller than Paul, and her right hand is raised in a gesture identical to his. But her dignity, importance, and teaching authority are all negated by having her eyes blinded and her hand scraped and burned off the wall (not iconoclasm, by the way, as only *her* eyes were obliterated).

To viewer left of Paul is a second female figure iconographically designated as a nubile virgin — her hair is unveiled and she listens to Paul's message, not with others out in the open but from a window in a red-brick house that encases her completely. Her name, "Thekla," is still — but barely — discernible to the left and right of her head.

Those three figures present a scene that summarizes a story which you, as viewer, are supposed to recognize. But you do not do so because, whatever about Paul, neither Theoklia nor Thekla — and Thekla, by the way, is the focal point of the fresco — is anywhere in your traditional New Testament. The textual version of that dramatic scene is in the Acts of Thecla, which is still extant as the opening chapters of the second-century Acts of Paul — hence it is often called the Acts of Paul and Thecla.

In those Acts — as in all the other second- and third-century Acts of the Apostles from outside the traditional New Testament — the challenge is celibate asceticism and most especially for women in a patriarchal world. Thecla, for example, is about thirteen years of age and would have been speedily married soon after her first menses. She would have passed, with or without her ultimate consent, from the power of her father to that of a husband at least twice her age.

Image and text visualize the dramatic moment when Thecla, having heard Paul preach the challenge of ascetic celibacy, decides to reject Thamyris, the man chosen to be her husband by parental authority. But such a decision — *by a teenage girl* — designates not just domestic disturbance but social subversion. Thecla ends up condemned to death in the arena but is saved by divine protection with not only all the women — pagan and Christian alike — on her side but even with a lioness fighting on her behalf against bear and lion.

You will, of course, find that Thecla story in the unit entitled "The Acts of Paul and Thecla" in this book, *A New New Testament*. But why is that inclusion important? Because if you do not know Thecla, you will not know Paul. You will not understand the thirteen letters *attributed* to him and making up half the texts *inside* the traditional New Testament.

Focus, for example, on the one text among those *attributed* letters that people seem to know even if they know nothing else about Paul. It is this sweeping indictment of what was clearly already in practice: "A woman must learn, listening in silence with all deference. I do not consent to them becoming teachers, or exercising authority over men; they ought not speak" (1 Timothy 2:11–12).

There is a massive scholarly consensus — based not externally on political correctness but internally on linguistic differences — that the three letters, 1–2 Timothy and Titus, were written well over a half century after Paul's death. They were post-, pseudo-, and even anti-Pauline compositions created in his name but reacting flatly to his radical views on equality for all those in the Christian community — whether they entered as Jews or gentiles, females or males, slaves or freeborns (Galatians 3:26–29). But what caused that reaction to female teaching authority?

The obvious answer is patriarchal dominance — men did not want women to be equal to them, let alone have any authority over them. That certainly explains those negative commands in 1 Timothy 2 that leaders cannot be female. It also explains those positive commands that Christian leaders must be male. But why does 1 Timothy also insist that those male leaders — be they first-level or second-level ones — be "married" and have "children" (3:2, 4, 12)?

The deeper problem for 1 Timothy is not just female pedagogy but ascetic celibacy. That is why it warns, in thoroughly nasty language, about those who "forbid marriage and enjoin abstinence from certain kinds of foods" (4:3). What frightens 1 Timothy's anonymous author(s) so profoundly is the challenge to Roman normalcy represented by Christian celibacy — especially by female celibates thereby out of male control and, most especially, by female teenagers thereby out of parental control. Thecla is the specter that haunts 1 Timothy.

In other words, to understand 1 Timothy you will have to look both inside and outside the New Testament: inside it, by looking at Paul's challenge of celibacy in 1 Corinthians 7; and outside it, by looking at Thecla's challenge of celibacy in *A New New Testament*. That is just a single case, but it touches on Paul, and, in action by him or reaction to him, he makes up half the traditional New Testament.

All Christians should know how important that challenge of ascetic celibacy was in our earliest traditions — and especially how it proclaimed the right for women to choose their lives despite patriarchal ascendancy. (Today and here we might not consider celibacy as a badge of freedom, but "today" and "here" are not normative for always and everywhere.)

I test that general principle concerning the traditional New Testament — that *you cannot know inside without knowing outside* — with one further example, from *A New New Testament*. It concerns the resurrection of Christ and therefore touches on the very heart of Christianity itself. I begin, once again, with an image — not a single instance in a hidden cave but one found on icons, frescoes, and mosaics from the Tiber to the Tigris and the Nevsky to the Nile. From ancient psalters to modern churches, among scenes of the life of Jesus, icons of the Twelve Great Feasts, and banners of Easter celebration, this image is how Eastern Christianity imagines "The Resurrection" of Christ. But you will not understand, will not even recognize, that image from anywhere in our traditional New Testament.

On the one hand, *Western* Christianity imagines the resurrection by showing Christ arising in muscular majesty — think Titian or Rubens — above sleeping or cowering tomb guards. He is magnificently alone and *individual* — as if to forget that he is not the first or last Jewish martyr to die on a Roman cross. You might be able to get that scenario by reading, say, Matthew.

On the other hand, Eastern Christianity depicts not an individual but a *communal* resurrection of Christ. It shows Christ, wounded, haloed, robed, and carrying a scroll in earlier examples but a cross in later ones. He is surrounded by a mandorla of heavenly light, stands on the bifold gates of Hades shaped into cross format, with broken locks and shattered bolts all around. He reaches out, grasps the hand of Adam — or Adam and Eve — and drags them forcibly to himself inside that aureole of radiant divinity.

You will never understand or even recognize that Eastern Christian iconography through studying the traditional New Testament. But you could do both from reading *A New New Testament* if you turn to Ode 42 in the section entitled "The Fourth Book of the Odes of Solomon." Read that Syrian Christian hymn from possibly as early as 100 CE. Read it slowly and carefully, thoughtfully and prayerfully, until you can see Christ's resurrection as communal rather than individual and as God's great peace-and-reconciliation covenant with our violence-scarred humanity. I would almost rest my case for having *A New New Testament* on the presence of that single early Christian Ode 42 within its covers.

I conclude by thinking — and asking you to think as well — about gain and loss. I gave you only two examples where I think our traditional New Testament has lost something precious. It would have been better, for example, to have both Timothy *and* Thecla in there as confrontational challenge rather than Timothy alone. Better for the New Testament, better for Christian history, better for women, and, yes, better also for men. That, surely, was loss.

Again, none of the Odes of Solomon are in the New Testament, and without their poignant poetry our Western vision of the resurrection of Christ has become severed from that of Eastern Christianity. That, too, is loss. As you read each single text in *A New New Testament,* ask yourself that same question: What has our traditional New Testament lost when it lost this text? At the end we may mourn, with apologies to Thomas Wolfe, like this: "O lost, and by the wind grieved, ghost, come back again." There may yet be other texts lost to us still, but here, in *A New New Testament,* at least we have the opportunity to consider that loss and, possibly, to move beyond it.

JOHN DOMINIC CROSSAN

Preface

WEEKNIGHT BIBLE STUDIES usually see groups numbering from five to twenty people. But on a Tuesday night in May 2012, some four hundred people sat together in the sanctuary of a Baptist church in a New York neighborhood eagerly awaiting the night's discussion. Many of those attendees were under the age of thirty-five; they were from various walks of life. They were all there to talk with me about scripture, but not a piece of familiar scripture, rather a book that wasn't even part of the New Testament. They had come to learn about the Gospel of Thomas.

Like many, most of those people had only recently learned that there was such a thing as the Gospel of Thomas. I began with the story of how it had been discovered in the sands of Egypt in the 1940s and then took what I knew from twenty years of introducing this and other discoveries from early Christianity to be the best next step. We simply read together parts of this new gospel, a gospel that was written in the very same century Jesus lived and died.

I asked that someone read a few verses, and a young woman in her thirties volunteered. She began: "Jesus said . . ." What followed was a teaching no one in the room had ever heard, let alone in church. She read only three sentences, but by the time she was midway through the passage, people were gasping, clapping, and shouting "Amen!"

As the night continued, we read numerous passages from Thomas's collection of Jesus's teachings, each one inciting delight, puzzlement, inspiration, and even tears of joy. Attendees questioned why they had never before heard this book and asked for more information about its discovery, provenance, and historical context. I had expected at least some people to be confused or offended, but of those who spoke, no such opinions arose. At the end of the evening there were three standing ovations, a prayer of blessing given over me by the pastor, and a reception line that lasted almost as long as the study.

It was this experience and some two hundred like it that made me ever more certain that the world needed to be made more familiar with many of the scriptures that had been, for one reason or another, excluded from the New Testament. We needed a new New Testament, one that benefited from the discoveries of the past century and that reconsidered the choices made (or not made) by bishops and councils of the fourth through sixth centuries. The Gospel of Thomas is in this *New New Testament,* as are nine other documents never before included in the traditional collection of Christian scripture. They have been added to the twenty-seven books in the New Testament to form *A New New Testament.* Each of them has freshness and depth that would make that Baptist church shout "Amen!," make those who left church long ago perk up and listen, and signal hope to those eager for their spiritual longings to be addressed.

Over the past 160 years, more than seventy-five previously unknown first- and second-century documents from the Christ movements have come to light. These manuscripts have been scientifically verified to be almost certainly as old as the manuscripts of the traditional New Testament. The titles alone pique one's curiosity: the Gospel of Mary (Magdalene), the Gospel of Truth, the Prayer of the Apostle Paul, the Gospel of Thomas, the Acts of Paul and Thecla, the Prayer of Thanksgiving, the Odes of Solomon, the Letter of Peter to Philip, the Secret Revelation of John, and The Thunder: Perfect Mind.

There are very few texts more influential on humankind than the twenty-seven books that we know collectively as the New Testament; the brilliant teachings, well-worn truths, and revolutionary stories they contain are still powerful today. But when placed in *A New New Testament* alongside ten new books from the early Christ movements, this traditional literature springs to life in new ways, sparkles with fresh comparisons and contrasts, and is supplemented where it has been found lacking.

This *New New Testament* opens the door to reciting the sermon on the mount alongside the newly discovered Gospel of Mary, in which Mary Magdalene courageously comforts all the disciples and teaches them things Jesus had taught only her. In addition to the traditional Revelation to John, it offers a very different Secret Revelation of John in which Christ also rescues the world from a vicious empire, not by end-of-the-world battles and curses that set the earth on fire, but by straightforward teaching about God's light and compassion. This *New New Testament* enables Jesus's words in the Gospel of John, "I am the good shepherd," to be read in the same sitting as the recently discovered The Thunder: Perfect Mind's assertion that "I am the first and the last. I am she who is honored and she who is mocked. I am the whore and the holy woman. I am the wife and the virgin."

The dilemma of the traditional New Testament in the twenty-first century is not just about people yawning in church, bored by the familiarity of the readings. In some ways the traditional New Testament's binding has broken open and is not coming back together easily. Every discovery of a previously unknown ancient scriptural document stretches the authority and strength of the traditional New Testament. Its contents spill sloppily onto its readers, staining and straining their lives with offensive and outmoded information: instructions for slaves to obey their masters, for wives to submit to their husbands, and for readers to think of Jews as coming from Satan.

It is not time to throw out the traditional New Testament, or to excise those parts that offend. Rather, the moment has arrived to add to it and rebind it. Without attempting to remove the ancient social prejudices from the lived fabric of the traditional New Testament texts, *A New New Testament* offers twenty-first-century readers a chance to reconsider, rethink, and reimagine the spiritual and historical content of early Christianity by expanding the writings.

This fresh mix of early Christian* books comes just in time. A deep spiritual longing has emerged over the past twenty-five years that can take great advantage of *A New New Testament*. Innumerable people are searching for alternative spiritual paths while still holding on to traditions of the past. Generations that have come of age in the past two decades want to integrate the traditional and the new. They seek something grounded in the familiar that they can nonetheless reinvent to call their own.

A New New Testament allows new perspectives on Christian beginnings, with all its values and its flaws. Like the works in the traditional New Testament, the added books of this *New New Testament* do not exhibit one particular point of view, nor were they written by one individual. These new works neither revolt against the contents of the more established gospels and letters, nor do they blandly mimic them. They tell new stories, from new perspectives, but they pulse with familiar passion and power in their depiction of spiritual experiences and deep quests for meaning.

A New New Testament invites the reader onto a serious, inspiring, and well-informed journey into the very early writings of those in the legacy of Jesus. It offers the chance to form new opinions about the earliest traditions of the Christ movements without the demands of later Christian doctrine or church organizations working to overwhelm with dogma or formal interpretations. Selected by a

---

* One particularly thorny vocabulary issue in the study of all this literature is the word cluster of *Christian, Christianity,* and *early Christianity.* There are several significant dimensions of this issue. A primary factor is that the word *Christian* occurs only three times in the entire existing New Testament. Another is that Jesus — in all books of the existing New Testament and this *New New Testament* — always considers himself and is considered by the authors as a "Jew." That is, Jesus is never anything but a Jew, and never a Christian or the founder of Christianity. Many twenty-first-century New Testament scholars also believe that most, if not all, of the authors of the existing New Testament considered themselves "Jewish." It is unclear when "Christianity" itself came into being as a separate movement from "Judaism." This also means — in keeping with the overwhelming majority of New Testament texts' lack of the term — that few people thought of themselves as "Christian" during the New Testament era.

By and large, I have addressed this larger vocabulary problem through another simplification that seems less problematic than the vocabulary issues described here. I have for the most part referred to all persons attached to these documents within the first two centuries as "the Christ movement," "the Christ movements," or the "Christ people." This has helped identify these people and books as related to the Christ figure without presuming that this meant they were really "Christians" or belonged to "Christianity," or — perhaps most egregious — did not belong to the traditions of Israel (in which all "Christ" terms are rooted). There are downsides to this approach. It fails to take into account that many of these "Christ" movements did not actually use the term *Christ.* For instance, that some of these movements referred only to Jesus (not Christ) is lost in my approach.

council of spiritual leaders — pastors and scholars, bishops and historians — it also includes new prayers from the first and second centuries, beckoning twenty-first-century readers to encounter and inhabit the meditations and practices of their predecessors.

As both a professor of the New Testament and a pastor to an active, engaged congregation, I have come to realize that the spiritual thirsts of our day need more nourishment. More than seventy-five books from the early Christ movements were discovered in the nineteenth and twentieth centuries. I reject the romanticized notion that the new discoveries always provide the best answers just as much as I worry about churches' strangleholds on what they deem unarguable truth about a certain kind of Jesus. Here, then, is a supplement to the usual fare. Here, thanks to the wise decisions of a twenty-first-century council, is a winsome — although not definitive — combination of the traditional New Testament and some key new additions. Here is a new New Testament, rich with all the treasures and foibles of the traditional collection and enriched by many new and occasionally flawed stories, teachings, songs, prayers, letters, and meditations. Here, then, is one new way of experiencing scriptural heritage, a project conceived in response to genuine yearning, created by a group of wise and concerned leaders, and brought now to be made new again by you.

Preface to the Translations

OUR PRIMARY TRANSLATION FOCUS has been on the new books included in *A New New Testament*. Up to now these works have been primarily translated in ways that align them with the categories of "heresy" and "gnosticism." This established approach uses esoteric and complicated terms that distinguish the new books from "orthodox" Christianity and portray "orthodox" Christianity as plainspoken and clear, but the new documents as secretive and obscure. One of the features of this process involves transliteration — the use of Greco-Coptic words, written in our Roman alphabet, that remain untranslated.

For this project we have avoided any assumptions that the new literature is somehow inferior or obscure. Throughout the translation of these texts we have tried to make sure that all words are rendered into English, both to make them more accessible and to bring them into a more direct relationship with their traditional New Testament counterparts. To this latter end, we have tried to use consistent language, where possible, among all the books in *A New New Testament*. In only one case, the translation of certain names of (usually) heavenly figures, have we kept both the transliteration and the English translation, in order to strengthen the real persona of these figures and, at the same time, to keep the actual meaning of their names in English.

All but one of the previously bound New Testament texts presented here are edited versions of the *Open English Bible* — a translation based on *The Twentieth Century New Testament*. We are deeply indebted to the innovative, public-oriented, careful translation and legal work done by the chief architect and copyright holder of the *Open English Bible,* Russell Allen. His devotion to making the works of the New Testament available to the larger public without constrictions of publishers' rights is heroic. In addition, the careful and collaborative way that Mr. Allen and the *Open English Bible* ensure that users of this translation can change it according to their own wisdom and translation skills makes the *Open English Bible* the most innovative biblical translation project in more than a century.

One of our major translation considerations has been how to address gendered language in both these ancient documents and our contemporary world. We have attempted to hold two values in creative tension throughout this work. First, we share the value of many translations of the New Testament from the past fifty years to make these texts more inclusive of women's experiences. Historically, *everyone* was signified by the male universal *he,* a move that effectively wrote much of women's experience out of both history and texts. And the authors of the male universal—while making everything look masculine—did realize that their male universal did include women. We have resolved that those women of the past need to become more visible, and women today must be able to find themselves in these works. However, we have not rescued the ancient text in every case from the discrimination against women in which it participates. Where parts of the text explicitly discriminate against women (for instance, when 1 Timothy goes out of its way to say that only men can be elders and bishops), we have not translated words like *man* with any implication of inclusion of women. On the other hand, in the many cases where obviously generic words or phrasing has used a male term to characterize a group of men and women, we have changed that term to something inclusive such as *human, person(s),* or *people.* So while making explicit efforts to uncover the women in the text, we also felt it important to show the language, experience, and expression of gendered experience in the early Christ movements. This has included a conscious effort to let the language of these people live in its innovation, prejudice, and compromise. This complex and nuanced translation in relationship to gender has had implications for the ways we used pronouns in the translation of the Coptic, Greek, and Syriac. In consultation with the publisher's senior editor, Jenna Johnson, we have chosen in our translation of pronouns to represent the implicit inclusion of women in the places where there are other indications that it does indeed include women with alternating masculine and feminine pronouns.

Much gratitude is extended to our translators—Karen King, for the Secret Revelation of John; Justin Lasser, for the Gospel of Thomas; and Elizabeth Miraglia, for the Odes of Solomon. Additional thanks to Alexis Waller for her work on the OEB, particularly the Gospel of Mark and 1, 2, and 3 John. My special thanks and immense gratitude go to Hal Taussig—for inviting me to be a part of this project, for his years of work on these texts, and most of all for his mentorship and conversation. I would not be doing this work without him.

One other complexity of translation needs to be explained. In the case of three of the "new" documents added to *A New New Testament,* no version of the otherwise standard chapter and verse format exists, so we have had to add our own chapters and versification to this edition. These three documents (the Gospel of Truth, The Thunder: Perfect Mind, and the Letter of Peter to Philip) have been made available to the public in various formats and translations without chapter and verse. In keeping with prior scholarly practice for such manuscripts, the reference system for these documents has generally been according to the column of the ancient manuscript accompanied by the line number of that column. So, for instance, a citation from the Gospel of Truth such as "18.36" has represented the eighteenth page of its Nag Hammadi manuscript and the thirty-sixth line. Since it seems quite possible that the readers of this *New New Testament* may have occasion to read these three documents in other publications and translations, we regret that our attempts to present both this column and line reference system and our new chapter and verse references on the same pages of these new documents have not been successful. We do think it very important that there be a chapter and verse system, because it breaks up the text into units that belong together rather than just the page/column and line, which do not really cohere with any organization of the thought of the text. So in these three documents we have forgone the more primitive column-and-line references in favor of the very first chapter and verse references.

CELENE LILLIE
Director of Translation
A New New Testament

Introducing A New New Testament

I T IS TIME FOR a new New Testament. A New Testament that causes people — inside and outside church — to lean forward with interest and engagement. This is meant to be that book. It contains astounding new material from the first-century Christ movements and places it alongside the traditional texts. Among its offerings are a new gospel whose primary character is a woman, a previously unknown collection of songs in Christ's voice lifting to God, another gospel with more than fifty new teachings from Jesus, and a prayer of the apostle Paul discovered in the sands of Egypt less than seventy years ago.

This *New New Testament* is not simply the product of one author. The ten added books have been chosen by a council of wise and nationally known spiritual leaders (listed on pages 555–558). An eclectic mix of bishops, rabbis, well-known authors, leaders of national churches, and women and men from African American, Native American, and European American backgrounds have studied many of the recent discoveries from the first two centuries, deliberated rigorously together, and chosen those new books.

What have these deliberations produced? Where did it come from? And what do readers need to know before immersing themselves in this new New Testament experience?

Where did these new books come from?

How could new books from the first centuries of Christianity, ones not in the New Testament, just suddenly appear? Where did they come from? And why aren't they in the New Testament to begin with? There is no simple answer to these questions. And these are not questions that need to be in the foreground of our experience of *A New New Testament*. So, they are addressed in a number of chapters that follow the scriptures included here, as a "Companion to *A New New Testament*: Basic Historical Background for This New Book of Books."

But there is a short answer to these important questions that can be summarized here. In the past hundred years a number of new works from the first centuries have been discovered in the desert sands of Egypt, the markets of Cairo, and the libraries of ancient monasteries. In some cases, scholars already knew about the existence of these books because they were mentioned in other, more familiar ancient texts, but the books themselves had never been found. In other cases, these newly found documents from the beginnings of Christianity had never before been heard of at all. In still other cases, some of these "new" documents have actually been in hand for quite a while but have been ignored, repressed, or known only to scholars.

There is no reason, then, to think that the Gospel of Thomas, which is not in the traditional New Testament, was read any less in the first and second centuries than the Gospel of John, which is in the traditional New Testament. Indeed, in the ancient world the Gospel of Thomas was distributed widely and translated into at least two languages. Early Christian writings that did not make it into the New Testament had, in their time, similar status to the works that did find their way into it. There was no "stamp of approval" until at least three hundred years after Jesus's birth.

Wait a minute! Wasn't the New Testament written, selected, and collected very soon after Jesus?

No. The New Testament did not exist for at least the first three hundred, if not five hundred, years after Jesus. Some of its books appear to have been written some twenty to thirty years after his death, but others probably not for at least 140 years after Jesus.

In the early centuries of Christianity the only hints of a sacred collection of texts are several lists of some gospels, letters, and apocalypses suggested for reading, with different Christ communities following different lists, and many communities not following any list. The second through fourth centuries after Jesus did see some actual bound books of collected early Christian works, but none of them are identical to, or even progenitors of, the New Testament. In other words, as is shown in more detail in the "Companion to *A New New Testament*" at the back of this book, these new additions to the New Testament existed for many years and during the crucial early period of Christianity alongside the books we know, without any privilege of one over any other, for a very long time. This "new" New Testament, then, in a very real way restores the kind of mix of early Christian documents about Jesus that existed in the first centuries.

The assumption that the existing New Testament was always the privileged, authorized book about Jesus is not true. The New Testament did not somehow descend from God after Jesus was gone. Christian churches spent centuries engaging in arguments and political deals to decide which early books would be included in their most sacred collections. This, of course, does not mean that the New Testament is fraudulent or less meaningful. It simply means that the historical record shows that collection to be a product of complex human negotiation over a long period of time.

So, if the New Testament as a collection of early Christian books did not come into existence in the first century, where did all these different books

*from the traditional New Testament and beyond it come from? And when
were they written?*

The introduction to each ancient text in *A New New Testament* gives an approximate date for when it might have been written. But it is difficult to know these dates exactly. None of these individual books make note of when they were written, and historians are left with many imponderables in dating them. It is reasonably clear that Paul's letters to the Galatians and Corinthians were written in the 50s CE (AD).* On the other hand, the Gospel of Luke could have been written anywhere from 60 CE to 140 CE, according to different historians. Many scholars now argue that the Gospel of Thomas (not included in the traditional New Testament but included in this *New New Testament*) was written much earlier than the Gospel of Luke. Later, we will look more closely at the difficulties and approximations of when the books in and outside of the traditional New Testament were written, in both the individual introductions to each ancient text and in the "Companion to *A New New Testament*."

The books inside and outside the traditional New Testament specify little about the conditions in which they were written, though from their hints at times, places, and real-life circumstances it is clear that they were written by and for particular people. The precise origins of the individual works of the traditional New Testament are in many cases just as elusive as the new additions to this new New Testament.

It can be shocking to learn just how many ambiguities and unknowns surround the origins of these documents, both familiar and new. However, it is worth stepping back from specific questions about individual texts to look at the bigger picture of the things we *do* know about them — because all of these documents have much in common. For instance, none of the traditional New Testament was written after 175 CE; so the 2012 council that chose the new books also did not allow books definitely written after 175 CE. Although there is little certainty about when, by whom, and for what these individual works were written, there are some general similarities in all of them. They were all — traditional and new — composed by and for people between 50 and 175 CE, somewhere around the Mediterranean Sea, with certain similar themes and within certain realities of life. All these books had a life of their own long before they were in the New Testament — not unlike the new books added to this new New Testament.

---

* The more traditional designation AD indicates the Latin phrase *Anno Domini,* which means "the Year of Our Lord." The more recent designation from the mid-twentieth century indicates the English phrase *Common Era.* I — like most biblical scholars — choose to use CE, so that this marking of history does not privilege Christian terminology or perspective, especially with its implicit put-down of Judaism.

Why are certain books in the traditional New Testament and others are not?

Many people acknowledge that the books of the New Testament were written and assembled by humans, but they still assume that some sort of reasonable criteria must have been in place to determine which books were included and which were not. The common assumption holds that the books that became the New Testament must have been in some way more true, more divinely inspired, or more historically accurate than the ones that weren't. One goal of *A New New Testament* is to rethink that misconception. The Gospel of Truth contains poetry about Jesus that is as beautiful as anything found in the traditional New Testament. The Gospel of Thomas records sayings of Jesus found nowhere else that are every bit as likely to have come from his lips as any of those in the New Testament. The Odes of Solomon provide us with more material from early Christian worship than the entire existing New Testament.

This *New New Testament* means to assist both the general public and scholars in getting beyond the overly simplistic readings of the existing New Testament and the new early Christian documents as either orthodox or heretical. Based on my experiences teaching the new documents and the existing New Testament side by side in churches and seminaries for the past twenty years, this project embodies a new way of thinking about what belongs in the heritage of early Christianity. It invites the reader to see how this new mix illuminates spiritual seeking, ethical issues, patterns of belief, and social practice. It calls for scholars and religious leaders to listen carefully to the way the public receives and responds to this new mix, and to provide fresh and solid ideas about how to make sense of the ways the various documents belong to each other and to the contemporary world.

What is in *A New New Testament?*

A New New Testament offers thirty-seven works of scripture from the early centuries of Christianity. It places new discoveries alongside familiar texts and groups them into six sections in an effort to create further contact and contours to their reading. These books include gospels, teachings, prayers, and prophecies.

A New New Testament also offers key summaries and introductions to each ancient book. These include discussions of their inspirations, important historical background, suggestions for ways to use the texts with and against the others in the collection, and potential meditations for broader and deeper understanding of the texts on a spiritual level.

Finally, after the last ancient book — the Secret Revelation of John — we present "A Companion to *A New New Testament*." These six chapters help the reader with major questions about how the new books were found, how the traditional New Testament came into being, what the new books have in common with each other and with the traditional ones, the specifics of how *A New New Testament* came into being, what twentieth- and twenty-first-century scholarship says about the new books, some of the meanings produced by reading the recently discovered and the traditional books together, and what the future of *A New New Testament* might be.

How was this new New Testament brought into being?

In the second through eighth centuries, early synods and councils often brought a group of spiritual leaders together to decide important issues.* In honor of this tradition, I invited spiritual leaders from across North America† to form a council that would decide which of the seventy-five or so additional early Christian documents should be collected together to create *A New New Testament*.‡ After more than six months of preparation, a group of nineteen such leaders convened in February of 2012 in New Orleans; the results of that invaluable discussion and decision-making process are what you hold in your hands. The names and brief biographies of the members of that council are listed in the back of this book, and the process of the council's deliberation is described in the "Companion to *A New New Testament*," also at the end.

As the bishops, authors, rabbis, and scholars of the New Orleans Council finished their work on a windswept day in 2012, they were tingling with excitement. They were confident of the integrity of their conversations and the literature they had just added to the traditional New Testament. Several worried that they had not added enough new books. All were certain that more discussion lay ahead and that this contribution would provide many opportunities for reconsidering how we imagine and encounter the story of Christianity. May your reading help this ongoing deliberation, as this new world of possibilities unfolds.

---

* Ironically only a few regional conferences of the first six centuries addressed the question of what should be in a New Testament. The first all-church council to declare the official contents of the New Testament was the Council of Trent in the sixteenth century.

† My experience is that the Bible means different things in different cultures. So in this initial effort, I decided to limit the scope of choice to those spiritual leaders who shared some cultural experiences. I do think that it may be possible for another "new" New Testament to be collected on an international basis. But this would require more wisdom and budget than I have had at my disposal.

‡ As is noted in the "Companion" chapters later in the book, some people suggested that this *New New Testament* eliminate some of the offensive books of the traditional New Testament. I do not deny that there are such books. For instance, I find the book of 1 Timothy tyrannical in its thoroughgoing attacks on women. However, it has seemed to me that in our times, our cultures are clearer on the need to add more books than to subtract them. So I have tried to err in this case on the side of caution.

How to Read A New New Testament

B Y AND LARGE, we can look to the ways in which people have approached the traditional New Testament as the best guide for coming to this new collection of books. But there are two problems with treating this new assemblage of texts in the usual ways. First of all, many people have never actually read the New Testament. They think they know what it says, or, in some cases, they have resisted reading it because of the way it has been preached at them. A vast number of even devoted Christians have never really read the New Testament and so have not accumulated the experiences and skills of reading any Bible to bring to reading *A New New Testament*.

Second, even those who have spent time reading the traditional New Testament sometimes find it quite difficult to understand its meaning or interpret its messages. The meanings of these texts are phrased in terms of the cultures of the ancient Mediterranean in which the books were written, and so they can sound to twenty-first-century readers as if they were written in somewhat of a foreign language. A huge gap lies between how people in this century and those in the first and second centuries understood themselves and their world. And perhaps the exalted status of the New Testament coupled with its inscrutable qualities make the reader feel less insightful or entitled to interpret the text.

Here are suggestions for four independent ways to read *A New New Testament*. Each kind of reading can draw out different dimensions of the texts, each of them can bring out a different feeling or meaning, so we should take each of them seriously.

1. **Read personally.** Read as if these documents matter deeply and immediately to you. Even if you are confused by some of the language, read as if the words might bring something to your friendships, your work, your family, and your inner life. Where there are stories, put yourself in them as a character, and see how they feel. Where there is a letter, imagine that it was written to you. If the document is a poem or a song, see what feelings and memories it conjures in you.

Reading personally does not necessarily mean that you have to agree with the document or that its instructions need to be followed. Nor does it mean that you should try to wring meaning out of every sentence or word. Reading personally can involve gratitude for the beauty and wisdom of the document or a dislike for what is being said, sometimes both, even within the same text. Most of all, this kind of reading simply invites us to respond through actively making connections to parts of our lives.

Reading personally does not necessarily produce solutions. But it does help us engage and seek meaning and to apply the text to our lives in ways that we might otherwise ignore or repress.

2. Read thoughtfully. Think about the time and social setting in which the document was written, who might have written it, and why. When these questions come up, stop to read other sources that reveal what life was like in the first and second centuries. Consult the introductions to the ancient texts and the "Companion" near the end of this book; all have been written with just these questions and issues in mind. A list of additional readings can be found both at the end of each introduction and in the larger list of recommended readings at the end of the book.

Ponder why the particular document was written. Think about what kind of person might have written each document.

Muse about the similarities and differences between the circumstances of our world and those of the ancient world. Notice how they affect what the particular document might have meant in the first century versus what it means in our time.

3. Read imaginatively. Open your memory, heart, and imagination to these texts. Let them affect you; let them surprise you. Let them trigger not so much your opinions but your curiosity, and let them send you into fantasy. Engage these texts the way you would read a good novel or watch a powerful film; let yourself be entertained by worlds that are different from yours. Give yourself freely to each text with the awareness that you can stop anytime if it becomes too powerful or takes you into territory that feels unpleasant or offensive.

Let the pictures in the text live in your mind or heart. If a document presents God as feminine or masculine, imagine how God might be as a female or male. Hear how the feminine God talks. Imagine how the masculine God feels about children. Think about how the masculine or feminine God relates to the elderly. If one of the documents has a story about a trip to a high mountain, picture the mountain for yourself or imagine yourself walking on it. If another document tells the story of someone being tortured, think of what twenty-first-century torture might correspond to it.

As you take in the text imaginatively, notice how it makes you feel. To what images or stories are you drawn? Which ones make you afraid? What in the text makes you feel joyful?

4. Read meditatively or prayerfully. Dwell on the words of the text that attract your attention. If certain words make you feel gratitude or warmth, go back over them and the ones around them again, lingering on them. Let them sink in. Similarly, if certain words are upsetting or offensive in the text, return to them and ask why they stir you up in this way. Notice what ideas in the document hold you or make you feel loved. Do not read further until you have received those feelings and acknowledged their place in you. Whether the words hold, repel, inspire, or confuse you, stay with them long enough to acknowledge their impact. Then let them go by giving thanks or releasing them into the universe. Let this release be an opening to a larger reality beyond you. Or, in the case of a challenging or frightening text, after acknowledging its impact on you, ask for safety or send the words of the text beyond you so that you feel safer.

In the case of the new texts that are explicit prayers, consider saying them out loud to help you linger over them.

Choosing Which Texts to Read When

Rarely does anyone read scripture from cover to cover. As you turn to the actual documents of this collection, do not expect to read them all either in their given sequence or without detours. They are too different, too demanding, and too rewarding for anyone to approach them in such a unilateral way and still reap their maximum benefits. You should anticipate coming back to some of the documents at a later time, reading various texts in alternate combinations, finding yourself at a stopping point, or wanting to ruminate on a particular text rather than forging ahead.

The power of this *New New Testament* comes in large part from the experience of reading new books and old books together. You might try this out near the beginning of your encounter with *A New New Testament* by first reading the opening sequence of the Prayer of Thanksgiving, the Gospel of Thomas, the Gospel of Matthew, and the Gospel of Mark. Each time you return to the collection, it is closest to the spirit of the project to read both old and new books in the same sitting. So you might read the Gospel of Thomas and the Gospel of Matthew together, or the Prayer of Thanksgiving and the Gospel of Mark. In each case you might notice some of the ways the books seem to belong together and some of the ways that they create tension with each other.

As with the traditional New Testament, it helps to be patient with yourself when material seems strange. Encounters with texts — old or new — that seem bizarre or outside your frame of reference can be negotiated in three basic ways: stop and think about the strangeness, make note of the strangeness but keep on reading, or skip the strange parts. A similar set of approaches can apply to material that seems so familiar that it is no longer engaging: stop to notice that it is boring or difficult to get excited about, make note of the boring sections, or skip the material that is too familiar.

The short introductions positioned right before each document are meant to give you background and context. Occasionally it also may be helpful to consult some of the material in "A Companion to *A New New Testament*" at the end of the book; keep in mind that these are available to fill out your reading.

When making longer-range choices of which documents to read and which to postpone reading, it may be helpful to note the overall organization of this book. The actual texts of *A New New Testament* are grouped and ordered more or less according to the conventions of the traditional New Testament — gospels, "acts," letters, poetry, and revelations. (These specific groupings of documents are explained in more detail in chapter 1 of the "Companion" at the back of the book.)

Although this book is structured similarly to the traditional New Testament, I have made two significant shifts to help readers who are interested in turning their reading into a spiritual process. First, each section of documents begins with a real prayer from the first two centuries of the Christ movements. I have split up the Prayer of Thanksgiving, the Prayer of the Apostle Paul, and the four books of the Odes of Solomon so that each section of books is framed by one part of these prayers. Second, I have made sure that the traditional and the new books occur alongside each other and are not segregated into the "old" and the "new." On one level, of course, this underlines the larger project of reading these texts together and giving them similar authority. But there is also a specific spiritual dimension of making sure they all stand together. Very often the old and the new interrupt one another in ways that draw attention to aspects of each text that had not been noticed before. When this happens, the new meaning of these documents is especially close. In the same way, the new and the old often reinforce one another to underline meanings that need to be emphasized.

Finally, in deciding what texts to read when, the overall structure of the whole book helps make note of particular kinds of literature. The way the books are divided up and grouped together can allow you to concentrate on material in which you have special interest or about which you have particular questions. For instance, if you are especially inclined to stories, the first two sections ("Gospels Featuring Jesus's Teachings" and "Gospels, Poems, and Songs Between Heaven and Earth") might best be read first. On the other hand, if you are drawn to the writings — both traditional and recently discovered — close to the figure of John, you might turn right away to the last section of *A New New Testament*: "Literature in the Tradition of John."

In the end, all advice for reading anything falls aside, and each of us brings particular gifts, insights, and inhibitions to what we read. So the final advice on how to read this book is to be open to the fresh spirit that brought it together and that stood behind so much of this powerful literature. With a light and open heart, approach this reading with joy, anticipation, and what beckons to you in the process.

The Books of
A New New Testament

AN ANCIENT PRAYER FROM THE
EARLY CHRIST MOVEMENTS

An Introduction to the Prayer of Thanksgiving

THIS PRAYER SPARKLES with evocative imagery. Pulsing with spiritual intimacy, its voice likely belongs to a very early layer of Christian spiritual practice, that of a community gathered for worship around a festive meal. For Christ followers — like most other groups of that day — such a meal contained a number of prayers, said at the beginning, in the middle, and at the end of the gathering. The New Orleans Council, which selected the ten new books for this collection, enthusiastically proposed that the Prayer of Thanksgiving should be included as the very first text in the volume. This would fulfill the council's wish that the reading of *A New New Testament* begin with a spiritual entrance into the world of the early Christ movements. There are very few prayers at all in the traditional New Testament, and the council felt strongly that the spiritual practices of these early Christ movements provided vital new perspectives on the beginnings of Christianity. With their emotional language and first-person expressions, prayers — and other spiritual practices — often provide more access to the felt dimensions of life than professions of belief and theology do.

This Prayer of Thanksgiving comes from the 1945 discovery of fifty-two documents, nearly all of them Christian, in Nag Hammadi, Egypt. Like all of the Nag Hammadi collection, it was written in the Coptic language. It is the only known manuscript with this exact text, but there are a number of other first-through-third-century Christian prayer texts that contain some of the same sentences and phrases. Neither its location nor its exact date of composition can be known. Its author is also unknown. The title affixed to the document, like many other titles of the ancient world, was added during the copying of the document for users much later.

The prayer does not explicitly refer to Jesus, but it does refer to the eating of a bloodless meal after the prayer, a practice that the Christ movements had in common with the traditions of Israel of that era. The theme of the prayer is thanksgiving, and some of the early Christ meals themselves were explicitly called *eucharists,* which is one of the Greek and Coptic words meaning "thanksgiving."

The language used to refer to God in the prayer is breathtaking for the modern ear: God is called "O name untroubled," "light of life," "womb of all that grows," "womb pregnant with the nature of the Father," and "never-ending endurance." This language demonstrates the fascinating openness of the nascent Christ movements in attributing to God both masculine and feminine character traits, especially in this focus on God having a womb through which creation happens. As seen in prayers from other new documents in this volume, early Christ followers seemed drawn to a prayer language that addressed God as a Father who had breasts from which humans could receive the symbolic milk.

This originality of expression shows the early Christ people as quite devoid of the religious rigidity or hierarchical conformity that would come to later Christian generations. It also shows that these early Christ people almost certainly used a variety of prayers for their festive meal "eucharists," not the lockstep formula of later Christianity. It can inspire twenty-first-century spiritual practice that is equally original, expressive, and outside the box of conventional practice and ideas. Or, this prayer's own wording directly offers an originality for those in our day who seek expressive and creative prayer.

Recommended Reading

Peter Dirkse and James Brashler, "The Prayer of Thanksgiving," pp. 375–77 in *The Coptic Gnostic Library: A Complete Edition of the Nag Hammadi Codices,* Volume III, general editor James M. Robinson

The Prayer of Thanksgiving

¹ This is the prayer they said:
We give thanks to you,
every life and heart stretches toward
   you,
O name untroubled,
honored with the name of God,
praised with the name of Father.
² To everyone and everything
comes the kindness of the Father,
and love
and desire.
³ And if there is a sweet and simple
   teaching,
it gifts us mind, word, and
   knowledge:
mind, that we may understand you;
word, that we may interpret you;
knowledge, that we may know you.
⁴ We rejoice and are enlightened by your
   knowledge.
We rejoice that you have taught us
   about yourself.
⁵ We rejoice that in the body
you have made us divine* through your
   knowledge.

⁶ The thanksgiving of the human who
   reaches you
is this alone:
that we know you.
⁷ We have known you,
O light of mind.
O light of life,
we have known you.
⁸ O womb of all that grows,
we have known you.
⁹ O womb pregnant with the nature of
   the Father,
we have known you.
¹⁰ O never-ending endurance of the
   Father who gives birth,
so we worship your goodness.
¹¹ One wish we ask:
we wish to be protected in knowledge.
¹² One protection we desire:
that we not stumble in this life.

¹³ When they said these things in prayer,
they welcomed one another, and they went
to eat their holy food, which had no blood
in it.

---

* Here *divine* can also be translated as "gods"; see Psalm 82:6; John 10:34–35.

GOSPELS FEATURING
JESUS'S TEACHINGS

An Introduction to the Gospel of Thomas

THE GOSPEL OF THOMAS provides a fresh look at Jesus as teacher, since its entire content consists of 114 sayings attributed to Jesus. These sayings are the same as or similar to about fifty in Matthew, Mark, or Luke, making more than fifty of them new to the ears of twenty-first-century readers. The Gospel of Thomas has drawn more scholarship and public attention than any other of the fifty-two Nag Hammadi documents.

The New Orleans Council wanted the Gospel of Thomas to be the first gospel in *A New New Testament,* because it is a near-perfect example of how these additional books offer both connections and contours: strong connections to the traditional New Testament and eye-popping new content not previously known.

The Gospel of Thomas was found along with fifty-one other, mostly Christian, manuscripts near the Egyptian town of Nag Hammadi in 1945. The Nag Hammadi copy is the only complete copy of this gospel and is written in Coptic, but since its discovery the existence of several other partial copies in Greek have also been identified. The existence of both Coptic and Greek versions indicates that this gospel was probably well known in a number of cultures in the ancient world. Scholars are deeply divided about whether the Gospel of Thomas as it exists in the Nag Hammadi manuscript comes from the first or second century. It seems quite possible that a significantly earlier version, even before Matthew, Mark, and Luke, could have existed. Although most of the manuscript evidence comes from Egypt, a number of scholars have suggested Syria as an original home for this gospel, because of similar content in Syria-based documents and because of the devotion of early Syrians to the figure of Thomas. Although the Gospel of Thomas itself indicates Thomas as the author in its opening, there is no consensus on who actually wrote the book. In the ancient world, authorship was regularly attributed falsely to leaders of previous generations, and this was clearly the case for Thomas and a number of other early Christian books.

One of the most remarkable aspects of the Gospel of Thomas lies in its form. It is a sayings gospel: it does not have an overall story of Jesus but simply offers a list of his teachings. These teachings are — like those in Matthew, Mark, and Luke — short and pithy parables, proverbs, and aphorisms. At first, scholars thought that the order of these sayings was arbitrary. Increased study of this gospel, however, now points to an overall organizing principle, but its exact shape and sense has not yet been deciphered.

Jesus, the Teacher

In a sayings gospels like Thomas, the main significance of Jesus is his role as a teacher. This dimension is worth dwelling on in order to notice how it both re-inforces and challenges some conventional pictures of Jesus. Jesus does teach a great deal in Matthew, Mark, Luke, and John; and he teaches very similar material in Thomas, Matthew, Mark, and Luke. But the picture of Jesus as teacher in Thomas does not include an emphasis on his saving death, his resurrection, or his healing. The meaning of Jesus comes from the wisdom he communicates, not from any special accomplishments, his position on earth or in heaven, or what fate or triumph he experiences. Here Jesus does not teach about his own significance, or about holy scriptures, but rather on issues of everyday life and practice. Per-haps the clearest theme is that of "the realm of God," which is a direct translation of a Coptic phrase that has most often been translated as "the kingdom of God." In Thomas, "the realm of God" is likened to particular life experiences. So, even when he draws on a term that seems somewhat religious or theological, he places it within the context of ordinary life. This is also true of Jesus's teachings in Matthew, Mark, and Luke, but not the gospels of John and Mary.

Thomas's approach is not at all unusual for ancient wisdom literature, which in-cludes many such documents, sometimes with the teacher named and sometimes without a designation of a speaker. Sometimes the meaning of the saying is clear and clever, as in Thomas 53: "His followers said to him, 'Is circumcision beneficial or not for us?' He said to them, 'If it were beneficial their father would beget them circumcised from their mother.'" Sometimes the teaching is poetic, pointed, and eloquent, as in Thomas 50: "If they say to you, 'Where have you come from?' say to them, 'We came from the light, the place where the light generated itself and es-tablished itself, and has been made manifest in their image.' If they say to you, 'Is it you?' say, 'We are its children.'" And sometimes the teaching is so pithy it raises more questions than answers, as in Thomas 42: "Jesus said, 'Be passersby.'"

So, these teachings are evocative, but not particularly practical. They are not meant to teach us how to build a house. Even while rooted in everyday experience, they are meant to get us thinking about the intangibles of life. This kind of process of gaining wisdom from one's own thought and experience is itself described in Thomas 70: "When you give birth to the one within you, that one will save you. If you do not have that one within you, that one will kill you."

The Realm of God in Thomas

As mentioned earlier, one might characterize the theme of Jesus's teachings in Thomas as "the realm of God." The realm of God is considered in Thomas to be primarily an earthly reality, describable, at least by comparison, in events and processes of ordinary life. This is also a major theme in the gospels of Matthew,

Mark, and Luke and the letters of Paul. Similarly to other early Christian literature, the realm of God here is also referred to as "the realm of heaven," but unique to Thomas is the phrase "the realm of the Father."

The more than fifteen teachings about the realm of God in Thomas include these:

If those who lead you proclaim to you: "The realm is in the sky," then the birds of the sky will enter before you. If they proclaim to you: "It is in the sea," then the fish will enter before you. Rather, the realm is within you and outside of you. (3)

The realm of the Father is compared to a woman carrying a jar filled with flour. While she was walking on the road a ways out, the handle of the jar broke. The flour emptied out along the road, but she did not realize it or recognize a problem. (97)

[The realm] will not come by looking for it. It will not be a matter of saying, "Here it is!" or "Look! There it is." Rather, the realm of the Father is spread out upon the earth, but people don't see it. (113)

These fresh teachings allow us to better see that Jesus's teachings about the realm of God may be far broader, even more creative, than is apparent when consulting only the traditional New Testament, and yet these lessons remain quite consistent with those well-worn teachings.

It's Not the End of the World You Need to Concentrate On, It's the Beginning

Much of early Christian literature pays attention to the impending end of the world. Images of cataclysmic destruction are found in everything from the Gospel of Matthew to the Revelation to John. The Gospel of Thomas not only ignores all such images but explicitly challenges the notion of the end of the world. In Thomas 18, when Jesus is asked by his disciples when the end will come, he answers: "Have you discovered the beginning that you ask about the end? For, in the place where the beginning is, there the end will be. Blessed is the one who takes a stand in the beginning. That one will know the end, and will not experience death."

This focus on the beginning takes on multiple images throughout Thomas. Focusing in Thomas 19 on five trees in the original garden, Jesus proclaims, "Blessed is the one who came into being from the beginning, before he came to be." In several other passages (21, 37) he evokes the nakedness of the Garden of Eden as a positive image. This dependence on the cosmic beginning is mirrored also in the life cycle of individuals in Jesus's teaching that "these little children are like those who enter the realm" (22). In 50, Jesus identifies humans as those who came from where the light itself came into being.

For the Gospel of Thomas the spiritual path of wisdom does not point toward

the end of time and the judgment day, nor does it hold up death as a crucial moment in the life of the individual. Instead, the origins of life and the world are the
real signs of God's purpose for human beings.

Thomas's Jesus makes twenty-first-century readers do a double or triple take.
Often these teachings sound very much like the standard gospels. On the other
hand, between or even in what appear to be traditional sayings, something very
new appears, making this gospel one that requires a fresh hearing and offers new
possibilities.

Recommended Reading

Stevan L. Davies, *The Gospel of Thomas and Christian Wisdom*
Elaine Pagels, *Beyond Belief: The Secret Gospel of Thomas*
Richard Valantasis, *The Gospel of Thomas*

The Gospel of Thomas

These are the veiled sayings which the living Jesus spoke and Judas, the Twin, Thomas wrote them down.

1 [1] And he said: "Whoever finds the meaning of these sayings will not experience death."

2 [1] Jesus said: "Let the one who seeks continue seeking until he finds. [2] And when that one finds he will be disturbed, and once that one is disturbed he will become awed, and will rule as a king over the all."

3 [1] Jesus said: "If those who lead you proclaim to you: 'The realm is in the sky,' then the birds of the sky will enter before you. If they proclaim to you: 'It is in the sea,' then the fish will enter before you. [2] Rather, the realm is within you and outside of you. [3] When you come to know yourselves, then you will be known, and you will realize that you are the children of the Living Father. [4] If, however, you do not come to know yourselves, then you dwell in poverty and you are the poverty."

4 [1] Jesus said: "The old person will not hesitate to ask a small child of seven days about the place of life, and the old one will live. [2] For many who are first will be last. [3] And they will come to be one alone."

5 [1] Jesus said: "Recognize what is right in front of your face, and what is hidden will be revealed to you. [2] For, there is nothing hidden that will not be revealed."

6 [1] His followers asked him: "Do you want us to fast? In what way should we fast? Should we give alms? What foods should we not eat?" [2] Jesus said, "Do not tell lies and do not do what you hate. [3] For all things are revealed before the presence of heaven."

7 [1] Jesus said: "Blessed is the lion which the person eats — and the lion becomes a person. And cursed is the person whom the lion eats — and the lion becomes a person."

8 [1] And he said: "The person compares to a wise fisherman: He cast his net into the sea. He drew it up from the sea full of little fish from below. And he found one large fish. The fisherman was wise. He cast the little fish into the sea. He chose the large fish without trouble. [2] Whoever has ears to hear, listen!"

9 [1] Jesus said: "Look, a sower went out with a handful of seeds and sowed them. Some fell on the road. The birds came and gathered them. Others fell on the rock. They did not take root in the soil or produce ears. And others fell among thorns. They choked the seed and were eaten by worms. And some fell upon good soil, and produced fruit up to the sky. Sixty per measure. One hundred and twenty per measure!"

10 [1] Jesus said: "I have cast fire upon the world. And behold! I watch over it until it burns."

11 [1] Jesus said: "This heaven will pass away and the one above it will pass away. [2] Those who are dead do not live and those who live will not die. In the days you ate what was dead you were making it alive. When you come to dwell in the light, what will you do? On the day you were one you became two. But when you become two, what will you do?"

12 [1] His followers said to Jesus: "We know that you will leave us. Who will become our leader?" [2] Jesus said to them: "In the place where you came from, you will go up to James the Righteous, for whom heaven and earth have come into being."

13 [1] Jesus said to his followers: "Compare and tell me whom I resemble." Simon Peter said to him: "You are like a righteous angel." Matthew said to him: "You are like a wise philosopher." Thomas said to him: "Teacher, my mouth will not permit me to say whom you resemble." Jesus said: "I am not your teacher — you are drunk. Because you drank from the bubbling spring that I have measured out." [2] And he took him and departed. He told him three sayings. When Thomas came back to his companions they asked him: "What did Jesus say to you?" Thomas said to them: "If I told you the sayings he told me, you would take up stones and cast them at me. And fire would burst out of those stones and burn you."

14 [1] Jesus said to them: "If you fast, you will produce sin for yourselves. And if you pray, you will be condemned. And if you give alms, you will do harm to your spirits. [2] And in whatever land you enter and in which you walk, if they receive you eat whatever is put before you, and heal the sick among them. [3] For, what goes into your mouth will not pollute you; rather, that which comes from your mouth will pollute you."

15 [1] Jesus said: "When you see one who was not born of woman, fall on your faces and worship him. That one is your Father."

16 [1] Jesus said: "Perhaps people think that it is peace that I have come to cast upon the world. But they do not know that it is rebellion that I have come to cast upon the earth: fire, sword, war! [2] For there will be five within a household: three against two, and two against three — father against son, and son against father, and they will stand alone."

17 [1] Jesus said: "I will give you what no eye has seen, what no ear has heard, what no hand has touched, and what has never encountered the human mind."

18 [1] His followers said to Jesus: "Tell us how our end will be." Jesus said: "Have you discovered the beginning that you ask about the end? For, in the place where the beginning is, there the end will be. [2] Blessed is the one who takes a stand in the beginning. That one will know the end, and will not experience death."

19 [1] Jesus said: "Blessed is the one who came into being from the beginning, before he came to be. [2] If you become my followers and listen to my sayings, these stones will become your servants. [3] For there are five trees in paradise, which remain unmoved summer and winter and whose leaves do not fall. Whoever knows them will not experience death."

20 [1] The disciples said to Jesus: "Tell us, what is the realm of heaven compared to?" He said: "It compares to a mustard seed smaller than all seeds. But when it falls on soil that is cultivated, it produces a large branch and becomes shelter for the birds of the sky."

21 [1] Mary said to Jesus: "Whom are your disciples like?" [2] He said: "They are like little children who have settled in a field that is not theirs. [3] When the owners of the field come, they will say, 'Give us back our field!' [4] But they will strip naked in front of them in order to abandon it, so that the field is returned to them. [5] That is why I say: 'If the householder knows that a thief is coming, he will keep watch before he comes. He will not let him break into his house and his estate to steal his possessions.' ⁶ But you, keep watch from the beginning of the world; gird up your loins. ⁷ Ready yourself with a great power so that the thieves do not find a way to get to you. Because they will find the necessities which you guard. ⁸ Let there be a person of understanding among you. When the grain ripened someone came quickly with a sickle and reaped it. ⁹ Whoever has ears, hear!"

22 ¹ Jesus saw little children being nursed. He said to his followers: "These little children are like those who enter the realm." ² They said to him: "Will we enter the realm as little children?" ³ Jesus said to them: "When you make the two one, and when you make the inside like the outside, and the outside like the inside, and the above like the below. And when you make the male and the female into a solitary one, so that the male is not male nor the female female. And when you make eyes in place of an eye, and a hand in place of a hand, and a foot in place of a foot, and an image in place of an image, then you will enter the realm."

23 ¹ Jesus said: "I will choose you, one from a thousand and two from ten thousand, and they will stand alone."

24 ¹ His followers said: "Show us the place where you are, because it is necessary that we seek it." He said to them: ² "Whoever has ears to hear, hear! ³ There is light within a person of light, and that one lights up the entire world. If that one does not shine, there is darkness."

25 ¹ Jesus said: "Love your brother or sister like your soul. Guard each of them like the pupil of your eye."

26 ¹ Jesus said: "You see the sliver in your brother's eye, but you fail to see the plank that is in your own eye. When you remove the plank from your own eye, then you will be able to see clearly enough to remove the sliver from your brother's eye."

27 ¹ Jesus said: "If you do not fast from the world you will not find the realm. If you do not make the sabbath a true sabbath, you will not see the Father."

28 ¹ Jesus said: "I took my stand in the midst of the world, and I was manifested to them in flesh. I found all of them drunk and none of them thirsting. And my soul throbbed for the children of humanity, for they are blind in their hearts and do not see. For blind they came into the world empty and seek also to leave the world empty. But right now they are merely drunk. When they sober up, then they will turn."

29 ¹ Jesus said: "If the flesh emerged from the spirit, it is a wonder. But if the spirit emerged from the body, that is a wonder of wonders! ² Yet, I wonder at how this great richness was placed in this poverty."

30 ¹ Jesus said: "Where there are three gods, they are Gods, where there are two or one, I am with them. ² Lift the stone, you will find me there. Split the piece of wood, I am there."

31 ¹ Jesus said: "No prophet is accepted in his or her own village. No physician heals those who know him."

32 ¹ Jesus said: "They are building a city upon a high mountain and fortifying it! It cannot fall — but it also cannot be hidden."

33 ¹ Jesus said: "What you hear with your ear declare with the other ear from your rooftops. ² For no one lights a lamp and puts it under a bushel, nor does one put it in a hidden place. Rather, that one puts it on a lamp stand so that everyone who enters and leaves will see its light."

34 [1] Jesus said: "If a blind person leads a blind person, both will fall into a pit."

35 [1] Jesus said: "It is not possible for someone to enter the house of a powerful man and take it by force without binding his hands. Only after binding the powerful man's hands will he loot the house."

36 [1] Jesus said, "Do not worry, from morning to evening and from evening to morning, about your food, about what you're going to eat, or about your clothing, what you are going to wear. [2] You are far better than the lilies, which do not card nor spin. [3] As for you when you have no clothes, what will you put on? Who might add to your status? [5] That one will give you your clothes."

37 [1] His disciples said: "When will you appear to us, and when will we see you?" [2] Jesus said: "When you strip naked without being ashamed, and take up your clothes and put them under your feet like little children, and tread on them. Then you will see the Child of the Living One and you will not be afraid."

38 [1] Jesus said: "Many times you longed to hear the sayings that I am telling you, and you have no other to hear them from. The days will come when you seek after me, but you will not find me."

39 [1] Jesus said: "The Pharisees and the scholars have taken the keys of knowledge and hidden them. They do not enter, nor do they permit those who desire to enter to enter. [2] As for you, be as cunning as snakes and as innocent as doves."

40 [1] Jesus said: "A grapevine has been planted outside the Father. Since it is not supported, it will be pulled up from the roots and will be destroyed."

41 [1] Jesus said: "Whoever has something in her hand, more will be given. And whoever has nothing, even the little that person has will be taken away from that person."

42 [1] Jesus said: "Be passersby."

43 [1] His followers said to him: "Who are you to say these things to us?" [2] "You do not realize who I am from what I say to you? Rather, you have become like the Judeans: they love the tree, but hate its fruit — and love its fruit, but hate the tree."

44 [1] Jesus said: "Whoever blasphemes against the Father will be forgiven. And whoever blasphemes against the Son will be forgiven. [2] But whoever blasphemes against the holy Spirit will not be forgiven, neither on earth nor in heaven."

45 [1] Jesus said: "Grapes are not harvested from thorns, nor are figs picked from thistles, for they do not bear fruit. [2] A good person brings forth good from his storehouse, a bad person brings forth evil from his corrupt storehouse which is in his heart, and he speaks evil. For out of abundance he produces evil."

46 [1] Jesus said: "From Adam to John the Baptizer, among those born of women, no one is honored more than John the Baptizer, so that his eyes need not be averted. [2] Yet, I have also said: 'Whoever among you becomes little will know the realm and will be honored more than John.'"

47 [1] Jesus said: "It is impossible for a person to mount two horses and to draw two bows. [2] And it is impossible for a servant to serve two masters, for he would honor the one and insult the other. [3] No one wants to drink aged wine and immediately wants to drink new wine. [4] And new wine is not poured into old wineskins, because they would burst. Nor is old wine poured into new wineskins, because it would spoil. [5] An old patch is not sewn onto a new garment, because a tear would result."

48 [1] Jesus said: "If two make peace with each other in the same house, they will say to the mountain, 'Move away!' and it will move."

49 [1] Jesus said: "Blessed are the solitary and chosen ones, for you will find the realm, for you are from it and will return there."

50 [1] Jesus said: "If they say to you, 'Where have you come from?' [2] say to them, 'We came from the light, the place where the light generated itself and established itself, and has been made manifest in their image.' If they say to you, 'Is it you?' say, 'We are its children, and we are the chosen of the Living Father.' [3] If they ask you, 'What is the sign of your Father in you?' say, 'It is movement and repose.'"

51 [1] His followers said to him: "When will the repose of the dead take place, and when will the new world come?" [2] He said to them: "That which you look for has come, but you did not recognize it."

52 [1] His followers said to him: "Twenty-four prophets have spoken in Israel, and all have spoken within you." [2] He said to them: "You have left out the Living One in your presence, and you spoke only about those who are dead."

53 [1] His followers said to him: "Is circumcision beneficial or not for us?" He said to them: "If it were beneficial their father would beget them circumcised from their mother. [2] Rather, true circumcision in spirit is entirely beneficial."

54 [1] Jesus said: "Blessed are the poor, for the realm of the sky is theirs."

55 [1] Jesus said: "Whoever does not hate her father and her mother cannot be a follower of mine. [2] And whoever does not hate his brothers and sisters and carry his cross as I do, will not be worthy of me."

56 [1] Jesus said: "Whoever has come to know the world has found a corpse. And whoever has found the world as a corpse, the world is not worthy of that one."

57 [1] Jesus said: "The realm of the Father compares to someone who had good seed. His enemy came in the night. He sowed a weed amid the good seed. The man did not permit them to pull up the weed. He said to them: 'When you go to pull up the weed you may also pull up the good seed. On the day of the harvest the weeds will be visible. Then you pull them up and burn them.'"

58 [1] Jesus said: "Blessed is the one who is disturbed by her discovery. That one has found life."

59 [1] Jesus said: "Look after the Living One while you are living, lest you die and seek to see that one. You will not find the power to see."

60 [1] He saw a Samaritan carrying a lamb on the way to Judea. He said to his followers: "He is surrounding the lamb." They said to him: "He does so in order to kill and eat it." He said to them: "While it is living he will not eat it. Rather, if he kills it, then it will become a corpse and then he can eat it." They said to him: "There is no other way?" He said to them: "You also, seek after a place of repose, lest you become corpses and get consumed."

61 [1] Jesus said: "Two will recline on a couch — one will die, the other will live!"

[2] Salome said: "Who are you to say such things while you recline upon my couch and eat from my table?" Jesus said to her: "I derive from the One who is equal to all. I was merely given by you that which is my Father's." "I am your follower." [2] "Because of this, I say: 'When a person becomes equal that person will be full of light.'"

62 [1] Jesus said: "I tell my secrets to those who are worthy of my secrets. Do not let your left hand know what your right hand is doing."

63 [1] Jesus said: "There was a rich man who had an abundance of money. He said: 'I shall put my money to use so that I may sow, reap, and plant and fill my storehouse so that I lack nothing.' Such were his intentions, but that very night he died! [2] Whoever has ears, hear!"

64 [1] Jesus said: "A man had guests. When he had prepared the dinner, he sent his slave to invite the guests. He came to the first person. He said: 'My master invites you.' He responded: 'I have money for some merchants who are coming to me this evening and I must place my orders. I cannot attend the dinner.' He went to another person. He said: 'My master invites you.' He responded: 'I just bought a house and am required for the day. I cannot attend.' He went to another person. He said: 'My master invites you.' He responded: 'My friend is getting married, and I am in charge of preparing the meal. I cannot attend the dinner.' He went to another person. He said: 'My master invites you.' He responded: 'I have purchased a field and am going to collect the rent. I cannot come. Please excuse me.' The slave left. He said to his master: 'The people you invited to the dinner have asked to be excused.' The master said to his slave: 'Go outside on the streets. Whoever you find, bring them in so that they may dine.' [2] Usurers

and merchants will not enter the places of my Father."

65 [1] Jesus said: "A usurer owned a vineyard. He leased it to some tenants so that they would work it and he take the fruit from their hands. He sent his slave to collect the fruit of the vineyard. They seized his slave. They beat him, almost to the point of death. The slave went back to his master and told him about what had happened. His master said: 'Perhaps they did not know him.' He sent another slave. The tenants beat that one as well. Then the master sent his son. He said: 'Perhaps they will be shamed before my son.' The tenants, since they knew he was the heir to the vineyard, seized him and killed him. [2] Whoever has ears, hear!"

66 [1] Jesus said: "Show me the stone that the builders rejected — that one is the cornerstone."

67 [1] Jesus said: "Whoever knows all, if she still needs herself, she still needs all."

68 [1] Jesus said: "Blessed are you when you are hated and persecuted. [2] For they will find no place where they persecuted you within."

69 [1] Jesus said: "Blessed are those who have been persecuted within their hearts. They are the ones who have truly known the Father. [2] Blessed are those who are hungry, for they are motivated to alleviate the belly of the one who desires."

70 [1] Jesus said: "When you give birth to the one within you, that one will save you. If you do not have that one within you, that one will kill you."

71 [1] Jesus said: "I will destroy this house and no one will be able to rebuild it."

72 [1] A man said to Jesus: "Tell my brothers to divide my father's possessions with me." He said to him: "Oh, sir, who has made me a divider?" He turned to his disciples and said: "I am not a divider, am I?"

73 [1] Jesus said: "The harvest is abundant, but the laborers are few. Pray to the master that he might send laborers to the harvest."

74 [1] He said: "Lord, there are many around the well, but there is nothing in it."

75 [1] Jesus said: "Many are standing at the door, but only the solitary ones will enter the bridal chamber."

76 [1] Jesus said: "The realm of the Father is compared to a merchant who had some merchandise. He found a pearl. That merchant was wise. He sold the merchandise. Then he purchased the pearl for himself alone. [2] You also, seek after his treasure, which does not perish, but endures — where neither moth approaches to eat it nor worm destroys."

77 [1] Jesus said: "I am the light which is above them all, I am the all. The all has come forth from me, and all has split open before me. [2] Lift the stone, you will find me there. Split the piece of wood, I am there."

78 [1] Jesus said: "Why have you come out to the field? To see a reed shaken by the wind and to see someone dressed in soft clothes like your kings and powerful men? They are dressed in soft clothes, but they don't know the truth."

79 [1] A woman in the crowd said to him: "Blessed is the womb that bore you and the breasts that nursed you." He said to her: "Blessed are those who have heard the word of the Father and have truly kept it. [2] For there will be days when you will say: 'Blessed is the womb that has not conceived, and the breasts which have not given milk.'"

80 [1] Jesus said: "Whoever has known the world has found the body. And whoever has found the body, the world is no longer worthy of that person."

81 [1] Jesus said: "Whoever has grown rich should rule. But whoever has power should renounce."

82 [1] Jesus said: "Whoever is near me is near the fire, and whoever is far from me is far from the realm."

83 [1] Jesus said: "The images are shown to humanity, and the light within them is hidden in the image of the Father's light. He will be shown but his image is hidden away in his light."

84 [1] Jesus said: "In the days when you looked at your resemblance you rejoiced. When, however, you look upon the images that came into being upon your emergence, which neither die nor manifest themselves, how much you will have to bear!"

85 [1] Jesus said: "Adam came into being from a great power and a great wealth. But he was not worthy of you. For, if he had been worthy of you, he would not have tasted death."

86 [1] Jesus said: "The foxes have their dens and the birds have their nests, but the Child of Humanity has no place to lay down his head and rest."

87 [1] Jesus said: "Damn the body that depends on a body; and damn the soul that depends on these two."

88 [1] Jesus said: "The messengers and the prophets will come to you. They will give you what is yours and you will give them what you have. You will say to yourselves: 'When will they come and take what is theirs?'"

89 [1] Jesus said: "Why do you wash the outside of the cup? Do you not understand that the one who created the inside is also the one who created the outside?"

90 [1] Jesus said: "Come to me, for my yoke is easy and my lordship is gentle. [2] And you will find rest for yourselves."

91 [1] They said to him: "Tell us who you are so that we may believe in you." [2] He said to them: "You read the face of the sky and the earth, but you do not know the one who is before you, nor do you know how to read this moment."

92 [1] Jesus said: "Seek and you will find. But that which you asked me about in those days I did not tell you, but I now desire to tell you, and you no longer seek to know."

93 [1] Jesus said: "Do not give what is holy to dogs, for they might toss them to the dung pile. Do not toss pearls to pigs, for they might trample them."

94 [1] Jesus said: "Whoever seeks, will find. Whoever knocks, they will open to that one."

95 [1] Jesus said: "If you have money, do not lend it at interest. Rather, lend it to someone who won't pay you back."

96 [1] Jesus said: "The realm of the Father is compared to a woman. She took a little yeast and hid it in dough. She made the loaves into leavened bread! [2] Whoever has ears, hear!"

97 [1] Jesus said: "The realm of the Father is compared to a woman carrying a jar filled with flour. While she was walking on the road a ways out, the handle of the jar broke. The flour emptied out along the road, but she did not realize it or recognize a problem."

98 [1] Jesus said: "The realm of the Father is compared to someone who wanted to kill a powerful man. He drew his sword in his house. He stabbed the wall in order to see whether his hand might hold steady. Then he killed the powerful man."

99 [1] His followers said to him: "Your brothers and your mother are standing outside." He said to them: "Those who do the will of my Father, they are my brothers and my mother. They are truly the ones who enter the realm of my Father."

100 [1] They showed Jesus a coin and said to him: "Caesar's people demand taxes from us." He said to them: "Give what is Caesar's to Caesar, give God what is God's. [2] And give me what is mine."

101 [1] Jesus said: "Whoever does not hate her father and her mother in the same way I do, cannot be a follower of mine. [2] And whoever does not love her father and her mother in the same way I do, cannot be a follower of mine. [3] For my mother birthed my body, but my true mother gave me life."

102 [1] Jesus said, "Damn the Pharisees for they resemble a dog resting in a manger with oxen, which neither eats nor permits the oxen to eat."

103 [1] Jesus said: "Blessed is the one who knows where the thieves are going to enter, so that he might arise and assemble his estate, and prepare himself."

104 [1] They said to Jesus: "Come, today let us pray and fast." Jesus said: "What sin have I committed, or where have I been defeated? Rather when the groom leaves the bridal chamber, then let them fast and pray."

105 [1] Jesus said: "Whoever knows mother and father will be called the child of a whore!"

106 [1] Jesus said: "When you make the two one, you will become children of humanity. And if you say: 'Mountain, move away!' it will move."

107 [1] Jesus said: "The realm compares to a shepherd who had a hundred sheep. One of them, the largest, went astray. He left the other ninety-nine, and he sought after that one until he found it. After such an effort, he said to the sheep: 'I love you more than the other ninety-nine.'"

108 [1] Jesus said: "Whoever drinks from my mouth will become like me. I myself will become that person, and what is hidden will be revealed to that person."

109 [1] Jesus said: "The realm compares to a man who had in his field a hidden treasure, but he was unaware of it. And after his death, he left it to his son. The son was also unaware of the treasure. He took the field and sold it. The one who bought the field went plowing and found the treasure. [2] He began to lend money at interest to those he loved."

110 [1] Jesus said: "Whoever has found the world and become rich should renounce the world."

111 [1] Jesus said: "The heavens and earth will be rolled up right before you. [2] And the one who lives from the Living One will not see death. [3] Does not Jesus say: 'Whoever has found oneself, the world is not worthy of that person'?"

112 [1] Jesus said: "Damn the flesh that depends on the soul, and damn the soul that depends on the flesh."

113 [1] His followers said to Jesus: "When will the realm come?" [2] "It will not come by looking for it. It will not be a matter of saying, 'Here it is!' or 'Look! There it is.' [3] Rather, the realm of the Father is spread out upon the earth, but people don't see it."

114 [1] Simon Peter said to them: "Let Mary leave us, for women do not deserve life." [2] Jesus said: "Look! I will lead her so that I might make her male, which will make her into a living spirit resembling you males. [3] For any woman that makes herself male will enter the realm of heaven."

An Introduction to the Gospel of Matthew

THOUGH IT IS POSITIONED IN THE TRADITIONAL New Testament as the first gospel, I have placed the Gospel of Matthew second in the gospels section of *A New New Testament*. This is meant to highlight the many similar teachings in Matthew and the Gospel of Thomas, which immediately precedes it, and to seriously reinforce the opinion of many scholars that Matthew was most likely preceded by other gospels like Thomas.

Most scholars place the writing of the Gospel of Matthew sometime in the 80s, fifty years after the death of Jesus. It is assumed to have been the second gospel written among those in the traditional New Testament. Often it is proposed that Matthew had the Gospel of Mark in hand and expanded it. In contrast to Mark, Matthew has stories about Jesus's birth and a more elaborate picture of Jesus's resurrection. Matthew's additional stories about Jesus's birth and resurrection are quite different from the stories found in the Gospel of Luke, but there are many teachings that occur in both Matthew and Luke but not in Mark and John. Although some speculate that Matthew was first written in Jesus's native tongue of Aramaic, the only existing ancient manuscripts are in Greek. The two most frequent proposals about where this gospel was written are Syrian Antioch and Galilee. Nothing is known directly about "Matthew" as a person. Indeed, the name "Matthew" occurs only in the book's title, which may have been added later.

A Strikingly Jewish Gospel

Only in Matthew does Jesus proclaim that every bit of Jewish Law (Torah) is valid. Indeed, Jesus announces that every punctuation mark of Torah must be obeyed (5:18–20). It is often hard for people to take this in, as many have been taught that the apostle Paul said that the Jewish Law was death. But Matthew is profoundly and insightfully devoted to Torah.

Jesus's adherence to this Law is portrayed as a deep spiritual devotion that is heartfelt and that can be redemptive for those who follow it. For Matthew's Jesus, subscribing to the Law means taking the true meaning of the Law into one's very person. In a very well-known series of challenges, Jesus says that the commandment not to murder really means one should not hate, the commandment not to commit adultery means not lusting in one's heart, and the commandment to love your neighbor needs to be understood as loving your enemies. In other words, the

Law or Torah is a call to deep, inner devotion to what is right in behavior, feelings, and attitude.

The Gospel of Matthew demonstrates its strong commitment to Judaism in many different ways. It tells the story of Jesus going through the water (of baptism), into the desert, and onto the mountain to give a sermon. This is an explicit participation in the people of Israel's exodus through the Red Sea, into the desert, and onto the mountain of Sinai to receive the Law. This gospel — in good Jewish fashion — has Jesus teaching about the realm of heaven rather than the realm of God (as in the other gospels and the writings of Paul) in order to minimize the explicit naming of God in vain. Matthew quotes the Hebrew Bible more than any other gospel.

In view of the many ways Christians have put down and done harm to Jewish people in the past 1,900 years, it is a treasure to have the New Testament include such an explicit endorsement and spiritually rich exploration of Judaism.

How to Live Together in a Jesus Community

How do we live together in a community with Jesus at its center? Of all the gospels, only Matthew shows Jesus teaching the process of those in community reconciling with one another. In these instances, a quarrel or conflict has erupted between people in the community. Jesus's response is not to say who is right and wrong in these disputes, such as "when presenting your gift at the altar, if even there you remember that your brother or sister has something against you" (5:23), or "If your brother or sister does wrong" (18:15). Rather, Jesus proposes a process of those in conflict solving the problem between themselves, or with the help of other community members.

Matthew has confidence in the followers of Jesus and their future. In contrast to the Gospel of Mark, in which they seem incapable of doing the right thing, in Matthew, Jesus praises the disciples and predicts a future for the Jesus community under their leadership: "At the new creation, 'when the Child of Humanity takes his seat on his throne of glory,' you who followed me will be seated on twelve thrones, as judges of the twelve tribes of Israel" (19:28). Similarly, only in Matthew does Jesus promise to give "the keys of the realm of heaven" to Peter (16:19). This gospel takes care, in ways that neither Mark nor John does, to tell Jesus's followers how to behave (how to pray and how to fast) in the coming time. Matthew's message eagerly describes the generation after Jesus as a time of community among his followers. The last words of Jesus in Matthew commission his followers to this future: "Go and make followers of all the nations, baptizing them" (28:19).

Matthew, then, is a special resource for communities and churches where there is conflict in times beyond the first century. Matthew's Jesus proves to be a companion, someone who can help those bumping heads or disputing right and wrong by encouraging building strong and clear processes for conflict resolution.

Recommended Reading

Warren Carter, *Matthew: Storyteller, Interpreter, Evangelist*
Warren Carter, *Matthew and Empire: Initial Explorations*
Craig Keener, *The Gospel of Matthew: A Socio-Rhetorical Commentary*

The Gospel of Matthew

The Birth, Parentage, and Infancy

1 [1] A genealogy of Jesus Christ, a descendant of David and Abraham. [2] Abraham was the father of Isaac, Isaac of Jacob, Jacob of Judah and his brothers, [3] Judah of Perez and Zerah, whose mother was Tamar, Perez of Hezron, Hezron of Ram, [4] Ram of Amminadab, Amminadab of Nashon, Nashon of Salmon, [5] Salmon of Boaz, whose mother was Rahab, Boaz of Obed, whose mother was Ruth, Obed of Jesse, [6] Jesse of David the King. David was the father of Solomon, whose mother was Uriah's widow, [7] Solomon of Rehoboam, Rehoboam of Abijah, Abijah of Asa, [8] Asa of Jehoshaphat, Jehoshaphat of Jehoram, Jehoram of Uzziah, [9] Uzziah of Jotham, Jotham of Ahaz, Ahaz of Hezekiah, [10] Hezekiah of Manasseh, Manasseh of Ammon, Ammon of Josiah, [11] Josiah of Jeconiah and his brothers, at the time of the Exile to Babylon. [12] After the Exile to Babylon — Jeconiah was the father of Shealtiel, Shealtiel of Zerubbabel, [13] Zerubbabel of Abiud, Abiud of Eliakim, Eliakim of Azor, [14] Azor of Zadok, Zadok of Achim, Achim of Eliud, [15] Eliud of Eleazar, Eleazar of Matthan, Matthan of Jacob, [16] Jacob of Joseph, the husband of Mary, who was the mother of Jesus, who is called "Christ." [17] So the whole number of generations from Abraham to David is fourteen; from David to the Exile to Babylon fourteen; and from the Exile to Babylon to the Christ fourteen.

[18] This is how Jesus Christ was born: His mother Mary was engaged to Joseph, but before the marriage took place, she found herself to be pregnant by the power of the holy Spirit. [19] Her husband, Joseph, was a just man and, since he did not want to disgrace her publicly, he resolved to put an end to their engagement privately. [20] He had been thinking this over, when an angel of the Lord appeared to him in a dream. "Joseph, son of David," the angel said, "do not be afraid to take Mary for your wife, for her child has been conceived by the power of the holy Spirit. [21] She will give birth to a son; his name will be Jesus, for he will save his people from their sins."

[22] All this happened in fulfillment of these words of the Lord in the prophet, where he says:

[23] "The young woman will conceive and
   will give birth to a son, and they will
   give him the name Immanuel"
— which means "God is with us."

[24] When Joseph woke up, he did as the angel of the Lord had directed him. [25] He made Mary his wife, but they did not sleep together until after the birth of her son; and he gave him the name Jesus.

2 [1] After the birth of Jesus at Bethlehem in Judea, in the reign of King Herod, some magi from the East arrived in Jerusalem, asking: [2] "Where is the newborn king of the Jews? For we saw his star in the east, and have come to worship him." [3] When King Herod heard of this, he was much troubled, and so, too, was all Jerusalem. [4] He called together all the chief priests and teachers of the Law in the nation, and questioned them as to where the Christ was to be born.

[5] "At Bethlehem in Judea," was their answer; "for it is said in the prophet:

'And you, Bethlehem in Judah's land,
   are in no way least among the chief
      cities of Judah;

for out of you will come a ruler —
who will shepherd my people Israel.'"

[7] Then Herod secretly sent for the magi, and found out from them the date of the appearance of the star; [8] and, sending them to Bethlehem, he said: "Go and make careful inquiries about the child, and, as soon as you have found him, bring me word so that I, too, can go and worship him." [9] The magi heard what the king had to say, and then continued their journey. The star which they had seen in the east led them on, until it reached and stood over the place where the child was. [10] At the sight of the star they were filled with great joy. [11] Entering the house, they saw the child with his mother, Mary, and fell at his feet and worshiped him. Then they opened their treasures and offered to the child presents of gold, frankincense, and myrrh. [12] But afterward, having been warned in a dream not to go back to Herod, they returned to their own country by another road.

[13] After they had left, an angel of the Lord appeared to Joseph in a dream, and said: "Get up, take the child and his mother, and flee to Egypt; and stay there until I tell you to return, for Herod is about to search for the child, to put him to death." [14] Joseph rose, and taking the child and his mother by night, went into Egypt, [15] and there he stayed until Herod's death; in fulfillment of these words of the Lord in the prophet, that say, "Out of Egypt I called my son."

[16] When Herod found out that the magi had tricked him, he flew into a rage. He sent and put to death all the boys in Bethlehem and the whole of that region, who were two years old or under, guided by the date which he had learned from the magi. [17] Then were fulfilled these words spoken in the prophet Jeremiah, that say:

[18] "A voice was heard in Ramah,
   weeping and mourning loudly;

Rachel, weeping for her children,
   refusing all comfort because they were
      dead."

[19] But on the death of Herod, an angel of the Lord appeared in a dream to Joseph in Egypt, and said: [20] "Get up, take the child and his mother, and go into the Land of Israel, for those who sought to take the child's life are dead." [21] Rising, he took the child and his mother, and went into the land of Israel. [22] But, hearing that Archelaus had succeeded his father Herod as king of Judea, he was afraid to go back there; and having been warned in a dream, he went into the part of the country called Galilee. [23] There he settled in the town of Nazareth, in fulfillment of these words in the prophets: "He will be called a Nazarene."

The Preparation

3 [1] About that time John the Baptizer first appeared, proclaiming in the wilderness of Judea: [2] "Repent, for the realm of heaven is at hand." [3] John was the one who was spoken of in the prophet Isaiah, where he says:

"The voice of one crying aloud in the
   wilderness:
'Make ready the way of the Lord,
make God's paths straight.'"

[4] John's clothes were made of camels' hair, with a leather strap round his waist, and his food was locusts and wild honey. [5] At that time Jerusalem, and all Judea, as well as the whole district of the Jordan, went out to him [6] and were baptized by him in the river Jordan, confessing their sins.

[7] But when John saw many of the Pharisees and Sadducees coming to receive his baptism, he said to them: "You children of snakes! Who has prompted you to seek refuge from the coming anger? [8] Bear fruits, then, that prove your repentance;

⁹ and do not think that you can say among yourselves, 'We have Abraham as our father,' for I tell you that out of these stones God is able to raise descendants for Abraham! ¹⁰ Already the ax is lying at the root of the trees. Therefore every tree that fails to bear good fruit will be cut down and thrown into the fire. ¹¹ I, indeed, bathe you with water of repentance; but the one coming after me is more powerful than I, and I am not fit even to carry his sandals. He will bathe you with the holy Spirit and with fire. ¹² His winnowing fan is in his hand, and he will clear his threshing floor, and store his grain in the barn, but the chaff he will burn with a fire that cannot be put out."

¹³ Then Jesus came from Galilee to the Jordan, to John, to be baptized by him. ¹⁴ But John tried to prevent him.

"I need to be baptized by you," he said, "so why have you come to me?"

¹⁵ "Drop this for now," Jesus answered; "this way makes it right." So John agreed.

¹⁶ After the baptism of Jesus, and just as he came up from the water, the skies opened, and he saw the Spirit of God descending, like a dove, and alighting on him, ¹⁷ and from the heavens there came a voice which said: "This is my dearly loved son, in whom I delight."

4 ¹ Then Jesus was led up into the wilderness by the Spirit to be tempted by the devil. ² And, after he had fasted for forty days and forty nights, he became hungry. ³ The Tempter came to him, and said: "If you are God's Child, tell these stones to become loaves of bread."

⁴ But Jesus answered: "It is written:

'It is not on bread alone that a person is
   to live, but on every word that comes
   from the mouth of God.'"

⁵ Then the devil took him to the holy city, and, placing him on the parapet of the Temple, said to him: ⁶ "If you are God's Child, throw yourself down, for it is written:

'He will give his angels commands
   about you,
and on their hands they will lift you up,
so you do not even strike your foot
   against a stone.'"

⁷ "It is also written," answered Jesus, 'You must not tempt the Lord your God.'"

⁸ The third time, the devil took Jesus to a very high mountain, and, showing him all the kingdoms of the world and their splendor, said to him: ⁹ "All these I will give you, if you will fall at my feet and worship me."

¹⁰ Then Jesus said to him: "Go away, Satan! For it is written, 'You must worship the Lord your God, and serve God only.'"

¹¹ Then the devil left him alone, and angels came and served him.

The Work in Galilee

¹² When Jesus heard that John had been committed to prison, he returned to Galilee. ¹³ Afterward, leaving Nazareth, he went and settled at Capernaum, which is by the side of the sea, within the borders of Zebulun and Naphtali, ¹⁴ in fulfillment of these words in the prophet Isaiah:

¹⁵ "The land of Zebulun and the land of
   Naphtali,
the land of the road by the sea, and
   beyond the Jordan,
with Galilee of the gentiles —

¹⁶ The people who were living in darkness
   have seen a great light,
and, for those who were living in the
   shadow-land of death,
a light has dawned!"

¹⁷ At that time Jesus began to proclaim, "Repent, for the realm of heaven is at hand."

¹⁸ As Jesus was walking along the shore of the Sea of Galilee, he saw two brothers — Simon, also known as Peter, and his brother Andrew — casting a net into the sea; for they were fishermen. ¹⁹ "Come and follow me," Jesus said, "and I will teach you to fish for people." ²⁰ The two men left their nets at once and followed him. ²¹ Going further on, he saw two other men who were also brothers, James, Zebedee's son, and his brother John, in their boat with their father, mending their nets. Jesus called them, ²² and they at once left their boat and their father, and followed him.

²³ Jesus went all through Galilee, teaching in their synagogues, proclaiming the good news of the realm, and curing every kind of disease and every kind of sickness among the people; ²⁴ and his reputation spread all through Syria. They brought to him all who were ill with any form of disease, or who were suffering pain — any who were either possessed by demons, or were epileptic, or paralyzed; and he cured them. ²⁵ He was followed by large crowds from Galilee, the district of the Ten Cities, Jerusalem, Judea, and from beyond the Jordan.

5 ¹ On seeing the crowds of people, Jesus went up the mountain; and, when he had taken his seat, his disciples came up to him; ² and he began to teach them, saying,

"Blessed are the poor in spirit,
for theirs is the realm of heaven.
Blessed are the mourners,
for they will be comforted.
Blessed are the gentle,
for they will inherit the earth.
Blessed are those who hunger and
    thirst for justice,
for they will be satisfied.
Blessed are the merciful,
for they will find mercy.
Blessed are the pure in heart,
for they will see God.

Blessed are the peacemakers,
for they will be called children of God.
¹⁰ Blessed are those who have been
    persecuted in the cause of
    righteousness,
for theirs is the realm of heaven.

¹¹ "Blessed are you when people insult you, and persecute you, and say all kinds of evil lies about you because of me. ¹² Be glad and rejoice, because your reward in heaven will be great; this is the way they persecuted the prophets who lived before you.

¹³ "You are salt for the world. But if salt becomes tasteless, how can it be made salty again? It is no longer good for anything, but is thrown away, and trampled underfoot by people. ¹⁴ It is you who are the light of the world. A town that stands on a hill cannot be hidden. ¹⁵ People do not light a lamp and put it under a basket, but on the lamp stand, where it gives light to everyone in the house. ¹⁶ Let your light so shine before people so that, seeing your good actions, they will praise your Father who is in heaven.

¹⁷ "Do not think that I have come to do away with the Law or the prophets; I have not come to do away with them, but to make them full. ¹⁸ For I tell you for sure, until the heavens and the earth disappear, not even the smallest letter, nor one stroke of a letter, will disappear from the Law until all is done. ¹⁹ Whoever, therefore, breaks one of these commandments, even the least of them, and teaches others to do so, will be called the least in the realm of heaven; but whoever keeps them, and teaches others to do so, will be called great in the realm of heaven. ²⁰ Indeed I tell you that, unless your righteousness exceeds that of the scholars, and Pharisees, you will never enter the realm of heaven.

²¹ "You have heard that to our ancestors it was said, 'You must not commit murder,' and 'Whoever commits murder will be brought to trial.' ²² But I say to you that

anyone who is angry at brother or sister will be brought to trial; and whoever insults brother or sister will be brought before the highest court, while whoever calls them a fool will be in danger of the fires of Gehenna. ²³ Therefore, when presenting your gift at the altar, if even there you remember that your brother or sister has something against you, ²⁴ leave your gift there, before the altar, go and be reconciled to this person first, then come and present your gift. ²⁵ Be ready to make friends quickly with your opponent, even when you meet him on your way to the court; otherwise he might hand you over to the judge, and the judge to the judicial officer, and you will be thrown into prison. ²⁶ I tell you, you will not come out until you have paid the last cent.

²⁷ "You have heard that it was said, 'You must not commit adultery.' ²⁸ But I say to you that anyone who looks at a woman and desires her has already committed adultery with her in his heart. ²⁹ If your right eye causes you to sin, take it out and throw it away. It would be best for you to lose one part of your body, and not to have the whole of it thrown into Gehenna. ³⁰ And, if your right hand causes you to sin, cut it off and throw it away. It would be best for you to lose one part of your body, and not to have the whole of it go down to Gehenna.

³¹ "It was also said, 'Let anyone who divorces his wife serve her with a notice of separation.' ³² But I say to you that anyone who divorces his wife, except on the ground of some serious sexual sin, makes her commit adultery; while anyone who marries her after her divorce is guilty of adultery. ³³ Again, you have heard that our ancestors were told, 'Do not break your oaths; keep your vows to the Lord.' ³⁴ But I say to you that you must not swear at all, either by heaven, since that is God's throne, ³⁵ or by the earth, since that is his footstool, or by Jerusalem, since that is the city of the great king. ³⁶ Nor should

you swear by your head, since you cannot make a single hair either white or black. ³⁷ Let your words be simply 'Yes' or 'No'; anything beyond this comes from what is evil.

³⁸ "You have heard that it was said, 'An eye for an eye and a tooth for a tooth.' ³⁹ But I say to you that you must not resist those who wrong you; but if anyone strikes you on the right cheek, turn the other to him also. ⁴⁰ If someone sues you for your shirt, let him have your cloak as well. ⁴¹ If you are forced to carry a pack for one mile, carry it two. ⁴² Give to anyone who asks and, if someone wants to borrow from you, do not turn him away.

⁴³ "You have heard that it was said, 'You must love your neighbor and hate your enemy.' ⁴⁴ But what I tell you is this: Love your enemies, and pray for those who persecute you, ⁴⁵ so that you may become children of your Father who is in heaven; for God causes the sun to rise on bad and good alike, and sends rain on the just and on the unjust. ⁴⁶ For, if you love only those who love you, what reward will you have? Even the tax collectors do this! ⁴⁷ And, if you only welcome your brothers and sisters, what are you doing more than others? Even the gentiles do this! ⁴⁸ You, then, must become complete — as your heavenly Father is complete.

6 ¹ "Take care not to perform your obligation to be fair in public in order to be seen by others; if you do, your Father who is in heaven has no reward for you. ² Therefore, when you do acts of mercy, do not have a trumpet blown in front of you, as hypocrites do in the synagogues and in the streets so that people will praise them. There, I tell you, is their reward! ³ But when you do acts of mercy, do not let your left hand know what your right hand is doing, ⁴ so that your mercy may be secret; and your Father, who sees what is in secret, will reward you.

⁵ "And, when you pray, you are not

to behave as hypocrites do. They like to pray standing in the synagogues and at the corners of the streets, so that people will see them. There, I tell you, is their reward! ⁶ But when one of you prays, let her go into her own room, shut the door, and pray to her Father who dwells in secret; and her Father, who sees what is secret, will reward her. ⁷ When praying, do not repeat the same words over and over again, as is done by the gentiles, who think that by using many words they will obtain a hearing. ⁸ Do not imitate them; for God, your Father, knows what you need before you ask him. ⁹ You, therefore, should pray like this:

Our Father, who is in heaven,
    may your name be held holy,
¹⁰ your kingdom come, your will be
        done —
    on earth, as in heaven.
¹¹ Give us today
    the bread that we will need;
¹² and forgive us our debts,
    as we have forgiven those to whom we
        are indebted;
¹³ and do not put us to the test,
    but deliver us from the evil one.

¹⁴ "For, if you forgive others their offenses, your heavenly Father will forgive you also; ¹⁵ but if you do not forgive others their offenses, not even your Father will forgive your offenses.

¹⁶ "And, when you fast, do not put on gloomy looks, as hypocrites do who disfigure their faces so that they may be seen by people to be fasting. That, I tell you, is their reward! ¹⁷ But when one of you fasts, let him scent his head and wash his face, ¹⁸ so that he may not be seen by people to be fasting, but by his Father who dwells in secret; and your Father, who sees what is secret, will reward you.

¹⁹ "Do not store up treasures for yourselves on earth, where moth and rust destroy, and where thieves break in and steal.

²⁰ But store up treasures for yourselves in heaven, where neither moth nor rust destroys, and where thieves do not break in or steal. ²¹ For where your treasure is, there will your heart be also. ²² The lamp of the body is the eye. If your eye is unclouded, your whole body will be lit up; ²³ but if your eye is diseased, your whole body will be darkened. And, if the light inside you is darkness, how intense must that darkness be! ²⁴ No one can serve two masters, for either she will hate one and love the other, or else will attach herself to one and despise the other. You cannot serve both God and money.

²⁵ "This is why I say to you: Do not be anxious about your life — what you can get to eat or drink, or about your body — what you can get to wear. Is not life more than food, and the body more than clothing? ²⁶ Look at the wild birds — they neither sow, nor reap, nor gather into barns; and yet your heavenly Father feeds them! Are you not more valuable than they? ²⁷ But which of you, by being anxious, can prolong your life a single moment? ²⁸ And why be anxious about clothing? Study the wild lilies and how they grow. They neither work nor spin; ²⁹ yet I tell you that even Solomon in all his splendor was not robed like one of these. ³⁰ If God so clothes even the grass of the field, which is living today and tomorrow will be thrown into the oven, will God not much more clothe you, you of little trust? ³¹ Do not then ask anxiously, 'What can we get to eat?' or 'What can we get to drink?' or 'What can we get to wear?' ³² All these are the things for which the nations are seeking, and your heavenly Father knows that you need them all. ³³ But first seek God's realm and God's justice, and all these things will be added for you. ³⁵ Therefore do not be anxious about tomorrow, for tomorrow will bring its own anxieties. Every day has trouble enough of its own.

7 ¹ "Do not judge and you will not be

judged. [2] For, just as you judge others, you will yourselves be judged, and the standard that you use will be used for you. [3] Why do you look at the speck of sawdust in your friend's eye, while you pay no attention at all to the plank of wood in yours? [4] How will you say to your friend, 'Let me take out the speck from your eye,' when all the time there is a plank in your own? [5] Hypocrite! Take out the plank from your own eye first, and then you will see clearly how to take out the speck from your friend's.

[6] "Do not give what is sacred to dogs. Do not throw your pearls before pigs; they will trample them underfoot and turn to attack you. [7] Ask, and it will be given to you; search, and you will find; knock, and the door will be opened to you. [8] For the person who asks receives, the person who searches finds, and the door will be opened to the person who knocks. [9] Who among you, when her child asks her for bread, will give the child a stone, [10] or when the child asks for a fish, will give a snake? [11] If you, then, wicked though you are, know how to give good gifts to your children, how much more will your Father in heaven give what is good to those who ask him!

[12] "Do to others whatever you would wish them to do to you; for that is the teaching of both the Law and the prophets. [13] Go in by the small gate. Broad and spacious is the road that leads to destruction, and those who go in by it are many; [14] for small is the gate, and narrow the road, which leads to life, and those who find it are few.

[15] "Beware of false prophets — people who come to you in the guise of sheep, but inside they are ravenous wolves. [16] By the fruit of their lives you will know them. Do people pick grapes from thornbushes, or figs from thistles? [17] So, too, every sound tree bears good fruit, while a worthless tree bears bad fruit. [18] A sound tree cannot produce bad fruit, nor can a worthless tree bear good fruit. [19] Every tree that fails to bear good fruit is cut down and thrown into the fire. [20] So it is by the fruit of their lives that you will know such people. [21] Not everyone who says to me, 'Master! Master!' will enter the realm of heaven, but only the person who does the will of my Father in heaven. [22] On that day many will say to me, 'Master, Master, was it not in your name that we prophesied, and in your name that we drove out demons, and in your name that we did many powerful deeds?' [23] And then I will say to them plainly, 'I never knew you. Go from my presence, you who live without the Law.'

[24] "Everyone, therefore, who listens to this teaching of mine and acts on it may be compared to a prudent person, who built his house on the rock. [25] The rain poured down, the rivers rose, the winds blew and beat on that house, but it did not fall, for its foundations were on rock. [26] Everyone who listens to this teaching of mine and does not act on it may be compared to a foolish person, who built his house on sand. [27] The rain poured down, the rivers rose, the winds blew and struck against that house, and it fell; and great was its downfall."

[28] By the time that Jesus had finished speaking, the crowd was filled with amazement at his teaching. [29] For he taught them like one who had authority, and not like their scholars.

8 [1] When he had come down from the hill, great crowds followed him. [2] He saw a person with a bad skin disease who came up, and bowed to the ground before him, and said: "Master, if only you are willing, you are able to make me clean." [3] Stretching out his hand, Jesus touched him, saying as he did so: "I am willing; become clean." Instantly he was made clean from his skin disease; [4] and then Jesus said to him: "Be careful not to say a word to anyone, but go and show yourself to the priest, and offer the gift directed by Moses, as evidence of your cure." [5] After he had entered Capernaum, a captain in the Roman army came up to him, entreating his help. [6] "Sir," he said, "my servant is lying ill at my house with a stroke of paralysis, and is suffering terribly."

[7] "I will come and heal him," answered Jesus. [8] "Sir," the captain went on, "I am unworthy to receive you under my roof; but only speak, and my servant will be cured. [9] For I myself am a man under the orders of others, with soldiers under me; and, if I say to one of them 'Go,' he goes, and to another 'Come,' he comes, and to my slave 'Do this,' he does it." [10] Jesus was surprised to hear this, and said to those who were following him: "Never, I tell you, in anyone in Israel have I met with such faith as this! [11] Yes, and many will come in from east and west and recline at the feast beside Abraham, Isaac, and Jacob, in the realm of heaven; [12] while the heirs to the realm will be banished into the darkness outside; there, there will be weeping and grinding of teeth." [13] Then Jesus said to the captain: "Go now, and it will be according to your faith." And the man was cured that very hour.

[14] When Jesus went into Peter's house, he saw Peter's mother-in-law prostrated with fever. [15] On his taking her hand, the fever left her, and she rose and began to take care of him. [16] In the evening the people brought to Jesus many who were possessed by demons; and he drove out the spirits with a word, and cured all who were ill, [17] in fulfillment of these words in the prophet Isaiah: "He took our illnesses on himself, and bore the burden of our diseases."

[18] Seeing a crowd around him, Jesus gave orders to go across. [19] A scholar came up to him, and said: "Teacher, I will follow you wherever you go."

[20] "Foxes have holes," answered Jesus, "and wild birds their nests, but the Child of Humanity has nowhere to lay his head." [21] "Master," said another, who was one of his followers, "let me first go and bury my father." [22] But Jesus answered: "Follow me, and leave the dead to bury their own dead." [23] Then he got into the boat, and his followers came along. [24] Suddenly so great a storm came up on the sea, that the waves broke right over the boat. But he was asleep; [25] and his followers came and roused him. "Master," they cried, "save us; we are lost!"

[26] "Why are you so timid?" he said. "You of little confidence!" Then he rose and rebuked the winds and the sea, and a great calm followed. [27] They were amazed, and exclaimed: "What kind of person is this, that even the winds and the sea obey him!"

[28] On getting to the other side — the country of the Gadarenes — he met two men who were possessed by demons, coming out of the tombs. They were so violent that no one was able to pass that way. [29] Suddenly they shrieked out: "What do you want with us, Child of God? Have you come here to torment us before our time?" [30] A long way off, there was a herd of many pigs, feeding; [31] and the demoniac spirits begged Jesus: "If you drive us out, send us into the herd of pigs."

[32] "Go," he said. The spirits came out, and entered the pigs; and the whole drove rushed down the steep slope into the sea, and died in the water. [33] At this the men who tended them ran away and went to the town, carrying the news of all that had occurred, and of what had happened to the possessed men. [34] At the news the whole town went out to meet Jesus, and, when they saw him, they entreated him to go away from their community.

9 [1] Afterward Jesus got into a boat, and, crossing over, came to his own town. [2] There some people brought to him a paralyzed man on a bed. When Jesus saw their confidence, he said to the man: "Courage, child! Your sins are forgiven." [3] Then some of the scholars said to themselves: "This man is blaspheming!" [4] Knowing their thoughts, Jesus said: "Why do you harbor such wicked thoughts? [5] Which is the easier — to say, 'Your sins are forgiven'? Or to say, 'Get up, and walk'? [6] But to show you that the Child of Humanity has power on earth to forgive sins" — then he said to the paralyzed man, "Get up, take up your bed, and return to your home." [7] The man got up and went to his home. [8] When the crowd saw this, they were awestruck, and praised God for giving such power to human beings.

[9] As Jesus went along, he saw a man, called Matthew, sitting in the tax office, and said to him: "Follow me." Matthew got up and followed him.

[10] And, later on, when he was having dinner in the house, a number of tax collectors and outcasts came in and reclined at dinner with Jesus and his followers. [11] When the Pharisees saw this, they said to his followers: "Why does your teacher eat in the company of tax collectors and outcasts?" [12] On hearing this, he said: "It is not those who are healthy who need a doctor, but those who are ill. [13] Go and learn what this means — 'I desire compassion, and not sacrifice'; for I did not come to call the well behaved, but the outcast." [14] Then John's followers came to him, and asked: "Why do we and the Pharisees fast while your followers do not?" [15] Jesus answered: "Can the groom's friends mourn as long as the groom is with them? But the days will come when the groom will be taken away from them, and they will fast then. [16] Nobody ever puts a piece of unshrunk cloth on an old garment; for such a patch tears away from the garment, and a worse tear is made. [17] Nor do people put new wine into old wineskins; for, if they do, the skins burst, and the wine runs out, and the skins are lost; but they put new wine into fresh skins, and so both are preserved."

[18] While Jesus was saying this, a president of a synagogue came up and bowed to the ground before him. "My daughter," he said, "has just died; but come and place your hand on her, and she will be restored to life." [19] So Jesus rose and followed him, and his followers went also. [20] But meanwhile a woman who had been suffering from a flow of blood for twelve years came up behind and touched the fringe of his cloak. [21] "If I only touch his clothes," she said to herself, "I will get well." [22] Turning and seeing her, Jesus said: "Courage, daughter! Your faith has delivered you." And at that very moment she became well. [23] When Jesus reached the president's house, seeing the flute players, and a number of people all in confusion, [24] he said: "Go away, the little girl is not dead; she is asleep." They began to laugh at him; [25] but when the people had been sent out, Jesus went in, and took the little girl's hand, and she rose. [26] The report of this spread through all that part of the country.

[27] As Jesus was passing on from there, he was followed by two blind men, who kept calling out: "Take pity on us, son of David!" [28] When he had gone indoors, the blind men came up to him; and Jesus asked them: "Do you believe that I am able to do this?" "Yes, Master!" they answered. [29] Then he touched their eyes, and said: "It will be according to your trust." [30] Then their eyes were opened. Jesus sternly cautioned them. "See that no one knows of it," he said. [31] But the men went out, and spread the news about him through all that part of the country. [32] Just as they were going out, some people brought up to Jesus a dumb man who was possessed by a demon; [33] and, as soon as the demon had been driven out, the dumb man spoke. The people were astonished at this, and exclaimed: "Nothing like this has ever been seen in Israel!" [34] But the Pharisees said: "He drives out the demons by the help of the chief of the demons."

[35] Jesus went around all the towns and the villages, teaching in their synagogues, proclaiming the good news of the realm, and curing every kind of disease and every kind of sickness. [36] But when he saw the crowds, his heart was moved with compassion for them, because they were distressed and harassed, "like sheep without a shepherd"; [37] and he said to his follow-

ers: "The harvest is abundant, but the laborers are few. [38] Therefore ask the owner of the harvest to send laborers to gather in the harvest."

10 [1] Calling twelve of his followers to him, he gave them authority over unclean spirits, so that they could drive them out, as well as the power of healing all kinds of disease and sickness. [2] The names of these twelve ambassadors are: first Simon, also known as Peter, and his brother Andrew; James the son of Zebedee, and his brother John; [3] Philip and Bartholomew; Thomas and Matthew the tax gatherer; James the son of Alphaeus, and Thaddaeus; [4] Simon the Zealot, and Judas Iscariot, who betrayed him.

[5] These twelve Jesus sent out as his messengers, after giving them these instructions: "Do not go to the gentiles, nor enter any Samaritan town, [6] but make your way rather to the lost sheep of the house of Israel. [7] On your way proclaim that the realm of heaven is at hand. [8] Heal the sick, raise the dead, make those with bad skin disease clean, drive out demons. You have received free of cost, give free of cost. [9] Do not provide yourselves with gold, or silver, or coins in your purses; [10] not even with a bag for the journey, or a change of clothes, or sandals, or even a staff; for the worker is worth his food. [11] Whatever town or village you visit, find out who is worthy in that place, and remain there until you leave. [12] As you enter the house, greet it. [13] Then, if the house is worthy, let your blessing rest on it, but if it is unworthy, let your blessing return on yourselves. [14] If no one welcomes you, or listens to what you say, as you leave that house or that town, shake off its dust from your feet. [15] I tell you, the doom of the land of Sodom and Gomorrah will be more bearable in the 'day of judgment' than the doom of that town.

[16] "Remember, I am sending you out as my messengers like sheep among wolves. So be as wise as snakes, and as blameless as doves. [17] Be on your guard against others, for they will betray you to courts of law, and scourge you in their synagogues; [18] and you will be brought before governors and kings for my sake so that you may witness before them and the nations. [19] Whenever they hand you over, do not be anxious as to how you will speak or what you will say, for what you will say will be given you at the moment; [20] for it will not be you who speak, but the breath of your Father that speaks within you. [21] Brother will betray brother to death, and the father his child; and children will turn against their parents, and cause them to be put to death; [22] and you will be hated by everyone because of me. Yet the person who endures to the end will be saved. [23] But when they persecute you in one town, escape to the next; for, I tell you, you will not have come to the end of the towns of Israel before the Child of Humanity comes. [24] A student is not above his teacher, nor a slave above his master. [25] It is enough for a student to become treated like his teacher, and a slave like his master. If the head of the house has been called Beelzebul, how much more the members of his household! [26] Do not, therefore, be afraid of them. There is nothing concealed which will not be revealed, nor anything hidden which will not become known. [27] What I tell you in the dark, say again in the light; and what is whispered in your ear, proclaim on the housetops. [28] Do not be afraid of those who kill the body, but are unable to kill the soul; rather be afraid of the one who is able to destroy both soul and body in Gehenna. [29] Are not two sparrows sold for one copper coin? Yet not one of them will fall to the ground without your Father's knowledge. [30] While as for you, even the hairs of your head are numbered. [31] Do not, therefore, be afraid; you are of more value than many sparrows. [32] Everyone, therefore, who will publicly acknowledge me, I, too, will acknowledge before my Father in heaven; [33] but if anyone publicly disowns

me, I, too, will disown him before my Father in heaven.

34 "Do not imagine that I have come to bring peace to the earth. I have come to bring, not peace, but sword. 35 For I have come to set 'son against father, and daughter against mother, and daughter-in-law against mother-in-law. 36 A person's enemies will be the members of her own household.' 37 Anyone who loves father or mother more than me is not worthy of me; and anyone who loves son or daughter more than me is not worthy of me. 38 Anyone who does not take his cross and follow in my steps is not worthy of me. 39 The person who has found her life will lose it, while the person who, for my sake, has lost her life will find it.

40 "Anyone who welcomes you is welcoming me; and anyone who welcomes me is welcoming the one who sent me. 41 The person who welcomes a prophet, because he is a prophet, will receive a prophet's reward; and anyone who welcomes a good person, because she is a good person, will receive a good person's reward. 42 And, if anyone gives so much as a cup of cold water to one of these little ones because she is my follower, I tell you that she will assuredly not lose her reward."

11 1 After Jesus had finished giving directions to these twelve followers, he left that place in order to teach and proclaim in their towns.

2 Now John had heard in prison what the Christ was doing, and he sent a message by his followers, 3 and asked, "Are you the one to come, or are we to look for someone else?" 4 The answer of Jesus was: "Go and report to John what you hear and see — 5 the blind recover their sight and the lame walk, those with severe skin disease are made clean and the deaf hear, the dead, too, are raised to life, and the good news is told to the poor. 6 Blessed is the person who finds no hindrance in me."

7 While they were returning, Jesus began to say to the crowds with reference to John: 8 "What did you go out into the wilderness to look at? A reed waving in the wind? If not, what did you go out to see? A man richly dressed? Why, those who wear rich things are to be found in the courts of kings! 9 What, then, did you go for? To see a prophet? Yes, I tell you, and far more than a prophet. 10 This is the one about whom it is written, 'I am sending my messenger ahead of you to prepare your way before you.' 11 I tell you, no one born of a woman has yet appeared who is greater than John the Baptizer; and yet the least in the realm of heaven is greater than he. 12 From the time of John the Baptizer to this very hour, the realm of heaven has been taken by force, and people using force have been seizing it. 13 For the teaching of all the prophets and of the Law continued until the time of John; 14 and — if you are ready to accept it — John is himself the Elijah who was destined to come. 15 Let the one who has ears hear. 16 But to what will I compare the present generation? It is like little children sitting in the marketplaces and calling out to their playmates, 17 'We have played the flute for you, but you have not danced; we have wailed, but you have not mourned.' 18 For, when John came, neither eating nor drinking, people said, 'He has a demon in him'; 19 and now that the Child of Humanity has come, eating and drinking, they are saying, 'Here is a glutton and a wine drinker, a friend of tax collectors and outcasts!' And yet Wisdom-Sophia* is vindicated by her actions."

---

* This name is hyphenated to cover two core meanings of the passage. The name Wisdom is used because that is the standard English translation. The name Sophia is used because that is the Greek word used for wisdom, because it connotes the name of a person, and since this text thinks of Wisdom as a person.

[20] Then Jesus began to reproach the towns in which most of his miracles had been done, because they had not repented: [21] "Alas for you, Chorazin! Alas for you, Bethsaida! For, if the miracles which were done in you had been done in Tyre and Sidon, they would have repented long ago in sackcloth and ashes. [22] Yet, I tell you, the doom of Tyre and Sidon will be more bearable in the day of judgment than yours. [23] And you, Capernaum! Will you 'exalt yourself to heaven'? 'You will go down to the place of death.' For, if the miracles which have been done in you had been done in Sodom, it would have been standing to this day. [24] Yet, I tell you, the doom of Sodom will be more bearable in the day of judgment than yours." [25] At that same time Jesus uttered the words: "I thank you, Father, Lord of heaven and earth, that, though you have hidden these things from the wise and learned, you have revealed them to the young ones! [26] Yes, Father, I thank you that this has seemed good to you. [27] Everything has been committed to me by my Father; nor does anyone fully know the Son, except the Father, or know the Father, except the Son and those to whom the Son may choose to reveal him. [28] Come to me, all you who work and are burdened, and I will give you rest! [29] Take my yoke on you, and learn from me, for I am gentle and humble, and you will find rest for your souls; [30] for my yoke is easy, and my burden is light."

12 [1] About the same time Jesus walked through the cornfields one sabbath. His followers were hungry, and began to pick some ears and eat them. [2] But when the Pharisees saw this, they said: "Look! Your followers are doing what it is not allowable to do on a sabbath!"

[3] "Have you not read," replied Jesus, "what David did, when he and his companions were hungry — [4] how he went into the house of God, and how they ate the consecrated bread, though it was not allowable for him or his companions to eat it, but only for the priests? [5] And have you not read in the Law that, on the sabbath, the priests in the Temple break the sabbath and yet are not guilty? [6] Here, however, I tell you, there is something greater than the Temple! [7] Had you learned the meaning of the words 'I desire compassion, and not sacrifice,' you would not have condemned those who are not guilty. [8] For the Child of Humanity is master of the sabbath."

[9] Passing on, he went into their synagogue, [10] and there he saw a man with a withered hand. Some people asked him whether it was allowable to heal on the sabbath — so that they might have a charge to bring against him. [11] But he said to them: "Which of you, if he had only one sheep, and that sheep fell into a pit on the sabbath, would not lay hold of it and pull it out? [12] How much more precious a person is than a sheep! Therefore it is allowable to do good on the sabbath." [13] Then he said to the man, "Stretch out your hand." He stretched it out; and it had become as sound as the other. [14] On coming out, the Pharisees plotted against him, to destroy him.

[15] Jesus, however, became aware of it, and went away from that place. A number of people followed him, and he healed them all; [16] but he warned them not to make him known, [17] in fulfillment of these words in the prophet Isaiah: [18] "Here is my chosen servant, whom I love and who pleases me! I will breathe my spirit on him, and he will announce a time of judgment to the nations. [19] He will not contend, nor cry aloud, neither will anyone hear his voice in the streets; [20] a bruised reed he will not break, and a smoldering wick he will not quench, until he has brought the judgment to a victorious result, [21] and on his name will the nations rest their hopes."

[22] Then some people brought to Jesus a possessed man, who was blind and dumb;

and he healed him, so that the man who had been dumb both talked and saw. [23] At this all the people were astounded. "Is it possible that this is the son of David?" they exclaimed. [24] But the Pharisees heard of it and said: "He drives out demons only by the help of Beelzebul, the chief of the demons." [25] He, however, was aware of what was passing in their minds, and said to them: "Any realm divided against itself becomes a desolation, and any town or household divided against itself will not last. [26] So, if Satan drives Satan out, he must be divided against himself; and how, then, can his realm last? [27] And, if it is by Beelzebul's help that I drive out demons, by whose help is it that your own sons drive them out? Therefore they will themselves be your judges. [28] But if it is by the spirit of God that I drive out demons, then the realm of God must already be upon you. [29] How, again, can anyone get into a strong man's house and carry off his goods, without first securing him? Not until then will he plunder his house. [30] Anyone who is not with me is against me, and the person who does not help me to gather is scattering. [31] Therefore, I tell you, people will be forgiven every sin and slander; but slander against the holy Spirit will not be forgiven. [32] Whoever speaks against the Child of Humanity will be forgiven, but whoever speaks against the holy Spirit will not be forgiven, either in the present age, or in the age to come.

[33] "You must assume either that both tree and fruit are good, or that both tree and fruit are worthless; since it is by its fruits that a tree is known. [34] You children of snakes! How can you, evil as you are, say anything good? For what fills the heart will rise to the lips. [35] A good person, from her good stores, produces good things; while a bad person, from her bad supplies, produces bad things. [36] I tell you that for every careless thing that people say, they must answer on the day of judgment. [37] For it is by your words that you

will be acquitted, and by your words that you will be condemned."

[38] At this point, some scholars and Pharisees spoke up. "Teacher," they said, "we want to see some sign from you."

[39] "It is a wicked and unfaithful generation," he answered, "that is asking for a sign, and no sign will be given it except the sign of the prophet Jonah. [40] For, just as Jonah was inside the sea monster three days and three nights, so will the Child of Humanity be three days and three nights in the heart of the earth. [41] At the judgment, the people of Nineveh will stand up with this generation, and will condemn it, because they repented at Jonah's proclamation; and here is more than a Jonah! [42] At the judgment the Queen of the South will rise up with the present generation, and will condemn it, because she came from the ends of the earth to listen to the wisdom of Solomon; and here is more than a Solomon! [43] No sooner does an unclean spirit leave a person, than it passes through places where there is no water, in search of rest, and does not find it. [44] Then it says, 'I will go back to the home which I left'; but on coming there, it finds it unoccupied, and swept, and put in order. [45] Then it goes and brings with it seven other spirits more wicked than itself, and they go in, and make their home there; and the last state of that person proves to be worse than the first. So, too, will it be with this wicked generation."

[46] While he was still speaking to the crowds, his mother and brothers were standing outside, asking to speak to him. [47] Someone told him this, and Jesus replied: [48] "Who is my mother? And who are my brothers?" [49] Then, stretching out his hands toward his followers, he said: "Here are my mother and my brothers! [50] For anyone who does the will of my Father in heaven is my brother and sister and mother."

13 [1] That same day, when Jesus had left

the house and was sitting by the sea, [2] such great crowds gathered around him, that he got into a boat, and sat in it, while all the people stood on the beach. [3] Then he told them much in parables. "A sower," he began, "went out to sow; and, [4] as he was sowing, some seed fell along the path, and the birds came and ate it up. [5] Some fell on rocky places, where it had not much soil, and, having no depth of soil, sprang up at once. [6] As soon as the sun had risen, it was scorched, and, having no root, withered away. [7] Some, again, fell into the brambles; but the brambles shot up and choked it. [8] Some, however, fell on good soil, and yielded a return, sometimes one hundred-, sometimes sixty-, sometimes thirtyfold. [9] Let those who have ears hear."

[10] Afterward his followers came to him, and said: "Why do you speak to them in parables?"

[11] "To you," answered Jesus, "the knowledge of the secrets of the realm of heaven has been imparted, but not to those. [12] For, to all who have, more will be given, and they will have abundance; but from all who have nothing, even what they have will be taken away. [13] That is why I speak to them in parables, because, though they have eyes, they do not see, and though they have ears, they do not hear or understand. [14] In them is being fulfilled that prophecy of Isaiah which says:

'You will hear with your ears without
    ever understanding,
and, though you have eyes, you will see
    without ever perceiving,
[15] for the heart of this people has grown
    dense,
and their ears are dull of hearing,
their eyes also have they closed;
Otherwise some day they might
    perceive with their eyes,
and with their ears they might hear,
and in their heart they might
    understand,

and might turn —
and they might be healed.'

[16] "But blessed are your eyes, for they see, and your ears, for they hear; [17] for I tell you that many prophets and good people have longed for the sight of the things which you are seeing, yet never saw them, and to hear the things which you are hearing, yet never heard them.

[18] "Listen, then, yourselves to the parable of the sower. [19] When anyone hears the message of the realm without understanding it, the evil one comes and snatches away what has been sown in their heart. This is the seed which was sown along the path. [20] By the seed which was sown on rocky places is meant the person who hears the message, and at once accepts it joyfully; [21] but, as he has no root, he stands for only a short time; and, when trouble or persecution arises because of the message, he falls away at once. [22] By the seed which was sown among the brambles is meant the person who hears the message, but the cares of the time and the glamour of wealth choke the message, so that it gives no return. [23] But by the seed which was sown on the good ground is meant the person who hears the message and understands it, and really yields a return, sometimes one hundred-, sometimes sixty-, sometimes thirtyfold."

[24] Another parable which Jesus told them was this: "The realm of heaven is compared to a person who sowed good seed in his field. [25] But while everyone was asleep, his enemy came and sowed weeds among the wheat, and then went away. [26] So, when the new wheat shot up, and ripened, the weeds made their appearance also. [27] The owner's slaves came to them, and said, 'Was it not good seed that you sowed in your field? Where, then, do the weeds in it come from?' [28] 'An enemy has done this,' was the owner's answer. 'Do you wish us, then,' they asked, 'to go and gather

them together?' [29] 'No,' said he, 'because while you are pulling up the weeds you might uproot the wheat with them. [30] Let both grow side by side until harvest; and then I will say to the reapers, 'Gather the weeds together first, and tie them in bundles for burning; but bring all the wheat into my barn.'"

[31] Another parable which he told them was this: "The realm of heaven is like a mustard seed, which a person took and sowed in his field. [32] This seed is smaller than all other seeds, but when it has grown up, it is larger than the herbs and becomes a tree, so that the wild birds come and roost in its branches."

[33] This was another parable which he related: "The realm of heaven is like some yeast which a woman took and covered up in three measures of flour, until the whole had risen." [34] Of all this Jesus spoke to the crowd in parables; indeed to them he used never to speak at all except in parables, [35] in fulfillment of these words in the prophet: "I will speak to you in parables; I will utter things kept secret since the foundation of the world."

[36] Then Jesus left the crowd, and went into the house. Presently his followers came to him, and said: "Explain to us the parable of the weeds in the field." [37] He answered: "The sower of the good seed is the Child of Humanity. [38] The field is the world. By the good seed is meant the people of the realm. The weeds are the children of wickedness, [39] and the enemy who sowed them is the devil. The harvest time is the close of the age, and the reapers are angels. [40] And, just as the weeds are gathered and burned, so it will be at the close of the age. [41] The Child of Humanity will send his angels, and they will gather from his realm all that hinders and those who live unlawfully, [42] and will throw them into the blazing furnace, where there will be weeping and grinding of teeth. [43] Then will the good shine like the sun in the realm of their Father. Let the one who has ears hear.

[44] "The realm of heaven is like a treasure hidden in a field, which a person found and hid again, and then, in delight, went and sold everything that he had, and bought that field.

[45] "Again, the realm of heaven is like a merchant in search of choice pearls. [46] Finding one of great value, he went and sold everything that he had, and bought it. [47] Or again, the realm of heaven is like a net which was cast into the sea, and caught fish of all kinds. [48] When it was full, they hauled it up on the beach, and sat down and sorted the good fish into baskets, but threw the worthless ones away. [49] So will it be at the close of the age. The angels will go out and separate the wicked from the good, [50] and will throw them into the blazing furnace, where there will be weeping and grinding of teeth.

[51] "Have you understood all this?" Jesus asked. "Yes," they answered. [52] Then he added: "So every scholar who has received instruction about the realm of heaven is like a householder who produces from the storeroom things both new and old."

[53] When Jesus had finished these parables, he withdrew from that place. [54] Going to his own part of the country, he taught the people in their synagogue in such a manner that they were deeply impressed. "Where did he get this wisdom?" they said, "and the miracles? [55] Is he not the carpenter's son? Is not his mother called Mary, and his brothers James, and Joseph, and Simon, and Judas? [56] And his sisters, too—are they not all living among us? Where, then, did he get all this?" [57] These things proved a hindrance to them. But Jesus said: "A prophet is not without honor, except in his own country and in his own house." [58] He did not work many miracles there, because of their want of loyalty.

14 [1] At that time Herod heard of the fame of Jesus, [2] and said to his attendants: "This must be John the Baptizer; he must be risen from the dead, and that is why these miraculous powers are active in him." [3] For Herod had arrested John, put him in chains, and shut him up in prison, to please Herodias, the wife of Herod's brother Philip. [4] For John had said to him, "You have no right to be living with her." [5] Yet, though Herod wanted to put him to death, he was afraid of the people, because they looked on John as a prophet. [6] But when Herod's birthday came, the daughter of Herodias danced before his guests, and so pleased Herod, [7] that he promised with an oath to give her whatever she asked. [8] Prompted by her mother, the girl said, "Give me here, on a dish, the head of John the Baptizer." [9] The king was distressed at this; yet, because of his oath and of the guests at his table, he ordered it to be given her. [10] He sent and beheaded John in the prison; [11] and his head was brought on a dish and given to the girl, and she took it to her mother. [12] Then John's followers came, and took the body away, and buried it; and went and told Jesus.

[13] When Jesus heard of it, he left privately in a boat to a lonely spot. The people, however, heard of his going, and followed him in crowds from the towns on foot. [14] On getting out of the boat, Jesus saw a great crowd, and his heart was moved at the sight of them; and he cured the sick among them. [15] In the evening the disciples came up to him, and said: "This is a lonely spot, and the day is now far advanced; send the crowds away so that they can go to the villages, and buy themselves food." [16] But Jesus said: "They need not go away; it is for you to give them something to eat." [17] "We have nothing here," they said, "except five loaves and two fishes." [18] "Bring them here to me," was his reply. [19] Jesus ordered the people to lie down on the grass; and, taking the five loaves and the two fish, he looked up to sky, and said

the blessing, and, after he had broken the loaves, gave them to his followers; and they gave them to the crowds. [20] Everyone was filled with what they had to eat, and they picked up enough of the broken pieces that were left to fill twelve baskets. [21] The men who ate were about five thousand in number, without counting women and children. [22] Immediately afterward Jesus made his followers get into a boat and cross over in advance of him, while he dismissed the crowds. [23] After dismissing the crowds, he went up the hill by himself to pray; and, when evening fell, he was there alone. [24] The boat was by this time some miles from shore, struggling in the waves, for there was a headwind. [25] Three hours after midnight, he came toward the disciples, walking on the water. [26] But when they saw him walking on the water, they were terrified. "It is a ghost," they exclaimed, and cried out in fear. [27] But Jesus at once spoke to them. "Courage!" he said. "It is I; do not be afraid!" [28] "Master," Peter exclaimed, "if it is you, tell me to come to you on the water." [29] Jesus said: "Come." So Peter got out of the boat, and walked on the water, and went toward Jesus; [30] but when he felt the wind, he was frightened, and, beginning to sink, cried out: "Master! Save me!" [31] Instantly Jesus stretched out his hand, and caught hold of him. "Your confidence is so small!" he said, "Why did you doubt?" [32] When they had gotten into the boat, the wind dropped. [33] But the men in the boat threw themselves on their faces before him, and said: "You are indeed a son of God."

[34] When they had crossed over, they landed at Gennesaret. [35] But the people of that place, recognizing Jesus, sent out to the whole country around, and brought to him all who were ill, [36] begging him merely to let them touch the fringe of his cloak; and all who touched were saved.

15 [1] Then some Pharisees and scholars came to Jesus, and said: [2] "How is it that your followers break the traditions of our ancestors? For they do not wash their hands when they eat food." [3] His reply was: "How is it that you on your side break God's commandments out of respect for your own traditions? [4] For God said, 'Honor your father and mother,' and 'Let the one who abuses his father or mother suffer death,' [5] but you say, 'Whenever anyone says to his father or mother, "Whatever of mine might have been of service to you is given to God," [6] he is in no way bound to honor his father.' In this way you have nullified the words of God for the sake of your traditions. [7] Hypocrites! It was well said by Isaiah when he prophesied about you: [8] 'This is a people that honor me with their lips, while their hearts are far removed from me; [9] but vainly do they worship me, for they teach but human precepts.'" [10] Then Jesus called the people to him, and said: "Listen, and mark my words. [11] It is not what enters a person's mouth that makes him unclean, but what comes out from his mouth — that makes him unclean!" [12] His followers came up to him, and said: "Do you know that the Pharisees were shocked on hearing what you said?"

[13] "Every plant," Jesus replied, "that my heavenly Father has not planted will be rooted up. [14] Let them be; they are but blind guides; and, if one blind person guides another, both of them will fall into a ditch." [15] Peter spoke up: "Explain this saying to us."

[16] "What, do even you understand nothing yet?" Jesus exclaimed. [17] "Do you not see that whatever goes into the mouth passes into the stomach, and is afterward expelled? [18] But the things that come out from the mouth proceed from the heart, and it is these that make a person unclean; [19] for out of the heart proceed bad thoughts — murder, adultery, sexual immorality, theft, perjury, slander. [20] These are the things that make a person unclean; but eating with unwashed hands does not make a person unclean."

[21] On going away from that place, Jesus went to the country around Tyre and Sidon. [22] There, a Canaanite woman of that district came out and began calling to Jesus: "Take pity on me, Master, son of David; my daughter is grievously possessed by a demon." [23] But Jesus did not say a word to her; and his followers came up and begged him to give in. "She keeps calling out after us," they said. [24] "I was not sent," he replied, "to anyone except the lost sheep of Israel." [25] But the woman came, and, bowing to the ground before him, said: "Master, help me."

[26] "It is not fair," he retorted, "to take the children's food and throw it to dogs." [27] "Yes, Master," she said, "but even dogs do feed on the scraps that fall from their owners' table."

[28] "Woman, your confidence is great," Jesus answered; "it will be as you wish!" And her daughter was healed that very hour.

[29] On leaving that place, Jesus went to the shore of the Sea of Galilee; and then went up the mountain, and sat down. [30] Great crowds of people came to him, bringing with them those who were lame, crippled, blind, or dumb, and many others. They put them down at his feet, and he healed them; [31] and the crowds were astonished when they saw the dumb talking, the cripples made sound, the lame walking about, and the blind with their sight restored; and they praised the God of Israel. [32] Afterward Jesus called his followers to him, and said: "My heart is moved at the sight of all these people, for they have already been with me three days and they have nothing to eat; and I am unwilling to send them away hungry; they might faint on the way home." [33] "Where can we," his followers asked, "in a lonely place find enough bread for such a crowd as this?"

[34] "How many loaves have you?" said Jesus. "Seven," they answered, "and a

few small fish." [35] Telling the crowd to recline on the ground, [36] he took the seven loaves and the fish, and, after giving thanks, broke them, and gave them to his followers; and they gave them to the crowds. [37] Everyone was satisfied with what they had to eat, and they picked up seven baskets full of the broken pieces left. [38] The men who ate were four thousand in number without counting women and children. [39] Then, after dismissing the crowds, he got into the boat, and went to the region of Magadan.

16 [1] Here the Pharisees and Sadducees came up, and, to test Jesus, requested him to show them some sign from the heavens. [2] But he answered: "In the evening you say, 'It will be fine weather, for the sky is as red as fire.' [3] But in the morning you say, 'Today it will be stormy, for the sky is as red as fire and threatening.' You learn to read the sky; yet you are unable to read the signs of the times! [4] A wicked and unfaithful generation is asking for a sign, but no sign will be given it except the sign of Jonah." So he left them and went away.

[5] Now his followers had crossed to the opposite shore, and had forgotten to take any bread. [6] Presently Jesus said to them: "Take care and be on your guard against the yeast of the Pharisees and Sadducees." [7] But the disciples began talking among themselves about their having brought no bread. [8] On noticing this, Jesus said: "Why are you talking among yourselves about your being short of bread, you of little trust? [9] Do you not yet see, nor remember the five loaves for the five thousand, and how many baskets you took away? [10] Nor yet the seven loaves for the four thousand, and how many basketfuls you took away? [11] How is it that you do not see that I was not speaking about bread? Be on your guard against the yeast of the Pharisees and Sadducees." [12] Then they understood that he had told them to be on their guard, not against the yeast of bread, but against

the teaching of the Pharisees and Sadducees.

[13] On coming into the neighborhood of Caesarea Philippi, Jesus asked his disciples this question: "Who do people say that the Child of Humanity is?" [14] "Some say John the Baptizer," they answered. "Others, however, say that he is Elijah, while others again say Jeremiah, or one of the prophets."

[15] "But you," he said, "who do you say that I am?" [16] To this Simon Peter answered: "You are the Anointed One, the Son of the living God."

[17] "Blessed are you, Simon, son of Jonah," Jesus replied. "For no human being has revealed this to you, but my Father who is in heaven. [18] Yes, and I say to you, your name is Peter—a Rock, and on this rock I will build my community, and the powers of the underworld will not prevail over it. [19] I will give you the keys of the realm of heaven. Whatever you bind on earth will be bound in heaven, and whatever you loose on earth will be loosed in heaven." [20] Then he charged his followers not to tell anyone that he was the Anointed One.

[21] At that time Jesus began to explain to his followers that he must go to Jerusalem, and undergo much suffering at the hands of the councilors, and chief priests, and scholars, and be put to death, and rise on the third day. [22] But Peter took Jesus aside, and began to rebuke him. "Master," he said, "please God that will never be your fate!" [23] Jesus, however, turning to Peter, said: "Out of my way, Satan! You are a hindrance to me; for you look at things, not as God does, but as people do." [24] Then Jesus said to his disciples: "If anyone wishes to walk in my steps, let him renounce self, and take up his cross, and follow me. [25] For whoever wishes to save her life will lose it, and whoever, for my sake, loses her life will find it. [26] What good will it do a person to gain the whole world, if she forfeits her life? Or what will a per-

son give that is of equal value with her life? [27] For the Child of Humanity is to come in his Father's glory, with his angels, and then he 'will give to everyone what his actions deserve.' [28] I tell you, some of those who are standing here will not know death until they have seen the Child of Humanity coming with his realm."

17 [1] Six days later, Jesus took with him Peter, and the brothers James and John, and led them up a high mountain alone. [2] There his appearance was transformed before their eyes; his face shone like the sun, and his clothes became as white as the light. [3] All at once Moses and Elijah appeared to them, talking with Jesus. [4] "Master," exclaimed Peter, interposing, "it is good to be here; if you wish, I will make three tents here, one for you, one for Moses, and one for Elijah." [5] While he was still speaking, a bright cloud enveloped them, and there was a voice from the cloud that said, "This is my dearly loved son, who brings me great joy; listen to him." [6] His followers, on hearing this, fell on their faces, greatly afraid. [7] But Jesus came and touched them, saying as he did so, "Rise up, and do not be afraid." [8] When they raised their eyes, they saw no one but Jesus himself alone. [9] As they were going down the mountainside, Jesus gave them this warning: "Do not speak of this vision to anyone, until the Child of Humanity has risen from the dead." [10] "How is it," they asked, "that scholars say that Elijah has to come first?"

[11] "Elijah indeed does come," Jesus replied, "and will restore everything; [12] and I tell you that Elijah has already come, and people have not recognized him, but have treated him just as they pleased. In the same way, too, the Child of Humanity is destined to undergo suffering at people's hands." [13] Then his followers understood that it was of John the Baptizer that he had spoken to them.

[14] When they came to the crowd, a man came up to Jesus, and, kneeling down before him, said: [15] "Master, take pity on my son, for he is epileptic and suffers terribly; indeed, he often falls into the fire and into the water. [16] I brought him to your followers, but they could not help him."

[17] "Faithless and perverse generation!" Jesus exclaimed. "How long must I be among you? How long must I have patience with you? Bring the boy here to me." [18] Then Jesus rebuked the demon, and it came out of the boy; and he was cured from that very hour. [19] Afterward his followers came up to Jesus, and asked him privately: "Why was it that we could not drive it out?"

[20] "Because you have so little confidence," he answered; "for, I tell you, if your confidence were only like a mustard seed, you could say to this mountain, 'Move from this place to that!' and it would be moved; and nothing would be impossible to you."

[22] While they were together in Galilee, he said to them: "The Child of Humanity is destined to be betrayed into human hands, [23] and they will put him to death, but on the third day he will rise." They were greatly distressed.

[24] After they had reached Capernaum, the collectors of the half drachma came up to Peter, and said: "Does not your Master pay the Temple tax?"

[25] "Yes," answered Peter. But on going into the house, before he could speak, Jesus said: "What do you think, Simon? From whom do earthly kings take taxes or tribute? From their sons, or from foreigners?" [26] "From foreigners," answered Peter. "Well then," continued Jesus, "their sons are exempt. [27] Still, so we don't offend them, go and throw a line into the sea; take the first fish that rises, open its mouth, and you will find in it a coin. Take that, and give it to the collectors for both of us."

18 [1] On the same occasion the disciples came to Jesus, and asked him: "Who is really the greatest in the realm of heaven?" [2] Jesus called a little child to him, and placed it in the middle of them, and then said: [3] "I tell you, unless you change and become like little children, you will not enter the realm of heaven at all. [4] Therefore, anyone who will humble himself like this child — that person will be the greatest in the realm of heaven. [5] And anyone who, for the sake of my name, welcomes even one little child like this, is welcoming me. [6] But if anyone hinders one of these little ones who trust in me, it would be best for him to be sunk in the depths of the sea with a great millstone hung around his neck. [7] Alas for the world with such hindering! There cannot but be hindrances but sorrow awaits the person who does the hindering!

[8] "If your hand or your foot hinders you, cut it off, and throw it away. It would be better for you to enter the life maimed or lame, than to have both hands, or both feet, and be thrown into the fire that never goes out. [9] If your eye hinders you, take it out, and throw it away. It would be better for you to enter the life with only one eye, than to have both eyes and be thrown into the fires of Gehenna. [10] Beware of despising one of these little ones, for in heaven, I tell you, their angels always see the face of my Father who is in heaven.

[12] "What think you? If a person has a hundred sheep, and one of them strays, will the person not leave the ninety-nine on the hills, and go and search for the one that is straying? [13] And, if he succeeds in finding it, I tell you that he rejoices more over that one sheep than over the ninety-nine which did not stray. [14] So, too, it is the will of my Father who is in heaven that not one of these little ones should be lost.

[15] "If your brother or sister does wrong, go to him and convince him of his fault when you are both alone. If he listens to you, you have won back the relationship. [16] But if he does not listen to you, take with you one or two others, so that on the evidence of two or three witnesses, every word may be put beyond dispute. [17] If he refuses to listen to them, speak to the assembly; and, if he also refuses to listen to the community, treat him as you would a gentile or a tax collector.

[18] "I tell you, all that you bind on earth will be bound in heaven, and all that you loose on earth will be loosed in heaven. [19] Again, I tell you that if two of you on earth agree to ask anything on earth, whatever it be, it will be granted you by my Father in heaven. [20] For where two or three have come together in my name, I am present with them."

[21] Then Peter came up, and said to Jesus: "Master, how often am I to forgive someone who wrongs me? As many as seven times?" [22] But Jesus answered: "Not seven times, but 'seventy times seven.' [23] Therefore the realm of heaven may be compared to a king who wished to settle accounts with his slaves. [24] When he had begun to do so, one of them was brought to him who owed him ten thousand bags of gold; [25] and, as he could not pay, his master ordered him to be sold toward the payment of the debt, together with his wife, and his children, and everything that he had. [26] The slave threw himself down on the ground before him and said, 'Have patience with me, and I will pay you all.' [27] The master was moved with compassion; and he let him go, and forgave him the debt. [28] But on going out, that same slave came upon one of his fellow slaves who owed him a hundred silver coins. Seizing him by the throat, he said, 'Pay what you owe me.' [29] His fellow slave threw himself on the ground and begged for mercy. 'Have patience with me,' he said, 'and I will pay you.' [30] But the other would not, but went and put him in prison until he should pay his debt. [31] When his fellow slaves saw what had happened, they were greatly distressed, and went to their master and laid the whole matter before him. [32] So the master sent for the slave,

and said to him, 'You wicked slave! When you begged me for mercy, I forgave you the whole of that debt. [33] Ought you not, also, to have shown mercy to your fellow slave, just as I showed mercy to you?' [34] Then his master, in anger, handed him over to the jailers, until he should pay the whole of his debt. [35] So, also, will my heavenly Father do to you, unless each one of you forgives your brother or sister from your heart."

The Journey to Jerusalem

19 [1] At the conclusion of this teaching, Jesus withdrew from Galilee, and went into the part of Judea which is on the other side of the Jordan. [2] Great crowds followed him, and he healed them there. [3] Presently some Pharisees came up to him, and, to test him, said: "Has a man the right to divorce his wife for every cause?"

[4] "Have you not read," replied Jesus, "that at the beginning the Creator 'made them male and female,' [5] and said, 'For this reason a man will leave his father and mother, and be united to his wife, and the man and his wife will become one'? [6] So that they are no longer two, but one. What God himself, then, has yoked together people must not separate." [7] "Why, then," they said, "did Moses direct that a man should 'serve his wife with a notice of separation and divorce her'?"

[8] "Moses, owing to the hardness of your hearts," answered Jesus, "permitted you to divorce your wives, but that was not so at the beginning. [9] But I tell you that anyone who divorces his wife, except on the ground of some serious sexual sin, and marries another woman, is guilty of adultery." [10] "If that," said his followers, "is the position of a man with regard to his wife, it is better not to marry."

[11] "It is not everyone," he replied, "who can accept this teaching, but only those who have been enabled to do so. [12] Some men, it is true, have from birth been made eunuchs, while others have been made eunuchs by people, and others again have made themselves eunuchs for the sake of the realm of heaven. Let him accept it who can."

[13] Then some little children were brought to Jesus, for him to place his hands on them, and pray; but the followers found fault with those who had brought them. [14] Jesus, however, said: "Let the little children come to me, and do not hinder them, for it is to such as these that the realm of heaven belongs." [15] So he placed his hands on them, and then went on his way.

[16] A man came up to Jesus, and said: "Teacher, what good thing must I do to obtain eternal life?"

[17] "Why ask me about goodness?" answered Jesus. "There is but One who is good. If you want to enter into life, keep the commandments." [18] "What commandments?" asked the man. "These," answered Jesus: "'You must not kill. You must not commit adultery. You must not steal. You must not say what is false about others. [19] Honor your father and your mother.' And 'You must love your neighbor as you love yourself.'" [20] "I have observed all these," said the young man. "What is still wanting in me?"

[21] "If you wish to be perfect," answered Jesus, "go and sell your property, and give to the poor, and you will have wealth in heaven; then come and follow me." [22] On hearing these words, the young man went away distressed, for he had great possessions. [23] At this, Jesus said to his disciples: "I tell you that a rich person will find it hard to enter the realm of heaven! [24] I say again, it is easier for a camel to get through a needle's eye than for a rich person to enter the realm of heaven!" [25] On hearing this, the disciples exclaimed in great astonishment: "Who then can possibly be saved?" [26] But Jesus looked at them, and said: "With people this is impossible, but with God everything is possible." Then Peter turned and said to Jesus: [27] "But we

—we left everything, and followed you; what, then, will we have?"

²⁸ "I tell you," answered Jesus, "that at the new creation, 'when the Child of Humanity takes his seat on his throne of glory,' you who followed me will be seated on twelve thrones, as judges of the twelve tribes of Israel. ²⁹ Everyone who has left houses, or brothers, or sisters, or father, or mother, or children, or land, for my sake, will receive many times as much, and will inherit life for the ages. ³⁰ But many who are first now will then be last, and those who are last will be first.

20 ¹ "For the realm of heaven is like an employer who went out in the early morning to hire laborers for his vineyard. ² He agreed with the laborers to pay them the standard daily rate of one denarius, and sent them into his vineyard. ³ On going out again, about nine o'clock, he saw some others standing in the marketplace, doing nothing. ⁴ 'You also may go into my vineyard,' he said, 'and I will pay you what is fair.' ⁵ So they went. Going out again about midday and about three o'clock, he did as before. ⁶ When he went out about five, he found some others standing there, and said to them, 'Why have you been standing here all day long, doing nothing?' ⁷ 'Because no one has hired us,' they answered. 'You also may go into my vineyard,' he said. ⁸ In the evening the owner of the vineyard said to his manager, 'Call the laborers, and pay them their wages, beginning with the last, and ending with the first.' ⁹ Now when those who had been hired about five o'clock went up, they received one denarius each. ¹⁰ So, when the first went up, they thought that they would receive more, but they also received one denarius each; ¹¹ at which they began to grumble at their employer. ¹² 'These last,' they said, 'have done only one hour's work, and yet you have put them on the same footing with us, who have borne the brunt of the day's work,

and the heat.' ¹³ 'My friend,' was his reply to one of them, 'I am not treating you unfairly. Did you not agree with me for one denarius? ¹⁴ Take what belongs to you, and go. I choose to give to this last man the same as to you. ¹⁵ Have I not the right to do as I choose with what is mine? Are you envious because I am generous?' ¹⁶ So those who are last will be first, and the first last."

¹⁷ When Jesus was on the point of going up to Jerusalem, he gathered the Twelve around him by themselves, and said to them as they were on their way: ¹⁸ "Listen! We are going up to Jerusalem; and there the Child of Humanity will be handed over to the chief priests and teachers of the Law, and they will condemn him to death, ¹⁹ and give him up to the gentiles for them to mock, and to scourge, and to crucify; and on the third day he will be raised up."

²⁰ Then the mother of Zebedee's sons came to him with her sons, bowing to the ground, and begging a favor. ²¹ "What is it that you want?" he asked. "I want you to say," she replied, "that in your realm these two sons of mine may sit, one on your right, and the other on your left."

²² "You do not know what you are asking," was Jesus's answer. "Can you drink the cup that I am to drink?" "Yes," they exclaimed, "we can."

²³ "You will indeed drink my cup," he said, "but as to a seat at my right and at my left — that is not mine to give, but it is for those for whom it has been prepared by my Father." ²⁴ On hearing of this, the ten others were very indignant about the two brothers. ²⁵ Jesus, however, called them to him, and said: "The rulers of the gentiles lord it over them as you know, and their high officials oppress them. ²⁶ Among you it will not be so. ²⁷ No, whoever wants to become great among you must be your servant, and whoever wants to take the first place among you must be your slave; ²⁸ just as the Child of Humanity came, not

to be served, but to serve, and to give his life as a ransom for many."

²⁹ As they were going out of Jericho, a great crowd followed him. ³⁰ Two blind men who were sitting by the roadside, hearing that Jesus was passing, called out: "Take pity on us, Master, son of David!" ³¹ The crowd told them to be quiet; but the men only called out the louder: "Take pity on us, Master, son of David!" ³² Then Jesus stopped and called them. "What do you want me to do for you?" he said. ³³ "Master," they replied, "we want our eyes to be opened." ³⁴ So Jesus, moved with compassion, touched their eyes, and immediately they recovered their sight, and followed him.

The Last Days

21 ¹ When they had almost reached Jerusalem, having come as far as Bethphage, on the Mount of Olives, Jesus sent on two followers. ² "Go to the village facing you," he said, "and you will immediately find a donkey tethered, with a colt by her side; untie her, and lead her here for me. ³ And, if anyone says anything to you, you are to say this: 'The Master wants them'; and the person will send them at once." ⁴ This happened in fulfillment of these words in the prophet: ⁵ "Say to the people of Zion — 'Your king is coming to you, gentle, and riding on a donkey, and on the colt of a beast of burden.'"

⁶ So the followers went and did as Jesus had directed them. ⁷ They led the donkey and the colt back, and, when they had put their cloaks on them, he seated himself on them. ⁸ The immense crowd of people spread their cloaks in the road, while some cut branches off the trees, and spread them on the road. ⁹ The crowds that led the way, as well as those that followed behind, kept shouting: "Hosanna to the son of David! Blessed is the one who comes in the name of the Lord! Hosanna in the highest!"

¹⁰ When he had entered Jerusalem, the whole city was stirred, and asked, ¹¹ "Who is this?" to which the crowd replied, "This is the prophet Jesus from Nazareth in Galilee."

¹² Jesus went into the Temple, and drove out all those who were buying and selling there. He overturned the tables of the moneychangers, and the seats of the pigeon dealers, ¹³ and said to them: "It is written, 'My house will be called a house of prayer'; but you are making it 'a den of robbers.'" ¹⁴ While he was still in the Temple, some blind and lame people came up to him, and he healed them. ¹⁵ But when the chief priests and the scholars saw the wonderful things that Jesus did, and the children who were calling out in the Temple "Hosanna to the son of David!" they were indignant, ¹⁶ and said to him: "Do you hear what they are saying?"

"Yes," answered Jesus; "but did you never read the words 'Out of the mouths of babes and sucklings you have called forth perfect praise'?"

¹⁷ Then he left them, and went out of the city to Bethany, and spent the night there.

¹⁸ The next morning, while returning to the city, he became hungry; ¹⁹ and, noticing a solitary fig tree by the roadside, he went up to it, but found nothing on it but leaves. So he said to it: "Never again will fruit be gathered off you." And suddenly the fruit tree withered up. ²⁰ When his followers saw this, they exclaimed in astonishment: "How suddenly the fig tree withered up!"

²¹ "I tell you," replied Jesus, "if you have confidence, without ever a doubt, you will do not only what has been done to the fig tree, but even if you should say to this hill, 'Be lifted up and hurled into the sea!' it would be done. ²² And whatever you ask for in your prayers will, if you have faith, be granted you."

²³ After Jesus had come into the Tem-

ple, the chief priests and the councilors of the nation came up to him as he was teaching, and said: "What authority have you to do these things? Who gave you this authority?"

²⁴ "I, too," said Jesus in reply, "will ask you one question; if you will give me an answer to it, then I, also, will tell you what authority I have to act as I do. ²⁵ It is about John's baptism. What was its origin? From heaven or from humans?" But they began arguing among themselves: "If we say 'from heaven,' he will say to us, 'Why then did you not believe him?' ²⁶ But if we say 'from humans,' we are afraid of the people, for everyone regards John as a prophet." ²⁷ So the answer they gave Jesus was: "We do not know."

"Then I," he said, "refuse to tell you what authority I have to do these things. ²⁸ What do you think of this? There was a man who had two sons. He went to the elder and said, 'Go and work in the vineyard today, my son.' ²⁹ 'I will not go,' he answered, but afterward thought better of it and went. ³⁰ Then the father went to the second son, and said the same. 'Certainly, sir,' he answered, but did not go. ³¹ Which of the two sons did as his father wished?" "The first," they said. "I tell you," added Jesus, "that tax collectors and prostitutes are going into the realm of God before you. ³² For when John came to you, walking in the path of justice, you did not believe him, but tax gatherers and prostitutes did; and yet you, though you saw this, even then did not think better of it, nor did you believe him.

³³ "Listen to another parable. A person, who was an employer, once planted a vineyard, put a fence around it, dug a winepress in it, built a tower, and then let it out to tenants and went abroad. ³⁴ When the time for the grape harvest drew near, he sent his slaves to the tenants, to collect his produce. ³⁵ But the tenants seized his slaves, beat one, killed another, and stoned a third. ³⁶ A second time the owner sent

some slaves, a larger number than before, and the tenants treated them in the same way. ³⁷ As a last resort he sent his son to them. 'They will respect my son,' he said. ³⁸ But the tenants, on seeing his son, said to each other, 'Here is the heir! Come, let us kill him, and get his inheritance.' ³⁹ So they seized him, and threw him outside the vineyard, and killed him. ⁴⁰ Now, when the owner of the vineyard comes, what will he do to those tenants?" ⁴¹ "Miserable wretches!" they exclaimed. "He will put them to a miserable death, and he will let out the vineyard to other tenants, who will deliver the produce at the proper times." ⁴² Then Jesus added: "Have you never read in the scriptures, 'The stone which the builders despised has now itself become the cornerstone; this has come from the Lord, and is marvelous in our eyes'? ⁴³ That, I tell you, is why the realm of God will be taken from you, and given to a people that does produce its fruit."

⁴⁵ After listening to these parables, the chief priests and the Pharisees saw that it was about them that he was speaking; ⁴⁶ yet, although eager to arrest him, they were afraid of the crowds, who regarded him as a prophet.

22 ¹ Once more Jesus spoke to them in parables. ² "The realm of heaven may be compared to a king who gave a banquet in honor of his son's wedding. ³ He sent his slaves to call those who had been invited to the banquet, but they were unwilling to come. ⁴ A second time he sent some slaves, with orders to say to those who had been invited, 'I have prepared my banquet, my cattle and fat beasts are killed, and everything is ready; come to the wedding.' ⁵ They, however, took no notice, but went off, one to his farm, another to his business; ⁶ while the rest, seizing his slaves, mistreated them and killed them. ⁷ The king, in anger, sent his troops, put those murderers to death, and set their city on fire. [8] Then he said to his slaves, 'The wedding is prepared, but those who were invited were not worthy. [9] So go to the crossroads, and invite everyone you find to the banquet.' [10] The slaves went out into the roads and collected all the people whom they found, whether bad or good; and the bridal hall was filled with guests. [11] But when the king went in to see his guests, he noticed there a man who had not put on a wedding robe. [12] So he said to him, 'My friend, how is it that you came in here without a wedding robe?' The man was speechless. [13] Then the king said to the attendants, 'Tie him hand and foot, and put him out into the darkness outside, where there will be weeping and grinding of teeth.' [14] For many are called, but few chosen."

[15] Then the Pharisees went away and conferred together as to how they might lay a trap for Jesus in the course of conversation. [16] They sent their followers to him, with the Herodians, to say to him: "Teacher, we know that you are an honest person, and that you teach the way of God honestly, and are not afraid of anyone; for you pay no regard to a person's position. [17] Tell us, then, what you think. Are we right in paying taxes to the emperor, or not?" [18] Perceiving their malice, Jesus answered: "Why are you testing me, you hypocrites? [19] Show me the coin with which the tax is paid." And, when they had brought him a coin, [20] he asked: "Whose head and title are these?" [21] "The emperor's," they answered; at which he said to them: "Then pay to the emperor what belongs to the emperor, and to God what belongs to God." [22] They wondered at his answer, and left him alone and went away.

[23] That same day some Sadducees came up to Jesus, maintaining that there is no resurrection. Their question was this: [24] "Teacher, Moses said, 'Should a man die without children, the man's brother will become the husband of the widow, and produce descendants for his brother.'

[25] Now we had living among us seven brothers, of whom the eldest married and died, and, as he had no family, left his wife to his brother. [26] The same thing happened to the second and the third brothers, and indeed to all the seven. [27] The woman herself died last of all. [28] At the resurrection, then, whose wife will she be out of the seven, all of them having been married to her?"

[29] "Your mistake," replied Jesus, "is due to your ignorance of the scriptures, and of the power of God. [30] For at the resurrection there is no marrying or being married, but all are as angels in heaven. [31] As to the resurrection of the dead, have you not read these words of God to you: [32] 'I am the God of Abraham, and the God of Isaac, and the God of Jacob'? He is not the God of dead people, but of the living." [33] The crowds who had been listening to him were greatly struck with his teaching.

[34] When the Pharisees heard that Jesus had silenced the Sadducees, they collected together. [35] Then one of them, to test him, asked this question: [36] "Teacher, what is the great commandment in the Law?" [37] His answer was: "'You must love the Lord your God with all your heart, and with all your soul, and with all your mind.' [38] This is the great first commandment. [39] The second, which is like it, is this: 'You must love your neighbor as you love yourself.' [40] On these two commandments hang all the Law and the prophets." [41] Before the Pharisees separated, Jesus put this question to them: [42] "What do you think about the Christ? Whose son is he?" "David's," they said. [43] "How is it, then," Jesus replied, "that David in spirit calls him 'Lord,' in the passage [44] 'The Lord said to my Lord: "Sit at my right hand, until I put your enemies beneath your feet"'? [45] Since, then, David calls him 'Lord,' how is he David's son?" [46] No one could say a word in answer; nor did anyone after that day venture to question him further.

23 ¹ Then Jesus, speaking to the crowds and to his followers, said: ² "The scholars and the Pharisees now occupy the chair of Moses. ³ Therefore practice and lay to heart everything that they say but do not practice what they do. ⁴ While they make up heavy loads and pile them on other people's shoulders, they decline, themselves, to lift a finger to move them. ⁵ All their actions are done to attract attention. They widen their headbands, and increase the size of their tassels, ⁶ and like to have the place of honor at dinner, and the best seats in the synagogues, ⁷ and to be greeted in the markets with respect, and to be called 'Rabbi' by everybody. ⁸ But do not allow yourselves to be called 'Rabbi,' for you have only one teacher, and you yourselves are all brothers and sisters. ⁹ And do not call anyone on the earth your 'Father,' for you have only one Father, the heavenly Father. ¹⁰ Nor must you allow yourselves to be called 'leaders,' for you have only one leader, the Christ. ¹¹ The person who wants to be the greatest among you must be your servant. ¹² Whoever exalts himself will be humbled, and whoever humbles herself will be exalted. ¹³ But alas for you, scholars and Pharisees, hypocrites that you are! You lock up the realm of heaven in people's faces. For you do not go in yourselves, nor allow those who try to go in to do so. ¹⁵ Alas for you, scholars and Pharisees, hypocrites that you are! You scour land and sea to make a single follower, and, when he is gained, you make him twice as deserving of Gehenna as you are yourselves. ¹⁶ Alas for you, you blind guides! You say, 'If any answer by the Temple, their oath counts for nothing; but if any swear by the gold of the Temple, their oath is binding them'! ¹⁷ Fools that you are and blind! Which is the more important? The gold? Or the Temple which has given sacredness to the gold? ¹⁸ You say, too, 'If anyone swears by the altar, his oath counts for nothing, but if anyone swears by the offering placed on it, his

oath is binding'! ¹⁹ Blind indeed! Which is the more important? The offering? Or the altar which gives sacredness to the offering? ²⁰ Therefore a person swearing by the altar swears by it and by all that is on it, ²¹ and a person swearing by the Temple swears by it and by him who dwells in it, ²² while a person swearing by heaven swears by the throne of God, and by the One who sits on it. ²³ Alas for you, scholars and Pharisees, hypocrites that you are! You pay tithes on mint, fennel, and caraway seed, and have neglected the weightier matters of the Law — justice, compassion, and good faith. These last you ought to have put into practice, without neglecting the first. ²⁴ You blind guides, to strain out a gnat and to swallow a camel! ²⁵ Alas for you, scholars and Pharisees, hypocrites that you are! You clean the outside of the cup and the dish, but inside they are filled with the results of greed and self-indulgence. ²⁶ You blind Pharisees! First clean the inside of the cup and the dish, so that the outside may become clean as well. ²⁷ Alas for you, scholars and Pharisees, hypocrites that you are! You are like whitewashed tombs, which indeed look beautiful outside, while inside they are filled with dead people's bones and all kinds of decay. ²⁸ It is the same with you. Outwardly, and to others, you have the look of good people, but inwardly you are full of hypocrisy and lawlessness. ²⁹ Alas for you, scholars and Pharisees, hypocrites that you are! You build the tombs of the prophets, and decorate the monuments of good people, ³⁰ and say, 'Had we been living in the days of our ancestors, we should have taken part in their murder of the prophets'! ³¹ By doing this you are furnishing evidence against yourselves that you are true children of the people who murdered the prophets. ³² Fill up the measure of your ancestors' guilt. ³³ You snakes and children of snakes! How can you escape being sentenced to Gehenna? ³⁴ That is why I send you prophets, wise people, and teachers of the Law, some of whom you will crucify and kill, and some of whom you will scourge in your synagogues, and persecute from town to town; [35] in order that every drop of innocent blood spilled on earth may fall on your heads, from the blood of innocent Abel down to that of Zechariah, Barachiah's son, whom you murdered between the sanctuary and the altar. [36] All this, I tell you, will come home to the present generation. [37] Jerusalem! Jerusalem! who slays the prophets and stones the messengers sent to her — Oh, how often have I wished to gather your children around me, as a hen gathers her brood under her wings, and you would not come! [38] Look, your house is left to you desolate! [39] For, I tell you, you will not see me again, until you say, 'Blessed is the one who comes in the name of the Lord!'"

24 [1] Leaving the Temple Courts, Jesus was walking away, when his followers came up to draw his attention to the Temple buildings. [2] "Do you see all these things?" he responded. "I tell you, not a single stone will be left here on another, which will not be thrown down." [3] While Jesus was sitting on the Mount of Olives, his followers came up to him privately and said: "Tell us when this will be, and what will be the sign of your coming, and of the close of the age." [4] Jesus replied to them: "See that no one leads you astray; [5] for, many will take my name, and come saying, 'I am the Christ,' and will lead many astray. [6] You will hear of wars and rumors of wars; take care not to be alarmed, for such things must occur; but the end is not yet here. [7] For nation will rise against nation and kingdom against kingdom, and there will be famines and earthquakes in various places. [8] All this, however, will be but the beginning of the birth pangs! [9] When that time comes, they will give you up to persecution, and will put you to death, and you will be hated by all nations because of me. [10] And then many will fall away, and

will betray one another, and hate one another. [11] Many false prophets, also, will appear and lead many astray; [12] and, owing to the increase of lawlessness, the love of most will grow cold. [13] Yet the person who endures to the end will be saved. [14] This good news of the realm will be proclaimed throughout the world as a witness to all nations; and then will come the end. [15] As soon, then, as you see the appalling desecration, mentioned by the prophet Daniel, standing in the Holy place" (the reader must consider what this means), [16] "then those in Judea must take refuge in the mountains; [17] and anyone on a housetop must not go down to get the things that are in the house; [18] nor must one who is on the farm turn back to get his cloak. [19] Alas for pregnant women, and for those who are nursing infants in those days! [20] Pray, too, that your flight may not take place in winter, nor on a sabbath; [21] for that will be a time of great distress, the like of which has not occurred from the beginning of the world down to the present time — no, nor ever will again. [22] Had not those days been limited, not a single soul would escape; but for the sake of the chosen a limit will be put to them. [23] At that time, if anyone should say to you, 'Look! Here is the Christ!' or 'Here he is!' do not believe it; [24] for false Christs and false prophets will arise, and will display great signs and marvels, so that, were it possible, even the chosen would be led astray. [25] Remember, I have told you beforehand. [26] Therefore, if people say to you, 'He is in the wilderness!' do not go out there; or 'He is in an inner room!' do not believe it; [27] for, just as lightning will start from the east and flash across to the west, so will it be with the coming of the Child of Humanity. [28] Wherever a dead body lies, there will the vultures flock. [29] Immediately after the distress of those days, the sun will be darkened, the moon will not give her light, the stars will fall from the heavens, and the forces of the heavens will be convulsed. [30] Then will appear the sign of the Child of Humanity in the heavens; and all the peoples of the earth will mourn, when they see the Child of Humanity coming on the clouds of the heavens, with power and great glory; [31] and he will send his angels, with a great trumpet, and they will gather the chosen around him from the four winds, from one end of heaven to the other.

[32] "Learn the lesson taught by the fig tree. As soon as its twigs are full of sap, and it is bursting into leaf, you know that summer is near. [33] And so may you, as soon as you see all these things, know that he is at your doors. [34] I tell you, even the present generation will not pass away, until all these things have taken place. [35] The sky and the earth will pass away, but my words will never pass away. [36] But about that day and hour, no one knows — not even the angels of heaven, nor the Son — but only the Father himself. [37] For, just as in the days of Noah, so will it be at the coming of the Child of Humanity. [38] In those days before the flood they went on eating and drinking, marrying and being married, up to the very day on which Noah entered the ark, [39] taking no notice until the flood came and swept them one and all away; and so will it be at the coming of the Child of Humanity. [40] At that time, of two men on a farm one will be taken and one left; [41] of two women grinding with the hand mill one will be taken and one left. [42] Therefore watch; for you cannot be sure on what day your Master is coming. [43] But this you do know, that had the owner of the house known at what time of night the thief was coming, he would have been on the watch, and would not have allowed his house to be broken into. [44] Therefore, you must also prepare, since it is just when you are least expecting him that the Child of Humanity will come. [45] Who, then, is that trustworthy, careful slave, who has been placed by his master over his household, to give them his food at the proper time?

[46] Happy will that slave be whom his master, when he comes home, will find doing this. [47] I tell you that his master will put him in charge of the whole of his property. [48] But should the slave be bad, and say to himself, 'My master is a long time in coming,' [49] and begins to beat the other slaves, and eat and drink with drunkards, [50] that slave's master will come on a day when he does not expect him, and at an hour of which he is unaware, [51] and will flog the slave severely, and assign him his place among the hypocrites, where there will be weeping and grinding of teeth.

25 [1] "Then the realm of heaven will be like ten bridesmaids who took their lamps and went out to meet the groom. [2] Five of them were foolish, and five were prudent. [3] The foolish ones took their lamps, but took no oil with them; [4] while the prudent ones, besides taking their lamps, took oil in their jars. [5] As the groom was late in coming, they all became drowsy, and slept. [6] But at midnight a shout was raised: 'The groom is coming! Come out to meet him!' [7] Then all the bridesmaids woke up and trimmed their lamps, [8] and the foolish said to the prudent, 'Give us some of your oil; our lamps are going out.' [9] But the prudent ones answered, 'No, there may not be enough for you and for us. Go instead to those who sell it, and buy for yourselves.' [10] But while they were on their way to buy it, the groom came; and the bridesmaids who were ready went in with him to the banquet, and the door was shut. [11] Afterward the other bridesmaids came. 'Sir, Sir,' they said, 'open the door to us!' [12] But the groom answered, 'I tell you, I do not know you.' [13] Therefore watch, since you know neither the day nor the hour.

[14] "For it is as though a man, going on his travels, called his slaves, and gave his property into their charge. [15] He gave five bags of gold to one, two to another, and one bag to a third, in proportion to the ability of each. Then he set out on his trav-

els. [16] The one who had received the five bags of gold went at once and traded with it, and made another five bags. [17] So, too, the one who had received the two bags of gold made another two bags. [18] But the one who had received the one bag went and dug a hole in the ground, and hid his master's money. [19] After a long time the master of those slaves returned, and settled accounts with them. [20] The one who had received the five bags of gold came up and brought five bags more. 'Sir,' he said, 'you entrusted me with five bags of gold; look, I have made another five bags!' [21] 'Well done, good, trustworthy slave!' said his master. 'You have been trustworthy with a small sum; now I will place a large one in your hands; come and share your master's joy!' [22] Then the one who had received the two bags of gold came up and said, 'Sir, you entrusted me with two bags; look, I have made another two!' [23] 'Well done, good, trustworthy slave!' said his master. 'You have been trustworthy with a small sum; now I will place a large one in your hands; come and share your master's joy!' [24] The man who had received the single bag of gold came up, too, and said, 'Sir, I knew that you were a hard man; you reap where you have not sown, and gather up where you have not winnowed; [25] and, in my fear, I went and hid your money in the ground; look, here is what belongs to you!' [26] 'You lazy, worthless slave!' was his master's reply. 'You knew that I reap where I have not sown, and gather up where I have not winnowed? [27] Then you ought to have placed my money in the hands of bankers, and I, on my return, should have received my money, with interest. [28] Therefore,' he continued, 'take away from him the one bag of gold, and give it to the one who has the ten bags. [29] For, to the one who has, more will be given, and that one will have abundance; but as for the one who has nothing, even what that one has will be taken away from him. [30] As for the useless slave, put him out into the darkness outside, where there will be weeping and grinding of teeth.

[31] "When the Child of Humanity has come in his glory and all the angels with him, then he will take his seat on his throne of glory; [32] and all the nations will be gathered before him, and he will separate the people — just as a shepherd separates sheep from goats — [33] placing the sheep on his right hand, and the goats on his left. [34] Then the king will say to those on his right, 'Come, you who are blessed by my Father, enter into possession of the realm prepared for you ever since the beginning of the world. [35] For, when I was hungry, you gave me food; when I was thirsty, you gave me drink; when I was a stranger, you took me to your homes; [36] when I was naked, you clothed me; when I fell ill, you visited me; and when I was in prison, you came to me.' [37] Then the righteous will answer, 'Lord, when did we see you hungry, and feed you? Or thirsty, and give you a drink? [38] When did we see you a stranger, and take you to our homes? Or naked, and clothe you? [39] When did we see you ill, or in prison, and come to you?' [40] And the king will reply, 'I tell you, as often as you did it to one of these my brothers or sisters, however unimportant she seemed, you did it to me.' [41] Then he will say to those on his left, 'Go from my presence, accursed, into the permanent fire which has been prepared for the devil and his angels. [42] For, when I was hungry, you gave me no food; when I was thirsty, you gave me no drink; [43] when I was a stranger, you did not take me to your homes; when I was naked, you did not clothe me; and, when I was ill and in prison, you did not visit me.' [44] Then they, in their turn, will answer, 'Lord, when did we see you hungry, or thirsty, or a stranger, or naked, or ill, or in prison, and did not supply your wants?' [45] And then he will reply, 'I tell you, as often as you failed to do it to one of these, however unimportant, you failed to do it to me.' [46] And these last will

go away into lasting correction, but the righteous into lasting life."

26 [1] When Jesus had finished teaching all of that, he said to his followers: [2] "You know that in two days' time the festival of the Passover will be here; and that the Child of Humanity is to be given up to be crucified." [3] Then the chief priests and the elders of the people met in the house of the high priest, who was called Caiaphas, [4] and plotted together to arrest Jesus by stealth and put him to death; [5] but they said: "Not during the festival, or the people may riot."

[6] After Jesus had reached Bethany, and while he was in the house of Simon, who had suffered from a bad skin disease, [7] a woman came up to him with an alabaster jar of very costly perfume, and poured the perfume on his head as he sat at the table. [8] His followers were indignant at seeing this. "What is this waste for?" they exclaimed. [9] "It could have been sold for a large sum, and the money given to poor people."

[10] "Why are you troubling the woman?" Jesus said, when he noticed it. "For this is a beautiful deed that she has done to me. [11] You always have the poor with you, but you will not always have me. [12] In pouring this perfume on my body, she has done it for my burial. [13] I tell you, wherever, in the whole world, this good news is proclaimed, what this woman has done will be told in memory of her."

[14] It was then that one of the Twelve, named Judas Iscariot, made his way to the chief priests, [15] and said, "What are you willing to give me, if I betray him to you?" The priests weighed him out thirty pieces of silver as payment. [16] So from that time he looked for an opportunity to betray him.

[17] On the first day of the festival of the unleavened bread, his followers came up to Jesus, and said: "Where do you wish

us to make preparations for you to eat the Passover?"

[18] "Go into the city to a certain man," he answered, "and say to him, 'The teacher says, "My time is near. I will keep the Passover with my followers at your house."'" [19] They did as Jesus directed them, and prepared the Passover. [20] In the evening Jesus took his place with the Twelve, [21] and, while they were eating, he said: "I tell you that one of you will betray me." [22] In great grief they began to say to him, one by one: "Can it be I, Master?"

[23] "The one who dipped his bread beside me in the dish," replied Jesus, "is the one who will betray me. [24] True, the Child of Humanity must go, as scripture says of him, yet alas for that person by whom the Child of Humanity is being betrayed! For that man it would be better never to have been born!" [25] Judas, who was betraying him, turned to him and said: "Can it be I, Rabbi?"

"It is you who say this," answered Jesus.

[26] While they were eating, Jesus took some bread, and, after saying the blessing, broke it and, as he gave it to his followers, said: "Take it and eat it; this is my body." [27] Then he took a cup, and, after saying the thanksgiving, gave it to them, with the words: "Drink from it, all of you; [28] for this is my blood of the covenant, which is poured out for many for the forgiveness of sins. [29] I tell you that I will never, after this, drink of wine, until that day when I will drink it new with you in the realm of my Father."

[30] They then sang a hymn, and went out to the Mount of Olives. [31] Then Jesus said to them: "Even you will all fall away from me tonight. Scripture says, 'I will strike down the shepherd, and the sheep of the flock will be scattered.' [32] But after I have risen, I will go before you into Galilee." [33] "If everyone else falls away from you," Peter answered, "I will never fall away!" [34] "I tell you," replied Jesus, "that this

very night, before the cock crows, you will disown me three times!" ³⁵ "Even if I must die with you," Peter exclaimed, "I will never disown you!" All the disciples spoke in the same way.

³⁶ Then Jesus came with them to a garden called Gethsemane, and he said to his disciples: "Sit down here while I go and pray over there." ³⁷ Taking with him Peter and the two sons of Zebedee, he began to show signs of sadness and deep distress of mind. ³⁸ "I am sad at heart," he said, "sad even to death; wait here and watch with me." ³⁹ Going on a little further, he threw himself on his face in prayer. "My Father," he said, "if it is possible, let me be spared this cup; only, not as I will, but as you will." ⁴⁰ Then he came to his disciples, and found them asleep. "What!" he said to Peter. "Could none of you watch with me for one hour? ⁴¹ Watch and pray so that you are not put to the test. True, the spirit is eager, but the flesh is weak." ⁴² Again, a second time, he went away and prayed. "My Father," he said, "if I cannot be spared this cup, but must drink it, your will be done!" ⁴³ And coming back again he found them asleep, for their eyes were heavy. ⁴⁴ So he left them, and went away again, and prayed a third time, again saying the same words. ⁴⁵ Then he came to his followers, and said: "Sleep on now, and rest yourselves. Look — my time is close at hand, and the Child of Humanity is being betrayed into the hands of wicked people. ⁴⁶ Up, and let us be going. Look! My betrayer is close at hand." ⁴⁷ And, while he was still speaking, Judas, who was one of the Twelve, came in sight; and with him was a great crowd of people, with swords and clubs, sent from the chief priests and elders of the people. ⁴⁸ Now the betrayer had arranged a signal with them. "The man whom I kiss," he had said, "will be the one; arrest him." ⁴⁹ So he went up to Jesus at once, and exclaimed: "Greetings, Rabbi!" and kissed him; ⁵⁰ at which Jesus said to him: "Friend, do what you have come for." The men went up, seized Jesus, and arrested him. ⁵¹ Suddenly one of those who were with Jesus stretched out his hand, and drew his sword, and striking the high priest's servant, cut off his ear. ⁵² "Sheathe your sword," Jesus said, "for all who draw the sword will be put to the sword. ⁵³ Do you think that I cannot ask my Father for help, when he would at once send to my aid more than twelve legions of angels? ⁵⁴ But in that case how would the scriptures be fulfilled, which say that this must be?" ⁵⁵ Jesus at the same time said to the crowds: "Have you come out, as if after a robber, with swords and clubs, to take me? I have sat teaching day after day in the Temple Courts, and yet you did not arrest me." ⁵⁶ The whole of this occurred in fulfillment of the scriptures of the prophets. Then his followers all forsook him and fled.

⁵⁷ Those who had arrested Jesus took him to Caiaphas, the high priest, where the scholars and the elders had assembled. ⁵⁸ Peter followed him at a distance as far as the courtyard of the offices, to see the end. ⁵⁹ Meanwhile the chief priests and the whole of the High Council were trying to get such false evidence against Jesus as would warrant putting him to death, ⁶⁰ but they did not find any, although many came forward with false evidence. Later on, however, two men came forward and said: ⁶¹ "This man said, 'I am able to destroy the Temple of God, and to build it in three days.'" ⁶² Then the high priest stood up, and said to Jesus: "Have you no answer? What is this evidence which these men are giving against you?" ⁶³ But Jesus remained silent. The high priest said to him: "I order you, by the living God, to tell us whether you are the Christ, the Son of God."

⁶⁴ "You say so," Jesus answered; "but I tell you all that hereafter you will see the Child of Humanity sitting on the right

hand of the Almighty, and coming on the clouds of the heavens." [65] Then the high priest tore his robes. "This is blasphemy!" he exclaimed. "Why do we want any more witnesses? You have just heard his blasphemy! [66] What is your decision?" They answered: "He deserves death." [67] Then they spat in his face, and struck him, while others dealt blows at him, saying as they did so: [68] "Now play the prophet for us, you Anointed One! Who was it that struck you?" [69] Peter, meanwhile, was sitting outside in the courtyard; and a maidservant came up to him, and exclaimed: "Why, you were with Jesus the Galilean!" [70] But Peter denied it before them all. "I do not know what you mean," he replied. [71] When he had gone out into the gateway, another servant saw him, and said to those who were there: "This man was with Jesus, the Nazarene!" [72] Again he denied it with an oath: "I do not know the man!" [73] But soon afterward those who were standing by came up and said to Peter: "You also are certainly one of them; why, even your way of speaking proves it!" [74] Then Peter said: "I swear that I do not know the man!" At that moment a cock crowed; [75] and Peter remembered the words which Jesus had said: 'Before a cock has crowed, you will disown me three times'; and he went outside, and wept bitterly.

27 [1] At daybreak all the chief priests and the elders of the people consulted together against Jesus, to bring about his death. [2] They tied him up and led him away, and gave him up to the governor, Pilate. [3] Then Judas, who betrayed him, seeing that Jesus was condemned, repented of what he had done, and returned the thirty pieces of silver to the chief priests and councilors. [4] "I did wrong in betraying a good man to his death," he said. "What has that to do with us?" they replied. "You must see to that yourself." [5] Judas flung down the pieces of silver in the Temple, and left; and went away and hanged himself.

[6] The chief priests took the pieces of silver, but they said: "We must not put them into the Temple treasury, because they are blood money." [7] So, after consultation, they bought with them the potter's field for a burial ground for foreigners; [8] and that is why that field is called the "Field of Blood" to this very day. [9] Then it was that these words spoken by the prophet Jeremiah were fulfilled: "They took the thirty pieces of silver, the price of him who was valued, whom some of the people of Israel valued, [10] and gave them for the Potter's field, as the Lord commanded me." [11] Meanwhile Jesus was brought before the governor. "Are you the king of the Jews?" asked the governor. "You are the one saying this," answered Jesus. [12] While charges were being brought against him by the chief priests and councilors, Jesus made no reply. [13] Then Pilate said to him: "Do you not hear how many accusations they are making against you?" [14] Yet Jesus made no reply — not even a single word; at which the governor was greatly astonished. [15] Now, at the festival, the governor was accustomed to grant the people the release of any one prisoner whom they might choose. [16] At that time they had a notorious prisoner called Barabbas. [17] So, when the people had collected, Pilate said to them: "Which do you wish me to release for you? Barabbas? Or Jesus who is called 'Anointed One'?" [18] For he knew that it was out of jealousy that they had given him up. [19] While he was still on the chair, his wife sent this message to him: "Do not have anything to do with that good man, for I have been very unhappy today because of a dream I had about him." [20] But the chief priests and the elders persuaded the crowds to ask for Barabbas, and to kill Jesus. [21] The governor, however, said to them: "Which of these two do you wish me to release for you?"

"Barabbas," they answered. [22] "What then," Pilate asked, "should I do with Jesus who is called 'the Anointed One'?" "Let him be crucified," they all replied. 23 "Why, what harm has he done?" he asked. But they kept shouting furiously: "Let him be crucified!" 24 When Pilate saw that his efforts were unavailing, but that, on the contrary, a riot was beginning, he took some water, and washed his hands in the sight of the crowd, saying as he did so: "I am not answerable for this bloodshed; you must see to it yourselves." 25 And all the people answered: "His blood be on our heads and on our children's!" 26 Then Pilate released Barabbas to them; but Jesus he scourged, and gave him up to be crucified.

27 After that, the governor's soldiers took Jesus with them into the government house, and gathered the whole garrison around him. 28 They stripped him, and put on him a purple military cloak, 29 and having twisted some thorns into a crown, put it on his head, and a rod in his right hand, and then, going down on their knees before him, they mocked him. "Long life to you, king of the Jews!" they said. 30 They spat at him and, taking the rod, kept striking him on the head; 31 and, when they had left off mocking him, they took off the cloak, and put his own clothes on him, and led him away to be crucified.

32 As they were on their way out, they came upon a man from Cyrene of the name of Simon; and they compelled him to go with them to carry the cross. 33 On reaching a place named Golgotha (that is, "The Place of the Skull"), 34 they gave him some wine to drink which had been mixed with gall; but after tasting it, Jesus refused to drink it. 35 When they had crucified him, they divided his clothes among them by casting lots. 36 Then they sat down, and kept watch over him there. 37 Above his head they fixed the accusation against him written out: "This is Jesus the king of the Judeans." 38 At the same time two robbers were crucified with him, one on the right, the other on the left. 39 The passersby railed at him, shaking their heads as

they said: 40 "You who destroy the Temple and build one in three days, save yourself! If you are God's Son, come down from the cross!" 41 In the same way the chief priests, with the scholars and elders, said in mockery: 42 "He saved others, but he cannot save himself! He is the 'king of Israel'! Let him come down from the cross now, and we will believe in him. 43 He has trusted in God; if God wants him, let him deliver him now; for he said, 'I am God's Son.'" 44 Even the robbers who were crucified with him insulted him in the same way. 45 After midday a darkness came over all the country, lasting until three in the afternoon. 46 About three Jesus called out loudly: *"Eloi, Eloi, lema sabacthani"* — that is to say, "My God, my God, why have you abandoned me?" 47 Some of those standing by heard this, and said: "The man is calling for Elijah!" 48 One of them immediately ran and took a sponge, and, filling it with common wine, put it on the end of a rod, and offered it to him to drink. 49 But the rest said: "Wait and let us see if Elijah is coming to save him." 50 But Jesus, uttering another loud cry, gave up his spirit. 51 Suddenly the Temple curtain was torn in two from top to bottom, the earth shook, the rocks were torn asunder, 52 the tombs opened, and the bodies of many of God's people who had fallen asleep rose, 53 and they, leaving their tombs, went, after the resurrection of Jesus, into the holy city, and appeared to many people. 54 The Roman captain, and the men with him who were watching Jesus, on seeing the earthquake and all that was happening, became greatly frightened and exclaimed: "This was really a son of God!" 55 There were many women there, watching from a distance, who had accompanied Jesus from Galilee and had been supporting him. 56 Among them were Mary of Magdala, Mary the mother of James and Joseph, and the mother of Zebedee's sons.

57 When evening had fallen, there came a rich man belonging to Ramah,

named Joseph, who had himself become a follower of Jesus. [58] He went to see Pilate, and asked for the body of Jesus. Pilate ordered it to be given him. [59] So Joseph took the body, and wrapped it in a clean linen sheet, [60] and laid it in his newly made tomb which he had cut in the rock; and, before he left, he rolled a great stone against the entrance of the tomb. [61] Mary of Magdala and the other Mary remained behind, sitting in front of the grave.

[62] The next day — that is, the day following the preparation day — the chief priests and Pharisees came in a body to Pilate, and said: [63] "Sir, we remember that during his lifetime, that impostor said, 'I will rise after three days.' [64] So order the tomb to be made secure until the third day. Otherwise his disciples may come and steal him, and then say to the people, 'He has risen from the dead,' which would be the latest fraud, even worse than the first."

[65] "You may have a guard," was Pilate's reply; "go and make the tomb as secure as you can." [66] So they went and made the tomb secure, by sealing the stone, in the presence of the guard.

The Risen Life

28 [1] After the sabbath, as the first day of the week began to dawn, Mary of Magdala and the other Mary had gone to look at the grave, [2] when suddenly a great earthquake occurred. For an angel of the Lord descended from the sky, and came and rolled away the stone, and seated himself on it. [3] His appearance was as dazzling as lightning, and his clothing was as white as snow; [4] and, in their terror of him, the men on guard trembled violently and became like dead men. [5] But the angel, addressing the women, said: "You need not be afraid. I know that it is Jesus, who was

crucified, for whom you are looking. [6] He is not here; for he has risen, as he said he would. Come, and see the place where he was lying; [7] and then go quickly and say to his followers, 'He has risen from the dead, and is going before you into Galilee; there you will see him.' Remember, I have told you." [8] They left the tomb quickly, in awe and great joy, and ran to tell the news to his followers. [9] Suddenly Jesus met them. "Greetings!" he said. The women went up to him, and clasped his feet, bowing to the ground before him. Then Jesus said to them: [10] "Do not be afraid; go and tell my brothers and sisters to set out for Galilee, and they will see me there." [11] While they were still on their way, some of the guard came into the city, and reported to the chief priests everything that had happened. [12] So they and the elders met and, after holding a consultation, gave a large sum of money to the soldiers, [13] and told them to say that his followers came in the night, and stole him while they were asleep. [14] "And should this matter come before the governor," they added, "we will satisfy him, and see that you have nothing to fear." [15] So the soldiers took the money, and did as they were instructed. This story spread among the people of Judea even until today.

[16] The eleven followers went to Galilee, to the mountain where Jesus told them to meet him; [17] and, when they saw him, they bowed to the ground before him; although some hesitated. [18] Then Jesus came up, and spoke to them, saying: "All authority in heaven and on the earth has been given to me. [19] Therefore go and make followers of all the nations, baptizing them into the name of the Father, the Son, and the holy Spirit, [20] and teaching them to lay to heart all the commands that I have given you; and, remember, I myself am with you every day until the close of the age."

An Introduction to the Gospel of Mark

OFTEN STANDING IN the shadows of the longer gospels of Matthew and Luke, Mark has only within the past century been recognized as a powerful and nuanced story on its own. This emergence of Mark as presenting a particular kind of vision of Jesus will be helped by other, less recognized gospels (like Thomas) standing alongside of it, in order to challenge the idea that Matthew and Luke are more authentic or fuller stories of Jesus.

The Gospel of Mark is generally thought of as the first gospel story, though both the Gospel of Thomas and the Gospel of Peter* may have actually preceded it. It is quite probable that both the Gospel of Matthew and the Gospel of Luke followed Mark's basic plot, and even much of Mark's story, often almost word for word. The gospel itself gives no information at all about its author, and even the name "Mark" in the title was probably added later. In effect, the author of this gospel is anonymous. Where and for whom this gospel was written are unknown, with early speculation citing Rome and more recent proposals pointing to Syria or Galilee. Although written in Greek with a number of grammatical weaknesses, Mark is composed with much subtlety, careful sequencing, and powerful meaning.

Its plot is stark and its scenes jagged with drama and pain. Broken bodies litter the story, with crippled, bleeding, and possessed people around almost every corner. Jesus himself is embattled almost from the beginning by enemies from Galilee and Jerusalem, even as he launches forth into the countryside to teach and to heal. He predicts his own death several times, and he eventually dies in agony at the hands of the Roman occupiers of Israel, crying out in protest against God's abandonment. The final scene of the gospel at the empty tomb of Jesus is also wrenching, as women who have followed Jesus discover that he has risen but run away frightened and tell no one the news. The pervasive loss and trauma in Mark, even in the midst of healings and occasional wonder, have led many to propose that it was written immediately prior to, during, or soon after the devastating reconquest of Israel by Rome in 68–70 CE, in which thousands of people were tortured and tens of thousands died.

---

* The Gospel of Peter, an extensive fragment of a gospel, contains extensive sections on the trial, death, and resurrection of Jesus. This document was discovered in the nineteenth century. It was not selected by the council for inclusion in *A New New Testament*.

Ragged Healing

In Mark, Jesus heals at almost every turn, from his first actions in Galilee until just before his entry into Jerusalem, where he is arrested and crucified. But the healings do not go smoothly. Some are contested and condemned by his opponents. At other times he is unable to heal, his ministrations need prompting from a foreign woman, or a blind man can't see correctly after Jesus tries to help him. Many times Jesus deflects credit for the healing by saying that the confidence of the sick person was the cause of the improvement. Still other times he tells people to keep quiet about the healing. Many of these events involve Jesus debating with and exorcising demons.

Mark's story highlights how starkly Jesus's healings contrast with his own fate on the cross. His enemies taunt him as he is dying: "He saved others, but he cannot save himself" (15:32). And, finally, Jesus himself is reduced to screaming angrily at God for having abandoned him. Mark's story of Jesus, the healer, seems to resist conclusions either that his power triumphantly wins or that he is a tragic failure. Both healing and loss persist.

Secret Son of God

Secrecy is a major element in Mark. Jesus regularly tells his followers or those whom he heals to keep secret what is happening and who he really is. When, during his baptism, God reveals that Jesus is God's Son, this message is addressed only to Jesus, and those around do not seem to hear it. Indeed, nearly all such revelations occur almost exclusively in private or in small groups. After Jesus's first parable in this gospel, he takes his followers aside and tells them that only they are to receive the "secret" of his teachings about the realm of God. When Peter seemingly gives Jesus his correct title of the "Anointed One" (often translated as "the Christ" or "the Messiah"), Jesus forbids him to tell anyone. And when the gospel ends, only the women know the secret of his resurrection.

This emphasis on secrecy in Mark has been much discussed, but there is no scholarly or theological consensus on what it means. It is, however, clear that it is a key element of Mark's overall understanding of the gospel. It could be part of Mark's focus on the pain and trauma from the Roman destruction in Galilee and Jerusalem and the desperate illness and poverty of the people. Mark's portrayal of Jesus as a secret divine agent lets both the devastation and the partial healing be recognized alongside each other, without the story turning either unrealistically triumphant or ultimately tragic. For twenty-first-century readers this jagged and incomplete picture of Jesus stands in helpful tension with the more resolved and triumphant versions of the story in Luke and John. The conventional church presentation of Jesus as a superman gives way to that of a relatively successful healer in the middle of trauma and, as such, offers positive, yet realistic, examples for the troubled twenty-first century.

Recommended Reading

Maia Kotrosits and Hal Taussig, *Marking Loss: Reading a Gospel Amidst Pain and Trauma*
Burton Mack, *A Myth of Innocence: The Gospel of Mark and Christian Origins*
Ched Myers, *Say to This Mountain: Mark's Story of Discipleship*

The Gospel of Mark

Prologue

1 ¹ The beginning of the good news of Jesus Christ.

² It is said in the prophet Isaiah: "Look! I am sending my messenger ahead of you; he will prepare your way. ³ The voice of one crying aloud in the wilderness, 'Make ready the way of the Lord, make God's paths straight.'"

And in fulfillment of this, John the Baptizer appeared in the wilderness proclaiming a bathing of repentance for the forgiveness of sins. ⁵ The whole of Judea as well as all the inhabitants of Jerusalem went out to him, and they were baptized by him in the river Jordan, confessing their sins.

⁶ John wore clothes made of camels' hair, with a leather strap around his waist, and lived on locusts and wild honey; ⁷ and he proclaimed: "There is coming after me one more powerful than I, and I am not fit even to stoop down and unfasten his sandals. ⁸ I have bathed you with water, but he will bathe you with the holy Spirit."

⁹ Now about that time Jesus came from Nazareth in Galilee and was baptized by John in the Jordan. ¹⁰ Just as he was coming up out of the water, he saw the sky split open and the Spirit like a dove descending on him, ¹¹ and from the sky came a voice: "You are my dearly loved child, in whom I delight."

¹² Immediately afterward the Spirit drove Jesus out into the wilderness; ¹³ and he was there in the wilderness forty days, tempted by Satan, and among the wild beasts, while the angels served him.

The Work in Galilee

¹⁴ After John was committed to prison, Jesus went to Galilee, proclaiming the good news of God: ¹⁵ "The time has come, and the realm of God is at hand; repent and believe the good news."

¹⁶ As Jesus was going along the shore of the Sea of Galilee, he saw Simon and his brother Andrew casting a net in the sea, for they were fishermen. ¹⁷ "Come and follow me," Jesus said, "and I will teach you to fish for people." ¹⁸ They left their nets at once, and followed him.

¹⁹ Going on a little further, he saw James, Zebedee's son, and his brother John, who also were in their boat mending the nets. ²⁰ Jesus called them at once, and they left their father Zebedee in the boat with the crew, and went after him.

²¹ They walked into Capernaum. On the next sabbath Jesus went into the synagogue and began to teach. ²² The people were amazed at his teaching, for he taught them like one who had authority, and not like the scholars. ²³ Now there was in their synagogue at the time a man under the power of an unclean spirit, who called out, ²⁴ "What do you want with us, Jesus of Nazareth? Have you come to destroy us? I know who you are — the holy one of God!" ²⁵ But Jesus rebuked the spirit, "Be quiet! Come out from him." ²⁶ The unclean spirit threw the man into a fit and with a loud cry came out from him. ²⁷ They were all so amazed that they kept asking, "What is this new teaching? He gives his commands with authority even to the unclean spirits, and they obey him!" ²⁸ And the fame of Jesus spread at once in all directions, through the whole of Galilee.

²⁹ As soon as they had come out from the synagogue, they went, with James and John, into the house of Simon and Andrew. ³⁰ Now Simon's mother-in-law was lying ill with fever, and they at once told

Jesus about her. [31] Jesus went up to her and, grasping her hand, raised her up; the fever left her, and she began to serve them.

[32] In the evening, after sunset, the people brought to Jesus all who were ill or possessed by demons; [33] and the whole town was gathered around the door. [34] Jesus cured many who were ill with various diseases, and he drove out many demons and would not permit them to speak, because they knew him to be the Christ.

[35] In the morning, long before daylight, Jesus rose and went out and, going to a lonely spot, there began to pray. [36] But Simon and his companions went out searching for him, [37] and when they found him, they exclaimed, "Everyone is looking for you!" [38] But Jesus said to them, "Let us go somewhere else, into the country towns nearby, so that I can make my proclamation in them also, for that was why I came." [39] And he went about making his proclamation in their synagogues all through Galilee and driving out the demons.

[40] One day a man with a skin disease came to Jesus and, falling on his knees, begged him for help. "If only you are willing," he said, "you are able to make me clean." [41] Moved with compassion, Jesus stretched out his hand and touched him, saying as he did so, "I am willing; become clean." [42] Instantly the disease left the man, and he became clean; [43] and then Jesus, after sternly warning him, immediately sent him away and said to him, [44] "Be careful not to say anything to anyone; but go and show yourself to the priest, and make the offerings for your cleansing directed by Moses as evidence of your cure." [45] The man, however, went away and began to speak about it publicly and to spread the story so widely that Jesus could no longer go openly into a town but stayed outside in lonely places; and people came to him from every direction.

2 [1] Some days later, when Jesus came back to Capernaum, the news spread that he was in a house there; [2] and so many people collected together that after a while there was no room for them even around the door; and he began to speak powerfully to them. [3] Some people came, bringing to him a paralyzed man who was being carried by four of them. [4] Being, however, unable to get him near to Jesus owing to the crowd, they removed the roofing above Jesus; and when they had made an opening, they let down the mat on which the paralyzed man was lying. [5] When Jesus saw their trust, he said to the man, "Child, your sins are forgiven."

[6] But some of the scholars who were sitting there were debating in their minds, [7] "Why does this man speak like this? He is blaspheming! Who can forgive sins except God?" [8] Jesus, at once intuitively aware that they were debating with themselves in this way, said to them, "Why are you debating in your minds about this? [9] Which is easier: To say to the paralyzed man, 'Your sins are forgiven'? Or to say, 'Get up, and take up your mat, and walk'? [10] But so you may know that the Child of Humanity has power to forgive sins on earth" — Here he said to the paralyzed man, [11] "To you I say, Get up, take up your mat, and return to your home." [12] The man got up and immediately took up his mat and went out before them all; at which they were amazed, and, as they praised God, they said, "We have never seen anything like this!"

[13] Jesus went out again to the sea, and all the people came to him, and he taught them. [14] As he went along, he saw Levi, the son of Alphaeus, sitting in the tax office and said to him, "Follow me." Levi got up and followed him.

[15] Later on he was in his house having dinner, and a number of tax collectors and outcasts took their places at the table with Jesus and his followers, for many of them were following him. [16] When the scholars belonging to the party of the Pharisees saw that he was eating in the company of such

people, they said to his followers, "He is eating in the company of tax collectors and outcasts!" [17] Hearing this, Jesus said, "It is not those who are healthy who need a doctor, but those who are ill. I did not come to call those who are just, but the outcast."

[18] Now John's followers and the Pharisees were fasting, and people came and asked Jesus, "Why is it that John's followers and the followers of the Pharisees fast, while yours do not?" [19] Jesus answered, "Can the groom's relatives fast, while the groom is with them? As long as they have the groom with them, they cannot fast. [20] But the days will come when the groom will be taken away from them, and they will fast then — when that day comes.

[21] "No one ever sews a piece of unshrunk cloth on an old garment; if she does, the patch tears away from it — the new from the old — and a worse tear is made. [22] And no one ever puts new wine into old wineskins; if she does, the wine will burst the skins, and both the wine and the skins are lost. But new wine is put into fresh skins."

[23] One sabbath, as Jesus was walking through the cornfields, his followers began to pick the ears as they went along. [24] "Look!" the Pharisees said to him. "Why are they doing what is not allowed on the sabbath?"

[25] "Have you never read," answered Jesus, "what David did when he was in need and hungry, he and his companions — [26] how he went into the house of God, in the time of Abiathar the high priest, and ate the consecrated bread, which only the priests are allowed to eat, and gave some to his comrades as well?"

[27] Then Jesus added, "The sabbath was made for people, and not people for the sabbath; [28] so the Child of Humanity is lord even of the sabbath."

3 [1] On another occasion Jesus went into the synagogue, where there was a man whose hand was withered. [2] And they watched Jesus closely, to see if he would heal the man on the sabbath, so that they might have a charge to bring against him. [3] "Stand out in the middle," Jesus said to the man with the withered hand; [4] and to the people he said, "Is it allowable to do good on the sabbath — or harm? To save a life or destroy it?" [5] As they remained silent, Jesus looked around at them in anger, grieving at the hardness of their hearts, and said to the man, "Stretch out your hand." The man stretched it out, and his hand was restored. [6] Immediately on leaving the synagogue, the Pharisees and the Herodians united in laying a plot against Jesus, to destroy him.

[7] Then Jesus went away with his followers to the sea, followed by a great number of people from Galilee. [8] All these people, hearing of all that he was doing, came to him from Judea, from Jerusalem, from Edom, from beyond the Jordan, and from the country around Tyre and Sidon. [9] So Jesus told his followers to keep a small boat close by, so that the crowd would not crush him. [10] For he had healed many of them, and so people kept crowding around him, so all who were sick might touch him, since many were infected. [11] The unclean spirits, too, whenever they caught sight of him, flung themselves down before him, and screamed out, "You are the Child of God!" [12] But he repeatedly warned them not to make him known.

[13] Jesus made his way up the mountain and called those whom he wished, and they went to him. [14] He appointed twelve — whom he also named "ambassadors" or "apostles"* — so that they might be with him, and that he might send them out as his messengers, to proclaim, [15] and

---

* The Greek word *apostolos* means "ambassador." We keep both words here to recognize the traditional word *apostle* while also showing what it means.

with power to drive out demons. [16] So he appointed the Twelve — Peter (which was the nickname that Jesus gave to Simon), [17] James, the son of Zebedee, and his brother John (to whom he gave the name of Boanerges, which means the "Sons of Thunder"), [18] Andrew, Philip, Bartholomew, Matthew, Thomas, James the son of Alphaeus, Thaddaeus, Simon the Canaanite, [19] and Judas Iscariot, the man who handed him over.

[20] Jesus went into a house; and again a crowd collected, so that they were not even able to eat their food. [21] When his relations heard of it, they went to take charge of him, for they said that he was out of his mind.

[22] The scholars who had come down from Jerusalem said, "He has Beelzebul in him! He drives the demons out by the help of their chief." [23] So Jesus called them to him and answered them in parables, "How can Satan drive out Satan? [24] When a realm is divided against itself, it cannot last; [25] and when a household is divided against itself, it will not be able to last. [26] So if Satan is in revolt against himself and is divided, he cannot last — his end has come!

[27] "No man who has gotten into a strong man's house can carry off his goods without first tying him up; and not until then will he plunder his house. [28] Truly I tell you that people will be forgiven everything — their sins, and all the slanders that they utter; [29] but whoever slanders the holy Spirit remains unforgiven to the end; that person is responsible forever." [30] This was said in reply to the charge that he had an unclean spirit in him. [31] His mother and his brothers came, and stood outside, and sent to ask him to come to them. [32] There was a crowd sitting around Jesus, and some of them said to him, "Look, your mother and your brothers are outside, asking for you."

[33] "Who is my mother? And my brothers?" was his reply. [34] Then he looked around on the people sitting in a circle around him, and said, "Here are my mother and my brothers! [35] Whoever does the will of God is my brother and sister and mother."

4 [1] Jesus again began to teach by the sea; and, as an immense crowd was gathering around him, he got into a boat and sat in it on the sea, while all the people were on the shore at the water's edge.

[2] Then he taught them much in parables. And in the course of his teaching he said to them,

[3] "Listen! A sower went out to sow; [4] and presently, as he was sowing, some of the seed fell along the path; and the birds came and ate it up. [5] Some fell on rocky ground where it had not much soil and, having no depth of soil, sprang up at once; [6] but when the sun rose, it was scorched, and, having no root, withered away. [7] Some of the seed fell among thorns; but the thorns shot up and completely choked it, and it yielded no return. [8] Some fell into good soil and, shooting up and growing, yielded a return, amounting to thirty-, sixty-, and even a hundredfold." [9] And Jesus said, "Let anyone who has ears to hear with hear."

[10] Afterward, when he was alone, his followers and the Twelve asked him about his parables, [11] and he said, "To you the secret of the realm of God has been imparted; but to those who are outside everything takes the form of parables so that [12] 'though they have eyes, they may see without perceiving; and though they have ears, they may hear without understanding; otherwise some day they might turn and be forgiven.'"

[13] And he said to them, "Do you not understand this parable? Then how will you understand all the other parables? [14] The sower sows the message. [15] The people meant by the seeds that fall along the path are these — where the message

is sown, but as soon as they have heard it, Satan immediately comes and carries away the message that has been sown in their hearts. [16] So, too, those meant by the seeds sown on the rocky places are the people who, when they have heard the message, at once accept it joyfully; [17] but, as they have no root, they stand only for a short time; and so, when trouble or an attack arises because of the message, they fall away at once. [18] Those meant by the seeds sown among the thorns are different; they are the people who hear the message, [19] but the cares of life, and the glamour of wealth, and cravings for many other things come in and completely choke the message, so that it gives no return. [20] But the people meant by the seeds sown on the good ground are those who hear the message, and welcome it, and yield a return, thirty-, sixty-, and even a hundredfold."

[21] And he said to them, "Is a lamp brought to be put under a basket or under the couch, instead of being put on the lamp stand? [22] There is nothing hidden that will not be revealed, and nothing is concealed that will not be brought into the open. [23] Let all who have ears to hear with hear."

[24] And he said to them, "Take care what you listen to. The standard you use will be used for you, and more will be added for you. [25] For to those who have, more will be given; while from those who have nothing, even what they have will be taken away."

[26] He also said, "This is what the realm of God is like — like a man who has scattered seed on the ground, [27] and then sleeps by night and rises by day, while the seed is shooting up and growing — he knows not how. [28] The ground bears the crop of itself — first the blade, then the ear, and then the full grain in the ear; [29] but as soon as the crop is ready, immediately he 'puts in the sickle because harvest has come.'"

[30] He also said, "To what can we liken the realm of God? [31] By what can we illustrate it? Perhaps by the growth of a mustard seed. This seed, when sown in the ground, though it is smaller than all other seeds, [32] yet when sown shoots up and becomes larger than any other herb and puts out great branches so that even 'the wild birds can nest in its shelter.'"

[33] With many such parables Jesus used to speak to the people of his message, as far as they were able to receive it; [34] and to them he never used to speak except in parables; but in private to his own followers he explained everything.

[35] In the evening of the same day, Jesus said to them, "Let us go across." [36] So, leaving the crowd behind, they took him with them, just as he was, in the boat; and there were other boats with him. [37] A great storm came, and the waves kept dashing into the boat, so that the boat was actually filling. [38] Jesus was in the stern asleep on the cushion, and they roused him and cried, "Teacher! Is it nothing to you that we are lost?" [39] Jesus rose and rebuked the wind, and said to the sea, "Hush! Be still!" Then the wind dropped, and a great calm followed. [40] "Why are you so afraid?" he exclaimed. "Have you no trust yet?" [41] But they were struck with great awe and said to one another, "Who can this be that even the wind and the sea obey him?"

5 [1] They came to the other side of the sea, to the country of the Gerasenes; [2] and as soon as Jesus had gotten out of the boat, he met a man coming out of the tombs who had an unclean spirit [3] and who made his home in the tombs. No one had ever been able to bind him, even with a chain; [4] for though he had been bound with fetters and chains many times, he had snapped the chains and broken the fetters to pieces, and no one could master him. [5] Night and day he was continually shrieking in the tombs and among the hills and cutting himself with stones. [6] Catching sight of Jesus from a distance, he ran and bowed to the ground before him, [7] shrieking out

in a loud voice, "What do you want with me, Jesus, son of the Most High God? For God's sake do not torment me!" [8] For Jesus had said, "Come out from the man, you unclean spirit." [9] And he asked him, "What is your name?" He said, "My name is Legion, for we are many." [10] And he begged Jesus again and again not to send them away out of that country.

[11] There was a large herd of pigs close by feeding on the hillside, [12] and the spirits begged him, "Send us into the pigs so that we can take possession of them." [13] He gave them leave. They came out and entered into the pigs, and the herd—about two thousand in number—rushed down the steep slope into the sea and were drowned in the sea.

[14] Then the men who tended them ran away and carried the news to the town and to the country around; and the people went to see what had happened. [15] When they came to Jesus, they found the possessed man sitting there, clothed and in his right mind—the man who had had the legion in him—and they were frightened. [16] Then those who had seen it explained to them what had happened to the possessed man, and about the pigs; [17] so they began to beg Jesus to leave their district.

[18] As Jesus was getting into the boat, the possessed man begged him to let him stay with him. [19] But Jesus refused. He said, "Go home to your people and tell them of all that the Lord has done for you and how he took pity on you." [20] So the man went and began to proclaim in the district of the Ten Cities all that Jesus had done for him, and everyone was amazed.

[21] By the time Jesus had crossed in the boat to the opposite shore, a great number of people had gathered to meet him and were standing by the sea. [22] One of the leaders of the synagogue, whose name was Jairus, came and, as soon as he saw Jesus, fell at his feet. [23] He begged him, "My little daughter is at the point of death. I beg you to come and place your hands on her

so that her life may be spared." [24] So Jesus went with him. A great number of people followed Jesus and kept pressing around him.

[25] There was a woman who for twelve years had suffered from a flow of blood. [26] She had undergone much at the hands of many doctors, spending all she had without obtaining any relief but, on the contrary, growing worse. [27] Having heard about Jesus, she came behind in the crowd and touched his clothes, [28] for she said, "If I can only touch his clothes, I will get well!" [29] At once the source of her flow of blood dried up, and she felt in her body that she was healed of her affliction. [30] Jesus knew in himself that the power had gone out from him, and turning back to the crowd, he said, "Who touched my clothes?"

[31] His followers said to him, "You see the people pressing around you, and you say, 'Who touched me?'" [32] But Jesus looked around to see who had done it. [33] Then the woman, in fear and trembling, knowing what had happened to her, came and threw herself down before him, and told him the whole truth. [34] He said to her, "Daughter, your confidence has delivered you. Go in peace and be healed from your affliction."

[35] Before he had finished speaking, some people came from the house of the leader of the synagogue and said, "Your daughter is dead! Why should you trouble the teacher further?" [36] But Jesus, overhearing what they were saying, said to the leader of the synagogue, "Do not be afraid, only have faith." [37] And he allowed no one to accompany him, except Peter, James, and John, the brother of James. [38] Presently they reached the president's house, where Jesus saw a scene of confusion—people weeping and wailing incessantly. [39] "Why this confusion and weeping?" he said on entering. "The little child is not dead, she is asleep." [40] They began to laugh at him, but he sent them all

out, and then, with the child's father and mother and his companions, went into the room where she was lying. ⁴¹ Taking her hand, Jesus said to her, *"Taleitha, koum!"* — which means, "Little girl, I am speaking to you — rise!" ⁴² The little girl stood up at once, and began to walk about; for she was twelve years old. And, as soon as they saw it, they were overwhelmed with amazement; ⁴³ but Jesus repeatedly cautioned them not to let anyone know of it, and told them to give her something to eat.

6 ¹ On leaving that place, Jesus, followed by his followers, went to his own part of the country. ² When the sabbath came, he began to teach in the synagogue, and many people who were listening to him were amazed. "Where did he get this?" they said, "And what is this wisdom that has been given him? And these powerful things he is doing? ³ Is he not the carpenter, the child of Mary, and the brother of James, and Joses, and Judas, and Simon? And are not his sisters, too, here among us?" This proved a hindrance to their trusting in him. ⁴ Then Jesus said to them, "A prophet is not without honor, except in his own country, and among his own relatives, and in his own house." ⁵ And he could not work any miracle there, beyond placing his hands on a few sick people and healing them. ⁶ And he marveled at their lack of trust. Jesus went around the villages, one after another, teaching.

⁷ He called the Twelve to him and began to send them out two by two, and gave them authority over unclean spirits. ⁸ He instructed them to take nothing but a staff for the journey — not even bread, or a bag, or coins in their purse; ⁹ but they were to wear sandals, and not to put on a second coat. ¹⁰ "Whenever you go to stay at a house," he said, "remain there until you leave that place. ¹¹ If a place does not welcome you or listen to you, as you go out of it shake off the dust that is on the soles of

your feet as a protest against them." ¹² So they set out and proclaimed the need of repentance. ¹³ They drove out many demons, and anointed with oil many who were infirm, and cured them.

¹⁴ Now King Herod heard of Jesus, for his name had become well known. People were saying, "John the Baptizer must have risen from the dead, and that is why these powers are active in him." ¹⁵ Others again said, "He is Elijah," and others, "He is a prophet, like one of the great prophets." ¹⁶ But when Herod heard of him, he said, "The man whom I beheaded — John — has been raised!"

¹⁷ For Herod himself had sent and arrested John, and put him in prison in chains, on account of Herodias, the wife of his brother Philip, because Herod had married her. ¹⁸ For John had said to Herod, "It is not right for you to have your brother's wife." ¹⁹ So Herodias was incensed against John and wanted to put him to death, but was unable to do so ²⁰ because Herod stood in fear of John, knowing him to be a righteous and holy man, and he protected him. He had listened to John, but still remained greatly perplexed, and yet he found pleasure in listening to him.

²¹ A suitable opportunity, however, occurred when Herod, on his birthday, gave a dinner for his high officials, and his generals, and the foremost men in Galilee. ²² When his daughter — that is, the daughter of Herodias — came in and danced, she delighted Herod and those who were dining with him. "Ask me for whatever you like," the king said to the girl, "and I will give it to you," ²³ and he swore to her that he would give her whatever she asked him — up to half his realm. ²⁴ The girl went out and said to her mother, "What must I ask for?"

"The head of John the Baptizer," answered her mother. ²⁵ So she went in as quickly as possible to the king and made her request. "I want you," she said, "to give me at once, on a dish, the head of John the Baptizer." [26] The king was much distressed, yet because of his oath and the guests at his table, he did not want to refuse her. [27] He immediately dispatched one of his bodyguards, with orders to bring John's head. The man went and beheaded John in the prison, [28] and, bringing his head on a dish, gave it to the girl, and the girl gave it to her mother.

[29] When John's followers heard of it, they came and took his body away, and laid it in a tomb.

[30] When the ambassadors came back to Jesus, they told him all that they had done and all that they had taught. [31] "Come by yourselves privately to a deserted place," he said, "and rest for a while" — for there were so many people coming and going that they had not time even to eat. [32] So they set off privately in their boat for a deserted place. [33] Many people saw them going, and recognized them, and from all the towns they flocked together to the place on foot, and got there before them. [34] On getting out of the boat, Jesus saw a great crowd, and his heart was moved at the sight of them, because they were "like sheep without a shepherd"; and he began to teach them many things. [35] When it grew late, his followers came up to him, and said, "This is a deserted place, and it is already late. [36] Send the people away, so that they may go to the farms and villages around and buy themselves something to eat." [37] But Jesus answered, "It is for you to give them something to eat." "Are we to go and spend almost a year's wages on bread," they asked, "to give them to eat?"

[38] "How many loaves have you?" he asked. "Go, and see." When they had found out, they told him, "Five, and two fish." [39] Jesus directed them to make all the people sit down on the green grass, in parties; [40] and they sat down in groups — in hundreds, and in fifties. [41] Taking the five loaves and the two fish, Jesus looked up to heaven, and said the blessing; he broke the loaves into pieces, and gave them to his followers for them to serve to the people, and he divided the two fish also among them all. [42] Everyone had sufficient to eat; [43] and they picked up enough broken pieces to fill twelve baskets, as well as some of the fish. [44] The people who ate the bread were five thousand in number.

[45] Immediately afterward Jesus made his followers get into the boat, and cross over in advance, in the direction of Bethsaida, while he himself was dismissing the crowd. [46] After he had taken leave of the people, he went away up the hill to pray. [47] When evening fell, the boat was out in the middle of the sea, and Jesus was on the shore alone. [48] Seeing them laboring at the oars — for the wind was against them — about three hours after midnight Jesus came toward them, walking on the water, intending to join them. [49] But when they saw him walking on the water, they thought it was a ghost, and cried out; [50] for all of them saw him, and were terrified. But Jesus at once spoke to them. "Courage!" he said. "It is I; do not be afraid!" [51] Then he got into the boat with them, and the wind dropped. The followers were utterly amazed, [52] for they had not understood about the loaves, their minds being slow to learn. [53] When they had crossed over, they landed at Gennesaret, and moored the boat. [54] But when they got out of the boat, the people, immediately recognizing Jesus, [55] hurried over the whole countryside, and began to carry about on mats those who were ill, wherever they heard he was. [56] So wherever he went — to villages, or towns, or farms — they would lay their sick in the marketplaces, begging him to let them touch only the fringe of his cloak; and all who touched were made well.

7 [1] One day the Pharisees and some of the scholars who had come from Jerusalem gathered around Jesus. [2] They had noticed that some of his followers ate their food with their hands defiled, by which they

meant unwashed. [3] (For the Pharisees, and indeed all Judeans, will not eat without first thoroughly washing their hands, holding in this to the tradition of the elders. [4] When they come from the market, they will not eat without first washing themselves; and there are many other traditions which they have inherited and hold to, such as washing cups, and jugs, and copper pans.) [5] So the Pharisees and the scholars asked Jesus this question: "How is it that your followers do not follow the tradition of the elders, but eat their bread with unclean hands?" [6] His answer was, "It was well said by Isaiah when he prophesied about you hypocrites in the words, 'This people honors me with their lips, while their hearts are far removed from me; [7] but vainly do they worship me, for they teach but human precepts.' [8] You neglect God's commandments and hold to human tradition. [9] Wisely do you set aside God's commandments," he exclaimed, "to keep your own tradition! [10] For while Moses said, 'Honor your father and your mother,' and 'Let anyone who abuses his father or mother suffer death,' [11] you say, 'If a person says to his father or mother, "Whatever of mine might have been of service to you is Korban"' (which means 'Given to God') — [12] why, then you do not allow him to do anything further for his father or mother! [13] In this way you nullify the words of God by your tradition, which you hand down; and you do many things like this."

[14] Then Jesus called the people to him again, and said, "Listen to me, all of you, and mark my words. [15] There is nothing external to a person, which by going into her can defile her; but the things that come out from a person are the things that defile her."

[17] When Jesus went indoors, away from the crowd, his followers began questioning him about this saying. [18] "What, do even you understand so little?" exclaimed Jesus. "Do you not see that there is nothing external to a person, which by going into a person, can defile her [19] because it does not pass into her heart, but into her stomach, and is afterward gotten rid of?" — in saying this Jesus pronounced all food "clean." [20] "It is what comes out from a person," he added, "that defiles her, [21] for it is from within, out of the hearts of people, that there come evil thoughts — sexual immorality, theft, murder, adultery, [22] greed, wickedness, deceit, indecency, envy, slander, haughtiness, folly; [23] all these wicked things come from within, and do defile a person."

[24] On leaving that place, Jesus went to the district of Tyre and Sidon. He went into a house, and did not wish anyone to know it, but could not escape notice. [25] For a woman, whose little daughter had an unclean spirit in her, heard of him immediately, and came and threw herself at his feet — [26] the woman was a Greek, from Syrophoenicia — and she begged him to drive the demon out of her daughter. [27] "Let the children be fed first," answered Jesus. "For it is not fair to take the children's food, and throw it to dogs."

[28] "Lord," she replied, "even the dogs under the table feed on the children's crumbs."

[29] "For saying that," he answered, "you may go. The demon has gone out of your daughter." [30] The woman went home, and found the child lying on her bed, and the demon gone.

[31] On returning from the district of Tyre, Jesus went, by way of Sidon, to the Sea of Galilee, across the district of the Ten Cities. [32] Some people brought to him a man who was deaf and almost mute, and they begged Jesus to place his hand on him. [33] Jesus took him aside from the crowd quietly, put his fingers into the man's ears, and touched his tongue with saliva. [34] Then, looking up to heaven, he sighed, and said to the man, *"Ephphatha!"* which means "Be opened." [35] The man's ears were opened, his tongue was released,

and he began to talk plainly. [36] Jesus insisted on their not telling anyone; but the more he insisted, the more perseveringly they made it known, [37] and a profound impression was made on the people. "He has done everything well!" they exclaimed. "He makes even the deaf hear and the mute speak!"

8 [1] About that time, when there was again a great crowd of people who had nothing to eat, Jesus called his followers to him and said, [2] "My heart is moved at the sight of all these people, for they have already been with me three days and they have nothing to eat; [3] and if I send them away to their homes hungry, they will faint on the way; and some of them have come a long distance."

[4] "Where will it be possible," his followers answered, "to get sufficient bread for these people here in the desert?"

[5] "How many loaves have you?" he asked. "Seven," they answered. [6] Jesus told the crowd to sit down on the ground. Then he took the seven loaves, and, after saying the thanksgiving, broke them, and gave them to his followers to serve out; and they served them out to the crowd. [7] They had also a few small fish; and, after he had said the blessing, he told the followers to serve out these as well. [8] The people ate and they were filled, and they picked up seven baskets full of the broken pieces that were left. [9] There were about four thousand people. Then Jesus dismissed them. [10] Immediately afterward, getting into the boat with his followers, Jesus went to the district of Dalmanutha.

[11] Here the Pharisees came out, and began to argue with Jesus, asking him for some sign from heaven, to test him. [12] Sighing deeply, Jesus said, "Why does this generation ask for a sign? I tell you, no sign will be given it." [13] So he left them to themselves, and, getting into the boat again, went away to the opposite shore.

[14] Now the followers had forgotten to take any bread with them, one loaf being all that they had in the boat. [15] So Jesus gave them this warning. "Take care," he said, "beware of the leaven of the Pharisees and the leaven of Herod." [16] They began talking to one another about their being short of bread; [17] and, noticing this, Jesus said to them, "Why are you talking about your being short of bread? Do you not yet see or understand? Are your minds still so slow to comprehend? [18] Though you have eyes, do you not see? And though you have ears, do you not hear? Do you not remember, [19] when I broke up the five loaves for the five thousand, how many baskets of broken pieces you picked up?"

"Twelve," they said. [20] "And when the seven for the four thousand, how many basketfuls of broken pieces did you pick up?"

"Seven," they said. [21] "Do you not understand now?" he repeated.

[22] They came to Bethsaida. There some people brought a blind man to Jesus, and begged him to touch him. [23] Taking the blind man's hand, Jesus led him to the outskirts of the village, and, when he had put saliva on the man's eyes, he placed his hands on him, and asked him, "Do you see anything?" [24] The man looked up, and said, "I see the people, for, as they walk about, they look to me like trees." [25] Then Jesus again placed his hands on the man's eyes; and the man saw clearly, his sight was restored, and he saw everything with perfect distinctness. [26] Jesus sent him to his home, and said, "Do not go even into the village."

[27] Afterward Jesus and his followers went into the villages around Caesarea Philippi; and on the way he asked his followers this question: "Who do people say that I am?"

[28] "John the Baptizer," they answered, "but others say Elijah, while others say one of the prophets."

[29] "But you," he asked, "who do you say that I am?" To this Peter replied, "You are the Anointed One." [30] At which Jesus

charged them not to say this about him to anyone. [31] Then he began to teach them that the Child of Humanity must undergo much suffering, and that he must be rejected by the elders, and the chief priests, and the scholars, and be put to death, and rise again after three days. [32] He said all this quite openly. But Peter took Jesus aside, and began to rebuke him. [33] Jesus, however, turning around and seeing his followers, rebuked Peter. "Out of my sight, Satan!" he exclaimed. "For you look at things, not as God does, but as people do."

[34] Calling the people and his followers to him, Jesus said, "If anyone wishes to walk in my steps, let him renounce self, take up his cross, and follow me. [35] For whoever wishes to save his life will lose it, and whoever, for my sake and for the sake of the good news, will lose his life will save it. [36] What good is it to a person to gain the whole world and forfeit his life? [37] For what could a person give that is of equal value with his life? [38] Whoever is ashamed of me and of my teaching, in this unfaithful and sinful generation, of that person will the Child of Humanity be ashamed, when he comes in his Father's glory with the holy messengers.

9 [1] "I tell you," he added, "that some of those who are standing here will not know death until they have seen the realm of God come in power."

[2] Six days later, Jesus took with him Peter, James, and John, and led them up a high mountain by themselves. There his appearance was transformed before their eyes, [3] and his clothes became of a more dazzling white than anyone on earth could bleach them. [4] And Elijah appeared to them, in company with Moses; and they were talking with Jesus. [5] "Rabbi," said Peter, interposing, "it is good to be here; let us make three tents, one for you, one for Moses, and one for Elijah." [6] For he did not know what to say, because they were much

afraid. [7] Then a cloud came down and overshadowed them, and from the cloud there came a voice: "This is my beloved Child; listen to him." [8] And suddenly, on looking around, they saw that there was now no one with them but Jesus alone.

[9] As they were going down the mountainside, Jesus cautioned them not to relate what they had seen to anyone, until after the Child of Humanity should have risen again from the dead. [10] They seized on these words and discussed with one another what this rising from the dead meant. [11] "How is it," they asked Jesus, "that our scholars say that Elijah has to come first?"

[12] "Elijah does indeed come first," answered Jesus, "and reestablish everything; and does not scripture speak, with regard to the Child of Humanity, of his undergoing much suffering and being utterly despised? [13] But I tell you that Elijah has come, and people have treated him just as they pleased, as it is written about him."

[14] When they came to the other followers, they saw a great crowd around them, and some scholars arguing with them. [15] But as soon as they saw Jesus, all the people, in great astonishment, ran up and greeted him. [16] "What are you arguing about with them?" Jesus asked. [17] "Teacher," answered a man in the crowd, "I brought my son to see you, as he has a mute spirit in him; [18] and, wherever it seizes him, it dashes him down; he foams at the mouth and grinds his teeth, and he is pining away. I asked your followers to drive the spirit out, but they failed."

[19] "Faithless generation!" exclaimed Jesus. "How long must I be with you? How long must I have patience with you? Bring the boy to me." [20] They brought him to Jesus; but no sooner did the boy see him than the spirit threw him into convulsions; and he fell on the ground, and rolled about, foaming at the mouth. [21] "How long has he been like this?" Jesus asked

the boy's father. ²² "From his childhood," he answered; "and it has often thrown him into fire and into water to put an end to his life; but if you can possibly do anything, take pity on us, and help us!" ²³ "Why say 'possibly'?" Jesus replied. "Everything is possible for one who has trust." ²⁴ The boy's father immediately cried out, "I have trust; help my want of trust!" ²⁵ But when Jesus saw that a crowd was quickly collecting, he rebuked the unclean spirit, "Deaf and mute spirit, it is I who command you. Come out from him and never enter him again." ²⁶ With a loud cry the spirit threw the boy into repeated convulsions, and then came out from him. The boy looked like a corpse, so that most of them said that he was dead. ²⁷ But Jesus took his hand, and lifted him; and he stood up.

²⁸ When Jesus had gone indoors, his followers asked him privately, "Why could we not drive it out?"

²⁹ "A spirit of this kind," he said, "can come out only by prayer."

³⁰ Leaving that place, Jesus and his followers went on their way through Galilee; but he did not want anyone to know it, ³¹ for he was instructing his followers, and telling them: "The Child of Humanity is being betrayed into the hands of his fellow men, and they will put him to death, but when he has been put to death, he will rise again after three days." ³² But the followers did not understand his meaning and were afraid to question him.

³³ They came to Capernaum. When Jesus had gone into the house, he asked them, "What were you discussing on the way?" ³⁴ But they were silent; for on the way they had been arguing with one another which was the greatest. ³⁵ Sitting down, Jesus called the Twelve and said, "If anyone wishes to be first, he must be last of all, and servant of all." ³⁶ Then Jesus took a little child, and placed it in the middle of them. Folding it in his arms, he said to them, ³⁷ "Anyone who, for the sake of my name, welcomes even a little child like this is welcoming me, and anyone who welcomes me is welcoming not me, but the one who sent me."

³⁸ "Teacher," said John, "we saw someone driving out demons by using your name, and we tried to prevent him, because he did not follow us."

³⁹ "None of you must prevent him," answered Jesus, "for no one who does a deed of power in my name will find it easy to speak evil of me. ⁴⁰ Whoever is not against us is for us. ⁴¹ Anyone who gives you a cup of water because you belong to Christ, I tell you, will assuredly not lose his reward.

⁴² "And, if anyone causes one of these little ones who trusts in me to stumble, it would be far better for him if he had been thrown into the sea with a great millstone around his neck. ⁴³ If your hand causes you to stumble, cut it off. It would be better for you to enter the life maimed, than to have both your hands and go into Gehenna, into the fire that cannot be put out. ⁴⁵ If your foot causes you to sin, cut it off. It would be better for you to enter the life lame, than to have both your feet and be thrown into Gehenna. ⁴⁷ If your eye causes you to sin, tear it out. It would be better for you to enter the realm of God with only one eye, than to have both eyes and be thrown into Gehenna, ⁴⁸ where 'their worm does not die, and the fire is not put out.'

⁴⁹ "For it is by fire that everyone will be salted.

⁵⁰ "Salt is good, but if the salt should lose its saltiness, what will you use to season it?

"You must have salt in yourselves, and live at peace with one another."

The Journey to Jerusalem

10 ¹ On leaving that place, Jesus went into the district of Judea on the other side of the Jordan. Crowds gathered about him

again; and again, as usual, he began teaching them. [2] Presently some Pharisees came up and, to test him, asked, "Has a husband the right to divorce his wife?"

[3] "What direction did Moses give you?" replied Jesus. [4] "Moses," they said, "permitted a man to draw up in writing a notice of separation and divorce his wife."

[5] "It was owing to the hardness of your hearts," said Jesus, "that Moses gave you this commandment; [6] but at the beginning of the Creation, God 'made them male and female.' [7] 'For this reason a man will leave his father and mother, [8] and the man and his wife will become one'; so that they are no longer two, but one. [9] What God himself, then, has yoked together no one must separate."

[10] When they were indoors, the followers asked him again about this, [11] and he said, "Anyone who divorces his wife and marries another woman commits adultery against his wife; [12] and if the woman divorces her husband and marries another man, she commits adultery."

[13] Some of the people were bringing little children to Jesus, for him to touch them; but the followers found fault with those who had brought them. [14] When, however, Jesus saw this, he was indignant. "Let the little children come to me," he said; "do not hinder them, for it is to the childlike that the realm of God belongs. [15] I tell you, unless a person receives the realm of God like a child, she will not enter it at all." [16] Then he folded the children in his arms, and, placing his hands on them, he blessed them.

[17] As Jesus was resuming his journey, a man came running up to him, and threw himself on his knees before him. "Good teacher," he asked, "what must I do to inherit eternal life?"

[18] "Why do you call me good?" answered Jesus. "No one is good but God. [19] You know the commandments: 'Do not kill. Do not commit adultery. Do not steal. Do not say what is false about others. Do not cheat. Honor your father and your mother.'"

[20] "Teacher," he replied, "I have observed all these from my childhood." [21] Jesus, looking at the man, loved him and said, "There is still one thing wanting in you; go and sell all that you have, and give to the poor, and you will have wealth in heaven; then come and follow me." [22] But the man's face clouded at these words, and he went away distressed, for he had great possessions.

[23] Then Jesus looked around, and said to his followers, "How hard it will be for people of wealth to enter the realm of God!" [24] The followers were amazed at his words. But Jesus said again, "My children, how hard a thing it is to enter the realm of God! [25] It is easier for a camel to get through a needle's eye than for a rich person to enter the realm of God."

[26] "Then who can be saved?" they exclaimed in the greatest astonishment. [27] Jesus looked at them, and answered, "With people it is impossible, but not with God; for everything is possible with God."

[28] "But we," began Peter, "we left everything and have followed you."

[29] "I tell you," said Jesus, "there is no one who has left house or brothers or sisters or mother or father or children or land for my sake and for the good news [30] who will not receive a hundred times as much, even now in the present — houses, and brothers, and sisters, and mothers, and children, and land — though not without persecutions, and, in the age that is coming, eternal life. [31] But many who are first now will then be last, and the last will be first."

[32] One day, when they were on their way, going up to Jerusalem, Jesus was walking in front of them, and they were amazed, while those who were following behind were afraid. Gathering the Twelve around him once more, Jesus began to tell them what was about to happen to him. [33] "Listen!" he said. "We are go-

ing up to Jerusalem; and there the Child of Humanity will be betrayed to the chief priests and the scholars, and they will condemn him to death, and they will give him up to the gentiles, ³⁴ who will mock him, spit on him, and scourge him, and put him to death; and after three days he will rise again."

³⁵ James and John, the two sons of Zebedee, went to Jesus, and said, "Teacher, we want you to do for us whatever we ask."

³⁶ "What do you want me to do for you?" he asked. ³⁷ "Grant us this," they answered, "to sit, one on your right, and the other on your left, in your glory."

³⁸ "You do not know what you are asking," Jesus said to them. "Can you drink the cup that I am to drink? Or receive the baptism that I am to receive?"

³⁹ "Yes," they answered, "we can."

"You will indeed drink the cup that I am to drink," Jesus said, "and receive the baptism that I am to receive, ⁴⁰ but as to a seat at my right or at my left — that is not mine to give, but it is for those for whom it has been prepared."

⁴¹ On hearing of this, the ten others were at first very indignant about James and John. ⁴² But Jesus called the ten to him, and said, "Those who are regarded as ruling among the gentiles lord it over them, as you know, and their great men oppress them. ⁴³ But among you it is not so. No, whoever wants to become great among you must be your servant, ⁴⁴ and whoever wants to take the first place among you must be the servant of all; ⁴⁵ for even the Child of Humanity came, not to be served, but to serve, and to give his life as a ransom for many."

⁴⁶ They came to Jericho. When Jesus was going out of the town with his followers and a large crowd, Bartimaeus, the son of Timaeus, a blind beggar, was sitting by the roadside. ⁴⁷ Hearing that it was Jesus of Nazareth, he began to call out, "Jesus, son of David, take pity on me." ⁴⁸ Many of the people kept telling him to be quiet,

but the man continued to call out all the louder, "Son of David, take pity on me." ⁴⁹ Then Jesus stopped. "Call him," he said. So they called the blind man. "Take heart!" they exclaimed. "Get up; he is calling you." ⁵⁰ The man threw off his cloak, sprang up, and came to Jesus. ⁵¹ "What do you want me to do for you?" said Jesus, addressing him. "My teacher," the blind man answered, "I want to recover my sight."

⁵² "You may go," Jesus said; "your confidence has delivered you." Immediately he recovered his sight, and began to follow Jesus along the road.

The Last Days

11 ¹ When they had almost reached Jerusalem, as far as Bethphage and Bethany, near the Mount of Olives, Jesus sent on two of his followers. ² "Go to the village facing you," he said, "and, as soon as you get there, you will find a foal tethered, which no one has ever ridden; untie it, and bring it. ³ And, if anyone says to you, 'Why are you doing that?' say, 'The Master wants it, and will be sure to send it back here at once.'" ⁴ The two went, and, finding a foal tethered outside a door in the street, they untied it. ⁵ Some of the bystanders said to them, "What are you doing, untying the foal?" ⁶ And the two followers answered as Jesus had told them; and they allowed them to go. ⁷ Then they brought the foal to Jesus, and, when they had laid their cloaks on it, he seated himself on it. ⁸ Many of the people spread their cloaks on the road, with some twigs which they had cut from the fields; ⁹ and those who led the way, as well as those who followed, kept shouting, "'God save him! Blessed is he who comes in the name of the Lord!' ¹⁰ Blessed is the coming realm of our father David! 'God save him from on high!'"

¹¹ Jesus entered Jerusalem, and went into the Temple; and, after looking around at everything, as it was already late, he went out to Bethany with the Twelve.

¹² The next day, after they had left Bethany, Jesus became hungry; ¹³ and, noticing a fig tree at a distance in leaf, he went to it to see if by any chance he could find something on it; but on coming up to it, he found nothing but leaves, for it was not the season for figs. ¹⁴ So he said to it, "May no one ever again eat of your fruit!" And his followers heard what he said.

¹⁵ They came to Jerusalem. Jesus went into the Temple, and began to drive out those who were buying and selling there. He overturned the tables of the money-changers, and the seats of the pigeon dealers, ¹⁶ and would not allow anyone to carry anything across the Temple. ¹⁷ Then he began to teach. "Does scripture not say," he asked, "'My house will be called a house of prayer for all the nations'? But you have made it a den of robbers." ¹⁸ Now the chief priests and the scholars heard this and began to look for some way of putting Jesus to death; for they were afraid of him, since all the people were so amazed by his teaching. ¹⁹ As soon as evening fell, Jesus and his followers went out of the city.

²⁰ As they passed by early in the morning, they noticed that the fig tree was withered up from the roots. ²¹ Then Peter recalled what had occurred. "Look, Rabbi," he exclaimed, "the fig tree which you doomed is withered up!"

²² "Have faith in God!" replied Jesus. ²³ "I tell you that if anyone should say to this hill, 'Be lifted up and hurled into the sea!' without ever a doubt in her mind, but in the faith that what she says will be done, she would find that it would be. ²⁴ And therefore I say to you, 'Have trust that whatever you ask for in prayer is already granted you, and you will find that it will be.'

²⁵ "And, whenever you stand up to pray, forgive any grievance that you have against anyone, so that your Father who is in heaven also may forgive you your offenses."

²⁷ They came to Jerusalem again. While Jesus was walking about in the Temple, the chief priests, the scholars, and the elders came up to him. ²⁸ "What authority have you to do these things?" they said. "Who gave you the authority to do them?"

²⁹ "I will put one question to you," said Jesus. "Answer me that, and then I will tell you what authority I have to act as I do. ³⁰ It is about John's baptism. Was it of divine or human origin? Answer me that." ³¹ They began arguing together. "If we say 'divine,' he will say, 'Why then did you not believe him?' ³² Yet can we say 'human'?" They were afraid of the people, for everyone regarded John as undoubtedly a prophet. ³³ So their answer to Jesus was: "We do not know."

"Then I," replied Jesus, "refuse to tell you what authority I have to do these things."

12 ¹ Jesus began to speak to them in parables. "A man once planted a vineyard, put a fence around it, dug a winepress, built a tower, and then let it out to tenants and went abroad. ² At the proper time he sent a slave to the tenants, to receive from them a share of the produce of the grape harvest; ³ but they seized him, and beat him, and sent him away empty-handed. ⁴ A second time the owner sent a slave to them; this man, too, the tenants struck on the head, and insulted. ⁵ He sent another, but him they killed; and so with many others — some they beat and some they killed. ⁶ He had still one son, who was very dear to him; and him he sent to them last of all. 'They will respect my son,' he said. ⁷ But those tenants said to one another, 'Here is the heir! Come, let us kill him, and his inheritance will be ours.' ⁸ So they seized him, and killed him, and threw his body outside the vineyard. ⁹ What will the owner of the vineyard do? He will come and destroy the tenants, and he will give the vineyard to others.

¹⁰ "Have you never read this passage of scripture: 'The stone which the builders despised has now itself become the cornerstone; ¹¹ this cornerstone has come from the Lord, and is marvelous in our eyes'?"

¹² After this they were eager to arrest him, but they were afraid of the crowd; for they saw that it was at them that he had aimed the parable. So they let him alone, and went away.

¹³ Afterward they sent to Jesus some of the Pharisees and some of the Herodians, to trap him in conversation. ¹⁴ These men came to him and said, "Teacher, we know that you are an honest man and are not afraid of anyone, for you pay no regard to a person's position, but teach the way of God honestly; are we right in paying taxes to the emperor, or not? ¹⁵ Should we pay, or should we not pay?" Knowing their hypocrisy, Jesus said to them, "Why are you testing me? Bring me a coin to look at." ¹⁶ And, when they had brought it, he asked, "Whose head and title are these?"

"The emperor's," they said; ¹⁷ and Jesus replied, "Pay to the emperor what belongs to the emperor, and to God what belongs to God." And they wondered at him.

¹⁸ Next came some Sadducees, who maintain that there is no resurrection. Their question was this: ¹⁹ "Teacher, in our scriptures Moses decreed that should a man's brother die, leaving a widow but no child, the man should take the widow as his wife, and raise up a family for his brother. ²⁰ There were once seven brothers, of whom the eldest took a wife, but died and left no family; ²¹ and the second took her, and died without family; and so did the third. ²² All the seven died and left no family. The woman herself died last of all. ²³ At the resurrection whose wife will she be, all seven brothers having had her as their wife?"

²⁴ "Is not the reason of your mistake," answered Jesus, "your ignorance of the scriptures and of the power of God? ²⁵ When people rise from the dead, there is no marrying or being married; but they are as angels in heaven.

²⁶ "As to the dead, and the fact that they rise, have you never read in the book of Moses, in the passage about the bush, how God spoke to him saying, 'I am the God of Abraham, and the God of Isaac, and the God of Jacob'? ²⁷ He is not God of dead people, but of living. You are greatly mistaken."

²⁸ Then came up one of the scholars who had heard their discussions. Knowing that Jesus had answered them wisely, he asked him this question: "What is the first of all the commandments?"

²⁹ "The first," answered Jesus, "is: 'Hear, Israel; the Lord our God is the one Lord; ³⁰ and you must love the Lord your God with all your heart, and with all your soul, and with all your mind, and with all your strength.' ³¹ The second is this: 'You must love your neighbor as you love yourself.' There is no commandment greater than these."

³² "Wisely answered, Teacher!" exclaimed the scholar. "It is true, as you say, that 'there is one God,' and that 'there is no other besides him'; ³³ and to 'love him with all one's heart, and with all one's understanding, and with all one's strength,' and to 'love one's neighbor as one loves oneself' is far beyond all 'burnt offerings and sacrifices.'" ³⁴ Seeing that he had answered with discernment, Jesus said to him, "You are not far from the realm of God."

After that no one ventured to question him further.

³⁵ While Jesus was teaching in the Temple, he asked, "How is it that the scholars say that the Christ is to be David's son? ³⁶ David said himself, speaking under the inspiration of the holy Spirit: 'The Lord said to my lord, "Sit at my right hand, until I put your enemies beneath your feet."'

[37] David himself calls him lord; how comes it, then, that he is to be his son?"

The large crowd listened to Jesus with delight. [38] In the course of his teaching, Jesus said, "See that you are on your guard against the scholars, who delight to walk about in long robes and to be greeted in the streets with respect, [39] and to have the best seats in the synagogues, and places of honor at dinner. [40] They are the men who rob widows of their homes, and make a pretense of saying long prayers. Their sentence will be all the heavier."

[41] Then Jesus sat down opposite the chests for the Temple offerings, and watched how the people put money into them. Many rich people were putting in large sums; [42] but one poor widow came and put in two small coins, worth very little. [43] Then, calling his followers to him, Jesus said, "I tell you that this poor widow has put in more than all the others who were putting money into the chests; [44] for everyone else put in something from what he had to spare, while she, in her need, put in all she had — everything that she had to live on."

13 [1] As Jesus was walking out of the Temple, one of his followers said to him, "Teacher, look what fine stones and buildings these are!"

[2] "Do you see these great buildings?" asked Jesus. "Not a single stone will be left here on another which will not be thrown down."

[3] When Jesus had sat down on the Mount of Olives, facing the Temple, Peter, James, John, and Andrew questioned him privately, [4] "Tell us when this will be, and what will be the sign when all this is drawing to its close."

[5] Then Jesus began, "See that no one leads you astray. [6] Many will take my name, and come saying, 'I am he,' and will lead many astray.

[7] "And, when you hear of wars and rumors of wars, do not be alarmed; such things must occur. But the end is not yet. [8] For 'nation will rise against nation, and realm against realm'; there will be earthquakes in various places; there will be famines. This will be but the beginning of the birth pangs.

[9] "See to yourselves! They will betray you to councils, and you will be beaten in synagogues; and you will be brought up before governors and kings for my sake, so that you can bear witness before them. [10] But the good news must first be proclaimed to every nation. [11] Whenever they betray you and hand you over for trial, do not be anxious beforehand as to what you will say, but say whatever is given you at the moment; for it will not be you who speak, but the holy Spirit. [12] Brother will betray brother to death, and the father his child; and children will turn against their parents, and cause them to be put to death; [13] and you will be hated by everyone because of me. Yet the person who endures to the end will be saved.

[14] "As soon, however, as you see 'the foul desecration' standing where it ought not" (the reader must consider what this means), "then those of you who are in Judea must take refuge in the mountains; [15] and a person on the housetop must not go down, or go in to get anything out of her house, [16] nor must one who is in the field turn back to get his cloak. [17] Woe to those who are pregnant and to those who are nursing infants in those days! [18] Pray, too, that this may not occur in winter. [19] For those days will be a time of distress, the like of which has not occurred from the beginning of God's creation until now — and never will again. [20] And had not the Lord put a limit to those days, not a single soul would be saved; but for the sake of God's own chosen people, he did limit them.

[21] "And at that time if anyone should say to you, 'Look, here is the Christ!' 'Look, there he is!' — do not believe it; [22] for false Christs and false prophets will arise, and

display signs and marvels, to lead astray, were it possible, even God's people. ²³ But see that you are on your guard! I have told you all this beforehand.

²⁴ "In those days, after that time of distress, 'the sun will be darkened, the moon will not give her light, ²⁵ the stars will be falling from the heavens,' and 'the powers in the heavens will be shaken.' ²⁶ Then will be seen the 'Child of Humanity coming in clouds' with great power and glory; ²⁷ and then he will send the angels, and gather his people from the four winds, from one end of the world to the other.

²⁸ "Learn the lesson taught by the fig tree. As soon as its branches are full of sap and it is bursting into leaf, you know that summer is near. ²⁹ And so may you, as soon as you see these things happening, know that he is at your doors. ³⁰ I tell you that even the present generation will not pass away, until all these things have taken place. ³¹ The heavens and the earth will pass away, but my words will not pass away.

³² "But about 'that day,' or 'the hour,' no one knows — not even the angels in heaven, nor yet the Child — but only the Father.

³³ "See that you are on the watch; for you do not know when the time will be. ³⁴ It is like a man going on a journey, who leaves his home, puts his slaves in charge — each having his and her special duty — and orders the porter to watch. ³⁵ Therefore watch, for you cannot be sure when the master of the house is coming — whether in the evening, at midnight, at daybreak, or in the morning — ³⁶ otherwise he might come suddenly and find you asleep. ³⁷ And what I say to you I say to all: Watch!"

14 ¹ It was now two days before the festival of the Passover and the unleavened bread. The chief priests and the scholars were looking for an opportunity to arrest Jesus by stealth, and to put him to death;

² for they said, "Not during the festival, or the people may riot."

³ When Jesus was still at Bethany, in the house of Simon the leper, while he was sitting at the table, a woman came with an alabaster jar of genuine spikenard perfume of great value. She broke the jar and poured the perfume on his head. ⁴ Some of those who were present said to one another indignantly, "Why has the perfume been wasted like this? ⁵ This perfume could have been sold for more than a year's wages, and the money given to the poor."

⁶ "Leave her alone," said Jesus, as they began to find fault with her, "why are you troubling her? This is a beautiful deed that she has done for me. ⁷ You always have the poor with you, and whenever you wish you can do good to them; but you will not always have me. ⁸ She has done what she could; she has perfumed my body beforehand for my burial. ⁹ And I tell you, wherever in the whole world the good news is proclaimed, what this woman has done will be told in memory of her."

¹⁰ After this, Judas Iscariot, one of the Twelve, went to the chief priests to betray Jesus to them. ¹¹ They were glad to hear what he said and promised to pay him. So he began looking for a good opportunity to betray Jesus.

¹² On the first day of the festival of the unleavened bread, when it was customary to kill the Passover lambs, his followers said to Jesus, "Where do you wish us to go and make preparations for your eating the Passover?" ¹³ Jesus sent forward two of his followers and said to them, "Go into the city, and there a man carrying a pitcher of water will meet you; follow him; ¹⁴ and, wherever he goes in, say to the owner of the house, 'The Teacher says, 'Where is my room where I am to eat the Passover with my followers?' ¹⁵ He will himself show you a large upstairs room, set out ready; and there make preparations for us." ¹⁶ So the followers set out and went into the city,

and found everything just as Jesus had told them; and they prepared the Passover.

¹⁷ In the evening he went there with the Twelve, ¹⁸ and when they had taken their places and were eating, Jesus said, "I tell you that one of you is going to betray me — one who is eating with me." ¹⁹ They were grieved at this, and began to say to him, one after another, "Can it be I?"

²⁰ "It is one of you twelve," said Jesus, "the one who is dipping his bread beside me into the dish. ²¹ True, the Child of Humanity must go, as scripture says of him, yet woe to that man by whom the Child of Humanity is being betrayed! For that man 'it would be better never to have been born!'"

²² While they were eating, Jesus took some bread, and, after saying the blessing, broke it, and gave it to them, and said, "Take it; this is my body." ²³ Then he took a cup, and, after giving thanks, gave it to them, and they all drank from it. ²⁴ "This is my blood of the covenant," he said, "which is poured out on behalf of many. ²⁵ I tell you that I will never again drink of the fruit of the vine, until that day when I will drink it new in the realm of God."

²⁶ They then sang a hymn and went out up the Mount of Olives. ²⁷ And Jesus said to them, "All of you will fall away; for scripture says, 'I will strike down the shepherd, and the sheep will be scattered.' ²⁸ Yet, after I have risen, I will go before you into Galilee."

²⁹ "Even if everyone else falls away," said Peter, "I will not."

³⁰ "I tell you," answered Jesus, "that you yourself today — yes, this very night — before the cock crows twice, will disown me three times." ³¹ But Peter vehemently protested, "Even if I must die with you, I will never disown you!" And they all said the same.

³² Presently they came to a place known as Gethsemane, and Jesus said to his followers, "Sit down here while I pray." ³³ He took with him Peter, James, and John; and began to show signs of great dismay and deep distress. ³⁴ "I am sad at heart," he said, "sad even to death; wait here, and watch." ³⁵ Going on a little further, he threw himself on the ground, and began to pray that if it were possible, he might be spared that hour. ³⁶ "Abba, Father," he said, "all things are possible to you; take away this cup from me; yet, not what I will, but what you will."

³⁷ Then he came and found them asleep. "Simon," he said to Peter, "are you asleep? Could you not watch for one hour? ³⁸ Watch and pray," he said to them all, "that you may not fall into temptation. True, the spirit is eager, but human nature is weak." ³⁹ Again he went away, and prayed in the same words; ⁴⁰ and coming back again he found them asleep, for their eyes were heavy; and they did not know what to say to him.

⁴¹ A third time he came, and said to them, "Sleep on now and rest yourselves. Enough! My time has come. Look, the Child of Humanity is being betrayed into the hands of wicked people. ⁴² Up, and let us be going. Look! My betrayer is close at hand."

⁴³ And just then, while he was still speaking, Judas, who was one of the Twelve, came up; and with him a crowd of people, with swords and clubs, sent by the chief priests, the scholars, and the elders. ⁴⁴ Now the betrayer had arranged a signal with them. "The man whom I kiss," he had said, "will be the one; arrest him and take him away safely." ⁴⁵ As soon as Judas came, he went up to Jesus at once, and said, "Rabbi!" and kissed him.

⁴⁶ Then the men seized Jesus, and arrested him.

⁴⁷ One of those who were standing by drew his sword, and struck at the high priest's servant, and cut off his ear. ⁴⁸ But Jesus spoke up, and said to the men, "Have you come out, as if after a robber, with swords and clubs, to take me? ⁴⁹ I have been among you day after day in the Tem-

ple teaching, and yet you did not arrest me; but this is in fulfillment of the scriptures." [50] And all of them forsook him, and fled. [51] One young man did indeed follow him, wrapped only in a linen sheet. They tried to arrest him; [52] but he left the sheet in their hands, and fled naked.

[53] Then they took Jesus to the high priest; and all the chief priests, the elders, and the scholars assembled. [54] Peter, who had followed Jesus at a distance into the courtyard of the high priest, was sitting there among the guards, warming himself at the blaze of the fire.

[55] Meanwhile the chief priest and the whole of the High Council were trying to get such evidence against Jesus as would warrant his being put to death, but they could not find any; [56] for, though there were many who gave false evidence against him, yet their evidence did not agree. [57] Presently some men stood up, and gave this false evidence against him: [58] "We ourselves heard him say, 'I will destroy this temple made with hands, and in three days build another made without hands.'" [59] Yet not even on that point did their evidence agree.

[60] Then the high priest stood forward, and questioned Jesus. "Have you no answer to make?" he asked. "What is this evidence which these men are giving against you?" [61] But Jesus remained silent, and made no answer.

A second time the high priest questioned him. "Are you," he asked, "the Anointed One, the Son of the Blessed One?"

[62] "I am," replied Jesus, "and you will all see the Child of Humanity sitting on the right hand of the Almighty, and 'coming in the clouds of heaven.'" [63] At this the high priest tore his vestments. "Why do we want any more witnesses?" he exclaimed. [64] "You heard his blasphemy. What is your verdict?" They all condemned him, declaring that he deserved death.

[65] Some of those present began to spit at him, and to blindfold his eyes, and strike him, saying, as they did so, "Now play the prophet!" and even the guards received him with blows.

[66] While Peter was in the courtyard down below, one of the high priest's maidservants came up; [67] and, seeing Peter warming himself, she looked closely at him, and exclaimed, "You were also with Jesus, the man from Nazareth!" [68] But Peter denied it. "I do not know or understand what you mean," he replied. Then he went out into the front courtyard; [69] and there the maidservant, on seeing him, began to say again to the bystanders, "This is one of them!" [70] But Peter again denied it.

Soon afterward the bystanders again said to him, "You certainly are one of them; you are a Galilean!" [71] But he said to them, "I swear that I do not know the man you are talking about! May God punish me if I am lying!" [72] At that moment, for the second time, a cock crowed; and Peter remembered the words that Jesus had said to him: "Before a cock has crowed twice, you will disown me three times"; and, as he thought of it, he began to weep.

15 [1] As soon as it was daylight, the chief priests, after holding a consultation with the elders and scholars — that is to say, the whole High Council — put Jesus in chains, and took him away, and gave him up to Pilate. [2] "Are you the king of the Jews?" asked Pilate. "You say so," replied Jesus. [3] Then the chief priests brought a number of charges against him. [4] So Pilate questioned Jesus again. "Have you no reply to make?" he asked. "See how many charges they are bringing against you." [5] But Jesus still made no reply whatever, so that Pilate was astonished.

[6] Now, at the feast, Pilate used to grant the people the release of any one prisoner whom they might ask for. [7] A man called Barabbas was in prison, with the rebels who had committed murder in the revolt. [8] So when the crowd went up and began to

ask Pilate to follow his usual custom, [9] he answered, "Do you want me to release the king of the Jews for you?" [10] For he was aware that it was out of jealousy that the chief priests had given Jesus up to him. [11] But the chief priests incited the crowd to get Barabbas released instead. [12] Pilate, however, spoke to them again: "What should I do then with the man whom you call the king of the Jews?" [13] Again they shouted, "Crucify him!"

[14] "Why, what harm has he done?" Pilate kept saying to them. But they shouted furiously, "Crucify him!" [15] And Pilate, wishing to satisfy the crowd, released Barabbas to them, and, after scourging Jesus, gave him up to be crucified.

[16] The soldiers then took Jesus away into the courtyard — that is, the governor's headquarters — and they called the whole garrison together. [17] They dressed him in a purple robe, and, having twisted a crown of thorns, put it on him, [18] and then began to salute him. "Hail, king of the Jews!" they said. [19] And they kept striking him on the head with a rod, spitting at him, and bowing to the ground before him, going down on their knees; [20] and, after mocking him, they took off the purple robe, and put his own clothes on him.

[21] They led Jesus out to crucify him; and they compelled a passerby, Simon from Cyrene, who was on his way in from the country, the father of Alexander and Rufus, to go with them to carry his cross. [22] They brought Jesus to the place which was known as Golgotha — a name which means "Place of a Skull." [23] There they offered him wine mixed with myrrh; but Jesus refused it. [24] Then they crucified him, and divided his clothes among them, casting lots for them, to settle what each should take.

[25] It was nine in the morning when they crucified him. [26] The words of the charge against him, written up over his head, read: "The King of the Jews." [27] And with him they crucified two bandits, one on the right, and the other on the left.

[29] The passersby railed at him, shaking their heads, as they said, "You who would destroy the Temple and build one in three days, [30] come down from the cross and save yourself!" [31] In the same way the chief priests, along with the scholars, said to one another in mockery, [32] "He saved others, but he cannot save himself! Let the Christ, the 'king of Israel,' come down from the cross now so that we can see it and believe." Even the men who had been crucified with Jesus insulted him.

[33] At midday, a darkness came over the whole country, lasting until three in the afternoon. [34] And, at three, Jesus called out loudly, *Eloi, Eloi, lama sabacthani?*" which means "My God, my God, why have you abandoned me?" [35] Some of those standing around heard this, and said, "Listen! He is calling for Elijah!" [36] And a man ran, and, soaking a sponge in sour wine, put it on the end of a reed, and offered it to him to drink, saying as he did so, "Wait and let us see if Elijah is coming to take him down." [37] But Jesus, giving a loud cry, expired. [38] The Temple curtain was torn in two from top to bottom. [39] The centurion who was standing facing Jesus, on seeing the way in which he expired, exclaimed, "This human being is God's Son. Really?"

[40] There were some women also watching from a distance, among them being Mary of Magdala, Mary the mother of James the younger and of Joses, and Salome — [41] all of whom used to accompany Jesus when he was in Galilee, and supported him; and there were many other women who had come up with him to Jerusalem.

[42] The evening had already fallen, when, as it was the preparation day — the day before the sabbath — [43] Joseph of Arimathea, a prominent member of the council, who was himself living in expectation of the realm of God, came and ven-

tured to go in to see Pilate, and to ask for the body of Jesus. [44] But Pilate was surprised to hear that he had already died. So he sent for the centurion, and asked if he were already dead; [45] and, on learning from the centurion that it was so, he gave the corpse to Joseph. [46] Joseph, having bought a linen sheet, took Jesus down, and wound the sheet around him, and laid him in a tomb which had been cut out of the rock; and then rolled a stone up against the entrance of the tomb. [47] Mary of Magdala and Mary the mother of Joses were watching to see where he was laid.

The Risen Life

16 [1] When the sabbath was over, Mary of Magdala, Mary the mother of James, and Salome bought some spices, so that they might go and anoint him. [2] And very early on the first day of the week they went to the tomb, after sunrise. [3] They were saying to one another, "Who will roll away the stone for us from the entrance of the tomb?" [4] But on looking up, they saw that the stone had already been rolled back; it was a very large one. [5] Going into the tomb, they saw a young man sitting on their right, in a white robe, and they were dismayed; but he said to them, [6] "Do not be dismayed; you are looking for Jesus of Nazareth, who has been crucified. He has been raised, he is not here! Look, here is the place they laid him. [7] But go, and say to his followers and to Peter, 'He is going before you into Galilee; there you will see him, as he told you.'" [8] They went out and fled from the tomb, for they were trembling and bewildered; and they did not say a word to anyone, for they were frightened.*

* The Gospel of Mark ends with verse 8 of chapter 16 in all the earliest manuscripts. A number of second- and third-century early Christian commentators defend this, despite the fact that later documents include one to three additional versions of the ending of Mark. I have kept the ending at 16:8, both in respect to the early manuscripts and in acknowledgment that the later additions are much less sensitive to the style and structure of the rest of Mark.

An Introduction to the Gospel of Luke and the Acts of the Apostles

THE GOSPEL OF LUKE and the Acts of the Apostles are perhaps best described as the big story that most people know about Jesus and the beginning of Christianity. In many ways the other quite diverse books of the traditional New Testament have most often found their meaning in how they fit with the grand narrative of Luke and Acts.

New Testament scholars are as unanimous as they can be that the Gospel of Luke and the Acts of the Apostles have the same author. Many lay readers of the Bible also know that these two books have the same author. What is not so well known is that upon close examination, Luke's gospel and the Acts of the Apostles are meant to be read together. For instance, the main plot of Luke focuses on Jesus traveling resolutely toward Jerusalem, where he knows he will die, while Acts picks up in Jerusalem after his death, proclaims Jesus's resurrection to the people of Jerusalem, and then narrates the expansion of this "complete" story of Jesus's message to the rest of the world. So this *New New Testament* presents Luke and Acts in the order and structure in which they were meant to be read.

Legend and conventional understanding name the common author of these two books "Luke," and he is often thought to have been Paul's companion. But the author's first-person self-introduction at the beginning of both books does not give a name. Nor do the earliest manuscripts consistently carry the title "The Gospel of Luke." It is generally thought that the name "Luke" came from speculation on passages about a "Luke" in Paul's letter to Philemon and the post-Pauline letters of Colossians and 2 Timothy.

Even if it may be overreaching to call with certainty the author of this pair of books "Luke," their style, elevated Greek, and structural unity provide a profile of the author. This author writes excellent Greek and is familiar with a range of literary traditions from the Greco-Roman world and Israel. Although both books refer to Hebrew Bible passages frequently, Acts portrays the emerging Christ traditions as the new inheritors of the traditions of Israel. Luke-Acts is perhaps the first formulation of the idea that became prevalent in later Christianity that Israel had forfeited the right to its traditions, and that the Christ movement deserved to take them over. One could surmise, then, that the author of Luke-Acts is a sophisticated Greco-Roman author, an idea not too far from "Luke, the beloved physician" mentioned in Colossians.

In the past twenty years many scholars have proposed that Luke-Acts was written somewhere between 110 and 135 CE, rather than the previously held idea of the

80s. Inasmuch as Luke-Acts was written nearer 120 CE, the author still could be a kind of sophisticated "Luke" from a Greco-Roman setting, but not a colleague of Paul, who probably died in the 60s.

Luke-Acts: The First Christian Epic

As the Christ movement entered the second century, its success and expansion throughout the Mediterranean called for someone to tell an epic story of how it began, in a way that would make it seem destined to flourish. Although the second century produced a number of books whose ambition was to chart the Christian movement as epic, Luke-Acts seems to have been one of the earliest and most extensive.

The structure of Luke-Acts shows such resolve. Luke is the only gospel to set Jesus's birth explicitly in terms of the grand history of Rome, showing exactly how Jesus's birth paralleled Augustus Caesar's and occurred at the end of Augustus's reign. Luke's story of Jesus's life has him setting his face toward Jerusalem, the holy city of Israel, now under Roman control (and by the time "Luke" wrote, a city that had been destroyed by Roman armies). So Jesus's death and resurrection occur in the holy city of Israel toward which Jesus had journeyed and whose eventual destruction was already known to Luke's readers.

Acts begins at the juncture of Jesus's resurrection and ascension into the sky, after having instructed his "ambassadors" (apostles) to spread his message to "the ends of the earth" (1:8). Acts then proceeds to narrate this expansion of the Christ movement. First, there is a series of stories of Peter as a chief apostle in Jerusalem accusing the leaders of Israel's traditions of having murdered Jesus, and then a story (which explicitly contradicts Paul's story of Peter's mission in Galatians 2:1–14) of Peter calling a Roman centurion and his family to be followers of Jesus. That is, in Acts, Peter endorses the extension of the Christ movement to the gentiles, all while confronting the leaders of Israel's traditions.

The rest of Acts shows Philip, others, and especially Paul taking the Christ message from Jerusalem to the ends of the earth, indeed to Rome, the capital of the known "world." Luke-Acts is structured to have Jesus move from the edges of Israel to its center in Jerusalem, whence he initiates the epic expansion of his movement to the rest of the world.

Poverty, Wealth, and Women in Luke-Acts

Luke-Acts is proactive in creating special portraits of the Christ movement's relationship to issues of poverty/wealth and women/men.

Luke's gospel shows Jesus to be more interested in the rift between rich and poor than any other gospel. Only in Luke does Jesus declare his mission to bring good news to the poor, liberty to the captives, and freedom for the oppressed (4:16–24).

Only in Luke does Jesus tell a story about a rich man who never gave to the beggar Lazarus but ended up in Gehenna, begging for the poor Lazarus to come from his home in the bosom of Abraham to relieve him from hellish torture (16:19–25). Only in Luke does Jesus companion his blessing of the poor with a cursing of the rich (6:20–24). In Acts, the people of the early Christ movement own everything in common, and anyone who withholds income from the community is struck dead by God (2:44–45; 4:32–37; 5:1–11). So Luke-Acts demonstrates dramatic solidarity with poor people. Yet occasionally this solidarity shows Luke as somewhat sympathetic to the rich as well. For instance, Luke does not use the story found in Matthew and Mark of Jesus telling the rich man to sell everything he has and give it all to the poor. Rather, Luke has a story of a chief tax collector who in response to Jesus agrees to give half of his property to the poor (19:1–10).

Luke frames issues of women and men together in a similar fashion. In eighteen different places Luke adds a woman character to a story or saying where Mark references only a man. Luke's story of Jesus's birth has an extended contrast between Mary, who believes the angel's promise of a miraculous birth, and the male priest Zacharias, who disbelieves a similar angelic promise. Acts also tells the only explicit story in the existing New Testament of a woman who is a disciple (9:36). Here, too, the dramatic commitment in Luke-Acts to women's participation has an underside. Luke is the only gospel that tells the story of Jesus scolding Martha as busy head of household and commending Mary for sitting silently at his feet. Acts does not have nearly as many women as Luke, and practically none in its last ten chapters, leaving the impression that women's broad participation may have been more valued in Jesus's generation than in the one where the apostles had authority.

Luke-Acts can be seen as proactive in addressing these issues of poverty, wealth, and gender that are still at stake in the twenty-first century. The complexity of these relationships in Luke-Acts invites attention today as well.

Recommended Reading

François Bovon, *Luke, the Theologian*
H. A. Conzelmann, *Acts of the Apostles: A Commentary*
Herman Hendrickx, *The Third Gospel for the Third World*
Richard Pervo, *Acts: A Commentary*
Richard Pervo, *The Mystery of Acts*
Turid Seim, *The Double Message: Patterns of Gender in Luke-Acts*

The Gospel of Luke

Dedication

1 ¹ To his Excellency, Theophilus.

Many attempts have been already made to draw up an account because of those events which have reached their conclusion among us, ² just as they were reported to us by those who from the beginning were eyewitnesses, bearers of the message. ³ And, therefore, I also, since I have followed all these things closely for some time, have resolved to write a connected presentation of them for you, ⁴ in order that you may be able to satisfy yourself of the truth of the story which you have heard from the lips of others.

Birth, Parentage, Infancy, and Boyhood

In the reign of Herod, king of Judea, there was a priest named Zechariah, who belonged to the division called after Abijah. His wife, whose name was Elizabeth, was also a descendant of Aaron. ⁶ They were both good people, who lived blameless lives, guiding their steps by all the commandments and ordinances of the Lord. ⁷ But they had no child, Elizabeth being barren; and both of them were advanced in years.

⁸ One day, when Zechariah was officiating as priest before God, during the turn of his division, ⁹ it fell to him by lot, in accordance with the practice among the priests, to go into the Temple of the Lord and burn incense; ¹⁰ and, as it was the Hour of Incense, the people were all praying outside. ¹¹ And an angel of the Lord appeared to him, standing on the right of the Altar of Incense. ¹² Zechariah was startled at the sight and was afraid. ¹³ But the angel said to him: "Do not be afraid, Zechariah; your prayer has been heard, and your wife Elizabeth will bear you a child, whom you will call by the name John. ¹⁴ He will be to you a joy and a delight; and many will rejoice over his birth. ¹⁵ For he will be great in the sight of the Lord; he will not drink any wine or strong drink, and he will be filled with the holy Spirit from the very hour of his birth, ¹⁶ and will reconcile many of the children of Israel to the Lord their God. ¹⁷ He will go before him in the spirit and with the power of Elijah, 'to reconcile fathers to their children' and the disobedient to the wisdom of the righteous, and so make ready for the Lord a people fit for him."

¹⁸ "How can I be sure of this?" Zechariah asked the angel. "For I am an old man and my wife is advanced in years."

¹⁹ "I am Gabriel," the angel answered, "who stands in the presence of God, and I have been sent to speak to you and to bring you this good news. ²⁰ And now you will be silent and unable to speak until the day when this takes place, because you did not believe what I said, though my words will be fulfilled in due course."

²¹ Meanwhile the people were watching for Zechariah, wondering at his remaining so long in the sanctuary. ²² When he came out, he was unable to speak to them, and they perceived that he had seen a vision there. But Zechariah kept making signs to them, and remained dumb. ²³ And, as soon as his term of service was finished, he returned home. ²⁴ After this his wife, Elizabeth, became pregnant and lived in seclusion for five months. ²⁵ "The Lord has done this for me," she said, "and has shown me kindness and taken away the public disgrace under which I have been living."

²⁶ Six months later the angel Gabriel was sent from God to a town in Galilee called Nazareth, ²⁷ to a young woman there who was engaged to a man named Joseph, a descendant of David. Her name was Mary. ²⁸ Gabriel came into her presence and greeted her, saying: "What joy! You have been shown great favor — the Lord is with you."

²⁹ Mary was much disturbed at his words, and was wondering to herself what such a greeting could mean, ³⁰ when the angel spoke again: "Do not be afraid, Mary, for you have found favor with God. ³¹ And now, you will conceive and give birth to a child, and you will give him the name Jesus. ³² The child will be great and will be called 'Child of the Most High,' and the Lord God will give him the throne of his ancestor David, ³³ and he will reign over the descendants of Jacob forever; and to his realm there will be no end."

³⁴ "How can this be?" Mary asked the angel. "For I have not known a man."

³⁵ "The holy Spirit will descend on you," answered the angel, "and the power of the Most High will overshadow you; and therefore the child will be called holy, and 'Son of God.' ³⁶ And Elizabeth, your cousin, is herself also expecting a child in her old age; and it is now the sixth month with her, though she is called barren; ³⁷ for no word from God can fail."

³⁸ "I am the slave of the Lord," exclaimed Mary; "let it be with me as you have said." Then the angel left her.

³⁹ Soon after this Mary set out, and made her way quickly into the hill country, to a town in Judah; ⁴⁰ and there she went into Zechariah's house and greeted Elizabeth. ⁴¹ When Elizabeth heard Mary's greeting, the child moved within her, and Elizabeth herself was filled with the holy Spirit, ⁴² and cried aloud: "Blessed are you among women, and blessed is the fruit of your womb! ⁴³ But how have I this honor, that the mother of my Lord should come to me? ⁴⁴ For, as soon as your greeting reached my ears, the child leaped within me with delight! ⁴⁵ Happy indeed is she who believed that the promise which she received from the Lord would be fulfilled."

⁴⁶ And Mary said:

"My soul exalts the Lord,
⁴⁷ my spirit delights in God my Savior;
⁴⁸ for he has remembered his humble
     slave;
   and from this hour all generations will
     count me happy!
⁴⁹ Great things has the Almighty done for
     me;
   and holy is his name.
⁵⁰ From age to age his compassion rests
   on those who fear him.
⁵¹ He has used the power of his arm;
   he scattered the proud of heart,
⁵² he overthrew princes from their
     thrones,
   and the humble he uplifted,
⁵³ the hungry he has loaded with good
     things,
   and the rich he sent away empty.

⁵⁴ He has stretched out his hand to his
     servant Israel,
   ever mindful of his mercy
⁵⁵ (as he promised to our ancestors)
   for Abraham and his race forever."

⁵⁶ Mary stayed with Elizabeth about three months, and then returned to her home. ⁵⁷ When Elizabeth's time came, she gave birth to a child; ⁵⁸ and her neighbors and relations, hearing of the great goodness of the Lord to her, came to share her joy. ⁵⁹ A week later they met to circumcise the child, and were about to call him "Zechariah" after his father, ⁶⁰ when his mother spoke up: "No, he is to be called John."

⁶¹ "You have no relation of that name!" they exclaimed; ⁶² and they made signs to the child's father, to find out what he wished the child to be called. ⁶³ Asking for a writing tablet, he wrote the words: "His

name is John." Everyone was surprised; [64] and immediately Zechariah recovered his voice and the use of his tongue, and began to bless God. [65] All their neighbors were awestruck at this; and throughout the hill country of Judea the whole story was much talked about; [66] and all who heard it kept it in mind, asking one another, "What can this child be destined to become?" For the hand of the Lord was with him.

[67] Then his father, Zechariah, was filled with the holy Spirit, and prophesied, saying:

[68] "Blessed is the Lord, the God of Israel,
who has visited his people and
accomplished their deliverance,
[69] and has raised up for us the strength of
our salvation
in the house of his servant David —

[70] as he promised by the lips of his holy
prophets of old —
[71] salvation from our enemies and from
the hands of all who hate us,
[72] showing compassion to our ancestors,
and mindful of God's holy covenant.

[73] This was the oath which he swore to
our father Abraham —
[74] that we should be rescued from the
hands of our enemies,
[75] and should serve him without fear in
holiness and justice,
in his presence all our days.

[76] And you, child, will be called prophet
of the Most High,
for you will go before the Lord to make
ready his way,
[77] to give his people the knowledge of
salvation
in the forgiveness of their sins,
[78] through the tender mercy of our God,
whereby the dawn will break on us
from heaven,
[79] to give light to those who live in
darkness and the shadow of death,

and guide our feet into the way of
peace."

[80] The child grew and became strong in spirit; and he lived in the desert until the time came for his appearance to Israel.

2 [1] About that time an edict was issued by the emperor Augustus that a census should be taken of the whole empire. [2] (This was the first census taken while Quirinius was governor of Syria.) [3] And everyone went to his own town to be registered. [4] Among others, Joseph went up from the town of Nazareth in Galilee to Bethlehem, the town of David, in Judea — because he belonged to the family and house of David — [5] to be registered with Mary, his engaged wife, who was pregnant. [6] While they were there her time came, [7] and she gave birth to her first child, a son. And because there was no room for them in the inn, she wrapped him in swaddling clothes and laid him in a manger. [8] In that same countryside were shepherds out in the open fields, watching their flocks that night, [9] when an angel of the Lord suddenly stood by them, and the glory of the Lord shone around them; and they were seized with fear. [10] "Have no fear," the angel said. "For I bring you good news of a great joy in store for all the nation. [11] This day there has been born to you, in the town of David, a Savior, who is Christ and Lord. [12] And this will be the sign for you. You will find the infant in swaddling clothes, and lying in a manger."
[13] Then suddenly there appeared with the angel a multitude of the heavenly army, praising God, and singing:

[14] "Glory to God on high,
and on earth peace among those in
whom he finds pleasure."

[15] Now, when the angels had left them and gone back to heaven, the shepherds said to one another: "Let us go at once to Bethlehem, and see this thing that has

happened, of which the Lord has told us."
16 So they went quickly, and found Mary
and Joseph, and the infant lying in a manger; 17 and, when they saw it, they told of
all that had been said to them about this
child. 18 All who heard the shepherds were
astonished at their story, 19 while Mary
treasured all that they said, and thought
about it often in her thoughts. 20 And the
shepherds went back, giving glory and
praise to God for all that they had heard
and seen, as it had been told them.

21 Eight days after the birth of the child,
when it was time to circumcise him, he received the name Jesus — the name given
him by the angel before his conception.

22 When the period of purification of
mother and child, required by the Law of
Moses, came to an end, his parents took
the child up to Jerusalem to present him
to the Lord, 23 in compliance with the Law
of the Lord that "every firstborn male will
be dedicated to the Lord," 24 and also to offer the sacrifice required by the Law of the
Lord — "a pair of turtledoves or two young
pigeons."

25 There was at that time in Jerusalem
a man named Simeon, a good and devout man, who lived in constant expectation of the consolation of Israel, and a holy
Spirit was on him. 26 It had been revealed
to him by the holy Spirit that he should
not die until he had seen the Lord's Christ.
27 Moved by the Spirit, Simeon came into
the Temple, and, when the parents brought
in the child Jesus, to do for him what was
customary under the Law, 28 Simeon himself took the child in his arms, and blessed
God, and said:

29 "Now, Master, release your slave,
    according to your word, in peace,
30 for my eyes have seen the salvation
31 which you have prepared in the sight of
    all nations —
32 a light of revelation to the gentiles,
    and to be the glory of your people
    Israel."

33 While the child's father and mother
were wondering at what was said about
him, 34 Simeon gave them his blessing,
and said to Mary, the child's mother: "This
child is appointed to be the cause of the
fall and rise of many in Israel, and to be
a sign much spoken against — 35 yes, the
sword will pierce your own heart — and
so the thoughts in many minds will be disclosed."

36 There was also a prophetess named
Hannah, a daughter of Phanuel and of
the tribe of Asher. She was far advanced
in years, having lived with her husband
for seven years after marriage, 37 and then
a widow, until she had reached the age
of eighty-four. She never left the Temple Courts, but, fasting and praying, worshiped God night and day. 38 At that moment she came up, and began publicly to
thank God and to speak about the child to
all who were looking for the deliverance of
Jerusalem.

39 When the child's parents had done
everything required by the Law of the
Lord, they returned to Galilee to their own
town of Nazareth. 40 The child grew and
became strong and wise, and the grace of
God was on him.

41 Every year the child's parents used
to go to Jerusalem at the Passover festival. 42 When Jesus was twelve years old,
they went according to custom to Jerusalem, 43 and had finished their visit; but
when they started to return, the boy Jesus remained behind in Jerusalem, without their knowing it. 44 Thinking that he
was with their fellow travelers, they went
one day's journey before searching for him
among their relations and acquaintances;
45 and then, as they did not find him, they
returned to Jerusalem, searching everywhere for him. 46 It was not until the third
day that they found him in the Temple, sitting among the teachers, now listening to
them, now asking them questions. 47 All
who listened to him marveled at his intelligence and his answers.

⁴⁸ They were overcome when they saw him, and his mother said to him: "My child, why have you treated us like this? Your father and I have been searching for you in great distress."

⁴⁹ "What made you search for me?" he answered. "Did you not know that I must be in my Father's house?" ⁵⁰ His parents did not understand what he meant. ⁵¹ He went down with them to Nazareth, and submitted himself to their control; and his mother treasured all that was said in her heart. ⁵² And Jesus grew in wisdom and the gracious presence of God and people as he also grew in years.

The Preparation

3 ¹ In the fifteenth year of the reign of the emperor Tiberius, when Pontius Pilate was governor of Judea, Herod ruler of Galilee, his brother Philip ruler of the territory comprising Ituraea and Trachonitis, and Lysanias ruler of Abilene, ² and when Annas and Caiaphas were high priests, a command from God came to John, the son of Zechariah, while he was in the wilderness. ³ And John went through the whole district of the Jordan, proclaiming a baptism of repentance, for the forgiveness of sins. ⁴ This was in fulfillment of what is said in the writings of the prophet Isaiah:

"The voice of one crying aloud in the
    wilderness:
'Make ready the way of the Lord,
make his paths straight.
Every chasm will be filled,
every mountain and hill will be leveled,
the winding ways will be straightened,
the rough roads made smooth,
and everyone will see the salvation of
    God.'"

⁷ And John said to the crowds that went to be baptized by him: "You children of snakes! Who has prompted you to seek refuge from the coming judgment? ⁸ Let your lives, then, prove your repentance; and do not begin to say among yourselves, 'Abraham is our ancestor,' for I tell you that out of these stones God is able to raise descendants for Abraham! ⁹ Already, indeed, the ax is lying at the root of the trees. Therefore every tree that fails to bear good fruit will be cut down and thrown into the fire."

¹⁰ "What are we to do then?" the people asked. ¹¹ "Let anyone who has two coats," answered John, "share with the person who has none; and anyone who has food do the same."

¹² Even tax collectors came to be baptized, and said to John: "Teacher, what are we to do?"

¹³ "Do not collect more than you have authority to demand," John answered. ¹⁴ And when some soldiers on active service asked, "And we—what are we to do?" he said: "Never use violence, or exact anything by false accusation; and be content with your pay."

¹⁵ Then, while the people were in suspense, and were all talking about whether John could be the Anointed One, ¹⁶ John, addressing them all, said: "I, indeed, wash you with water; but there is coming one more powerful than I, and I am not fit even to unfasten his sandals. He will bathe you with the holy Spirit and with fire. ¹⁷ His winnowing fan is in his hand so that he may clear his threshing floor, and store the grain in his barn, but the chaff he will burn with a fire that cannot be put out."

¹⁸ And so with many different appeals John proclaimed good news to the people. ¹⁹ But Prince Herod, being rebuked by John respecting Herodias, the wife of Herod's brother, and for all the evil things that he had done, ²⁰ crowned them all by shutting John up in prison.

²¹ Now after the baptism of all the people, and when Jesus had been baptized and was still praying, the heavens opened, ²² and the holy Spirit descended, in a bodily form, like a dove, on him, and

from the heavens came a voice: "You are my dearly loved child; you bring me great joy."

²³ When beginning his work, Jesus was about thirty years old. He was regarded as the son of Joseph, whose ancestors were:

Eli, ²⁴ Mattith, Levi, Melchiah, Janna, Joseph, ²⁵ Mattithiah, Amos, Nahum, Azaliah, Nogah, ²⁶ Mattith, Mattithiah, Shimei, Joseph, Josheh, ²⁷ Johanan, Rhesa, Zerubbabel, Shealtiel, Neriah, ²⁸ Melchiah, Addi, Cosam, Elmodam, Er, ²⁹ Joshua, Eliezer, Joram, Mattith, Levi, ³⁰ Simeon, Judah, Joseph, Jonam, Eliakim, ³¹ Meleah, Menan, Mattithiah, Nathan, David, ³² Jesse, Obed, Boaz, Salah, Nahshon, ³³ Amminadab, Arni, Hezron, Perez, Judah, ³⁴ Jacob, Isaac, Abraham, Terah, Nahor, ³⁵ Serug, Reu, Peleg, Eber, Shelah, ³⁶ Kenan, Arpachshad, Shem, Noah, Lamech, ³⁷ Methuselah, Enoch, Jared, Mahalalel, Kenan, ³⁸ Enosh, Seth, and Adam the son of God.

4 ¹ On returning from the Jordan, full of the holy Spirit, Jesus was led in the spirit through the wilderness for forty days, tempted by the devil.

² All that time he ate nothing; and, when it was over, he became hungry. ³ So the devil said to him: "If you are God's Child, tell this stone to become a loaf of bread." ⁴ And Jesus answered him: "It is written, 'It is not on bread alone that a person is to live.'"

⁵ And the devil led Jesus up, and showing him in a single moment all the kingdoms of the earth, said to him: ⁶ "I will give you all this power, and the splendor of them; for it has been given into my hands and I give it to whom I wish. ⁷ If you worship me, it will all be yours." ⁸ And Jesus answered him: "It is written, 'You should worship the Lord your God, and be in service to him only.'"

⁹ The devil next led him into Jerusalem, and, placing him on the parapet of the Temple, said: "If you are God's Child, throw yourself down from here, ¹⁰ for it is written, 'He will give his angels commands about you, to guard you safely,' ¹¹ and 'On their hands they will lift you up, otherwise you might strike your foot against a stone.'" ¹² But Jesus answered him: "It is said, 'You must not put the Lord your God to the test.'"

¹³ When he had tried every way to put him to the test, the devil left Jesus, until another opportunity.

The Work in Galilee

¹⁴ Moved by the power of the Spirit, Jesus returned to Galilee. Reports about him spread through all that region; ¹⁵ and he began to teach in their synagogues, and was honored by everyone.

¹⁶ Coming to Nazareth, where he had been brought up, Jesus, as was his custom, went on the sabbath into the synagogue, and stood up to read the scriptures. ¹⁷ He was given the book of the prophet Isaiah; and Jesus opened the book and found the place where it says:

¹⁸ "The Spirit of the Lord is on me,
  for he has consecrated me to bring
    good news to poor people,
  he has sent me to proclaim release to
    captives and restoration of sight to
    the blind,
  to set the oppressed at liberty,
¹⁹ to proclaim a year of favor from the
    Lord."

²⁰ Then, closing the book and returning it to the attendant, he sat down. The eyes of all in the synagogue were fixed on him, ²¹ and Jesus began:

"This very day this passage has been fulfilled in your hearing."

²² All who were present spoke well of him, and were astonished at the beautiful words that fell from his lips. "Is he not Joseph's son?" they asked. ²³ "Doubtless," said Jesus, "you will remind me of the

saying, 'Doctor, cure yourself'; and you will say, 'Do here in your own country all that we have heard that has been done at Capernaum.' ²⁴ I tell you," he continued, "that no prophet is acceptable in his own country. ²⁵ There were, doubtless, many widows in Israel in Elijah's days, when the heavens were closed for three years and six months, and a severe famine prevailed throughout the country; ²⁶ and yet it was not to one of them that Elijah was sent, but to a widow at Zarephath in Sidonia. ²⁷ And there were many in Israel with skin diseases in the time of the prophet Elisha, yet it was not one of them who was made clean, but Naaman the Syrian." ²⁸ All the people in the synagogue, as they listened to this, became enraged. ²⁹ Starting up, they drove Jesus out of the town, and led him to the brow of the hill on which their town stood, intending to hurl him down. ³⁰ But he passed through the middle of the crowd and went on his way.

³¹ Then Jesus went down to Capernaum, a city in Galilee. On the sabbath he taught the people. ³² They were amazed at his teaching, because his words were spoken with authority. ³³ In the synagogue there was a man with the spirit of an unclean demon in him, who called out loudly: ³⁴ "Stop! What do you want with us, Jesus of Nazareth? Have you come to destroy us? I know who you are—the Holy One of God!" ³⁵ But Jesus rebuked it. "Be silent! Come out from him," he said. The demon flung the man down in the middle of the people, and then came out from him, without causing him further harm. ³⁶ And they were all lost in amazement, and kept saying to one another: "What words are these? For he gives his commands to the unclean spirits with a marvelous authority, and they come out." ³⁷ And rumors about Jesus traveled through every place in the surrounding countryside.

³⁸ On leaving the synagogue, Jesus went into Simon's house. Now Simon's mother-in-law was suffering from a severe attack of fever, and they asked Jesus to do something for her. ³⁹ Bending over her, he rebuked the fever; the fever left her, and she immediately got up and began to serve them. ⁴⁰ At sunset, all who had friends suffering from various diseases took them to Jesus; and he placed his hands on every one of them and healed them. ⁴¹ And even demons came out from many people, screaming, 'You are the Child of God.' Jesus rebuked them, and would not allow them to speak, because they knew that he was the Christ.

⁴² At daybreak, Jesus went out and walked to a lonely spot. But crowds of people began to look for him; and they came to where he was and tried to detain him and prevent his leaving them. ⁴³ Jesus, however, said to them: "I must take the good news of the realm of God to the other towns also, for that was why I was sent." ⁴⁴ And he continued to make his proclamation in the synagogues of Judea.

5 ¹ Once, when the people were pressing around Jesus as they listened to God's message, he happened to be standing by the shore of the Lake of Gennesaret, and saw two boats close to the shore. ² The fishermen had gone away from them and were washing the nets. ³ So, getting into one of the boats, which belonged to Simon, Jesus asked him to push off a little way from the shore, and then sat down and taught the people from the boat. ⁴ When he had finished speaking, he said to Simon: "Push off into deep water, and throw out your nets for a haul."

⁵ "We have been hard at work all night, sir," answered Simon, "and have not caught anything, but if you say so, I will throw out the nets." ⁶ They did so, and enclosed such a great shoal of fish that their nets began to break. ⁷ So they signaled to their partners in the other boat to come and help them; and they came and filled both the boats so full of fish that they were almost sinking. ⁸ When Simon Peter saw this, he threw

himself down at Jesus's knees, exclaiming: "Master, leave me, for I am a sinful man!" [9] For he and all who were with him were lost in amazement at the haul of fish which they had made; [10] and so, too, were James and John, Zebedee's sons, who were Simon's partners. "Do not be afraid," Jesus said to Simon; "from today you will catch people." [11] And, when they had brought their boats to shore, they left everything, and followed him.

[12] On one occasion Jesus was staying in a town, when he saw a man who was covered with a skin disease. When the man saw Jesus, he threw himself on his face and implored his help: "Master, if only you are willing, you are able to make me clean." [13] Stretching out his hand, Jesus touched him, saying as he did so: "I am willing; become clean."

Instantly the disease left the man; [14] and then Jesus impressed on him that he was not to say a word to anyone, "but," he added, "set out and show yourself to the priest, and make the offerings for your cleansing, in the manner directed by Moses, as evidence of your having been healed." [15] However, the story about Jesus spread all the more, and great crowds came together to listen to him, and to be cured of their illnesses; [16] but Jesus tended to withdraw to lonely places and pray.

[17] On one of those days, when Jesus was teaching, some Pharisees and scholars were sitting nearby. (They had come from all the villages in Galilee and Judea, and from Jerusalem; and the power of the Lord was on Jesus, so that he could heal.) [18] And there some men brought on a bed a man who was paralyzed. They tried to get him in and lay him before Jesus; [19] but finding no way of getting him in owing to the crowd, they went up on the roof and lowered him through the tiles, with his pallet, into the middle of the people and in front of Jesus. [20] When he saw their faith, Jesus said: "Friend, your sins have been forgiven." [21] The scholars and the Pharisees began debating about this. "Who is this man who speaks so blasphemously?" they asked. "Who can forgive sins except God?"

[22] When Jesus became aware of their thoughts, he turned to them and exclaimed: "What are you thinking among yourselves? [23] Which is the easier: To say, 'Your sins have been forgiven you'? Or to say, 'Get up, and walk'? [24] But so that you may know that the Child of Humanity has power on earth to forgive sins" — he spoke to the paralyzed man: "To you I say, Get up, and take up your pallet, and go to your home." [25] Instantly the man stood up before their eyes, took up what he had been lying on, and went to his home, praising God. [26] The people, one and all, were lost in amazement, and praised God; and in great awe they said: "We have seen strange things today!"

[27] After this, Jesus went out; and he noticed a tax collector, named Levi, sitting in the tax office, and said to him: "Follow me." [28] Levi left everything and got up and followed him. [29] And Levi gave a great entertainment at his house, in honor of Jesus; and a large number of tax gatherers and others were having dinner with them.

[30] The Pharisees and the teachers of the Law belonging to their party complained of this to his followers. [31] In answer Jesus said: "It is not those who are well who need a doctor, but those who are ill. [32] I have not come to call the righteous, but the outcast, to repent."

[33] "John's followers," they said to him, "often fast and say prayers, and so do the followers of the Pharisees, while yours are eating and drinking!"

[34] But Jesus answered them: "Can you make the groom's friends fast while the groom is with them? [35] But the days will come — a time when the groom will be taken away from them; and they will fast then, when those days come." [36] Then, as an illustration, Jesus said to them: "No one ever tears a piece from a new garment and puts it on an old one; for, if she does, she

will not only tear the new garment, but the piece from the new one will not match the old. [37] And no one puts new wine into old wineskins; for, if she does, the new wine will burst the skins, and the wine itself will run out, and the skins be lost. [38] But new wine must be put into fresh skins. [39] No one after drinking old wine wishes for new. 'No,' they say, 'the old is excellent.'"

6 [1] One sabbath Jesus was walking through cornfields, and his followers were picking the ears, and rubbing them in their hands, and eating them. [2] "Why are you doing what it is not allowable to do on the sabbath?" asked some of the Pharisees. [3] Jesus's answer was: "Have you not read even of what David did, when he was hungry, he and his companions — [4] that he went into the house of God, and took the consecrated bread and ate it, and gave some to his companions, though only the priests are allowed to eat it?" [5] Then Jesus added: "The Child of Humanity is lord even of the sabbath."

[6] On another sabbath Jesus went into the synagogue and taught; and there was a man there whose right hand was withered. [7] The scholars and the Pharisees watched Jesus closely, to see if he would heal on the sabbath, so that they might find a charge to bring against him. [8] He, however, knew what was in the their minds, and said to the man whose hand was withered: "Stand up and come out into the middle." The man stood up; [9] and Jesus said to them: "I ask you, is it allowable to do good on the sabbath — or harm? To save a life, or let it perish?" [10] Then, looking around at them all, he said to the man: "Stretch out your hand." The man did so; and his hand had become well. [11] But the scholars and the Pharisees became furious, and consulted together what they could do to Jesus.

[12] Now about that time, Jesus went out, up the hill, to pray, and spent the whole night in prayer to God. [13] When day came, he summoned his followers, and chose twelve of them, whom he also named "ambassadors." [14] They were Simon (whom Jesus also named Peter), and his brother Andrew, James, John, Philip, Bartholomew, [15] Matthew, Thomas, James son of Alphaeus, Simon known as the Zealot, [16] Judas son of James, and Judas Iscariot, who proved a traitor. [17] Afterward Jesus came down the hill with them and took his stand on a level place. With him was a large crowd of his followers, and great numbers of people from the whole of Judea, Jerusalem, and the coast district of Tyre and Sidon, [18] who had come to hear him and to be restored to health. Those, too, who were troubled with unclean spirits were healed; [19] and everyone in the crowd was trying to touch him, because a power went out from him which restored them all.

[20] Then, raising his eyes and looking at his followers, he said:

> "Blessed are you who are poor, for
>   yours is the realm of God.
> [21] Blessed are you who hunger now, for
>   you will be satisfied.
> Blessed are you who weep now, for you
>   will laugh.
> [22] Blessed are you when people hate you,
>   and when they expel you from among
>   them,
> and insult you,
> and reject your name as criminal —
> because of the Child of Humanity.

[23] "Then be glad and dance for joy, for be sure that your reward in heaven will be great; for that is what their ancestors did to the prophets. [24] But

> 'cursed are you who are rich,'
>   for you have had your comforts in full.
> [25] Cursed are you who are full now,
>   for you will hunger.
> Cursed are you who laugh now,
>   for you will mourn and weep.
> [26] Cursed are you when everyone speaks
>   well of you;

for this is what their ancestors did to
the false prophets.

²⁷ "But to you who are listening I say
—love your enemies, show kindness to
those who hate you, ²⁸ bless those who
curse you, pray for those who insult you.
²⁹ When someone gives one of you a blow
on the cheek, offer the other cheek as well;
and, when anyone takes away your cloak,
do not keep back your coat either. ³⁰ Give
to everyone who asks of you; and, when
anyone takes away what is yours, do not
demand its return. ³¹ Do to others as you
wish them to do to you.

³² "If you love only those who love you,
what thanks will be due to you? Why, even
the bad people love those who love them!
³³ For, if you show kindness only to those
who show kindness to you, what thanks
will be due to you? Even bad people do
that! ³⁴ If you lend only to those from
whom you expect to get something, what
thanks will be due to you? Even bad people lend to their compatriots in the hope
of getting as much in return! ³⁵ But love
your enemies, and show them kindness,
and lend to them, never expecting a return. Then your reward will be great, and
you will be children of the Most High, for
he himself is kind to the thankless and the
bad.

³⁶ "Be compassionate—even as your
Father is compassionate. ³⁷ Do not judge,
and you will not be judged; do not condemn, and you will not be condemned.
Forgive, and you will be forgiven. ³⁸ Give,
and it will be given to you. A generous
measure, pressed and shaken down, and
running over, will they pour into your lap;
for the standard you use will be the standard used for you."

³⁹ Then he told them a parable: "Can
one blind person guide another? Will they
not both fall into a ditch? ⁴⁰ Students are
not above their teacher; yet every finished
student will be like his teacher. ⁴¹ And why

do you look at the speck of sawdust in
someone's eye, while you pay no attention
at all to the plank of wood in your own?
⁴² How can you say to your friend, 'Friend,
let me take out the speck in your eye,'
while you yourself do not see the plank in
your own? Hypocrite! Take out the plank
from your own eye first, and then you will
see clearly how to take out the speck in
your friend's. ⁴³ There is no such thing as
a good tree bearing worthless fruit, or, on
the other hand, a worthless tree bearing
good fruit. ⁴⁴ For every tree is known by
its own fruit. People do not gather figs off
thornbushes, nor pick a bunch of grapes
from weeds. ⁴⁵ A good person, from the
good stores of her heart, brings out what
is good; while a bad person, from her bad
stores, brings out what is bad. For what
fills someone's heart will rise to her lips.
⁴⁶ Why do you call me 'Master! Master!'
and yet fail to do what I tell you? ⁴⁷ Everyone who comes to me and listens to my
teaching and acts on it—I will show you
to whom he may be compared. ⁴⁸ He
may be compared to a person building a
house, who dug, and went deep, and laid
the foundation on the rock. Then, when a
flood came, the river swept down on that
house, but had no power to shake it, because it had been built well. ⁴⁹ But those
who have listened and not acted on what
they have heard may be compared to a
person who built a house on the ground
without any foundation. The river swept
down on it, and the house immediately
collapsed; and great was the crash that followed."

7 ¹ After Jesus brought to a conclusion all
that he had then had to say to the people,
he entered Capernaum.

² A captain in the Roman army had a
slave whom he liked, and who was seriously ill—almost at the point of death.
³ And, hearing about Jesus, he sent some
Judean elders to him, with the request that

he would come and save his slave's life. [4] When they found Jesus, they earnestly implored him to do so. "He deserves the favor from you," they said, [5] "for he is devoted to our nation, and himself built our synagogue for us." [6] So Jesus went with them. But when he was no great distance from the house, the captain sent some friends with the message: "Do not trouble yourself, sir; for I am unworthy to receive you under my roof. [7] That was why I did not even venture to come to you myself; but speak, and let my attendant be healed. [8] For I myself am a person under the orders of others, with soldiers under me; and if I say to one of them 'Go,' he goes, and to another 'Come,' he comes, and to my slave 'Do this,' he does it." [9] Jesus was surprised to hear these words from him; and, turning to the crowd which was following him, he said: "I tell you, nowhere in Israel have I met with such faith as this!" [10] And, when the messengers returned to the house, they found the slave recovered.

[11] Shortly after, Jesus went to a town called Nain, his followers and a great crowd going with him. [12] Just as he approached the gate of the town, there was a dead man being carried out — an only son, and his mother was a widow. A large number of the people of the town were with her. [13] When he saw her, the Master was moved with compassion for her, and he said to her: "Do not weep." [14] Then he went up and touched the bier, and the bearers stopped; and Jesus said: "Young man, I am speaking to you — rise!" [15] The dead man sat up and began to talk, and Jesus restored him to his mother. [16] Everyone was awestruck and began praising God. "A great prophet has arisen among us," they said; "and God has visited his people."

[17] And this story about Jesus spread all through Judea, and in the neighboring countries as well.

[18] All these events were reported to John by his followers. [19] So he summoned two of them, and sent them to the Master to ask, "Are you the one to come, or are we to look for someone else?"

[20] When these men found Jesus, they said: "John the Baptist has sent us to you to ask, 'Are you the one to come, or are we to look for somebody else?'" [21] At that very time Jesus had healed many people of diseases, afflictions, and evil spirits, and had given many blind people their sight. [22] So his answer to the question was: "Go and report to John what you have witnessed and heard — the blind recover their sight, the lame walk, those with terrible skin ailments are made clean, and the deaf hear, the dead are raised to life, the good news is told to the poor. [23] And blessed is the person who finds no hindrance in me."

[24] When John's messengers had left, Jesus, speaking to the crowds, began to say with reference to John: [25] "What did you go out into the wilderness to look at? A reed waving in the wind? If not, what did you go out to see? A man dressed in rich clothing? Why, those who are accustomed to fine clothes and luxury live in royal palaces. [26] What then did you go to see? A prophet? Yes, I tell you, and far more than a prophet. [27] This is the man of whom it is written:

'I am sending my messenger ahead of you,
and he will prepare your way before you.'

[28] "There is, I tell you, no one born of a woman who is greater than John; and yet the least in the realm of God is greater than he."

[29] (All the people, when they heard this, and even the tax collectors, having accepted John's baptism, acknowledged the justice of God. [30] But the Pharisees and the scholars, having rejected John's bap-

tism, frustrated God's purpose in regard to them.)

³¹ "To what then should I compare the people of the present generation? What are they like? ³² They are like some little children who are sitting in the marketplace and calling out to one another: 'We have played the flute for you, but you have not danced; we have wailed, but you have not wept!' ³³ For now that John the Baptizer has come, not eating bread or drinking wine, you are saying, 'He has a demon in him'; ³⁴ and now that the Child of Humanity has come, eating and drinking, you are saying, 'Here is a glutton and a wine drinker, a friend of tax collectors and outcasts.' ³⁵ And yet Wisdom-Sofia is vindicated by all her children."

³⁶ One of the Pharisees asked Jesus to dine with him, so Jesus went to his house and took his place at the table. ³⁷ Just then a woman who was an outcast in the town, having heard that Jesus was eating in the Pharisee's house, brought an alabaster jar of perfume, ³⁸ and placed herself behind Jesus, near his feet, weeping. Then she began to make his feet wet with her tears, and she dried them with the hair of her head, repeatedly kissing his feet and anointing them with the perfume.

³⁹ When the Pharisee who had invited Jesus saw this, he said to himself: "Had this man been a prophet, he would have known who, and what sort of woman, this is who is touching him, and that she is an outcast." ⁴⁰ But, addressing him, Jesus said: "Simon, I have something to say to you."

"Go ahead, Teacher," Simon answered; and Jesus began: ⁴¹ "There were two people who were in debt to a moneylender; one owed five hundred silver coins, and the other fifty. ⁴² As they were unable to pay, he forgave them both. Which of them, do you think, will love him the more?"

⁴³ "I suppose," answered Simon, "it will be the man to whom he forgave the greater debt."

"You are right," said Jesus, ⁴⁴ and then,

turning to the woman, he said to Simon: "Do you see this woman? I came into your house — you gave me no water for my feet, but she has made my feet wet with her tears and dried them with her hair. ⁴⁵ You did not give me one kiss, but she, from the moment I came in, has not ceased to kiss my feet. ⁴⁶ You did not anoint even my head with oil, but she has anointed my feet with perfume. ⁴⁷ And for this, I tell you, her sins, many as they are, have been pardoned, because she has loved greatly; but one who has little pardoned him, loves but little." ⁴⁸ Then he said to the woman: "Your sins have been pardoned." ⁴⁹ The other guests began to say to one another: "Who is this man who even pardons sins?" ⁵⁰ But Jesus said to the woman: "Your trust has delivered you; go, and peace be with you."

8 ¹ Shortly afterward, Jesus went on a journey through the towns and villages, proclaiming the good news of the realm of God. With him went the Twelve, ² as well as some women who had been healed of wicked spirits and of infirmities. They were Mary, known as Mary of Magdala (from whom seven demons had been expelled), ³ and Joanna (the wife of Herod's steward, Chuza), and Susannah, and many others — all of whom provided for them out of their own resources.

⁴ Once, when a great crowd was collecting, and when the people of town after town were flocking to Jesus, he spoke to them in the form of a parable: ⁵ "The sower went out to sow his seed; and, as he was sowing, some of the seed fell along the path and was trampled on; and the wild birds ate it up. ⁶ Other seed fell on rock, and, as soon as it began to grow, having no moisture, withered away. ⁷ Other seed fell in the middle of thorns, but the thorns grew up with it and choked it entirely. ⁸ Other seed fell into good soil, and grew, and gave a hundredfold return." After saying this, Jesus cried aloud: "Let those who have ears to hear with hear."

[9] His followers asked Jesus the meaning of this parable. [10] "To you," he said, "the knowledge of the realm of God has been imparted, but to others in parables only, so that though they have eyes, they may not see, and though they have ears, they may not understand. [11] This is the parable: The seed is God's message. [12] By the seed which fell along the path is meant those who hear the message; but then comes the devil and carries away the message from their minds, to prevent their trusting it and being saved. [13] By the seed which fell on the rock is meant those who, as soon as they hear the message, welcome it joyfully; but they have no root, and trust it only for a time, and, when the time of trial comes, they draw back. [14] By that which fell among the thorns is meant those who hear the message, but who, as they go on their way, are completely choked by this world's cares and wealth and pleasures, and bring nothing to fullness. [15] But by that in the good ground is meant those who, having heard the message, listen in the goodness and beauty of their hearts, and patiently yield a plentiful return.

[16] "No one sets light to a lamp and then covers it with a bowl or puts it underneath a couch, but they put it on a lamp stand, so that anyone who comes in may see the light. [17] Nothing is hidden which will not be brought into the light of day, not ever kept secret which will not become known and come into the light of day. [18] Take care, then, how you listen. For, to all those who have, more will be given; while from all those who have nothing, even what they seem to have will be taken away."

[19] Presently Jesus's mother and brothers came where he was, but they were not able to join him because of the crowd. [20] So word was brought to him: "Your mother and your brothers are standing outside, wanting to see you." [21] His reply, spoken to them all, was: "My mother and my brothers are those who listen to God's teaching and do what it says."

[22] One day about that time, he got into a boat with his followers and said to them: "Let us go across the lake." [23] So they put off. While they were sailing, Jesus fell asleep. A squall swept down on the lake, and their boat was filling and they were in danger. [24] So they came and roused him. "Master, Master," they cried, "we are lost!" Jesus rose and rebuked the wind and the rushing waves, and they fell, and a calm followed. [25] "Where is your confidence?" he exclaimed. But in great awe and amazement they said to one another: "Who can this be, who commands even the winds and the waves, and they obey him?"

[26] And they reached the country of the Gerasenes, which is on the opposite side to Galilee; [27] and, on getting ashore, he met a man who had demons in him, coming out of the town. For a long time this man had worn no clothing, and he had not lived in a house, but in the tombs. [28] Catching sight of Jesus, he shrieked and threw himself down before him, and in a loud voice exclaimed: "What do you want with me, Jesus, Child of the Most High God? I beg you not to torment me." [29] For Jesus was commanding the foul spirit to come out from the man. On many occasions it had seized him, and, even when secured with chains and fetters, and watched, he would break through anything that bound him, and be driven by the demon into the wilderness.

[30] "What is your name?" Jesus asked.

"Legion," he answered (for many demons had taken possession of him); [31] and the demons begged Jesus not to order them away into the bottomless pit. [32] There was a herd of many pigs close by, feeding on the hillside; and the demons begged Jesus to give them leave to enter into them. He gave them leave. [33] They came out from the man and took possession of the pigs; and the herd rushed down the steep slope into the lake and were drowned. [34] When the men who tended them saw what had happened, they ran away, and carried the news to the town, and to the country around. ³⁵ The people went out to see what had happened, and, when they came to Jesus, they found the man from whom the demons had gone out, sitting, clothed and in his right mind, at Jesus's feet; and they were awestruck. ³⁶ Those who had seen it told them how the possessed man had been delivered. ³⁷ Then all the people in the region of the Gerasenes asked Jesus to leave them, for they were terrified. Jesus got into a boat and returned. ³⁸ The man from whom the demons had gone out begged Jesus to let him be with him; but Jesus sent him away. ³⁹ "Go back to your home," he said, "and relate the story of all that God has done for you." So the man went through the whole town and proclaimed, as he went, all that Jesus had done for him.

⁴⁰ On his return, Jesus was welcomed by the people; for everyone was looking out for him. ⁴¹ And a man named Jairus, who was a resident of the synagogue, came to Jesus, and threw himself at Jesus's feet, with entreaties that he would come to his house, ⁴² because his only daughter, who was about twelve years old, was dying. As Jesus was going, the people were pressing closely around him. ⁴³ And a woman who had suffered from hemorrhage for twelve years, and whom no one could heal, ⁴⁴ came up behind him and touched the fringe of his cloak. Instantly the hemorrhage ceased.

⁴⁵ "Who touched me?" Jesus asked; and, while everyone was denying having done so, Peter exclaimed: "Why, sir, the people are crowding around you and pressing against you!"

⁴⁶ "Somebody touched me," said Jesus; "for I felt that power had gone out from me." ⁴⁷ Then the woman, when she saw that she was discovered, came forward trembling, and threw herself down before him; and, in the presence of all the people,

she told him her reason for touching him, and that she had been healed instantly.

⁴⁸ "Daughter," he said, "your confidence has saved you. Go, and peace be with you."

⁴⁹ Before he had finished speaking, someone came from the house of the president of the synagogue and said: "Your daughter is dead! Do not trouble the teacher further." ⁵⁰ But Jesus, hearing this, spoke to the president: "Do not be afraid; only have confidence, and she will yet be delivered." ⁵¹ When he reached the house, he did not allow anyone to go in with him, except Peter, John, and James, and the child's father and mother. ⁵² And everyone was weeping and mourning for her.

"Do not weep," Jesus said, "she is not dead; she is asleep." ⁵³ They began to laugh at him, for they knew that she was dead. ⁵⁴ But, taking her by the hand, Jesus said in a loud voice: "Child, get up!" ⁵⁵ The child's spirit returned to her, and she instantly stood up; and Jesus ordered them to give her something to eat. ⁵⁶ Her parents were amazed, but Jesus impressed on them that they were not to tell anyone what had happened.

9 ¹ Jesus called the Twelve together, and gave them power and authority over all demons, as well as to heal diseases. ² He sent them out as his messengers, to proclaim the realm of God, and to heal. ³ "Do not," he said to them, "take anything for your journey; not even a staff, or a bag, or bread, or any money, or a change of clothes with you. ⁴ Whatever house you go to stay in, remain there, and leave from that place. ⁵ If people do not welcome you, as you leave that town, shake even the dust off your feet, as a protest against them." ⁶ Then they set out and went from village to village, telling the good news and curing people everywhere.

⁷ Prince Herod heard of all that was happening, and was perplexed, because it was said by some that John must be risen

from the dead. [8] Some again said that Elijah had appeared, and others that one of the prophets of old had risen again. [9] But Herod himself said: "John I beheaded; but who is this of whom I hear such things?" And he endeavored to see him.

[10] When the ambassadors returned, they related to him all that they had done. Then Jesus went privately to a town called Bethsaida, taking them with him. [11] But the people recognized him and followed him in crowds; and Jesus welcomed them and spoke to them about the realm of God, while he healed those who were in need. [12] The day was drawing to a close, when the Twelve came up to him, and said: "Send the crowd away, so that they may make their way to the villages and farms around about, and find themselves lodgings and provisions, for we are in a lonely spot here." [13] But he said: "It is for you to give them something to eat."

"We have not more than five loaves and two fishes," they answered, "unless indeed we are to go and buy food for all these people." [14] (For the men among them were about five thousand.) "Have them recline in groups," he said to his followers, "about fifty in each." [15] This they did, and got all the people reclined. [16] Taking the five loaves and the two fishes, Jesus looked up to heaven and said the blessing over them. Then he broke them in pieces, and gave them to his followers to set before the people. [17] Everyone was satisfied with what they had to eat, and what was left of the broken pieces was picked up — twelve baskets.

[18] Afterward, when he was alone, praying, his followers joined him, and he asked them this question: "Who do the people say that I am?"

[19] "John the Baptizer," was their answer; "others, however, say that you are Elijah, while others say that one of the ancient prophets has risen again."

[20] "But you," he went on, "who do you say that I am?" And to this Peter answered: "The Anointed One of God."

[21] Jesus, however, strictly charged them not to say this to anyone; [22] he told them that the Child of Humanity must undergo much suffering, and be rejected by the elders, and chief priests, and scholars, and be put to death, and rise on the third day. [23] And to everyone he said: "If anyone wishes to walk in my steps, let him renounce self, and take up his cross daily, and follow me. [24] For whoever wishes to save his life will lose it, and whoever, for my sake, loses his life — that person will save it. [25] What good does it do someone if, when he has gained the whole world, he has lost or forfeited himself? [26] Whoever is ashamed of me and of my teaching, the Child of Humanity will be ashamed of him, when he comes in his glory and the glory of the Father and of the holy angels. [27] Indeed, I tell you, some who are standing here will not know death, until they have seen the realm of God."

[28] About eight days after speaking these words, Jesus went up the mountain to pray, taking with him Peter, John, and James. [29] As he was praying, the aspect of his face was changed, and his clothing became of a glittering whiteness. [30] And all at once two men were talking with Jesus; they were Moses and Elijah, [31] appearing in a glorified state, and spoke of his departure, which was going to take place at Jerusalem. [32] Peter and his companions had been overpowered by sleep but, suddenly becoming wide awake, they saw his glory and the two men who were standing beside him.

[33] And, as they were disappearing from him, Peter exclaimed: "Sir, it is good to be here; let us make three tents, one for you, and one for Moses, and one for Elijah." He did not know what he was saying; [34] and, while he was speaking, a cloud came down and enveloped them; and they were afraid, as they passed into the cloud; [35] and from

the cloud came a voice which said: "This is my Child, the chosen one; listen to him." [36] And, as the voice ceased, Jesus was found alone. They kept silence, and told no one about any of the things that they had seen.

[37] The next day, when they had come down from the mountain, a great crowd met him. [38] And just then a man in the crowd shouted out: "Teacher, I entreat you to look at my son, for he is my only child; [39] all at once a spirit will seize him, suddenly shriek, and throw him into convulsions until he foams, and will leave him only when he is utterly exhausted. [40] I begged your followers to drive the spirit out, but they could not."

[41] "Faithless and perverse generation!" Jesus exclaimed. "How long must I be with you and have patience with you? Lead your son here." [42] While the boy was coming up to Jesus, the demon dashed him down and threw him into convulsions. But Jesus rebuked the unclean spirit, and healed the boy, and gave him back to his father. [43] And all present were struck with awe at the greatness of God.

In the midst of the general wonder at all that Jesus was doing, he said to his followers:

[44] "Listen carefully to my words. For the Child of Humanity is destined to be betrayed into the hands of people." [45] But his followers did not understand the meaning of this; it had been concealed from them so that they did not see it, and they were afraid to question him as to what he meant.

[46] A discussion arose among the disciples as to which of them was the greatest; [47] and Jesus, knowing of the discussion that was occupying their thoughts, took hold of a little child, and placed it beside him, [48] and then said to them: "Anyone who, for the sake of my name, welcomes even this little child is welcoming me; and anyone who welcomes me is welcoming the one who sent me. For whoever is least among you all — that person is great."

[49] John said: "Sir, we saw a man driving out demons by using your name, and we tried to prevent him, because he does not follow you with us."

[50] "None of you must prevent him," Jesus said to John; "whoever is not against you is for you."

The Journey to Jerusalem

[51] As the days before his being taken up were growing few, he set his face resolutely in the direction of Jerusalem; and he sent on messengers in advance. [52] On their way, they went into a Samaritan village to make preparations for him, [53] but the people there did not welcome him, because his face was set in the direction of Jerusalem. [54] When James and John saw this, they said: "Master, do you wish us to call for fire to come down from the sky and consume them?" [55] But Jesus turned and rebuked them. [56] And they made their way to another village.

[57] And, while they were on their way, a man said to Jesus: "I will follow you wherever you go."

[58] "Foxes have holes," he replied, "and wild birds their nests, but the Child of Humanity has nowhere to lay his head." [59] To another Jesus said: "Follow me."

"Let me first go and bury my father," he said. [60] But he said: "Leave the dead to bury their dead; but go yourself and carry far and wide the news of the realm of God."

[61] "Master," said another, "I will follow you; but first let me say goodbye to my family." [62] But Jesus answered: "No one who looks back, after putting his hand to the plow, is fitted for the realm of God."

10 [1] After this, the Master appointed seventy-two, and sent them on as his messengers, two by two, in advance, to every town and place that he was himself intending to visit.

2 "The harvest," he said, "is abundant, but the laborers are few. Therefore pray to the owner of the harvest to send laborers to gather in his harvest. 3 Now, go. Remember, I am sending you out like lambs among wolves. 4 Do not take a purse with you, or a bag, or sandals; and do not stop to greet anyone on your journey. 5 Whatever house you go to stay at, begin by praying for a blessing on it. 6 Then, if anyone there is deserving of a blessing, your blessing will rest on him; but if not, it will come back on yourselves. 7 Remain at that same house, and eat and drink whatever they offer you; for the worker is worth his wages. Do not keep changing from one house to another. 8 Whatever town you visit, if the people welcome you, eat what is set before you; 9 heal the sick there, and tell people, 'The realm of God is close at hand.' 10 But whatever town you go to visit, if the people do not welcome you, go out into its streets and say, 11 'We wipe off the dust of your town which has clung to our feet; still, be assured that the realm of God is close at hand.' 12 I tell you that the doom of Sodom will be more bearable on that day than the doom of that town. 13 Alas for you, Chorazin! Alas for you, Bethsaida! For, if the miracles which have been done in you had been done in Tyre and Sidon, they would have sat in sackcloth and ashes and repented long ago. 14 Yet the doom of Tyre and Sidon will be more bearable at the judgment than yours. 15 And you, Capernaum! Will you 'exalt yourself to heaven'? 'You will go down to the place of death.' 16 Anyone who listens to you is listening to me, and anyone who rejects you is rejecting me; while the person who rejects me is rejecting him who sent me."

17 When the seventy-two returned, they exclaimed joyfully: "Master, even the demons submit to us when we use your name." 18 And Jesus replied: "I have had visions of Satan, fallen, like lightning from the heavens. 19 Remember, I have given you the power to trample on snakes and scorpions, and to meet all the strength of the enemy. Nothing will ever harm you in any way. 20 Yet do not rejoice in the fact that the spirits submit to you, but rejoice that your names have been enrolled in heaven."

21 At that same time, moved to exultation by the holy Spirit, he said:

"I thank you, Father, Lord of heaven and earth, that though you have hidden these things from the wise and learned, you have revealed them to the very young! Yes, Father, I thank you that this has seemed good to you.

22 "Everything has been committed to me by my Father; nor does anyone know who the Son is, except the Father, or who the Father is, except the Son and those to whom the Son may choose to reveal him."

23 Then, turning to his disciples, Jesus said to them alone: "Blessed are the eyes that see what you are seeing; 24 for, I tell you, many prophets and kings wished for the sight of the things which you are seeing, yet never heard them."

25 Just then a student of the Law came forward to test Jesus further. "Teacher," he said, "what must I do if I am to gain life through the ages?"

26 "What is said in the Law?" he answered. "What do you read there?" 27 His reply was:

"'You must love the Lord your God
    with all your heart, and with all your
    soul, and with all your strength,
    and with all your mind; and your
    neighbor as you love yourself.'"

28 "You have answered right," said Jesus; "do that, and you will live." 29 But the man, wanting to justify himself, said to Jesus: "And who is my neighbor?"

30 To which Jesus replied: "A man was

once going down from Jerusalem to Jericho when he fell into the hands of robbers, who stripped him of everything, and beat him, and went away leaving him half dead. [31] As it chanced, a priest was going down by that road. He saw the man, but passed by on the opposite side. [32] A Levite, too, did the same; he came up to the spot, but when he saw the man, passed by on the opposite side. [33] But a Samaritan, traveling that way, came upon the man, and, when he saw him, he was moved with compassion. [34] He went to him and bound up his wounds, dressing them with oil and wine, and then put him on his own mule, and brought him to an inn, and took care of him. [35] The next day he took out two silver coins and gave them to the innkeeper. 'Take care of him,' he said, 'and whatever more you may spend I myself will repay you on my way back.' [36] Now which, do you think, of these three," asked Jesus, "proved himself a neighbor to the one who fell into the robbers' hands?"

[37] "The one that took pity on him," was the answer; at which Jesus said: "Go and do the same yourself."

[38] As they continued their journey, Jesus came to a village, where a woman named Martha welcomed him to her house. [39] She had a sister called Mary, who seated herself at the Master's feet, and listened to his teaching; [40] but Martha was distracted by the many preparations that she was making. So she went up to Jesus and said: "Master, do you approve of my sister's leaving me to make preparations alone? Tell her to help me."

[41] "Martha, Martha," replied the Master, "you are anxious and trouble yourself about many things; [42] but only a few are necessary, or rather one. Mary has chosen the good part, and it will not be taken away from her."

11 [1] One day Jesus was at a certain place praying, and, when he had finished, one of his followers said to him: "Master, teach us to pray, as John taught his followers."

[2] "When you pray," Jesus answered, "say:

'Father,
May your name be held holy,
your realm come.
  Give us each day the bread that we will
    need;
  and forgive us our sins,
  for we ourselves forgive everyone who
    is in debt to us;
  and do not put us to the test.'"

[5] Jesus also said to them: "Suppose that one of you who has a friend were to go to her in the middle of the night and say, 'Friend, lend me three loaves, [6] for a friend of mine has arrived at my house after a journey, and I have nothing to offer him.' [7] And suppose that the other should answer from inside, 'Do not trouble me; the door is already fastened, and my children and I are in bed; I cannot get up and give you anything'; [8] I tell you that even though she will not get up and give her anything because she is a friend, yet because of her persistence she will rouse herself and give her what she wants.

[9] "And so I say to you: Ask, and it will be given you; search, and you will find; knock, and the door will be opened to you. [10] For the person who asks receives, everyone who searches finds, and to the person who knocks the door will be opened. [11] What father among you, if his son asks him for a fish, will give him a snake instead, [12] or, if he asks for an egg, will give him a scorpion? [13] If you, then, wicked though you are, know how to give good gifts to your children, how much more will the Father in heaven give the holy Spirit to those who ask him!"

[14] Once Jesus was driving out a dumb demon, and, when the demon had gone out, the dumb man spoke. The people

were amazed at this; [15] but some of them said: "He drives out demons by the help of Beelzebul, the chief of the demons"; [16] while others, to test him, asked him for some sign from the heavens. [17] Jesus himself, however, was aware of what they were thinking, and said to them: "Any kingdom wholly divided against itself becomes a desolation; and a divided house falls. [18] So, too, if Satan is wholly divided against himself, how can his kingdom last? Yet you say that I drive out demons by the help of Beelzebul. [19] But if it is by Beelzebul's help that I drive out demons, by whose help is it that your own sons drive them out? Therefore they will themselves be your judges. [20] But if it is by the hand of God that I drive out demons, then the realm of God must already be upon you. [21] When a strong man is keeping guard, fully armed, over his own mansion, his property is in safety; [22] but when one still stronger has attacked and overpowered him, he takes away all the weapons on which the other had relied, and divides his spoil. [23] Whoever is not with me is against me, and the person who does not help me to gather is scattering. [24] No sooner does an unclean spirit leave someone, than it passes through places where there is no water, in search of rest; and finding none, it says, 'I will go back to the home which I left'; [25] but on coming there, it finds it unoccupied, swept, and put in order. [26] Then it goes and brings with it seven other spirits more wicked than itself, and they go in, and make their home there; and the last state of that person proves to be worse than the first." [27] As Jesus was saying this, a woman in the crowd, raising her voice, exclaimed: "Blessed is the womb that bore you and the breasts that fed you!" [28] But Jesus replied: "More blessed are those who listen to God's message and keep it."

[29] As the crowds increased, he began to speak: "This generation is a wicked generation. It is asking for a sign, but no sign will be given it except the sign of Jonah. [30] For, as Jonah became a sign to the people of Nineveh, so will the Child of Humanity be to this generation. [31] At the judgment the Queen of the South will rise up with the people of this generation, and will condemn them, because she came from the ends of the earth to listen to the wisdom of Solomon; and here is more than a Solomon! [32] At the judgment the men of Nineveh will stand up with this generation, and will condemn it, because they repented at Jonah's proclamation; and here is more than a Jonah! [33] No one sets light to a lamp, and then puts it in the cellar or under a basket, but he puts it on the lamp stand, so that anyone who comes in may see the light. [34] The lamp of the body is your eye. When your eye is unclouded, your whole body also is lit up; but as soon as your eye is diseased, your body also is darkened. [35] Take care, therefore, that the inner light is not darkness. [36] If, then, your whole body is lit up, and no corner of it darkened, the whole will be lit up, just as when a lamp gives you light by its brilliance."

[37] As he finished speaking, a Pharisee asked him to breakfast with him, and Jesus went in and took his place at the table. [38] The Pharisee noticed, to his astonishment, that Jesus omitted the washing before the meal. [39] But the Master said to him: "You Pharisees do, it is true, clean the outside of the cup and of the plate, but inside you yourselves are filled with greed and wickedness. [40] Fools! Did not the maker of the outside make the inside too? [41] Only give away what is in them in charity, and at once you have the whole clean. [42] But cursed be you Pharisees! You pay tithes on mint, rue, and herbs of all kinds, and pass over justice and love to God. These last you ought to have put into practice without neglecting the first. [43] Cursed be you Pharisees! You delight to have the front seat in the synagogues,

and to be greeted in the markets with respect. ⁴⁴ Cursed be you! You are like unsuspected graves, over which people walk unawares."

⁴⁵ Here one of the scholars interrupted him by saying: "Teacher, when you say this, you are insulting us also." ⁴⁶ But Jesus went on: "Cursed be you, too, you scholars! You load people with loads that are too heavy to carry, but do not, yourselves, touch them with one of your fingers. ⁴⁷ Cursed be you! You build the monuments of the prophets whom your ancestors killed. ⁴⁸ You are actually witnesses to your ancestors' acts and show your approval of them, because, while they killed the prophets, you build tombs for them. ⁴⁹ That is why the Wisdom of God said: 'I will send to them prophets and messengers, ⁵⁰ some of whom they will persecute and kill, in order that the blood of all the prophets that has been spilled since the creation of the world may be exacted from this generation — ⁵¹ from the blood of Abel down to the blood of Zechariah, who was slain between the altar and the house of God.' Yes, I tell you, it will be exacted from this generation. ⁵² Alas for you scholars! You have taken away the key of the door of knowledge. You have not gone in yourselves and you have hindered those who try to go in."

⁵³ When he left the house, the scholars and the Pharisees began to press him hard and question him closely on many subjects, ⁵⁴ laying traps for him, so as to seize on anything that he might say.

12 ¹ Meanwhile the people had gathered in thousands, so that they trod on one another, when he, addressing himself first to his followers, began by saying to them: "Be on your guard against the leaven — that is, the hypocrisy — of the Pharisees. ² There is nothing, however covered up, which will not be uncovered, nor anything kept secret which will not become known. ³ So all that you have said in the dark will be heard in the light, and what you have spoken in the ear, within closed doors, will be proclaimed on the housetops. ⁴ To you who are my friends I say, Do not be afraid of those who kill the body, but after that can do no more. ⁵ I will show you of whom you should be afraid. Be afraid of the one who, after killing you, has the power to fling you into Gehenna. Yes, I say, be afraid of him. ⁶ Are not five sparrows sold for two copper coins? Yet not one of them has escaped God's notice. ⁷ No, even the hairs of your head are all numbered. Do not be afraid; you are of more value than many sparrows. ⁸ Everyone, I tell you, who publicly acknowledges me, the Child of Humanity also will acknowledge before God's angels; ⁹ but the person who publicly disowns me will be altogether disowned before God's angels. ¹⁰ Everyone who will say anything against the Child of Humanity will be forgiven, but for the person who slanders the holy Spirit there will be no forgiveness. ¹¹ Whenever they take you before the synagogue or the magistrates or other authorities, do not be anxious as to how you will defend yourselves, or what your defense will be, or what you will say; ¹² for the holy Spirit will show you at the moment what you ought to say."

¹³ "Teacher," a man in the crowd said to Jesus, "tell my brother to share the property with me." ¹⁴ But Jesus said to him: "Man, who made me a judge or an arbiter between you?" ¹⁵ And then he added: "Take care to keep yourselves free from every form of possessiveness; for even in the height of his prosperity a person's true life does not depend on what he has."

¹⁶ Then Jesus told them this parable: "There was once a rich man whose land was very fertile; ¹⁷ and he began to ask himself, 'What will I do, for I have nowhere to store my crops? ¹⁸ This is what I will do,' he said; 'I will pull down my barns and build larger ones, and store all my grain and my goods in them; ¹⁹ and I will say to myself, Now you have plenty of

good things put by for many years; take your ease, eat, drink, and enjoy yourself.' ²⁰ But God said to the man, 'Fool! This very night your life is being demanded; and as for all you have prepared — who will have it?' ²¹ So it is with those who lay by wealth for themselves and are not rich in God."

²² And Jesus said to his disciples: "That is why I say to you, Do not be anxious about the life here — what you can get to eat; nor yet about your body — what you can get to wear. ²³ For life is more than food, and the body more than its clothes. ²⁴ Think of the ravens — they neither sow nor reap; they have neither storehouse nor barn; and yet God feeds them! And how much more precious are you than birds! ²⁵ But which of you, by being anxious, can prolong your life a moment? ²⁶ And, if you cannot do even the smallest thing, why be anxious about other things? ²⁷ Think of the lilies, and how they grow. They neither toil nor spin; yet, I tell you, even Solomon in all his splendor was not robed like one of these. ²⁸ If, even in the field, God so clothes the grass which is living today and tomorrow will be thrown into the oven, how much more will he clothe you, you of little faith! ²⁹ And you — do not be always seeking what you can get to eat or what you can get to drink; and do not waver. ³⁰ These are the things which all the nations of the world are seeking, and your Father knows that you need them. ³¹ No, seek God's realm, and these things will be added for you. ³² So do not be afraid, my little flock, for your Father has been pleased to give you the realm.

³³ "Sell what belongs to you, and give compassionately. Make yourselves purses that will not wear out — an inexhaustible treasure in heaven, where no thief comes near, or moth works ruin. ³⁴ For where your treasure is, there also will your heart be. ³⁵ Make yourselves ready, with your lamps alight; ³⁶ and be like people who are waiting for their master's return from his wedding, so that when he comes and knocks, they may open the door for him at once. ³⁷ Happy are those slaves whom, on his return, the master will find watching. I tell you that he will make himself ready, and have them take their places at the table, and will come and serve them. ³⁸ Whether it is late at night, or in the early morning that he comes, if he finds all as it should be, then happy are they. ³⁹ This you do know, that had the owner of the house known at what time the thief was coming, he would have been on the watch, and would not have let his house be broken into. ⁴⁰ You must also prepare, for when you are least expecting him the Child of Humanity will come."

⁴¹ "Master," said Peter, "are you telling this parable with reference to us or to everyone?"

⁴² "Who, then," replied the Master, "is that trustworthy steward, the careful man, who will be placed by his master over his establishment, to give rations at the proper time? ⁴³ Happy will that slave be whom his master, when he comes home, will find doing this. ⁴⁴ His master, I tell you, will put him in charge of the whole of his property. ⁴⁵ But should that slave say to himself, 'My master is a long time coming,' and begin to beat the menservants and the maidservants, and to eat and drink and get drunk, ⁴⁶ that slave's master will come on a day when he does not expect him, and at an hour of which he is unaware, and will flog him severely and assign him his place among the untrustworthy. ⁴⁷ The slave who knows his master's wishes and yet does not prepare and act accordingly will receive many lashes; ⁴⁸ while one who does not know his master's wishes, but acts so as to deserve a flogging, will receive but few. From everyone to whom much has been given much will be expected, and from the man to whom much has been entrusted the more will be demanded. ⁴⁹ I came to cast fire on the earth; and how I wish that it were already blazing. ⁵⁰ There

is a baptism that I must undergo, and how great is my distress until it is over! ⁵¹ Do you think that I am here to give peace on earth? No, I tell you, but to cause division. ⁵² For from this time, if there are five people in a house, they will be divided, three against two, and two against three.

⁵³ "Father will be opposed to son and son to father, mother to daughter and daughter to mother, mother-in-law to her daughter-in-law and daughter-in-law to her mother-in-law."

⁵⁴ And to the people Jesus said: "When you see a cloud rising in the west, you say at once, 'There is a storm coming,' and come it does. ⁵⁵ And when you see that the wind is in the south, you say, 'It will be burning hot,' and so it proves. ⁵⁶ Hypocrites! You know how to judge the earth and the sky; how is it, then, that you cannot judge this time? ⁵⁷ Why do not you yourselves decide what is right? ⁵⁸ When, for instance, you are going with your opponent before a magistrate, on your way to the court do your best to make a deal with him; otherwise he might drag you before the judge, then the judge will hand you over to the bailiff of the court, and the bailiff throw you into prison. ⁵⁹ You will not, I tell you, come out until you have paid the very last cent."

13 ¹ Just at that time some people had come to tell Jesus about the Galileans, whose blood Pilate had mingled with the blood of their sacrifices. ² "Do you suppose," he replied, "that because these Galileans have suffered in this way, they were worse sinners than any other Galileans? ³ No, I tell you; but unless you repent, you will all perish as they did. ⁴ Or those eighteen men at Siloam on whom the tower fell, killing them all, do you suppose that they were worse offenders than any other inhabitants of Jerusalem? ⁵ No, I tell you; but unless you repent, you will all perish in the same manner."

⁶ And he told them this parable: "A man who had a fig tree growing in his vineyard came to look for fruit on it, but could not find any. ⁷ So he said to his gardener, 'Three years now I have come to look for fruit on this fig tree, without finding any! Cut it down. Why should it rob the soil?' ⁸ 'Leave it this one year more, sir,' the man answered, 'until I have dug around it and manured it. ⁹ Then, if it bears in future, well and good; but if not, you can have it cut down.'"

¹⁰ Jesus was teaching on a sabbath in one of the synagogues, ¹¹ and he saw before him a woman who for eighteen years had suffered from weakness owing to her having a spirit in her. She was bent double, and was wholly unable to raise herself. ¹² When Jesus saw her, he called her to him, and said: "Woman, you are released from your weakness." ¹³ He placed his hands on her, and she was instantly made straight, and began to praise God. ¹⁴ But the president of the synagogue, indignant that Jesus had healed on the sabbath, intervened and said to the people: "There are six days on which work ought to be done; come to be cured on one of those, and not on the sabbath."

¹⁵ "You hypocrites!" the Master answered him. "Does not every one of you let your ox or your donkey loose from its manger, and take it out to drink, on the sabbath? ¹⁶ But this woman, a daughter of Abraham, who has been kept in bondage by Satan for now eighteen years, ought not she to have been released from her bondage on the sabbath?" ¹⁷ As he said this, his opponents all felt ashamed; but all the people rejoiced to see all the wonderful things that he was doing.

¹⁸ So Jesus said: "What is the realm of God like? And to what can I liken it? ¹⁹ It is like a mustard seed which a person took and put in the garden. The seed grew and became a tree, and 'the wild birds roosted in its branches.'" ²⁰ And again Jesus said: "To what can I liken the realm of God? ²¹ It is like some yeast which a woman

took and covered in three pecks of flour, until the whole had risen."

²² Jesus went through towns and villages, teaching as he went, and making his way toward Jerusalem. ²³ "Master," someone asked, "are there but few who will be saved?" And Jesus answered: ²⁴ "Strive to go in by the small door. Many, I tell you, will seek to go in, but they will not be able, ²⁵ when once the master of the house has gotten up and shut the door, while you begin to say, as you stand outside and knock, 'Sir, open the door for us.' His answer will be: 'I do not know where you come from.' ²⁶ Then you will begin to say, 'We have eaten and drunk in your presence, and you have taught in our streets,' and his reply will be: ²⁷ 'I do not know where you come from. Leave my presence, all you who are living in wickedness.' ²⁸ There, there will be weeping and grinding of teeth, when you see Abraham, Isaac, and Jacob, and all the prophets, in the realm of God, while you yourselves are being driven outside. ²⁹ People will come from east and west, and from north and south, and take their places at the banquet in the realm of God. ³⁰ There are those who are last now who will then be first, and those who are first now who will then be last!"

³¹ Just then some Pharisees came up to Jesus and said: "Go away and leave this place, for Herod wants to kill you." ³² But Jesus answered: "Go and say to that fox, 'Look you, I am driving out demons and will be healing today and tomorrow, and on the third day I will have finished.' ³³ But today and tomorrow and the day after I must go on my way, because it cannot be that a prophet should meet his end outside Jerusalem. ³⁴ Jerusalem! Jerusalem! You who slay the prophets and stone the messengers sent to you — Oh, how often have I wished to gather your children around me, as a hen takes her brood under her wings, and you would not come! ³⁵ Verily your house is left to you desolate! And never, I tell you, will you see me, until you say,

'Blessed is the one who comes in the name of the Lord.'"

14 ¹ On one occasion, as Jesus was going on a sabbath into the house of one of the leading Pharisees to dine, they were watching him closely. ² There he saw before him a man who was suffering from dropsy. ³ "Is it allowable," said Jesus, addressing the students of the Law and the Pharisees, "to heal on the sabbath, or is it not?" ⁴ They remained silent. Jesus took hold of him and healed him, and sent him away. ⁵ And he said to them: "Which of you, finding that your child or your ox has fallen into a well, will not immediately pull it out on the sabbath day?" ⁶ And they could not make any answer to that.

⁷ Observing that the guests were choosing the best places for themselves, Jesus told them this parable: ⁸ "When you are invited by anyone to a wedding banquet, do not recline yourself in the best place. Someone of higher rank might have been invited by your host; ⁹ and the host who invited you both will come and say to you, 'Make room for this person,' and then you will begin in confusion to take the lowest place. ¹⁰ No, when you are invited, go and take the lowest place, so that when the host who has invited you comes, he may say to you, 'Friend, come higher up'; and then you will be honored in the eyes of all your fellow guests. ¹¹ For all persons who exalt themselves will be humbled, and those who humble themselves will be exalted."

¹² Then Jesus went on to say to the man who had invited him: "When you give a meal or a dinner, do not ask your friends, or your brothers or sisters, or your relations, or rich neighbors, because they might invite you in return, and so you should be repaid. ¹³ No, when you entertain, invite the poor, the crippled, the lame, the blind; ¹⁴ and then you will be happy indeed, since they cannot reward

you; for you will be rewarded at the resurrection of the good."

¹⁵ One of the guests heard what he said and exclaimed: "Happy will be the person who will eat bread in the realm of God!" ¹⁶ But he said to him: "A man was once giving a great dinner. He invited many people, ¹⁷ and sent his slave, when it was time for the dinner, to say to those who had been invited, 'Come, for everything is now ready.' ¹⁸ They all with one accord began to ask to be excused. The first said to the servant, 'I have bought a field and am obliged to go and look at it. I must ask you to consider me excused.' ¹⁹ The next said, 'I have bought five pairs of bullocks, and I am on my way to try them. I must ask you to consider me excused'; ²⁰ while the next said, 'I am just married, and for that reason I am unable to come.' ²¹ On his return the servant told his master all these answers. Then in anger the owner of the house said to his servant, 'Go out at once into the streets and alleys of the town, and bring in here the poor, and the crippled, and the blind, and the lame.' ²² Presently the slave said, 'Sir, your order has been carried out, and still there is room.' ²³ 'Go out,' the master said, 'into the roads and hedgerows, and make people come in, so that my house may be filled; ²⁴ for I tell you all that not one of those people who were invited will taste my dinner.'"

²⁵ One day, when great crowds of people were walking with Jesus, he turned and said to them: ²⁶ "If anyone comes to me and does not hate his father, and mother, and wife, and children, and brothers, and sisters, yes and even his life, he can be no follower of mine. ²⁷ Whoever does not carry his own cross, and walk in my steps, can be no follower of mine. ²⁸ Why, which of you, when you want to build a tower, does not first sit down and reckon the cost, to see if you have enough to complete it? ²⁹ Otherwise, if you have laid the foundation and are not able to finish it, everyone who sees it will laugh at you, ³⁰ and say, 'Here is a person who began to build and was not able to finish!' ³¹ Or what king, when he is setting out to fight another king, does not first sit down and consider if with ten thousand men he is able to meet one who is coming against him with twenty thousand? ³² And if he cannot, then, while the other is still at a distance, he sends envoys and asks for terms of peace. ³³ And so with every one of you who does not bid farewell to all you have — you cannot be a follower of mine. ³⁴ Yes, salt is good; but if the salt itself should lose its strength, what will be used to season it? ³⁵ It is not fit either for the land or for the manure heap. People throw it away. Let those who have ears to hear with hear!"

15 ¹ The tax collectors and the outcasts were all drawing near to Jesus to listen to him; ² but the Pharisees and the scholars found fault.

"This man always welcomes outcasts, and takes meals with them!" they complained.

³ So Jesus told them this parable: ⁴ "Who among you who has a hundred sheep, and has lost one of them, does not leave the ninety-nine out in the open country, and go after the lost sheep until he finds it? ⁵ And, when he has found it, he puts it on his shoulders rejoicing; ⁶ and, on reaching home, he calls his friends and his neighbors together, and says, 'Come and rejoice with me, for I have found my sheep which was lost.' ⁷ So, I tell you, there will be more rejoicing in heaven over one outcast who repents, than over ninety-nine good people, who have no need to repent. ⁸ Or again, what woman who has ten silver coins, if she loses one of them, does not light a lamp, and sweep the house, and search carefully until she finds it? ⁹ And, when she has found it, she calls her friends and neighbors together, and says, 'Come and rejoice with me, for I have found the coin which I lost.' ¹⁰ So, I tell you, there is

rejoicing in the presence of God's angels over one outcast who repents."

¹¹ Then Jesus continued: "A man had two sons; ¹² and the younger of them said to his father, 'Father, give me my share of the inheritance.' So the father divided the property between them. ¹³ A few days later the younger son got together all that he had, and went away into a distant land; and there he squandered his inheritance by leading a life of debauchery. ¹⁴ After he had spent all that he had, there was a severe famine through all that country, and he began to be in actual want. ¹⁵ So he went and engaged himself to one of the people of that country, who sent him into his fields to tend pigs. ¹⁶ He even longed to satisfy his hunger with the bean pods on which the pigs were feeding; and no one gave him anything. ¹⁷ But when he came to himself, he said, 'How many of my father's hired servants have more bread than they can eat, while here am I starving to death! ¹⁸ I will get up and go to my father, and say to him, "Father, I sinned against heaven and against you; ¹⁹ I am no longer fit to be called your son; make me one of your hired servants."' ²⁰ And he got up and went to his father. But while he was still a long way off, his father saw him and was deeply moved; he ran and threw his arms around his neck and kissed him. ²¹ 'Father,' the son said, 'I sinned against heaven and against you; I am no longer fit to be called your son; make me one of your hired servants.' ²² But the father turned to his servants and said, 'Be quick and fetch a robe — the very best — and put it on him; give him a ring for his finger and sandals for his feet; ²³ and bring the fattened calf and kill it, and let us eat and make merry; ²⁴ for here is my son who was dead, and is alive again, was lost, and is found.' So they began making merry. ²⁵ Meanwhile the elder son was out in the fields; but on coming home, when he got near the house, he heard music and dancing, ²⁶ and he called one of the servants and asked what it all meant. ²⁷ 'Your brother has come back,' the servant told him, 'and your father has killed the fattened calf, because he has him back safe and sound.' ²⁸ This made him angry, and he would not go in. But his father came out and begged him to do so. ²⁹ 'No,' he said to his father, 'look at all the years I have been serving you, without ever once disobeying you, and yet you have never given me even a young goat, so that I might have a party with my friends. ³⁰ But no sooner has this son of yours come, who has eaten up your property in the company of prostitutes, than you have killed the fattened calf for him.' ³¹ 'Child,' the father answered, 'you are always with me, and everything that I have is yours. ³² We could but make merry and rejoice, for here is your brother who was dead, and is alive; who was lost, and is found.'"

16 ¹ He said to his disciples: "There was a rich man who had a steward; and this steward was maliciously accused of wasting his estate. ² So the master called him and said, 'What is this that I hear about you? Give in your accounts, for you cannot act as steward any longer.' ³ 'What am I to do,' the steward asked himself, 'now that my master is taking the steward's place away from me? I have not strength to dig, and I am ashamed to beg. ⁴ I know what I will do, so that as soon as I am turned out of my stewardship, people may welcome me into their homes.' ⁵ One by one he called up his master's debtors. 'How much do you owe my master?' he asked of the first. ⁶ 'Four hundred and forty gallons of oil,' answered the man. 'Here is your agreement,' he said; 'sit down at once and make it two hundred and twenty.' ⁷ And you, the steward said to the next, 'how much do you owe?' 'Seventy quarters of wheat,' he replied. 'Here is your agreement,' the steward said; 'make it fifty-six.' ⁸ His master complimented this dishonest steward on the shrewdness of his action. And indeed children of the world are shrewder in dealing with their compatriots than the children of light. [9] And I say to you, 'Win friends for yourselves with your tainted money,' so that when it comes to an end, there may be a welcome for you in dwellings of the ages. [10] The person who is trustworthy in the smallest matter is trustworthy in a great one also; and the person who is dishonest in the smallest matter is dishonest in a great one also. [11] So, if you have proved untrustworthy with the tainted money, who will trust you with the true? [12] And, if you have proved untrustworthy with what does not belong to you, who will give you what is really your own? [13] Servants cannot serve two masters, for either they will hate one and love the other, or else they will attach themselves to one and despise the other. You cannot serve both God and money."

[14] All this was said within hearing of the Pharisees, who were lovers of money, and they began to sneer at Jesus.

[15] "You," said Jesus, "are the ones who justify yourselves before the world, but God can read your hearts; and what is highly esteemed among people may be an abomination in the sight of God. [16] The Law and the prophets sufficed until the time of John. Since then the good news of the realm of God has been told, and everybody has been forcing his way into it. [17] It would be easier for the heavens and the earth to disappear than for one stroke of a letter in the Law to be lost. [18] Everyone who divorces his wife and marries another woman is an adulterer, and the man who marries a divorced woman is an adulterer. [19] There was once a rich man who dressed in purple robes and fine linen, and feasted every day in great splendor. [20] Near his gateway there had been laid a beggar named Lazarus, who was covered with sores, [21] and who longed to satisfy his hunger with what fell from the rich man's table. Even the dogs came and licked his sores. [22] After a time the beggar died, and was taken by the angels to be with Abraham. The rich man also died and was bur-

ied. [23] In the place of death he looked up in his torment, and saw Abraham at a distance and Lazarus reclining with him. [24] So he called out, 'Pity me, Father Abraham, and send Lazarus to dip the tip of his finger in water and cool my tongue, for I am suffering agony in this flame.' [25] 'Child,' answered Abraham, 'remember that you in your lifetime received what you thought desirable, just as Lazarus received what was not desirable; but now he has his consolation here, while you are suffering agony. [26] And not only that, but between you and us there lies a great chasm, so that those who wish to pass from here to you cannot, nor can they cross from there to us.' [27] 'Then, Father,' he said, 'I beg you to send Lazarus to my father's house — [28] for I have five brothers — to warn them, so that they may not come to this place of torture also.' [29] 'They have the writings of Moses and the prophets,' replied Abraham; 'let them listen to them.' [30] 'But, Father Abraham,' he urged, 'if someone from the dead were to go to them, they would repent.' [31] 'If they do not listen to Moses and the prophets,' answered Abraham, 'they will not be persuaded, even if someone were to rise from the dead.'"

17 [1] Jesus said to his disciples: "It is inevitable that there should be hindrances, but sorrow awaits the person who causes the hindrance! [2] It would be good for him if he had been flung into the sea with a millstone around his neck, rather than that he should prove a trap for even one of these little ones. [3] Be on your guard! If your brother or sister does wrong, rebuke him or her; but if he or she repents, forgive him or her. [4] Even if he or she wrongs you seven times a day, but turns to you every time and says, 'I am sorry,' you must forgive him or her."

[5] "Give us more faith," said the ambassadors to the Master; [6] but the Master said: "If your faith were only like a mustard seed, you could say to this mulberry tree,

'Be uprooted and planted in the sea,' and it would obey you. ⁷ Which of you, if he had a slave plowing, or tending the sheep, would say to him, when he came in from the fields, 'Come at once and take your place at the table,' ⁸ instead of saying, 'Prepare my dinner, and then make yourself ready and serve me while I am eating and drinking, and after that you will eat and drink yourself'? ⁹ Does he feel grateful to his slave for doing what he is told? ¹⁰ And so with you — when you have done all that you have been told, still say, 'We are but useless slaves; we have done no more than we ought to have done.'"

¹¹ On the way to Jerusalem Jesus passed between Samaria and Galilee. ¹² As he was entering a village, ten people with virulent skin disease met him. ¹³ Standing still, some distance off, they called out loudly: "Jesus! Master! Pity us!" ¹⁴ When Jesus saw them, he said: "Go and show yourselves to the priest." And, as they were on their way, they were made clean. ¹⁵ One of them, finding he was healed, came back, praising God loudly, ¹⁶ and threw himself on his face at Jesus's feet, thanking him for what he had done; and this man was a Samaritan. ¹⁷ "Were not all the ten made clean?" exclaimed Jesus. "But the nine — where are they? ¹⁸ Were there none to come back and praise God except this foreigner? ¹⁹ Get up," he said to him, "and go on your way. Your confidence has delivered you."

²⁰ Being once asked by the Pharisees when the realm of God was to come, he answered: "The realm of God does not come in a way that can be grasped, ²¹ nor will people say, 'Look, here it is!' or 'There it is!'; for the realm of God is among you! ²² The day will come," he said to his followers, "when you will long to see but one of the days of the Child of Humanity, and will not see it. ²³ People will say to you, 'There he is!' or 'Here he is!' Do not go and follow them. ²⁴ For, just as lightning will lighten and flare from one side of the heavens to the other, so will it be

with the Child of Humanity. ²⁵ But first he must undergo much suffering, and he must be rejected by the present generation. ²⁶ As it was in the days of Noah, so will it be again in the days of the Child of Humanity. ²⁷ They were eating and drinking and marrying and being married, up to the very day on which Noah entered the ark, and then the flood came and destroyed them all. ²⁸ So, too, in the days of Lot. People were eating, drinking, buying, selling, planting, building; ²⁹ but on the very day on which Lot came out of Sodom, it rained fire and sulfur from the skies and destroyed them all. ³⁰ It will be the same on the day on which the Child of Humanity reveals himself. ³¹ On that day, if a person is on her housetop and her goods in the house, she must not go down to get them; nor again must one who is on the farm turn back. ³² Remember Lot's wife. ³³ Whoever is eager to get the most out of her life will lose it; but whoever will lose it will preserve it. ³⁴ On that night, I tell you, of two people on the same bed, one will be taken and the other left; ³⁵ of two women grinding grain together, one will be taken and the other left."

³⁷ "Where will it be, Master?" asked his followers. "Where there is a body," said Jesus, "there will the vultures flock."

18 ¹ He told his disciples a parable to show them that they should always pray and never despair. ² "There was," he said, "in a certain town a judge who had no fear of God nor regard for people. ³ In the same town there was a widow who went to him again and again, and said, 'Grant me justice against my opponent.' ⁴ For a time the judge refused, but afterward he said to himself, 'Although I am without fear of God or regard for people, ⁵ yet, as this widow is so troublesome, I will grant her justice, to stop her from plaguing me with her endless visits.'" ⁶ Then the Master added: "Listen to what this iniquitous judge says! ⁷ And will God not see that his own people, who cry to him night and day, have justice done them — though he holds his hand? [8] God will, I tell you, give them justice soon enough! Yet, when the Child of Humanity comes, will he find faith on earth?"

[9] Another time, speaking to people who were satisfied that they were righteous, and who regarded everyone else with scorn, he told this parable: [10] "Two people went up into the Temple to pray. One was a Pharisee and the other a tax collector. [11] The Pharisee stood forward and began praying to himself in this way: 'God, I thank you that I am not like other people — thieves, rogues, adulterers — or even like this tax collector. [12] I fast twice a week, and give a tenth of everything I get to God.' [13] Meanwhile the tax collector stood at a distance, not venturing even to raise his eyes to heaven; but he kept striking his breast and saying, 'God, be compassionate with me, a sinner.' [14] This man, I tell you, went home reconciled, rather than the other; for everyone who exalts himself will be humbled, while everyone who humbles himself will be exalted."

[15] Some of the people were bringing even their babies to Jesus, for him to touch them; but when his followers saw it, they began to find fault with those who had brought them. [16] Jesus, however, called the little children to him. "Let the little children come to me," he said, "and do not hinder them; for it is to such as these that the realm of God belongs. [17] I tell you, unless a person receives the realm of God like a child, that person will not enter it at all."

[18] And one of the rulers asked Jesus this question: "Good Teacher, what must I do if I am to gain life through the ages?"

[19] "Why do you call me good?" answered Jesus. "No one is good but God. [20] You know the commandments: 'Do not commit adultery. Do not kill. Do not steal. Do not say what is false about others. Honor your father and your mother.'"

[21] "I have observed all these," he replied, "from childhood." [22] Hearing this, Jesus said to him: "There is one thing still lacking in you; sell everything that you have, and distribute to the poor, and you will have wealth in heaven; then come and follow me." [23] But the man became greatly distressed on hearing this, for he was extremely rich. [24] Seeing this, Jesus said to his disciples: "How hard it is for the wealthy to enter the realm of God! [25] It is easier, indeed, for a camel to get through a needle's eye than for a rich person to enter the realm of God!"

[26] "Then who can be saved?" asked those who heard this. [27] But he said: "What is impossible with people is possible with God."

[28] "But we," said Peter, "we left what belonged to us and followed you."

[29] "I tell you," he answered, "that there is no one who has left house, or wife, or brothers, or parents, or children, for the sake of the realm of God [30] who will not receive many times as much in the present, and in the age that is coming, life through the ages."

[31] Gathering the Twelve around him, Jesus said to them: "Listen! We are going up to Jerusalem; and there everything that is written in the prophets will be done to the Child of Humanity. [32] For he will be given up to the gentiles, mocked, insulted, and spat on; [33] they will scourge him, and then put him to death; and on the third day he will rise again." [34] They did not comprehend any of this; his meaning was unintelligible to them, and they did not understand what he was saying.

[35] As he was getting near Jericho, a blind man was sitting by the roadside, begging. [36] Hearing a crowd going by, the man asked what was the matter; [37] and, when people told him that Jesus of Nazareth was passing, [38] he shouted out: "Jesus, son of David, take pity on me!" [39] Those who were in front kept telling him to be quiet, but he continued to call out the louder: "Son of David, take pity on me!"

⁴⁰ Then Jesus stopped and ordered the man to be brought to him. And, when he had come close up to him, Jesus asked him: ⁴¹ "What do you want me to do for you?"

"Master," he said, "I want to recover my sight." ⁴² And Jesus said: "Recover your sight, your confidence has delivered you." ⁴³ Instantly he recovered his sight, and began to follow Jesus, praising God. And all the people, on seeing it, gave glory to God.

19 ¹ He entered Jericho and made his way through the town. ² There was a man there, known by the name of Zacchaeus, who was a chief tax collector and a rich man. ³ He tried to see what Jesus was like; but, being short, he was unable to do so because of the crowd. ⁴ So he ran on ahead and climbed into a sycamore tree, to see Jesus, for he knew that he must pass that way. ⁵ When Jesus came to the place, he looked up and said to him: "Zacchaeus, be quick and come down, for I am to stay at your house today." ⁶ So Zacchaeus got down quickly, and joyfully welcomed him. ⁷ On seeing this, everyone began to complain: "He has gone to stay with an outcast." ⁸ But Zacchaeus stood forward and said to the Master: "Listen, Master! I will give half my property to the poor, and, if I have defrauded anyone of anything, I will give him back four times as much."

⁹ "Salvation has come to this house today," answered Jesus, "for even this person is a son of Abraham. ¹⁰ The Child of Humanity has come to search for those who are lost and to save them."

¹¹ As the people were listening to this, he went on to tell them a parable. He did so because he was near Jerusalem, and because they thought that the realm of God was going to be proclaimed at once. ¹² He said: "A nobleman once went to a distant country to receive his appointment as king and then return. ¹³ He called ten of his slaves and gave them ten pounds of silver each, and told them to trade with them during his absence. ¹⁴ But his subjects hated him and sent envoys after him to say, 'We will not have this man as our king.' ¹⁵ On his return, after having been appointed king, he directed that the slaves to whom he had given his money should be summoned, so that he might learn what amount of trade they had done. ¹⁶ The first came up, and said, 'Sir, your ten pounds have made a hundred.' ¹⁷ 'Well done, good slave!' exclaimed the master. 'As you have proved trustworthy in a very small matter, I appoint you governor over ten towns.' ¹⁸ When the second came, he said, 'Your ten pounds, sir, have produced fifty.' ¹⁹ So the master said to him, 'And you I appoint over five towns.' ²⁰ Another slave also came and said, 'Sir, here are your ten pounds; I have kept them put away in a handkerchief. ²¹ For I was afraid of you, because you are a stern man. You take what you have not planted, and reap what you have not sown.' ²² The master answered, 'Out of your own mouth I judge you, you worthless slave. You knew that I am a stern man, that I take what I have not planted, and reap what I have not sown. ²³ Then why did you not put my money into a bank? And I, on my return, could have claimed it with interest. ²⁴ Take away from him the ten pounds,' he said to those standing by, 'and give them to the one who has the hundred.' ²⁵ 'But, sir,' they said, 'he has a hundred pounds already!' ²⁶ 'I tell you,' he answered, 'that to him who has, more will be given, but from him who has nothing, even what he has will be taken away. ²⁷ But as for my enemies, these men who would not have me as their king, bring them here and put them to death in my presence.'"

²⁸ After saying this, Jesus went on in front, going up to Jerusalem.

The Last Days

²⁹ It was when he had almost reached Bethphage and Bethany, near the Mount of Olives, that he sent on two of his follow-

ers. ³⁰ "Go to the village facing us," he said, "and, when you get there, you will find a colt tethered, which no one has yet ridden; untie it and lead it here. ³¹ And, if anybody asks you, 'Why are you untying it?' you are to say this: 'The Master wants it.'" ³² So the two who were sent went and found it as Jesus had told them. ³³ While they were untying the colt, the owners asked them, "Why are you untying the colt?" ³⁴ And the two disciples answered, "The Master wants it." ³⁵ Then they led it back to Jesus, and threw their cloaks on the foal and put Jesus on it. ³⁶ As he went along, the people kept spreading their cloaks in the road. ³⁷ When he had almost reached the place where the road led down the Mount of Olives, every one of the many followers began in their joy to praise God loudly for all the powerful deeds that they had seen:

³⁸ "Blessed is the one who comes —
     our king — in the name of the Lord!
   Peace in heaven,
   and glory on high."

³⁹ Some of the Pharisees in the crowd said to him: "Teacher, restrain your disciples." ⁴⁰ But Jesus answered: "I tell you that if they are silent, the stones will call out."

⁴¹ When he drew near, on seeing the city, he wept over it, and said: ⁴² "If only you had known, while yet there was time — even you — the things that make for peace! But now they have been hidden from your sight. ⁴³ For a time is coming when your enemies will surround you with earthworks, and encircle you, and hem you in on all sides; ⁴⁴ they will trample you down and your children within you, and they will not leave in you one stone on another, because you did not know the time of your visitation."

⁴⁵ Jesus went into the Temple Courts and began to drive out those who were selling, ⁴⁶ saying as he did so: "It is written: 'My house will be a house of prayer; but you have made it a den of robbers.'"

⁴⁷ Jesus continued to teach each day in the Temple; but the chief priests and teachers of the Law were eager to take his life, and so also were the leaders of the people. ⁴⁸ Yet they could not see what to do, for the people all hung on his words.

20 ¹ On one of these days, when Jesus was teaching the people in the Temple Courts and telling the good news, the chief priests and scholars, joined by the elders, confronted him, ² and addressing him, said: "Tell us what authority you have to do these things. Who is it who has given you this authority?"

³ "I, too," he said in reply, "will ask you one question. Give me an answer to it. ⁴ It is about John's baptism — was it of divine or of human origin?" ⁵ But they began arguing together: "If we say 'divine,' he will say, 'Why did you not believe him?' ⁶ But if we say 'human,' the people will all stone us, for they are persuaded that John was a prophet." ⁷ So they answered that they did not know its origin. ⁸ "Then I," said Jesus, "refuse to tell you what authority I have to do these things."

⁹ But Jesus began to tell the people this parable: "A man once planted a vineyard, and then let it out to tenants, and went abroad for a long while. ¹⁰ At the proper time he sent a slave to the tenants, so that they could give him a share of the produce of the vineyard. The tenants, however, beat him and sent him away empty-handed. ¹¹ The owner afterward sent another slave; but the tenants beat and insulted this man, too, and sent him away empty-handed. ¹² He sent a third; but they wounded this man also, and threw him outside. ¹³ 'What should I do?' said the owner of the vineyard. 'I will send my son, who is very dear to me. Perhaps they will respect him.' ¹⁴ But on seeing him, the tenants consulted with one another. 'Here is the heir!' they said. 'Let us kill him, and then the inheritance will become ours.' ¹⁵ So they threw him outside the vineyard and killed him.

"Now what will the owner of the vineyard do to them? ¹⁶ He will come and put those tenants to death, and will let the vineyard to others."

"Heaven forbid!" they exclaimed when they heard it. ¹⁷ But Jesus looked at them and said: "What then is the meaning of this passage:

'The stone which the builders despised has now itself become the cornerstone.'

¹⁸ "Everyone who falls on that stone will be dashed to pieces, while anyone on whom it falls — it will scatter him as dust."

¹⁹ After this the scholars and the chief priest were eager to lay hands on him then and there, but they were afraid of the people; for they saw that it was at them that he had aimed this parable. ²⁰ Having watched for their opportunity, they afterward sent some spies, who pretended to be good men, to catch him in the course of conversation, and so enable them to give him up to the governor's jurisdiction and authority. ²¹ They asked him a question. They said: "Teacher, we know that you are right in what you say and teach, and that you do not take any account of a person's position, but teach the way of God honestly; ²² are we right in paying tribute to the emperor or not?" ²³ Seeing through their deceitfulness, Jesus said to them: ²⁴ "Show me a coin. Whose head and title are on it?"

²⁵ "The emperor's," they said; and Jesus replied: "Well, then, pay to the emperor what belongs to the emperor, and to God what belongs to God." ²⁶ They could not lay hold of this answer before the people; and, in their wonder at his reply, they held their tongues.

²⁷ Presently there came up some Sadducees, who maintain that there is no resurrection. Their question was this: ²⁸ "Teacher, Moses laid down for us in his writings that

'Should a man's married brother die, and should he be childless, the man should take the widow as his wife, and raise up a family for his brother.'

²⁹ "Well, there were once seven brothers, of whom the eldest, after taking a wife, died childless. ³⁰ The second and third brothers both took her as their wife; ³¹ and so, too, did all seven — dying without children. ³² The woman herself was the last to die. ³³ About the woman, then — at the resurrection, whose wife is she to be, all seven brothers having had her as their wife?"

³⁴ "The men and women of this world," said Jesus, "marry and are given in marriage; ³⁵ but for those who are thought worthy to attain to that other world and the resurrection from the dead, there is no marrying or being married, ³⁶ nor indeed can they die again, for they are like angels and, having shared in the resurrection, they are God's children. ³⁷ As to the fact that the dead rise, even Moses indicated that, in the passage about the bush, when he calls the Lord:

'The God of Abraham, and the God of Isaac, and the God of Jacob.'

³⁸ "Now he is not God of dead people, but of living. For in his sight all are alive."

³⁹ "Well said, Teacher!" exclaimed some of the teachers of the Law, ⁴⁰ for they did not venture to question him any further. ⁴¹ But Jesus said to them: "How is it that people say that the Christ is David's son? ⁴² For David, in the book of Psalms, says himself:

'The Lord said to my lord: "Sit at my right hand,
⁴³ until I put your enemies as a stool for your feet."'

⁴⁴ "David, then, calls him 'lord,' so how is he David's son?"

⁴⁵ While all the people were listening, Jesus said to the disciples: ⁴⁶ "Be on your guard against the teachers of the Law, who delight to walk about in long robes, and like to be greeted in the streets with respect, and to have the best seats in the synagogues, and places of honor at dinner.

[47] These are the men who rob widows of their houses, and make a pretense of saying long prayers. Their sentence will be all the heavier."

21 [1] Looking up, Jesus saw the rich people putting their gifts into the chests for the Temple offerings. [2] He saw, too, a widow in poor circumstances putting two small coins into them. [3] "I tell you," he said, "that this poor widow has put in more than all the others; [4] for everyone else here put in something from what he had to spare, while she, in her need, has put in all she had to live on."

[5] When some of them spoke about the Temple being decorated with beautiful stones and votive offerings, Jesus said: [6] "As for these things that you are looking at, a time is coming when not one stone will be left on another here, which will not be thrown down." [7] So his followers questioned Jesus: "But, Teacher, when will this be? And what sign will there be when this is near?"

[8] And Jesus said: "See that you are not led astray; for many will take my name, and come saying, 'I am the one,' and 'The time is close at hand.' Do not follow them. [9] And, when you hear of wars and disturbances, do not be terrified, for these things must occur first; but the end will not come at once." [10] Then he said to them: "Nation will rise against nation and kingdom against kingdom. [11] And there will be great earthquakes, and plagues and famines in various places, and there will be terrible appearances and signs in the heavens. [12] Before all this, they will lay hands on you and persecute you, and they will betray you to synagogues and put you in prison, when you will be brought before kings and governors for the sake of my name. [13] Then will be your opportunity of witnessing for me. [14] Make up your minds, therefore, not to prepare your defense; [15] for I will myself give you words,

and a wisdom which all your opponents together will be unable to resist or defy. [16] You will be betrayed even by your parents and brothers and sisters and relations and friends, and they will cause some of you to be put to death, [17] and you will be hated by everyone because of my name. [18] Yet not a single hair of your heads will be lost! [19] By your endurance you will win yourselves life. [20] As soon, however, as you see Jerusalem surrounded by armed camps, then you may know that the hour of her desecration is at hand. [21] Then those of you who are in Judea must take refuge in the mountains, those who are in the city must leave at once, and those who are in the country places must not go into it. [22] For these are to be the days of vengeance, when all that is written will be fulfilled. [23] Alas for pregnant women, and for those who are nursing infants in those days! For there will be great suffering in the land, and anger against this people. [24] They will fall by the edge of the sword, and will be taken prisoners to every land, and Jerusalem will be under the heel of the gentiles, until their day is over. [25] There will be signs, too, in the sun and moon and stars, and on the earth despair among the nations, in their dismay at the roar of the sea and the surge. [26] People's hearts will fail them through dread of what is coming upon the world; for the forces of the heavens will be convulsed. [27] Then will be seen the Child of Humanity coming in a cloud with power and great glory. [28] And, when these things begin to occur, look upward and lift your heads, for your deliverance will be at hand."

[29] Then he taught them a lesson, saying: "Look at the fig tree and all the other trees. [30] As soon as they shoot, you know, as you look at them, without being told, that summer is near. [31] And so may you, as soon as you see these things happening, know that the realm of God is near. [32] I tell you that even the present generation will not pass

away until all has taken place. [33] The sky and the earth will pass away, but my words will never pass away. [34] Be on your guard or your minds will become dulled by debauchery or drunkenness or the anxieties of life, and that day will close on you suddenly like a trap. [35] For come it will on all who are living upon the face of the whole earth. [36] Be on the watch at all times, and pray that you may have strength to escape all that is destined to happen, and to stand in the presence of the Child of Humanity."

[37] During the days, Jesus continued to teach in the Temple Courts, but he went out and spent the nights on the hill called the Mount of Olives. [38] And all the people would get up early in the morning and come to listen to him in the Temple.

22 [1] The feast of the unleavened bread, known as the Passover, was near. [2] The chief priest and the scholars were looking for an opportunity to destroy him, for they were afraid of the people.

[3] Now Satan took possession of Judas, who was known as Iscariot, and who belonged to the Twelve; [4] and he went and discussed with the chief priests and officers in charge at the Temple the best way of betraying Jesus to them. [5] They were glad of this, and agreed to pay him. [6] So Judas assented, and looked for an opportunity to betray Jesus to them, in the absence of a crowd.

[7] When the day of the festival of the unleavened bread came, on which the Passover sacrifice occurred, [8] he sent forward Peter and John, saying to them: "Go and make preparations for our eating the Passover."

[9] "Where do you wish us to make preparations?" they asked. [10] "Listen," he answered, "when you have gotten into the city, a man carrying a pitcher of water will meet you; follow him into whatever house he enters; [11] and you will say to the owner of the house, 'The Teacher says to you,

"Where is the room where I am to eat the Passover with my disciples?"' [12] The man will show you a large upstairs room, with couches; there make preparations."

[13] So they went on, and found everything just as Jesus had told them, and they prepared the Passover.

[14] When the time came, Jesus reclined at dinner, and the ambassadors with him. [15] "I have most earnestly wished," he said, "to eat this Passover with you before I suffer. [16] For I tell you that I am not eating it, until it has had its fulfillment in the realm of God." [17] Then, on receiving a cup, after saying the thanksgiving, he said: [18] "Take this and share it among you. For I tell you that I will not, after today, drink of the fruit of the vine, until the realm of God comes." [19] Then Jesus took some bread, and, after saying the thanksgiving, broke it and gave to them, with the words: "This is my body. [20] Do this in my memory." He did the same with the cup after the supper, and said, "This cup is the new covenant in my blood poured out for you. [21] Yet see! The hand of the man who is betraying me is beside me on the table! [22] True, the Child of Humanity is passing by the way ordained for him, yet alas for that one by whom he is being betrayed!" [23] Then they began questioning one another which of them it could be who was going to do this.

[24] And a dispute arose among them as to which of them was to be regarded as the greatest. [25] Jesus, however, said: "The kings of the gentiles lord it over them, and those with authority are styled 'benefactors.' [26] But with you it must not be so. No, let the greatest among you become like the youngest, and him who leads like him who serves. [27] Which is the greater — the master at the table or his servant? Is it not the master at the table? Yet I myself am among you as one who serves. [28] You are the ones who have stood by me in my trials; [29] and, just as my Father has assigned me a realm, I assign you places, [30] so that you may eat

and drink at my table in my realm, and be seated on twelve thrones as judges of the twelve tribes of Israel. [31] Simon! Simon! Listen. Satan has his wish to sift you all like wheat, [32] but I prayed for you, Simon, that your faith should not fail. And you, when you have returned to me, are to strengthen the others."

[33] "Master," said Peter, "with you I am ready to go both to prison and to death."

[34] "I tell you, Peter," replied Jesus, "the cock will not crow today until you have disowned all knowledge of me three times." [35] Then he said to them all: "When I sent you out as my messengers, without either purse, or bag, or sandals, were you in need of anything?"

"No; nothing," they answered. [36] "Now, however," he said, "the one who has a purse must take it and her bag as well; and the one who does not have a sword must sell his cloak and buy one. [37] For, I tell you, that which is written must be fulfilled in me, which says, 'He was counted among the godless'; indeed all that refers to me is finding its fulfillment."

[38] "Master," they exclaimed, "look, here are two swords!"

"That is enough!" he said.

[39] He then went out, and made his way as usual to the Mount of Olives, followed by his disciples. [40] And, when he reached the spot, he said to them: "Pray that you may not fall into temptation." [41] Then he withdrew about a stone's throw, and knelt down and began to pray. [42] "Father," he said, "if it pleases you, spare me this cup; only, not my will but your will be done." [43] Presently there appeared to him an angel from heaven, who strengthened him. [44] And, as his anguish became intense, he prayed still more earnestly, while his sweat was like great drops of blood falling on the ground. [45] Then he rose from praying, and came to the disciples and found them sleeping out of grief. [46] "Why are you asleep?" he asked them. "Rise and pray so that you are not put to the test." [47] While

he was still speaking, a crowd appeared, led by the man called Judas, who was one of the Twelve. Judas approached Jesus, to kiss him; [48] at which Jesus said to him: "Judas, is it by a kiss that you betray the Child of Humanity?" [49] But when those who were around him saw what was going to happen, they exclaimed: "Master, should we use our swords?" [50] And one of them struck the high priest's servant and cut off his right ear; [51] at which Jesus said: "Let me at least do this"; and, touching his ear, he healed the wound. [52] Then, turning to the chief priests and captains in charge at the Temple and the elders who had come for him, he said: "Have you come out, as if after a robber, with swords and clubs? [53] When I was with you day after day in the Temple, you did not lay hands on me; but now your time has come, and the power of darkness."

[54] Those who had taken Jesus prisoner took him away into the house of the high priest. Peter followed at a distance. [55] But when they had lit a fire in the center of the courtyard and had all sat down there, Peter seated himself in the middle of them. [56] Presently a maidservant saw him sitting near the blaze of the fire. Fixing her eyes on him, she said: "Why, this man was one of his companions!" [57] But Peter denied it. "I do not know him," he replied. [58] A little while afterward someone else saw him and said: "Why, you are one of them!"

"No," Peter said, "I am not." [59] About an hour later another one declared positively: "This person also was certainly with him. Why, he is a Galilean!" [60] But Peter said: "I do not know what you are speaking about." Instantly, while he was still speaking, a cock crowed. [61] And the Master turned and looked at Peter; and Peter remembered the words that the Master had said to him: "Before a cock has crowed today, you will disown me three times"; [62] and he went outside and wept bitterly.

[63] The men who held Jesus kept making sport of him and beating him. [64] They

blindfolded him and then questioned him. "Now play the prophet," they said; "who was it that struck you?" [65] And they heaped many other insults on him.

[66] At daybreak the National Council met — both the chief priests and the teachers of the Law — and took Jesus before their High Council. [67] "If you are the Christ," they said, "tell us so."

"If I tell you," replied Jesus, "you will not believe me; [68] and if I question you, you will not answer. [69] But from this hour 'the Child of Humanity will be seated on the right hand of God's power.'"

[70] "Are you, then, the Child of God?" they all asked. "It is you who say that I am," he answered. [71] At this they exclaimed: "Why do we want any more evidence? We have heard it ourselves from his own lips!"

23 [1] Then they all rose in a body and led him before Pilate. [2] And they began to accuse him: "This is someone whom we found misleading our people, opposing paying taxes to the emperor, and giving out that he himself is the Anointed One, a king."

[3] "Are you the king of the Judeans?" Pilate asked him. "It is you who say it," he replied. [4] But Pilate, turning to the chief priests and the people, said: "I do not see anything to find fault with in this man." [5] But they insisted: "He is stirring up the people by his teaching all through Judea; he began with Galilee and has now come here." [6] Hearing this, Pilate asked if the man was a Galilean; [7] and, having satisfied himself that Jesus came under Herod's jurisdiction, he sent him to Herod, who also was in Jerusalem at the time. [8] When Herod saw Jesus, he was exceedingly pleased, for he had been wanting to see him for a long time, having heard a great deal about him; and he was hoping to see some sign given by him. [9] So he questioned him at some length, but Jesus made no reply. [10] Meanwhile the chief priests and the scholars stood by and vehemently accused him. [11] And Herod, with his soldiers, treated Jesus with scorn; he mocked him by throwing a gorgeous robe around him, and then sent him back to Pilate. [12] And Herod and Pilate became friends that very day, for before that there had been ill will between them.

[13] So Pilate summoned the chief priests, and the leaders, and the people, [14] and said to them: "You brought this man before me charged with misleading the people; and yet, for my part, though I examined him before you, I did not find this man to blame for any of the things of which you accuse him; [15] nor did Herod either; for he has sent him back to us. And, as a fact, he has not done anything deserving death; [16] so I will have him whipped, and then release him." [18] But they began to shout as one man: "Get rid of him, but release Barabbas for us." [19] (Barabbas was a man who had been put in prison for a riot that had broken out in the city and for murder.) [20] Pilate, however, wanting to release Jesus, called to them again; [21] but they kept calling out: "Crucify, crucify him!"

[22] "Why, what harm has this man done?" Pilate said to them for the third time. "I have found nothing in him for which he could be condemned to death. So I will have him scourged, and then release him." [23] But they persisted in loudly demanding his crucifixion; and their shouts kept getting louder. [24] Pilate decided that their demand should be granted. [25] He released the one who had been put in prison for riot and murder, as they demanded, and gave Jesus up to be dealt with as they pleased.

[26] And, as they were leading Jesus away, they laid hold of Simon from Cyrene, who was on his way in from the country, and they put the cross on his shoulders, for him to carry it behind Jesus. [27] There was a great crowd of people following him, many being women who were beating their breasts and wailing for him. [28] So Je-

sus turned and said to them: "Women of Jerusalem, do not weep for me, but weep for yourselves and for your children. 29 A time, I tell you, is coming when it will be said, 'Happy are the women who are barren, and the wombs which have never borne children, and the breasts that have never nursed!' 30 At that time people will begin to say to the mountains, 'Fall on us,' and to the hills, 'Cover us.' 31 If what you see is done while the tree is green, what will happen when it is dry?" 32 There were two others also, criminals, led out to be executed with Jesus. 33 When they had reached the place called "The Skull," there they crucified Jesus and the criminals, one on the right, and one on the left. 34 Then Jesus said: "Father, forgive them; they do not know what they are doing." His clothes they divided among them by casting lots. 35 Meanwhile the people stood looking on. Even the leaders said with a sneer: "He saved others, let him save himself, if he is God's Christ, his chosen one." 36 The soldiers, too, came up in mockery, bringing him common wine, 37 and saying as they did so: "If you are the king of the Judeans, save yourself." 38 Above him were the words

"This is the king of the Judeans."

39 One of the criminals who were hanging beside Jesus railed at him. "Are you not the Anointed One? Save yourself and us," he said. 40 But the other rebuked him. "Have you not," he said, "any fear of God, now that you are under the same sentence? 41 And we justly so, for we are only reaping our deserts, but this man has not done anything wrong. 42 Jesus," he went on, "do not forget me when you have come to your realm." 43 And Jesus answered: "I tell you, this very day you will be with me in paradise."

44 It was nearly midday when a darkness came over the whole country, lasting until three in the afternoon, 45 the sun's light having failed; and the Temple curtain was torn down the middle. 46 Then Jesus, with a loud cry, said: "Father, into your hands I commit my spirit." And with these words he breathed his last. 47 The Roman captain, on seeing what had happened, praised God, exclaiming: "This was a good human being!" 48 All the people who had collected to see the spectacle watched what occurred, and then went home beating their breasts. 49 All his friends had been standing at a distance, as did the women who accompanied him from Galilee, watching all this.

50 Now there was a man of the name of Joseph, who was a member of the Council, and who bore a good and upright character. 51 (This man had not assented to the decision and action of the Council.) He belonged to Aramathaea, a town in Judea, and lived in expectation of the realm of God. 52 He now went to see Pilate, and asked for the body of Jesus; 53 and, when he had taken it down, he wrapped it in a linen sheet, and laid him in a tomb cut out of stone, in which no one had yet been buried. 54 It was the preparation day, and just before the sabbath began. 55 The women who had accompanied Jesus from Galilee followed, and saw the tomb and how the body of Jesus was laid, 56 and then went home, and prepared spices and perfumes.

The Risen Life

During the sabbath they rested, as directed by the commandment.

24 1 But very early on the first day of the week they went to the tomb, taking with them the spices that they had prepared. 2 They found that the stone had been rolled away from the tomb; 3 and, on going into it, they could not find the body. 4 While they were at a loss to account for this, all at once two men stood beside them, in dazzling clothing. 5 But when in their fear the women bowed their faces to

the ground, the men said to them: "Why are you looking among the dead for him who is living? ⁶ Remember how he spoke to you before he left Galilee—⁷ how he said that the Child of Humanity must be betrayed into the hands of wicked men, and be crucified, and rise again on the third day." ⁸ Then they remembered his words, ⁹ and, on returning from the tomb, they told all this to the Eleven and to all the rest. ¹⁰ There were Mary of Magdala, and Joanna, and Mary, the mother of James. The other women, too, spoke about this to Jesus's ambassadors. ¹¹ What they said seemed mere nonsense, and they did not believe them.

¹³ It happened that very day that two of them were going to a village called Emmaus, which was about seven miles from Jerusalem, ¹⁴ talking together, as they went, about all that had just taken place. ¹⁵ While they were talking about these things and discussing them, Jesus himself came up and went on their way with them; ¹⁶ but their eyes were blinded so that they could not recognize him. ¹⁷ "What is this that you are saying to each other as you walk along?" Jesus asked. They stopped, with sad looks on their faces, ¹⁸ and then one of them, whose name was Cleopas, said to Jesus: "You must be the only person in Jerusalem not to have heard of the things that have happened there within the last few days."

¹⁹ "What things do you mean?" asked Jesus. "Why, about Jesus of Nazareth," they answered, "who, in the eyes of God and all the people, was a prophet, whose power was felt in both his words and actions; ²⁰ and how the chief priests and our leaders gave him up to be sentenced to death, and afterward crucified him. ²¹ But we were hoping that he was the one to set Israel free; yes, and besides all this, it is now three days since these things occurred. ²² And what is more, some of the women among us have greatly astonished us. They went to the tomb at daybreak ²³ and, not finding the body of Jesus there, came and told us that they had seen a vision of angels who told them that he was alive. ²⁴ So some of our number went to the tomb and found everything just as the women had said; but they did not see him at all."

²⁵ Then he said to them: "You slow and hardhearted people, slow to accept all that the prophets have said! ²⁶ Was not the Christ bound to undergo this suffering before entering into his glory?" ²⁷ Then, beginning with Moses and all the prophets, he explained to them all through the writings the passages that referred to himself. ²⁸ When they got near the village to which they were walking, Jesus appeared to be going further; ²⁹ but they pressed him not to do so. "Stay with us," they said, "for it is getting toward evening, and the sun is already low." So Jesus went in to stay with them. ³⁰ After he had reclined with them at the meal, he took the bread and said the blessing, and broke it, and gave it to them. ³¹ Then their eyes were opened and they recognized him; but he disappeared from their sight. ³² "How our hearts glowed," his followers said to each other, "while he was talking to us on the road, and when he explained the writings to us!"

³³ Then they immediately got up and returned to Jerusalem, where they found the Eleven and their companions all together, ³⁴ who told them that the Master had really risen, and had appeared to Simon. ³⁵ So they also related what had happened during their walk, and how they had recognized Jesus at the breaking of the bread. ³⁶ While they were still talking about these things, he himself stood among them. ³⁷ In their terror and alarm they thought they saw a spirit, ³⁸ but he said to them: "Why are you so startled? And why do doubts arise in your minds? ³⁹ Look at my hands and my feet, and you will know that it is I. Feel me, and look at me, for a spirit has not flesh and bones, as you see that I have." ⁴⁰ Saying this, he

showed them his hands and feet. [41] While they were still unable to believe it all, overcome with joy, and were wondering if it were true, Jesus said to them: "Have you anything here to eat?" [42] They handed him a piece of broiled fish, [43] and he took it and ate it before their eyes. [44] "This is what I told you," he said, "when I was still with you — that everything that had been written about me in the Law of Moses, the prophets, and the psalms was to be fulfilled."

[45] Then he enabled them to understand the meaning of the writings, saying to them: [46] "It is written that the Anointed One should suffer, and that he should rise again from the dead on the third day, [47] and that repentance for forgiveness of sins should be proclaimed on his authority to all the nations — beginning at Jerusalem. [48] You yourselves are to be witnesses to all this. [49] And now I am myself about to send you that which my Father has promised. But you must remain in the city until you have been invested with power from above."

[50] After this, Jesus led them out as far as Bethany, and there raised his hands and blessed them. [51] As he was blessing them, he left them. [52] They returned to Jerusalem full of joy; [53] and they were constantly in the Temple, praising God.

The Acts of the Apostles

The Doings of the Ambassadors Peter and John

1 ¹ The first account which I drew up, Theophilus, dealt with all that Jesus did and taught from the very first, ² down to that day on which he was taken up to heaven, after he had, by the help of the holy Spirit, given instructions to the ambassadors whom he had chosen. ³ With abundant proofs, he showed himself to them, still living, after his death; appearing to them from time to time during forty days, and speaking of all that related to the realm of God. ⁴ And once, when he had gathered them together, he charged them not to leave Jerusalem, but to wait there for the fulfillment of the Father's promise — "that promise," he said, "of which you have heard me speak; ⁵ for, while John baptized with water, you will be baptized with the holy Spirit before many days have passed."

⁶ So, when they had met together, they asked Jesus this question: "Master, is this the time when you intend to reestablish the kingdom for Israel?" ⁷ His answer was: "It is not for you to know times or hours, for the Father has reserved these for his own decision; ⁸ but you will receive power, when the holy Spirit will have descended on you, and will be witnesses for me not only in Jerusalem, but throughout Judea and Samaria, and to the ends of the earth."

⁹ No sooner had Jesus said this than he was caught up before their eyes, and a cloud received him from their sight. ¹⁰ While they were still gazing up into the sky, as he went, suddenly two men, clothed in white, stood beside them, ¹¹ and said: "People of Galilee, why are you standing here looking up into the sky? This same Jesus, who has been taken from you into the heavens, will come in the same way in which you have seen him go into the heavens."

¹² Then they returned to Jerusalem from the hill called Olivet, which is about three-quarters of a mile from the city. ¹³ When they reached Jerusalem, they went to the upstairs room, where they were staying. Staying there were Peter, John, James, and Andrew, Philip and Thomas, Bartholomew and Matthew, James the son of Alphaeus, Simon the Zealot, and Judas the son of James. ¹⁴ They all united in devoting themselves to prayer, and so did some women, and Mary, the mother of Jesus, and his brothers.

¹⁵ About this time, at a meeting of the Lord's followers, when there were about a hundred and twenty present, Peter rose to speak. ¹⁶ "Brothers," he said, "it was necessary the writing should be fulfilled, which the holy Spirit made by the lips of David about Judas, who acted as guide to the men that arrested Jesus, ¹⁷ for he was one of our number and had his part allotted him in this work of ours." ¹⁸ (This man had bought a piece of land with the price of his treachery; and, falling heavily, his body had burst open, and all his bowels protruded. ¹⁹ This became known to everyone living in Jerusalem, so that the field came to be called, in their language, "Akeldama," which means the "Field of Blood.")

²⁰ "For in the book of Psalms it is said:

'Reduce his encampment to ruin,
and let no one live in it';

and also:

'His office let another take.'

²¹ "Therefore, from among the men who have been with us all the time that Jesus, our Master, went in and out among us — ²² from his baptism by John down to that day on which he was taken from us — someone must be found to join us as a witness of his resurrection." ²³ So they put forward two men, Joseph called Barsabas, whose other name was Justus, and Matthias; ²⁴ and they offered this prayer:

"Lord, who reads all hearts, show which of these two men you have chosen ²⁵ to take the place in this work of ambassador, which Judas has abandoned, to go to his proper place."

²⁶ Then they drew lots between them; and, the lot having fallen on Matthias, he was added to the number of the eleven ambassadors.

2 ¹ In the course of the festival of Pentecost they had all met together, ² when suddenly there came from the sky a noise like a strong wind rushing by; it filled the whole house in which they were sitting. ³ Then there appeared tongues of what seemed to be flame, separating, so that one settled on each of them; ⁴ and they were all filled with the holy Spirit, and began to speak with strange tongues as the Spirit prompted their utterances.

⁵ Now there were then staying in Jerusalem religious Judeans from every country in the world; ⁶ and, when this sound was heard, numbers of people collected, in the greatest excitement, because each of them heard the followers speaking in his own language. ⁷ They were utterly amazed, and kept asking in astonishment:

"What! Are not all these people who are speaking Galileans? ⁸ Then how is it that each of us hears them in our own language? ⁹ Some of us are Parthians, some Medes, some Elamites; and some of us live in Mesopotamia, in Judea and Cappadocia, in Pontus and Roman Asia, ¹⁰ in Phrygia and Pamphylia, in Egypt and the

districts of Libya adjoining Cyrene; some of us are visitors from Rome, ¹¹ either Judeans by birth or converts, and some are Cretans and Arabians — yet we all alike hear them speaking in our own tongues of the great things that God has done." ¹² They were all utterly amazed and bewildered.

"What does it mean?" they asked one another. ¹³ But there were some who said with a sneer: "They have had too much new wine."

¹⁴ Then Peter, surrounded by the Eleven, stood up, and, raising his voice, addressed the crowd. "People of Judea," he began, "and all you who are staying in Jerusalem, let me tell you what this means. Mark well my words. ¹⁵ These people are not drunk, as you suppose; for it is only now nine in the morning! No! ¹⁶ This is what is spoken of in the prophet Joel:

¹⁷ 'It will come about in the last days,'
    God says,
  'that I will pour out my Spirit on all
    humanity;
  your sons and your daughters will
    become prophets,
  your young men will see visions,
  and your old men dream dreams;
¹⁸ yes, even on the slaves — for they are
    mine — both men and women,
  I will in those days pour out my Spirit,
  and they will become prophets;
¹⁹ and I will show wonders in the heavens
    above,
  and signs on the earth below —
  blood and fire and mist of smoke;
²⁰ the sun will become darkness,
  and the moon blood red,
  before the day of the Lord comes — that
    great and awful day.
²¹ Then will everyone who invokes the
    name of the Lord be saved.'

²² "People of Israel, listen to what I am saying. Jesus of Nazareth, a man whose

mission from God to you was proved by miracles, wonders, and signs, which God showed among you through him, as you know full well — 23 he, I say, in accordance with God's definite plan and with his previous knowledge, was betrayed, and you, by the hands of lawless men, nailed him to a cross and put him to death. 24 But God released him from the pangs of death and raised him to life, it being impossible for death to retain its hold on him. 25 Indeed he was the one David was referring to when he said:

'I have had the Lord ever before my
　eyes,
for he stands at my right hand, so that I
　should not be disquieted.
26 Therefore my heart was cheered, and
　my tongue told its delight;
yes, even my body, too, will rest in
　hope;
27 for you will not abandon my soul to the
　place of death,
nor surrender me, your holy one, to
　undergo corruption.
28 You have shown me the path to life,
you will fill me with gladness in your
　presence.'

29 "Brothers and sisters, I can speak to you the more confidently about the patriarch David, because he is dead and buried, and his tomb is here among us to this very day. 30 David, then, prophet as he was, knowing that God 'had solemnly sworn to him to set one of his descendants on his throne,' looked into the future, 31 and referred to the resurrection of the Christ when he said that 'he had not been abandoned to the place of death, nor had his body undergone corruption.' 32 It was this Jesus, whom God raised to life; and of that we are ourselves all witnesses. 33 And now that he has been exalted to the right hand of God, and has received from the Father the promised gift of the holy Spirit, he has begun to pour out that gift, as you yourselves now see and hear. 34 It was not David who went up into heaven; for he himself says:

'The Lord said to my master: "Sit on
　my right hand,
35 until I put your enemies as a footstool
　under your feet."'

36 "So let the whole nation of Israel know beyond all doubt that God has made him both Lord and Christ — this Jesus whom you crucified."

37 When the people heard this, they were conscience-smitten, and said to Peter and the rest of the ambassadors: "Friends, what can we do?"

38 "Repent," answered Peter, "and be baptized every one of you in the faith of Jesus Christ for the forgiveness of your sins; and then you will receive the gift of the holy Spirit. 39 For the promise is for you and for your children, and also for all those now far away, who may be called by the Lord our God."

40 Peter spoke to them for a long time using many other arguments and pleaded with them: "Save yourselves from the perverse spirit of this age." 41 So those who accepted his teaching were baptized, and about three thousand people joined the followers on that day alone. 42 They devoted themselves to the teaching of the ambassadors and to the common life of the church, to the breaking of the bread and to the prayers.

43 A deep impression was made on everyone, and many wonders and signs were done at the hands of the ambassadors. 44 All who became believers in Christ held everything for the common use; 45 they sold their property and their goods, and shared the proceeds among them all, according to their individual needs. 46 Every day they devoted themselves to meeting together in the Tem-

ple, and to the breaking of bread at their homes, while they partook of their food in simple-hearted gladness, praising God, and winning the goodwill of all the people. [47] And the Lord daily added to their company those who were in the path of salvation.

3 [1] One day, as Peter and John were going up into the Temple for the three o'clock prayers, a man who had been lame from his birth was being carried by. [2] This man used to be set down every day at the gate of the Temple called "the Beautiful Gate," to beg of those who went in. [3] Seeing Peter and John on the point of entering, he asked them to give him something. [4] Peter fixed his eyes on him, and so did John, and then Peter said: "Look at us."

[5] The man was all attention, expecting to get something from them; [6] but Peter added: "I have no gold or silver, but I give you what I have. In the name of Jesus Christ of Nazareth, get up and walk." [7] Grasping the lame man by the right hand, Peter lifted him up. Instantly the man's feet and ankles became strong, [8] and, leaping up, he stood and began to walk about, and then went with them into the Temple, walking, and leaping, and praising God. [9] All the people saw him walking about and praising God; [10] and, when they recognized him as the man who used to sit begging at the Beautiful Gate of the Temple, they were utterly astonished and amazed at what had happened to him. [11] While the man still clung to Peter and John, the people all quickly gathered around them in the colonnade named after Solomon, in the greatest astonishment.

[12] On seeing this, Peter said to the people: "People of Israel, why are you surprised at this? And why do you stare at us, as though we, by any power or piety of our own, had enabled this man to walk? [13] The God of Abraham, Isaac, and Jacob, the God of our ancestors, has done honor to his servant Jesus — him whom you gave up and disowned before Pilate, when he had decided to set him free. [14] You, I say, disowned the holy and righteous one, and asked for the release of a murderer! [15] The guide to life you put to death! But God raised him from the dead — and of that we are ourselves witnesses. [16] And it is by faith in the name of Jesus that this man, whom you all see and know, has — by his name — been made strong. Yes, it is the confidence inspired by Jesus that has made this healing of the man complete, before the eyes of you all. [17] And yet, my friends, I know that you acted as you did from ignorance, and your rulers also. [18] But it was in this way that God fulfilled all that he had long ago foretold, as to the sufferings of his Christ, by the lips of all the prophets. [19] Therefore, repent and turn so that your sins may be wiped away; so that happier times may come from the Lord himself, [20] and so that he may send you, in Jesus, your long-appointed Christ Jesus. [21] But heaven must be his home, until the days of the universal restoration, of which God has spoken by the lips of his holy prophets from the very first. [22] Moses himself said:

"'The Lord your God will raise up from among yourselves a prophet, as he raised me. To him you will listen whenever he speaks to you. [23] And it will be that should anyone among the people not listen to that prophet, he will be utterly cut off.'

[24] "Yes, and all the prophets from Samuel onward, and all their successors who had a message to deliver, told of these days. [25] You yourselves are the heirs of the prophets, and heirs, too, of the covenant which God made with your ancestors, when he said to Abraham:

"'In your descendants will all the nations of the earth be blessed.'

[26] "For you, first, God raised up his servant, and sent him to bless you, by turning each one of you from your wicked ways."

4 [1] While Peter and John were still speaking to the people, the chief priest, with the officer in charge at the Temple and the Sadducees, came up to them, [2] much annoyed because they were teaching the people, and because, through Jesus, they were preaching the resurrection from the dead. [3] They arrested them, and, as it was already evening, had them placed in custody until the next day. [4] Many, however, of those who had heard their message became believers in Christ, the number of the men alone amounting to about five thousand.

[5] The next day, a meeting of the leaders of the people, the elders, and the teachers of the Law was held in Jerusalem. [6] There were present Annas the high priest, Caiaphas, John, Alexander, and all who were of high-priestly rank. [7] They had Peter and John brought before them, and questioned them.

"By what power," they asked, "or in whose name have you done this thing?" [8] Then Peter, filled with the holy Spirit, said: "Leaders of the people and councilors, [9] since we are on trial today for a kind act done to a helpless man, and are asked in what way the man here before you has been healed, [10] let me tell you all and all the people of Israel, that it is by the name of Jesus Christ of Nazareth, whom you crucified and whom God raised from the dead — it is, I say, by his name that this one stands here before you lame no longer. [11] Jesus is 'the stone which, scorned by you the builders, has yet become the cornerstone.' [12] And salvation is in him alone; for there is no other name in the whole world, given to people, by which we must be saved."

[13] When the Council saw how boldly Peter and John spoke, and found that they were uneducated men of humble station, they were surprised, and realized that they had been companions of Jesus. [14] But when they looked at the person who had been healed, standing there with them, they had nothing to say. [15] So they ordered them out of court, and then began consulting together.

[16] "What are we to do to these people?" they asked one another. "That a remarkable sign has been given through them is obvious to everyone living in Jerusalem, and we cannot deny it. [17] But to prevent this thing from spreading further among the people, let us warn them not to speak in this name anymore to anyone."

[18] So they called them in, and ordered them not to speak or teach in the name of Jesus.

[19] But Peter and John replied: "Whether it is right, in the sight of God, to listen to you rather than to God — [20] judge for yourselves, for we cannot help speaking of what we have seen and heard." [21] However, after further warnings, the Council set them at liberty, not seeing any safe way of punishing them, because of the people, for they were all praising God for what had occurred; [22] for the person who was the subject of this miraculous healing was more than forty years old.

[23] After they had been set at liberty, the ambassadors went to their friends and told them what the chief priests and the councilors had said to them. [24] All who heard their story, moved by a common impulse, raised their voices to God in prayer:

"Sovereign Lord, it is you who has made the heavens, the earth, the sea, and everything that is in them, [25] and who, by the lips of our ancestor, your servant David, who spoke under the influence of the holy Spirit, have said:

'Why did the nations rage,
  and the peoples form vain designs?
[26] The kings of the earth set their
    array,
  and its rulers gathered together,
  against the Lord and against his
    Anointed One.'

27 "There have indeed gathered together in this city against your holy servant Jesus, whom you have consecrated the Christ, not Herod and Pontius Pilate only, but the nations and the people of Israel besides — 28 yet only to do what you, by your power and of your own will, did long ago destine to be done. 29 Now, therefore, Lord, mark their threats, and enable your slaves, with all fearlessness, to tell your message, 30 while you stretch out your hand to heal, and cause signs and wonders to take place through the name of your holy servant Jesus."

31 When their prayer was ended, the place in which they were assembled was shaken; and they were all filled with the holy Spirit, and began to tell God's message fearlessly.

32 The whole body of those who had become believers were of one heart and soul. Not one of them claimed any goods as their own, but everything was held for the common use. 33 The ambassadors continued with great power to bear their testimony to the resurrection of the Lord Jesus, and God's blessing rested on them all abundantly. 34 Nor was there anyone in need among them, for all who were owners of land or houses sold them, and brought the proceeds of the sales 35 and laid them at the ambassadors' feet; and then everyone received a share in proportion to his wants. 36 A Levite of Cyprian birth, named Joseph (who had received from the ambassadors the additional name of "Barnabas" — which means "the Consoler"), 37 sold a farm that belonged to him, and brought the money and laid it at the ambassadors' feet.

5 1 There was, however, a man named Ananias, who, with his wife Sapphira, sold some property, 2 and, with her connivance, kept back some of the proceeds. He brought only a part and laid it at the ambassadors' feet.

3 "Ananias," Peter exclaimed, "how is it that Satan has so taken possession of your heart that you have lied to the holy Spirit, and kept back a part of the money paid for the land? 4 While it was unsold, was it not your own? And after it was sold, was the money not at your own disposal? How did you come to think of such a thing? You have lied, not to people, but to God!"

5 As Ananias heard these words, he fell down dead; and everyone who heard of it was appalled. 6 The young men got up, and, winding the body in a sheet, carried it out and buried it.

7 After an interval of about three hours his wife came in, not knowing what had happened. 8 "Is it true," Peter asked, addressing her, "that you sold your land for such a sum?"

"Yes," she answered, "we did." 9 Then Peter said: "How did you come to agree to provoke the Spirit of the Lord? Listen! The footsteps of those who have buried your husband are at the door; and they will carry you out too."

10 Instantly Sapphira fell down dead at Peter's feet. On coming in, the young men found her dead; so they carried her out and buried her by her husband's side. 11 The whole church and all who heard of these events were appalled.

12 Many signs and wonders continued to occur among the people, through the hands of the ambassadors, whose custom it was to meet all together in the Colonnade of Solomon; 13 but of the rest no one ventured to join them. On the other hand, the people were full of their praise, 14 and still larger numbers, both of men and women, as they became believers in the Lord, were added to their number. 15 The consequence was that people would bring out their sick even into the streets, and lay them on mattresses and mats, in the hope that as Peter came by, at least his shadow might fall on some one of them. 16 Besides this, the inhabitants of the towns around Jerusalem flocked into the city, bringing with them their sick and those who

were troubled by unclean spirits; and they healed everyone.

[17] At this the high priest was roused to action, and he and all his supporters (who formed the party of the Sadducees), moved by jealousy, [18] arrested the ambassadors, and had them placed in jail. [19] An angel of the Lord, however, opened the prison doors at night and led them out. [20] "Go," he said, "and stand in the Temple, and tell the people the whole message of this new life." [21] When they heard this, they went at daybreak into the Temple, and began to teach. The high priest and his party, on their arrival, summoned the High Council, including all the leaders of the people among the Israelites, and sent to the jail to fetch the ambassadors. [22] But when the officers got there, they did not find them in the prison; so they returned and reported that [23] while they had found the prison barred securely and the guards posted at the doors, yet, on opening them, they had not found anyone inside. [24] When the officer in charge at the Temple and the chief priests heard their story, they were perplexed as to what all this would lead to. [25] Presently, however, someone came and told them that the men whom they had put in prison were actually standing in the Temple, teaching the people. [26] Then the officer went with his assistants and fetched them — without using violence, for they were afraid of being stoned by the people — [27] and then brought them before the Council. The high priest demanded an explanation from them.

[28] "We gave you strict orders," he said, "not to teach in this name. Yet you have actually flooded Jerusalem with your teaching, and you want to make us responsible for the death of this one."

[29] To this Peter and the ambassadors replied: "We must obey God rather than people. [30] The God of our ancestors raised Jesus, whom you put to death by hanging him on a cross. [31] It is this Jesus whom God has exalted to his right hand, to be a guide and a Savior, to give Israel repentance and forgiveness of sins. [32] And we are witness to the truth of this, and so is the holy Spirit — the gift of God to those who obey him."

[33] The members of the Council became frantic with rage on hearing this, and were for putting them to death. [34] But Gamaliel, a Pharisee, who was a doctor of the Law and who was held in universal respect, rose in the Council, and directed that they should be taken out of court for a little while.

[35] He then said: "People of Israel, take care as to what you intend to do with these people. [36] For not long ago Theudas appeared, professing to be somebody, and was joined by a body of some four hundred men. But he was killed; and all his followers scattered and dwindled away. [37] After him, Judas the Galilean appeared at the time of the census, and induced people to follow him; yet he, too, perished and all his followers were dispersed. [38] And, in this present case, my advice to you is not to interfere with these men, but to let them alone, for, if their designs and their work are merely of human origin, they will come to an end; [39] but if they are of divine origin, you will be powerless to put an end to them — or else you may find yourselves fighting against God!"

[40] The Council followed his advice, and, calling the ambassadors in, had them flogged, and then, after cautioning them not to speak in the name of Jesus, set them free. [41] But they left the Council, rejoicing that they had been thought worthy to suffer disgrace for that name; [42] and never for a single day, either in the Temple or in private houses, did they cease to teach, or to tell the good news of Jesus, the Christ.

6 [1] About this time, when the number of the followers was constantly increasing, complaints were made by the Greek speakers against the Hebrew speakers, that their widows were being overlooked in the daily distribution. [2] The Twelve, therefore, called together the general body of the followers and said to them: "It is not good for us to see to the distribution at the tables and neglect God's message. [3] Therefore, friends, look for seven men of reputation among yourselves, wise and spiritually minded, and we will appoint them to attend to this matter; [4] while we, for our part, will devote ourselves to prayer, and to the delivery of the message."

[5] This proposal was unanimously agreed to; and the followers chose Stephen — a man full of faith and of the holy Spirit — and Philip, Prochorus, Nicanor, Timon, Parmenas, and Nicholas of Antioch, a former convert to Judaism; [6] and they brought them to the ambassadors, who, after praying, placed their hands on them.

[7] So God's message spread, and the number of the followers continued to increase rapidly in Jerusalem, and a large body of the priests accepted this trust.

[8] Meanwhile Stephen, filled with grace and power, was showing great wonders and signs among the people. [9] But some members of the Synagogue of the Freed Slaves (as it was called), Cyrenians, Alexandrians, and visitors from Cilicia and Roman Asia, were roused to action and began disputing with Stephen; [10] yet they were quite unable to withstand the wisdom and the inspiration with which he spoke. [11] Then they induced some men to assert that they had heard Stephen saying blasphemous things against Moses, and against God; [12] and they stirred up the people, as well as the elders and the scholars, and set on Stephen, and arrested him, and brought him before the High Council. [13] There they produced witnesses who gave false evidence.

"This person," they said, "is incessantly saying things against this holy place and the Law; [14] indeed, we have heard him declare that this Jesus of Nazareth will destroy this place, and change the customs handed down to us by Moses." [15] The eyes of all the members of the Council were riveted on Stephen, and they saw his face looking like the face of an angel.

7 [1] Then the high priest asked: "Is this true?" [2] Stephen replied: "Brothers and fathers, hear what I have to say. God, who manifests himself in the glory, appeared to our ancestor Abraham when he was in Mesopotamia, and before he settled in Haran, and said to him: [3] 'Leave your country and your kindred, and come into the country that I will show you.' [4] And so Abraham left the country of the Chaldaeans and settled in Haran; and from there, after his father's death, God caused him to migrate into this country, in which you are now living. [5] God did not at that time give him any part of it, not even a foot of ground. But he promised to give him possession of it and his descendants after him, though at that time he had no child. [6] God's words were these: 'Abraham's descendants will live in a foreign country, where they will be enslaved and mistreated for four hundred years. [7] But I myself will judge the nation, to which they will be enslaved,' God said, 'and after that they will leave the country and worship me in this place.' [8] Then God made with Abraham the covenant of circumcision; and under it Abraham became the father of Isaac, and circumcised him when he was eight days old; and Isaac became the father of Jacob; and Jacob of the twelve patriarchs. [9] The patriarchs, out of jealousy, sold Joseph into slavery in Egypt; but God was with him, [10] and delivered him out of all his troubles, and enabled him to win favor and show wisdom before Pharaoh, king of Egypt, who appointed him governor of Egypt and of his whole household. [11] Then a famine spread over the whole of Egypt and Canaan, causing great distress, and our ancestors could find no food. [12] Hearing, however, that there was corn in Egypt, Jacob sent our ancestors there on their first visit. [13] In the course of their second visit, Joseph revealed himself to his brothers, and his family became known to Pharaoh. [14] Then Joseph sent an urgent invitation to his father Jacob and to his relations, seventy-five persons in all; [15] and so Jacob went down into Egypt. There he died, and our ancestors also, [16] and their bodies were removed to Shechem, and laid in the tomb which Abraham had bought for a sum of money from the sons of Hamor in Shechem. [17] As the time drew near for the fulfillment of the promise which God had made to Abraham, the people increased largely in numbers in Egypt, [18] until a new king, who knew nothing of Joseph, came to the throne. [19] This king acted deceitfully toward our race and mistreated our ancestors, making them abandon their own infants, so that they should not be reared. [20] It was just at this time that Moses was born. He was an exceedingly beautiful child, and for three months was brought up in his own father's house; [21] and, when he was abandoned, the daughter of Pharaoh found him and brought him up as her own son. [22] So Moses was educated in all the learning of the Egyptians, and proved his ability by both his words and his actions. [23] When he was in his fortieth year, he resolved to visit his fellow Israelites; [24] and, seeing an Israelite ill treated, he defended him, and avenged the man who was being wronged by striking down the Egyptian. [25] He thought his own people would understand that God was using him to save them; but they failed to do so. [26] The next day he again appeared on the scene, when some of them were fighting, and tried to make peace between them. 'Men,' he said, 'you are brothers; how is it that you are mistreating one another?' [27] But the man who was mistreating his fellow workman pushed Moses aside, saying, 'Who made you a ruler and judge over us? [28] Do you mean to make away with me as you did yesterday with that Egyptian?' [29] At these words Moses took to flight, and

became an exile in Midian; and there he had two sons born to him. [30] Forty years had passed when there appeared to him, in the desert of Mount Sinai, an angel in a flame of fire in a bush. [31] When Moses saw it, he was astonished at the vision; but on his going nearer to look at it more closely, the voice of the Lord was heard to say, [32] 'I am the God of your ancestors, the God of Abraham, Isaac, and Jacob.' Moses trembled, and did not dare to look. [33] Then the Lord said to him, 'Take your sandals off your feet, for the spot where you are standing is holy ground. [34] I have seen the oppression of my people who are in Egypt, and heard their groans, and I have come down to deliver them. Come now and I will send you into Egypt.' [35] This same Moses, whom they had disowned with the words 'Who made you a ruler and a judge?' was the man whom God sent to be both a ruler and a deliverer, under the guidance of the angel that had appeared to him in the bush. [36] He it was who led them out, after he had shown wonders and signs in Egypt, in the Red Sea, and in the desert during forty years. [37] This was the Moses who said to the people of Israel, 'God will raise up for you, from among yourselves, a prophet, as he raised up me.' [38] He, too, it was who was present at the assembly in the desert, with the angel who talked to him on Mount Sinai, and with our ancestors, and who received living truths to impart to you. [39] Yet our ancestors refused him obedience; more than that, they rejected him, and in their hearts turned back to Egypt, [40] while they said to Aaron, 'Make us gods who will lead the way for us, since, as for this Moses who has brought us out of Egypt, we do not know what has become of him.' [41] That was the time when they made the calf and offered sacrifice to their idol, and held festivities in honor of their own handiwork! [42] So God turned from them and left them to the worship of the Starry Host, as is written in the book of the prophets:

'Did you offer victims and sacrifices to
   me, house of Israel,
all those forty years in the desert?
[43] You took with you the tent where
   Moloch is worshiped
and the star of the god Rephan —
   the images which you had made to
   worship.
Therefore I will exile you beyond
   Babylon.'

[44] "Our ancestors had the tent where
they worshiped God in the desert, constructed, just as he who spoke to Moses had directed him to make it, after the
model which he had seen. [45] This tent,
which was handed down to them, was
brought into this country by our ancestors who accompanied Joshua (at the conquest of the nations that God drove out
before their advance), and remained here
until the time of David. [46] David found favor with God, and prayed that he might
provide the God of Jacob with a place to
reside. [47] But it was Solomon who built a
house for God. [48] Yet it is not in buildings
made by hands that the Most High dwells.
As the prophet says:

[49] 'The heavens are a throne for me,
   and the earth a stool for my feet.
What manner of house will you build
   me, saith the Lord,
   or what place is there where I may rest?
[50] Was it not my hand that made all these
   things?'

[51] "Stubborn race, heathen in heart and
ears, you are forever resisting the holy
Spirit; your ancestors did it, and you are
doing it still. [52] Which of the prophets escaped persecution at their hands? They
killed those who foretold the coming of
the righteous one; of whom you, in your
turn, have now become the betrayers and
murderers — [53] you who received the Law
as transmitted by angels and yet failed to
keep it."

[54] As they listened to this, the Council
grew frantic with rage, and gnashed their
teeth at Stephen. [55] He, filled as he was
with the holy Spirit, fixed his eyes intently
on the heavens, and saw the glory of God
and Jesus standing at God's right hand.
[56] "Look," he exclaimed, "I see heaven
open and the Child of Humanity standing at God's right hand!" [57] At this, with
a loud shout, they stopped their ears and
all rushed on him, forced him outside the
city, [58] and began to stone him, the witnesses laying their clothes at the feet of
a young man named Saul. [59] And they
stoned Stephen, while he cried to the Lord:
"Lord Jesus! Receive my spirit!" [60] Falling
on his knees, he called out loudly: "Lord!
Do not charge them with this sin"; and
with these words he fell asleep.

8 [1] Saul approved of his being put to
death.

On that very day a great persecution
broke out against the church which was
in Jerusalem; and its members, with the
exception of the ambassadors, were all
scattered over the districts of Judea and
Samaria. [2] Some devoted men buried Stephen, with loud lamentations for him.
[3] But Saul began to devastate the church;
he entered house after house, dragged out
men and women alike, and threw them
into prison.

[4] Now those who were scattered in different directions went from place to place
proclaiming the good news. [5] Philip went
down to a city in Samaria, and there began to preach the Anointed One. [6] The
people, one and all, listened attentively
to what Philip told them, when they
heard of, and saw, the miracles which
he was working. [7] For there were many
instances of people with unclean spirits, where the spirits, with loud screams,
came out of them; [8] and many who were
paralyzed or lame were healed, so that
there was great rejoicing throughout that
city. [9] There was staying in the city a man

named Simon, who had been practicing magic there and astonishing the Samaritan people, giving himself out to be some great being. [10] Everyone, high and low, paid attention to him. "This man," they used to say, "must be that power of God which people call great." [11] And they paid attention to him because they had for a long time been enthused about his magic arts. [12] However, when they came to trust Philip, as he told them the good news about the realm of God and the name of Jesus Christ, they were baptized, both men and women. [13] Even Simon believed, and after his baptism attached himself to Philip, and was in his turn astonished at seeing signs and great miracles constantly occurring.

[14] When the ambassadors at Jerusalem heard that the Samaritans had welcomed God's message, they sent Peter and John to them; [15] and they, on their arrival, prayed that the Samaritans might receive the holy Spirit. [16] (As yet the Spirit had not descended on any of them; they had only been baptized into the faith of the Lord Jesus.) [17] Then Peter and John placed their hands on them, and they received the holy Spirit.

[18] When Simon saw that it was through the placing of the ambassadors' hands on them that the Spirit was given, he brought them a sum of money and said: [19] "Give me also this power of yours, so that if I place my hands on anyone, that person may receive the holy Spirit."

[20] "A curse on you and on your money," Peter exclaimed, "for thinking that God's free gift can be bought with gold! [21] You have no share or part in our message, for your heart is not right with God. [22] Therefore repent of this wickedness of yours, and pray to the Lord that, if possible, you may be forgiven for such a thought; [23] for I see that you have fallen into the bitterness of envy and the fetters of sin."

[24] "Pray to the Lord for me, all of you," Simon answered, "so that none of the things you have spoken of may happen to me."

[25] Peter and John, having borne their testimony and delivered the Lord's message, returned to Jerusalem, telling the good news, as they went, in many Samaritan villages.

[26] Meanwhile an angel of the Lord had said to Philip: "Set out on a journey southward, along the road that runs down from Jerusalem to Gaza." (It is now deserted.) [27] So Philip set out on a journey; and on his way he came on an official of high rank, in the service of Candace, queen of the Abyssinians. He was a eunuch, and had been to Jerusalem to worship, [28] and was now on his way home, sitting in his carriage and reading the prophet Isaiah.

[29] The Spirit said to Philip: "Go up to the carriage over there and keep close to it." [30] So Philip ran up, and he heard the Abyssinian reading the prophet Isaiah.

"Do you understand what you are reading?" he asked. [31] "How can I," the other answered, "unless someone will explain it to me?" and he invited Philip to get up and sit by his side. [32] The passage of scripture which he was reading was this:

"Like a sheep, he was led away to
    slaughter,
and as a lamb is dumb in the hands of
    its shearer,
so he refrains from opening his lips.
[33] He was humiliated and justice was
    denied him.
Who will tell the story of his
    generation?
For his life is cut off from earth."

[34] "Now," said the eunuch, addressing Philip, "tell me, of whom is the prophet speaking? Of himself, or of someone else?" [35] Then Philip began, and, taking this passage as his text, told him the good news about Jesus.

[36] Presently, as they were going along the road, they came to some water, and

the eunuch exclaimed: "Look! Here is water; what is to prevent my being baptized?" [38] So he ordered the carriage to stop, and they went down into the water — both Philip and the eunuch — and Philip baptized him. [39] But when they came up out of the water, the Spirit of the Lord caught Philip away, and the eunuch saw no more of him; for he continued his journey with a joyful heart. [40] But Philip was found at Ashdod, and, as he went on his way, he told the good news in all the towns through which he passed, until he came to Caesarea.

9 [1] Meanwhile Saul, still breathing murderous threats against the followers of the Lord, went to the high priest, [2] and asked him to give him letters to the Judean congregations at Damascus, authorizing him, if he found there any supporters of the cause, whether men or women, to have them put in chains and brought to Jerusalem.

[3] While on his journey, as he was nearing Damascus, suddenly a light from the heavens flashed around him. [4] He fell to the ground and heard a voice saying to him, "Saul, Saul, why are you persecuting me?"

[5] "Who are you, Lord?" he asked.

"I am Jesus, whom you are persecuting," the voice answered. [6] "Yet stand up and go into the city, and you will be told what you must do."

[7] The men traveling with Saul were meanwhile standing speechless; they heard the sound of the voice, but saw no one. [8] When Saul got up from the ground, though his eyes were open, he could see nothing. So he was led by the hand, and they brought him into Damascus; [9] and for three days he was unable to see, and took nothing either to eat or to drink.

[10] Now there was at Damascus a follower named Ananias, to whom, in a vision, the Lord said: "Ananias."

"Yes, Lord," he answered. [11] "Go at once," said the Lord, "to the 'Straight Street,' and ask at Judas's house for a man named Saul, from Tarsus. He is at this moment praying, [12] and he has seen, in a vision, a man named Ananias coming in and placing his hands on him, so that he may recover his sight."

[13] "Lord," exclaimed Ananias, "I have heard from many people about this man — how much harm he has done at Jerusalem to your people there. [14] And here, too, he holds authority from the chief priests to put in chains all those who invoke your name." [15] But the Lord said to him: "Go, for this one is my chosen instrument to uphold my name before the gentiles and their kings, and the people of Israel. [16] I will myself show him all that he has to suffer for my name."

[17] So Ananias went, entered the house, and, placing his hands on Saul, said: "Saul, my brother, I have been sent by the Lord — by Jesus, who appeared to you on your way here — so that you may recover your sight and be filled with the holy Spirit." [18] Instantly it seemed as if a film fell from Saul's eyes, and his sight was restored. Then he got up and was baptized, [19] and, after he had taken food, he felt his strength return.

Saul stayed for some days with the followers who were at Damascus, [20] and at once began in the synagogues to proclaim Jesus as the Child of God. [21] All who heard him were amazed.

"Is this not," they asked, "the one who worked havoc in Jerusalem among those that invoke this name, and who had also come here for the express purpose of having such persons put in chains and taken before the chief priests?" [22] Saul's influence, however, kept steadily increasing, and he confounded the Judean people who lived in Damascus by the proofs that he gave that Jesus was the Anointed One.

[23] After some time some of them laid a plot to kill Saul, [24] but it became known to him. They even watched the gates day and

night, to kill him; [25] but his followers let him down by night through an opening in the wall, lowering him in a basket.

[26] On his arrival in Jerusalem, Saul attempted to join the followers, but they were all afraid of him, as they did not believe that he was really a follower. [27] Barnabas, however, taking him by the hand, brought him to the ambassadors, and told them the whole story of how Saul on his journey had seen the Lord, and how the Lord had talked to him, and how in Damascus he had spoken out fearlessly in the name of Jesus. [28] After that, Saul remained in Jerusalem; and he spoke fearlessly in the name of the Lord, [29] talking and arguing with the Greek speakers, who, however, made attempts to kill him. [30] But when the followers found this out, they took him down to Caesarea, and sent him on his way to Tarsus.

[31] And so it came about that the churches throughout Judea, Galilee, and Samaria enjoyed peace and became firmly established; and, ordering their life by respect for the Lord and the help of the holy Spirit, it increased in numbers.

[32] Peter, while traveling from place to place throughout the country, went down to visit the people of Christ living at Lydda. [33] There he found a man named Aeneas, who had been bedridden for eight years with paralysis. [34] "Aeneas," Peter said to him, "Jesus Christ heals you. Get up, and make your bed." Aeneas got up at once; [35] and all the inhabitants of Lydda and of the Plain of Sharon saw him, and came over to the Lord's side.

[36] At Jaffa there lived a follower whose name was Tabitha, which is in Greek *Dorcas* — "Gazelle." Her life was spent in doing good and giving to those in need. [37] Just at that time she was taken ill, and died; and they had washed her body and laid it out in an upstairs room. [38] Jaffa was near Lydda, and the followers, having heard that Peter was at Lydda, sent two men with the request that he come to them without delay. [39] Peter returned with them at once. On his arrival, he was taken upstairs, and all the widows came around him in tears, showing the coats and other clothing which Dorcas had made while she was among them. [40] But Peter sent everybody out of the room, and knelt down and prayed. Then, turning to the body, he said: "Tabitha! Stand up."

She opened her eyes, and, seeing Peter, sat up. [41] Giving her his hand, Peter raised her up, and, calling in the widows and others of Christ's people, presented her to them alive. [42] This became known all through Jaffa, and numbers of people came to believe in the Lord. [43] And Peter stayed some days at Jaffa with a tanner named Simon.

10 [1] At Caesarea there was a man named Cornelius, a captain in the regiment known as the "Italian Regiment," [2] a devout person and one who reverenced God, with all his household. He was liberal in giving to the people, and prayed to God constantly. [3] One afternoon, about three o'clock, he distinctly saw in a vision an angel from God come to him, and call him by name. [4] Cornelius fixed his eyes on him and, in great alarm, said: "What is it, Lord?"

"Your prayers and your works of mercy," the angel answered, "have been an acceptable offering to God. [5] And now, send messengers to Jaffa and fetch a man called Simon, who is also known as Peter. [6] He is lodging with a tanner named Simon, who has a house near the sea."

[7] When the angel who had spoken to him had gone, Cornelius called two slaves and a respectful soldier, who was one of his constant attendants, [8] and, after telling them the whole story, sent them to Jaffa.

[9] On the next day, while these men were on their way, just as they were nearing the town, Peter went up on the housetop about midday to pray. [10] He became hungry and wanted something to eat; but while it was

being prepared, he fell into a trance, [11] and saw that the sky opened, and that something like a great sail was descending, let down by its four corners toward the earth. [12] In it were all kinds of quadrupeds, reptiles, and birds. [13] Then he was aware of a voice which said, "Stand up, Peter, kill something, and eat."

[14] "No, Lord, I cannot," answered Peter, "for I have never eaten anything common and unclean." [15] Again he was aware of a voice which said, "What God has pronounced clean, do not regard as defiled." [16] This happened three times, and then suddenly it was all taken up into the heavens.

[17] While Peter was still perplexed as to the meaning of the vision that he had seen, the men sent by Cornelius, having inquired the way to Simon's house, came up to the gate, [18] and called out and asked if the Simon, who was also known as Peter, was lodging there. [19] Peter was still pondering over the vision, when the Spirit said to him: "There are two men looking for you at this moment. [20] Go down at once and do not hesitate to go with them, for I have sent them."

[21] Peter went down to the men and said: "I am the person you are looking for. What is your reason for coming?"

[22] The men replied: "Our captain, Cornelius, a pious man who reverences God and is well spoken of by the whole Judean nation, has been instructed by a holy angel to send for you to his house, and to listen to what you have to say." [23] So Peter invited them in and entertained them.

The next day he lost no time in setting out with them, accompanied by some of the Lord's followers from Jaffa; [24] and the day following he entered Caesarea. Cornelius was expecting them, and had invited his relations and intimate friends to meet them. [25] So, when Peter entered the city, Cornelius met him, and, throwing himself at Peter's feet, bowed to the ground. [26] Peter, however, lifted him up, saying as he did so: "Stand up, I am only human like yourself."

[27] Talking with him as he went, Peter entered the house, where he found a large gathering of people, to whom he said: [28] "You are doubtless aware that it is forbidden for a Judean to be intimate with a foreigner, or even to enter his house; and yet God has shown me that I ought not to call anyone common or 'unclean.' [29] That was why I came when I was sent for, without raising any objection. And now I ask your reason for sending for me."

[30] "Just three days ago this very hour," Cornelius said, "I was in my house, saying the afternoon prayers, when a man in dazzling clothing suddenly stood before me. [31] 'Cornelius,' he said, 'your prayer has been heard, and your works of compassion have been accepted by God. [32] Therefore send to Jaffa, and invite the Simon, who is also known as Peter, to come here. He is lodging in the house of Simon the tanner, near the sea.' [33] Accordingly I sent to you at once, and you have been so good as to come. And now we are all here in the presence of God, to listen to all that you have been instructed by the Lord to say." [34] Then Peter began.

"I see, beyond all doubt," he said, "that 'God does not show partiality,' [35] but that in every nation he who reverences him and does what is right is acceptable to him. [36] God has sent a message to the Israelites and told them, through Jesus Christ, the good news of peace — and Jesus is Lord of all! [37] You yourselves know the story which spread through all Judea, how, beginning from Galilee, after the baptism which John proclaimed — [38] the story, I mean, of Jesus of Nazareth, and how God consecrated him his Anointed by imbuing him with the holy Spirit and with power; and how he went about doing good and healing all who were under the power of the devil, because God was with him. [39] We are ourselves, too, witnesses to all that he did in Judea and in Jerusalem; yet they put him to death by hanging him on a cross! [40] This Jesus God raised on the third day, and enabled him to appear, [41] not indeed to everyone, but to witnesses chosen beforehand by God — to us, who ate and drank with him after his resurrection from the dead. [42] Further, God charged us to proclaim to the people, and solemnly affirm, that it is Jesus who has been appointed by God judge of the living and the dead. [43] To him it is that all the prophets bear witness, when they say that everyone who believes in him receives through his name forgiveness of sins."

[44] Before Peter had finished saying these words, the holy Spirit fell on all who were listening to the message. [45] Those circumcised who had come with Peter were amazed that the gift of the holy Spirit had been bestowed even on the gentiles; [46] for they heard them speaking with "tongues" and extolling God. At this Peter asked: [47] "Can anyone refuse the water for the baptism of these people, now that they have received the holy Spirit as we did ourselves?" [48] And he directed that they should be baptized in the faith of Jesus Christ; after which they asked him to stay there a few days longer.

11 [1] The ambassadors and the followers throughout Judea heard that even the gentiles had welcomed God's message. [2] But when Peter went up to Jerusalem, those who were circumcised began to confront him, [3] on the ground that he had visited people who were not circumcised, and had taken meals with them. [4] So Peter began to relate the facts to them as they had occurred. [5] "I was in the town of Jaffa," he said, "and was praying; and, while in a trance, I saw a vision. There was something like a great sail descending, let down by its four corners out of the heavens; and it came right down to me. [6] Looking intently at it, I began to distinguish quadrupeds, wild beasts, reptiles, and birds; [7] and I also heard a voice saying to me, 'Stand up, Peter, kill something and eat.' [8] 'No, Lord, I cannot,' I answered, 'for nothing "defiled" or "unclean" has ever passed my lips.' [9] Then a second time there came a voice from the heavens. 'What God has pronounced "clean,"' it said, 'you must not call "defiled."' [10] This happened three times, and then all was drawn up again into the heavens. [11] At that moment three men, who had been sent from Caesarea to see me, came up to the house in which we were. [12] The Spirit told me to go with them without hesitation. These six companions also went with me. And, when we came into the man's house, [13] he told us how he had seen the angel standing in his house, and how the angel had said to him, 'Send to Jaffa and fetch the Simon, who is also known as Peter; [14] for he will tell you truths, which will prove the means of salvation to you and all your household.' [15] I had but just begun to speak," continued Peter, "when the holy Spirit fell on them, exactly as on us at the first; [16] and I recalled the saying of the Master: 'John baptized with water, but you will be baptized with the holy Spirit.' [17] Since then, God has given them the very same gift as he gave us when we became believers in Jesus Christ the Master — who was I that I could thwart God?"

[18] On hearing this statement, they said no more, but broke out into praise of God. "So even to the gentiles," they exclaimed, "God has granted the repentance which leads to life!"

[19] Now those who had been scattered in different directions, in consequence of the persecution that followed the death of Stephen, went as far as Phoenicia, Cyprus, and Antioch, telling the message — but only to Judeans. [20] Some of them, however, who were men of Cyprus and Cyrene, on coming to Antioch, addressed themselves also to the Greeks, telling them the good news about the Lord Jesus. [21] The power of the Lord was with them, so that a great number who had

learned to believe came over to the Lord's side. ²² The news about them reached the ears of the church at Jerusalem, and they sent Barnabas to Antioch. ²³ On coming there he saw to his great joy these tokens of the loving kindness of God, and encouraged them all to make up their minds to be faithful to the Lord — ²⁴ for Barnabas was a good man and full of the holy Spirit and of faith — and a large number of people took their stand on the Lord's side. ²⁵ Afterward Barnabas left for Tarsus to look for Saul; ²⁶ and, when he had found him, he brought him to Antioch. And so it came about that for a whole year, they attended the meetings of the church there, and taught a large number of people; and it was in Antioch that the followers were first called "Christians."

²⁷ During this time, some prophets came to Antioch from Jerusalem. ²⁸ One of them, named Agabus, came forward and, under the influence of the Spirit, foretold a great famine that was to spread over all the world — a famine which occurred in the reign of Claudius. ²⁹ So the followers, without exception, determined, in proportion to their means, to send something to help the followers living in Judea. ³⁰ And this they did, sending it to the officers of the church by the hands of Barnabas and Saul.

12 ¹ It was at that time that King Herod began to mistreat some of the members of the church. ² He had James, the brother of John, beheaded; ³ and, when he saw that the Judeans were pleased with this, he proceeded to arrest Peter also. (This was during the festival of the unleavened bread.) ⁴ After seizing Peter, Herod put him in prison, and entrusted him to the keeping of four guards of four soldiers each, intending, after the Passover, to bring him up before the people. ⁵ So Peter was kept in prison, but meanwhile the prayers of the church were being earnestly offered to God on his behalf. ⁶ Just when Herod was

intending to bring him before the people, on that very night Peter was asleep between two soldiers, chained to them both, while there were sentries in front of the door, guarding the prison. ⁷ Suddenly an angel of the Lord stood by him, and a light shone in the cell. The angel struck Peter on the side, and roused him with the words: "Get up quickly." ⁸ The chains dropped from his wrists, and then the angel said: "Put on your girdle and sandals." When Peter had done so, the angel added: "Throw your cloak around you and follow me."

⁹ Peter followed him out, not knowing that what was happening under the angel's guidance was real, but thinking that he was seeing a vision. ¹⁰ Passing the first guard, and then the second, they came to the iron gate leading into the city, which opened to them of itself; and, when they had passed through that, and had walked along one street, all at once the angel left him.

¹¹ Then Peter came to himself and said: "Now I know beyond all doubt that the Lord has sent his angel, and has rescued me from Herod's hands and from all that the Judean people have been expecting." ¹² As soon as he realized what had happened, he went to the house of Mary, the mother of John who was also known as Mark, where a number of people were gathered together, praying. ¹³ On his knocking at the door in the gate, a maidservant, named Rhoda, came to answer it. ¹⁴ She recognized Peter's voice, but in her joy left the gate unopened, and ran in, and told them that Peter was standing outside.

¹⁵ "You are mad!" they exclaimed. But when she persisted that it was so, they said: "It must be his spirit!"

¹⁶ Meanwhile Peter went on knocking, and, when they opened the gate and saw him, they were amazed. ¹⁷ Peter signed to them with his hand to be silent, and then told them how the Lord had brought him out of the prison, adding: "Tell James and

the others all this." Then he left the house, and went away to another place.

[18] In the morning there was a great stir among the soldiers — what could have become of Peter? [19] And, when Herod had made further search for him and failed to find him, he closely questioned the guard, and ordered them away to execution. Then he went down from Judea to stay at Caesarea.

[20] It happened that Herod was deeply offended with the people of Tyre and Sidon, but they went in a body to him, and, having succeeded in winning over Blastus, the chamberlain, they begged Herod for a reconciliation, because their country was dependent on the king for its food supply. [21] On an appointed day Herod, wearing his state robes, seated himself on his throne, and delivered an oration. [22] The people kept shouting: "It is the voice of God, and not of a person!"

[23] Instantly an angel of the Lord struck him, because he did not give God the glory; and he was attacked with worms, and died. [24] Meanwhile the Lord's message kept extending, and spreading far and wide.

[25] When Barnabas and Saul had carried out their mission, they returned to Jerusalem, and took with them John, who was also known as Mark.

Doings of the Ambassador Paul

13 [1] Among the members of the church at Antioch there were several prophets and teachers — Barnabas, Simeon who was known by the name of "Black," Lucius of Cyrene, Manaen, foster brother of Prince Herod, and Saul. [2] While they were engaged in the worship of the Lord and were fasting, the holy Spirit said: "Set apart for me Barnabas and Saul, for the work to which I have called them." [3] Accordingly, after fasting and prayer, they placed their hands on them and dismissed them.

[4] Barnabas and Saul, sent on this mission, as they were, by the holy Spirit, went down to Seleucia, and from there sailed to Cyprus. [5] On reaching Salamis, they began to tell the message of God in the Judean synagogues; and they had John with them as an assistant. [6] After passing through the whole island, they reached Paphos, where they found a magician who pretended to be a prophet — a Judean by birth, whose name was Barjoshua. [7] He was at the court of the governor, Sergius Paulus, a man of intelligence, who sent for Barnabas and Saul and asked to be told God's message. [8] But Elymas, the magician (for that is the meaning of the word), opposed them, eager to divert the governor's attention from the faith. [9] However, Saul (who is the same as Paul), full of the holy Spirit, fixed his eyes on him and said: [10] "You incarnation of deceit and all fraud! You child of the devil! You opponent of all that is good! Will you never cease to divert the straight paths of the Lord? Listen! [11] The hand of the Lord is on you even now, and you will be blind for a time and unable to see the sun." Immediately a mist and darkness fell on him, and he went feeling about for someone to guide him. [12] When the governor saw what had happened, he came to trust in Christ, being greatly impressed by the teaching about the Lord.

[13] After this, Paul and his companions set sail from Paphos and went to Perga in Pamphylia, where John left them and returned to Jerusalem. [14] The others went on from Perga and arrived at Antioch in Pisidia. There they went into the synagogue on the sabbath and took their seats. [15] After the reading of the Law and the prophets, the president of the synagogue sent them this message: "Friends, if you have any helpful words to address to the people, now is the time to speak." [16] So Paul rose and, motioning with his hand, said:

"People of Israel and God-fearers, hear what I have to say. [17] The God of this people Israel chose our ancestors, and during their stay in Egypt increased the prosperity of the people, and then with uplifted arm brought them out from that land. [18] For about forty years he bore with them in the desert; [19] then, after destroying seven heathen nations in Canaan, he allotted their land to this people — [20] for about four hundred and fifty years. In later times he gave them judges, of whom the prophet Samuel was the last. [21] And, when they demanded a king, God gave them Saul the son of Kish, a man of the tribe of Benjamin, who reigned for forty years. [22] After removing him, he raised David to the throne, and bore this testimony to him: 'In David, the son of Jesse, I have found a man after my own heart, who will carry out all my purposes.' [23] It was from this man's descendants that God, in accordance with his promise, gave Israel a Savior — Jesus; [24] John having first proclaimed, before the appearance of Jesus, a baptism of repentance for all the people of Israel. [25] As John was drawing toward the end of his career, he said, 'What do you suppose that I am? I am not the Anointed One. But there is one coming after me whose sandal I am not worthy to untie.' [26] Brothers and sisters, descendants of Abraham, and all those among you who worship God, it was to us that the message of this salvation was sent. [27] The people of Jerusalem and their leaders, failing to recognize Jesus, and not understanding the utterances of the prophets that are read every sabbath, fulfilled them by condemning him. [28] They found no grounds at all for putting him to death, and yet demanded his execution from Pilate; [29] and, after carrying out everything written about him, they took Jesus down from the cross, and laid him in a tomb. [30] But God raised him from the dead; [31] and he appeared for many days to those who had gone up with him from Galilee to Jerusalem, and who are now witnesses for him to the people. [32] We also have good news to tell you, about the promise made to our ancestors — [33] that our children

have had this promise completely fulfilled to them by God, by his raising Jesus. That is just what is said in the second Psalm:

'You are my Son; this day I have
     become your Father.'

[34] "As to his raising Jesus from the dead, never again to return to corruption, this is what is said:

'I will give to you the sacred promises
     made to David.'

[35] "And, therefore, in another Psalm it is said:

'You will not give up the holy One to
     undergo corruption.'

[36] "David, after obediently doing God's will in his own time, fell asleep and was laid by the side of his ancestors, and did undergo corruption; [37] but Jesus, whom God raised from the dead, did not undergo corruption. [38] I would, therefore, like you to know, friends, that through Jesus forgiveness of sins is being proclaimed to you, [39] and that, in union with him, everyone who believes in him is absolved from every sin from which under the Law of Moses you could not be absolved. [40] Beware, therefore, that what is said in the prophets does not come true of you:

[41] 'Look, you despisers, and wonder, and
     perish;
   for I am doing a deed in your days —
   a deed which, though told you in full,
     you will never believe.'"

[42] As Paul and Barnabas were leaving the synagogue, the people begged for a repetition of this teaching on the next sabbath. [43] After the congregation had dispersed, many of the Judeans, and the converts who joined in their worship, fol-

lowed Paul and Barnabas, who talked with them and urged them to continue to rely on the loving kindness of God.

⁴⁴ On the following sabbath, almost all the city gathered to hear God's message. ⁴⁵ But the sight of the crowds of people filled the minds of the Judeans with jealousy, and they kept contradicting Paul's statements in violent language. ⁴⁶ Then Paul and Barnabas spoke out fearlessly, and said:

"It was necessary that the message of God should be told to you first; but since you reject it and reckon yourselves not worthy of the eternal life — we turn to the gentiles! ⁴⁷ For this is the Lord's command to us:

'I have destined you for a light to the
    gentiles,
a means of salvation to the ends of the
    earth.'"

⁴⁸ On hearing this, the gentiles were glad and extolled God's message; and all those who had been enrolled for eternal life became believers in Christ; ⁴⁹ and the Lord's message was carried throughout that district. ⁵⁰ But the Judeans incited the women of high social standing who worshiped with them, and the leaders of the town, and started a persecution against Paul and Barnabas, and drove them out of their neighborhood. ⁵¹ They, however, shook the dust off their feet in protest, ⁵² and went to Iconium, leaving the followers full of joy and of the holy Spirit.

14 ¹ The same thing occurred in Iconium, where Paul and Barnabas went into the Judean synagogue, and spoke in such a way that a great number of both Judeans and Greeks trusted. ² But the Judeans who refused to believe stirred up the gentiles, and poisoned their minds against the Lord's followers. ³ Therefore Paul and Barnabas spent a long time there, and

spoke out fearlessly, relying on God, who confirmed the message of his love by permitting signs and wonders to take place at their hands. ⁴ But the townspeople were divided, some siding with the Judeans, some with the ambassadors; ⁵ and, when there was an attempt on the part of both gentiles and Judeans, with their leaders, to resort to violence and to stone them, ⁶ they heard of it, and took refuge in Lystra and Derbe, towns in Lycaonia, and in the district around, ⁷ and there they continued to tell the good news.

⁸ In the streets of Lystra there used to sit a man who had no power in his feet; he had been lame from his birth, and had never walked. ⁹ This man was listening to Paul speaking, when Paul, fixing his eyes on him, and seeing that he had the faith to be healed, ¹⁰ said loudly: "Stand upright on your feet."

The man leaped up, and began walking about, ¹¹ and the crowd, seeing what Paul had done, called out in the Lycaonian language: "The gods have come down to us in human form." ¹² So they called Barnabas "Zeus," and Paul "Hermes," because he took the lead in speaking; ¹³ and the priest of Zeus-beyond-the-Walls, accompanied by the crowd, brought bullocks and garlands to the gates, with the intention of offering sacrifices. ¹⁴ But when the ambassadors Barnabas and Paul heard of it, they tore their clothes and rushed out into the crowd.

"Friends, why are you doing this?" they shouted. ¹⁵ "We are only people like yourselves, and we have come with the good news that you should turn away from these follies to a living God, who made the heavens, the earth, the sea, and everything that is in them. ¹⁶ In bygone times he permitted all the nations to go their own ways. ¹⁷ Yet he has not failed to give you, in the good he does, some revelation of himself — sending you from the sky rain and fruitful seasons, and gladdening your hearts with plenty and good cheer." [18] Even with this appeal they could hardly restrain the people from offering sacrifice to them.

[19] Presently, however, there came some Judeans from Antioch and Iconium who, after they had won over the people, stoned Paul, and dragged him out of the town, thinking him to be dead. [20] But when the followers had gathered around him, he got up and went back into the town; the next day he went with Barnabas to Derbe. [21] After telling the good news throughout that town, and making a number of converts, they returned to Lystra, Iconium, and Antioch, [22] reassuring the minds of the followers, urging them to remain true to the faith, and showing that it is only through many troubles that we can enter the realm of God. [23] They also appointed officers for them in every church, and, after prayer and fasting, commended them to the Lord in whom they had learned to believe. [24] Paul and Barnabas then went through Pisidia, and came into Pamphylia, [25] and, after telling the message at Perga, went down to Attaleia. [26] From there they sailed to Antioch — the place where they had been committed to the gracious care of God for the work which they had now finished. [27] After their arrival, they gathered the church together, and gave an account of all that God had helped them to do, and especially how he had opened to the gentiles the door of faith; [28] and at Antioch they stayed with the followers for a considerable time.

15 [1] But certain persons came down from Judea, and began to teach the Lord's followers that unless they were circumcised, in accordance with the custom required by Moses, they could not be saved. [2] This gave rise to a serious dispute, and much discussion, between Paul and Barnabas and these people, and it was therefore settled that Paul and Barnabas and others of their number should go up to Je-

rusalem, to consult the ambassadors and officers about the matter under discussion.

[3] The church, therefore, sent them on their journey, and they made their way through Phoenicia and Samaria, telling the story of the conversion of the gentiles, to the great joy of all the followers. [4] On their arrival at Jerusalem, they were welcomed by the church, as well as by the ambassadors and the officers, and gave an account of all that God had helped them to do. [5] Some of the Pharisees' party, however, who had become believers in Christ came forward and declared that they were bound to circumcise converts and to direct them to observe the Law of Moses. [6] The ambassadors and the officers held a meeting to consider this question. [7] After much discussion, Peter rose and said:

"You, my friends, know well that long ago God singled me out — that through my lips the gentiles should hear the message of the good news, and become believers in Christ. [8] Now God, who reads all hearts, declared his acceptance of the gentiles by giving them the holy Spirit, just as he did to us. [9] He made no distinction between them and us, when he purified their hearts by their faith. [10] Why, then, do you now provoke God, by putting on the necks of these followers a yoke which neither our ancestors nor we were able to bear? [11] No, it is through the loving kindness of the Lord Jesus that we, just as they do, believe that we have been saved."

[12] Every voice in the assembly was hushed, as they listened to Barnabas and Paul, while they gave an account of all the signs and wonders which God had shown among the gentiles through them. [13] After they had finished speaking, James addressed the Council.

"Friends," he began, "hear what I have to say. [14] Simon has described the manner in which God first visited the gentiles, in order to take from among them a people to bear his name. ¹⁵ And that is in harmony with the words of the prophets, where they say:

¹⁶ "'After this I will return;
and I will rebuild the house of David
which has fallen—
its ruins I will rebuild,
and will set it up once more;
¹⁷ that so the rest of humankind may
earnestly seek the Lord—
even all the gentiles on whom my name
has been bestowed."
¹⁸ Says the Lord, as he does these things,
foreknown from of old.'

¹⁹ "In my judgment, therefore, we should not add to the difficulties of those gentiles who are turning to God, ²⁰ but we should write to them to abstain from food that has been polluted by being sacrificed to idols, from uncleanness, from eating the flesh of strangled animals, and from blood. ²¹ For in every town, for generations past, there have been those who proclaim Moses, read as he is in the synagogues every sabbath."

²² It was then decided by the ambassadors and the officers, with the assent of the whole church, to choose some of their number, and send them to Antioch with Paul and Barnabas. Those chosen were Judas (called Barsabas) and Silas, who were leaders among the community. ²³ They were bearers of the following letter:

"The ambassadors, and the elders who are the officers of the church, send their greetings to the followers of the Lord of gentile birth in Antioch, Syria, and Cilicia. ²⁴ As we had heard that some of our number had upset you by their assertions, and unsettled your minds—without instructions from us—²⁵ we met and decided to choose certain men and send them to you with our dear friends Barnabas and Paul, ²⁶ who have risked their lives for the name of our Lord, Jesus Christ. ²⁷ We are accordingly sending Judas and Silas, and

they will tell you by word of mouth what we are now writing. ²⁸ We have, therefore, decided, under the guidance of the holy Spirit, to lay no further burden on you beyond these necessary conditions—²⁹ that you abstain from food offered to idols, from blood, from eating the flesh of strangled animals, and from impurity. If you guard yourselves against such things, it will be well with you. Farewell."

³⁰ So the bearers of this letter were sent on their way, and went down to Antioch. There they called a meeting of all the followers, ³¹ and delivered the letter, the reading of which caused great rejoicing by its encouraging contents. ³² Judas and Silas, who were themselves prophets, further encouraged them by many an address, and strengthened their faith. ³³ After some stay, they were dismissed with kind farewells from the followers, and returned to those who had sent them.

³⁵ Paul and Barnabas, however, remained in Antioch, where they taught and, with the help of many others, told the good news of the Lord's message. ³⁶ Sometime after this, Paul said to Barnabas: "Let us go back and visit the Lord's followers in every town in which we have told the Lord's message, and see how they are prospering." ³⁷ Barnabas wished to take with them John, whose other name was Mark; ³⁸ but Paul felt that they ought not to take with them the man who had deserted them in Pamphylia, and had not gone on with them to their work. ³⁹ This caused such unpleasant feeling between them that they parted ways, Barnabas taking Mark and sailing for Cyprus, ⁴⁰ while Paul chose Silas for his companion and, after he had been committed by the followers to the gracious care of the Lord, ⁴¹ started on his journey and went through Syria and Cilicia, strengthening the churches in the faith.

16 ¹ Among other places Paul went to Derbe and Lystra. At the latter place they

found a follower named Timothy, whose mother was a faithful Judean, while his father was a Greek, [2] and who was well spoken of by the followers of the Lord in Lystra and Iconium. [3] Wishing to take this man with him on his journey, Paul had him circumcised out of consideration for the Judeans in that neighborhood, for they all knew that his father had been a Greek. [4] As they traveled from town to town, they gave the followers the decisions which had been reached by the ambassadors and officers at Jerusalem, for them to observe.

[5] So the churches grew stronger in confidence, and increased in numbers from day to day.

[6] They next went through the Phrygian district of Galatia, but were restrained by the holy Spirit from delivering the message in Roman Asia. [7] When they reached the borders of Mysia, they attempted to go into Bithynia, but the spirit of Jesus did not permit them. [8] Passing through Mysia, they went down to Troas; [9] and there one night Paul saw a vision. A Macedonian was standing and appealing to him: "Come over to Macedonia and help us." [10] So, immediately after Paul had seen the vision, we looked for an opportunity to cross over to Macedonia, concluding that God had summoned us to tell the good news to the people there.

[11] Accordingly we set sail from Troas, and ran before the wind to Samothrace, reaching Neapolis the next day. [12] From there we made our way to Philippi, which is the principal city of that part of Macedonia, and also a Roman settlement.

In that city we spent several days. [13] On the sabbath we went outside the gate to the riverside, where we supposed there would be a place of prayer; and we sat down and talked to the women who were gathered there. [14] Among them was a woman named Lydia, belonging to Thyatira, a dealer in purple cloth, who was accustomed to join in the worship of God.

The Lord touched this woman's heart, so that she gave attention to the message delivered by Paul, [15] and, when she and her household had been baptized, she urged us to become her guests.

"If you credit me," she said, "with trust in the Lord, come and stay in my house." And she insisted on our doing so.

[16] One day, as we were on our way to the place of prayer, we were met by a girl possessed by a divining spirit, who made large profits for her masters by fortune-telling. [17] This girl followed Paul and the rest of us, calling: "These men are slaves of the Most High God, and they are bringing you news of a way to salvation." [18] She had been doing this for several days when Paul, much vexed, turned and said to the spirit within her: "In the name of Jesus Christ I command you to leave her." That very moment the spirit left her.

[19] When her masters saw that there was no hope of further profit from her, they seized Paul and Silas, dragged them into the public square to the authorities, [20] and took them before the magistrates.

"These men are causing a great disturbance in our town," they complained. [21] "They are Judeans, and they are teaching customs which it is not right for us, as Romans, to sanction or adopt."

[22] The mob rose as one person against them, and the magistrates stripped them of their clothing and ordered them to be beaten with rods. [23] After beating them severely, the magistrates put them in prison, with orders to the jailer to keep them in safe custody. [24] On receiving so strict an order, the governor put them into the inner cell, and fastened their feet in the stocks. [25] About midnight, while Paul and Silas were praying and singing hymns to God, and while the prisoners were listening to them, [26] suddenly there was an earthquake of such violence that the jail was shaken to its foundations; all the doors flew open, and all the prisoners' chains were loosened. [27] Roused from his

sleep, and seeing the prison doors open, the governor drew his sword, intending to kill himself, in the belief that the prisoners had escaped. [28] But Paul called out loudly: "Do not harm yourself; we are all here."

[29] Calling for a light, the governor rushed in, and flung himself trembling at the feet of Paul and Silas. [30] Then he led them out, and said: "What must I do to be saved?"

[31] "Trust in Jesus, our Lord," they replied, "and you will be saved, you and your household too." [32] Then they spoke to him of God's message, and to all his household as well. [33] And that very hour of the night he took them and washed their wounds, and he himself and everyone belonging to him were baptized without delay. [34] Afterward he took them up to his house and set before them something to eat, rejoicing that he, with all his household, had come to trust in God.

[35] In the morning the magistrates sent the police with an order for the men to be discharged. [36] The jailer told Paul of his instructions. "The magistrates have sent an order for your discharge," he said, "so you had better leave the place at once and go quietly away."

[37] But Paul's answer to them was: "They have flogged us in public without trial, though we are Roman citizens, and they have put us in prison, and now they are for sending us out secretly! No, indeed! Let them come and take us out themselves." [38] The police reported his words to the magistrates, who, on hearing that Paul and Silas were Roman citizens, were alarmed, [39] and went to the prison, and did their best to conciliate them. Then they took them out, and begged them to leave the city. [40] When Paul and Silas left the prison, they went to Lydia's house, and, after they had seen the brothers and sisters and encouraged them, they left the place.

17 [1] After passing through Amphipolis and Apollonia, Paul and Silas came to Thessalonica. Here the Judeans had a synagogue; [2] and, following his usual custom, Paul joined them, and for three sabbaths addressed them, drawing his arguments from that which is written. [3] He laid before them and explained that the Christ must undergo suffering and rise from the dead; and "It is this man," he declared, "who is the Anointed One—this Jesus about whom I am telling you."

[4] Some of the people were convinced, and threw in their lot with Paul and Silas, as did also a large body of Greeks who were accustomed to join in the Judean services, and a great number of influential women. [5] But the Judean leaders, becoming jealous, engaged some worthless fellows from the streets, and, getting a mob together, kept the city in an uproar. They attacked Jason's house, with the intention of bringing Paul and Silas before the Popular Assembly; [6] and, not finding them there, they proceeded to drag Jason and some of the brothers and sisters before the city magistrates, shouting out:

"These people, who have turned the world upside down, have now come here, [7] and have been harbored by Jason! They have broken Caesar's edicts by saying that someone else is king—a man called Jesus!"

[8] On hearing this, the people and the city magistrates were much concerned; [9] and, before letting them go, they took bail from Jason and the others. [10] That very night the followers sent Paul and Silas off to Beroea; and on reaching that place, they went to the Judean synagogue. [11] These Judeans of Beroea were better disposed than those in Thessalonica, for they welcomed the message with great readiness, and daily examined the writings to see if what was said was true. [12] As a consequence, many of them came to trust in Christ, besides a considerable number of Greek women of position, and men also. [13] But when the Judean leaders in Thessalonica found out that God's message

had been delivered by Paul at Beroea, they came there too, exciting and disturbing the people. [14] The followers immediately arranged for Paul to go away to the coast, but both Silas and Timothy stayed behind in Beroea. [15] Those who escorted Paul took him as far as Athens, and, after receiving a message for Silas and Timothy to join him as quickly as possible, they started on their return.

[16] While Paul was waiting for them at Athens, his heart was stirred at seeing the whole city full of idols. [17] So he argued in the synagogue with the Judeans and with those outside the traditions of Israel who joined in their worship, as well as daily in the public square with those who happened to be there. [18] Among others, some Epicurean and Stoic philosophers joined issue with him. Some asked, "What is this parrot wanting to make out?" while others said, "He seems to be a proclaimer of foreign deities." (This was because he was telling the good news about Jesus and the resurrection.) [19] So they laid hold of him and took him to the Areopagus.

"May we hear," they asked, "what new teaching this is which you are giving? [20] For you are bringing some strange things to our notice, and we should like to know what they mean." [21] (All Athenians and the foreigners staying in the city found no time for anything else but telling, or listening to, the latest new idea.)

[22] So Paul took his stand in the middle of the court, and said: "People of Athens, on every hand I see signs of your being very devout. [23] For as I was going about, looking at your sacred shrines, I came upon an altar with this inscription: 'To an Unknown God.' What, therefore, you worship in ignorance, that I am now proclaiming to you. [24] The God who made the world and all things that are in it — he, Lord as he is of heaven and earth — does not live in temples made by hands, [25] nor yet do human hands minister to his wants,

as though he needed anything, since he himself gives, to all, life, and breath, and all things. [26] Out of one, he made all races of the earth's surface — fixing a time for their rise and fall, and the limits of their settlements — [27] that they might search for God, if by any means they might feel their way to him and find him. And yet he is not really far from any one of us; [28] for in him we live and move and are. To use the words of some of your own poets:

'We are all God's people.'

[29] "Therefore, as the people of God, we must not think that the deity has any resemblance to anything made of gold, or silver, or stone — a work of human art and imagination. [30] True, God looked with indulgence on the days of people's ignorance, but now he is announcing to everyone everywhere the need for repentance, [31] because he has fixed a day on which he intends to 'judge the world with justice,' by a man whom he has appointed — and of this he has given all people a pledge by raising this man from the dead."

[32] On hearing of a resurrection of the dead, some began jeering, but others said that they wanted to hear what he had to say about that another time. [33] And so Paul left them. [34] There were, however, some people who joined him, and became believers. Among them were Dionysius, a member of the court of Areopagus, a woman named Damaris, and several others.

18 [1] On leaving Athens, Paul next went to Corinth. [2] There he met a Judean of the name of Aquila, from Pontus, who, with his wife Priscilla, had lately come from Italy, in consequence of the order which had been issued by the emperor Claudius for all Judeans to leave Rome. Paul paid them a visit, [3] and, since their trade was the same as his, he stayed and worked with them — their trade was tent-making. [4] Every sabbath Paul gave addresses in the synagogue, trying to convince both Judeans and Greeks.

[5] But when Silas and Timothy had come down from Macedonia, Paul devoted himself entirely to delivering the message, earnestly maintaining before the Judeans that Jesus was the Anointed One. [6] However, as they set themselves against him and became abusive, Paul shook his clothes in protest and said to them: "Your blood be on your own heads. My conscience is clear. From this time forward I will go to the gentiles."

[7] So he left, and went to the house of a certain Titius Justus, who was God-fearing, and whose house was next door to the synagogue. [8] Crispus, the president of the synagogue, came to trust in the Lord, and so did all his household; and many of the Corinthians, as they listened to Paul, trusted and were baptized. [9] One night the Lord said to Paul, in a vision: "Have no fear, but continue to speak, and refuse to be silenced; [10] for I am with you, and no one will do you harm, for I have many people in this city." [11] So he settled there for a year and a half, and taught God's message among them.

[12] While Gallio was governor of Greece, some of the Judean leaders made a combined attack on Paul, and brought him before the Governor's Bench, [13] charging him with persuading people to worship God in a way forbidden by the Law. [14] Just as Paul was on the point of speaking, Gallio said to them:

"If this were a case of misdemeanor or some serious crime, there would be some reason for my listening patiently to you; [15] but since it is a dispute about words, and names, and your own Law, you must see to it yourselves. I do not choose to be a judge in such matters."

[16] Saying this, he drove them back from the judgment bench. [17] Then they all set on Sosthenes, the president of the synagogue, and beat him in front of the bench, but Gallio did not trouble himself about any of these things.

[18] Paul remained there some time after this, and then took leave of the followers, and sailed to Syria with Priscilla and Aquila, but not before his head had been shaved at Cenchreae, because he was under a vow. [19] They put into Ephesus, and there Paul, leaving his companions, went into the synagogue and addressed the Judeans. [20] When they asked him to prolong his stay, he declined, saying, however, [21] as he took his leave, "I will come back again to you, please God," and then set sail from Ephesus. [22] On reaching Caesarea, he went up to Jerusalem and exchanged greetings with the church, and then went down to Antioch. [23] After making some stay in Antioch, he set out on a tour through the Phrygian district of Galatia, strengthening all the followers as he went.

[24] Meanwhile there had come to Ephesus an Alexandrian Judean named Apollos, an eloquent man who was well versed in the writings. [25] He had been well instructed in the cause of the Lord, and with burning zeal he spoke of and taught carefully about Jesus, though he knew of no baptism but John's. [26] This man began to speak out fearlessly in the synagogue; and when Priscilla and Aquila heard him, they took him home and explained the Way to him more carefully still. [27] When he wanted to cross to Greece, the brothers and sisters furthered his plans, and wrote to the followers there to welcome him. On his arrival he proved of great assistance to those who had, through loving kindness, become believers, [28] for he vigorously confuted the Judeans, publicly proving by the writings that Jesus was the Christ.

19 [1] While Apollos was at Corinth, Paul passed through the inland districts of Roman Asia, and went to Ephesus. There he found some followers, of whom he asked: [2] "Did you, when you became believers, receive the holy Spirit?"

"No," they answered, "we did not even hear that there was a holy Spirit."

[3] "What then was your baptism?" Paul asked. They replied, "With John's baptism." [4] "John's baptism was a baptism of repentance," rejoined Paul, "and John told the people, speaking of the one coming after him, that they should believe in that one — that is, in Jesus."

[5] On hearing this, they were baptized into the name of the Lord Jesus, [6] and, after Paul had placed his hands on them, the holy Spirit descended on them, and they began to speak with tongues and to prophesy. [7] There were about twelve of them in all.

[8] He went to the synagogue there, and for three months spoke out fearlessly, giving addresses and trying to convince his hearers about the realm of God. [9] Some of them, however, hardened their hearts and refused to believe, denouncing the Way before the people. So Paul left them and withdrew his followers, and gave daily addresses in the lecture hall of Tyrannus. [10] This went on for two years, so that all who lived in Roman Asia, Judeans and Greeks alike, heard the Lord's message.

[11] God did miracles of no ordinary kind by Paul's hands; [12] so that people would carry home to the sick handkerchiefs or aprons that had touched his body, and their diseases would leave them and the wicked spirits go out of them. [13] An attempt was made by some itinerant Judeans who were exorcists to use the name of the Lord Jesus over those who had wicked spirits in them.

"I order you," they would say, "by the Jesus whom Paul preaches." [14] The seven sons of Sceva, a Judean chief priest, were doing this; [15] but the wicked spirit answered them: "Jesus I acknowledge, and Paul I know, but you — who are you?"

[16] Then the man in whom this wicked spirit was, sprang on them, mastered both of them, and so completely overpowered them, that they fled out of the house, stripped of their clothes and wounded. [17] This incident came to the knowledge of all the Judeans and Greeks living at Ephesus; they were all awestruck, and the name of the Lord Jesus was held in the highest honor. [18] Many, too, of those who had become believers in Christ came with a full confession of their practices; [19] while a number of people who had practiced magic collected their books and burned them publicly; and on reckoning up the price of these, they found it amounted to fifty thousand silver coins. [20] So irresistibly did the Lord's message spread and prevail.

[21] Sometime after these events Paul resolved to go through Macedonia and Greece, and then make his way to Jerusalem. "And after I have been there," he said, "I must visit Rome also." [22] So he sent to Macedonia two of his helpers, Timothy and Erastus, while he himself stayed for some time longer in Roman Asia.

[23] Just about that time a great disturbance arose in the Way. [24] A silversmith named Demetrius, who made silver models of the shrine of Artemis, and so gave a great deal of work to the artisans, [25] got these men together, as well as the workmen engaged in similar occupations, and said:

"Men, you know that our prosperity depends on this work, [26] and you see and hear that not only at Ephesus, but in almost the whole of Roman Asia, this Paul has convinced and won over great numbers of people by his assertion that those gods which are made by hands are not gods at all. [27] So that not only is this business of ours likely to fall into discredit, but there is the further danger that the temple of the great goddess Artemis will be thought nothing of, and that she herself will be deprived of her splendor — though all Roman Asia and the whole world worship her."

²⁸ When they heard this, the men were greatly enraged, and began shouting: "Great is Artemis of the Ephesians!" ²⁹ The commotion spread through the whole city, and the people rushed together into the amphitheater, dragging with them Gaius and Aristarchus, two Macedonians who were Paul's traveling companions. ³⁰ Paul wished to go into the amphitheater and face the people, but the followers would not let him, ³¹ while some of the chief religious officials of the province, who were friendly to him, sent repeated entreaties to him not to trust himself inside. ³² Meanwhile some were shouting one thing and some another, for the Assembly was all in confusion, most of those present not even knowing why they had met. ³³ But some of the crowd prompted Alexander, whom several of the Judean leaders had pushed to the front, and he waved his hand to show that he wanted to speak in their defense to the people. ³⁴ However, when they recognized him as a Judean, one cry broke from them all, and they continued shouting for two hours: "Great is Artemis of the Ephesians!"

³⁵ When the recorder had succeeded in quieting the crowd, he said: "People of Ephesus, who is there, I ask you, who needs to be told that this city of Ephesus is the warden of the temple of the great Artemis, and of the statue which fell down from Zeus? ³⁶ As these are undeniable facts, you ought to keep calm and do nothing rash; ³⁷ for you have brought these men here, though they are neither robbers of temples nor blasphemers of our goddess. ³⁸ If, however, Demetrius and the artisans who are acting with him have a charge to make against anyone, there are court days and there are magistrates; let both parties take legal proceedings. ³⁹ But if you want anything more, it will have to be settled in the regular Assembly. ⁴⁰ For I tell you that we are in danger of being pro-

ceeded against for today's riot, there being nothing to account for it; and in that case we will be at a loss to give any reason for this disorderly gathering."

⁴¹ With these words he dismissed the Assembly.

20 ¹ When the uproar had ceased, Paul sent for the followers, and, with encouraging words, bade them goodbye, and started on his journey to Macedonia. ² After going through those districts and speaking many encouraging words to the followers, he went into Greece, where he stayed three months. ³ He was about to sail to Syria, when he learned that a plot had been laid against him by several of the Judean leaders; so he decided to return by way of Macedonia. ⁴ He was accompanied by Sopater, the son of Pyrrhus, of Beroea, Aristarchus and Secundus from Thessalonica, Gaius of Derbe, and Timothy, as well as by Tychicus and Trophimus of Roman Asia. ⁵ These people went to Troas and waited for us there, ⁶ while we ourselves sailed from Philippi after the Passover, and joined them five days later at Troas, where we stayed for a week.

⁷ On the first day of the week, when we had met for the breaking of bread, Paul, who was intending to leave the next day, began to address those who were present, and prolonged his address until midnight. ⁸ There were a good many lamps in the upstairs room, where we had met; ⁹ and a young man named Eutychus, sitting at the window, was gradually overcome with great drowsiness, as Paul continued his address. At last, quite overpowered by his drowsiness, he fell from the third story to the ground, and was picked up for dead. ¹⁰ But Paul went down, threw himself on him, and put his arms around him.

"Do not be alarmed," he said, "he is still alive." ¹¹ Then he went upstairs; and, after breaking and partaking of the bread, he talked with them at great length until daybreak, and then left. ¹² Meanwhile they had taken the lad away alive, and were greatly comforted.

[13] We started first, went on board ship, and sailed for Assos, intending to take Paul on board there. This was by his own arrangement, as he intended to go by land himself. [14] So, when he met us at Assos, we took him on board and went on to Mitylene. [15] The day after we had sailed from there, we arrived off Chios, touched at Samos the following day, and the next day reached Miletus; [16] for Paul had decided to sail past Ephesus, so as to avoid spending much time in Roman Asia. He was making haste to reach Jerusalem, if possible, by the Pentecost festival.

[17] From Miletus, however, he sent to Ephesus and invited the officers of the church to meet him; [18] and, when they came, he said to them: "You know well the life that I always led among you from the very first day that I set foot in Roman Asia, [19] serving the Lord, as I did, in all humility, amid the tears and trials which fell to my lot through the plots of some of the Judean leaders. [20] I never shrank from telling you anything that could be helpful to you, or from teaching you both in public and in private. [21] I earnestly pointed both Judeans and Greeks to the repentance that leads to God, and to faith in Jesus, our Lord. [22] And now, under spiritual constraint, I am here on my way to Jerusalem, not knowing what will happen to me there, [23] except that in town after town the holy Spirit plainly declares to me that imprisonment and troubles await me. [24] But I count my life of no value to myself, if only I may complete the course marked out for me, and the task that was allotted me by the Lord Jesus — which was to declare the good news of the love of God. [25] And now, I tell you, I know that none of you will ever see my face again — you among whom I have gone about proclaiming the realm. [26] Therefore I declare to you this day that my conscience is clear in regard

to the fate of any of you, [27] for I have not shrunk from announcing the whole purpose of God regarding you. [28] Be watchful over yourselves, and over the whole flock of which the holy Spirit has placed you in charge, to shepherd the church of God, which he won for himself at the cost of his life. [29] I know that, after my departure, merciless wolves will get in among you who will not spare the flock; [30] and from among yourselves, too, people will arise who will teach perversions of truth, so as to draw away the followers after them. [31] Therefore, be on your guard, remembering how for three years, night and day, I never ceased, even with tears, to warn each one of you. [32] And now I commend you to the Lord and to the message of his grace — a message which has the power to build up your characters, and to give you your place among all those who are becoming holy. [33] I have never coveted anyone's gold or silver or clothing. [34] You, yourselves, know that these hands of mine provided not only for my own wants, but for my companions also. [35] I left nothing undone to show you that, laboring as I labored, you ought to help the weak, and to remember the words of the Lord Jesus, how he said himself, 'It is more blessed to give than to receive.'" [36] When Paul had finished speaking, he knelt down and prayed with them all. [37] All were in tears; and throwing their arms around Paul's neck, they kissed him again and again, [38] grieving most of all over what he said — that they would never see his face again. Then they escorted him to the ship.

21 [1] When we had torn ourselves away and had set sail, we ran before the wind to Cos; the next day we came to Rhodes, and from there to Patara, [2] where we found a ship crossing to Phoenicia, and went on board and set sail. [3] After sighting Cyprus and leaving it on the left, we sailed to Syria, and put into Tyre, where the ship was to

discharge her cargo. [4] There we found the followers and stayed a week with them. Speaking under the influence of the Spirit, they warned Paul not to set foot in Jerusalem. [5] However, when we had come to the end of our visit, we went on our way, all the followers with their wives and children escorting us out of the city. We knelt down on the beach, and prayed, [6] and then said goodbye to one another; after which we went on board, and they returned home.

[7] After we had made the run from Tyre, we landed at Ptolemais, and exchanged greetings with the followers there, and spent a day with them. [8] The next day we left, and reached Caesarea, where we went to the house of Philip, the missionary, who was one of "the Seven," and stayed with him. [9] He had four unmarried daughters, who had the gift of prophecy. [10] During our visit, which lasted several days, a prophet named Agabus came down from Judea. [11] He came to see us, and, taking Paul's belt, and binding his own feet and hands with it, said: "This is what the holy Spirit says: 'The man to whom this belt belongs will be bound like this by the Judeans in Jerusalem, and they will give him up to the gentiles.'" [12] When we heard that, we and the people of the place began to entreat Paul not to go up to Jerusalem.

[13] It was then that Paul made the reply: "Why are you weeping and breaking my heart like this? For my part, I am ready not only to be bound, but even to suffer death at Jerusalem for the name of the Lord Jesus." [14] So, as he would not be persuaded, we said no more to him, only adding, "The Lord's will be done."

[15] At the end of our visit, we made our preparations, and started on our way up to Jerusalem. [16] Some of the followers from Caesarea went with us, and brought Mnason with them, a Cypriot follower of long standing, with whom we were to stay. [17] On our arrival at Jerusalem, the followers of the Lord there gave us a hearty welcome; [18] and the next day Paul went with us to see James, and all the officers of the church were present. [19] After greeting them, Paul related in detail all that God had done among the gentiles through his efforts; [20] and, when they had heard it, they began praising God, and said to Paul:

"You see, brother, that those of our people who have become believers may be numbered by the thousands, and they are all naturally earnest in upholding the Law. [21] Now they have heard it said about you, that you teach all of our people in foreign countries to forsake Moses, for you tell them not to circumcise their children or even to observe Judean customs. [22] Well now, as they are certain to hear of your arrival, do what we are going to suggest. [23] We have four men here, who have of their own accord put themselves under a vow. [24] Join these men, share their purification, and bear their expenses, so that they may shave their heads; and then all will see that there is no truth in what they have been told about you, but that, on the contrary, you yourself rule your life in obedience to the Law. [25] As to the gentiles who have come to trust, we have sent our decision that they should avoid food offered to idols, and blood, and the flesh of strangled animals, and impurity."

[26] Paul joined the men, and the next day shared their purification, and went into the Temple, and gave notice of the expiration of the period of purification when the usual offering should have been made on behalf of each of them.

[27] But just as the seven days were drawing to a close, some of the Judean people from Roman Asia caught sight of Paul in the Temple, and caused great excitement among all the people present, by seizing Paul and shouting: [28] "People of Israel! Help! This is the man who teaches everyone everywhere against our people, our Law, and this place; and, what is more, he

has actually brought Greeks into the Temple and defiled this sacred place." ²⁹ (For they had previously seen Trophimus the Ephesian in Paul's company in the city, and were under the belief that Paul had taken him into the Temple.)

³⁰ The whole city was stirred, and the people quickly collected, seized Paul, and dragged him out of the Temple, when the doors were immediately shut. ³¹ They were bent on killing him, when it was reported to the officer commanding the garrison that all Jerusalem was in commotion. ³² He instantly got together some officers and soldiers, and charged down on the crowd, who, when they saw the commanding officer and his soldiers, stopped beating Paul. ³³ Then he went up to Paul, arrested him, ordered him to be doubly chained, and proceeded to inquire who he was, and what he had been doing. ³⁴ Some of the crowd said one thing, and some another; and, as he could get no definite reply because of the uproar, he ordered Paul to be taken into the barracks. ³⁵ When Paul reached the steps, he was actually being carried by the soldiers, owing to the violence of the mob; ³⁶ for the people were following in a mass, shouting out: "Kill him!"

³⁷ Just as he was about to be taken into the fort, Paul said to the commanding officer: "May I speak to you?"

"Do you know Greek?" asked the commanding officer. ³⁸ "Are you not, then, the Egyptian who some time ago raised an insurrection and led the four thousand bandits out into the wilderness?"

³⁹ "No," said Paul, "I am a Judean of Tarsus in Cilicia, a citizen of a city of some note; and I beg you to give me permission to speak to the people."

⁴⁰ The commanding officer gave his permission, and Paul, standing on the steps, made signs with his hand to the people, and, when comparative silence had been obtained, he said to them in Hebrew:

22 ¹ "Brothers and fathers, listen to the defense which I am about to make." ² When they heard that he was speaking to them in Hebrew, they were still more quiet; and Paul went on:

³ "I am a Judean, from Tarsus in Cilicia, but I was brought up in this city under the teaching of Gamaliel, and educated in accordance with the strict system of our ancestral Law. I was as zealous in God's service as any of you who are here today. ⁴ In my persecution of this cause I did not stop even at the taking of life. I put in chains, and imprisoned, men and women alike — ⁵ and to that the high priest himself and all the Council can testify. For I had letters of introduction from them to our fellow Judeans at Damascus, and I was on my way to that place, to bring those whom I might find there prisoners to Jerusalem for punishment. ⁶ While I was still on my way, just as I was getting close to Damascus, about midday, suddenly there flashed from the heavens a great light all around me. ⁷ I fell to the ground, and heard a voice saying to me, 'Saul, Saul, why are you persecuting me?' ⁸ 'Who are you, Lord?' I replied. Then the voice said, 'I am Jesus of Nazareth whom you are persecuting.' ⁹ The men with me saw the light, but did not hear the speaker's voice. ¹⁰ Then I said, 'What am I to do, Lord?' 'Get up and go into Damascus,' the Lord said to me, 'and there you will be told all that you have been appointed to do.' ¹¹ In consequence of that dazzling light I could not see, but my companions held me by the hand, until I reached Damascus. ¹² There a man named Ananias, a strict observer of our Law, well spoken of by all the Judean inhabitants, came to see me. ¹³ Standing close to me, he said, 'Saul, my brother, recover your sight.' And then and there I recovered my sight and looked up at him. ¹⁴ Then he said, 'The God of our ancestors has appointed you to learn his will, and to see the righteous one, and to hear words from his lips;

[15] for you will be a witness for him to all the world of what you have just seen and heard. [16] And now why wait any longer? Be baptized at once, wash away your sins, and invoke his name.' [17] After my return to Jerusalem, while I was praying one day in the Temple, I fell into a trance, [18] and saw Jesus saying to me, 'Make haste and leave Jerusalem at once, because they will not accept your testimony about me.' [19] 'Lord,' I answered, 'these people know that I used to imprison and scourge, in synagogue after synagogue, those who believed in you; [20] and, when the blood of your martyr Stephen was being shed, I was myself standing by, approving of his death, and took charge of the clothes of those who were murdering him. [21] But Jesus said to me, 'Go; for I will send you to the gentiles far away.'"

[22] Up to this point the people had been listening to Paul, but at these words they called out: "Kill him! A fellow like this ought not to have been allowed to live!" [23] As they were shouting, tearing off their clothes, and throwing dust in the air, [24] the commanding officer ordered Paul to be taken into the fort, and directed that he should be examined under the lash so that he might find out the reason for their outcry against him.

[25] But just as they had tied him up to be scourged, Paul said to the captain standing near: "Is it legal for you to scourge a Roman citizen, unconvicted?" [26] On hearing this, the captain went and reported it to the commanding officer. "Do you know what you are doing?" he said. "This man is a Roman citizen." [27] So the commanding officer went up to Paul and said: "Tell me, are you a Roman citizen?"

"Yes," replied Paul. [28] "I had to pay a heavy price for my position as citizen," said the officer. "I am one by birth," rejoined Paul.

[29] The men who were to have examined Paul immediately drew back, and the officer, finding that Paul was a Roman citizen, was alarmed at having put him in chains.

[30] On the next day the commanding officer, wishing to find out the real reason why Paul was denounced by the Judean leaders, had his chains taken off, and directed the chief priests and the whole of the High Council to assemble, and then took Paul down and brought him before them.

23 [1] Paul fixed his eyes on the Council, and began:

"Brothers, for my part, I have always ordered my life before God, with a clear conscience, up to this very day." [2] At this, the high priest Ananias ordered the attendants standing near to strike him on the mouth; [3] Paul turned to him and said:

"God will strike you, you whitewashed wall! Are you sitting there to try me in accordance with law, and yet, in defiance of law, order me to be struck?" [4] The people standing near said to Paul: "Do you know that you are insulting God's high priest?"

[5] "I did not know, brothers, that it was the high priest," said Paul, "for it is written:

'Of the ruler of your people you should speak no ill.'"

[6] Noticing that some of those present were Sadducees and others Pharisees, Paul called out in the Council: "Brothers, I am a Pharisee and a son of Pharisees. It is on the question of hope for the dead and of their resurrection that I am on trial."

[7] As soon as he said this, a dispute arose between the Pharisees and the Sadducees; and there was a sharp division of opinion among those present. [8] (For Sadducees say there is no such thing as a resurrection, and that there is neither angel nor spirit, while Pharisees believe in both.) [9] So a great uproar ensued, and some of the scholars belonging to the Pharisees' party stood up and hotly protested: "We

find nothing whatever wrong in this person. Suppose a spirit did speak to him, or an angel." [10] The dispute was becoming so violent that the commanding officer, fearing that Paul would be torn in pieces between them, ordered the guard to go down and rescue him from them, and take him into the fort.

[11] That night the Lord came and stood by Paul, and said: "Courage! You have borne witness for me in Jerusalem and you must bear witness in Rome also." [12] In the morning some Judean men combined together, and took an oath that they would not eat or drink until they had killed Paul. [13] There were more than forty in the plot; [14] and they went to the chief priests and the elders, and said: "We have taken a solemn oath not to touch food until we have killed Paul. [15] So we want you now, with the consent of the Council, to suggest to the commanding officer that he should bring Paul down before you, as though you intended to go more fully into his case; but before he comes here, we will be ready to make away with him."

[16] However, the son of Paul's sister, hearing of the plot, went to the fort, and on being admitted, told Paul about it. [17] Paul called one of the captains of the garrison and asked him to take the lad to the commanding officer, as he had something to tell him. [18] The captain went with the young man to the commanding officer, and said: "The prisoner Paul called me and asked me to bring this lad to you, as he has something to tell you."

[19] The commanding officer took the young man by the hand, and, stepping aside, asked what it was he had to tell him. [20] "Some men have agreed," answered the lad, "to ask you to bring Paul down before the Council tomorrow, on the plea of your making further inquiry into his case. [21] But do not let them persuade you, for more than forty of them are lying in wait for him, who have taken an oath that they

will not eat or drink until they have made away with him; and they are at this very moment in readiness, counting on your promise." [22] The commanding officer then dismissed the young man, cautioning him not to mention to anybody that he had given him that information. [23] Then he called two captains, and ordered them to have two hundred soldiers ready to go to Caesarea, as well as seventy troopers and two hundred lancers, by nine o'clock that night, [24] and to have horses ready for Paul to ride, so that they might take him safely to Felix, the governor. [25] He also wrote a letter along these lines:

[26] "Claudius Lysias sends his compliments to His Excellency Felix the Governor. [27] The man whom I send with this had been seized by some Judeans, and was on the point of being killed by them, when I came upon them with the force under my command, and rescued him, as I learned that he was a Roman citizen. [28] Wanting to know exactly the basis of the charges they made against him, I brought him before their Council, [29] when I found that their charges were connected with questions of their own Law, and that there was nothing alleged involving either death or imprisonment. [30] Having, however, information of a plot against the man, which was about to be put into execution, I am sending him to you at once, and I have also directed his accusers to prosecute him before you."

[31] The soldiers, in accordance with their orders, took charge of Paul and conducted him by night to Antipatris; [32] and on the next day, leaving the troopers to go on with him, they returned to the fort. [33] On arriving at Caesarea, the troopers delivered the letter to the governor, and brought Paul before him. [34] As soon as Felix had read the letter, he inquired to what province Paul belonged, and, learning that he came from Cilicia, he said: [35] "I will hear all you have to say as soon as your accusers have arrived." And he ordered Paul

to be kept under guard in Herod's government house.

24 [1] Five days afterward the high priest Ananias came down with some of the elders and a lawyer named Tertullus. They presented evidence with the governor against Paul; [2] and, when the hearing commenced, Tertullus began his speech for the prosecution. [3] "We owe it to your Excellency," he said, "that we are enjoying profound peace, and we owe it to your foresight that this nation is constantly securing reforms — advantages which we very gratefully accept at all times and places. [4] But — not to be tedious — I beg you, with your accustomed fairness, to listen to a brief statement of our case. [5] We have found this man a public pest; he is one who stirs up disputes among our people all the world over, and is a ringleader of the Nazarene devotees. [6] He even attempted to desecrate the Temple itself, but we caught him; [8] and you will be able, by examining him on all these points, to satisfy yourself as to the charges which we are bringing against him."

[9] The Judean crowd also joined in the attack and bore out his statements. [10] On a sign from the governor, Paul made this reply:

"Knowing, as I do, for how many years you have acted as judge to this nation, it is with confidence that I undertake my own defense. [11] For you can easily verify that it is not more than twelve days ago that I went up to worship at Jerusalem, [12] where my prosecutors never found me holding discussions with anyone, or causing a crowd to collect — either in the Temple, or in the synagogues, or about the city; [13] and they cannot establish the charges which they are now making against me. [14] This, however, I do acknowledge to you, that it is as one who trusts in the Way, which they describe as contentious, that I worship the God of my ancestors. At the same time, I believe everything that is in accordance with the Law and that is written in the prophets; [15] and I have a hope that rests in God — a hope which they also cherish — that there will one day be a resurrection of good and bad alike. [16] This being so, I strive at all times to keep my conscience clear before both God and people. [17] After some years' absence I had come to bring relief money to my nation, and to make offerings; [18] and it was while engaged in this that they found me in the Temple, after completing a period of purification, but not with any crowd or disorder. [19] There were, however, some Judeans from Roman Asia who ought to have been here before you, and to have made any charge that they may have against me — [20] or else let my opponents here say what they found wrong in me when I was before the Council, [21] except as to the one sentence that I shouted out as I stood among them: 'It is about the resurrection of the dead that I am on trial before you today.'"

[22] Felix, however, adjourned the case — though he had a fairly accurate knowledge of all that concerned the cause — with the promise: "When Lysias, the commanding officer, comes down, I will give my decision in your case." [23] So he gave orders to the captain in charge of Paul to keep him in custody, but to relax the regulations, and not to prevent any of his personal friends from attending to his wants.

[24] Some days later Felix came with his wife Drusilla, who was herself a Judeaness, and, sending for Paul, listened to what he had to say about faith in Christ Jesus. [25] But while Paul was speaking at length about righteousness, self-control, and the coming judgment, Felix started to be afraid, and interrupted him: "Go for the present, but when I find an opportunity, I will send for you again." [26] He was hoping, too, for a bribe from Paul, and so he used to send for him frequently and talk with

him. ²⁷ But after the lapse of two years, Felix was succeeded by Porcius Festus; and, wishing to gain popularity with the Judean leaders, he left Paul a prisoner.

25 ¹ Three days after Festus had arrived in his province, he left Caesarea and went up to Jerusalem. ² There the chief priests and the leaders among the Judeans presented an argument before him against Paul, ³ and asked a favor of him, to Paul's injury — to have Paul brought to Jerusalem. All the while they were plotting to make away with him on the road. ⁴ But Festus answered that Paul was in prison at Caesarea, and that he himself would be leaving for that place shortly.

⁵ "So let the powerful people among you," he said, "go down with me, and if there is anything amiss in the man, charge him formally with it." ⁶ After staying among them some eight or ten days, Festus went down to Caesarea. The next day he took his seat on the bench, and ordered Paul to be brought before him. ⁷ On Paul's appearance, the Judean leaders who had come down from Jerusalem surrounded him, and made many serious charges, which they failed to establish. ⁸ Paul's answer to the charge was: "I have not committed any offense against the Judean Law, or the Temple, or the emperor." ⁹ But as Festus wished to gain popularity with the Judeans, he interrupted Paul with the question:

"Are you willing to go up to Jerusalem and be tried on these charges before me there?"

¹⁰ "No," replied Paul, "I am standing at the emperor's court, where I ought to be tried. I have not wronged the Judeans, as you yourself are well aware. ¹¹ If, however, I am breaking the law and have committed any offense deserving death, I do not ask to escape the penalty; but if there is nothing in the accusations of these people, no one has the power to give me up to them. I appeal to the emperor."

¹² Festus, after conferring with his Council, answered: "You have appealed to the emperor; to the emperor you will go."

¹³ Some days later King Agrippa and Bernice came down to Caesarea, and paid a visit of congratulation to Festus; ¹⁴ and, as they were staying there for several days, Festus laid Paul's case before the king. "There is a man here," he said, "left a prisoner by Felix, ¹⁵ about whom, when I came to Jerusalem, the Judean chief priest and the elders presented evidence, demanding judgment against him. ¹⁶ My answer to them was, that it was not the practice of Romans to give up anyone to his accusers until the accused had met them face-to-face, and had also had an opportunity of answering the charges brought against him. ¹⁷ So they met here, and without loss of time I took my seat on the bench the very next day, and ordered the man to be brought before me. ¹⁸ But when his accusers came forward, they brought no charge of wrongdoing such as I had expected; ¹⁹ but I found that there were certain questions in dispute between them about their own practices, and about some dead man called Jesus, whom Paul declared to be alive. ²⁰ And, as I was at a loss how to inquire into questions of this kind, I asked Paul if he were willing to go up to Jerusalem, and be put on trial there. ²¹ Paul, however, appealed to have his case reserved for the consideration of his August Majesty, so I ordered him to be detained in custody, until I could send him to the emperor."

²² "I should like to hear this man myself," Agrippa said to Festus.

"You will hear him tomorrow," Festus answered.

²³ So the next day, when Agrippa and Bernice had come in full state and had entered the Audience Chamber, with the superior officers and the principal people of the city, by the order of Festus Paul was brought before them. ²⁴ Then Festus said: "King Agrippa, and all here present, you

see before you the man about whom the whole Judean people have applied to me, both at Jerusalem and here, loudly asserting that he ought not to be allowed to live. [25] I found, however, that he had not done anything deserving death; so, as he had himself appealed to his August Majesty, I decided to send him. [26] But I have nothing definite to write about him to my Imperial Master; and for that reason I have brought him before you all, and especially before you, King Agrippa, that, after examining him, I may have something to write. [27] For it seems to me absurd to send a prisoner without at the same time stating the charges made against him."

26 [1] Turning to Paul, Agrippa said: "You are at liberty to speak for yourself." Then Paul stretched out his hand and began his defense. [2] "I have been congratulating myself, King Agrippa," he said, "that it is before you that I have to make my defense today, with regard to all the charges brought against me by my own people, [3] especially as you are so well versed in all the customs and questions of the Judean world. I beg you therefore to give me a patient hearing. [4] My life, then, from youth upward, was passed, from the very first, among my own nation, and in Jerusalem, and is within the knowledge of all Judeans; [5] and they have always known — if they choose to give evidence — that, in accordance with the very strictest form of our traditions, I lived as a true Pharisee. [6] Even now, it is because of my hope in the promise given by God to our ancestors that I stand here on trial — [7] a promise which our twelve tribes, by earnest service night and day, hope to see fulfilled. It is for this hope, your Majesty, that I am accused — and by Judeans themselves! [8] Why do you all hold it incredible that God should raise the dead? [9] I myself, it is true, once thought it my duty to oppose in every way the name of Jesus of Nazareth; [10] and I actually did so at Jerusalem. Acting on the authority of

the chief priests, I myself threw many of these holy people into prison, and, when it was proposed to put them to death, I gave my vote for it. [11] Time after time, in every synagogue, I tried by punishments to force them to blaspheme. So frantic was I against them that I pursued them even to towns beyond our borders. [12] It was while I was traveling to Damascus on an errand of this kind, entrusted with full powers by the chief priests, [13] that at midday, your Majesty, I saw right in my path, coming from the heavens, a light brighter than the glare of the sun, which shone all around me and those traveling with me. [14] We all fell to the ground, and then I heard a voice saying to me in Hebrew: 'Saul, Saul, why are you persecuting me? By kicking against the goad you are punishing yourself.' [15] 'Who are you, Lord?' I asked. And the Lord said: 'I am Jesus, whom you are persecuting; [16] but get up and stand upright; for I have appeared to you in order to appoint you a servant and a witness of those revelations of me which you have already had, and of those in which I will yet appear to you, [17] since I am choosing you out from your own people and from the gentiles, to whom I now send you, [18] to open their eyes, and to turn them from darkness to light, and from the power of Satan to God; so that they may receive pardon for their sins, and a place among those who have become God's people, by faith in me.' [19] After that, King Agrippa, I did not fail to obey the heavenly vision; [20] on the contrary, first to those at Damascus and Jerusalem, and then through the whole of Judea, and to the gentiles as well, I began to preach repentance and conversion to God, and a life befitting that repentance. [21] This is why some men seized me in the Temple, and made attempts on my life. [22] However, I have received help from God to this very day, and so stand here, and bear my testimony to high and low alike — without adding a word to what the prophets, as well as Moses, declared should happen — [23] that the Anointed One must suffer, and that by rising from the dead, he was destined to be the first to bring news of light, not only to our nation, but also to the gentiles."

[24] While Paul was making this defense, Festus called out loudly: "You are mad, Paul; your great learning is driving you mad."

[25] "I am not mad, your Excellency," he replied; "on the contrary, the statements that I am making are true and sober. [26] Indeed, the king knows about these matters, so I speak before him without constraint. I am sure that there is nothing whatever of what I have been telling him that has escaped his attention; for all this has not been done in a corner. [27] King Agrippa, do you believe the prophets? I know you do."

[28] But Agrippa said to Paul: "You are soon trying to make a Christian of me!"

[29] "Whether it is soon or late," answered Paul, "I pray to God that not only you, but all who are listening to me, might today become just what I am myself — except for these chains!" [30] Then the king rose, with the governor and Bernice and those who had been sitting with them, [31] and, after retiring, discussed the case among themselves. "There is nothing," they said, "deserving death or imprisonment in this man's conduct"; [32] and, speaking to Festus, Agrippa added: "The man might have been discharged, if he had not appealed to the emperor."

27 [1] As it was decided that we were to sail to Italy, Paul and some other prisoners were put in charge of a captain of the Augustan Guard, named Julius. [2] We went on board a ship from Adramyttium, which was on the point of sailing to the ports along the coast of Roman Asia, and put to sea. Aristarchus, a Macedonian from Thessalonica, went with us. [3] The next day we put in to Sidon, where Julius treated Paul in a friendly manner, and allowed him to go to see his friends and receive their hospitality. [4] Putting to sea again, we sailed under the lee of Cyprus, because the wind was against us; [5] and, after crossing the sea of Cilicia and Pamphylia, we reached Myra in Lycia. [6] There the Roman officer found an Alexandrian ship on her way to Italy, and put us on board of her. [7] For several days our progress was slow, and it was only with difficulty that we arrived off Cnidus. As the wind was still unfavorable when we came off Cape Salmone, we sailed under the lee of Crete, [8] and with difficulty, by keeping close in shore, we reached a place called "Fair Havens," near which was the town of Lasea.

[9] This had taken a considerable time, and sailing was already dangerous, for the fast was already over; and so Paul gave this warning. [10] "My friends," he said, "I see that this voyage will be attended with injury and much damage, not only to the cargo and the ship, but to our own lives also."

[11] The Roman officer, however, was more influenced by the captain and the owner than by what was said by Paul. [12] And, as the harbor was not a suitable one to winter in, the majority were in favor of continuing the voyage, in hope of being able to reach Phoenix, and winter there. Phoenix was a Cretan harbor, open to the northeast and southeast. [13] So, when a light wind sprang up from the south, thinking that they had found their opportunity, they weighed anchor and kept along the coast of Crete, close in shore. [14] But shortly afterward a hurricane came down on us off the land — a northeaster, as it is called. [15] The ship was caught by it and was unable to keep her head to the wind, so we had to give way and let her drive before it. [16] Running under the lee of a small island called Cauda, we only just managed to secure the ship's boat, [17] and, after hoisting it on board, the men frapped the ship. But, afraid of being driven on to the Syrtis Sands, they lowered the yard,

and then drifted. [18] So violently were we tossed about by the storm that the next day they began throwing the cargo overboard, [19] and, on the following day, threw out the ship's tackle with their own hands. [20] As neither sun nor stars were visible for several days, and as the gale still continued severe, all hope of our being saved was at last abandoned.

[21] It was then, when they had gone a long time without food, that Paul came forward, and said: "My friends, you should have listened to me, and not have sailed from Crete and so incurred this injury and damage. [22] Yet, even as things are, I beg you not to lose courage, for there will not be a single life lost among you — only the ship. [23] For last night an angel of the God to whom I belong, and whom I serve, stood by me, and said: [24] 'Have no fear, Paul; you must appear before the emperor, and God himself has given you the lives of all sailing with you.' [25] Therefore, courage, my friends! For I believe God, that everything will happen exactly as I have been told. [26] We will, however, have to be driven on some island."

[27] It was now the fourteenth night of the storm, and we were drifting about in the Adriatic Sea, when, about midnight, the sailors began to suspect that they were drawing near land. [28] So they took soundings, and found twenty fathoms of water. After waiting a little, they took soundings again, and found fifteen fathoms. [29] Then, as they were afraid of our being driven on some rocky coast, they let go four anchors from the stern, and longed for daylight. [30] The sailors wanted to leave the ship, and had lowered the boat, on pretense of running out anchors from the bows, [31] when Paul said to the Roman officer and his men: "Unless the sailors remain on board, you cannot be saved." [32] So the soldiers cut the ropes which held the boat, and let her drift away. [33] In the interval before daybreak Paul kept urging them all to take something to eat.

"It is a fortnight today," he said, "that, owing to your anxiety, you have gone without food, taking nothing. [34] So I beg you to take something to eat; your safety depends on it, for not one of you will lose even a hair of his head." [35] With these words he took some bread, and, after saying the thanksgiving to God before them all, broke it in pieces, and began to eat; [36] and the men all felt cheered and had something to eat themselves. [37] There were about seventy-six of us on board, all told. [38] After satisfying their hunger, they further lightened the ship by throwing the grain into the sea. [39] When daylight came, they could not make out what land it was, but, observing a creek in which there was a beach, they consulted as to whether they could run the ship safely into it. [40] Then they cast off, and abandoned the anchors, and at the same time unlashed the gear of the steering oars, hoisted the foresail to the wind, and made for the beach. [41] They got, however, into a kind of channel, and there ran the ship aground. The bows stuck fast and could not be moved, while the stern began breaking up under the strain. [42] The advice of the soldiers was that the prisoners should be killed, so that none of them could swim away and make their escape. [43] But the Roman officer, anxious to save Paul, prevented their carrying out their intention, and ordered that those who could swim should be the first to jump into the sea and try to reach the shore; [44] and that the rest should follow, some on planks, and others on different pieces of the ship. In these various ways everyone managed to get safely ashore.

28

[1] When we were all safe, we found that the island was called Malta. [2] The island's people showed us marked kindness, for they lit a fire and took us all under shelter, because it had come on to rain and was cold. [3] Paul had gathered a quantity of dry sticks and laid them on the fire, when a poisonous snake, driven out by the heat,

fastened on his hand. [4] When the islanders saw the creature hanging from his hand, they said to one another: "Evidently this person is a murderer, for though he has been saved from the sea, Justice has not allowed him to live." [5] However, Paul shook the creature off into the fire and took no harm. [6] The islanders were expecting inflammation to set in, or that he would suddenly fall dead; but after waiting for a long time, and seeing that there was nothing amiss with him, they changed their minds and said that he was a god.

[7] In that neighborhood there was an estate belonging to the head of the island, whose name was Publius. He took us up to his house, and for three days entertained us most courteously. [8] It happened that the father of Publius was lying ill of fever and dysentery. So Paul went to see him; and, after praying, he placed his hands on him and healed him. [9] After this, all the people in the island who had any illness came to Paul, and were healed. [10] They also presented us with many gifts, and when we set sail they put necessary supplies on board.

[11] After three months, we set sail in a ship that had wintered in the island. She was an Alexandrian vessel, and had the twin sons of Zeus for her figurehead. [12] We put in at Syracuse and stayed there three days, [13] and from there we worked to windward and so got to Rhegium. A day later a south wind sprang up and took us to Puteoli in two days. [14] There we found some of the Lord's followers, and were urged to stay a week with them; after which we went on to Rome. [15] The followers there had heard about us, and came out as far as the Market of Appius and the Three Taverns to meet us. At the sight of them Paul thanked God and was much cheered. [16] On our reaching Rome, Paul was allowed to live by himself, except for the soldier who was in charge of him.

[17] Three days after our arrival, Paul invited the leading Judeans to meet him; and, when they came, he said: "Brothers, although I had done nothing hostile to the interests of our nation or to our ancestral customs, yet I was sent from Jerusalem as a prisoner, and handed over to the Romans. [18] The Romans, when they had examined me, were ready to release me, because there was nothing in my conduct deserving death. [19] But as the Judean leaders opposed my release, I was compelled to appeal to the emperor — not, indeed, that I had any charge to make against my own nation. [20] This, then, is my reason for urging you to come to see me and talk with me; because it is for the sake of the hope of Israel that I am here in chains."

[21] "We," was their reply, "have not had any letter about you from Judea, nor have any of our fellow Judeans come and reported or said anything bad about you. [22] But we will be glad to hear from you what your views are, for, with regard to this sect, we are well aware that it is spoken against on all sides."

[23] They then fixed a day with him, and came to the place where he was staying, in even larger numbers, when Paul proceeded to lay the subject before them. He bore his testimony to the realm of God, and tried to convince them about Jesus, by arguments drawn from the Law of Moses and from the prophets — speaking from morning until evening. [24] Some were inclined to accept what he said; others, however, rejected it. [25] So, as they disagreed among themselves, they began to disperse, Paul adding only:

"True, indeed, was the declaration made by the holy Spirit, through the prophet Isaiah to your ancestors:

[26] 'Go to this nation and say,
    "You will hear with your ears without
        ever understanding,
    and, though you have eyes, you will
        see without ever perceiving."
[27] For the mind of this nation has grown
        dense,

and their ears are dull of hearing,
their eyes also have they closed;
otherwise someday they might see
     with their eyes,
and with their ears they might
     hear,
and in their mind they might
     understand, and might turn —
and I might heal them.'

[28] "Understand, then, that this salvation of God was sent for the gentiles; and they will listen."

[30] For two whole years Paul stayed in a house which he rented for himself, welcoming all who came to see him, [31] proclaiming the realm of God, and teaching about the Lord Jesus Christ, with perfect fearlessness, unmolested.

GOSPELS, POEMS, AND SONGS
BETWEEN HEAVEN AND EARTH

An Introduction to the First Book of
the Odes of Solomon

T HE ODES OF SOLOMON are simultaneously one of the most significant discoveries of early Christian literature and one of the most ignored discoveries of early Christian literature in the past two hundred years. Found in piles of research in a well-traveled and expert scholar's office in the early twentieth century, they have been published since shortly after their "discovery." They are indisputably the largest trove of early Christian worship material ever found in one document, which is almost a third the size of the Bible's book of 150 psalms. The New Orleans Council eagerly chose to include these odes, both for their beautiful and evocative language and in order to make *A New New Testament* a strong witness to actual material from the worship of some early Christ movements.

These forty-one "songs" of early Christianity are most likely a collection from different communities over a period of time and therefore have no unified authorship. However, they do represent a certain kind of early Christianity in their beliefs, practices, and ways of framing the world. They look and sound very much like the psalms of the Hebrew scriptures, except that they have regular references to the Word, the Light, the Lord, and the Son of God in ways that indicate that they belong to some kind of Christ movement; that is, they are definitely "psalms" of a "Christian" character, although they never use the name "Jesus," and rarely even the title "Christ" or "Anointed One."

The title, "The Odes of Solomon" — probably added to the document later than its assemblage — cannot, of course, refer to the author of this collection (since Solomon lived a thousand years before) but serves rather as an affirmation of a strong and intimate connection between this part of early "Christianity" and the traditions of Israel. This document represents a collection of different odes from different communities, making "Solomon" something like the psalms' figure of "David." It is also difficult to identify a date of composition for the odes. Most commentators think they came early, with the past thirty years of scholarship pointing more toward the first century than the second. The place of composition is also unclear. The closeness to the psalms of the Hebrew scriptures suggests a "Christ" movement with very strong ties to the traditions of Israel. The odes' language of Syriac points toward Syria. It is not clear whether the odes were ever transcribed in Greek or Aramaic, but the fine poetic style indicates a real possibility that they may originally have been in Syriac.

The "Christ" figure often speaks in these odes, which means that early Christ people who sang them took on the identity of "Christ." This identification of the singers with the "Christ" is complemented by the content of the odes in which the "Christ" is a cosmic figure who makes humans one with God.

Because the odes, as a collection, do not represent one authorship, the New Orleans Council proposed that they could be broken up into distinct smaller collections; in *A New New Testament* four distinct parts of the Odes of Solomon are placed with different groups of documents. In keeping with the council's and my interest in making the reading of *A New New Testament* as worshipful as possible, these groups provide a spiritual preamble to the documents that follow. The First Book of the Odes of Solomon contains Odes 1 and 3–12 (Ode 2 was missing from the manuscript). The second book contain Odes 13–22; the third, Odes 23–32; and the fourth, Odes 33–42.

The First Book of the Odes of Solomon bubbles over with creative combinations of voices. It has a variety of perspectives on the relationships of the author(s) of the odes, the Christ figure, and God. Some of these odes are spoken and/or sung in the voice of the composer. Others are in the voice of the Christ and in the first person. Still others are probably in the first person of God. Some are spoken in the third person as a description of the relationship between God and the human singer(s). And some shift from one voice to the other in the middle of the song. In this way the reader/singer of these odes experiences them as a kind of multivoiced chorus in which various solos emerge and recede.

Ode 3 is a love poem to the "Lord." In this case, the "Lord" is the Christ figure, and the love between the composer or singer(s) and the Lord is expressed as a unification: "Because I love the one who is the Child, I will become a child" (3:7b). Odes 11 (in the first person) and 12 (in the third person) also express a merging of two persons in love. It is not completely clear whether these two persons are the "Christ" and God, the odist and the "Christ," or the odist and God. It is quite possible that these odes are meant to evoke all of these communions between persons.

Ode 8 opens with seven verses of invitation to praise. Then the voice changes to that of the "Christ," who speaks directly of his experience, and who also invites humans to "recognize my knowledge" and "love me with gentleness" (8:11). The direct invitation from "Christ" for such a loving relationship becomes more intimate as "he" describes the origins and substance of this relationship:

Even from before, when they did not yet exist,
I knew them,
And I imprinted a seal on their faces.
I fashioned their members,
And I presented my own breasts for them,
So they could drink my own consecrated milk, that through it
    they might live. (8:13–14)

Here, too, the communion of the Christ with those singing the odes becomes particularly intense as the worshipers sing in the voice of the Christ inviting them to love him and receive his nourishment.

Overall, these eleven odes ring with enthusiasm and happiness in the merging relationship of God, "Christ," and human. As Ode 7 says, "The course of Joy over the Beloved . . . produces of her fruits without obstacle" (7:1). Many twenty-first-century readers will find in these odes an almost ecstatic combination of human and divine perspectives. The interweaving of the voices calls forth the possibility of real music. Because the actual first- or second-century music for these odes has been lost, they beckon now for twenty-first-century melodies that match the powerful combination of realities portrayed in the words.

Recommended Reading

James Charlesworth, *The Odes of Solomon: The Syriac Texts Edited with Translation and Notes*
M. Franzmann, *The Odes of Solomon: An Analysis of the Poetical Structure and Form*
J. R. Harris and A. Mingana, *The Odes and Psalms of Solomon*

The First Book of the Odes of Solomon

Ode 1

¹ The Lord is upon my head like a crown,
   And I will not be without him.
² The crown of truth was braided for me
   And caused your branches to bloom
within me.
³ For it is not a barren crown that never
blooms
⁴ But you live upon my head
   And blossomed down upon me.
⁵ Your fruits are full and overflowing
   They are full of your salvation.

Ode 3

¹ I put on the love* of the Lord
² And his members are with him,
   And I am raised up by them, and he
loves me.
³ Indeed I would not have known [how]
to love the Lord,
   Except that he had continuously loved
me.
⁴ Who is able to recognize love
   Except the one who has been loved?
⁵² I cherish the Beloved and my whole self
loves him and
   Wherever his rest is, I am also there.
⁶ I will not be rejected,
   Because there is no suspicion with
the Lord, the Most High and Compassionate.
⁷ I have been joined [to the Lord] because
the lover has found the one who is beloved,
   Because I love the one who is the Child,
I will become a child.

⁸ Truly, whoever is united to the one who
does not die, neither will he die.
⁹ And the one who delights in the Life will
become alive.
¹⁰ This is the Spirit of the Lord, who is not
deceitful,
   Who instructs humanity† so that they
might recognize his paths.
¹¹ Be wise, understanding, and awakened.
Halleluiah.

Ode 4

¹ My God, no one conceals your holy
place,
   Nor will anyone change it and put it in
another place,
² Because there is no one ruling over it,
   Indeed you conceived of your sanctuary before you made the [other] places.
³ The older one will not be overshadowed
by those who are younger than it.
   Lord, you have given your heart to the
ones who have faith.
⁴ You will never be empty,
   Nor will you be without fruits.
⁵ For one moment of your faith
   Is more excellent than all of the days
and years.
⁶ For who will put on your bounty and
still be denied?
⁷ Because your seal‡ is known,
   And your creatures are known to it.
⁸ And your forces hold it,
   The great chosen angels are clothed
with it.
⁹ You have given us your intimacy;

---

* This type of love is deeply intertwined with compassion; meaning changes only with different
conjugations.
† Literally, "sons of men."
‡ This can sometimes indicate the cross.

It was not that you were lost from us,
  But rather that we were lost from you.
¹⁰ Sprinkle upon us your drops,
  And open your abundant springs,
which flow [with] milk and honey for us.
¹¹ Indeed there is no regret with you,
  Such that you would lament over anything which you have promised,
¹² But the result was clear to you.
¹³ Surely what you have given, you have
given freely,
  So that you will not change and take
them back again later.
¹⁴ For as God, everything was clear to you,
  And was established in the beginning
in your presence.
¹⁵ You, Lord, have made all.
Halleluiah.

Ode 5

¹ Lord, I profess you
  Because I love you.
² Most High, do not abandon me,
  Because you are my hope.
³ I have freely received your kindness,
  May I be kept alive by it.
⁴ My tormentors will come; do not let
them see me.
⁵ Let a cloud of darkness fall over their
eyes,
  And a vapor of dark mist eclipse them.
⁶ And let there be no light for them, by
which they might see,
  So that they will not seize me.
⁷ Let their mind become swollen,
  And let whatever they have devised return upon their own heads.
⁸ Truly they have devised a judgment,
  But it was not for them [to do].*
⁹ They prepared themselves wickedly,
  And they were found empty.
¹⁰ Indeed my hope is upon the Lord,

I will not fear.
¹¹ And because the Lord is my redemption,
  I will not fear.
¹² And he is as a crown upon my head,
  I will not be moved.
¹³ And even if everything else should be
shaken,
  I will stand.
¹⁴ If whatever is visible should perish,
  I will not die,
¹⁵ Because the Lord is with me,
  And I am with him.

Ode 6

¹ As the wind passes through the lyre,
  The strings speak.
² So also the spirit† of the Lord speaks
through my members,
  And I speak through his love.
³ For he ruins whatever is rejected,
  Yet everything is of the Lord.
⁴ Indeed it was so from the beginning,
  And [will be] until the end.
⁵ So that nothing will be hostile,
  And nothing will rise up against
him.
⁶ The Lord increased his knowledge
  He was eager that those things which
have been given to us through his kindness be known.
⁷ And he gave his glory to us, on account
of his name.
  Our spirits praise his holy Spirit.
⁸ For a stream went out, and became a
river, great and broad.
  Truly it flooded everything, broke it up,
and brought it to the Temple.
⁹ Neither were the impediments of hu-
manity‡ able to dam it,
  Nor the skills of those who usually restrain waters.

---

* I believe the odist means that the tormentors have assumed a duty that was not their own.
† This noun is identical to what I have translated as "wind."
‡ Literally, "sons of men."

¹⁰ For it came over the whole face of the earth,
  And filled everything.
¹¹ All of the thirsty ones upon the earth drank,
  And the thirst was diminished and quenched.
¹² The drink was given from the Most High,
¹³ Therefore, happy are the ministers* of that drink,
  Those who have been trusted with his waters.
¹⁴ They have revived dry lips,
  And raised the broken will.
¹⁵ And the lives that were near passing away,
  They held back from death.
¹⁶ And the members that have fallen,
  They have set right and sustained.
¹⁷ They gave strength to their coming,
  And light for their eyes,
¹⁸ Because everyone recognized them in the Lord,
  And they lived in the living water of eternity.
Halleluiah.

Ode 7

¹ As the course of anger over irreverence
  So also is the course of Joy over the Beloved
  Which produces of her† fruits without obstacle.
² My joy is the Lord and my course is toward him,
  My journey is beautiful.
³ For there is a helper for me, the Lord.
  He has made his entire self known to me, without grudge, by extension.
  Indeed his kindness has shrunk his immensity.

⁴ He became like me, so that I might receive him.
  He seemed like me in form so that I would put him on.
⁵ So I did not tremble when I saw him,
  Because he was compassionate to me.
⁶ He became like my [own] nature, so that I might join with him,
  And as my image so that I would not turn back from him.
⁷ The Father of perception
  Is the word of understanding.
⁸ The one who created wisdom
  Is wiser than the creations.
⁹ The one who created me when I did not exist,
  Knew what I would do while I existed.
¹⁰ Because of this, that one was compassionate to me with abundant mercy,
  And allowed me to seek him, to receive from his own sacrifice,
¹¹ Because he is the one who is not consumed,
  The whole burnt offering of the generations, and their Father.
¹² The Father has the Lord appear to those who are his own,
  So that they might recognize the one who made them,
  So that they might not suppose that they exist of themselves.
¹³ For he has set his way to knowledge.
  Expanded her, lengthened her, brought her to all fullness,
¹⁴ And set over her traces of light,
  She went out from the beginning until the end.
¹⁵ For the Lord was cultivated by the Father,
  And was pleased with the child.
¹⁶ Because of his breaking loose‡ the Lord will contain everything,

---

* In the sense of both "management" and "holy service."
† Refers to "course."
‡ This can also mean "salvation," "redemption," "ransom."

And the Most High will be recognized in the consecrated ones:

¹⁷ To announce to those who have songs of the coming of the Lord,

So that they may go out to meet him and praise him.

¹⁸ The ones who see will go out before him,

And they will be seen before him.

¹⁹ They will praise the Lord through love,

Because he is near and sees.

²⁰ Also hate will be removed from the earth,

And will sink alongside jealousy.

²¹ For ignorance was destroyed by her,

Because the recognition of the Lord came to her.*

²² Let the singers sing of the kindness of the Lord Most High,

Let them bring their psalms.

²³ Let their hearts be as the day,

And their chants as the great beauty of the Lord.

²⁴ Let there be no one that is without knowledge,

And who is without voice.

²⁵ For he gave a mouth to creation,

To open the voice of the mouth toward him

And praise him.

²⁶ Acknowledge his strength,

Demonstrate his kindness.

Ode 8

¹ Open; open your hearts to the dancing joy of the Lord

And let your love abound from heart to lips:

² In order to bring forth fruits for the Lord, a holy life,

And to speak with attention in his light.

³ Stand and be restored,

All of you who were once flattened.

⁴ Speak, you who were silent,

Because your mouth has been opened.

⁵ From now on be lifted up, you who were destroyed

Since your justice has been raised.

⁶ For the Right Hand of the Lord is with you all,

And she will be a helper for you.

⁷ Peace was prepared for you,

Before what may be your war.

[Christ speaks]

⁸ Hear the word of truth, and

Receive the knowledge of the Most High.

⁹ Your flesh may not understand what I say to you,

Nor your clothing what I show you.

¹⁰ Keep my mystery, you who are kept by it.

Keep my faith, you who are kept by it.

¹¹ Recognize my knowledge, you who, in truth, know me.

Love me with gentleness, those who love.

¹² For I do not turn my face from my own,

Because I recognize them.

¹³ Even from before, when they did not yet exist,

I knew them,

And I imprinted a seal on their faces.

¹⁴ I fashioned their members,

And I presented my own breasts for them,

So they could drink my own consecrated milk, that through it they might live.

¹⁵ I am delighted by them,

And am not confused by them.

¹⁶ For they are my own creation,

The force of my thoughts.

¹⁷ Who, therefore, will stand against my creation?

Moreover, who is defiant to them?

¹⁸ I willed and formed both mind and heart,

And they are my own,

---

* Refers to "earth."

By my own Right Hand I have written my chosen things.

¹⁹ My justice goes before them,

They will not be separated from my name

Because it is with them.

[Odist speaks]

²⁰ Seek and satiate [them],

And remain in the compassion of the Lord,

²¹ Those who are loved by the beloved,

And those who are protected by the one who lives,

And who are released by the one who was broken.

²² You shall be found without corruption in all the generations,

On account of the name of your Father. Halleluiah.

Ode 9

¹ Open your ears,

And I will speak to you.

² Give your entire self to me,

So that I may give my entire self to you.

³ The word of the Lord and his desires,

The holy thought which he has considered about his Anointed One.

⁴ For your lives are in the will of the Lord,

His consciousness is the life of eternity,

And your fullness is without corruption.

⁵ Grow rich in God the Father,

And receive the understanding of the Most High;

Be strong, and be saved by his abundance.

⁶ Indeed I announce peace to you, his unstained ones,

So that those of you who listen, do not fall in war.

⁷ Moreover that those who know him will not perish,

And that those who have received will not be confused.

⁸ Truth is an eternal crown,

Happy are those who set it upon their head.

⁹ It is a precious, heavy stone,

In fact the wars were because of the crown.

¹⁰ Justice has taken it,

And given it to you.

¹¹ Set the crown in the true covenant of the Lord,

And all of those who are blameless will be inscribed in his book.

¹² For their book is your victory,

And she sees you before her, and desires that you will be redeemed. Halleluiah.

Ode 10

¹ The Lord has directed my mouth with his word,

And opened my heart with his light.

² And he has caused his immortal life to dwell in me,

And allowed me to sound the fruit of his peace.

³ In order to restore the lives of those willing to come to him,

And to capture a precious captivity to freedom.

[Christ speaks]

⁴ I grew up and became strong and the world was taken captive,

It was for me, for the glory of the Most High and of God, my Father.

⁵ The peoples who had been scattered were gathered,

Yet I was not defiled by my affections,*

Because they praised me in the heights.

⁶ And vestiges of light were established upon their hearts,

And they lived according to my life and they were saved,

---

* This same root can mean "sin," and it is likely that both meanings are intended.

And they became my people* forever. Halleluiah.

Ode 11

¹ My heart was circumcised, and its flower appeared,
 And in it kindness sprouted,
 And produced fruits for the Lord.
² For the Most High circumcised me with his holy Spirit,
 He revealed to him [self] my innermost parts,
 And filled me from his love.
³ The Lord's circumcising was a redemption for me,
 And I ran in the path, in his peace,
 In the way of Truth.
⁴ From the beginning and until the end
 I received his knowledge.
⁵ I was established upon the rock of Truth,
 Where he set me.
⁶ Then speaking waters from the fountain of the Lord
 Touched my lips, without envy.
⁷ I drank, and I was intoxicated
 By the living waters that do not die.
⁸ But my intoxication was not without knowledge,
 Rather I abandoned emptiness.
⁹ I turned toward the Most High, my God,
 And I flourished in his gifts.
¹⁰ I abandoned the insanity cast down upon the earth,
 Stripped it off, and threw it away from me.
¹¹ Then the Lord renewed me in his garment,
 And established me in his light.
¹² And from above he restored me without blemish,
 I was as the earth which is sprouting and lush in her fruits.

¹³ And the Lord is like the sun
 On the face of the earth.
¹⁴ My eyes were illuminated,
 And my face took in the dew.
¹⁵ My breath was made sweet
 in the sweet fragrance of the Lord.
¹⁶ He brought me into his paradise,
 In which is the store of the lusciousness† of the Lord.
 I saw trees that were ripe and bearing fruit
 And their crown was grown naturally.
 Their branches were blooming, and their fruits were beaming.
 Their roots were from immortal earth.
 The joyful river irrigates them,
 And circles around those of the land of eternal life.
¹⁷ Then I kneeled down to the Lord because of his splendor,
¹⁸ And I said, "Lord, they are blessed,
 The ones who have planted in your earth,
 And those who have a place for themselves in your paradise,
¹⁹ And who grow in the sprouting of your trees,
 And who turn away from darkness toward light.
²⁰ See! All of your laborers are beautiful,
 Who do kind, excellent deeds,
 And turn back from wickedness to your sweetness.
²¹ They turned away from themselves the bitterness of the trees
 When they were planted in your earth.
²² Everything became like your remnant.
 Blessed are the workers of your waters
 And the eternal memory of your faithful workers.
²³ Indeed there is a great deal of space in your paradise,
 Yet there is nothing idle in it.

---

* Or "with me."
† The same root as "sweetness."

Instead everything is full of fruit.
24 Praise to you, God, the delight of eternal paradise.

Ode 12

1 He has filled me with words of Truth,
So that I may speak for him.
2 And as the flow of the waters, Truth flows from my mouth,
And my lips tell of his fruits.
3 He has made his knowledge to abound in me,
Because the mouth of the Lord is the true Word,
And the door of his Light.
4 And the Most High has given it to the generations:
The expounders of his beauty,
The speakers of his glory,
The confessors of his thought,
And the sanctifiers of his deeds.
5 For the lightness of the word is without narration,
And as the narrative, so also is the swiftness and sharpness,
Its progression is endless.
6 And it never falls, but stands continually,
And no one knows its descent or its journey.
7 For as his formation is, so also is his expectation,
Indeed he is light and the dawn of thought.
8 The generations spoke to one another through him,
And those that were silent were able to speak.
9 From him came love and worth,
And they spoke, one to the other, that which was theirs.
10 And they were made right by the Word,
And they recognized the one who made them
Because they were in unison,
11 Because the mouth of the Most High spoke to them
And its exposition ran by his hand.
12 And the dwelling of the Word is humanity,
And his truth is love.
13 They are blessed, those who by his hand have known everything
And who recognized the Lord by his Truth.
Halleluiah.

An Introduction to
The Thunder: Perfect Mind

WITH THE EXCEPTION OF THE Gospel of Thomas, no other Nag Hammadi document has been received with as much excitement in the twentieth and twenty-first centuries as The Thunder: Perfect Mind. The artistic community has been most active in receiving Thunder. Nobel Prize–winning novelist Toni Morrison has used Thunder citations as the epigraph to her novels *Jazz* and *Parade*. Umberto Eco discussed it in his novel *Foucault's Pendulum*. Julie Dash's award-winning feature film *Daughters of the Dust* opens with a long citation from Thunder, accompanied by beautiful and haunting images. And Thunder's text anchors a 2005 film by Academy Award–winning director Ridley Scott and his daughter Jordon Scott. Numerous music groups and composers have set it to music.

Only one manuscript of The Thunder: Perfect Mind exists. It was found at Nag Hammadi with fifty-one other documents. There is no mention of Thunder in any other known piece of ancient literature. So this discovery at Nag Hammadi is monumental.

There is no indication of an author in the Nag Hammadi pages, and the title, as in many other documents from early Christianity, seems to have been added later. The meaning of the book's title has remained inscrutable and awaits new ideas emerging from its active use in our day. It is possible that Thunder was composed in Egypt, as it was found there and Egypt is the only location mentioned in the text. Many scholars assume that Thunder was originally in Greek, like most early Christian letters and gospels. But recent work on its Coptic text suggests the possibility that Coptic is its original language, highlighting again its possible origin in Egypt. Most difficult is approximating the time of Thunder's composition. The possibilities range from the first century BCE to the third century CE. Recent close study of Thunder has also concluded that column 21, the last of its nine manuscript pages, was almost certainly written later than the rest of the text, most probably in the third century.

The national spiritual leaders in the New Orleans Council expressed delight and surprise as they read Thunder. For the most part it was new to them, and it received positive votes from everyone. This enthusiasm for the way Thunder's divine and mostly feminine voice makes creative room for all kinds of human experience led a number of the council members to propose that Thunder should be the very first thing to be read in *A New New Testament*. As a subcommittee of the council worked more thoroughly on the order of this collection, the place of Thunder eventually lodged in the section on "Gospels, Poems, and Songs Between Heaven and Earth."

Although found in a collection of Christian documents, Thunder itself does not refer to Jesus or Christ at all. This is also true of 3 John in the traditional New Testament, and the Letter of James mentions Jesus only twice. The divine self-proclaiming voice of Thunder is most like the voice of Jesus in the Gospel of John. Like John's Jesus, who is a divine figure both powerful and humiliated, Thunder's divine voice speaks simultaneously of its own deep pain and its glorious boldness:

> I am the first and the last
> I am she who is honored and she who is mocked
> I am the whore and the holy woman
> I am the wife and the virgin
> I am the mother and the daughter
> I am the limbs of my mother
> I am a sterile woman and she has many children . . .
> I am both awareness and obliviousness
> I am humiliation and pride
> I am without shame
> I am ashamed . . .
> Do not be arrogant to me when I am thrown to the ground . . .
> Do not laugh at me in the lowest places
> Do not throw me down among those slaughtered viciously . . .
> I am she who exists in all fears and in trembling boldness
> I am she who is timid . . .
> (1:5–7; 2:7–8, 12, 14–15, 18–19)

Besides the Gospel of John's Jesus and Thunder, no other ancient (or modern) divine voice presents itself as simultaneously both so glorious and so humiliated.

Of course, Thunder's primarily feminine voice shocks and amazes most twenty-first-century readers. Close attention to this gendered dimension of Thunder's self-proclamation points to two striking aspects:

1. The roles and situations with which Thunder identifies correspond to a very wide range of women's roles in the ancient (and modern) world. By associating herself with so many different women characters, Thunder breaks down the many ways in which the ancient world stereotyped women as glorious, shameful, corrupt, powerful, and opaque. This voice does not seem to allow itself to be caricatured in the ways women were/are. In this way, Thunder both associates women with the divine in unexpected ways and makes herself more real relative to life's challenges, promises, and ironies. Of course, it is exactly this dynamic in Thunder that has already made it so popular in twenty-first-century media, art, and feminism.

2. Although most translations of the past thirty years have not attended to this, the Coptic (and the translation used in *A New New Testament*) scrambles Thunder's gender a bit. Although she speaks primarily as a feminine divine figure, occasionally she speaks as a masculine divine figure. This is similar to Jesus in the gospels of John and Matthew, and Paul's First Letter to the Corinthians, where Jesus is actively associated with the feminine figure of divine Wisdom and as such becomes a person both feminine and masculine. This is also the case in the way Jesus and the Spirit are described in the Odes of Solomon. This more diffuse engenderedness opens up for the twenty-first-century reader a space where highly prescribed Western ideas of what is feminine or masculine are challenged. It offers readers today the chance to identify with Jesus and Thunder without rehearsing and reinforcing the long-held Western ideas of a defended and prescribed femininity and masculinity. Here the twentieth- and twenty-first-century "queer movements"* have much to offer in understanding these ancient portraits of Thunder and Jesus.

A New New Testament is likely to be Thunder's first major coming-out party in the modern world. Although it has remained mostly unknown to the public since its discovery at Nag Hammadi in the mid-twentieth century, wherever it has surfaced in literature and art it has met with excited surprise.

A Note on Chapter and Verse Numbering

Since this text is so "new," no version of the otherwise standard chapter and verse format exists. So we have had to add our own chapter and versification to this edition. The Thunder: Perfect Mind has been made available to the public in various formats and translations without chapter and verse over the past thirty years. We do think it also very important that there be a chapter and verse system, since it breaks up the text into units that belong together. We do, however, want to alert readers that the relatively frequent availability of this text in non–chapter and verse form or in the ancient manuscript form of simply noting the column and line numbers of the original document does not match our new chapter and verse format.

---

* Some twenty-first-century readers may not know that for many lesbian, gay, bisexual, and transgender people of our day the word *queer,* which originally was an insult to people of these sexual orientations, is now used as a positive term. In this way the term *queer* has come to mean the volatility of sexual orientation and gender in human beings, and it signals a deep receptivity to the vagueness and multiplicity of sexual identity. The term *queer* is now also used widely in literature and is even a relatively frequent term for some scholars of the New Testament and early Christianity. See, for instance, the books of Judith Butler (for general treatment) and Stephen Moore (for its meaning in the interpretation of the New Testament and early Christianity).

Recommended Reading

Anne McGuire, The Thunder: Perfect Mind website: http://www.stoa.org/diotima/anthology/
thunder.shtml
Anne McGuire, "Thunder, Perfect Mind," pp. 39–54 in *Searching the Scriptures*, Volume 2:
A Feminist Commentary
Hal Taussig, Jared Calaway, Maia Kotrosits, Celene Lillie, and Justin Lasser, *The Thunder: Perfect
Mind: A New Translation and Introduction*

The Thunder: Perfect Mind

1 ¹ I was sent out from power
I came to those pondering me
And I was found among those seeking me
² Look at me, all you who contemplate me
Audience, hear me
Those expecting me, receive me
³ Don't chase me from your sight
Don't let your voice or your hearing hate me
⁴ Don't ignore me any place, any time
Be careful. Do not ignore me
⁵ I am the first and the last
I am she who is honored and she who is mocked
I am the whore and the holy woman
⁶ I am the wife and the virgin
I am he the mother and the daughter
I am the limbs of my mother
⁷ I am a sterile woman and she has many children
I am she whose wedding is extravagant and I didn't have a husband
⁸ I am the midwife and she who hasn't given birth
I am the comfort of my labor pains
⁹ I am the bride and the bridegroom
And it is my husband who gave birth to me
I am my father's mother,
My husband's sister, and he is my child
¹⁰ I am the slave woman of him who served me
I am she, the lord
of my child
¹¹ But it is he who gave birth to me at the wrong time
And he is my child born at the right time
And my power is from within him

¹² I am the staff of his youthful power
And he is the baton of my old womanhood
Whatever he wants happens to me
2 ¹ I am the silence never found
And the idea infinitely recalled
² I am the voice with countless sounds
And the thousand guises of the word
I am the speaking of my name
³ You who loathe me why do you love me and loathe the ones who love me?
⁴ You who deny me, confess me
You who confess me, deny me
⁵ You who speak the truth about me, lie about me
You who lie about me, speak the truth about me
⁶ You who know me, ignore me
You who ignore me, know me
⁷ I am both awareness and obliviousness
I am humiliation and pride
⁸ I am without shame
I am ashamed
⁹ I am security and I am fear
I am war and peace
¹⁰ Pay attention to me
I am she who is disgraced and she who is important

¹¹ Pay attention to me, to my impoverishment and to my extravagance
¹² Do not be arrogant to me when I am thrown to the ground
You will find me among the expected
¹³ Do not stare at me in the shit pile, leaving me discarded
You will find me in the kingdoms
¹⁴ Do not stare at me when I am thrown out among the condemned
Do not laugh at me in the lowest places

¹⁵ Do not throw me down among those slaughtered viciously

¹⁶ I myself am compassionate

And I am cruel

Watch out!

Do not hate my compliance and do not love my restraint

¹⁷ In my weakness do not strip me bare

Do not be afraid of my power

¹⁸ Why do you despise my fear and curse my pride?

I am she who exists in all fears and in trembling boldness

¹⁹ I am she who is timid

And I am safe in a comfortable place

I am witless, and I am wise

3 ¹ Why did you hate me with your schemes?

² I shall shut my mouth among those whose mouths are shut

And then I will show up and speak

³ Why then did you hate me, you Greeks?

Because I am a barbarian among barbarians?

⁴ I am the wisdom of the Greeks and the knowledge of the barbarians

I am the deliberation of both the Greeks and barbarians

⁵ I am he whose image is multiple in Egypt

And she who is without an image among the barbarians

⁶ I am she who was hated in every place

And she who was loved in every place

⁷ I am she whom they call life

And you all called death

⁸ I am she whom they call law

And you all called lawlessness

⁹ I am she whom you chased and she whom you captured

¹⁰ I am she whom you scattered

And you have gathered me together

¹¹ I am she before whom you were ashamed

And you have been shameless to me

¹² I am she who does not celebrate festivals

And I am she whose festivals are spectacular

¹³ I, I am without God

And I am she whose God is magnificent

¹⁴ I am he the one you thought about and you detested me

I am not learned, and they learn from me

¹⁵ I am she whom you detested and yet you think about me

¹⁶ I am he from whom you hid

And you appear to me

¹⁷ Wherever you hide yourselves, I myself will appear . . .

¹⁸ Receive me with understanding and heartache

Take me from the disgraced and crushed places

¹⁹ Rob from those who are good, even though in disgrace

4 ¹ Bring me in shame, to yourselves, out of shame

With or without shame

² Blame the parts of me within yourselves

³ Come toward me, you who know me

And you who know the parts of me

⁴ Assemble the great among the small and earliest creatures

⁵ Advance toward childhood

Do not hate it because it is small and insignificant

⁶ Don't reject the small parts of greatness because they are small

Since smallness is recognized from within greatness

⁷ Why do you curse me and revere me?

You wounded me and you relented

⁸ Don't separate me from the first ones

Throw away no one

Turn away no . . .

⁹ I know those

And the ones after these know me

¹⁰ I am the mind and the rest
I am the learning from my search
And the discovery of those seeking me
¹¹ The command of those who ask about me
And the power of powers
In my understanding of the angels
Who were sent on my word
¹² And the Gods in God, according to my design
And spirits of all men who exist with me
And the women who live in me
¹³ I am she who is revered and adored
And she who is reviled with contempt
¹⁴ I am peace and war exists because of me
I am a foreigner and a citizen of the city
¹⁵ I am being
I am she who is nothing
¹⁶ Those who do not participate in my presence, don't know me
Those who share in my being know me
¹⁷ Those who are close to me, did not know me
Those who are far from me, knew me
¹⁸ On the day that I am close to you, you are far away from me
And on the day that I am far away from you, I am close to you
¹⁹ I . . . of the heart . . . of the natures
I am he . . . of the creation of spirits . . . request of the souls . . .
²⁰ control and the uncontrollable
I am the coming together and the falling apart
I am the enduring and the disintegration
²¹ I am down in the dirt and they come up to me
I am judgment and acquittal
²² I myself am without sin, and the root of sin is from within me
I appear to be lust but inside is self-control
²³ I am what anyone can hear but no one can say

I am a mute that does not speak and my words are endless
²⁴ Hear me in tenderness, learn from me in roughness
I am she who shouts out and I am thrown down on the ground
²⁵ I am the one who prepares the bread and my mind within
I am the knowledge of my name
²⁶ I am she who shouts out and it is I that listens
I appear . . . and walk in . . . seal
²⁷ I am he . . . the defense
I am she they call truth, and violation
You honor me . . . and you whisper against me
²⁸ You conquered ones: judge them before they judge you
Because the judge and favoritism exist in you
²⁹ If he condemns you, who will release you?
If he releases you, who can detain you?
³⁰ Since what is your inside is your outside
And the one who shapes your outside is he who shaped your inside
³¹ And what you see on the outside, you see revealed on the inside
It is your clothing
³² Hear me, audience, and learn from my words, you who know me
I am what everyone can hear and no one can say
³³ I am the name of the sound and the sound of the name
I am the sign of writing and disclosure of difference

Appendix

5 ¹ And I . . . light . . . and
Hearers . . . to you . . . the great power
² And . . . will not move the name . . .
. . . he who created me
But I will speak his name
the name

It is he who created me
But I will speak his name
3 Look then at his pronouncements and all the writings that have been completed
Listen then, audience
And also you angels
4 Along with those who have been sent
And spirits who have risen from among the dead
5 For I am he who exists alone

And no one judges me
6 Since many sweet ideas exist in all kinds of sin,
Uncontrollable and condemning passions
7 And passing pleasures that people have
Until they become sober and go up to their resting place,
8 And they will find me in that place
They will live and they will not die again

An Introduction to the Gospel of John

S TRIKINGLY DIFFERENT FROM the gospels of Thomas, Matthew, Mark, and
Luke, the Gospel of John begins its story of Jesus with a poem portraying him
as an everlasting figure at one with God. In John, Jesus exists before the creation
of anything and then strides through Galilee and Jerusalem with the authority of
a divine figure. This very distinct gospel seems to have been written from within
a movement that felt both powerful and embattled from all sides. Not unlike The
Thunder: Perfect Mind, John portrays a cosmic figure in the crosshairs of human
trauma, loss, and potential.

The author is not identified in the text, and the title itself is probably later than
the gospel. The book is thought to have been written in the 90s CE. Speculations
on where it was written vary from Palestine to Asia Minor. It is written in Greek.

This gospel is organized primarily around paired units of what it calls the "signs"
(its particular word for Jesus's healings and feeding of the five thousand) and long
speeches of Jesus. Each sign/miracle is followed by a speech from Jesus. Almost all
of his speeches use an ancient formula for a divine figure revealing who he or she
is. The formula begins with "I am . . ." and, in the case of the Gospel of John, con-
cludes with phrases like "the bread of life," "the resurrection and the life," and "the
good shepherd." Jesus does not speak like this at all in Matthew, Mark, or Luke,
and he does so sparingly in the Gospel of Thomas.

Living in God

The Gospel of John makes a steady case for people to be a part of God. This invitation comes through a number of poetic images. Often Jesus describes a dynamic in
which people are in him, he is in God, and God is in him. In this elliptical connection, people are in God by virtue of their being in Jesus (14:20). Jesus explains this
in chapter 15 in terms of his being the vine and people being the branches and then
extends this comparison: "If you keep my commandments, you will remain in my
love; just as I have kept my Father's commandments and remain in his love" (15:10).

This relationship among Jesus, people, and God seems very similar to the way
Jesus in John talks about the Advocate, which is sometimes called the holy Spirit
or the Spirit of Truth: "[Jesus said,] and I will ask the Father, and he will give you
another helper, to be with you always — the spirit of truth . . . you recognize it, because it is with you, and is in you" (14:16, 17b). This same interlocking identity
among Jesus, people, Spirit, and God occurs in the story itself. Throughout there
is an unnamed man called the one "whom Jesus loved." In John he is the only male

follower of Jesus who is with Jesus at the cross, he reclines with Jesus on the same couch at the last supper, and he is the first person to arrive at Jesus's tomb. This person seems to share Jesus's life in a way that resembles how Jesus describes the intimate relationship among people, himself, and God.

Women Who Speak

In contrast to Matthew, Mark, and Luke, the Gospel of John has more fully formed women characters. Jesus's mother in a story about a wedding actively disputes what Jesus should do, and she tries to manage his dealings with the servants. The Canaanite woman Jesus meets at the well has an extended discussion with him, perhaps the longest in the gospel. Both Mary and Martha of Bethany (who are described as two of the three characters in the gospel whom Jesus loves) confront, beg, and debate Jesus. Jesus talks to his mother while he is on the cross. And Mary Magdalene is the first person to see Jesus after he has risen and has a conversation with him in the garden near the tomb.

These women are not particularly sexualized by the Gospel of John, nor are they nameless, as they are generally in Matthew, Mark, and Luke. This portrait of women gives a broader range of ways to relate to them and to identify with them. It raises the possibility that women in the communities for whom this gospel was written were themselves leaders. It is the gospel that most clearly poses the likelihood that women were leaders in Jesus's own association. And it provides a model for women today to play central roles in society and Christianity.

Recommended Reading

Warren Carter, *John: Storyteller, Interpreter, Evangelist*
Warren Carter, *John and Empire: Initial Explorations*
Bruce Malina and Richard Rohrbaugh, *Social Science Commentary on the Gospel of John*

The Gospel of John

Introduction

1 ¹ In the beginning the Word was;
and the Word was with God;
and the Word was God.

² The Word was in the beginning with
God;

³ through the Word all things came into
being
and nothing came into being apart
from the Word.

⁴ That which came into being in the
Word was life
and the life was the light of humanity;
⁵ and the light shines in the darkness,
and the darkness never overpowered
it.

⁶ There appeared a man sent from God,
whose name was John;

⁷ he came as a witness — to bear witness
to the light
so that through him everyone might
believe.

⁸ He was not the light,
but he came to bear witness to the light.

⁹ That was the true light which
enlightens everyone coming into the
world.

¹⁰ He was coming into the world;
and through him the world came into
being —
yet the world did not know him.

¹¹ He came to his own —
yet his own did not receive him.

¹² But to all who did receive him he gave
power to become children of God —
to those who trust in his name,

¹³ not through blood, nor through will of
the flesh, nor through the desires of
men
but through birth from God.

¹⁴ And the Word became flesh, and lived
among us.

We saw his glory — the glory of the
only Child from the Father,
full of grace and truth.

¹⁵ John bears witness to him; he cries
aloud,
"This is the one of whom I said
The one coming after me is now ahead
of me,
because he was before me;

¹⁶ out of his fullness we have all received,
grace upon grace;

¹⁷ for the Law was given through Moses,
grace and truth came through Jesus
Christ.

¹⁸ No one has ever seen God;
the only Son and God, the one very
close to the Father
who made him known."

The Preparation

¹⁹ When the Judeans sent priests and Levites to ask John, "Who are you?" ²⁰ he told them clearly and simply: "I am not the Anointed One." ²¹ "What then?" they asked. "Are you Elijah?"

"No," he said, "I am not."

"Are you the prophet?" He answered, "No."

²² "Who then are you?" they continued; "tell us so that we have an answer to give to those who have sent us. What do you say about yourself?"

²³ "I," he answered, "am:

'The voice of one crying aloud in the
wilderness — prepare a way for the
Lord, make his paths straight,'

as the prophet Isaiah said."

²⁴ These men had been sent from the Pharisees; ²⁵ and their next question was:

"Why then do you cleanse, if you are not the Christ, nor Elijah, nor yet the prophet?" [26] John's answer was: "I baptize with water, but among you stands one whom you do not know; [27] he is coming after me, yet I am not worthy even to unfasten his sandal." [28] This happened at Bethany, across the Jordan, where John was baptizing.

[29] The next day John saw Jesus coming toward him, and exclaimed: "Here is the Lamb of God, who takes away the sin of the world! [30] I was talking about him when I said, 'After me there is coming one who ranks ahead of me, because before I was born he already was.' [31] I did not know who he was, but I have come cleansing with water to make him known to Israel." [32] John also said:

"I saw the Spirit come down from heaven like a dove and rest on him. [33] I myself did not know him, but the one who sent me to baptize with water, he said to me, 'The one on whom you see the Spirit descending, and remaining on him — it is he who cleanses with the holy Spirit.' [34] This I have seen myself, and I have declared that he is the Child of God."

[35] The next day, when John was standing with two of his followers, [36] he looked at Jesus as he passed and exclaimed: "There is the Lamb of God!" [37] The two followers heard him say this, and followed Jesus. [38] But Jesus turned around, and saw them following. "What are you looking for?" he asked. They answered, "Rabbi" (which means "teacher"), "where are you staying?"

[39] "Come, and you will see," he replied. So they went, and saw where he was staying, and spent that day with him.

It was then about four in the afternoon. [40] One of the two, who heard what John said and followed Jesus, was Andrew, Simon Peter's brother. [41] He first found his own brother Simon, and said to him: "We have found the Messiah!" (a word which means "Christ"). [42] Then he brought him to Jesus. Fixing his eyes on him, Jesus said: "You are Simon, the son of John; you will be called Cephas" (which means "Rock").

[43] The following day Jesus decided to leave for Galilee. He found Philip, and said to him: "Follow me." [44] Philip was from Bethsaida, the same town as Andrew and Peter. [45] He found Nathanael and said to him: "We have found him of whom Moses wrote in the Law, and of whom the prophets also wrote — Jesus of Nazareth, Joseph's son!"

[46] "Can anything good come out of Nazareth?" asked Nathanael. "Come and see," replied Philip. [47] When Jesus saw Nathanael coming toward him, he said: "Here is a true Israelite, in whom there is no deceit!"

[48] "How do you know me?" asked Nathanael. "Even before Philip called you," replied Jesus, "when you were under the fig tree, I saw you."

[49] "Rabbi," Nathanael exclaimed, "you are the Son of God, you are king of Israel!"

[50] "Do you believe in me," asked Jesus, "because I told you that I saw you under the fig tree? You will see greater things than those! [51] In truth I tell you," he added, "you will all see heaven open, and 'the angels of God ascending and descending' on the Child of Humanity."

The Work in Judaea, Galilee, and Samaria

2 [1] Two days after this there was a wedding at Cana in Galilee, and Jesus's mother was there. [2] Jesus himself, too, with his followers, was invited to the wedding. [3] And, when the wine ran short, his mother said to him: "They have no wine left."

[4] "Woman, what do you want with me?" answered Jesus. "My time has not come yet." [5] His mother said to the servants: "Do whatever he tells you." [6] There were standing there six stone water jars, in accordance with the Judean rule of "purifi-

cation," each holding twenty or thirty gallons.

⁷ Jesus said to the servants: "Fill the water jars with water." ⁸ And, when they had filled them to the brim, he added: "Now take some out, and carry it to the president of the feast." The servants did so. ⁹ And, when the president of the feast had tasted the water which had now become wine, not knowing where it had come from — although the servants who had taken out the water knew — ¹⁰ he called the groom and said to him: "Everyone puts good wine out first, and inferior wine afterward, when his guests have drunk freely; but you have kept back the good wine till now!" ¹¹ This, the first sign of his mission, Jesus gave at Cana in Galilee, and by it revealed his glory; and his followers believed in him.

¹² After this, Jesus went down to Capernaum — he, his mother, his brothers, and his followers; but they stayed there only a few days.

¹³ Then, as the Judeans' Passover was near, Jesus went up to Jerusalem. ¹⁴ In the Temple he found people who were selling cattle, sheep, and pigeons, and the money-changers at their tables. ¹⁵ So he made a whip of cords, and drove them all out of the Temple, and the sheep and cattle as well; he scattered the money of the money-changers, and overturned their tables, ¹⁶ and said to the pigeon dealers: "Take these things away. Do not turn my Father's house into a market house." ¹⁷ His followers remembered that it is written: "Passion for your house will consume me."

¹⁸ Then the Judeans asked Jesus: "What sign are you going to show us, that you should act in this way?"

¹⁹ "Destroy this temple," was his answer, "and I will raise it in three days."

²⁰ "This Temple," the Judeans replied, "has been forty-six years in building, and are you going to raise it in three days?" ²¹ But Jesus was speaking of his body as a temple. ²² Afterward, when he had risen from the dead, his followers remembered that he had said this; and they trusted the writing, and the words which he had spoken.

²³ While he was in Jerusalem, during the Passover festival, many came to trust in him, when they saw the signs that he was giving. ²⁴ But Jesus did not put himself in their power because he knew what was in their hearts. ²⁵ He did not need any information about the people because he could read what was in humans.

3 ¹ Now there was a Pharisee named Nicodemus, who was a ruler among the Judeans. ² He came to Jesus by night, and said to him: "Rabbi, we know that you are a teacher come from God; for no one could give such signs as you are giving, unless God were with him." ³ "In truth I tell you," Jesus answered, "unless a person is born from above, she cannot see the realm of God."

⁴ "How can a person," asked Nicodemus, "be born when she is old? Is it possible to go back into the womb again and be born a second time?"

⁵ "In truth I tell you," answered Jesus, "unless a person is born through water and spirit, she cannot enter the realm of God. ⁶ That which is born of the flesh is flesh and that which is born of the spirit is spirit. ⁷ Do not wonder at my telling you that you all need to be born from above. ⁸ The wind blows wherever it wants, and you can hear the sound it makes, but you do not know where it comes from, or where it goes; it is the same with everyone who is born of the spirit."

⁹ "How can that be?" asked Nicodemus. ¹⁰ "What! You the teacher of Israel," Jesus answered, "and yet do not understand this! ¹¹ In truth I tell you that we speak of what we know, and state what we have seen; and yet you do not accept our statements. ¹² If, when I tell you earthly things, you do not believe me, how will you believe me when I tell you of heavenly things? ¹³ No one has ascended to heaven, except him who de-

scended from heaven — the Child of Humanity himself. [14] And, as Moses lifted up the snake in the desert, so must the Child of Humanity be lifted up; [15] so that everyone who trusts in him may have life through the generations."

[16] For God so loved the world, that he gave his only Child, so that everyone who believes in him may not be lost, but have life through the ages. [17] For God did not send his Son into the world to condemn the world, but so that the world might be saved through him. [18] The person who believes in him escapes condemnation, while the person who does not believe in him is already condemned, because he has not believed in the only Child of God. [19] The ground of his condemnation is this, that though the light has come into the world, people preferred the darkness to the light, because their actions were wicked. [20] For the person who lives an evil life hates the light, and will not come to it, fearing that his actions will be exposed; [21] but the person who lives by the truth comes into the light, so it can be clearly seen that God is in all he does.

[22] After this, Jesus went with his disciples into the country parts of Judea; and there he stayed with them, and baptized. [23] John, also, was baptizing at Aenon near Salim, because there was much water there; and people were constantly coming and being washed. [24] For John had not yet been imprisoned. [25] Now a discussion arose between some of John's followers and a Judean on the subject of cleansing; [26] and the followers came to John and said: "Rabbi, the man who was with you on the other side of the Jordan, and to whom you have yourself borne testimony — he, also, is baptizing, and everybody is going to him." [27] John's answer was: "A person can gain nothing but what is given him from heaven. [28] You are yourselves witnesses that I said, 'I am not the Anointed One,' but 'I have been sent before him as a messenger.' [29] It is the groom

who has the bride; but the groom's friend, who stands by and listens to him, is filled with joy when he hears the groom's voice. This joy I have felt to the full. [30] He must become greater, and I less."

[31] The one who comes from above is above all others; but a child of earth is earthly, and his teaching is earthly, too. The one who comes from heaven is above all others. [32] He states what he has seen and what he heard, and yet no one accepts his statement. [33] They who did accept his statement confirm the fact that God is true. [34] For the one whom God sent gives us God's own teaching, for God does not limit the gift of the spirit. [35] The Father loves his Child, and has put everything in his hands. [36] The person who trusts in the Son has life through all ages, while a person who rejects the Son will not even see that life, but remains under "God's displeasure."

4 [1] Now, when Jesus heard that the Pharisees had been told that he was making and baptizing more followers than John [2] (though it was not Jesus himself, but his followers, who baptized), [3] he left Judea, and set out again for Galilee. [4] He had to pass through Samaria, [5] and, on his way, he came to a Samaritan town called Shechem, near the plot of land that Jacob gave to his son Joseph. [6] Jacob's well was there, and Jesus, being tired after his journey, sat down beside the source, just as he was. It was then about midday. [7] A woman of Samaria came to draw water; and Jesus said to her, "Give me some to drink," [8] for his disciples had gone into the town to buy food. [9] "How is it," replied the Samaritan woman, "that you who are a Judean ask for water from a Samaritan woman like me?" (for Jews do not associate with Samaritans). [10] "If you knew of the gift of God," replied Jesus, "and who it is that is saying to you, 'Give me some water,' you would have asked him, and he would have given you living water."

¹¹ "You have no bucket, sir, and the well is deep," she said; "from where do you have this living water? ¹² Surely you are not greater than our ancestor Jacob who gave us the well, and used to drink from it himself, and his sons, and his cattle!"

¹³ "All who drink of this water," replied Jesus, "will be thirsty again; ¹⁴ but whoever once drinks of the water that I will give him will never thirst anymore; but the water that I will give him will become a spring welling up within him — a source of life through the ages."

¹⁵ "Give me this water, sir," said the woman, "so that I may not be thirsty, nor have to come all the way here to draw water."

¹⁶ "Go and call your husband," said Jesus, "and then come back."

¹⁷ "I have no husband," answered the woman. "You are right in saying, 'I have no husband,'" replied Jesus, ¹⁸ "for you have had five husbands, and the man with whom you are now living is not your husband; in saying that, you have spoken the truth."

¹⁹ "I see, sir, that you are a prophet!" exclaimed the woman. ²⁰ "It was on this mountain that our ancestors worshiped; and yet you Judeans say that the proper place for worship is in Jerusalem."

²¹ "Believe me," replied Jesus, "a time is coming when it will be neither on this mountain nor in Jerusalem that you will worship the Father. ²² You Samaritans do not know what you worship; we know what we worship, for salvation comes from the Judeans. ²³ But a time is coming, indeed it is already here, when the true worshipers will worship the Father spiritually and truly; for such are the worshipers that the Father desires. ²⁴ God is spirit; and those who worship him must worship in spirit and in truth."

²⁵ "I know," answered the woman, "that the Anointed One, who is called the Christ, is coming; when once he has come, he will tell us everything."

²⁶ "I am that one," Jesus said to her, "I who am speaking to you." ²⁷ At this moment his followers came up, and were surprised to find him talking with a woman; but none of them asked, "What do you want?" or "Why are you talking with her?" ²⁸ So the woman, leaving her pitcher, went back to the town, and said to the people: ²⁹ "Come and see someone who has told me everything that I have done. Can he be the Anointed One?" ³⁰ And the people left the town and went to see Jesus.

³¹ Meanwhile the followers kept saying to him: "Take something to eat, Rabbi."

³² "I have food to eat," he answered, "of which you know nothing."

³³ "Can anyone have brought him anything to eat?" the followers said to one another. ³⁴ "My food," replied Jesus, "is to do the will of the one who sent me, and to complete his work. ³⁵ Do you not say that there are four months to harvest? Why, look up, and see how white the fields are for harvest! ³⁶ Already the reaper is receiving wages and gathering in sheaves for life through the generations, so that sower and reaper rejoice together. ³⁷ For here the proverb holds good — 'One sows, another reaps.' ³⁸ I have sent you to reap that on which you have spent no labor; others have labored, and you have reaped the results of their labor."

³⁹ Many from that town came to believe in Jesus — Samaritans though they were — because the woman had said: "He has told me everything that I have done." ⁴⁰ And, when these Samaritans had come to Jesus, they begged him to stay with them, and he stayed there two days. ⁴¹ But far more came to believe in him because of what he said himself, ⁴² and they said to the woman: "It is no longer because of what you say that we trust in him, for we have heard him ourselves and know that he really is the Savior of the world."

⁴³ After these two days Jesus went on to Galilee; ⁴⁴ for he himself declared that a prophet is not honored in his own coun-

try. ⁴⁵ When he entered Galilee, the Galileans welcomed him, for they had seen all that he did at Jerusalem during the festival, at which they also had been present. ⁴⁶ So Jesus came again to Cana in Galilee, where he had turned the water into wine. Now there was an official whose son was lying ill at Capernaum. ⁴⁷ When this man heard that Jesus had returned from Judea to Galilee, he went to him, and begged him to come down and heal his son; for he was at the point of death. ⁴⁸ Jesus answered: "Unless you all see signs and wonders, you will not believe."

⁴⁹ "Sir," said the official, "come down before my child dies." And Jesus answered: "Go, your son is living." ⁵⁰ The man believed what Jesus said to him, and went; ⁵¹ and, while he was on his way down, his slaves met him, and told him that his child was living. ⁵² So he asked them at what time the boy began to get better. "It was yesterday, about one o'clock," they said, "that the fever left him." ⁵³ By this the father knew that it was at the very time when Jesus had said to him, "Your son is living"; and he himself, with all his household, believed in Jesus. ⁵⁴ This was the second occasion on which Jesus gave a sign of his mission on coming from Judea to Galilee.

5 ¹ Sometime after this there was a Judean festival; and Jesus went up to Jerusalem. ² There is in Jerusalem, near the sheep gate, a bath with five colonnades around it. It is called in Hebrew *Bethesda*. ³ In these colonnades a large number of sick people were lying — blind, lame, and crippled. ⁵ One man who was there had been crippled for thirty-eight years. ⁶ Jesus saw the man lying there, and, finding that he had been in this state a long time, said to him: "Do you wish to be healthy again?"

⁷ "I have no one, sir," the sick man answered, "to put me into the bath when there is a troubling of the water, and, while I am getting to it, someone else steps down before me."

⁸ "Stand up," said Jesus, "take up your mat, and walk." ⁹ The man was cured immediately, and took up his mat and began walking. ¹⁰ Now it was the sabbath. So the Judeans said to the man who had been healed: "This is the sabbath; you must not carry your mat."

¹¹ "The man who healed me," he answered, "said to me, 'Take up your mat and walk.'"

¹² "Who was it," they asked, "that said to you, 'Take up your mat and walk'?" ¹³ But the man who had been restored did not know who it was; for Jesus had moved away, because there was a crowd there. ¹⁴ Afterward he found the man in the Temple, and said to him: "You are healed now; do not sin again, or something worse may happen to you."

¹⁵ The man went away, and told the authorities that it was Jesus who had healed him. ¹⁶ And that was why they began to persecute Jesus — because he did things of this kind on the sabbath. ¹⁷ But Jesus replied: "My Father works to this very hour, and I work also." ¹⁸ This made the Judeans all the more eager to kill him, because not only was he doing away with the sabbath, but he actually called God his own Father — putting himself on an equality with God. ¹⁹ So Jesus made this further reply: "In truth I tell you, the Child can do nothing of himself; he does only what he sees the Father doing; whatever the Father does, the Son does also. ²⁰ For the Father loves his Son, and shows him everything that he is doing; and he will show him still greater things — so that you will be filled with wonder. ²¹ For, just as the Father raises the dead and gives them life, so also the Son gives life to whom he pleases. ²² The Father himself does not judge anyone, but has entrusted the work of judging entirely to his Son, ²³ so that everyone may honor the Son, just as they honor the Father. The person who does not honor the Son fails to honor the Father who sent him. ²⁴ In truth I tell you that the person

who listens to my message and believes the One who sent me has life through the ages, and does not come under condemnation, but has already passed out of death into life. ²⁵ In truth I tell you that a time is coming, indeed it is already here, when the dead will listen to the voice of the Child of God, and when those who listen will live. ²⁶ For, just as the Father has inherent life within him, so also he has granted to the Child to have inherent life within him; ²⁷ and, because he is a Child of Humanity, he has also given him authority to act as judge. ²⁸ Do not wonder at this; for the time is coming when all who are in their graves will hear his voice, ²⁹ and will come out — those who have done good rising to life, and those who have lived evil lives rising for condemnation. ³⁰ I can do nothing of myself; I judge as I am taught; and the judgment that I give is just, because my aim is not to do my own will, but the will of him who sent me.

³¹ "If I bear testimony to myself, my testimony is not trustworthy; ³² it is another who bears testimony to me, and I know that the testimony which that one bears to me is trustworthy. ³³ You have yourselves sent to John, and he has testified to the truth. ³⁴ But the testimony which I receive is not from people; I am saying this for your salvation. ³⁵ That one was a lamp burning and shining, and you were ready to rejoice, for a time, in his light. ³⁶ But the testimony which I have is of greater weight than John's; for the work that the Father has given me to carry out — the work that I am doing — is in itself proof that the Father has sent me. ³⁷ The Father who has sent me has himself borne testimony to me. You have neither listened to his voice, nor seen his form; ³⁸ and you have not taken his message home to your hearts, because you do not trust the one whom he sent. ³⁹ You search the writings, because you think that in them you have life through the ages; and, though it is those writings that bear testimony to

me, ⁴⁰ you refuse to come to me to have life.

⁴¹ "I do not receive honor from people, ⁴² but I know this of you, that you have not the love of God in yourselves. ⁴³ I have come in my Father's name, and you do not receive me; if another comes in his own name, you will receive him. ⁴⁴ How can you trust in me, when you receive honor from one another and do not desire the honor which comes from the one God? ⁴⁵ Do not think that I will accuse you to the Father; your accuser is Moses, on whom you have been resting your hopes. ⁴⁶ For, had you believed Moses, you would have believed me, for it was of me that Moses wrote; ⁴⁷ but if you do not believe his writings, how will you believe my teaching?"

6 ¹ After this, Jesus crossed the Sea of Galilee — otherwise called the Lake of Tiberias. ² A great crowd of people, however, followed him, because they saw the signs in his work among those who were sick. ³ Jesus went up the hill, and sat down there with his followers. ⁴ It was near the time of the Judean festival of the Passover. ⁵ Looking up, and noticing that a great crowd was coming toward him, Jesus said to Philip: "Where are we to buy bread for these people to eat?" ⁶ He said this to test him, for he himself knew what he meant to do. ⁷ "Even if we spent a year's wages on bread," answered Philip, "it would not be enough for each of them to have a little."

⁸ "There is a boy here," said Andrew, another of his followers, Simon Peter's brother, ⁹ "who has five barley loaves and two fishes; but what is that for so many?"

¹⁰ "Make the people recline," said Jesus. It was a grassy spot; so the people, who numbered about five thousand, lay back, ¹¹ and then Jesus took the loaves, and, after saying thanks, distributed them to those who were lying down; and the same with the fish, giving the people as much as they wanted. ¹² When they were satisfied, Jesus

said to his followers: "Collect the broken pieces that are left, so that nothing may be wasted." [13] His followers did so, and filled twelve baskets with the pieces of the five barley loaves, which were left after all had eaten.

[14] When the people saw the signs which Jesus gave, they said: "This is certainly the prophet who was to come into the world." [15] But Jesus, having discovered that they were intending to come and carry him off to make him king, went again up the hill alone.

[16] When evening fell, his followers went down to the sea, [17] and, getting into a boat, began to cross to Capernaum. By this time darkness had set in, and Jesus had not yet come back to them; [18] the sea, too, was getting rough, for a strong wind was blowing. [19] When they had rowed three or four miles, they caught sight of him walking on the water and approaching the boat, and they were frightened. [20] But Jesus said to them: "It is I; do not be afraid!" [21] And after this they were glad to take him into the boat; and the boat at once arrived at the shore, for which they had been making.

[22] The people who remained on the farther side of the sea had seen that only one boat had been there, and that Jesus had not gone into it with his followers, but that they had left without him. [23] Some boats, however, had come from Tiberias, from near the spot where they had eaten the bread. [24] So, on the next day, when the people saw that Jesus was not there, or his followers either, they themselves got into the boats, and went to Capernaum to look for him. [25] And, when they found him on the other side of the sea, they said: "When did you get here, Rabbi?"

[26] "In truth I tell you," answered Jesus, "it is not because of the signs which you saw that you are looking for me, but because you had the bread to eat and were satisfied. [27] Work, not for the food that perishes, but for the food that lasts from generation to generation, which the Child of Humanity will give you; for on him the Father — God himself — has set the seal of his approval."

[28] "How," they asked, "are we to do the work that God wants us to do?"

[29] "The work that God wants you to do," answered Jesus, "is to trust in the one whom God sent."

[30] "What sign, then," they asked, "are you giving, which we may see, and so trust you? What is the work that you are doing? [31] Our ancestors had the manna to eat in the desert; as it is written, 'He gave them bread from heaven to eat.'"

[32] "In truth I tell you," replied Jesus, "Moses did not give you the bread from heaven, but my Father does give you the bread from heaven; [33] for the bread that God gives is that which comes down from heaven, and gives life to the world."

[34] "Master," they exclaimed, "give us that bread always!"

[35] "I am the bread of life," Jesus said to them; "whoever comes to me will never be hungry, and whoever believes in me will never thirst again. [36] But as I have said already, you have seen me, and yet you do not trust me. [37] All those whom the Father gives me will come to me; and no one who comes to me will I ever turn away. [38] For I have come down from heaven, to do, not my own will, but the will of him who sent me; [39] and his will is this — that I should not lose anything he has given me, but should raise it up at the last day. [40] For it is the will of my Father that everyone who sees the Son, and trusts in him, should have life from age to age; and I myself will raise him up at the last day."

[41] The Judeans began murmuring against Jesus for saying, "I am the bread which came down from heaven." [42] "Is this not Jesus, Joseph's son," they asked, "whose father and mother we know? How is it that he now says that he has come down from heaven?"

[43] "Do not murmur among yourselves," said Jesus in reply. [44] "No one can come to

me unless the Father who sent me draws him to me; and I will raise that one up at the last day. ⁴⁵ It is said in the prophets, 'And they will all be taught by God.' Everyone who is taught by the Father and learns from him comes to me. ⁴⁶ Not that anyone has seen the Father, except the one who is by God's side — he has seen the Father. ⁴⁷ In truth I tell you, the person who trusts in me has eternal life. ⁴⁸ I am the bread of life. ⁴⁹ Your ancestors ate the manna in the desert, and yet died. ⁵⁰ The bread that comes down from heaven is such that whoever eats of it will never die. ⁵¹ I am the living bread that has come down from heaven. Anyone eating of this bread will live into the ages; and the bread that I will give is my flesh, which I will give for the life of the world."

⁵² The Judeans began disputing with one another: "How is it possible for this man to give us his flesh to eat?"

⁵³ "In truth I tell you," answered Jesus, "unless you eat the flesh of the Child of Humanity, and drink his blood, you have not life within you. ⁵⁴ Everyone who takes my flesh for her food, and drinks my blood, has life through the generations; and I will raise her up at the last day. ⁵⁵ For my flesh is true food, and my blood true drink. ⁵⁶ Everyone who takes my flesh for her food, and drinks my blood, remains in me, and I in her. ⁵⁷ As the Living Father sent me, and as I live because the Father lives, so the person who takes me for her food will live because I live. ⁵⁸ That is the bread which has come down from heaven — not such as your ancestors ate, and yet died; the person who takes this bread for her food will live from generation to generation."

⁵⁹ All this Jesus said in a synagogue, when he was teaching in Capernaum. ⁶⁰ On hearing it, many of his followers said: "This is harsh teaching! Who can bear to listen to it?" ⁶¹ But Jesus, aware that his followers were murmuring about it, said to them: ⁶² "Is this a hindrance to you? What, then, if you should see the Child of Humanity ascending where he was before? ⁶³ It is the spirit that gives life; the flesh achieves nothing. The teaching that I have been giving you is spirit and life. ⁶⁴ Yet there are some of you who do not trust in me." For Jesus knew from the first who they were that did not believe in him, and who it was that would betray him; ⁶⁵ and he added: "This is why I told you that none can come to me, except as it is given to them by the Father." ⁶⁶ After this many of his followers gave up, and did not go about with him any longer. ⁶⁷ So Jesus said to the Twelve: "Do you also wish to leave me?" ⁶⁸ But Simon Peter answered: "Master, to whom would we go? You have the words of life from age to age; ⁶⁹ and we have learned to trust and to know that you are the Holy One of God.

⁷⁰ "Did not I myself choose you as the Twelve?" replied Jesus. "And yet, even of you, one is playing a devil." ⁷¹ He meant Judas, the son of Simon Iscariot, who was about to betray him, though he was one of the Twelve.

7 ¹ After this, Jesus went about in Galilee, for he would not do so in Judea, because the Judeans were eager to put him to death. ² When the Judean festival of Tabernacles was near, ³ his brothers said to him: "Leave this part of the country, and go into Judea, so that your followers may see the work that you are doing. ⁴ For no one does a thing privately, if he is seeking to be widely known. Since you do these things, you should show yourself publicly to the world." ⁵ For even his brothers did not believe in him.

⁶ "My time," answered Jesus, "is not come yet, but your time is always here. ⁷ The world cannot hate you, but it does hate me, because I testify that its ways are evil. ⁸ Go yourselves up to the festival; I am not going to this festival, because my time has not yet come." ⁹ After telling them this, he stayed on in Galilee.

[10] But when his brothers had gone up to the festival, Jesus also went up — not publicly, but secretly. [11] The Judeans were looking for him at the festival and asking, "Where is he?"; [12] and there were many whispers about him among the people, some saying, "He is a good man"; others: "No! He is leading the people astray." [13] No one, however, spoke freely about him, because they were afraid of the Judeans.

[14] About the middle of the festival week, Jesus went up into the Temple, and began teaching. [15] The Judeans were astonished. "How has this man learned to read," they asked, "when he has never studied?" [16] So, in reply, Jesus said: "My teaching is not my own; it is his who sent me. [17] If anyone has the will to do God's will, he will find out whether my teaching is from God, or whether I speak on my own authority. [18] The person who speaks on his own authority seeks honor for himself; but the person who seeks the honor of the one that sent him is sincere, and there is nothing false in him. [19] Was it not Moses who gave you the Law? Yet not one of you obeys it! Why are you seeking to put me to death?"

[20] "You must be possessed by a demon!" the people exclaimed. "Who is seeking to put you to death?"

[21] "There was one thing I did," replied Jesus, "at which you are all still amazed. [22] Moses gave you circumcision — it was not from Moses, but from the patriarchs — and you circumcise on the Sabbath. [23] When a man receives circumcision on a sabbath to prevent the Law of Moses from being broken, how can you be angry with me for making a man sound and well on a sabbath? [24] Do not judge by appearances; judge justly." [25] At this some of the people of Jerusalem exclaimed: "Is this not the man whom they are seeking to put to death? [26] Yet here he is, speaking out boldly, and they say nothing to him! Is it possible that our leaders have really discovered that he is the Christ? [27] Yet we know where this man is from; but when the Anointed One comes, no one will be able to tell where he is from." [28] Therefore, Jesus, as he was teaching in the Temple, raised his voice and said: "Yes; you know me and you know where I am from. Yet I have not come on my own authority, but the one who sent me may be trusted; and him you do not know. [29] I do know him, for it is from him that I have come, and he sent me." [30] So they sought to arrest him; but no one touched him, for his time had not come yet. [31] Many of the people, however, believed in him. "When the Christ comes," they said, "will he give more signs of his mission than this man has given?" [32] The Pharisees heard the people whispering about him in this way, and so the Pharisees sent officers to arrest him; [33] at which Jesus said: "I will be with you but a little longer, and then I am going to the one who sent me. [34] You will look for me, and you will not find me; and you will not be able to come where I will be."

[35] "Where is this man going," the people asked one another, "that we would not find him? Will he go to the Greeks, and teach the Greeks? [36] What does he mean by saying, 'You will look for me, and you will not find me; and you will not be able to come where I will be'?"

[37] On the last and greatest day of the festival, Jesus, who was standing by, exclaimed: "If anyone thirsts, let her come to me, and drink. Let anyone who trusts in me come and drink. [38] As it is written, 'From his heart streams of live water will flow.'" [39] By this he meant the Spirit, which those who had believed in him were to receive; for the Spirit had not yet come, because Jesus had not yet been exalted. [40] Some of the listening crowd said, "This one is really the prophet." [41] And others said, "This one is the Anointed One," but still others said, "Would the Christ come from Galilee? [42] "Is it not written that it is of the race of David, and from Bethlehem, the village to which David belonged, that the

Anointed One is to come?" [43] So there was a sharp division among the people because of Jesus. [44] Some of them wanted to arrest him, and yet no one touched him. [45] When the officers returned to the chief priests and Pharisees, they were asked: "Why have you not brought him?"

[46] "No one ever spoke as he speaks!" they answered. [47] "What! Have you been led astray too?" the Pharisees replied. [48] "Have any of our rulers believed in him, or any of the Pharisees? [49] As for these people who do not know the Law—they are cursed!" [50] But one of their number, Nicodemus, who before this had been to see Jesus, said to them: [51] "Does our Law pass judgment on a person without first giving him a hearing, and finding out what he has been doing?"

[52] "Are you also from Galilee?" they retorted. "Search, and you will find that no prophet is to arise in Galilee!"

[53] And everyone went home

8 [1] except Jesus, who went to the Mount of Olives. [2] * But he went again into the Temple early in the morning, and all the people came to him; and he sat down and taught them. [3] Presently, however, the scholars and the Pharisees brought a woman who had been caught in adultery, and placed her in the middle of the Court, [4] and said to Jesus:

"Teacher, this woman was found in the act of adultery. Now Moses, [5] in the Law, commanded us to stone such women to death; what do you say?"

[6] They said this to test him, in order to have a charge to bring against him. But Jesus stooped down, and wrote on the ground with his finger. [7] However, as they continued asking him, he raised himself, and said:

"Let the person among you who has never done wrong throw the first stone at her." [8] And again he stooped down, and wrote on the ground. [9] When they heard that, they went out one by one, beginning with the eldest; and Jesus was left alone with the woman in the middle of the Court. [10] Raising himself, Jesus said to her:

"Woman, where are they? Did no one condemn you?"

[11] "No one, sir," she answered.

"Neither do I condemn you," said Jesus. "Go, and do not sin again."

[12] Jesus again addressed the people. "I am the light of the world," he said. "The person who follows me will not walk in darkness, but will have the light of life."

[13] "You are bearing testimony to yourself!" exclaimed the Pharisees; "your testimony is not true."

[14] "Even if I bear testimony to myself," answered Jesus, "my testimony is true; for I know where I came from, and where I am going; but you do not know where I come from, nor where I am going. [15] You judge according to the flesh; I judge no one. [16] Yet, even if I judge, my judgment would be true; because I am not alone, but the Father who sent me is with me. [17] Why, in your Law it is said that the testimony of two persons is trustworthy. [18] I, who bear testimony to myself, am one, and the Father who sent me also bears testimony to me." [19] "Where is your father, then?" they asked. "You know neither me nor my Father," replied Jesus. "If you had known me, you would have also known my Father." [20] These statements Jesus made in the Treasury, while teaching in the Temple Courts. Yet no one arrested him, for his time had not then come.

[21] Jesus again spoke to the people. "I am going away," he said, "and you will look for

---

* John 8:2–11 does not exist in the earliest manuscripts of the Gospel of John and is written in an entirely different style. This passage is inserted here in some later manuscripts from an ancient source and is found either after John 7:53 or after Luke 21:38 or elsewhere.

me, but you will die in your sin; you cannot come where I am going."

²² "Is he going to kill himself," the people exclaimed, "that he says, 'You cannot go where I am going'?" ²³ "You," added Jesus, "are from below, I am from above; you are of this world, I am not; ²⁴ and so I told you that you would die in your sins, for, unless you believe that I am, you will die in your sins."

²⁵ "Who are you?" they asked. "Why ask exactly what I have been telling you?" said Jesus. ²⁶ "I have still much that concerns you to speak of and to pass judgment on; yet the one who sent me may be trusted, and I speak to the world only of the things which I have heard from him." ²⁷ They did not understand that he meant the Father. ²⁸ So Jesus added: "When you have lifted up the Child of Humanity, then you will understand that I am, and that I do nothing of myself, but that I say just what the Father has taught me. ²⁹ Moreover, he who sent me is with me; he has not left me alone; for I always do what pleases him." ³⁰ While he was speaking in this way, many came to believe in him. ³¹ So Jesus went on to say to those who had believed him: "If you remain constant to my message, you are truly my followers; ³² and you find out the truth, and the truth will set you free."

³³ "We are descendants of Abraham," was their answer, "and have never yet been in slavery to anyone. What do you mean by saying, 'You will be set free'?" ³⁴ "In truth I tell you," replied Jesus, "everyone who sins is a slave to sin. ³⁵ And a slave does not remain in the home always; but a son remains always. ³⁶ If, then, the Son sets you free, you will be free indeed! ³⁷ I know that you are descendants of Abraham; yet you are seeking to put me to death, because my message finds no place in your hearts. ³⁸ I tell you what I have myself seen in the presence of my Father; and you, in the same way, do what you have learned from your father."

³⁹ "Our father is Abraham," was their answer. "If you are Abraham's children," replied Jesus, "do what Abraham did. ⁴⁰ But as it is, you are seeking to put me to death — a man who has told you the truth as he heard it from God. Abraham did not act in that way. ⁴¹ You are doing what your own father does."

"We are not bastards," they said; "we have one Father — God himself."

⁴² "If God were your Father," Jesus replied, "you would have loved me, for I came out from God, and now am here; and I have not come of myself, but he sent me. ⁴³ How is it that you do not understand what I say? It is because you cannot bear to listen to my message. ⁴⁴ As for you, you are children of your father the devil, and you are determined to do what your father loves to do. He was a murderer from the first, and did not stand by the truth, because there is no truth in him. Whenever he lies, he does what is natural to him, because he is a liar, and the father of lying. ⁴⁵ But as for me, it is because I speak the truth to you that you do not believe me. ⁴⁶ Which of you can convict me of sin? Why then do you not believe me, if I am speaking truth? ⁴⁷ The person who comes from God listens to God's teaching; the reason why you do not listen is because you do not come from God."

⁴⁸ "Are we not right, after all," replied the people, "in saying that you are a Samaritan, and are possessed by a demon?"

⁴⁹ "I am not possessed by a demon," Jesus answered, "but I am honoring my Father; and yet you dishonor me. ⁵⁰ Not that I am seeking honor for myself; there is one who is seeking my honor, and that one does the judging. ⁵¹ In truth I tell you, if anyone lays my message to heart, he will never see death."

⁵² "Now we are sure that you are possessed by a demon," the Judeans replied. "Abraham died, and so did the prophets; and yet you say, 'If anyone keeps my message, he will never know death.' ⁵³ Are you

greater than our ancestor Abraham, who died? And the prophets died too. Whom do you make yourself out to be?"

[54] "If I do honor to myself," answered Jesus, "such honor counts for nothing. It is my Father who does me honor—and you say that he is your God; [55] and yet you have not learned to know him; but I know him; and, if I were to say that I do not know him, I should be a liar like you; but I do know him, and I keep his word. [56] Your ancestor Abraham rejoiced that he would see my day; and he did see it, and was glad."

[57] "You are not fifty years old yet," the people exclaimed, "and have you seen Abraham?"

[58] "In truth I tell you," replied Jesus, "before Abraham existed, I am." [59] At this they took up stones to throw at him; but Jesus hid himself, and left the Temple.

9 [1] As Jesus passed by, he saw someone who had been blind from his birth. [2] "Rabbi," asked his followers, "who was it that sinned, this one or his parents, that he was born blind?"

[3] "Neither the person nor the parents," replied Jesus; "but he was born blind so that the work of God should be made plain in him. [4] We must do the work of the one who sent me, while it is day; night is coming, when no one can work. [5] As long as I am in the world, I am the light of the world." [6] Saying this, Jesus spat on the ground, made clay with the saliva, and put it on the man's eyes. [7] "Go," he said, "and wash your eyes in the Bath of Siloam" (a word which means "messenger"). So he went and washed his eyes, and returned able to see. [8] His neighbors, and those who had formerly known him by sight as a beggar, exclaimed: "Is this not the man who used to sit and beg?"

[9] "Yes," some said, "it is"; while others said: "No, but he is like him." The man himself said: "I am he."

[10] "How did you get your sight, then?"

they asked. [11] "The man whom they call Jesus," he answered, "made clay, and anointed my eyes, and said to me, 'Go to Siloam and wash your eyes.' So I went and washed my eyes, and gained my sight."

[12] "Where is he?" they asked. "I do not know," he answered. [13] They took the man who had been blind to the Pharisees. [14] Now it was a sabbath when Jesus made the clay and gave him his sight. [15] So the Pharisees also questioned the man as to how he had gained his sight. "He put clay on my eyes," he answered, "and I washed them, and I can see."

[16] "The man cannot be from God," said some of the Pharisees, "for he does not keep the sabbath."

"How is it possible," retorted others, "for a bad man to give signs like this?" [17] So there was a difference of opinion among them, and they again questioned the man. "What do you yourself say about him, for it is to you that he has given sight?" He said, "He is a prophet." [18] The Judeans, however, refused to believe that he had been blind and had gained his sight, until they had called his parents and questioned them. [19] "Is this your son," they asked, "who you say was born blind? If so, how is it that he can see now?"

[20] "We know that this is our son," answered the parents, "and that he was born blind; [21] but how it is that he can see now we do not know; nor do we know who it was that gave him his sight. Ask him—he is old enough—he will tell you about himself." [22] His parents spoke in this way because they were afraid of the Judeans; for the Judeans had already agreed that if anyone should acknowledge Jesus as the Anointed One, he should be expelled from their synagogues. [23] This was why his parents said, "He is old enough; ask him." [24] So the Judeans again called the man who had been blind, and said to him: "Give God the praise; we know that this is a bad man."

[25] "I know nothing about his being

a bad man," he replied; "one thing I do know, that although I was blind, now I can see."

²⁶ "What did he do to you?" they asked. "How did he give you your sight?"

²⁷ "I told you just now," he answered, "and you did not listen. Why do you want to hear it again? Surely you also do not want to become his followers?"

²⁸ "You are his follower," they retorted scornfully; "but we are followers of Moses. ²⁹ We know that God spoke to Moses; but as for this one, we do not know where he comes from."

³⁰ "Well," the man replied, "this is very strange; you do not know where he comes from, and yet he has given me my sight! ³¹ We know that God never listens to bad people, but when a person is God-fearing and does God's will, God listens to her. ³² Since the world began, such a thing was never heard of as anyone's giving sight to a person born blind. ³³ If this man had not been from God, he could not have done anything at all."

³⁴ "You," they retorted, "were born totally depraved; and are you trying to teach us?" So they expelled him. ³⁵ Jesus heard of their having put him out; and, when he had found the man, he asked: "Do you trust in the Child of Humanity?"

³⁶ "Tell me who he is, sir," he replied, "so that I may believe in him."

³⁷ "Not only have you seen him," said Jesus, "but it is he who is now speaking to you."

³⁸ "Then, sir, I do trust," said the man, bowing to the ground before him; ³⁹ and Jesus added: "It was to judge that I came into this world, in order that those who cannot see should see, and that those who can see should become blind." ⁴⁰ Hearing this, some of the Pharisees who were with him said: "Then are we blind too?"

⁴¹ "If you had been blind," replied Jesus, "you would have had no sin to answer for; but as it is, you say, 'We can see,' and so your sin remains.

10 ¹ "In truth I tell you, whoever does not go into the sheepfold through the door, but climbs up at some other place, that person is a thief and a robber; ² but the person who goes in through the door is shepherd to the sheep. ³ For him the watchman opens the door; and the sheep listen to his voice; and he calls his own sheep by name, and leads them out. ⁴ When he has brought them all out, he walks in front of them, and his sheep follow him, because they know his voice. ⁵ They will not follow a stranger, but will run away from him; because they do not know a stranger's voice." ⁶ This was the allegory that Jesus told them, but they did not understand of what he was speaking. ⁷ So he continued: "In truth I tell you, I am the door for the sheep. ⁸ All who came before me were thieves and robbers; but the sheep did not listen to them. ⁹ I am the door; the one who goes in through me will be safe, and will go in and out and find pasture. ¹⁰ The thief comes only to steal, to kill, and to destroy; I have come so that they may have life, and may have it in greater fullness. ¹¹ I am the good shepherd. The good shepherd lays down his life for his sheep. ¹² The hired man who is not a shepherd, and who does not own the sheep, when he sees a wolf coming, leaves them and runs away; then the wolf seizes them, and scatters the flock. ¹³ He does this because he is only a hired man and does not care about the sheep. ¹⁴ I am the good shepherd; and I know my sheep, and my sheep know me — ¹⁵ just as the Father knows me and I know the Father — and I lay down my life for the sheep. ¹⁶ I have other sheep besides, which do not belong to this fold; I must lead them also, and they will listen to my voice; and they will become one flock under one shepherd. ¹⁷ This is why the Father loves me, because I lay down my life — to receive it again. ¹⁸ No one took it from me, but I lay it down of myself. I have authority to lay it down, and I have authority to receive it again. This is the command which I received from my Father." ¹⁹ In consequence of these words a difference of opinion again arose among the people. ²⁰ Many of them said: "He is possessed by a demon and is mad; why do you listen to him?" ²¹ Others said: "This is not the teaching of one who is possessed by a demon. Can a demon give sight to the blind?"

²² Soon after this the festival of the Re-dedication was held at Jerusalem. ²³ It was winter; and Jesus was walking in the Temple Courts, in the Colonnade of Solomon, ²⁴ when the people gathered around him, and said: "How long are you going to keep us in suspense? If you are the Christ, tell us so frankly."

²⁵ "I have told you so," replied Jesus, "and you do not trust me. The work that I am doing in my Father's name bears testimony to me. ²⁶ But you do not believe me, because you are not of my flock. ²⁷ My sheep listen to my voice; I know them, and they follow me; ²⁸ and I give them life from generation to generation, and they will not be lost; nor will anyone snatch them out of my hands. ²⁹ What my Father has entrusted to me is more than all else; and no one can snatch anything out of the Father's hands. ³⁰ The Father and I are one."

³¹ Some of the people again brought stones to throw at him; ³² and seeing this, Jesus said: "I have done before your eyes many good actions, inspired by the Father; for which of them would you stone me?"

³³ "It is not for any good action that we would stone you," they answered, "but for blasphemy; and because you, who are only a human being, make yourself out to be God."

³⁴ "Are there not," replied Jesus, "these words in your Law: 'I said, "You are gods"'? ³⁵ If those to whom God's word was addressed were said to be 'gods' — and scripture cannot be set aside — ³⁶ do you say of one whom the Father has commissioned and sent as his messenger to the world, 'You are blaspheming,' because I said 'I am

God's Son'? ³⁷ If I am not doing the work that my Father is doing, do not believe me; ³⁸ if I am doing it, even though you do not believe me, believe what that work shows; so that you may understand, and understand more and more clearly, that the Father is in me, and I am in the Father." ³⁹ They again sought to arrest him; but he escaped their hands.

⁴⁰ Then he again crossed the Jordan to the place where John used to baptize at first, and stayed there some time, during which many people came to see him. ⁴¹ "John gave no sign," they said; "but everything that he said about this one was true." ⁴² And many learned to trust in Jesus there.

11 ¹ Now a man named Lazarus, of Bethany, was lying ill; he belonged to the same village as Mary and her sister Martha. ² This Mary, whose brother Lazarus was ill, was the Mary who anointed the Master with perfume, and wiped his feet with her hair. ³ The sisters, therefore, sent this message to Jesus: "Master, the one you love is ill"; ⁴ and, when Jesus heard it, he said: "This illness is not to end in death, but is to redound to the glory of God, in order that the Child of God may be glorified through it." ⁵ Jesus loved Martha and her sister, and Lazarus. ⁶ Yet, when he heard of the illness of Lazarus, he still stayed two days in the place where he was. ⁷ Then, after that, he said to his followers: "Let us go to Judea again."

⁸ "Rabbi," they replied, "the Judeans there were but just now seeking to stone you; and are you going there again?"

⁹ "Are there not twelve hours in the day?" answered Jesus. "If someone walks about in the daytime, she does not stumble, because she can see light; ¹⁰ but if she walks about at night, she stumbles, because she does not have light." ¹¹ And, when he had said this, he added: "Our friend Lazarus has fallen asleep; but I am going so that I may wake him."

¹² "If he has fallen asleep, Master, he will get well," said his followers. ¹³ But Jesus meant that he was dead; they, however, supposed that he was speaking of sleep. ¹⁴ Then he said to them plainly: "Lazarus is dead; ¹⁵ and I am glad for your sakes that I was not there, so that you may learn to trust me. But let us go to him." ¹⁶ At this, Thomas, who was called "The Twin," said to his fellow followers: "Let us go too, so that we may die with him." ¹⁷ When Jesus reached the place, he found that Lazarus had been four days in the tomb already. ¹⁸ Bethany being only about two miles from Jerusalem, ¹⁹ a number of the people had come there to comfort Martha and Mary because of their brother's death. ²⁰ When Martha heard that Jesus was coming, she went to meet him; but Mary sat quietly at home. ²¹ "Master," Martha said to Jesus, "if you had been here, my brother would not have died. ²² Even now, I know that God will grant you whatever you ask him."

²³ "Your brother will rise to life," said Jesus. ²⁴ "I know that he will," replied Martha, "in the resurrection at the last day."

²⁵ "I am the resurrection and the life," said Jesus. "Anyone who believes in me will live, even when having died; ²⁶ and the one who lives and trusts in me will never die. Do you believe this?"

²⁷ "Yes, Master," she answered; "I believe that you are the Anointed One, the Son of God, the one coming into the world." ²⁸ After saying this, Martha went and called her sister Mary, and whispered: "The Teacher is here, and is asking for you." ²⁹ As soon as Mary heard that, she got up quickly, and went to meet him. ³⁰ Jesus had not then come into the village, but was still at the place where Martha had met him. ³¹ So the Judeans, who were in the house with Mary, comforting her, when they saw her get up quickly and go out, followed her, thinking that she was going to the tomb to weep there. ³² When Mary came where Jesus was and saw him,

she threw herself at his feet. "Master," she exclaimed, "if you had been here, my brother would not have died!" ³³ When Jesus saw her weeping, and the Judeans who had come with her weeping also, he groaned deeply, and was greatly distressed. ³⁴ "Where have you buried him?" he asked. "Come and see, Master," they answered. ³⁵ Jesus burst into tears. ³⁶ "How he must have loved him!" the Judeans exclaimed; ³⁷ but some of them said: "Could not this man, who gave sight to the blind man, have also prevented Lazarus from dying?" ³⁸ Again groaning inwardly, Jesus came to the tomb. It was a cave, and a stone lay against the mouth of it. ³⁹ "Move the stone away," said Jesus. "Master," said Martha, the sister of the dead man, "by this time the smell must be offensive, for this is the fourth day since his death."

⁴⁰ "Did I not tell you," replied Jesus, "that if you would believe in me, you should see the glory of God?" ⁴¹ So they moved the stone away; and Jesus, with uplifted eyes, said:

"Father, I thank you that you have heard my prayer; ⁴² I know that you always hear me; but I say this for the sake of the people standing near, so that they may believe that you have sent me."

⁴³ Then, after saying this, Jesus called in a loud voice: "Lazarus! Come out!" ⁴⁴ The dead man came out, wrapped hand and foot in a winding sheet; his face, too, had been wrapped in a cloth. "Set him free," said Jesus, "and let him go."

⁴⁵ In consequence of this, many of the Judeans who had come to visit Mary and had seen what Jesus did, learned to trust in him. ⁴⁶ Some of them, however, went to the Pharisees, and told them what he had done. ⁴⁷ The chief priests and the Pharisees called a meeting of the High Council, and said: "What are we to do, now that this man is giving so many signs? ⁴⁸ If we let him alone as we are doing, everyone will believe in him; and the Romans will come and will take from us both our city

and our nation." [49] One of them, however, Caiaphas, who was high priest that year, said to them: [50] "You are utterly mistaken. You do not consider that it is better for you that one person should die for the people, rather than the whole nation should be destroyed." [51] Now he did not say this of his own accord; but as high priest that year, he prophesied that Jesus was to die for the nation — [52] and not for the nation only, but also that he might unite the children of God now scattered far and wide. [53] So from that day they plotted to put Jesus to death.

[54] In consequence of this, Jesus did not go about publicly among the people anymore, but left that area, and went into the country bordering on the wilderness, to a town called Ephraim, where he stayed with his followers. [55] But the Judean festival of the Passover was near; and many people had gone up from the country to Jerusalem, for their purification, before the festival began. [56] So they looked for Jesus there, and said to one another, as they stood in the Temple: "What do you think? Do you think he will come to the festival?" [57] The chief priests and the Pharisees had already issued orders that if anyone learned where Jesus was, he should give information, so that they might arrest him.

The Last Days

12 [1] Six days before the Passover Jesus came to Bethany, where Lazarus, whom he had raised from the dead, was living. [2] There a supper was given in his honor at which Martha waited, while Lazarus was reclining with him. [3] So Mary took a pound of choice spikenard perfume of great value, and anointed the feet of Jesus with it, and then wiped them with her hair. The whole house was filled with the scent of the perfume. [4] One of the followers, Judas Iscariot, who was about to betray Jesus, asked: [5] "Why was not this perfume sold for a year's wages, and the money given to poor people?" [6] He said this, not because he cared for the poor, but because he was a thief, and, being in charge of the purse, used to take what was put in it. [7] "Leave her alone," said Jesus, "so that she may keep it until the day when my body is being prepared for burial. [8] The poor you always have with you, but you will not always have me."

[9] Now great numbers of people found out that Jesus was at Bethany; and they came there, not only because of him, but also to see Lazarus, whom he had raised from the dead. [10] The chief priests, however, plotted to put Lazarus, as well as Jesus, to death, [11] because it was owing to him that many of the Judeans had left them, and were becoming believers in Jesus. [12] On the following day great numbers of people who had come to the festival, hearing that Jesus was on his way to Jerusalem, took palm branches, [13] and went out to meet him, shouting as they went: "Hosanna! Blessed is the one who comes in the name of the Lord — the king of Israel!" [14] Having found a young ass, Jesus seated himself on it, in accordance with what had been written: [15] "Fear not, people of Zion; your king is coming to you, sitting on the colt of a donkey." [16] His followers did not understand all this at first; but when Jesus had been exalted, then they remembered that these things had been said of him in the writings, and that they had done these things for him. [17] Meanwhile the people who were with him when he called Lazarus out of the tomb and raised him from the dead were telling what they had seen. [18] This, indeed, was why the crowd met him — because people had heard that he had given this sign. [19] So the Pharisees said to one another: "You see that you are gaining nothing! Why, all the world has run after him!"

[20] Among those who were going up to worship at the festival were some Greeks, [21] who went to Philip of Bethsaida in

Galilee, and said: "Sir, we wish to see Jesus." [22] Philip went and told Andrew, and then together they went and told Jesus. [23] This was his reply: "The time has come for the Child of Humanity to be exalted. [24] In truth I tell you, unless a grain of wheat falls into the ground and dies, it remains a single grain; but if it dies, it becomes fruitful. [25] A person who loves her life loses it; while someone who hates her life in the present world will preserve it for life through the ages. [26] If someone is ready to serve me, let her follow me; and where I am, there my servant will be also. If a person is ready to serve me, my Father will honor her. [27] Now I am distressed at heart and what can I say? Father, bring me safe through this hour — yet it was for this reason that I came to this hour — [28] Father, glorify your own name." At this there came a voice from heaven, which said: "I have already glorified it, and I will glorify it again." [29] The crowd of bystanders who heard the sound said that it was thundering. Others said: "An angel has been speaking to him."

[30] "It was not for my sake that the voice came," said Jesus, "but for yours. [31] Now this world is judged. Now the ruler of this world will be driven out; [32] and I, when I am lifted up from the earth, will draw all people to myself." [33] By these words he indicated what death he was destined to die. [34] "We," replied the people, "have learned from the Law that the Anointed One is to remain forever; how is it, then, that you say that the Child of Humanity must be lifted up? Who is this Child of Humanity?"

[35] "Only a little while longer," answered Jesus, "will you have the light among you. Travel on while you have the light, so that darkness may not overtake you; the one who travels in the darkness does not know where he is going. [36] While you still have the light, trust in the light, so that you may be children of light." After he had said this, Jesus went away, and hid himself

from them. [37] But though Jesus had given so many signs of his mission before their eyes, they did not believe in him, [38] in fulfillment of the words of the prophet Isaiah, where he says: "Lord, who has believed our teaching? And to whom has the might of the Lord been revealed?" [39] The reason why they were unable to believe is given by Isaiah elsewhere, in these words: [40] "He has blinded their eyes, and blunted their mind, so that they should not see with their eyes, and perceive with their mind, and changing their ways, be healed by me." [41] Isaiah said this, because he saw his glory; and it was of him that he spoke. [42] Yet for all this, even among the rulers there were many who came to believe in Jesus; but because of the Pharisees, they did not acknowledge it, because they were afraid that they should be expelled from their synagogues; [43] for they valued honor from people more than honor from God. [44] But Jesus had proclaimed: "They who trust in me trust, not in me, but in the one who sent me; [45] and the one who sees me sees the one who sent me. [46] I have come as a light into the world, so that no one who believes in me should remain in the darkness. [47] When anyone hears my teaching and pays no heed to it, I am not his judge; for I came not to judge the world, but to save the world. [48] The one who rejects me, and disregards my teaching, has a judge already — the message which I have delivered will itself be his judge at the last day. [49] For I have not delivered it on my own authority; but the Father, who sent me, has himself given me his command as to what I should say, and what message I should deliver. [50] And I know that life through the generations lies in keeping his command. Therefore, whatever I say, I say only what the Father has taught me."

13 [1] Before the Passover festival began, Jesus knew that the time had come for him to leave the world and go to the Father. He had loved those who were his own in the world, and he loved them to the last. [2] The devil had already put the thought of betraying Jesus into the mind of Judas Iscariot, the son of Simon; [3] and at supper, Jesus — although knowing that the Father had put everything into his hands, and that he had come from God, and was to return to God — [4] rose from his place, and, taking off his upper garments, tied a towel around his waist. [5] He then poured some water into the basin, and began to wash his followers' feet, and to wipe them with the towel which was tied around him. [6] When he came to Simon Peter, Peter said: "You, Master! Are you going to wash my feet?"

[7] "You do not understand now what I am doing," replied Jesus, "but you will learn by and by."

[8] "You will never wash my feet!" exclaimed Peter. "Unless I wash you," answered Jesus, "you have nothing in common with me."

[9] "Then, Master, not my feet only," exclaimed Simon Peter, "but also my hands and my head."

[10] "He who has bathed," replied Jesus, "has no need to wash, unless it be his feet, but is altogether clean; and you," he said to the followers, "are clean, yet not all of you." [11] For he knew who was going to betray him, and that was why he said, "You are not all clean." [12] When he had washed their feet, and had put on his upper garments and taken his place, he spoke to them again. "Do you understand what I have been doing to you?" he asked. [13] "You yourselves call me 'the Teacher' and 'the Master,' and you are right, for I am both. [14] If I, then — 'the Master' and 'the Teacher' — have washed your feet, you also ought to wash one another's feet; [15] for I have given you an example, so that you may do just as I have done to you. [16] In truth I tell you, a slave is not greater than his master, nor yet an ambassador than the one who sends him. [17] Now that you know these things, happy are you if you do them. [18] I am not speaking about all of you. I

know whom I have chosen; but this is in fulfillment of the words of scripture: 'He that is eating my bread has lifted his heel against me.' [19] For the future I will tell you of things before they take place, so that when they take place, you may believe that I am. [20] In truth I tell you, the one who receives anyone that I send receives me; and the person who receives me receives him who sent me." [21] After saying this, Jesus was much troubled, and said solemnly: "In truth I tell you that it is one of you who will betray me." [22] The disciples looked at one another, wondering whom he meant. [23] Reclining next to Jesus, in the place on his right hand, was the follower whom Jesus loved. [24] So Simon Peter made signs to that follower: "Ask who it is that he means." [25] Being in this position, that disciple leaned back on Jesus's chest, and asked him: "Who is it, Master?"

[26] "It is the one," answered Jesus, "to whom I will give a piece of bread after dipping it in the dish." And, when Jesus had dipped the bread, he took it and gave it to Judas, the son of Simon Iscariot; [27] and it was then, after he had received it, that Satan took possession of him. So Jesus said to him: "Do at once what you are going to do." [28] But no one at the table understood why he said this to Judas. [29] Some thought that as Judas kept the purse, Jesus meant that he was to buy some things needed for the festival, or to give something to the poor. [30] After taking the piece of bread, Judas went out immediately; and it was night.

[31] When Judas had gone out, Jesus said: "Now the Child of Humanity has been exalted, and God has been glorified through him; [32] and God will exalt him with himself — yes, he will exalt him forthwith. [33] Children, I am to be with you but a little while longer. You will look for me; and what I said to the Judeans — 'You cannot come where I am going' — I now say to you. [34] I give you a new commandment — love one another; love one an-

other as I have loved you. ³⁵ It is by this that everyone will recognize you as my followers — by your loving one another."

³⁶ "Where are you going, Master?" asked Peter. "I am going where you cannot now follow me," answered Jesus, "but you will follow me later."

³⁷ "Why cannot I follow you now, Master?" asked Peter. "I will lay down my life for you."

³⁸ "Will you lay down your life for me?" replied Jesus. "In truth I tell you, the cock will not crow until you have disowned me three times.

14 ¹ "Do not let your hearts be troubled. You trust in God; trust also in me. ² In my Father's home there are many dwellings. If it had not been so, I should have told you, for I am going to prepare a place for you. ³ And, since I go and prepare a place for you, I will return and take you to be with me, so that you may be where I am; ⁴ and you know the way to the place where I am going."

⁵ "We do not know where you are going, Master," said Thomas, "so how can we know the way?" ⁶ Jesus answered: "I am the way, and the truth, and the life; no one comes to the Father except through me. ⁷ If you recognize me, you will know my Father also; from now on you know him, indeed you have already seen him."

⁸ "Master, show us the Father," said Philip, "and we will be satisfied."

⁹ "Have I been all this time among you," said Jesus, "and yet you, Philip, have not recognized me? The person who has seen me has seen the Father; how can you say, then, 'Show us the Father'? ¹⁰ Do you not believe that I am in the Father, and the Father in me? In giving you my teaching I am not speaking on my own authority; but the Father himself, living in me, does his own work. ¹¹ Believe me," he said to them all, "when I say that I am in the Father and the Father in me, or else believe me because of the works themselves. ¹² In truth I tell you,

the person who believes in me will herself do the work that I am doing; and she will do greater work still, because I am going to the Father. ¹³ Whatever you ask in my name, I will do, so that the Father may be glorified in the Son. ¹⁴ If you ask anything in my name, I will do it. ¹⁵ If you love me, you will keep my commandments, ¹⁶ and I will ask the Father, and he will give you another helper, to be with you always — the spirit of truth. ¹⁷ The world cannot receive this Spirit, because it does not see it or recognize it, but you recognize it, because it is with you, and is in you. ¹⁸ I will not leave you bereaved; I will come to you. ¹⁹ In a little while the world will see me no more, but you will still see me; because I am living, you will be living also. ²⁰ At that time you will recognize that I am in the Father, and you in me, and I in you. ²¹ It is they who have my commandments and keep them that love me; and the person who loves me will be loved by my Father, and I will love her, and will reveal myself to her."

²² "What has happened, Master," said Judas (not Judas Iscariot), "that you are going to reveal yourself to us, and not to the world?"

²³ "Whoever loves me," Jesus answered, "will keep my word; and my Father will love her, and we will come to her and make our home with her. ²⁴ The person who does not love me will not keep my words; and the message to which you are listening is not my own, but comes from the Father who sent me. ²⁵ I have told you all this while still with you, ²⁶ but the helper — the holy Spirit whom the Father will send in my name — will teach you all things, and will recall to your minds all that I have said to you. ²⁷ Peace be with you! My own peace I give you. But I do not give to you as the world gives. Do not let your hearts be troubled, or dismayed. ²⁸ You heard me say that I was going away and would return to you. If you loved me, you would be glad that I am going to the Father, because the Father is greater than I. ²⁹ And this I

have told you now before it happens, so that when it does happen, you may trust in me. [30] I will not talk with you much more, for the ruler of the world is coming. He has nothing in common with me; [31] but he is coming so that the world may see that I love the Father, and that I do as the Father commanded me. Come, let us be going.

15 [1] "I am the true vine, and my Father is the vine grower. [2] Any unfruitful branch in me he cuts off, and he prunes every fruitful branch, so that it may bear more fruit. [3] You are already pruned because of the message that I have given you. [4] Remain in me, as I in you. As a branch cannot bear fruit by itself, unless it remains united to the vine; no more can you, unless you remain united to me. [5] I am the vine, you are the branches. The one remaining in me, and I in him, bears fruit plentifully; for you can do nothing apart from me. [6] If anyone does not remain united to me, he is thrown away, as a branch would be, and withers up. Such branches are collected and thrown into the fire, and are burned. [7] If you remain in me, and my words remain in you, ask whatever you wish, and it will be yours. [8] It is to the glory of my Father that you should bear much fruit and be my followers. [9] As the Father has loved me, so have I loved you; remain in my love. [10] If you keep my commandments, you will remain in my love; just as I have kept my Father's commandments and remain in his love. [11] I have told you all this so that my own joy may be in you, and that your joy may be complete. [12] This is my command—love one another, as I have loved you. [13] No one can give greater love than by laying down his life for his friends. [14] And you are my friends. If you do what I command you, [15] I no longer call you slaves, because a slave does not know what his master is doing; but I have called you friends, because I made known to you everything that I learned from my Father. [16] It was not you who chose me, but I who chose you, and I appointed you to go and bear fruit—fruit that should remain, so that the Father might grant you whatever you ask in my name. [17] I am giving you these commands that you may love one another. [18] If the world hates you, you know that it has first hated me. [19] If you belonged to the world, the world would love its own. Because you do not belong to the world, but I have chosen you out of the world—that is why the world hates you. [20] Remember what I said to you: A slave is not greater than his master. If they have persecuted me, they will also persecute you; if they have kept my word, they will keep yours as well. [21] But they will do all this to you because of my name, for they do not know him who sent me. [22] If I had not come and spoken to them, they would have had no sin to answer for; but as it is, they have no excuse for their sin. [23] The person who hates me hates my Father also. [24] If I had not done among them such work as no one else ever did, they would have had no sin to answer for; but as it is, they have seen and hated both me and my Father. [25] And so is fulfilled what is said in their Law: 'They hated me without cause.' [26] But when the helper comes, whom I will send to you from the Father, the Spirit of Truth—who comes from the Father—will bear testimony to me; [27] yes, and you also are to bear testimony, because you have been with me from the first.

16 [1] "I have spoken to you in this way so that you may not falter. [2] They will expel you from their synagogues; indeed the time is coming when anyone who kills you will think that he is making an offering to God. [3] He will do this, because he has not learned to know the Father, or even me. [4] But I have spoken to you of these things so that when the time for them comes, you may remember that I told you about them myself. [5] I did not tell you all this at first, because I was with you. But now I am to return to him who sent me; and yet not one of you asks me, 'Where are you going?' [6] although your hearts are full of sorrow at all that I have been saying to you. [7] Yet I am only telling you the truth; it is for your good that I should go away. For otherwise the helper will never come to you, but if I leave you, I will send him to you. [8] And he, when he comes, will bring conviction to the world as to sin, and as to righteousness, and as to judgment; [9] as to sin, for people do not believe in me; [10] as to righteousness, for I am going to the Father, and you will see me no longer; [11] as to judgment, for the ruler of this world has been condemned. [12] I have still much to say to you, but you cannot bear it now. [13] Yet on arrival, the Spirit of Truth will guide you into all truth; for this one will not speak on its own authority, but will speak of all that it hears; and will tell you of the things that are to come. [14] This one will glorify me, and will take of what is mine, and will tell it to you. [15] Everything that the Father has is mine; that is why I said that the helper takes of what is mine, and will tell it to you. [16] In a little while you will no longer see me; and then in a little while you will see me." [17] At this some of his followers said to one another: "What does he mean by saying to us, 'In a little while you will not see me, and then in a little while you will see me indeed'; and by saying, 'Because I am going to the Father'? [18] What does he mean by 'in a little while'?" they said; "we do not know what he is speaking about." [19] Jesus saw that they were wanting to ask him a question, and said: "Are you trying to find out from one another what I meant by saying, 'In a little while you will not see me; and then in a little while you will see me indeed'? [20] In truth I tell you that you will weep and mourn, and the world will rejoice; you will suffer pain, but your pain will turn to joy. [21] A woman in labor is in pain because her time has come; but no sooner is the child born, than she forgets her trouble in her joy that a child has been born into the

world. [22] You, in the same way, are sorry now; but I will see you again, and your hearts will rejoice, and no one will rob you of your joy. [23] And at that time you will not ask me anything; in truth I tell you, if you ask the Father for anything, he will grant it to you in my name. [24] So far you have not asked for anything in my name; ask, and you will receive, so that your joy may be complete. [25] I have spoken to you of all this in veiled figures of speech; a time is coming, however, when I will not speak any longer to you in these figures of speech, but will tell you about the Father plainly. [26] You will ask, at that time, in my name; and I do not say that I will intercede with the Father for you; [27] for the Father himself loves you, because you have loved me, and have believed that I came from the Father. [28] I came out from the Father, and have come into the world; and now I am to leave the world, and go to the Father."

[29] "At last," exclaimed the disciples, "you are using plain words and not speaking in figures at all. [30] Now we are sure that you know everything, and need not wait for anyone to question you. This makes us trust that you did come from God."

[31] "Do you believe that already?" Jesus answered. [32] "Listen! A time is coming — indeed it has already come — when you are to be scattered, each going your own way, and to leave me alone; and yet I am not alone, because the Father is with me. [33] I have spoken to you in this way so that in me you may find peace. In the world you will find trouble; yet, take courage! I have conquered the world."

17 [1] After saying this, Jesus raised his eyes heavenward, and said:

"Father, the hour has come; glorify your Child, so that your Child may glorify you; [2] even as you gave him power over all humanity, so that he may give eternal life to all those whom you have given him. [3] And life from generation to generation is this — to know you the one true God, and Jesus Christ whom you have sent. [4] I have glorified you on earth by completing the work which you have given me to do; [5] and now do you glorify me, Father, at your own side, with the glory which I had at your side before the world began. [6] I have revealed your name to those whom you gave me from the world; they were your own, and you gave them to me; and they have laid your message to heart. [7] They recognize now that everything that you gave me was from you; [8] for I have given them the teaching which you gave me, and they received it, and clearly understood that I came from you, and they trusted that you sent me. [9] I intercede for them; I am not interceding for the world, but for those whom you have given me, for they belong to you — [10] all that is mine is yours, and all that is yours is mine — and I am glorified in them. [11] Now I am to be in this world no longer, but they are still to be in the world, and I am to come to you. Holy Father, keep them true to your name which you have given me, so that they may be one, as we are. [12] While I was with them, I kept them true to your name, and I have guarded them; and not one of them has been lost, except that one destined to be lost — in fulfillment of the writings. [13] But now I am to come to you; and I am speaking like this, while still in the world, so that they may have my own joy, in all its fullness. [14] I have given them your message; and the world hated them, because they do not belong to the world, even as I do not belong to the world. [15] I do not ask you to take them out of the world, but to keep them from evil. [16] They do not belong to the world, even as I do not belong to the world. [17] Make them holy in truth; your word is truth. [18] Just as you have sent me, so I send them as my messengers to the world. [19] And it is for their sakes that I am giving myself in holiness, so that they also may become truly holy. [20] But it is not only for them that I am interceding, but

also for those who trust me through their message, [21] that they all may be one — that as you, Father, are in me and I am in you, so that they may be in us and that the world may trust that it was you who sent me. [22] I have given them the glory which you have given me, so that they may be one as we are one — [23] I in them and you in me — that so they may be perfected in oneness, and so that the world may know that you have sent me, and that you have loved them as you have loved me. [24] Father, my desire for all those whom you have given me is that they may be with me where I am, so that they may see the glory which you have given me; for you did love me before the beginning of the world. [25] Righteous Father, though the world did not know you, I knew you; and these people knew that you have sent me. [26] I have made you known to them, and will do so still; that the love that you have had for me may be in them, and that I may be in them."

18 [1] When Jesus had said this, he went out with his followers and crossed the Kedron valley to a place where there was a garden, into which he and his followers went. [2] The place was well known to Judas, the betrayer, for Jesus and his followers had often met there. [3] So Judas, who had obtained soldiers from the Roman garrison, and some police officers from the chief priests and the Pharisees, came there with lanterns, torches, and weapons. [4] Jesus, aware of all that was coming upon him, went to meet them, and said to them: "For whom are you looking?"

[5] "Jesus of Nazareth," was their answer. "Here I am," he said. (Judas, the betrayer, was also standing with them.) [6] When Jesus said, 'I am,' they drew back and fell to the ground. [7] So he again asked for whom they were looking, and they answered: "Jesus of Nazareth."

[8] "I have already told you that I am he," replied Jesus, "so, if it is for me that you

are looking, let these people go." [9] This was in fulfillment of his words: "Of those whom you have given me I have not lost one." [10] At this, Simon Peter, who had a sword with him, drew it, and struck the high priest's slave, and cut off his right ear. The slave's name was Malchus. [11] But Jesus said to Peter: "Sheathe your sword. Should I not drink the cup which the Father has given me?"

[12] So the soldiers of the garrison, with their commanding officer and the Judean police, arrested Jesus and bound him, [13] and took him first of all to Annas. Annas was the father-in-law of Caiaphas, who was high priest that year. [14] It was Caiaphas who had counseled the Judeans that it was best that one person should die for the people. [15] Meanwhile Simon Peter followed Jesus, and so did another follower. That one, being well known to the high priest, went with Jesus into the high priest's courtyard, [16] while Peter stood outside by the door. Presently the other follower — the one well known to the high priest — went out and spoke to the porteress, and brought Peter in. [17] So the maidservant said to Peter: "Are you not also one of this person's followers?"

"No, I am not," he said. [18] The servants and police officers were standing around a charcoal fire (which they had made because it was cold), and were warming themselves. Peter, too, was with them, standing and warming himself. [19] The high priest questioned Jesus about his followers and about his teaching. [20] "For my part," answered Jesus, "I have spoken to all the world openly. I always taught in some synagogue, or in the Temple, places where everyone assembles, and I never spoke of anything in secret. [21] Why question me? Question those who have listened to me as to what I have spoken about to them. They must know what I said." [22] When Jesus said this, one of the police officers who was standing near gave him a blow with his hand. "Do you answer the high priest

like that?" he exclaimed. [23] "If I said anything wrong, give evidence about it," replied Jesus; "but if not, why do you strike me?" [24] Annas sent him bound to Caiaphas the high priest. [25] Meanwhile Simon Peter was standing there, warming himself; so they said to him: "Are you not also one of his followers?" Peter denied it. "No, I am not," he said. [26] One of the high priest's servants, a relation of the man whose ear Peter had cut off, exclaimed: "Did not I myself see you with him in the garden?" [27] Peter again denied it; and at that moment a cock crowed.

[28] From Caiaphas they took Jesus to the government house. It was early in the morning. But they did not enter the government house themselves, otherwise they might become unclean, and so be unable to eat the Passover. [29] Therefore Pilate came outside to speak to them. "What charge do you bring against this man?" he asked. [30] "If he had not been a criminal, we should not have given him up to you," they answered. [31] "Take him yourselves," said Pilate, "and try him by your own Law."

"We have no power to put anyone to death," the authorities replied — [32] in fulfillment of what Jesus had said when indicating the death that he was destined to die. [33] After that, Pilate went into the government house again, and calling Jesus up, asked him: "Are you the king of the Judeans?"

[34] "Do you ask me that yourself," replied Jesus, "or did others say it to you about me?"

[35] "Do you take me for a Judean?" was Pilate's answer. "It is your own people and the chief priests who have given you up to me. What have you done?"

[36] "My realm," replied Jesus, "is not of this world. If it had been so, my servants would be doing their utmost to prevent my being given up to the Judeans; but my realm is not here."

[37] "So you are a king after all!" exclaimed Pilate. "It is you who say that I

am a king," answered Jesus. "I was born for this, I have come into the world for this — to bear testimony to the truth. Everyone who is on the side of truth listens to my voice." ³⁸ "What is truth?" exclaimed Pilate. After saying this, he went out to the crowd again, and said: "For my part, I find nothing with which he can be charged." ³⁹ It is, however, the custom for me to grant you the release of one man at the Passover festival. Do you wish for the release of the king of the Judeans?"

⁴⁰ "No, not this man," they shouted again, "but Barabbas!" This Barabbas was a robber.

19 ¹ After that, Pilate had Jesus scourged. ² The soldiers made a crown with some thorns and put it on his head and threw a purple robe around him. ³ They kept coming up to him and saying: "Long live the king of the Judeans!" and they gave him blow after blow with their hands. ⁴ Pilate again came outside, and said to the people: "Look! I am bringing him out to you, so that you may know that I find nothing with which he can be charged." ⁵ Then Jesus came outside, wearing the crown of thorns and the purple robe; and Pilate said to them: "Here is the human one!" ⁶ When the chief priests and the police officers saw him, they shouted: "Crucify him! Crucify him!"

"Take him yourselves and crucify him," said Pilate. "For my part, I find nothing with which he can be charged."

⁷ "But we," replied the Judeans, "have a Law, under which he deserves death for making himself out to be the Son of God." ⁸ When Pilate heard what they said, he became still more alarmed; ⁹ and, going into the government house again, he said to Jesus: "Where do you come from?" ¹⁰ But Jesus made no reply. So Pilate said to him: "Do you refuse to speak to me? Do you not know that I have power to release you, and have power to crucify you?"

¹¹ "You would have no power over me at all," answered Jesus, "if it had not been given you from above; and, therefore, the man who betrayed me to you is guilty of the greater sin." ¹² This made Pilate anxious to release him; but the crowd shouted: "If you release that man, you are no friend of the emperor! Anyone who makes himself out to be a king is setting himself against the emperor!" ¹³ On hearing what they said, Pilate brought Jesus out, and took his seat on the judgment bench at a place called "The Stone Pavement" — in Hebrew *Gabbatha*. ¹⁴ It was the Passover preparation day, and about noon. Then he said to the crowd: "Here is your king!" ¹⁵ At that the people shouted: "Kill him! Kill him! Crucify him!"

"What! Should I crucify your king?" exclaimed Pilate. "We have no king but the emperor," replied the chief priests; ¹⁶ so Pilate gave Jesus up to them to be crucified.

So they took Jesus; ¹⁷ and he went out, carrying his cross himself, to the location called "The Place of a Skull," or, in Hebrew, *Golgotha*. ¹⁸ There they crucified him, and two others with him — one on each side, and Jesus between them. ¹⁹ Pilate also had these words written and put up over the cross: "Jesus of Nazareth, the King of the Judeans." ²⁰ These words were read by many people, because the place where Jesus was crucified was near the city; and they were written in Hebrew, Latin, and Greek. ²¹ The chief priests said to Pilate: "Do not write 'The King of the Judeans,' but write what he said: 'I am the king of the Judeans.'" ²² But Pilate answered: "What I have written, I have written."

²³ When the soldiers had crucified Jesus, they took his clothes and divided them into four shares — a share for each soldier — and they took the coat also. The coat had no seam, being woven in one piece from top to bottom. ²⁴ So they said to one another: "Do not let us tear it, but let us cast lots for it, to see who will have

it." This was in fulfillment of the words of scripture:

> "They shared my clothes among them,
>   and over my clothing they cast lots."

That was what the soldiers did. ²⁵ Meanwhile near the cross of Jesus were standing his mother and his mother's sister, as well as Mary the wife of Clopas and Mary of Magdala. ²⁶ When Jesus saw his mother, and the follower whom he loved, standing near, he said to his mother: "This is your child." ²⁷ Then he said to that follower: "This is your mother." And from that very hour the follower took her to live in his house.

²⁸ Afterward, knowing that everything was now finished, Jesus said, in fulfillment of the words in the writings: "I am thirsty." ²⁹ There was a bowl standing there full of common wine; so they put a sponge soaked in the wine on the end of a hyssop stalk, and held it up to his mouth. ³⁰ When Jesus had received the wine, he exclaimed: "It is finished!" Then, bowing his head, he handed over his spirit. ³¹ It was the preparation day, and so, to prevent the bodies from remaining on the crosses during the sabbath (for that sabbath was an important day), the Judeans asked Pilate to have the legs broken and the bodies removed. ³² Accordingly the soldiers came and broke the legs of the first man, and then those of the other who had been crucified with Jesus; ³³ but on coming to him, when they saw that he was already dead, they did not break his legs. ³⁴ One of the soldiers, however, pierced his side with a spear, and blood and water immediately flowed from it. ³⁵ This is the statement of one who actually saw it — and his statement may be relied on, and he knows that he is speaking the truth — and it is given in order that you might believe. ³⁶ For all this happened in fulfillment of the words of the writing: "Not one of its bones will be broken." ³⁷ And there is another passage which says: "They will look on him whom they pierced." ³⁸ After this, Joseph of Arimathea, a follower of Jesus — but a secret one, owing to his fear of the Judeans — begged Pilate's permission to remove the body of Jesus. Pilate gave him leave; so Joseph went and removed the body. ³⁹ Nicodemus, too — the man who had formerly visited Jesus by night — came with a roll of myrrh and aloes, weighing nearly a hundred pounds. ⁴⁰ They took the body of Jesus, and wound it in linen with the spices, according to the Judean mode of burial. ⁴¹ At the place where Jesus had been crucified there was a garden, and in the garden a newly made tomb in which no one had ever been laid. ⁴² And so, because of its being the preparation day, and as the tomb was close at hand, they laid Jesus there.

The Risen Life

20 ¹ On the first day of the week, early in the morning, while it was still dark, Mary of Magdala went to the tomb, and saw that the stone had been removed. ² So she came running to Simon Peter, and to that other disciple whom Jesus loved, and said to them: "They have taken away the Master out of the tomb, and we do not know where they have laid him!" ³ So Peter started off with that other disciple, and they went to the tomb. ⁴ The two began running together; but the other disciple ran faster than Peter, and reached the tomb first. ⁵ Stooping down, he saw the linen wrappings lying there, but did not go in. ⁶ Presently Simon Peter came following behind him, and went into the tomb; and he looked at the linen wrappings lying there, ⁷ and the cloth which had been on Jesus's head, not lying with the wrappings, but rolled up on one side, separately. ⁸ Then the other disciple, who had reached the tomb first, went inside too, and he saw for himself and believed. ⁹ For they did not then understand the writing which says that Jesus must rise again from the dead. [10] The disciples then returned to their companions.

[11] Meanwhile Mary was standing close outside the tomb, weeping. Still weeping, she leaned forward into the tomb, [12] and saw two angels clothed in white sitting there, where the body of Jesus had been lying, one where the head and the other where the feet had been. [13] "Why are you weeping?" asked the angels. "They have taken my Master away," she answered, "and I do not know where they have laid him." [14] After saying this, she turned around, and looked at Jesus standing there, but she did not know that it was Jesus. [15] "Why are you weeping? Whom are you seeking?" he asked. Supposing him to be the gardener, Mary answered: "If it was you, sir, who carried him away, tell me where you have laid him, and I will take him away myself."

[16] "Mary!" said Jesus. She turned around, and exclaimed in Hebrew: *"Rabboni!"* (which is to say, "Teacher"). [17] "Do not touch me," Jesus said; "for I have not yet ascended to the Father. But go to my brothers, and tell them that I am ascending to my Father and their Father, my God and their God." [18] Mary of Magdala went and told the disciples that she had seen the Master, and that he had said this to her.

[19] In the evening of the same day — the first day of the week — after the doors of the room in which his followers were had been shut because they were afraid of the Judeans, Jesus came and stood among them and said: "Peace be with you"; [20] after which he showed them his hands and his side. The disciples were filled with joy when they saw the Master. [21] Again Jesus said to them: "Peace be with you. As the Father has sent me, so I am sending you." [22] After saying this, he breathed on them, and said: "Receive the holy Spirit; [23] if you forgive anyone's sins, they have been forgiven; and, if you retain them, they have been retained."

[24] But Thomas, one of the Twelve, called "The Twin," was not with them when Jesus came; [25] so the rest of his followers said to him: "We have seen the Master!"

"Unless I see the marks of the nails in his hands," he exclaimed, "and put my finger into the marks, and put my hand into his side, I will not believe it." [26] A week later the disciples were again in the house, and Thomas with them. After the doors had been shut, Jesus came and stood among them, and said: "Peace be with you." [27] Then he said to Thomas: "Place your finger here, and look at my hands; and place your hand here, and put it into my side; and do not refuse to trust, but believe." [28] And Thomas exclaimed: "My Master, and my God!"

[29] "Is it because you have seen me that you have believed?" said Jesus. "Blessed are they who have not seen, and yet have trusted!"

[30] There were many other signs that Jesus gave in presence of his followers which are not recorded in this book; [31] but these have been recorded so that you may believe that Jesus is the Anointed One, the Son of God — and that in your believing, you may have life through his name.

21 [1] Later on, Jesus showed himself again to his followers by the Sea of Tiberias. [2] It was in this way: Simon Peter, Thomas, who was called "The Twin," Nathanael of Cana in Galilee, Zebedee's sons, and two other followers of Jesus were together, when Simon Peter said: [3] "I am going fishing."

"We will come with you," said the others. They went out and got into the boat, but caught nothing that night. [4] Just as day was breaking, Jesus came and stood on the beach; but his followers did not know that it was Jesus. [5] "Children," he said, "have you anything to eat?"

"No," they answered. [6] "Cast your net to the right of the boat," he said, "and you will find fish." So they cast the net, and now they could not haul it in because of the quantity of fish. [7] The follower whom Jesus loved said to Peter: "It is the Master!" When Simon Peter heard that it was the Master, he fastened his coat around him (for he was nude), and threw himself into the sea. [8] But the rest of his followers came in the boat (for they were only about a hundred yards from shore), dragging the net full of fish. [9] When they had come ashore, they found a charcoal fire ready, with some fish already on it, and some bread as well. [10] "Bring some of the fish which you have just caught," said Jesus. [11] So Simon Peter got into the boat and hauled the net ashore full of large fish, a hundred and fifty-three of them; and yet, although there were so many, the net had not been torn. [12] And Jesus said to them: "Come and breakfast." Not one of the disciples ventured to ask him who he was, knowing that it was the Master. [13] Jesus went and took the bread and gave it to them, and the fish too. [14] This was the third time that Jesus showed himself to the disciples after he had risen from the dead.

[15] When breakfast was over, Jesus said to Simon Peter: "Simon, son of John, do you love me more than the others?"

"Yes, Master," he answered, "you know that I love you."

"Feed my lambs," said Jesus. [16] Then, a second time, Jesus asked: "Simon, son of John, do you love me?"

"Yes, Master," he answered, "you know that I am your friend."

"Tend my sheep," said Jesus. [17] The third time, Jesus said to him: "Simon, son of John, do you love me?" Peter was hurt at his third question being 'Do you love me?' and exclaimed: "Master, you know everything! You can tell that I love you."

"Feed my sheep," said Jesus. [18] "In truth I tell you," he continued, "when you were young, you used to put on your own belt, and walk wherever you wished; but when you have grown old, you will have to stretch out your hands, while someone else puts on your belt, and takes you where you do not wish." [19] Jesus said this to show the death by which Peter was to glorify God, and then he added: "Follow me." [20] Peter turned around, and saw the follower whom Jesus loved following—the one who at the supper leaned back on the Master's chest, and asked him who it was who would betray him. [21] Seeing him, Peter said to Jesus: "Master, what about this one?"

[22] "If it is my will that he should wait until I come," answered Jesus, "what has that to do with you? Follow me yourself." [23] So the report spread among his followers that that follower was not to die; yet Jesus did not say that he was not to die, but said, "If it is my will that he should wait until I come, what has that to do with you?"

[24] It is this follower who states these things, and who recorded them; and we know that his statement is true.

[25] There are many other things which Jesus did; but if every one of them were to be recorded in detail, not even the world itself would hold the books that would be written.

An Introduction to the Gospel of Mary

T HE GOSPEL OF MARY — although not well known to the general public — has burst open new possibilities for many over the past twenty-five years. It is the first and only known gospel whose main figure is a woman. This figure of Mary (most likely Magdalene) is portrayed as a confidante of Jesus, someone familiar with Greek philosophy, and a (somewhat controversial) leader of the disciples after Jesus leaves them.

This gospel was most likely written sometime between 80 and 180 CE — as early as the Gospel of Matthew or the Letter to the Ephesians and as late as the heresy fighter Irenaeus. Church historian Karen King places it around 120, or around the time many now situate the Gospel of Luke. Almost certainly not written by Mary herself, the gospel has a distinctly Greek cultural flavor, even though the only known copies are in Coptic. Both discovered manuscripts of the gospel are incomplete. One is missing almost ten pages, the other almost twelve. This break in the text is also footnoted in the copy found in *A New New Testament*.

The New Orleans Council gave the Gospel of Mary its highest number of votes. Although some members expressed doubts about a book with so much of its content missing, the parts that remained were seen as crucial for understanding Christianity's beginnings and meanings for today.

The Child of Humanity Exists Within You

The Blessed One . . . said . . . "Beware that no one lead you astray saying, 'Look over here!' Or 'Look over there!' For the Child of Humanity is within you. . . ."
Mary . . . said, . . . "Let us praise his greatness, for he has prepared us and made us Humans. . . ."
Levi . . . said, . . . "We should clothe ourselves with the perfect Human, acquire it for ourselves as he commanded us, and proclaim the good news. . . ."
(4:1–4; 5:4–8; 10:7–12)

At the heart of the Gospel of Mary is a throbbing enthusiasm for becoming a true human being. For this ancient gospel, Jesus is the Savior because he teaches people how to welcome true humanity into themselves. None of the preceding quotations from the Gospel of Mary point to how Jesus saves them, forgives them, or makes them holy. Rather, the focus of these teachings is on being real human beings.

In many ways this gospel makes the promise of becoming real human beings in the most excited and clearest way of any early Christian gospel. Jesus is the "Child of Humanity," according to his own teaching. Mary Magdalene, who in this gospel has been taught many things that Jesus taught no one else, says that Jesus's primary purpose is making "us" "human beings." Levi, who defends Mary after Peter and Andrew have criticized her, says that the "good news" is about being clothed in "the perfect Human."

For many twenty-first-century readers this emphasis on the goodness of humanity, proclaimed in an early Christian gospel, comes as a surprise. So often Christianity has been understood as praising God and judging humanity. In much Christian piety humans are pictured as the lost and wretched person of "Amazing Grace." TV evangelists and popes alike portray humans as so thoroughly deserving of God's condemnation that only the bloody sacrifice of Jesus can make things right.

This is simply not the portrait of humanity in the Gospel of Mary. Here Jesus and his followers are united in perfect humanity. The good news is not in escaping one's human identity but in embracing it.

Nor does this gospel treat Jesus's death as a key to salvation. His death is not an act of atonement, but rather an event to overcome through the teachings Jesus told Mary.

This message can be very good news to many people who have been told in one way or another that they are hopeless and shameful as humans. The Gospel of Mary's invitation to clothe oneself with "the perfect Human" breaks out of both secular cynicism and Christian condemnation, allowing people to see their humanity not as cursed or meaningless, but as powerful and good.

It is tempting to think of this new gospel in its embrace of humanity as quite different from the other gospels of early Christianity. Although the message in the Gospel of Mary may be expressed in particularly striking images, it actually is quite similar to the gospels of Matthew, Mark, Luke, John, and Thomas. The language of corrupt and condemned humanity is mostly a product of later Christianity after the gospels had been completed. The guilt-laden humanity of later theologians such as Augustine and Martin Luther is hardly present in any early gospels.

The gospels of Matthew, Mark, and Luke all show Jesus teaching "good news" about the "realm" (or "kingdom") of God which is "at hand" or "among you." Indeed, Jesus's words in the Gospel of Mary about the child of true humanity are strikingly similar to his words about the realm of God in Luke: "The realm of God does not come in a way that can be grasped, nor will people say, 'Look, here it is!' or 'There it is!'; for the realm of God is among you!" (17:20–21).

The Gospel of Mary's celebration of humanity then reclaims a larger message from early Christianity that has been hidden by later Christian doctrines about sin and corruption. This newly discovered gospel's dramatic embrace of what good news human existence embodies is certain to confuse guilt- or shame-focused

Christians of more recent times. At the same time, it can serve as a way to redis-cover a similar message in the other gospels. Or, for still others who are wary of anything in the traditional New Testament, the Gospel of Mary's affirmation of the goodness of humanity may be the first time such a message is associated with Jesus.

The Main Character of This Gospel Is a Woman

This gospel focuses on Mary Magdalene. She is portrayed as one of Jesus's closest associates. She consoles the rest of the disciples as they fear that they might be cru-cified as Jesus was. Mary's authority stems from both her closeness to Jesus and the fact that Jesus has told her things that he told no one else. There is no suggestion in the story of physical or sexual intimacy between Jesus and Mary. Indeed, the focus is on an intellectual and spiritual connection between them. The idea of a sexual relationship between Jesus and Mary is almost certainly a modern fixation, not an ancient notion.

This gospel not only concentrates on Mary Magdalene, but its story points di-rectly to Mary's authority as a woman leader. Both Andrew and Peter challenge her teaching about Jesus, and Peter explicitly doubts its validity because she is a woman. Here the modern interest in women claiming authority resonates with the ancient one.

The plot of this contest between men and women for authority in the early churches is both subtle and appealing for the twenty-first-century reader, for whom such questions are very much alive. Levi comes to the defense of Mary after she is criticized. And, in the end, the message according to Mary is proclaimed to the larger world.

On the other hand, there also seems to be some ambivalence in the way this gos-pel's ending handles Mary's authority. First of all, the ending shows only a small minority following Mary's teaching about Jesus. Perhaps more disturbing is that Mary seems to lose her voice at the end of the gospel. She cries and gives only a sentence response to Peter's and Andrew's rebukes. Then Levi takes on the role of defending her. And even though her point of view carries the day, it is not at all clear that she herself goes out to teach.

The importance of the Gospel of Mary for today's worldwide negotiation of rights and roles for women cannot be underestimated. That an early Christian writing presents a major female figure whose leadership is actively disputed by the apostles introduces a dramatic new dimension to Christian understanding of women's authority. Even with the consideration of the important ambiguities at the end of the Gospel of Mary, this document still turns the tables on claims like that of the Vatican that women cannot be priests because there were no women disciples.

But it turns out that classic statements from the earliest Christian documents do not all put women down. Many have puzzled, for instance, how Paul both says that there was neither male nor female, but all are one in Christ, and still instructs the women to be silent in the Corinthian gatherings. Additional investigations have queried what the Acts of the Apostles means by calling a woman a "disciple." After the past forty years of scholarship, few scholars of early Christianity now doubt that this movement had significant women's leadership.

In this mix it is very important to notice the real possibility that the Gospel of Mary was written around the same time as both the Gospel of Luke and the First Letter to Timothy. Both of these New Testament works pay very explicit attention to the roles of women, but in strikingly different ways. First Timothy criticizes certain women in leadership as gossips and offensive in their dress, while encouraging them to be childbearing wives and attentive to their husbands. On the other hand, the Gospel of Luke adds many women to its story in an apparent dramatic appreciation of women, portrays women as supporting Jesus financially, and underlines that women were the first to see and believe Jesus's resurrection.

Certain kinds of Christians today appeal to the Paul who wants the Corinthian women to be silent and draw the conclusion that women should not become ministers or priests. Others appeal to the Acts of the Apostles and other texts — even other texts authored by Paul — to show that early Christianity had women in recognized leadership roles. Whatever material is used from these very early Christian documents, the debate is not just about what happened in the first century. Rather, it is also very much about legitimate women's leadership today. Without resolving the issue, the Gospel of Mary complicates this debate about women's authority. Its picture of Mary Magdalene as an insightful and courageous leader who was a close spiritual companion of Jesus opens up space for new ways of thinking about women's roles. It undermines conservative Christian claims that Jesus's exclusively male disciples offer the only model for leadership. It takes another chink out of closed systems of male succession and invites people into structures where women exercise a variety of leadership roles.

Uniting with God: The Ascent of the Soul

One of the most tantalizing dimensions of the Gospel of Mary is the almost four missing pages in the middle of the document. At that point in the gospel, Mary has announced that Jesus gave her special teachings, and the disciples have asked her to tell them those teachings. She begins to teach . . . and then the document breaks off for the better part of three pages.

When the document picks up again, Mary is still telling the disciples about these special teachings from Jesus that they have not heard. She seems to be near the end of a story about the soul as it ascends toward God. Mary then narrates how certain "powers" are trying to stop the soul from ascending. At one point Desire stops the soul and tries to prevent it from proceeding toward God. At another point Ignorance makes a similar challenge. Other powers, such as Anger, Darkness, and Flesh, also make it difficult for the soul's journey. In each case the soul outwits its opponents and continues its ascent.

To the twenty-first-century mind, the idea of a soul ascending to God is perhaps most often understood as something that happens after death. This does not seem to be the case in the Gospel of Mary. Indeed, the conversation between the soul and Desire makes it clear that this challenge is going on in relationship to the soul's struggle to be its true self. Nor does it seem to be that the ascent of the soul is about afterlife in many other early Christian writings. For instance, Paul writes in 2 Corinthians that he once made a journey into the second heaven and returned to his regular life.

In many ancient documents, stories about ascending to God are actually about a person's spiritual process while living. This, of course, makes a great deal of sense for the Gospel of Mary's story of the ascent of the soul as well. Desire and Ignorance trying to stop a soul from uniting with God makes much more sense as a way of talking about the possibilities and problems of someone in the middle of life trying to connect with God.

This can be true today as well. For instance, one of the powers that challenge the soul in the Gospel of Mary is Anger. Anger in human experience—although sometimes helpful—often stands in the way of people experiencing the presence of God or peace of mind. Anger can be addictive and can prevent one from unfolding as a fuller person. And because anger can also help a person grow, deciding how to deal with one's own anger always involves the kind of negotiation pictured in the Gospel of Mary's debate between the powers and the ascending soul.

Relating to desire can be similar. In many cases desire holds precious personal promise and imagination that allow people to break through discouragement toward something new. Or sometimes desire can help preserve specific hopes from the past and keep those possibilities alive. On the other hand, desire can become an obsession and prevent people from thinking clearly about their lives. In almost all cases desire is a complicated mix of authentic longing and internalizations of loss and ambition. So, the Gospel of Mary's picture of a soul negotiating with Desire makes sense in our own experience.

In the Gospel of Mary, God is clearly defined as "the good"; that is, the ascent of the soul in this gospel is about one's journey toward goodness in one's inner consciousness, one's behavior, and one's relationships. This gospel charts a personal process of the struggle for goodness. This process is not naïve or obvious. Rather, it takes seriously the ways things like desire, anger, and materiality can both help and hurt people's efforts to be "good."

"There Is No Such Thing as Sin"

> Peter said to him, "Since you have explained everything to us, tell us one other thing. What is the sin of the world?"
>
> The Savior said, "There is no sin, but it is you who make sin when you do the things that are like the nature of adultery, which is called 'sin.' That is why the Good came into your midst, coming to the good which belongs to every nature, in order to restore it to its root." (3:1–6)

For people of the twenty-first century, Jesus saying, "There is no sin" comes as a shock. Christianity is known around the world for its confrontation with people concerning their sinfulness. Conservative Christians aren't the only ones who hold up sexual activities, lawlessness, dishonesty, and cruelty as examples of the sinfulness of humankind. Nor does Christianity's reputation for being sin-based come just from doctrinal Christianity's trumpeting of "original sin" as a way of talking about humanity's natural depravity. Liberal Christians also often condemn people or society for the sinfulness of social injustice. It is nearly impossible for people of our time to think about Christianity without sin.

For Jesus in the Gospel of Mary, sin is an illusion. It has no objective reality. It is only the way people think that gives sin importance. If one rejects the notion of sin, the Savior says, one allows the Good to come forward and take its rightful place as a guide to how to become a true human being.

At first blush, one could then see this as an example of why the Gospel of Mary should be considered a "heretical" writing, according to any Christian standard. Although many Christians and non-Christians reject the Christian emphasis on sin, it may very well seem reasonable to say that the rejection of sin entirely simply cannot belong to any valid form of Christianity.

Such a conclusion may, however, not at all be the whole picture. Upon a closer look, one can see this statement of the Gospel of Mary as belonging to a larger cluster of early Christian statements, even in the traditional New Testament. There is an important layer of expressions that seem to be saying something quite similar to this gospel's proclamation that there is no such thing as sin.

Indeed, in some parts of the traditional New Testament the rejection of sin's reality might be seen as being even stronger than the one in the Gospel of Mary. For instance, Paul's Letter to the Romans contains the following conclusion to a particular section about baptism and resurrection: "For the death that he died was a death to sin, once and for all. But the life that he now lives, he lives for God. So let it be with you — regard yourselves as dead to sin, but as living for God, in Christ Jesus" (6:10–11). A paraphrase of this might go something like this: Christ's death ended any chance of him sinning, so that the new life he now lives (as resurrected) is completely for God. So you also are free from sin and alive to God.

The Gospel of Mary's rejection of the notion of sin is like these other statements from the Letter to the Romans, as well as Colossians and Ephesians. They focus on the radical new quality of life in Christ, which makes sin negligible. This, then, does not naïvely reject concern about personal responsibility, but it does seem to distance itself from assertions that all humans are hopelessly corrupt.

The Gospel of Mary's language about sin is fresh and striking for twenty-first-century reading. It would probably not have been as surprising to the readers of the likes of Romans, Colossians, and Ephesians. As such, the Gospel of Mary provides both new insight and connection to many traditional parts of the New Testament.

Recommended Reading

Melanie Johnson Debaufre and Jane Schaberg, *Mary Magdalene Understood*
Karen King, *The Gospel of Mary of Magdala: Jesus and the First Woman Apostle*
Jane Schaberg, *The Resurrection of Mary Magdalene: Legends, Apocrypha, and the Christian Testament*

The Gospel of Mary

1

The Savior Teaches About Matter, Sin, and the Good

2 ¹ "Will* matter then be destroyed or not?" ² The Savior said, "All natures, all forms, all creatures exist in and with one another, ³ and they will be resolved again into their own roots. ⁴ For the nature of matter is released into the roots of its nature. ⁵ Those who have ears to hear, let them hear!"

3 ¹ Peter said to him, "Since you have explained everything to us, tell us one other thing. ² What is the sin of the world?"

³ The Savior said, "There is no sin, ⁴ but it is you who make sin when you do the things that are like the nature of adultery, which is called 'sin.' ⁵ That is why the Good came into your midst, coming to the good which belongs to every nature, ⁶ in order to restore it to its root."

⁷ Then he continued. He said, "This is why you become sick and die ⁸ for you love what deceives you. ⁹ One who understands, let him understand! ¹⁰ Matter gives birth to a passion that has no likeness because it proceeds from what is contrary to nature. ¹¹ Then there arises a disturbance in the whole body. ¹² Because of this I said to you, 'You shall become satisfied, and not be persuaded. You shall be joined in the presence of the likeness of nature.' ¹³ Those who have ears to hear, let them hear!"

The Savior Departs

4 ¹ When the Blessed One had said these things, he greeted them all, saying, "Peace be with you! ² Bear my peace within yourselves! ³ Beware that no one lead you astray ⁴ saying, 'Look over here!' Or 'Look over there!' ⁵ For the Child of Humanity is within you! ⁶ Follow it! ⁷ Those who seek it will find it. ⁸ Go then and proclaim the good news of the realm. ⁹ Do not lay down any rules beyond what I determined for you, ¹⁰ nor give a law like the lawgiver, lest you be confined by it." ¹¹ When he had said this, he departed.

Mary Comforts the Other Followers

5 ¹ But they were pained. They wept greatly, saying, ² "How shall we go to the nations and proclaim the good news of the Child of Humanity? ³ If they did not spare him, how will they spare us?"

⁴ Then Mary stood up. She greeted them all, and said to her brothers and sisters, ⁵ "Do not weep and be pained, nor doubt, ⁶ for all his grace will be with you and shelter you. ⁷ But rather let us praise his greatness, ⁸ for he has prepared us and made us Humans." ⁹ When Mary said this, she turned their heart to the Good, ¹⁰ and they began to discuss the words of the Savior.

Mary's Vision of the Savior

6 ¹ Peter said to Mary, "Sister, we know that the Savior loved you more than the rest of the women. ² Tell us the words of

---

* Pages 1–6 of the manuscript are missing. The text begins abruptly here.

the Savior which you remember, which you know and we do not, nor have we heard them." [3] Mary answered and said, "What is hidden from you I will tell you." [4] And she began to say to them these words.

7 [1] "I," she said, "I saw the Lord in a vision [2] and I said to him, 'Lord, I saw you today in a vision.' [3] He answered and said to me, 'Blessed are you that you did not waver at seeing me. [4] For where the mind is, there is the treasure.' [5] I said to him, 'Lord, now, does one who sees the vision see it with the soul or with the spirit?' [6] The Savior answered and said, 'One does not see with the soul or with the spirit, [7] but the mind which is between the two sees the vision.'"

8[*]

The Ascent of the Soul

9 [1] "And Desire said, [2] 'I did not see you go down, but now I see you go up. [3] Why do you lie, since you belong to me?' [4] The Soul answered and said, 'I saw you. You did not see me or know me. [5] I lived as a garment [6] and you did not know me.' [7] When the Soul had said this, it went away rejoicing greatly.

[8] "Again the Soul came to the third Power, which is called Ignorance. [9] It closely examined the Soul, saying, 'Where are you going? [10] You are ruled by wickedness. [11] You are ruled — [12] do not judge!' [13] And the Soul said, 'Why do you judge me since I have not judged? [14] I was ruled though I have not ruled. [15] I was not known. But I have known that all things are being released, both those belonging to earth and those belonging to heaven.' [16] "When the Soul had left the third

Power desolate, it went upward and saw the fourth Power. [17] It had seven forms. [18] The first form is Darkness; [19] the second Desire; [20] the third Ignorance; [21] the fourth Eagerness for Death; [22] the fifth is the Realm of the Flesh; [23] the sixth is the Foolish Wisdom of the Flesh; [24] the seventh is Wrathful Wisdom. [25] These are the seven Powers of Wrath. [26] They asked the Soul, 'Where are you coming from, human-killer, and where are you going you place-destroyer?' [27] The Soul answered and said, 'What rules me has been slain, and what turns me has been destroyed, and my desire has been filled, and ignorance has died. [28] In a world I was released from a world, and in a mold from a higher mold, and from the chain of forgetfulness which is temporal. [29] From this hour on, at the time of the season of the generations, I will rest in silence.'"

[30] After Mary said this, she was silent, [31] since it was to this point that the Savior had spoken with her.

The Followers Argue About Mary's Teaching

10 [1] But Andrew responded and said to the brothers and sisters, "Say what you will about what she has said, [2] I do not believe that the Savior said this, for certainly these teachings are strange ideas." [3] Peter responded and spoke concerning these same things. He questioned them about the Savior, "Did he really speak with a woman without our knowing about it? [4] Are we to turn around and all listen to her? Did he choose her over us?"

[5] Then Mary wept and said to Peter, "My brother, Peter, what are you thinking? [6] Do you think that I have thought this up

---

[*] Pages 11–14 of the manuscript are missing. The missing pages most likely contain a part of the Savior's recounting of the soul's journey to God, which is still being presented when the text picks up.

myself in my heart, or that I am telling lies about the Savior?" [7] Levi responded and said to Peter, "Peter, you have always been an angry person. [8] Now I see you contending against the woman like the adversaries. [9] But if the Savior made her worthy, who are you, then, to reject her? [10] Surely the Savior's knowledge of her is trustworthy. That is why he loved her more than us.

[11] Rather, let us be ashamed. We should clothe ourselves with the perfect Human, acquire it for ourselves as he commanded us, [12] and proclaim the good news, [13] not laying down any other rule or other law beyond what the Savior said."

[14] After he had said these things, they started going out to teach and proclaim.*

[15] The Good News according to Mary.

---

* There are two partial manuscripts of the Gospel of Mary, which mostly complement and reinforce one another. In this ending we have followed the longer manuscript, the Papyrun Berolinnensis 8502.1. There is another, somewhat different ending in the shorter manuscript, the Papyrus Oxyrhunchus 3525. That ending goes like this: "After he had said these things, Levi left and began to announce the good news."

An Introduction to the Gospel of Truth

T HE GOOD NEWS OF TRUTH IS JOY" are the first words of this document, and they convey the power of the whole document, which brims with a sense of aliveness, engagement, contemplation, and inner richness. Unlike the gospels of Matthew, Mary, Mark, Luke, and John, the Gospel of Truth does not have a central story. Instead, it is like a meandering stream that bursts its banks unpredictably. As it overflows with joy, fulfillment, and sensuousness, this gospel by turns sounds like a poem, a letter, or an ecstatic sermon. For example, chapter 19 combines the ecstatic and the poetic: "The Father is sweet and within his desire is goodness. . . . The Father's children are his fragrance for they are from the beauty of his face. Because of this, the Father loves his fragrance and discloses it everywhere, and when it mixes with matter it gives his fragrance to the light" (19:1, 4–5).

The New Orleans Council was drawn to this lushness of language. Attracted especially to the way this gospel integrates beauty and desire into its picture of life with God, members of the council by and large rejected previous scholarship's allegation that the Gospel of Truth is disembodied and too focused on the knowledge of God.

The Gospel of Truth seems to offer enough different strands of early Christian teaching that it probably was not written before 80 CE and could have been written as late as 160 CE. Its general grasp of different kinds of early Christian expression makes it difficult to place in one particular milieu or culture. The Nag Hammadi collection has two copies of this gospel, and there are substantial differences between the manuscripts' contents. These differences, the broad range of perspectives in the gospel, and a reference to this document by the late second-century Christian bishop Irenaeus indicate that the Gospel of Truth was probably quite well known around the Mediterranean. Some scholars think that it was authored by the well-known early Christian thinker Valentinus (who was accused of heresy), but as no other writings of Valentinus survive, it is impossible to know. The title of the book is most likely based on the first words of the gospel about truth, a common way of giving titles to otherwise title-less works in ancient Christianity. The concept of "truth" is not particularly accentuated in the book.

Jesus in the Gospel of Truth

The Gospel of Truth's portrait of Jesus is full of old and new details and at the same time unique in the way all these details enthusiastically gush forth. One of the major meditations on the meaning of Jesus in early Christianity, it contains many dimensions, including a strong awareness of Jesus as a teacher of parables, developed references to him as the Word in ways comparable to the Gospel of John, calling him "the Mother," an extended portrait of Jesus's cosmic role as the one whose teachings corrected the Transgression that made all humanity ignorant, and significant attention to the meaning of Jesus's death. All of these aspects relate to other early Christian traditions, but the Gospel of Truth gives each of them a poetic twist. For instance, Jesus's death on the cross is imagined with him being nailed to a tree and thus becoming the fruit of the Father's knowledge and (in another section of the gospel) as the publication of the book of life.

When speaking of Jesus as God's Son, Truth summarizes Jesus's cosmic contributions this way: "He spoke new things while speaking what is in the Father's heart and brought out the faultless Word. When the light had spoken through his mouth and voice, which gave birth to life, he gave them thought and understanding, compassion and salvation, and the spirit of power in the Father's boundlessness and sweetness. He did away with torture and torment . . ." (16:6–8).

Human Fulfillment, Joy, and Engagement

The Gospel of Truth takes seriously human pain and error but concentrates on affirming the ways the goodness and beauty of life continue to overflow everywhere. The Son revealed to people who God is, which "became a way for those who strayed and knowledge for those who were ignorant, discovery for those searching and strength for those who were shaken, purity for those who were defiled" (16:10). The results are that "the Father is within them and they are in the Father. They are full and undivided from the one who is truly good. They need nothing at all, but they are at rest, fresh in spirit, and will listen to their root" (27:6–8). For the Gospel of Truth this is not a beatific vision of heaven, but one of humans fully alive in the present moment.

This allows them to become engaged and hear the gospel's mandate: "Speak of the day from above which has no night and of the perfect light that does not set. Say then from the heart that you are the perfect day and within you dwells the light that never ends. Speak of the truth with those who seek it and of knowledge with those who have sinned through their transgressions. Strengthen the feet of those who stumble and stretch your hands to those who are weak. Feed those who are hungry and give rest to the weary" (17:10–14).

Without ignoring issues of conflict and difficulty, the Gospel of Truth is perhaps the most joyous and ecstatic book from early Christianity. It provides a stunning contrast to the kinds of twenty-first-century Christianity that feature condemnation and dark prophecies.

A Note on Chapter and Verse Numbering

Since this text is so "new," no version of the otherwise standard chapter and verse format exists. So we have had to add our own chapter and versification to this edition. The Gospel of Truth has been made available to the public in various formats and translations without chapter and verse over the past thirty years. We do think it also very important that there be a chapter and verse system, because it breaks up the text into units that belong together. We do, however, want to alert readers that the availability of this text in non–chapter and verse form or in the ancient manuscript form of simply noting the column and line numbers of the original document does not match our new chapter and verse format.

Recommended Reading

Harold Attridge and George MacRae, "The Gospel of Truth: Introduction," in *The Coptic Gnostic Library*, Volume I
Ronald Cameron, editor, *The Other Gospels: Non-Canonical Gospel Texts*
Helmut Koester, *Ancient Christian Gospels*
Jacqueline Williams, *Biblical Interpretation in the Gnostic Gospel of Truth from Nag Hammadi*

The Gospel of Truth

1 ¹ The good news of truth is joy for those who have received grace from the Father of the truth, that they might know him through the power of the Word which has come from the fullness and is in the thought and mind of the Father. ² They speak about this one as "Savior," the name given to the work he is to do to redeem those who had not known the Father. ³ And the name "good news" is the revelation of hope, for this is the discovery of those who seek him.

Transgression and Forgetfulness

2 ¹ All things have searched for the one from whom they have come. ² All things were within him — the uncontainable, incomprehensible one who surpasses all thought. ³ Ignorance of the Father produced disturbance and fear, and disturbance enveloped like a mist so that no one was able to see. ⁴ In this way Transgression found strength, and she fashioned materiality with emptiness. ⁵ She did not know the truth and became a molded form, preparing — in power and beauty — a substitute for truth. ⁶ This was not humiliating for the uncontainable, incomprehensible one, for disturbance and forgetfulness and molded forms are lies, while the established truth is unchanging, undisturbed, and beyond beauty. ⁷ Therefore, disregard Transgression because this one has no root. ⁸ She was in a mist concerning the Father, preparing the works of forgetfulness and fear, and by them, to gather the ones in the middle and take them captive.

3 ¹ The forgetfulness of Transgression was not revealed; it was not with the Father. ² Forgetfulness did come from the Father, though if it came into being it was because of him. ³ What comes into being in him is knowledge, which appeared so that forgetfulness might be dissolved and the Father might be known. ⁴ Forgetfulness came into being because the Father was not known, so when the Father comes to be known, forgetfulness, from that time on, will not exist.

The Good News and Hidden Mystery of Jesus

4 ¹ This is the good news of the one whom they seek, revealed to those filled through the mercies of the Father. ² Through the hidden mystery, Jesus Christ shone to the ones in the darkness of forgetfulness. ³ He enlightened them and showed them a way. The way he taught them is truth. ⁴ Because of this Transgression was angry with him and pursued him. She was distressed by him and left barren.

⁵ He was nailed to a tree and became the fruit of the Father's knowledge. ⁶ It did not cause destruction when it was eaten, but it caused those who ate it to come into being and find contentment within its discovery. ⁷ And he discovered them in himself, and they discovered him in themselves — the uncontainable, the unknowable Father, the one who is full and made all things. ⁸ All things are in him and all things have need of him.

5 ¹ Though he kept their fullness within himself, which he did not give to everything, the Father was not jealous. ² For what jealousy is there between him and his members? [3] For if the generations had received their fullness, they would not be able to come to the Father. [4] He kept their fullness within himself, giving it them to bring back to him with full, unified knowledge. [5] He is the one who ordered all things and all things are in him. [6] Everything was in need of him, like someone who is not known but desires to be known and loved. [7] For what do all things need if not knowledge of the Father?

[8] He became a guide, at rest and at leisure. He came into their midst and spoke a teacher's words in places of learning. [9] Those thinking themselves wise tested him, but he reproached them because they were empty and hated him for they were not truly wise. [10] After all these, the little children came — those to whom knowledge of the Father belongs. [11] When they had been strengthened, they learned about the Father's face. [12] They knew and they were known, they were glorified and they glorified.

The Living Book of the Living

6 [1] In their hearts the living book of the living was revealed. [2] It was written in the thought and mind of the Father and, since the beginning of all things, was in his incomprehensibility. [3] This book was impossible to take because it was placed there for the one to take it to be killed. [4] No one would have appeared from among those who trust in salvation if that book had not appeared. [5] Because of this, the compassionate, faithful Jesus was patient. [6] He accepted sufferings until he took up that book, since he knows that his death is life for many.

[7] Like a will not yet opened, the fortune of the dead master's house is hidden; so too all things which were hidden while the Father of everything was invisible, but which come from within him, from whom every way comes forth. [8] Because of this, Jesus appeared and clothed himself in that book. [9] He was nailed to a tree and published as the Father's edict on the cross. Oh, what a great teaching! [10] He drew himself down from death, clothing himself in never-ending life. [11] He stripped off the perishable rags and put on imperishability, which no one can take away from him.

7 [1] When he entered empty ways of fear, he passed through those stripped by forgetfulness. [2] He is knowledge and fullness, and he promises the things that are in the heart and teaches those who will learn. [3] And those who will learn are the living who are written in the book of the living. [4] They learn about themselves and receive instruction from the Father and return to him again. [5] Since the fullness of all things is in the Father, all things must go up to him. [6] Then, if they have knowledge, they receive what is their own and he draws them to him. [7] For they who are ignorant are in need and their need is great, since they need what will fill them. [8] Since the fullness of all things dwells in the Father, all things must go up to him and each one receives what is hers. [9] He already inscribed these things, having prepared to give them to those who came from him.

The Father Calls the Names of Those with Knowledge

8 [1] Those whose names he already knew were called at the end, so that those who have knowledge are the ones whose names the Father recites. [2] For those whose names have not been spoken are ignorant. [3] How could they hear if their names had not been called? [4] For those who are ignorant until the end are creatures of forgetfulness and will dissolve with it. [5] If not, why do these arrogant

ones have no name? ⁶ Why do they have no voice? ⁷ So, those who have knowledge are from above; and if called, they hear and answer, turning to the one who called them and going up to him. ⁸ They know how they were called, have knowledge and do the will of the one who called them. ⁹ They want to please him, they find rest — their names become their own. ¹⁰ Those who have knowledge in this way know where they come from and where they are going. ¹¹ They know as ones who having become drunk, have turned from drunkenness and returned to themselves, setting themselves right.

9 ¹ He has brought back many from Transgression. ² He went before them to the places they had moved from when they followed Transgression because of the depth of the one who surrounds every place, though nothing surrounds him. ³ It is a great wonder that they were in the Father without knowing him and that they were able to leave by themselves, since they were not able to receive and know the one whom they were in. ⁴ He revealed his will as knowledge in accordance with it and all its bounty. ⁵ This is the knowledge of the living book which he revealed to the generations at the end as his letters, showing how they are not places of voices nor letters without sound, so that one might read them and think of something empty, but they are letters of truth — they speak and know themselves. ⁶ Each letter is filled with truth, like a perfect book, for they are letters gathered in unity, gathered by the Father for the generations, so that by his letter they might know the Father.

The Father's Word

10 ¹ His Wisdom* meditates on the Word and his teaching speaks it, his knowledge reveals it and his patience is a crown upon it. ² His joy is in harmony with it and his glory has exulted it. ³ His manner has revealed it and his rest has received it. ⁴ His love made a body for it and his trust has embraced it. ⁵ In this way the Word of the Father walks in creation, as the fruit of his heart and the face of his love. ⁶ It bears all things and chooses all things, and it receives the face of all things and purifies them, bringing them back to the Father, to the Mother, Jesus of boundless sweetness.

⁷ The Father opens his bosom and his bosom is the holy Spirit. ⁸ He reveals his hidden self — his hidden self is his Child — so that through the compassion of the Father the generations might know him and end their strenuous search for the Father, resting in him and knowing that this is rest. ⁹ He has filled need and dissolved appearance — the appearance of need is the world in which he served. ¹⁰ For the place where there is envy and struggle is in need, but the place where there is oneness is full. ¹¹ Since need came into being because the Father was not known, when the Father is known, from that moment on, need will no longer exist. ¹² As ignorance dissolves when one gains knowledge of another and darkness dissolves when the light appears, so too need dissolves in fullness. ¹³ So from that moment on appearance is no longer manifest, but dissolved in union with oneness.

11 ¹ Now their works lie scattered, but in time oneness will make the places full.

---

* In many places in the both traditional and newly added books of *A New New Testament,* we have translated this as "Wisdom-Sophia" in order to indicate that this figure who is meditating is a divine feminine being. The Greek and Greco-Coptic word *Sophia* has several meanings, only one of which includes the sense that "Wisdom" is a divine feminine being. This indeed is the case here as well, but the translator of this document has preferred simply the translation "Wisdom."

[2] In oneness all will return to themselves, within knowledge purifying themselves from multiplicity into oneness, devouring matter within themselves like fire, and darkness by light, death by life. [3] If indeed these things have happened to each one of us, it is necessary for us to think about all things so that this house might be holy and tranquil in oneness.

The Parable of the Jars

12 [1] It is like people who moved from one house to another. [2] They had some jars that were not good in places and they broke. [3] And the owner of the house suffered no loss, but she rejoiced for in place of the bad jars there were full ones that were perfect. [4] For this is the judgment which has come from above and has judged everyone. [5] It is a double-edged sword, drawn and cutting on this side and that. [6] The Word, which was within the hearts of those who speak it, came into their midst. [7] It is not simply a sound, but it became embodied. [8] A great disturbance happened within some of the jars for some were empty and others half full, some supplied and others poured out, some purified and others in pieces. [9] All ways were shaken and disturbed because they had no order or stability. [10] Transgression was anxious, not knowing what to do. [11] She suffered and mourned and tore at herself for she did not know anything. [12] And knowledge, which is the destructions of her and all her bounty, came near. [13] Transgression is empty — there is nothing within her.

The Coming of Truth and Nightmare of Ignorance

13 [1] Truth came into their midst and all its bounty knew it. [2] They welcomed the Father in truth and perfect power that joins them with the Father. [3] For everyone loves truth, because truth is the Father's mouth, his tongue the holy Spirit. [4] Whoever clings to the truth clings to the Father's mouth and by his tongue will receive the holy Spirit. [5] This is the manifestation of the Father and the revelation to his generations. [6] He revealed what was hidden of himself and explained it. [7] For who exists if not for the Father alone? [8] All ways are his bounty and know that they have come from him like children in a mature person. [9] They had not yet taken form or received a name. [10] The Father gives birth to each one, and they receive form through his knowledge. [11] For though they were in him, they did not know him. [12] The Father is full — he knows every way within himself. [13] If he desires something, that which he desires appears, and he gives it form and a name. [14] He gives it a name and brings into being those who before existing were ignorant of the one who created them.

14 [1] I am not saying that those who have not yet come to be are nothing, but they come into being when the one who desires their existence makes them appear. [2] He knows what he will produce before anything appears. [3] But the fruit which has not yet appeared knows nothing and does nothing. [4] Therefore, all ways that exist in the Father come from the one who exists, the one who establishes them from what does not exist. [5] For that which has no root has no fruit, and though thinking, "I have come into being," it will perish by itself. [6] Because of this, that which does not exist at all will never exist. [7] What, then, does he want them to think of themselves? [8] It is this: "I have come into being like the shadows and ghosts of the night." [9] When the light shines on the fear endured, the person knows it was nothing.

[10] They did not know the Father whom they did not see. [11] Since there was fear and confusion and instability and divisions, there were many illusions at work among

them. [12] And there was empty ignorance as if they were sleeping and found themselves in disturbing dreams — running someplace or powerless while pursued, coming to blows or themselves beaten, falling from heights or flying through air without wings. [13] Or sometimes as if people are trying to kill them or they are killing their neighbors, smeared with their blood. [14] Until the time, after having all these dreams, they awaken. [15] Those in the midst of all this confusion see nothing for these things are nothing.

15 [1] Such are those who cast ignorance from themselves like sleep. [2] They do not consider it anything or its works as real things, but leave them behind like a dream in the night. [3] Knowledge of the Father they value as the dawn. [4] Each one acted as if asleep when he was without knowledge. [5] And this is the way he comes to knowledge — as if awakened. [6] Good for the one who returns to one's self and awakens. [7] Blessed is the one who has opened the eyes of the blind. [8] And when this one awakened, the Spirit pursued in haste. [9] Having given its hand to those spread on the ground, it set them on their feet — for they had not yet arisen.

Knowledge of the Father and Revelation of the Child

16 [1] Knowledge of the Father and the revelation of his Child gave them means of knowing. [2] For when they saw him and heard him, he let them taste him and smell him and touch the beloved Child. [3] When he appeared, telling them about the Father — the uncontainable one — he breathed into them what is in the thought, doing his will. [4] When they received the light, many turned to him, for the material ones were strangers, and they did not see his image and did not know him. [5] For

he came in the form of flesh and nothing blocked his path, for incorruptibility is ungraspable.

[6] He spoke new things while speaking what is in the Father's heart and brought out the faultless Word. [7] When the light had spoken through his mouth and voice, which gave birth to life, he gave them thought and understanding, compassion and salvation, and the spirit of power in the Father's boundlessness and sweetness. [8] He did away with torture and torment for they caused those needing compassion, those in transgression and bonds, to stray from his face. [9] He dissolved them with power and reproached them with knowledge. [10] He became a way for those who strayed and knowledge for those who were ignorant, discovery for those searching and strength for those who were shaken, purity for those who were defiled.

The Parable of the Sheep

17 [1] He is the shepherd who left behind the ninety-nine sheep that had not strayed, and went and searched for the one who had gone astray. [2] He rejoiced when he found it, for ninety-nine is a number in the left hand which holds it. [3] When the one is found, the whole number moves to the right hand. In this way, what is in need of one — that is, the whole right hand — draws that which it needs and takes it from the left hand and moves it to the right so the number becomes one hundred. [4] This is the sign of the sound of the numbers. This is the Father.

[5] Even on the sabbath he worked for the sheep he found fallen in the pit. [6] He saved the life of the sheep — he brought it up from the pit. [7] Understand this in your hearts, children of the heart's knowledge. [8] For what is the sabbath? [9] A day on which it is inappropriate for salvation to be idle. [10] Speak of the day from above which has no night and of the per-

fect light that does not set. [11] Say then from the heart that you are the perfect day and within you dwells the light that never ends. [12] Speak of the truth with those who seek it and of knowledge with those who have sinned through their transgressions. [13] Strengthen the feet of those who stumble and stretch your hands to those who are weak. [14] Feed those who are hungry and give rest to the weary. [15] Raise those who wish to arise and awaken those who sleep — for you all are understanding drawn forth. [16] If strength does these things, strength becomes stronger.

18 [1] Be concerned with yourselves. [2] Do not be concerned with things you have cast from yourselves. [3] Do not return to eat what you have vomited. [4] Do not be rotten. [5] Do not be worms, for you have already shaken it off. [6] Do not become a place for the devil, for you have already left him barren. [7] Do not strengthen barriers that are falling away for support. [8] For the lawless one is nothing. [9] Treat one as this more fiercely than the just. [10] For the lawless person does his works as a lawless one and the just person does his work among others. [11] Do then what the Father desires, for you are from him.

The Father's Sweetness

19 [1] For the Father is sweet and within his desire is goodness. [2] He knows what is yours in which you might find rest. [3] For by the fruits one knows what is yours. [4] The Father's children are his fragrance for they are from the beauty of his face. [5] Because of this, the Father loves his fragrance and discloses it everywhere, and when it mixes with matter it gives his fragrance to the light. [6] And in his tranquil-

ity he makes it surpass every form and every sound. [7] For ears do not smell the fragrance, but it is breath and spirit* that smells and draws the fragrance to itself, is immersed† in the Father's fragrance. [8] It harbors it and takes it to the place it came from, from the first fragrance which has become cold — something in psychic form. [9] It is like cold water which has flowed into loose earth. [10] Those who see it think it is simply earth. [11] Afterward, it evaporates and dissolves again; when a breath of wind draws it, it becomes warm. [12] So the cold fragrances are from division. [13] Trust came for this reason — to dissolve division. [14] And it brought the warm fullness of love so that the cold might not return and that there might be a unity of perfect thought.

The Good News of Fullness

20 [1] This is the Word of the good news of the discovery of fullness for those who await the salvation coming from above. [2] Their hope, toward which they stretch, is stretching toward them — they whose image is light with no shadow in it. [3] Then, at this time, fullness is about to come. [4] The need of matter did not come through the boundlessness of the Father, who came to give time to need. [5] Of course no one is able to say that the imperishable one would come in this way. [6] The Father's depth was multiplied and Trangression's thought did not come through him. [7] It is a thing that falls and a thing easily set upright in the discovery of the one who has (already) come to that which he wants to return. [8] For the return is called repentance.

[9] This is the reason imperishability breathed out. [10] It followed the one who

---

* The Greek word here, *pneuma,* expresses both "breath" and "spirit."

† The Coptic word here, *ōms,* can be associated with baptism.

sinned so that the sinner might rest. [11] For forgiveness is what remains for the light in the midst of need, the Word of fullness. [12] For the physician rushes to the place where there is sickness because that is the physician's desire. [13] The one in need, then, does not hide it—for one has what the other needs. [14] So fullness—which has no need but fills need—gives from itself to fill each person's need so that she might receive grace. [15] When one was in need she had no grace. [16] Because of this, a contracting happens in the place where there was no grace. [17] When that which was contracted was received, it was revealed that the one in need was fullness. [18] This is the discovery of the light of truth which rose upon one like this—that it is unchanging.

21 [1] For this reason, they said of Christ the Anointed One, in their midst: "Seek, and those who are troubled will return, and he will anoint them with ointment." [2] The ointment is the mercy of the Father, who will have mercy on them. [3] Those who are anointed are full. [4] For full jars are the ones that are usually coated.* [5] But when the coating of one is dissolved, it is emptied and the cause of its lack is the place where the ointment is released. [6] For a breath of wind, and the power with it, draws it. [7] But from the one not lacking, no coating is removed nor is it emptied, but what it lacks the perfect Father fills again. [8] He is good. He knows his seedlings for he sowed them in his paradise. And his paradise is his place of rest. [9] This is the fullness of the Father's thought, and these are the words of his meditation. [10] Each of his words is the work of his one desire in the revelation of his Word. [11] Since they were in the depths of his thought, the Word—which was the first to come forth—revealed them along with mind, which speaks the one Word in silent grace. [12] It was called "thought" since they dwelled in it before being revealed. [13] It happened that he was first to come forth when the desire of the one who desired willed it. [14] And desire is what the Father rests in and what pleases him.

22 [1] Nothing happens without him nor does anything happen without the Father's desire, but his desire is incomprehensible. [2] His footprint is desire and no one can know him nor does he exist for people to observe in order to grasp him. [3] But when he desires, what he desires is this—even if the sight does not please them in any way before God—the desire of the Father. [4] For he knows the beginning of all and their end—for at their end he will greet their faces. [5] And the end is the acceptance of knowledge about the one who is hidden. [6] And this one is the Father, from whom the beginning came and to whom all will return. [7] They have come forth from him and appeared for the glory and joy of his name.

The Name of the Father

23 [1] The name of the Father is the Child. [2] It was he who, in the beginning, gave a name to the one who came from him, who was himself. [3] And he birthed him as a child. [4] He gave him his name which belonged to him. [5] All that exists with him belongs to the Father. [6] The name belongs to him; the child belongs to him. [7] It is possible to see the Child, but the name

---

* The Coptic word here, *tōhs*, expresses both "anointing" and "pouring" or "smearing," connecting the covering or sealing of the jars with anointing.

cannot be seen for it alone is the mystery of the invisible, which comes to ears completely filled with it by him. [8] For they do not speak the Father's name, but it is revealed through a child. [9] In this way, the name is great.

[10] Who, then, can recite his name — the great name — except for him alone to whom the name belongs, and the children of the name, in whom the Father's name rests and in turn who rest themselves in his name? [11] Since the Father is not begotten, he alone is the one who birthed him to himself as a name before he set the generations in order, so that the name of the Father might have authority over them as Lord. [12] This is the name of truth which is secure in his command in perfect power. [13] For the name is not simply words or name-making, but his name is invisible.

24 [1] He gave a name to him alone for he alone saw him. [2] It is he alone who has the power to name him. [3] For one who does not exist has no name — for what name is given to one who does not exist? [4] One who exists also exists with his name — he alone knows it and alone has given him a name. [5] "The Father is the Child" is his name. He did not hide it in himself, but it existed. [6] The Child alone gave a name. The name, then, belongs to the Father, as the name of the Father is the Child. [7] Since where would compassion find a name outside the Father?

[8] No doubt they will say to their neighbor, "Who gives a name to the one who existed before himself? [9] Do children not receive names from the ones who birthed them?" [10] First, we should think about this — what is the name? It is the name in truth. [11] It, then, is the name from the Father for it is the decisive name. [12] He did not receive the name on loan, like others, according to the form in which each one is created. [13] This is the decisive name. There is no

one else who gave it to him. [14] But he is unnamable, indescribable, until the time when the one who is full spoke of him alone.

25 [1] He is the one who has power to speak his name and see him. [2] It pleased him that his beloved name should be his child and gave the name to him who came forth from the depths. [3] He told his secret, knowing that the Father is without evil. [4] Because of this, he brought him forth to speak about both the place and his resting place from which he had come, and to glorify the fullness, the greatness of this name, and the sweetness of the Father.

The Place of Fullness and Rest

26 [1] Each one will speak about the place he came from and will hasten to return again to the place he was made to stand, and to taste from that place, receiving nourishment and growth. [2] This place of rest is his fullness. [3] All the Father's bounties are fullnesses — the root of his bounty is in the one who caused all of them to grow from within himself. [4] He gave them their destinies. Each one appears so that through her own thought they might be filled. [5] For the place to which they send their thought — that place is the root, which takes them above all the heights to the Father.

[6] They hold his head, which is rest for them, and they grasp him, approaching him as if to receive kisses from his face. [7] But they do not reveal this. For they did not exalt themselves or need the Father's glory. [8] They did not think of him as small or bitter or wrathful. He is without evil, tranquil, and sweet. [9] He knows all ways before they exist, and has no need of instruction.

27 [1] This is the way of those who hold something of the immeasurable greatness from above. ² They stretch toward the full one alone, who is a Mother for them.* ³ They do not descend into Hades nor do they have envy or groaning. ⁴ They do not have death within themselves, but they rest in the one who rests. ⁵ They are not troubled or twisted around the truth, but they are truth. ⁶ And the Father is within them and they are in the Father. ⁷ They are full and undivided from the one who is truly good. ⁸ They need nothing at all, but they are at rest, fresh in spirit, and will listen to their root. ⁹ They will concern themselves with those things in which they will find their root and not suffer loss to their souls. ¹⁰ This is the place of the blessed. This is their place.

¹¹ May others in their places know that it is inappropriate for me, having come to the place of rest, to say another thing. ¹² It is there I shall dwell and be engaged in every moment with the Father of all things and the true brothers and sisters upon whom the love of the Father flows and in whose midst no need of him exists. ¹³ They are the ones who appear in truth and dwell in true and never-ending life. ¹⁴ They speak of the perfect light, filled with the Father's seed, which is in his heart and in the fullness. ¹⁵ His spirit rejoices in it and glorifies the one in whom it dwells. ¹⁶ He is good and his children are full and worthy of his name. ¹⁷ For he is the Father and it is children like this that he loves.

---

* Or "who is there for them."

THE WRITINGS OF PAUL
AND AN INTRODUCTORY PRAYER

An Introduction to the Prayer of the Apostle Paul

THIS PRAYER IS ON the first page of the first codex of the Nag Hammadi collection. As such, it clearly served as a spiritual exercise for readers of the other fifty-one documents. The evocative language of the prayer seeks healing, gives deep praise, and wishes for unity with God and Jesus; all of this most likely indicates that it was a prayer used in many settings long before the Nag Hammadi collection was put together in the fourth century. The document found at Hammadi is, however, the only copy of this prayer.

It is unlikely that the prayer comes from Paul himself. In the seven authentic letters of Paul, no reference is made either to this prayer or to the general contents and ideas of the prayer. Within a generation of his death, Paul became a legend, and the traditional New Testament includes books written in his name that were probably not written by him; it is not unusual for early Christian literature to be attributed to Paul. One might think of this prayer in relationship to the historical person of Paul in the same way as the Letter to the Ephesians, which also carries his name but was most likely not written by him. The prayer — written in Coptic — could be dated as early as 75 CE or as late as 250 CE.

The members of the New Orleans Council were nearly unanimously in favor of including this prayer, mostly to give the reader an additional aid to reading this New Testament prayerfully, as there are so few early Christian prayers in the traditional New Testament. The council saw it as a spiritually helpful way to begin the material related to Paul.

This prayer is unusual for early Christianity in that it is spoken in the first person singular. Usually first- and second-century prayers were voiced as "we," not "I." The content of the prayer weaves tightly together the gestures of praise and request. God is praised as mind, treasury, fullness, preexistent, powerful, glorious, and great. The one who prays seeks a deep union with Jesus Christ as God's blessed, chosen, firstborn, and mystery of God's house.

For readers today who use spiritual practice as a part of their reading of scriptures, it is recommended that the Prayer of the Apostle Paul be read before each of the letters of Paul in this section. Indeed, there remains the possibility that this prayer could be read with profit before any of the books of A New New Testament.

Recommended Reading

Dieter Mueller, "The Prayer of the Apostle Paul (Introduction)," from The Nag Hammadi Library, edited by James M. Robinson

The Prayer of the Apostle* Paul

1 Grant me your mercy,
 my Redeemer, redeem me,
 for I am yours —
 the one who has come from you.
2 You are my mind —
 birth me.
3 You are my treasure —
 open for me.
4 You are my fullness —
 receive me.
5 You are my rest —
 give me unrestrained maturity.
6 I pray to you who exists and preexists,
 in the name raised up above every
 name,
 through Jesus Christ,
 the Lord of lords,
 the King of ages.
7 Give me your gifts without regret,
 through the Child of Humanity,
 the Spirit,
 the Advocate of truth.
8 Give me authority, I ask you.
 Give healing to my body when I ask
 you,
 through the one who brings good
 news,
 and redeem my soul, enlightened and
 eternal,

and my spirit,
and open my mind
to the firstborn Child
of the fullness of grace.
9 Grant what no angel's eye has
 seen,
and no ruler's ear has heard,
and what has not entered into the
 human heart,
which became angelic
and was molded in the image of the
 living God
when it was formed in the beginning.
10 I have trust and hope.
And place upon me your
beloved, chosen, and blessed greatness,
the firstborn,
the first brought forth,
the amazing mystery of your house.
11 For yours is
the power and the glory,
and the praise and the greatness,
forever and ever.
Amen.
The Prayer of the Ambassador Paul.
In peace,
Christ is Holy.

---

* The standard name of this book is the Prayer of the Apostle Paul. In general our translation team has translated the Greek *apostolos* as the less transliterated and more accurate English "ambassador." But here in the title we keep the name of the book as it is commonly known in scholarly literature.

An Introduction to the Letter to the Romans

O FTEN UNDERSTOOD AS the most mature and systematic of Paul's letters, Romans pieces together something of a proposal for the bigger picture of God's call to a mix of ethnicities and stations in life. Viewing Romans this way underestimates its quality as a particular address to a particular set of people in a specific place, but its scope does seem to match the largeness Rome and its people imagined for itself.

This is a real letter, observing standard forms, and is addressed to what are probably several different groups of Christ people in the vicinity of Rome. The authenticity of Paul as the author has not been questioned. It was probably written in the mid- to late 50s CE, before Paul ever was in Rome. I have kept this letter at the head of Paul's correspondence, where it is also found in the traditional New Testament.

Paul calls himself an "ambassador" (apostle),* even though in other circles that word is often reserved for followers of Jesus who knew him while he lived, something Paul does not claim for himself. Contrary to understandings of Paul for much of Christian history, scholarship of the past several generations tends to posit that Paul always thought of himself as belonging to the traditions of Israel and did not think of himself as a Christian. Rather, he appears to have thought that Christ enabled the gentiles to belong genuinely to the larger constellation of traditions of Israel.

The Trust of Jesus

This letter focuses on a contrast between Law and trust (or faith) as key to relationships among humans and between humans and God. Jesus is the model of trust/faith, showing those both inside and outside the traditions of Israel a way to live beyond shame and sin. God's judgment and justice for all are transformed into grace through the event of Jesus's death on the cross. Inasmuch as one lives in Christ, one claims trust in God as the freeing dynamic for peoples of all kinds. The trust in God Jesus demonstrated in his death opens a way for all people to live without fear and intimidation.

The Law (probably best thought of as some combination of the laws of Israel and Rome) is what condemns humans to slavery and shame. The Law prescribes be-

---

* The Greek word *apostolos*, often translated (or better put, transliterated) as "apostle," means "one who is sent" and is used throughout Greek literature to designate a messenger or, in the case of an important messenger, an "ambassador."

havior as the key to human life, rather than dependence on the grace of God. The power of life in Christ is especially visible when people are baptized. "Through sharing his death in our baptism, we were buried with him; that just as Christ was raised from the dead by a manifestation of the Father's power, so we also may live a new life. . . . regard yourselves as dead to sin, but as living for God, in Christ Jesus" (6:4, 11). This is for Paul a life full of trust and without shame in the here and now, applicable to all who would enter into God through Christ.

Israel Forever

Paul criticizes many of the practices within Israel's traditions, but contrary to many conventional Christian impressions of the medieval and modern era he affirms in Romans that Israel will always be God's people. In Paul's view, Israel's status as God's people has been dramatically expanded to include all gentiles who would claim Jesus's trust in God as their own. Paul is in vehement disagreement with those within the traditions of Israel who do not accept this radical expansion. But Paul refuses to condemn Israel's status in the eyes of God, and "from the standpoint of God's selection, they are dear to him for the sake of the patriarchs. For God never regrets his gifts or his call [of Israel]" (11:28–29).

Within this framework, however, there are many changes. Gentiles in Christ are not required to be circumcised, as was previously the Law. There are other traditions of Israel that also need to be taken more symbolically than literally. The key figure in Israel's traditions here is Abraham, who belonged to Israel before the Law from Moses ever existed. Abraham, then, is the major figure in Israel's traditions that Paul uses to make the Christ people's belonging to Israel clear while distancing them from Moses, the lawgiver.

Eating Together Across Ethnic Boundaries

In chapters 14 and 15 Paul deals with a specific problem of the Roman Christ assemblies: how to celebrate their regular meal together in Christ. In some contrast to Paul's instructions to the Corinthians, here in Rome the problem with their meal practice is not so much the words used, but the kind of food shared. Among the Christ people in Rome, some (most likely gentiles) are eating meat, and some (most likely those living more deeply in the traditions of Israel) are not eating meat, but just vegetables and bread.

Paul sides here with those more deeply in the traditions of Israel, not because of any inherent virtue of their traditions as much as a way for them all to come together as one people. Paul instructs everyone to eat only vegetables, so that there will not be any conflict about food. In this regard, he evokes Jesus's teachings about the realm of God by saying that "the realm of God does not consist of eating and drinking, but of righteousness and peace and gladness through the presence of the holy Spirit" (14:17).

The Letter to the Romans — when understood within Paul's own life situation rather than as a part of later Christian doctrine — remains a key entry point into his message for twenty-first-century readers. It shines with his affirmation of human freedom and goes far beyond what much Christian dogma has focused on in trying to make this letter into a system of belief about the nature of God and humans.

Recommended Reading

Paul Achtemeier, *Romans: Interpretation: A Bible Commentary for Teaching and Preaching*
Robert Jewett, *Romans: A Commentary*
Stanley Stowers, *A Rereading of Romans: Justice, Jews, and Gentiles*

The Letter to the Romans

Introduction

1 ¹ To all in Rome who are dear to God and have been called to be holy, from Paul, a slave of Jesus Christ, who has been called to become an ambassador of Christ Jesus, and has been set apart for God's good news. ² This good news God promised long ago through his prophets in the holy scriptures, ³ concerning his Child, Jesus Christ, our Lord; who, as to flesh, was born of David's lineage, ⁴ but as to the spirit of holiness within him, was designated Son of God by his resurrection from the dead. ⁵ Through him we received the gift of the office of ambassador, to win trust among all nations for his name. ⁶ And in these nations you yourselves have been called to Jesus Christ.

⁷ Grace and deep peace to you from God, our Father, and the Lord Jesus Christ.

⁸ First, I thank my God through Jesus Christ about you all, because the report of your confidence is spreading throughout the world. ⁹ God, to whom I offer my spiritual worship as I tell the good news of his Child, is my witness how constantly I mention you when I pray, ¹⁰ asking that, if he be willing, I may someday at last find the way open to visit you. ¹¹ For I long to see you, in order to impart to you some spiritual gift and so give you fresh strength — ¹² or rather that both you and I may find encouragement in each other's trust. ¹³ I do want you to know, my friends, that I have many times intended coming to see you — but until now I have been prevented — that I might find among you some fruit of my labors, as I have already among the other nations.

¹⁴ I have a duty to both the Greek and the barbarian, to both the cultured and the ignorant. ¹⁵ And so, for my part, I am ready to tell good news to you also who are in Rome.

¹⁶ For I am not ashamed of the good news; it is the power of God which brings salvation to everyone who trusts, to the Judean first, and to the Greek. ¹⁷ For in it there is a revelation of the divine righteousness from trust and leading into trust; as scripture says, "Through trusting the righteous will come alive."

¹⁸ There is a revelation from heaven of the divine wrath against every form of ungodliness and wickedness on the part of those people who, by their wicked lives, are stifling the truth. ¹⁹ This is so, because what can be known about God is plain to them; for God himself has made it plain. ²⁰ For ever since the creation of the universe God's invisible attributes — his everlasting power and divinity — are to be seen and studied in his works, so that people have no excuse; ²¹ because, although they learned to know God, yet they did not offer him as God either praise or thanksgiving. Their speculations about him proved futile, and their undiscerning hearts were darkened. ²² Professing to be wise, they showed themselves fools; ²³ and they transformed the glory of the immortal God into the likeness of mortal humans, and of birds, and beasts, and reptiles.

²⁴ Therefore God abandoned them to impurity, letting them follow the cravings of their hearts, until they dishonored their own bodies; ²⁵ for they had substituted a lie for the truth about God, and had reverenced and worshiped created things more than the Creator, who is to be praised forever. Amen. ²⁶ That, I say, is why God abandoned them to degrading passions. Even the women among them perverted the natural use of their bodies to the un-

natural; [27] while the men, disregarding that for which women were intended by nature, were consumed with passion for one another. Men indulged in vile practices with men, and incurred in their own persons the inevitable penalty for their error.

[28] Then, as they would not keep God before their minds, God abandoned them to depraved thoughts, so that they did all kinds of shameful things. [29] They reveled in every form of wickedness, evil, greed, vice. Their lives were full of envy, murder, quarreling, treachery, malice. [30] They became back-biters, slanderers, impious, insolent, and boastful. They devised new sins. They disobeyed their parents. [31] They were undiscerning, untrustworthy, without natural affection or pity. [32] Well aware of God's decree, that those who do such things deserve to die, not only are they guilty of them themselves, but they even applaud those who do them.

2 [1] Therefore you have nothing to say in your own defense, whoever you are who set yourself up as a judge. In judging others you condemn yourself, for you who set yourself up as a judge do the very same things. [2] And we know that God's judgment falls unerringly on those who do them. [3] You who judge those that do such things and yet are yourself guilty of them—do you suppose that you of all people will escape God's judgment? [4] Or do you think lightly of his abundant kindness, patience, and forbearance, not realizing that his kindness is meant to lead you to repentance? [5] Hardhearted and impenitent as you are, you are storing up for yourself wrath on the day of wrath, when God's justice as a judge will be revealed; [6] for "he will give to everyone what her actions deserve." [7] To those who, by perseverance in doing good, aim at glory, honor, and all that is imperishable, he will give life through the ages; [8] while as to those who are factious, and disobedient to truth but

obedient to evil, wrath and anger, distress and despair, [9] will fall on every human being who persists in wrongdoing—on the Judean first, but also on the Greek. [10] But there will be glory, honor, and peace for everyone who does right—for the Judean first, but also for the Greek, [11] since God shows no partiality. [12] All who, when they sin, are without Law will also perish without Law; while all who, when they sin, are under Law will be judged as being under Law. [13] It is not those who hear the words of a law that are righteous before God, but it is those who obey it that will be pronounced righteous. [14] When gentiles, who have no Law, do instinctively what the Law requires, they, though they have no Law, are a law to themselves; [15] for they show the demands of the Law written on their hearts; their consciences corroborating it, while in their thoughts they argue either in self-accusation or, it may be, in self-defense—[16] on the day when God passes judgment on people's inmost lives, as the good news that I tell declares that he will do through Christ Jesus.

[17] But perhaps you bear a Judean name and are relying on Law, and boast of belonging to God, and understand his will, [18] and, having been carefully instructed from the Law, have learned to appreciate the finer moral distinctions. [19] Perhaps you are confident that you are a guide to the blind, a light to those who are in the dark, an instructor of the unintelligent, [20] and a teacher of the childish, because in the Law you possess the outline of all knowledge and truth. [21] Why, then, you teacher of others, do you not teach yourself? Do you teach against stealing, and yet steal? [22] Do you forbid adultery, and yet commit adultery? Do you loathe idols, and yet plunder temples? [23] Boasting, as you do, of your Law, do you dishonor God by breaking the Law? [24] For, as it is written, "The gentiles insult God's name because of you"! [25] Circumcision has its value, if you are obeying the Law. But if you are a

breaker of the Law, your circumcision is no better than uncircumcision. [26] If, then, an uncircumcised man pays regard to the requirements of the Law, will he not, although not circumcised, be regarded by God as if he were? [27] Indeed, the man who, owing to his birth, remains uncircumcised, and yet scrupulously obeys the Law, will condemn you, who, for all your written Law and your circumcision, are yet a breaker of the Law. [28] For a man who is only a Judean outwardly is not a real Judean; nor is outward bodily circumcision real circumcision. The real Judean is the person who is a Judean in soul; [29] and the real circumcision is the circumcision of the heart, a spiritual and not a literal thing. Such a person wins praise from God, though not from people.

3 [1] What is the advantage, then, of being a Judean? Or what is the good of circumcision? [2] Great in every way. First of all, because the Judeans were entrusted with God's utterances. [3] What follows then? Some, no doubt, showed a lack of faith; but will their lack of faith make God break faith? Heaven forbid! [4] God must prove true, though everyone prove a liar! As it is written, "That you may be pronounced righteous in what you say, and gain your cause when people would judge you."

[5] But what if our wrongdoing makes God's righteousness all the clearer? Will God be wrong in inflicting punishment? (I can but speak as a person.) Heaven forbid! [6] Otherwise how can God judge the world?

[7] But if my falsehood redounds to the glory of God, by making his truthfulness more apparent, why am I like others, still condemned as a sinner? [8] Why should we not say—as some people slanderously assert that we do say—"Let us do evil that good may come"? The condemnation of such people is indeed just!

[9] What follows, then? Are we Judeans in any way superior to others? Not at all.

Our indictment against both Judeans and Greeks was that all alike were in subjection to sin. [10] As it is written:

"There is not even one who is
      righteous,
[11] not one who understands,
not one who is searching for God!
[12] They have all gone astray;
they have one and all become
      depraved;
there is no one who is doing
      good—no, not one!"
[13] "Their throats are like opened graves;
they deceive with their tongues."
"The venom of snakes lies behind their
      lips,"
[14] "And their mouths are full of bitter
      curses."
[15] "Swift are their feet to shed blood.
[16] Distress and trouble dog their steps,
[17] and the path of peace they do not
      know."
[18] "The fear of God is not before their
      eyes."

[19] Now we know that everything said in the Law is addressed to those who are under its authority, in order that every mouth may be closed, and to bring the whole world under God's judgment. [20] For no human being will be pronounced righteous before God as the result of obedience to Law; for it is Law that shows what sin is.

[21] But now, quite apart from Law, the divine righteousness stands revealed, and to it the Law and the prophets bear witness—[22] the divine righteousness which is bestowed, through faith in Jesus Christ, on all, without distinction, who believe in him. [23] For all have sinned, and all fall short of God's glorious ideal, [24] but in his loving kindness, are being freely pronounced righteous through the deliverance found in Christ Jesus. [25] For God set him before the world, to be, by the shedding of his blood, a means of reconcilia-

tion through faith. And this God did to prove his righteousness, and because, in his forbearance, he had passed over the sins that people had previously committed; ²⁶ as a proof, I repeat, at the present time, of his own righteousness, that he might be justice in our eyes, and might pronounce righteous the person who takes a stand on trusting in Jesus.

²⁷ What, then, becomes of our boasting? It is excluded. By what sort of Law? A Law requiring obedience? No, a Law requiring trust.

²⁸ For we conclude that a person is pronounced righteous on the ground of faith, quite apart from obedience to Law. ²⁹ Or can it be that God is the God only of the Judeans? Is he not also the God of the gentiles? ³⁰ Yes, of the gentiles also, since there is only one God, and he will pronounce those who are circumcised righteous as the result of faith, and also those who are uncircumcised on their showing the same faith.

³¹ Do we, then, use this faith to abolish Law? Heaven forbid! No, we establish Law.

4 ¹ What then, it may be asked, are we to say about Abraham, the ancestor of our nation? ² If he was pronounced righteous as the result of obedience, then he has something to boast of. Yes, but not before God. ³ For what are the words of the writings? "Abraham had faith in God, and his trust was regarded by God as righteousness." ⁴ Now wages are regarded as due to the person who works, not as a favor, but as a debt; ⁵ while, as for the person who does not rely on his obedience, but has faith in the one who can pronounce the godless righteous, his trust is regarded by God as righteousness.

⁶ In precisely the same way David speaks of the blessing pronounced on the person who is regarded by God as righteous apart from actions: ⁷ "Blessed are those whose wrongdoings have been forgiven and over whose sins a veil has been

drawn! ⁸ Blessed the one whom the Lord will never regard as sinful!" ⁹ Is this blessing, then, pronounced on the circumcised only or on the uncircumcised as well? We say that "Abraham's faith was regarded by God as righteousness." ¹⁰ Under what circumstances, then, did this take place? After his circumcision or before it? ¹¹ Not after, but before. And it was as a sign of this that he received circumcision — to show the righteousness due to the faith of an uncircumcised man — in order that he might be the father of all who have faith in God even when uncircumcised, so that they also may be regarded by God as righteous. ¹² He is as well the father of the circumcised — to those who are not only circumcised, but who also follow our father Abraham in that faith which he had while still uncircumcised. ¹³ For the promise that he should inherit the world did not come to Abraham or his descendants through Law, but through the righteousness due to faith. ¹⁴ If those who take their stand on Law are to inherit the world, then faith is robbed of its meaning and the promise comes to nothing! ¹⁵ Law entails punishment; but where no Law exists, no breach of it is possible. ¹⁶ That is why everything is made to depend on faith: so that everything may be God's gift, and in order that the fulfillment of the promise may be made certain for all Abraham's descendants — not only for those who take their stand on the Law, but also for those who take their stand on the trust of Abraham. (He is the father of us all; ¹⁷ as it is written, "I have made you the Father of many nations.") And this they do in the sight of that God in whom Abraham had faith, and who gives life to the dead, and speaks of what does not yet exist as if it did. ¹⁸ With no ground for hope, Abraham, sustained by hope, put faith in God; in order that in fulfillment of the words "So many will your descendants be," he might become "the father of many nations." ¹⁹ Though he was nearly a hundred years old, yet his faith did not fail him, even when he thought of his own body, then utterly worn out, and remembered that Sarah was past bearing children. ²⁰ He was not led by lack of trust to doubt God's promise. ²¹ On the contrary, his faith gave him strength; and he praised God, in the firm conviction that what God has promised he is also able to carry out. ²² And therefore his faith was regarded as righteousness. ²³ Now these words — it was regarded as righteousness — were not written with reference to Abraham only; ²⁴ but also with reference to us. Our faith, too, will be regarded by God in the same light, if we trust in him who raised Jesus, our Lord, from the dead. ²⁵ For Jesus was given up to death to atone for our offenses, and was raised to life that we might be pronounced righteous.

5 ¹ Therefore, having been pronounced righteous as the result of faith, let us enjoy peace with God through Jesus Christ, our Lord. ² It is through him that, by reason of our trust, we have obtained admission to that place in God's favor in which we now stand. So let us exult in our hope of attaining God's glorious ideal. ³ And not only that, but let us also exult in our troubles; ⁴ for we know that trouble develops endurance, and endurance strength of character, and strength of character hope, ⁵ and that hope never disappoints. For the love of God has filled our hearts through the holy Spirit which was given us; ⁶ seeing that while we were still powerless, Christ, in God's good time, died on behalf of the godless. ⁷ Even for an upright person scarcely anyone will die. For a really good person perhaps someone might even dare to die. ⁸ But God puts his love for us beyond all doubt by the fact that Christ died on our behalf while we were still sinners. ⁹ Much more, then, now that we have been pronounced righteous by virtue of the shedding of his blood, will we be saved through him from the wrath of God. ¹⁰ For if, when we were God's enemies, we

were reconciled to him through the death of his Son, much more, now that we have become reconciled, will we be saved by virtue of Christ's life. ¹¹ And not only that, but we exult in God, through Jesus Christ, our Lord, through whom we have now obtained this reconciliation.

¹² Therefore, just as sin came into the world through one man, and through sin came death; so, also, death spread to all humanity, because every person has sinned. ¹³ Even before the time of the Law there was sin in the world; but sin cannot be charged against someone where no Law exists. ¹⁴ Yet, from Adam to Moses, death reigned even over those whose sin was not a breach of a Law, as Adam's was. And Adam foreshadows the One to come. ¹⁵ But there is a contrast between Adam's offense and God's gracious gift. For, if by reason of the offense of the one man the whole race died, far more were the loving kindness of God, and the gift given in the loving kindness of the one man, Jesus Christ, lavished on the whole race. ¹⁶ There is a contrast, too, between the gift and the results of the one man's sin. The judgment, which followed on the one man's sin, resulted in condemnation, but God's gracious gift, which followed on many offenses, resulted in a decree of righteousness. ¹⁷ For if, by reason of the offense of the one person, death reigned through that one man, far more will those on whom God's grace and his gift of righteousness are lavished find life, and reign through the one man, Jesus Christ. ¹⁸ Briefly, then, just as a single offense resulted for all humanity in condemnation, so, too, a single decree of righteousness resulted for all humanity in that declaration of righteousness which brings life. ¹⁹ For, as through the disobedience of the one person the whole race was rendered sinful, so, too, through the obedience of the one, the whole race will be rendered righteous. ²⁰ Law was introduced in order that offenses might be multiplied. But where

sins were multiplied, the loving kindness of God was lavished the more, [21] in order that, just as sin had reigned in the realm of death, so, too, might grace reign through righteousness, and result in life from generation to generation, through Jesus Christ, our Lord.

6 [1] What are we to say, then? Are we to continue to sin, in order that God's loving kindness may be multiplied? [2] Heaven forbid! We became dead to sin, and how can we go on living in it? [3] Or can it be that you do not know that all of us who were baptized in Christ Jesus in our baptism shared his death? [4] Consequently, through sharing his death in our baptism, we were buried with him; that just as Christ was raised from the dead by a manifestation of the Father's power, so we also may live a new life. [5] If we have become united with him in dying this death, surely we are also united with him by his resurrection. [6] We recognize the truth that our old self was crucified with Christ, in order that the body, the stronghold of sin, might be rendered powerless, so that we should no longer be slaves to sin. [7] For the person who has so died has been pronounced righteous and released from sin. [8] And our belief is that as we have shared Christ's death, we will also share his life. [9] We know, indeed, that Christ, having once risen from the dead, will not die again. Death has power over him no longer. [10] For the death that he died was a death to sin, once and for all. But the life that he now lives, he lives for God. [11] So let it be with you — regard yourselves as dead to sin, but as living for God, in Christ Jesus. [12] Therefore do not let sin reign in your mortal bodies and compel you to obey its cravings. [13] Do not offer any part of your bodies to sin, in the cause of unrighteousness, but once for all offer yourselves to God (as those who, though once dead, now have life), and devote every part of your bodies to the cause of righteousness. [14] For sin will not lord it over you. You are living under the reign, not of Law, but of love.

[15] What follows, then? Are we to sin because we are living under the reign of love and not of Law? Heaven forbid! [16] Surely you know that when you offer yourselves as servants, to obey anyone, you are the slaves of the person whom you obey, whether the service be a service to sin which leads to death, or a service to duty which leads to righteousness. [17] God be thanked that though you were once slaves of sin, yet you learned to give hearty obedience to that form of teaching under which you were placed. [18] Set free from the control of sin, you became slaves to righteousness. [19] I can but speak as people do because of the weakness of your earthly nature. Once you offered every part of your bodies to the service of impurity, and of wickedness, which leads to further wickedness. Now, in the same way, offer them to the service of righteousness, which leads to holiness. [20] While you were still servants of sin, you were free as regards righteousness. [21] But what were the fruits that you reaped from those things of which you are now ashamed? For the end of such things is death. [22] But now that you have been set free from the control of sin, and have become slaves to God, the fruit that you reap is an ever-increasing holiness, and life through the ages. [23] The wages of sin are death, but the gift of God is life from generation to generation, in Christ Jesus, our Lord.

7 [1] Surely, friends, you know (for I am speaking to people who know what Law means) that Law has power over a person only as long as she lives. [2] For example, by Law a married woman is bound to her husband while he is living; but if her husband dies, she is set free from the Law that bound her to him. [3] If, then, during her husband's lifetime, she unites herself to another man, she will be called an adulteress; but if her husband dies, the Law has

no further hold on her, nor, if she unites herself to another man, is she an adulteress. ⁴ And so with you, my friends; as far as the Law was concerned, you underwent death in the crucified body of the Christ, so that you might be united to another, to him who was raised from the dead, in order that our lives might bear fruit for God. ⁵ When we were living merely earthly lives, our sinful passions, aroused by the Law, were active in every part of our bodies, with the result that our lives bore fruit for death. ⁶ But now we are set free from the Law, because we are dead to that which once kept us under restraint; and so we serve under new, spiritual conditions, and not under old, written regulations.

⁷ What are we to say, then? That Law and sin are the same thing? Heaven forbid! On the contrary, I should not have learned what sin is, had it not been for Law. If the Law did not say, "You must not covet," I should not know what it is to covet. ⁸ But sin took advantage of the commandment to arouse in me every form of covetousness, for where there is no consciousness of Law, sin shows no sign of life. ⁹ There was a time when I myself, unconscious of Law, was alive; but when the commandment was brought home to me, sin sprang into life, while I died! ¹⁰ The commandment that should have meant life I found to result in death! ¹¹ Sin took advantage of the commandment to deceive me, and used it to bring about my death. ¹² And so the Law is holy, and each commandment is also holy, and just, and good. ¹³ Did, then, a thing which in itself was good involve death in my case? Heaven forbid! It was sin that involved death; so that by its use of what I regarded as good to bring about my death, its true nature might appear; and in this way the commandment showed how intensely sinful sin is. ¹⁴ We know that the Law is spiritual, but I am earthly — sold into slavery to sin. ¹⁵ I do not understand my own actions. For I am so far from habitually doing what I want to

do, that I find myself doing the thing that I hate. ¹⁶ But when I do what I want not to do, I am admitting that the Law is right. ¹⁷ This being so, the action is no longer my own, but is done by the sin which is within me. ¹⁸ I know that there is nothing good in me — I mean in my earthly nature. For, although it is easy for me to want to do right, to act rightly is not easy. ¹⁹ I fail to do the good thing that I want to do, but the bad thing that I want not to do — that I habitually do. ²⁰ But when I do the thing that I want not to do, the action is no longer my own, but is done by the sin which is within me. ²¹ This, then, is the Law that I find — when I want to do right, wrong presents itself! ²² At heart I delight in the Law of God; ²³ but throughout my body I see a different law, one which is in conflict with the Law accepted by my reason, and which endeavors to make me a prisoner to that law of sin which exists throughout my body. ²⁴ Miserable man that I am! Who will deliver me from the body that is bringing me to this death? ²⁵ Thank God, there is deliverance through Jesus Christ, our Lord! Well then, for myself, with my reason I serve the Law of God, but with my earthly nature the law of sin.

8 ¹ There is, therefore, now no condemnation for those who are in union with Christ Jesus; ² for through your union with Christ Jesus, the Law of the life-giving Spirit has set you free from the law of sin and death. ³ What Law could not do, insofar as our earthly nature weakened its action, God did, by sending his own Child, with a nature resembling our sinful nature, to atone for sin. He condemned sin in that earthly nature, ⁴ so that the requirements of the Law might be satisfied in us who live now in obedience, not to our earthly nature, but to the Spirit. ⁵ They who follow their earthly nature are earthly minded, while they who follow the Spirit are spiritually minded. ⁶ To be earthly minded means death, to be spiritually minded means life and peace; [7] because to be earthly minded is to be an enemy to God, for such a mind does not submit to the Law of God, nor indeed can it do so. [8] They who are earthly cannot please God. [9] You, however, are not earthly but spiritual, since the Spirit of God lives within you. Unless a person has the Spirit of Christ, he does not belong to Christ; [10] but if Christ is within you, then, though the body is dead as a consequence of sin, the spirit is life as a consequence of righteousness. [11] And, if the Spirit of him who raised Jesus from the dead lives within you, he who raised Christ Jesus from the dead will give life even to your mortal bodies, through his Spirit living within you.

[12] So then, friends, we owe nothing to our earthly nature, that we should live in obedience to it. [13] If you live in obedience to your earthly nature, you will inevitably die; but if, by the power of the Spirit, you put an end to the evil habits of the body, you will live. [14] All who are guided by the Spirit of God are children of God. [15] For you did not receive the spirit of a slave, to fill you once more with fear, but the spirit of a child which leads us to cry, 'Abba, our Father.' [16] The Spirit himself unites with our spirits in bearing witness to our being God's children, [17] and if children, then heirs — heirs of God, and joint heirs with Christ, since we share Christ's sufferings in order that we may also share his glory.

[18] I do not count the sufferings of our present life worthy of mention when compared with the glory that is to be revealed and bestowed on us. [19] All nature awaits with eager expectation the appearing of the children of God. [20] For Nature was made subject to imperfection — not by its own choice, but owing to him who made it so — [21] yet not without the hope that someday Nature, also, will be set free from enslavement to decay, and will attain to the freedom which will mark the glory of the children of God. [22] We know, indeed, that all Nature alike has been groaning in the pains of labor to this very hour. [23] And not Nature only; but we ourselves also, though we have already a first gift of the Spirit — we ourselves are inwardly groaning, while we eagerly await our full adoption as children — the redemption of our bodies. [24] By our hope we were saved. But the thing hoped for is no longer an object of hope when it is before our eyes; for who hopes for what is before her eyes? [25] But when we hope for what is not before our eyes, then we wait for it with patience.

[26] So, also, the Spirit supports us in our weakness. We do not even know how to pray as we should; but the Spirit himself pleads for us in sighs that can find no utterance. [27] Yet he who searches all our hearts knows what the Spirit's meaning is, because the pleadings of the Spirit for Christ's people are in accordance with his will. [28] But we do know that God causes all things to work together for the good of those who love him — those who have received the call in accordance with his purpose. [29] For those whom God chose from the first he also destined from the first to be transformed into likeness to his Child, so that his Child might be the eldest among many brothers and sisters. [30] And those whom God destined for this he also called; and those whom he called he also pronounced righteous; and those whom he pronounced righteous he also brought to glory.

[31] What are we to say, then, in the light of all this?

If God is on our side, who can there be against us?

[32] God did not withhold his own Child, but gave him up on behalf of us all; will he not, then, with him, freely give us all things?

[33] Who will bring a charge against any of God's people? He who pronounces them righteous is God!

[34] Who is there to condemn them? He who died for us is Christ Jesus — or, rather, it was he who was raised from the dead,

and who is now at God's right hand and is even pleading on our behalf!

[35] What is there to separate us from the love of the Christ? Will trouble, or difficulty, or persecution, or hunger, or nakedness, or danger, or the sword?

[36] Scripture says, "For your sake we are being killed all the day long, we are regarded as sheep to be slaughtered." [37] Yet amid all these things we more than conquer through him who loved us! [38] For I am persuaded that neither death, nor life, nor angels, nor archangels, nor the present, nor the future, nor any powers, [39] nor height, nor depth, nor any other created thing, will be able to separate us from the love of God revealed in Christ Jesus, our Lord!

Gentiles and Judeans

9 [1] I am speaking the truth as one in union with the Anointed One; it is no lie; and my conscience, enlightened by the holy Spirit, [2] bears me out when I say that there is a great weight of sorrow on me and that my heart is never free from pain. [3] I could wish that I were myself accursed and severed from the Anointed One, for the sake of my people — my own flesh and blood. [4] For they are Israelites, and theirs are the adoption as children, the visible presence, the covenants, the revealed Law, the Temple worship, and the promises. [5] They are descended from the patriarchs; and, as far as his human nature was concerned, from them came the Christ — he who is supreme over all things, God forever blessed. Amen.

[6] Not that God's Word has failed. For it is not all who are descended from Israel who are true Israelites; [7] nor, because they are Abraham's descendants, are they all his children; but: "It is Isaac's children who will be called your descendants." [8] This means that it is not the children born in the course of nature who are God's children, but it is the children born in ful-

fillment of the Promise who are to be regarded as Abraham's descendants. [9] For these words are the words of a promise: "About this time I will come, and Sarah will have a son." [10] Nor is that all. There is also the case of Rebecca, when she was about to bear children to our ancestor Isaac. [11] For in order that the purpose of God, working through selection, might not fail — a selection depending, not on obedience, but on his call — Rebecca was told, before her children were born and before they had done anything either right or wrong, [12] that "the elder would be a servant to the younger." [13] The words of scripture are: "I loved Jacob, but I hated Esau."

[14] What are we to say, then? Is God guilty of injustice? Heaven forbid! [15] For his words to Moses are: "I will take pity on whom I take pity, and be merciful to whom I am merciful." [16] So, then, all depends, not on human wishes or human efforts, but on God's mercy. [17] In scripture, again, it is said to Pharaoh, "It was for this purpose that I raised you to the throne, to show my power by my dealings with you, and to make my name known throughout the world." [18] So, then, where God wills, he takes pity, and where he wills, he hardens the heart. [19] Perhaps you will say to me, "How can anyone still be blamed? For who withstands his purpose?" [20] I might rather ask, "Who are you who are arguing with God?" Does a thing which a person has molded say to the person who has molded it, "Why did you make me like this?" [21] Has not the potter absolute power over her clay, so that out of the same lump she makes one thing for better and another for common use? [22] And what if God, intending to reveal his displeasure and make his power known, bore most patiently with the objects of his displeasure, though they were fit only to be destroyed, [23] so as to make known his surpassing glory in dealing with the objects of his mercy, whom he prepared beforehand for glory, [24] and whom he called — even us — not only from

among the Judeans but from among the gentiles also! ²⁵ This, indeed, is what he says in the book of Hosea: "Those who were not my people, I will call my people, and those who were unloved I will love. ²⁶ And in the place where it was said to them, 'You are not my people,' they will be called children of the living God." ²⁷ And Isaiah cries aloud over Israel: "Though the children of Israel are like the sand of the sea in number, only a remnant of them will escape! ²⁸ For the Lord will execute his sentence on the world, fully and without delay." ²⁹ It is as Isaiah foretold: "Had not the Lord of Hosts spared some few of our race to us, we should have become like Sodom and been made to resemble Gomorrah."

³⁰ What are we to say, then? Why, that gentiles, who were not in search of righteousness, secured it — a righteousness which was the result of faith; ³¹ while Israel, which was in search of a Law which would ensure righteousness, failed to discover one. ³² And why? Because they looked to obedience, and not to faith, to secure it. They stumbled over "'the stumbling block." ³³ As scripture says, "See, I place a stumbling block in Zion — a Rock which will prove a hindrance; and those who trust in him will have no cause for shame."

10 ¹ My friends, my heart's desire and prayer to God for my people are for their salvation. ² I can testify that they are zealous for the honor of God; but they are not guided by true insight, ³ for, in their ignorance of the divine righteousness, and in their eagerness to set up a righteousness of their own, they refused to accept with submission the divine righteousness. ⁴ For Christ has brought Law to an end, so that righteousness may be obtained by everyone who believes in him. ⁵ For Moses writes that, as for the righteousness which results from Law, "those who practice it will find life through it."

⁶ But the righteousness which results from faith finds expression in these words: "Do not say to yourself, 'Who will go up into heaven?'" — which means to bring Christ down — ⁷ "or 'Who will go down into the depths below?'" — which means to bring Christ up from the dead. ⁸ No, but what does it say? "The message of faith" which we proclaim. ⁹ For, if with your lips you acknowledge the truth of the message that Jesus is Lord, and believe in your heart that God raised him from the dead, you will be saved. ¹⁰ For with their hearts people believe and so attain to righteousness, while with their lips they make their profession of faith and so find salvation. ¹¹ As the passage of scripture says, "No one who believes in him will have any cause for shame." ¹² For no distinction is made between the Judean and the Greek, for all have the same Lord, and he is bountiful to all who invoke him. ¹³ For "everyone who invokes the name of the Lord will be saved." ¹⁴ But how, it may be asked, are they to invoke one in whom they have not learned to believe? And how are they to believe in one whose words they have not heard? And how are they to hear his words unless someone proclaims him? ¹⁵ And how is anyone to proclaim him unless he is sent as his messenger? As scripture says, "How beautiful are the feet of those who bring good news!"

¹⁶ Still, it may be said, everyone did not give heed to the good news. No, for Isaiah asks, "Lord, who has believed our teaching?" ¹⁷ And so we gather, faith is a result of teaching, and the teaching comes in the message of Christ. ¹⁸ But I ask, "Is it possible that people have never heard?" No, indeed, for "Their voices spread through all the earth, and their message to the ends of the world." ¹⁹ But again I ask, Did not the people of Israel understand? First there is Moses, who says, "I, the Lord, will stir you to rivalry with a nation which is no nation; against an undiscerning nation I will arouse your anger." ²⁰ And Isaiah says

boldly, "I was found by those who were not seeking me; I made myself known to those who were not inquiring of me." [21] But of the people of Israel he says, "All day long I have stretched out my hands to a people who disobey and contradict."

11 [1] I ask, then, "Has God rejected his people?" Heaven forbid! For I myself am an Israelite, a descendant of Abraham, of the tribe of Benjamin. [2] God has not rejected his people, whom he chose from the first. Have you forgotten the words of scripture in the story of Elijah — how he appeals to God against Israel? [3] "Lord, they have killed your prophets, they have pulled down your altars, and I only am left; and now they are eager to take my life." [4] But what was the divine response? "I have kept for myself seven thousand who have never bowed the knee to Baal." [5] And so in our own time, too, there is to be found a remnant of our nation selected by God in love. [6] But if in love, then no longer as a result of obedience. Otherwise love would cease to be love. [7] What follows from this? Why, that Israel as a nation failed to secure what it was seeking, while those whom God selected did secure it. [8] The rest grew callous; as scripture says, "God has given them a deadness of mind — eyes that are not to see and ears that are not to hear — and it is so to this very day." [9] David, too, says, "May their feasts prove a snare and a trap to them — a hindrance and a retribution; [10] may their eyes be darkened, so that they cannot see; and do you always make their backs to bend." [11] I ask then, "Was their stumbling to result in their fall?" Heaven forbid! On the contrary, through their falling away salvation has reached the gentiles, to stir the rivalry of Israel. [12] And, if their falling away has enriched the world, and their failure has enriched the gentiles, how much more will result from their full restoration!

[13] But I am speaking to you who were gentiles. [14] Being myself an ambassador to the gentiles, I exalt my office, in the hope that I may stir my countrymen to rivalry, and so save some of them. [15] For, if their being cast aside has meant the reconciliation of the world, what will their reception mean, but life from the dead? [16] If the first handful of dough is holy, so is the whole mass; and if the root is holy, so are the branches. [17] Some, however, of the branches were broken off, and you, who were only a wild olive, were grafted in among them, and came to share with them the root which is the source of the richness of the cultivated olive. [18] Yet do not exult over the other branches. But if you do exult over them, remember that you do not support the root, but that the root supports you. [19] But branches, you will say, were broken off, so that I might be grafted in. [20] True; it was because of their want of faith that they were broken off, and it is because of your faith that you are standing. Do not think too highly of yourself, but beware. [21] For, if God did not spare the natural branches, neither will he spare you. [22] See, then, both the goodness and the severity of God — his severity toward those who fell, and his goodness toward you, provided that you continue to confide in that goodness; otherwise you, also, will be cut off. [23] And they, too, if they do not continue in their unbelief, will be grafted in; for God has it in his power to graft them in again. [24] If you were cut off from your natural stock — a wild olive — and were grafted, contrary to the course of nature, on a good olive, much more will they — the natural branches — be grafted back into their parent tree.

[25] My friends, so that you do not think too highly of yourselves, I want you to recognize the truth, hitherto hidden, that the callousness which has come over Israel is only partial, and will continue only until the whole gentile world has been gathered in. [26] And then all Israel will be saved. As scripture says, "From Zion will come the Deliverer; he will banish ungodliness

from Jacob. ²⁷ And they will see the fulfillment of my covenant, when I have taken
away their sins." ²⁸ From the standpoint of
the good news, the Judeans are God's enemies for your sake; but from the standpoint of God's selection, they are dear to
him for the sake of the patriarchs. ²⁹ For
God never regrets his gifts or his call.
³⁰ Just as you at one time were disobedient
to him, but have now found mercy in the
day of their disobedience; ³¹ so, too, they
have now become disobedient in your day
of mercy, in order that they also in their
turn may now find mercy. ³² For God has
given all alike over to disobedience, that to
all alike he may show mercy. ³³ Oh! The
unfathomable wisdom and knowledge of
God! How inscrutable are his judgments,
how untraceable his ways! ³⁴ "Who has
ever comprehended the mind of the Lord?
Who has ever become his counselor?
³⁵ Or who has first given to him, so that
he may claim a reward?" ³⁶ For all things
are from him, through him, and for him.
And to him be all glory forever and ever!
Amen.

Advice on Daily Life

12 ¹ I entreat you, then, friends, by the
mercies of God, to offer your bodies as
a living and holy sacrifice, acceptable to
God, for this is your rational worship.
² Do not conform to the fashion of this
world; but be transformed by the complete
change that has come over your minds,
so that you may discern what God's will
is — all that is good, acceptable, and perfect.

³ In fulfillment of the charge with which
I have been entrusted, I tell every one of
you not to think more highly of yourself
than you ought to think, but to think until you learn to think soberly — in accordance with the measure of faith that God
has allotted to each. ⁴ For, just as in the human body there is a union of many parts,
and each part has its own function, ⁵ so

we, by our union in Christ, many though
we are, form but one body, and individually we are related one to another as its
parts. ⁶ Since our gifts differ in accordance
with the particular charge entrusted to us,
if our gift is to preach, let our preaching
correspond to our faith; ⁷ if it is to minister to others, let us devote ourselves to our
ministry; the teacher to her teaching, ⁸ the
counselor to her counsel. Let the person
who gives in charity do so with a generous heart; let the person who is in authority exercise due diligence; let the person
who shows kindness do so in a cheerful
spirit. ⁹ Let your love be sincere. Hate the
wrong; cling to the right. ¹⁰ In the love of
the community of the Lord's followers, be
affectionate to one another; in showing respect, set an example of deference to one
another; ¹¹ never flagging in zeal; fervent
in spirit; serving the Master; ¹² rejoicing
in your hope; steadfast under persecu-
tion; persevering in prayer; ¹³ relieving the
wants of the Anointed One's people; de-
voted to hospitality. ¹⁴ Bless your persecutors — bless and never curse. ¹⁵ Rejoice
with those who are rejoicing, and weep
with those who are weeping. ¹⁶ Let the
same spirit of sympathy animate you all,
not a spirit of pride; enjoy the company of
ordinary people. Do not think too highly
of yourselves. ¹⁷ Never return injury for
injury. Aim at doing what everyone will
recognize as honorable. ¹⁸ If it is possible, as far as rests with you, live peaceably
with everyone. ¹⁹ Never avenge yourselves,
dear friends, but make way for the wrath
of God; for scripture declares, "'It is for
me to avenge, I will requite,' says the Lord."
²⁰ Rather, "If your enemy is hungry, feed
him; if he is thirsty, give him to drink. By
doing this you will heap coals of fire on his
head." ²¹ Never be conquered by evil, but
conquer evil with good.

13 ¹ Let everyone obey the supreme authorities. For no authority exists except by
the will of God, and the existing authori-

ties have been appointed by God. [2] Therefore those who set themselves against the authorities are resisting God's appointment, and those who resist will bring a judgment on themselves. [3] A good action has nothing to fear from rulers; a bad action has. Do you want to have no reason to fear the authorities? Then do what is good, and you will win their praise. [4] For they are God's servants appointed for your good. But if you do what is wrong, you may well be afraid; for the sword they carry is not without meaning! They are God's servants to inflict his punishments on those who do wrong. [5] You are bound, therefore, to obey, not only through fear of God's punishments, but also as a matter of conscience. [6] This, too, is the reason for your paying taxes; for the officials are God's officers, devoting themselves to this special work. [7] In all cases pay what is due from you — tribute where tribute is due, taxes where taxes are due, respect where respect is due, and honor where honor is due.

[8] Owe nothing to anyone except love; for they who love their neighbor have satisfied the Law. [9] The commandments — "You must not commit adultery. You must not kill. You must not steal. You must not covet," and whatever other commandment there is — are all summed up in the words "You must love your neighbor as you love yourself." [10] Love never wrongs a neighbor. Therefore love fully satisfies the Law. [11] This I say, because you know the crisis that we have reached, for the time has already come for you to rouse yourselves from sleep; our salvation is nearer now than when we accepted the faith.

[12] The night is almost gone; the day is near. Therefore let us have done with the deeds of darkness, and arm ourselves with the weapons of light. [13] Being in the light of day, let us live becomingly, not in revelry and drunkenness, not in lust and licentiousness, not in quarreling and jealousy. [14] No! Arm yourselves with the spirit of the Lord Jesus Christ, and spend no thought on your earthly nature, to satisfy its cravings.

14 [1] As for those whose faith is weak, always receive them as friends, but not for the purpose of passing judgment on their scruples. [2] One person's faith permits of their eating food of all kinds, while another whose faith is weak eats only vegetable food. [3] The person who eats meat must not despise the person who abstains from it; nor must the person who abstains from eating meat pass judgment on the one who eats it, for God himself has received them both. [4] Who are you, that you should pass judgment on the servant of another? Her standing or falling concerns her own master. And stand she will, for her master can enable her to stand. [5] Again, one person considers some days to be more sacred than others, while another considers all days to be alike. Everyone ought to be fully convinced in her own mind. [6] The person who observes a day, observes it to the Master's honor. They, again, who eat meat eat it to the Master's honor, for they give thanks to God; while the person who abstains from it abstains from it to the Master's honor, and also gives thanks to God. [7] There is not one of us whose life concerns ourself alone, and not one of us whose death concerns ourself alone; [8] for, if we live, our life is for the Master, and, if we die, our death is for the Master. Whether, then, we live or die we belong to the Master. [9] The purpose for which Christ died and came back to life was this — that he might be Lord over both the dead and the living. [10] I would ask the one, "Why do you judge other followers of the Lord?" And I would ask the other, "Why do you despise them?" For we will all stand before the court of God. [11] For scripture says, "'As surely as I live,' says the Lord, 'every knee will bend before me; and every tongue will make acknowledgment to God.'" [12] So, then, each one of us will have to render account of herself to God.

[13] Let us, then, cease to judge one another. Rather let this be your resolve — never to place a stumbling block or an obstacle in the way of a fellow follower of the Lord. [14] Through my union with the Lord Jesus, I know and am persuaded that nothing is "defiling in itself." A thing is "defiling" only to the person who holds it to be so. [15] If, for the sake of what you eat, you wound your fellow follower's feelings, your life has ceased to be ruled by love. Do not, by what you eat, ruin someone for whom Christ died! [16] Do not let what is right for you become a matter of reproach. [17] For the realm of God does not consist of eating and drinking, but of righteousness and peace and gladness through the presence of the holy Spirit. [18] The person who serves the Christ in this way pleases God, and wins the approval of his fellows. [19] Therefore our efforts should be directed toward all that makes for peace and the mutual building up of character. [20] Do not undo God's work for the sake of what you eat. Though everything is "clean," yet, if a person eats so as to put a stumbling block in the way of others, he does wrong. [21] The right course is to abstain from meat or wine or, indeed, anything that is a stumbling block to your fellow follower of the Lord. [22] As for yourself — keep this faith of yours to yourself, as in the presence of God. Happy the person who never has to condemn himself in regard to something he thinks right! [23] The person, however, who has misgivings stands condemned if he still eats, because his doing so is not the result of faith. And anything not done as the result of faith is a sin.

15 [1] We, the strong, ought to take on our own shoulders the weaknesses of those who are not strong, and not merely to please ourselves. [2] Let each of us please our neighbor for our neighbor's good, to help in the building up of his character. [3] Even the Anointed One did not please himself! On the contrary, as scripture says of him, "The reproaches of those who were reproaching you fell upon me." [4] Whatever was written in the scriptures in days gone by was written for our instruction, so that through patient endurance, and through the encouragement drawn from the scriptures, we might hold fast to our hope. [5] And may God, the giver of this patience and this encouragement, grant you to be united in sympathy in the Anointed One, [6] so that with one heart and one voice you may praise the God and Father of Jesus Christ, our Lord. [7] Therefore always receive one another as friends, just as the Anointed One himself received us, to the glory of God. [8] For I tell you that Christ, in vindication of God's truthfulness, has become a minister of the covenant of circumcision, so that he may fulfill the promises made to our ancestors, [9] and that the gentiles also may praise God for his mercy. As scripture says, "Therefore will I make acknowledgment to you among the gentiles and sing in honor of your name." [10] And again it says, "Rejoice, you gentiles, with God's people." [11] And yet again, "Praise the Lord, all you gentiles, and let all peoples sing his praises." [12] Again, Isaiah says, "There will be a Scion of the house of Jesse, One who is to arise to rule the gentiles; on him will the gentiles rest their hopes." [13] May God, who inspires our hope, grant you perfect happiness and peace in your faith, until you are filled with this hope by the power of the holy Spirit.

[14] I am persuaded, my friends — yes, I, Paul, with regard to you — that you are yourselves full of kindness, furnished with all Christian learning, and well able to give advice to one another. [15] But in parts of this letter I have expressed myself somewhat boldly — by way of refreshing your memories — [16] because of the charge with

which God has entrusted me, that I should be a minister of Christ Jesus to go to the gentiles — that I should act as a priest of God's good news, so that the offering up of the gentiles may be an acceptable sacrifice, consecrated by the holy Spirit. [17] It is, then, through my union with Christ Jesus that I have a proud confidence in my work for God. [18] For I will not dare to speak of anything but what Christ has done through me to win the obedience of the gentiles — [19] by my words and actions, through the power displayed in signs and marvels, and through the power of the holy Spirit. And so, starting from Jerusalem and its neighborhood, and going as far as Illyria, I have told in full the good news of the Christ; [20] yet always with the ambition to tell the good news where Christ's name had not previously been heard, so as to avoid building on another's foundations. [21] But as scripture says, "They to whom he had never been proclaimed will see; and they who have never heard will understand!"

Conclusion

[22] That is why I have so often been prevented from coming to you. [23] But now there are no further openings for me in these parts, and I have for several years been longing to come to you whenever I may be going to Spain. [24] For my hope is to visit you on my journey, and then to be sent on my way by you, after I have first partly satisfied myself by seeing something of you. [25] Just now, however, I am on my way to Jerusalem, to take help to the Anointed One's people there. [26] For Macedonia and Greece have been glad to make a collection for the poor among Christ's people at Jerusalem. [27] Yes, they were glad to do so; and indeed it is a duty which they owe to them. For the gentile converts who have shared their spiritual blessings are in duty bound to minister to them in the things of this world. [28] When I have set-

tled this matter, and have secured to the poor at Jerusalem the enjoyment of these benefits, I will go, by way of you, to Spain. [29] And I know that when I come to you, it will be with a full measure of blessing from the Anointed One.

[30] I beg you, then, friends, by Jesus Christ, our Lord, and by the love inspired by the Spirit, to join me in earnest prayer to God on my behalf. [31] Pray that I may be rescued from those in Judea who reject the faith, and that the help which I am taking to Jerusalem may prove acceptable to the Anointed One's people; [32] so that, God willing, I may be able to come to you with a joyful heart, and enjoy some rest among you. [33] May God, the giver of peace, be with you all. Amen.

16 [1] I commend to your care our sister Phoebe, who is a minister of the church at Cenchreae; [2] and I ask you to give her a trustworthy welcome — one worthy of Christ's people — and to aid her in any matter in which she may need your assistance. She has proved herself a staunch friend and protector of mine and to many others.

[3] Give my greeting to Prisca and Aquila, my fellow workers in the cause of Christ Jesus, [4] who risked their own lives to save mine. It is not I alone who thank them, but all the churches among the gentiles thank them also. [5] Give my greeting, also, to the church that meets at their house, as well as to my dear friend Epaenetus, one of the first in Roman Asia to believe in the Anointed One; [6] to Mary, who worked hard for you; [7] to Andronicus and Junia, fellow Judeans and once my fellow prisoners, who are people of note among the ambassadors, and who belonged to the Anointed One before I did; [8] to my dear friend in the Lord Ampliatus; [9] to Urban, our fellow worker in the cause of the Anointed One, and to my dear friend Stachys; [10] to that proved servant of Christ Apelles; to the household of Aristo-

bulus; [11] to my countryman Herodion; to those in the household of Narcissus who belong to the Lord; [12] to Tryphaena and Tryphosa, who have worked hard for the Master; to my dear friend Persis, for she has done much hard work for the Master; [13] to that eminent servant of the Lord Rufus, and to his mother, who has been a mother to me also; [14] to Asyncritus, Phlegon, Hermes, Patrobas, Hermas, and our friends with them; [15] also to Philologus and Julia, Nereus and his sister, and Olympas, and to all Christ's people who are with them. [16] Greet one another with a sacred kiss. All the churches of the Anointed One send you greetings.

[17] I beg you, friends, to be on your guard against people who, by disregarding the teaching which you received, cause divisions and create difficulties; dissociate yourselves from them. [18] For such persons are not serving the Anointed One, our Master, but are slaves to their own appetites; and, by their smooth words and flattery, they deceive simple-minded people. [19] Everyone has heard of your ready obedience. It is true that I am very happy about you, but I want you to be well versed in all that is good, and innocent of all that is bad. [20] And God, the giver of peace, will before long crush Satan under your feet.

May the blessing of Jesus, our Lord, be with you.

[21] Timothy, my fellow worker, sends you his greetings, and Lucius, Jason, and Sosipater, my countrymen, send theirs.

[22] I, Tertius, who am writing this letter, greet you in the Lord.

[23] My host Gaius, who extends his hospitality to the whole church, sends you his greeting; and Erastus, the city treasurer, and Quartus, our dear friend, add theirs.

[25] Now to the One who is able to strengthen you, as promised in the good news entrusted to me and in the proclamation of Jesus Christ, in accordance with the revelation of that hidden purpose, which in past ages was kept secret but now has been revealed [26] and, in obedience to the command of the immortal God, made known through the writings of the prophets to all nations, to secure submission to the faith — [27] to him, I say, the wise and only God, be ascribed, through Jesus Christ, all glory forever and ever. Amen.

An Introduction to the First Letter
to the Corinthians

WRITTEN NEAR THE beginning of what was probably an extended correspondence between Paul and Christ assemblies in the Macedonian city
of Corinth, 1 Corinthians is one of the most expressive and detailed documents of
early Christianity in its breadth of subject matter and emotions about the life of
the first generation of gentile Christ communities. The situations treated in 1 Corinthians include deciding whether to use the civil court system to settle a Christ
community dispute, assessing speaking in tongues, thinking about whether an old
man and a young woman should live together, evaluating the value of philosophy, wondering how important baptism is, deciding whether to be celibate or married, collecting money for Jerusalem, debating behavior at the weekly communal
meals, deciding where to shop for meat, making sense of being humiliated, trying to stand up for oneself, finding out what love means, thinking about the fate of
those who die, and arguing about men's and women's places in the community and
the world. Paul wrote this letter in Greek in the early 50s CE.

Paul calls himself an "ambassador" (apostle),* even though in other circles that
word is often reserved for followers of Jesus who knew him while he lived. Paul
never claims that he knew Jesus of Nazareth in person. Contrary to understandings of Paul for much of Christian history, scholarship of the past several generations tends to think that Paul always thought of himself as belonging to the traditions of Israel and not as a Christian. Rather, he appears to have thought that
Christ enabled the gentiles to belong genuinely to the larger constellation of traditions of Israel.

Paul knows many of the people in the Corinthian Christ assemblies and has affectionate and combative relationships with their leaders. He is also aware that
other Christ movement leaders such as Apollos and Peter are influencing the Corinthian Christ groups. He has had to delay his return to see them. He wants the
best for the Corinthians and works hard to cajole, influence, and intimidate them
into his positions about how to be in community.

---

* The Greek word *apostolos,* often translated (or better put, transliterated) as "apostle," means
"one who is sent" and is used throughout Greek literature to designate a messenger or, in the case
of an important messenger, an "ambassador."

The Body of Christ

Paul presents the "body of Christ" to the Corinthian assemblies as a concept and an image of social and spiritual connection. He is concerned that their weekly meals together show respect for one another and invoke connectedness in Christ. He pushes them to respect one another's dietary principles and to express themselves in ways that build up the social body. For Paul such respect and expression include setting severe limits on women speaking at the meals. This is a sure sign that the Corinthian Christ assemblies already had women in articulate leadership during their meals together.

Sharing bread and wine together was a way of participating in the social body of Christ. Songs, prayers, teachings, and food all contributed to making up a social body of Judeans as well as Greeks, slaves as well as free people. Paul is enamored of the way all kinds of different people make up this body of Christ, and he articulates the ways these different parts of the social body should interrelate. His vision of and personal participation in this unity in Christ both poetically evoke a symphony of differences in one connected group and shock with some of his prejudices.

The Resurrection

Although in his Letter to the Romans Paul proposed that resurrection is a participation of Christ people in the present time as demonstrated in their freedom from shame and corruption, in 1 Corinthians he concentrates on the meaning of the resurrection relative to those who have died or will die. In chapter 15 he affirms that after his death, Christ appeared to many people, including, and "last of all," Paul himself. He uses Christ's appearance after death to assert that there is resurrection for the dead.

This affirmation of a resurrection for the dead seems to have surprised the Corinthians, who probably believed in the resurrection as a mode of present reality, in a way similar to Paul's own expression in Romans. Explaining the importance of a resurrection for the dead occasions Paul to make two proposals: the resurrection of the dead is bodily, and a "spiritual body" is raised after death. The notion of a spiritual body accords with ancient notions of "spirit," which included a physical aspect, although one less dense than other forms of physical existence. For Paul, in both the present and future life, Christ's resurrection defeats the finality of death.

The rootedness of 1 Corinthians in all kinds of specific dilemmas of the first century shows a daily commitment to the spiritual freedom in Christ's body that Paul recommends. Its evocation of everyday realities points toward a similar possibility in the specific dilemmas of twenty-first-century life.

Recommended Reading

Dale B. Martin, *The Corinthian Body*
Jerome Murphy-O'Connor, *St. Paul's Corinth: Texts and Archaeology*
Antoinette Clark Wire, *The Corinthian Women Prophets*

The First Letter to the Corinthians

Introduction

1 ¹ To the church of God in Corinth, to those who have been consecrated by union with Christ Jesus and called to become his people, and also to all, wherever they may be, who invoke the name of our Lord Jesus Christ—their Master and ours, ² from Paul, who has been called to be an ambassador of Jesus Christ by the will of God, and from Sosthenes, our fellow follower of the Lord. ³ May God, our Father, and the Lord Jesus Christ bless you and give you peace. ⁴ I always thank God about you for the blessing bestowed on you in Christ Jesus. ⁵ For through union with him you were enriched in every way—in your power to proclaim, and in your knowledge of the truth—⁶ and so became yourselves a confirmation of my testimony to the Anointed One. ⁷ There is no gift in which you are deficient, while waiting for the appearing of our Lord Jesus Christ. ⁸ And God himself will strengthen you to the end, so that at the day of our Lord Jesus Christ you may be found blameless. ⁹ God will not fail you, and it is he who called you into communion with his Child, Jesus Christ, our Lord.

The State of the Church at Corinth

¹⁰ But I appeal to you, my friends, by the name of our Lord Jesus Christ, to agree in what you profess, and not to allow divisions to exist among you, but to be united—of one mind and of one opinion. ¹¹ For I have been informed, my friends, by the members of Chloe's household, that party feeling exists among you. ¹² I mean this: that every one of you says either "I follow Paul," or "I Apollos," or "I Cephas," or "I Christ." ¹³ You have torn the Anointed One in pieces! Was it Paul who was crucified for you? Or were you baptized into the faith of Paul? ¹⁴ I am thankful that I did not baptize any of you except Crispus and Gaius, ¹⁵ so that no one can say that you were baptized into my faith. ¹⁶ I baptized also the household of Stephanas. I do not know that I baptized anyone else. ¹⁷ My mission from the Anointed One was not to baptize, but to tell the good news; not, however, in the language of philosophy, in case the cross of the Christ should be robbed of its meaning.

¹⁸ The message of the cross is indeed mere folly to those who are in the path to ruin, but to us who are in the path of salvation it is the power of God. ¹⁹ For scripture says:

> "I will bring the philosophy of the
> philosophers to naught, and the
> shrewdness of the shrewd I will
> bring to nothing."

²⁰ Where is the philosopher? Where the teacher of the Law? Where the disputant of today? Has God not shown the world's philosophy to be folly? ²¹ For since the world, in God's wisdom, did not by its philosophy learn to know God, God saw fit, by the "folly" of our proclamation, to save those who believe in the Anointed One! ²² While Judeans ask for miraculous signs, and Greeks study philosophy, ²³ we are proclaiming Christ crucified—to the Judeans an obstacle, to the gentiles mere folly, ²⁴ but to those who have received the call, whether Judeans or Greeks, Christ, the power of God and the wisdom of God! ²⁵ For God's "folly" is wiser than people,

and God's "weakness" is stronger than people.

²⁶ Look at the facts of your call, friends. There are not many among you who are wise, as people reckon wisdom, not many who are influential, not many who are high-born; ²⁷ but God chose what the world counts foolish to put its wise to shame, and God chose what the world counts weak to put its strong to shame, ²⁸ and God chose what the world counts poor and insignificant — things that to it are unreal — to bring its "realities" to nothing, ²⁹ so that in his presence no one should boast. ³⁰ But you, by your union with Christ Jesus, belong to God; and Christ, by God's will, became not only our wisdom, but also our righteousness, holiness, and deliverance, ³¹ so that — in the words of scripture —

"Let him who boasts make his boast of
   the Lord!"

2 ¹ For my own part, friends, when I came to you, it was with no display of eloquence or philosophy that I came to tell the hidden purpose of God; ² for I had determined that while with you, I would forget everything but Jesus Christ — and him crucified! ³ Indeed, when I came among you, I was weak, and full of fears, and in great anxiety. ⁴ My message and my proclamation were not delivered in the persuasive language of philosophy, but were accompanied by the manifestation of spiritual power, ⁵ so that your faith should be based, not on human wisdom, but on the power of God.

⁶ Yet there is a wisdom that we teach to those whose faith is matured, but it is not the philosophy of today, or of the lead-ers of today — whose downfall is at hand. ⁷ No, it is a divine Wisdom-Sophia* that we teach, one concerned with the hidden purpose of God — that long hidden Wisdom-Sophia which God, before time began, destined for our glory. ⁸ She was not recognized by the leaders of today; for, had they recognized this Wisdom-Sophia, they would not have crucified our glorified Lord. ⁹ It is what scripture speaks of as:

"What eye never saw, nor ear ever
   heard,
what never entered people's minds —
even all that God has prepared for
   those who love him."

¹⁰ Yet to us God revealed it through his Spirit; for the Spirit fathoms all things, even the inmost depths of God's being. ¹¹ For what person is there who knows what a person is, except the person's own spirit within her? So, also, no one comprehends what God is, except the Spirit of God. ¹² And as for us, it is not the spirit of the world that we have received, but the Spirit that comes from God, so that we may realize the blessings given to us by him. ¹³ And we speak of these gifts, not in language taught by human philosophy, but in language taught by the Spirit, explaining spiritual things in spiritual words. ¹⁴ The merely intellectual person rejects the teaching of the Spirit of God; for to her it is mere folly; she cannot grasp it, because it is to be understood only by spiritual insight. ¹⁵ But the person with spiritual insight is able to understand everything, although she herself is understood by no one. ¹⁶ For "who has so comprehended the mind of the Lord as to be able to instruct

---

* This treatment of "wisdom" relies on the divine person of Wisdom portrayed in Proverbs 1–9, Matthew 11, and James 3. The Greek word for "wisdom" is *sophia*. In this way the Greek word and its English translation are used together to indicate the personhood of Wisdom in these verses.

him?" We, however, have the mind of the Anointed One.

3 [1] But I, my friends, could not speak to you as people with spiritual insight, but only as worldly minded — mere infants in the faith of Christ. [2] I fed you with milk, not with solid food, for you were not then able to take it.

No, and even now you are not able; you are still worldly. [3] While there exist among you jealousy and party feeling, is it not true that you are worldly, and are acting merely as other people do? [4] When one says, "I follow Paul," and another, "I follow Apollos," are you not like other people? [5] What, I ask, is Apollos? Or what is Paul? Servants through whom you were led to accept the faith; and that only as the Lord helped each of you. [6] I planted, and Apollos watered, but it was God who caused the growth. [7] Therefore neither the one who plants, nor the one who waters, counts for anything, but only God who causes the growth. [8] In this the person who plants and the person who waters are one; yet each will receive his own reward in proportion to his own labor. [9] For we are God's fellow workers; you are God's harvest field, God's building.

[10] In fulfillment of the charge which God had entrusted to me, I laid the foundation like a skillful master; but someone else is now building on it. Let everyone take care how they build; [11] for no one can lay any other foundation than the one already laid — Jesus Christ. [12] Whatever is used by those who build on this foundation, whether gold, silver, costly stones, wood, hay, or straw, [13] the quality of each person's work will become known, for the day will make it plain; because that day is to be ushered in with fire, and the fire itself will test the quality of everyone's work. [14] If anyone's work, built on that foundation, still remains, the builder will gain a reward. [15] If anyone's work is burned up,

the builder will suffer loss; though he himself will escape, but only as one who has passed through fire.

[16] Do you not know that you are God's temple, and that God's spirit has its home in you? [17] If anyone destroys the temple of God, God will destroy him; for the temple of God is sacred, and so also are you.

[18] Let no one deceive himself. If anyone among you imagines that, as regards this world, he is wise, let him become a "fool," that he may become wise. [19] For in God's sight this world's wisdom is folly. Scripture tells of

"One who catches the wise in their own craftiness."

[20] And it says again:

"The Lord sees how fruitless are the deliberations of the wise."

[21] Therefore let no one boast about people; for all things are yours — [22] whether Paul, or Apollos, or Cephas, or the world, or life, or death, or the present, or the future — all things are yours! [23] But you are Christ's and Christ is God's.

4 [1] Let people look on us as Christ's servants, and as stewards of the hidden truths of God. [2] Now what we look for in stewards is that they should be trustworthy. [3] But it weighs very little with me that I am judged by you or by any human tribunal. No, I do not even judge myself; [4] for, though I am conscious of nothing against myself, that does not prove me innocent. It is the Lord who is my judge. [5] Therefore do not pass judgment before the time, but wait until the Lord comes. He will throw light on what is now dark and obscure, and will reveal the motives in people's minds; and then everyone will receive due praise from God.

[6] All this, friends, I have, for your sakes,

applied to Apollos and myself, so that from our example, you may learn to observe the precept, "Keep to what is written," that none of you may speak boastfully of one teacher to the disparagement of another. [7] For who makes any one of you superior to others? And what have you that was not given you? But if you received it as a gift, why do you boast as if you had not? [8] Are you all so soon satisfied? Are you so soon rich? Have you begun to reign without us? Would indeed that you had, so that we also might reign with you! [9] For, as it seems to me, God has exhibited us, the apostles, last of all, as people doomed to death. We are made a spectacle to the universe, both to angels and to people! [10] We, for Christ's sake, are "fools," but you, by your union with Christ, are people of discernment. We are weak, but you are strong. You are honored, but we are despised. [11] To this very hour we go hungry, thirsty, and naked; we are beaten; we are homeless; [12] we work hard, toiling with our own hands. We meet abuse with blessings, we meet persecution with endurance, [13] we meet slander with gentle appeals. We have been treated as the scum of the earth, the vilest of the vile, to this very hour.

[14] It is with no wish to shame you that I am writing like this; but to warn you as my own dear children. [15] Though you may have thousands of instructors in the faith of Christ, yet you have not many fathers. It was I who, through union with Christ Jesus, became your father by means of the good news. [16] Therefore I entreat you — follow my example. [17] This is my reason for sending Timothy to you. He is my own dear faithful child in the Master's service, and he will remind you of my methods of teaching the faith of Christ Jesus — methods which I follow everywhere in every church.

[18] Some, I hear, are puffed up with pride, thinking that I am not coming to you. [19] But come to you I will, and that

soon, if it please the Lord; and then I will find out, not what words these people use who are so puffed up, but what power they possess; [20] for the realm of God is based, not on words, but on power. [21] What do you wish? Am I to come to you with a rod, or in a loving and gentle spirit?

5 [1] There is a widespread report respecting a case of immorality among you, and that, too, of a kind that does not occur even among the gentiles — a man, I hear, is living with his father's wife! [2] Instead of grieving over it and taking steps for the expulsion of the man who has done this thing, is it possible that you are still puffed up? [3] For I myself, though absent in body, have been present with you in spirit, and in the name of our Lord Jesus I have already passed judgment, just as if I had been present, on the man who has acted in this way. [4] I have decided — having been present in spirit at your meetings, when the power of the Lord Jesus was with us — [5] to deliver such a man as this over to Satan, that what is sensual in him may be destroyed, so that his spirit may be saved at the day of the Lord. [6] Your boasting is unseemly. Do you not know that even a little leaven leavens all the dough? [7] Get rid entirely of the old leaven, so that you may be like new dough — free from leaven, as in truth you are. For our Passover lamb is already sacrificed — Christ himself; [8] therefore let us keep our festival, not with the leaven of former days, nor with the leaven of vice and wickedness, but with the unleavened bread of sincerity and truth.

[9] I told you, in my letter, not to associate with immoral people — [10] not, of course, meaning people of the world who are immoral, or who are covetous and grasping, or who worship idols; for then you would have to leave the world altogether. [11] But as things are, I say that you are not to associate with anyone who, although a follower of Christ in name, is immoral, or covetous,

or an idolater, or abusive, or a drunkard, or grasping—no, not even to sit down to eat with such people. [12] What have I to do with judging those outside the church? Is it not for you to judge those who are within the church, [13] while God judges those who are outside? "Put away the wicked from among you."

6 [1] Can it be that when one of you has a dispute with another, you dare to have your case tried before the heathen, instead of before Christ's people? [2] Do you not know that Christ's people will try the world? And if the world is to be tried by you, are you unfit to try the most trivial cases? [3] Do you not know that we are to try angels—to say nothing of the affairs of this life? [4] Why, then, if you have cases relating to the affairs of this life, do you try them before those who carry no weight with the church? To your shame I ask it. [5] Can it be that there is not one among you wise enough to decide between two of your fellow followers? [6] Must a follower sue a fellow follower? In front of unbelievers? [7] To begin with, it is undoubtedly a loss to you to have lawsuits with one another. Why not rather let yourselves be wronged? Why not rather let yourselves be cheated? [8] Instead of this, you wrong and cheat others yourselves—yes, even other followers! [9] Do you not know that wrongdoers will have no share in God's kingdom? Do not be deceived. No one who is immoral, or an idolater, or an adulterer, or licentious, or a sexual pervert, [10] or a thief, or covetous, or a drunkard, or abusive, or grasping, will have any share in God's kingdom. [11] Such some of you used to be; but you washed yourselves clean. You became Christ's people! You were pronounced righteous through the name of our Lord Jesus Christ, and through the Spirit of our God!

[12] Everything is allowable for me! Yes, but everything is not profitable. Every-thing is allowable for me! Yes, but for my part, I will not let myself be enslaved by anything. [13] Food exists for the stomach, and the stomach for food; but God will put an end to both the one and the other. The body, however, exists, not for immorality, but for the Lord, and the Lord for the body; [14] and, as God has raised the Lord, so he will raise up us also by the exercise of his power. [15] Do you not know that your bodies are Christ's members? Am I, then, to take the members that belong to the Anointed One and make them the members of a prostitute? Heaven forbid! [16] Or do you not know that a man who unites himself with a prostitute is one with her in body (for "the two," it is said, "will become one"); [17] while a man who is united with the Lord is one with him in spirit? [18] Shun all immorality. Every other sin that people commit is something outside the body; but an immoral person sins against his own body. [19] Again, do you not know that your body is a shrine of the holy Spirit that is within you—the Spirit which you have from God? [20] Moreover, you are not your own masters; you were bought, and the price was paid. Therefore, honor God in your bodies.

Answers to Questions Asked by the Church at Corinth

7 [1] With reference to the subjects about which you wrote to me: It is good for a man to remain single. [2] But, owing to the prevalence of immorality, I advise every man to have his own wife, and every woman her husband. [3] A husband should give his wife her due, and a wife her husband. [4] It is not the wife, but the husband, who exercises power over her body; and so, too, it is not the husband, but the wife, who exercises power over his body. [5] Do not deprive each other of what is due—unless it is only for a time and by mutual con-

sent, so that your minds may be free for prayer until you again live as man and wife — otherwise Satan might take advantage of your want of self-control and tempt you. [6] I say this, however, as a concession, not as a command. [7] I should wish everyone to be just what I am myself. But everyone has his own gift from God — one in one way, and one in another.

[8] My advice, then, to those who are not married, and to widows, is this: It would be good for them to remain as I am myself. [9] But if they cannot control themselves, let them marry, for it is better to marry than to be consumed with passion. [10] To those who are married my direction is — yet it is not mine, but the Master's — that a woman is not to leave her husband [11] (if she has done so, let her remain as she is, or else be reconciled to her husband) and also that a man is not to divorce his wife. [12] To all others I say — I, not the Master — If a follower of the Lord is married to a woman who is an unbeliever but willing to live with him, he should not divorce her; [13] and a woman who is married to a man who is an unbeliever but willing to live with her should not divorce her husband. [14] For, through his wife, the husband who is an unbeliever has become associated with the Anointed One's people; and the wife who is an unbeliever has become associated with Christ's people through the Lord's follower whom she has married. Otherwise your children would be "defiled," but as it is, they belong to Christ's people. [15] However, if the unbeliever wishes to be separated, let him be so. Under such circumstances neither is bound; God has called you to live in peace. [16] How can you tell, wife, whether you may not save your husband? And how can you tell, husband, whether you may not save your wife?

[17] In any case, a person should continue to live in the condition which the Lord has allotted to him, and in which he was when God called him. This is the rule that I lay down in every church. [18] Was a man already circumcised when he was called? Then he should not efface his circumcision. Has a man been called when uncircumcised? Then he should not be circumcised. [19] Circumcision is nothing; the want of it is nothing; but to keep the commands of God is everything. [20] Let everyone remain in that condition of life in which they were when the call came to them. [21] Were you a slave when you were called? Do not let that trouble you. No, even if you are able to gain your freedom, still do your best. [22] For the person who was a slave when he was called to the Master's service is the Master's freedman; so, too, the person who was free when called is the Anointed One's slave. [23] You were bought, and the price was paid. Do not let yourselves become slaves to people. [24] Friends, let everyone remain in the condition in which they were when they were called, in close communion with God.

[25] With regard to unmarried women, I have no command from the Master to give you, but I tell you my opinion, and the Master in his mercy has made me worthy to be trusted. [26] I think, then, that in view of the time of suffering that has now come upon us, what I have already said is best — that a man should remain as he is. [27] Are you married to a wife? Then do not seek to be separated. Are you separated from a wife? Then do not seek for a wife. [28] Still, if you should marry, that is not wrong; nor, if a young woman marries, is that wrong. But those who marry will have much trouble to bear, and my wish is to spare you. [29] What I mean, friends, is this: The time is short. Meanwhile, let those who have wives live as if they had none, [30] those who are weeping as if not weeping, those who are rejoicing as if not rejoicing, those who buy as if not possessing, [31] and those who use the good things of the world as using them sparingly; for this world as we see it is passing away. [32] I want you to be free from anxiety. The unmarried man is anxious about the Mas-

ter's cause, desiring to please him; ³³ while the married man is anxious about worldly matters, desiring to please his wife; ³⁴ and so his interests are divided. Again, the unmarried woman, whether she is old or young, is anxious about the Master's cause, striving to be pure both in body and in spirit, while the married woman is anxious about worldly matters, desiring to please her husband. ³⁵ I say this for your own benefit, not with any intention of putting a halter around your necks, but in order to secure for the Master seemly and constant devotion, free from all distraction.

³⁶ If, however, a father thinks that he is not acting fairly by his unmarried daughter, when she is past her youth, and if under these circumstances her marriage ought to take place, let him act as he thinks right. He is doing nothing wrong — let the marriage take place. ³⁷ On the other hand, a father who has definitely made up his mind, and is under no compulsion, but is free to carry out his own wishes, and who has come to the decision, in his own mind, to keep his unmarried daughter at home, will be doing right. ³⁸ In short, the one who consents to his daughter's marriage is doing right, and yet the other will be doing better.

³⁹ A wife is bound to her husband as long as he lives; but if the husband should pass to his rest, the widow is free to marry anyone she wishes, provided he is a believer. ⁴⁰ Yet she will be happier if she remains as she is — in my opinion, for I think that I also have the Spirit of God.

8 ¹ With reference to food that has been offered in sacrifice to idols — we are aware that all of us have knowledge! Knowledge breeds conceit, while love builds up character. ² If someone thinks that she knows anything, she has not yet reached that knowledge which she ought to have reached. ³ On the other hand, if a person loves God, she is known by God. ⁴ With reference, then, to eating food that has

been offered to idols — we are aware that an idol is nothing in the world, and that there is no God but one. ⁵ Even supposing that there are so-called "gods" either in heaven or on earth — and there are many such "gods" and "lords" — ⁶ yet for us there is only one God, the Father, from whom all things come (and for him we live), and one Lord, Jesus Christ, through whom all things come (and through him we live). ⁷ Still, it is not everyone who has this knowledge. Some people, because of their association with idols, continued down to the present time, eat the food as food offered to an idol; and their consciences, while still weak, are dulled. ⁸ What we eat, however, will not bring us nearer to God. We lose nothing by not eating this food, and we gain nothing by eating it. ⁹ But take care that this right of yours does not become in any way a stumbling block to the weak. ¹⁰ For if someone should see you who possess this knowledge feasting in an idol's temple, will not her conscience, if she is weak, become so hardened that she, too, will eat food offered to idols? ¹¹ And so, through this knowledge of yours, the weak person is ruined — someone for whose sake Christ died! ¹² In this way, by sinning against your fellow followers of the Lord and injuring their consciences, while still weak, you sin against Christ. ¹³ Therefore, if what I eat makes a follower of the Lord fall, rather than make her fall, I will never eat meat again.

9 ¹ Am I not free? Am I not an apostle? Have I not seen our Lord Jesus? Are not you yourselves my work achieved in union with the Lord? ² If I am not an apostle to others, yet at least I am to you; for you are the seal that stamps me as an apostle in union with the Lord. ³ The defense that I make to my critics is this: ⁴ Have we not a right to food and drink? ⁵ Have we not a right to take a wife with us, if she is a believer, as the other apostles and the Master's brothers and Cephas all do? ⁶ Or is it only Barnabas and I who have no right to give up working for our bread? [7] Does anyone ever serve as a soldier at his own expense? Does anyone plant a vineyard and not eat its produce? Or does anyone look after a herd and not drink the milk? [8] Am I, in all this, speaking only from the human standpoint? Does not the Law also say the same? [9] For in the Law of Moses it is said:

> "You should not muzzle a bullock while it is treading out the grain."

Is it the bullocks that God is thinking of? [10] Or is it not said entirely for our sakes? Surely it was written for our sakes, for the plowman ought not to plow, nor the thrasher to thrash, without expecting a share of the grain. [11] Since we, then, sowed spiritual seed for you, is it too much that we should reap from you an earthly harvest? [12] If others share in this right over you, do not we even more? Still we did not avail ourselves of this right. No, we endure anything rather than impede the progress of the good news of the Christ. [13] Do you not know that those who do the work of the Temple live on what comes from the Temple, and that those who serve at the altar share the offerings with the altar? [14] So, too, the Master has appointed that those who tell the good news should get their living from the good news. [15] I, however, have not availed myself of any of these rights. I am not saying this to secure such an arrangement for myself; indeed, I would far rather die—nobody will make my boast a vain one! [16] If I tell the good news, I have nothing to boast of, for I can but do so. Woe is me if I do not tell it! [17] If I do this work willingly, I have a reward; but if unwillingly, I have been charged to perform a duty. [18] What is my reward, then? To present the good news free of all cost, and so make but a sparing use of the rights which it gives me.

[19] Although I was entirely free, yet, to win as many converts as possible, I made myself everyone's slave. [20] To the Judeans I became like a Judean, to win Judeans. To those who are subject to Law I became like a man subject to Law—though I was not myself subject to Law—to win those who are subject to Law. [21] To those who have no Law I became like a man who has no Law—not that I am free from God's Law; no, for I am under Christ's Law—to win those who have no Law. [22] To the weak I became weak, to win the weak. I have become all things to all people, so as at all costs to save some. [23] And I do everything for the sake of the good news, so that with them I may share in its blessings.

[24] Do you not know that on a racecourse, though all run, yet only one wins the prize? Run in such a way that you may win. [25] Every athlete exercises self-restraint in everything; they, indeed, for a crown that fades, we for one that is unfading. [26] I, therefore, run with no uncertain aim. I box—not like a man hitting the air. [27] No, I bruise my body and make it my slave, so that I, who have called others to the contest, will not myself be rejected.

10 [1] I want you to bear in mind, friends, that all our ancestors were beneath the cloud, and all passed through the sea; [2] that in the cloud and in the sea they all underwent baptism as followers of Moses; [3] and that they all ate the same supernatural food, [4] and all drank the same supernatural water, for they used to drink from a supernatural rock which followed them, and that rock was the Christ. [5] Yet with most of them God was displeased; for they were "struck down in the desert." [6] Now these things happened as warnings to us, to teach us not to long for evil things as our forefathers longed. [7] Do not become idolaters, as some of them became. Scripture says:

> "The people sat down to eat and drink, and stood up to dance."

[8] Nor let us act immorally, as some of them acted, with the result that twenty-three thousand of them fell dead in a single day. [9] Nor let us try the patience of the Lord too far, as some of them tried it, with the result that they "were, one after another, destroyed by the snakes." [10] And do not murmur, as some of them murmured, and so "were destroyed by the angel of death." [11] These things happened to them by way of warning, and were recorded to serve as a caution to us, in whose days the close of the ages has come.

[12] Therefore let the person who thinks that she stands take care that she does not fall. [13] No temptation has come upon you that is not common to all humanity. God will not fail you, and he will not allow you to be tempted beyond your strength; but when he sends the temptation, he will also provide the way of escape, so that you may have strength to endure.

[14] Therefore, my dear friends, shun the worship of idols. [15] I speak to you as man of discernment; form your own judgment about what I am saying. [16] In the cup of blessing which we bless, is there not a sharing in the blood of the Christ? And in the bread which we break, is there not a sharing in the body of the Christ? [17] The bread is one, and we, though many, are one body; for we all partake of that one bread. [18] Look at the people of Israel. Do those who eat the sacrifices not share with the altar? [19] What do I mean? That an offering made to an idol, or the idol itself, is anything? [20] No; what I say is that the sacrifices offered by the gentiles "are offered to demons and to a being who is no God," and I do not want you to share with demons. [21] You cannot drink both the Cup of the Lord and the cup of demons. You cannot partake at the Table of the Lord and at the table of demons. [22] Or "are we to rouse the jealousy of the Lord?" Are we stronger than he?

[23] Everything is allowable! Yes, but everything is not profitable. Everything is allowable! Yes, but everything does not build up character. [24] A person must not study her own interests, but the interests of others.

[25] Eat anything that is sold in the market, without making inquiries to satisfy your scruples; [26] for "the earth, with all that is in it, belongs to the Lord." [27] If an unbeliever invites you to her house and you consent to go, eat anything that is put before you, without making inquiries to satisfy your scruples. [28] But if anyone should say to you, "This has been offered in sacrifice to an idol," then, for the sake of the speaker and her scruples, do not eat it. [29] I do not say "your" scruples, but "hers." For why should the freedom that I claim be condemned by the scruples of another? [30] If, for my part, I take the food thankfully, why should I be abused for eating that for which I give thanks?

[31] Whether, then, you eat or drink or whatever you do, do everything to the honor of God. [32] Do not cause offense either to Judeans or Greeks or to the church of God; [33] for I, also, try to please everybody in everything, not seeking my own advantage, but do what is best for others, so that they may be saved.

11 [1] Imitate me, as I myself imitate Christ. [2] I praise you, indeed, because you never forget me, and are keeping my injunctions in mind, exactly as I laid them on you. [3] But I am anxious that you should understand that the Anointed One is the head of every man, that man is the head of woman, and that God is the head of the Christ. [4] Any man who keeps his head covered, when praying or preaching in public, dishonors him who is his head; [5] while any woman who prays or preaches in public bareheaded dishonors him who is her head; for that is to make herself like one of the shameless women who shave their heads. [6] Indeed, if a woman does not keep her head covered, she may as well cut her hair short. But since to cut her hair short, or shave it off, marks her as one of the shameless women, let her keep her head covered. [7] A man ought not to have his head covered, for he has been from the beginning "the likeness of God" and the reflection of his glory, but woman is the reflection of man's glory. [8] For it was not man who was taken from woman, but woman who was taken from man. [9] Besides, man was not created for the sake of woman, but woman for the sake of man. [10] And, therefore, a woman ought to wear on her head a symbol of her subjection, because of the presence of the angels. [11] Still, when in union with the Lord, woman is not independent of man, or man of woman; [12] for just as woman came from man, so man comes by means of woman; and all things come from God. [13] Judge for yourselves. Is it fitting that a woman should pray to God in public with her head uncovered? [14] Does not Nature herself teach us that while for a man to wear his hair long is degrading to him, [15] a woman's long hair is her glory? Her hair has been given her to serve as a covering. [16] If, however, anyone still thinks it right to contest the point — well, we have no such custom, nor have the churches of God.

[17] In giving directions on the next subject, I cannot praise you; because your meetings do more harm than good. [18] To begin with, I hear you and, to some extent, I believe it. [19] Indeed, there must be actual parties among you, for so only will the people of real worth become known. [20] When you meet together, as I understand, it is not possible to eat the Lord's Supper; [21] for, as you eat, each of you tries to secure his own supper first, with the result that one has too little to eat, and another has too much to drink! [22] Have you no houses in which you can eat and drink? Or are you trying to show your contempt for the church of God, and to humiliate the poor? What can I say to you? Should I praise you? In this matter I cannot praise

you. [23] For I myself received from the Lord the account which I have in turn given to you — how the Lord Jesus, on the very night of his betrayal, took some bread, [24] and, after saying the thanksgiving, broke it and said, "This is my own body given on your behalf. Do this in memory of me." [25] And in the same way with the cup, after supper, saying, "This cup is the new covenant made by my blood. Do this, whenever you drink it, in memory of me." [26] For whenever you eat this bread and drink the cup, you proclaim the Lord's death — until he comes. [27] Therefore, whoever eats the bread, or drinks the Lord's cup, in an irreverent spirit, will have to answer for an offense against the Lord's body and blood. [28] Let everyone look into his own heart, and only then eat of the bread and drink from the cup. [29] For the person who eats and drinks brings a judgment on himself by his eating and drinking, when he does not discern the body. [30] That is why so many among you are weak and ill, and why some are sleeping. [31] But if we judged ourselves rightly, we should not be judged. [32] Yet, in being judged by the Lord, we are undergoing discipline, so that we may not have judgment passed on us with the rest of the world. [33] Therefore, my friends, when you meet together to eat the Supper, wait for one another. [34] If anyone is hungry, let him eat at home, so that your meetings may not bring a judgment on you. The other details I will settle when I come.

12 [1] In the next place, friends, I do not want you to be ignorant about spiritual gifts. [2] You know that there was a time when you were gentiles, going astray after idols that could not speak, just as you happened to be led. [3] Therefore I tell you plainly that no one who speaks under the influence of the Spirit of God says, "Jesus is accursed," and that no one can say, "Jesus is Lord," except under the influence of the holy Spirit. [4] Gifts differ, but the Spirit is the same; [5] ways of serving differ, yet the Master is the same; [6] results differ, yet the God who brings about every result is in every case the same. [7] To each of us there is given spiritual illumination for the general good. [8] To one is given the power to speak with wisdom through the Spirit; to another the power to speak with knowledge, due to the same Spirit; [9] to another faith by the same Spirit; to another power to cure diseases by the one Spirit; to another supernatural powers; [10] to another the gift of preaching; to another the gift of distinguishing between true and false inspiration; to another varieties of the gift of "tongues"; to another the power to interpret "tongues." [11] All these result from one and the same Spirit, who distributes his gifts to each individually as he wills.

[12] For just as the human body is one whole, and yet has many parts, and all its parts, many though they are, form but one body, so it is with the Anointed One; [13] for it was by one Spirit that we were all baptized to form one body, whether Judeans or Greeks, slaves or free, and were all imbued with one Spirit. [14] The human body, I repeat, consists not of one part, but of many. [15] If the foot says, "Since I am not a hand, I do not belong to the body," it does not because of that cease to belong to the body. [16] Or if the ear says, "Since I am not an eye, I do not belong to the body," it does not because of that cease to belong to the body. [17] If all the body were an eye, where would the hearing be? If it were all hearing, where would the sense of smell be? [18] But in fact God has placed each individual part just where he thought fit in the body. [19] If, however, they all made up only one part, where would the body be? [20] But in fact, although it has many parts, there is only one body. [21] The eye cannot say to the hand, "I do not need you," nor, again, the head to the feet, "I do not need you." [22] No! Those parts of the body that seem naturally the weaker are indispensable; [23] and those

parts which we deem less honorable we surround with special honor; and our ungraceful parts receive a special grace which our graceful parts do not require. [24] Yes, God has so constructed the body — by giving a special honor to the part that lacks it — [25] as to secure that there should be no disunion in the body, but that the parts should show the same care for one another. [26] If one part suffers, all the others suffer with it, and if one part has honor done it, all the others share its joy. [27] Together you are the body of Christ, and individually its parts. [28] In the church God has appointed, first, ambassadors, secondly preachers, thirdly teachers; then he has given supernatural powers, then power to cure diseases, aptness for helping others, capacity to govern, varieties of the gift of "tongues." [29] Can everyone be an ambassador? Can everyone be a preacher? Can everyone be a teacher? Can everyone have supernatural powers? [30] Can everyone have power to cure diseases? Can everyone speak in "tongues"? Can everyone interpret them? [31] Strive for the greater gifts.

Yet I can still show you a way that is beyond all comparison the best.

13 [1] Though I speak in the "tongues" of people, or even of angels, yet have not love, I have become mere echoing brass, or a clanging cymbal! [2] Even though I have the gift of preaching, and fathom all hidden truths and all the depths of knowledge; even though I have such faith as might move mountains, yet have not love, I am nothing! [3] Even though I dole my substance to the poor, even though I sacrifice my body in order to boast, yet have not love, it avails me nothing! [4] Love is longsuffering, and kind; love is never envious, never boastful, never conceited, never behaves unbecomingly; [5] love is never selfseeking, never provoked, never reckons up her wrongs; [6] love never rejoices at evil, but rejoices in the triumph of truth;

[7] love bears with all things, ever trustful, ever hopeful, ever patient. [8] Love never fails. But whether it be the gift of preaching, it will be done with; whether it be the gift of "tongues," it will cease; whether it be knowledge, it, too, will be done with. [9] For our knowledge is incomplete, and our preaching is incomplete, [10] but when the perfect has come, that which is incomplete will be done with. [11] When I was a child, I talked as a child, I felt as a child, I reasoned as a child; now that I am a man, I have done with childish ways. [12] As yet we see, in a mirror, dimly, but then — face-to-face! As yet my knowledge is incomplete, but then I will know in full, as I have been fully known. [13] Meanwhile faith, hope, and love endure — these three, but the greatest of these is love.

14 [1] Seek this love earnestly, and strive for spiritual gifts, above all for the gift of preaching. [2] The person who, when speaking, uses the gift of "tongues" is speaking, not to people, but to God, for no one understands her; yet in spirit she is speaking of hidden truths. [3] But those who preach are speaking to their fellow men and women words that will build up faith, and give them comfort and encouragement. [4] Those who, when speaking, use the gift of "tongues" build up their own faith, while those who preach build up the faith of the church. [5] Now I want you all to speak in "tongues," but much more I wish that you should preach. A preacher is worth more than one who speaks in "tongues," unless she interprets her words, so that the faith of the church may be built up. [6] This being so, friends, what good will I do you, if I come to you and speak in "tongues," unless my words convey some revelation, or knowledge, or take the form of preaching or teaching? [7] Even with inanimate things, such as a flute or a harp, though they produce sounds, yet unless the notes are quite distinct, how can the tune played on the flute or the harp be recognized? [8] If the bugle sounds a doubtful call, who will prepare for battle? [9] And so with you; unless, in using the gift of "tongues," you utter intelligible words, how can what you say be understood? You will be speaking to the winds! [10] There is, for instance, a certain number of different languages in the world, and not one of them fails to convey meaning. [11] If, however, I do not happen to know the language, I will be a foreigner to those who speak it, and they will be foreigners to me. [12] And so with you; since you are striving for spiritual gifts, be eager to excel in such as will build up the faith of the church. [13] Therefore let her who, when speaking, uses the gift of "tongues" pray for ability to interpret them. [14] If, when praying, I use the gift of "tongues," my spirit indeed prays, but my mind is a blank. [15] What, then, is my conclusion? Simply this — I will pray with my spirit, but with my mind as well; I will sing with my spirit, but with my mind as well. [16] If you bless God with your spirit only, how can people in the congregation who are without your gift say "Amen" to your thanksgiving? They do not know what you are saying! [17] Your thanksgiving may be excellent, but the other is not helped by it. [18] Thank God, I use the gift of "tongues" more than any of you. [19] But at a meeting of the church I would rather speak five words with my mind, and so teach others, than ten thousand words when using the gift of "tongues."

[20] My friends, do not show yourselves children in understanding. In wickedness be infants, but in understanding show yourselves adults. [21] It is said in the Law:

> "In strange tongues and by the lips of strangers will I speak to this people, but even then they will not listen to me, says the Lord."

[22] Therefore the gift of the "tongues" is

intended as a sign, not for those who believe in Christ, but for those who do not, while the gift of preaching is intended as a sign, not for those who do not believe in Christ, but for those who do. ²³ So, when the whole church meets, if all present use the gift of "tongues," and some people who are without the gift, or who are unbelievers, come in, will they not say that you are mad? ²⁴ While, if all those present use the gift of preaching, and an unbeliever, or someone without the gift, comes in, he is convinced of his sinfulness by them all, he is called to account by them all; ²⁵ the secrets of his heart are revealed, and then, throwing himself on his face, he will worship God, and declare, "God is indeed among you!"

²⁶ What do I suggest, then, friends? Whenever you meet for worship, each of you comes, either with a hymn, or a lesson, or a revelation, or the gift of "tongues," or the interpretation of them; let everything be directed to the building up of faith. ²⁷ If any of you use the gift of "tongues," not more than two, or at the most three, should do so — each speaking in his turn — and someone should interpret them. ²⁸ If there is no one able to interpret what is said, he should not speak to the community, but speak only to himself and to God. ²⁹ Of preachers two or three should speak, and the rest should weigh well what is said. ³⁰ But if some revelation is made to another person as he sits there, the first speaker should stop. ³¹ For you can all preach in turn, so that all may learn some lesson and all receive encouragement. ³² (The spirit that moves the preachers is within the preachers' control; ³³ for God is not a God of disorder, but of peace.) This custom prevails in all the churches of Christ's people.

³⁴ At the meetings of the church women should remain silent, for they are not allowed to speak in public; they should take a subordinate place, as the Law itself directs. ³⁵ If they want information on any point, they should ask their husbands about it at home; for it is unbecoming for a married woman to speak at a meeting of the church. ³⁶ What! Did God's message to the world originate with you? Or did it find its way to none but you?

³⁷ If anyone thinks that he has the gift of preaching or any other spiritual gift, let him recognize that what I am now saying to you is a command from the Lord. ³⁸ Anyone who ignores it may be ignored. ³⁹ Therefore, my friends, strive for the gift of preaching, and yet do not forbid speaking in "tongues." ⁴⁰ Let everything be done in a proper and orderly manner.

The Teaching Regarding the Resurrection of the Dead

15 ¹ Next, friends, I would like to remind you of the good news which I told you, and which you received — the good news on which you have taken your stand, ² and by means of which you are being saved. I would like to remind you of the words that I used in telling it to you, since you are still holding fast to it, and since it was not in vain that you became believers in Christ. ³ For at the very beginning of my teaching I gave you the account which I had myself received — that the Anointed One died for our sins (as the scriptures had foretold), ⁴ that he was buried, that on the third day he was raised (as the scriptures had foretold), ⁵ and that he appeared to Cephas, and then to the Twelve. ⁶ After that, he appeared to more than five hundred of his followers at one time, most of whom are still alive, though some have gone to their rest. ⁷ After that, he appeared to James, and then to all the apostles. ⁸ Last of all, he appeared even to me, who am, as it were, the abortion. ⁹ For I am the meanest of the ambassadors, I who am unworthy of the name of "ambassador," because

I persecuted the church of God. [10] But it is through the love of God that I am what I am, and the love that he showed me has not been wasted. No, I have toiled harder than any of them, and yet it was not I, but the love of God working with me. [11] Whether, then, it was I or whether it was they, this we proclaim, and this you believed.

[12] Now, if it is proclaimed of the Anointed One that he has been raised from the dead, how is it that some of you say that there is no such thing as a resurrection of the dead? [13] But if there is no such thing as a resurrection of the dead, then even Christ has not been raised; [14] and if Christ has not been raised, then our proclamation is without meaning, and our faith without meaning also! [15] Yes, and we are being proved to have borne false testimony about God; for we testified of God that he raised the Christ, whom he did not raise, if, indeed, the dead do not rise! [16] For, if the dead do not rise, then even Christ himself has not been raised, [17] and if Christ has not been raised, your faith is folly — your sins are on you still! [18] Yes, and they who have passed to their rest in union with Christ perished! [19] If all that we have done has been to place our hope in Christ for this life, then we of all people are the most to be pitied.

[20] But in truth, Christ has been raised from the dead, the first fruits of those who are at rest. [21] For, since through a man there is death, so, too, through a man there is a resurrection of the dead. [22] For as through union with Adam all die, so through union with the Christ will all be made to live. [23] But each in their proper order — Christ the first fruits; afterward, at his coming, those who belong to the Christ. [24] Then will come the end — when he surrenders the kingdom to his God and Father, having overthrown all other rule and all other authority and power. [25] For he must reign until God "has put all his enemies under his feet." [26] The last enemy to be overthrown is death; [27] for God has placed all things under Christ's feet. (But when it is said that all things have been placed under Christ, it is plain that God is excepted who placed everything under him.) [28] And, when everything has been placed under him, the Son will place himself under God who placed everything under him, so that God may be all in all! [29] Again, what good will they be doing who are baptized on behalf of the dead? If it is true that the dead do not rise, why are people baptized on their behalf? [30] Why, too, do we risk our lives every hour? [31] Daily I face death — I swear it, friends, by the pride in you that I feel through my union with Christ Jesus, our Lord. [32] If with only human hopes I had fought in the arena at Ephesus, what should I have gained by it? If the dead do not rise, then "Let us eat and drink, for tomorrow we will die"! [33] Do not be deceived.

"Good character is marred by evil company."

[34] Wake up to a righteous life, and cease to sin. There are some who have no true knowledge of God. I speak in this way to shame you.

[35] Someone, however, may ask, "How do the dead rise? And in what body will they come?" [36] You foolish person! The seed you yourself sow does not come to life, unless it dies! [37] And when you sow, you sow not the body that will be, but a mere grain — perhaps of wheat, or something else. [38] God gives it the body that he pleases — to each seed its special body. [39] All forms of life are not the same; there is one for people, another for beasts, another for birds, and another for fishes. [40] There are heavenly bodies, and earthly bodies; but the beauty of the heavenly bodies is not the beauty of the earthly. [41] There is a beauty of the sun, and a beauty of the moon, and a beauty of the stars; for even star differs from star in beauty. [42] It is the

same with the resurrection of the dead. Sown a mortal body, it rises immortal; sown disfigured, it rises beautiful; [43] sown weak, it rises strong; sown a human body, it rises a spiritual body. [44] As surely as there is a human body, there is also a spiritual body. [45] That is what is meant by the words "Adam, the first man, became a human being"; the last Adam became a life-giving spirit. [46] That which comes first is not the spiritual, but the human; afterward comes the spiritual; [47] the first man was from the dust of the earth; the second man from heaven. [48] Those who are of the dust are like him who came from the dust; and those who are of heaven are like him who came from heaven. [49] And as we have borne the likeness of him who came from the dust, so let us bear the likeness of him who came from heaven. [50] This I say, friends — flesh and blood can have no share in the realm of God, nor can the perishable share the imperishable. [51] Listen, I will tell you God's hidden purpose! We will not all have passed to our rest, but we will all be transformed — in a moment, in the twinkling of an eye, [52] at the last trumpet call; for the trumpet will sound, and the dead will rise immortal, and we, also, will be transformed. [53] For this perishable body of ours must put on an imperishable form, and this dying body a deathless form. [54] And, when this dying body has put on its deathless form, then indeed will the words of scripture come true:

[55] "Death has been swallowed up
in victory! Where, death, is your
victory? Where, death, is your
sting?"

[56] It is sin that gives death its sting, and it is the Law that gives sin its power. [57] But thanks be to God, who gives us the victory, through Jesus Christ, our Lord. [58] Therefore, my dear friends, stand firm, unshaken, always diligent in the Lord's work, for you know that in union with him, your toil is not in vain.

Conclusion

16 [1] With reference to the collection for Christ's people, I want you to follow the instructions that I gave to the churches in Galatia. [2] On the first day of every week each of you should put by what she can afford, so that no collections need be made after I have come. [3] On my arrival, I will send any persons whom you may authorize by letter to carry your gift to Jerusalem; [4] and, if it appears to be worthwhile for me to go also, they will go with me.

[5] I will come to you as soon as I have been through Macedonia — for I am going through Macedonia — [6] and I will probably make some stay with you or, perhaps, remain for the winter, so that you may yourselves send me on my way, wherever I may be going. [7] I do not propose to pay you a visit in passing now, for I hope to stay with you for some time, if the Lord permits. [8] I intend, however, staying at Ephesus until the festival at the close of the harvest; [9] for a great opening for active work has presented itself, and there are many opponents.

[10] If Timothy comes, take care that he has no cause for feeling anxious while he is with you. He is doing the Master's work no less than I am. [11] No one, therefore, should slight him. See him safely on his way to me, for I am expecting him with some of our friends.

[12] As for our friend Apollos, I have often urged him to go to you with the others. He has, however, been very unwilling to do so as yet; but he will go as soon as he finds a good opportunity.

[13] Be watchful; stand firm in your faith; be brave; be strong. [14] Let everything you do be done in a loving spirit.

[15] I have another request to make of you, friends. You remember Stephanas and his household, and that they were the

first fruits gathered in from Greece, and set themselves to serve Christ's people. [16] I want you, on your part, to show deference to such people as these, as well as to every fellow laborer and earnest worker. [17] I am glad Stephanas and Fortunatus and Achaicus have come, for they have made up for your absence; [18] they have cheered my heart, and your hearts also. Recognize the worth of such people as these.

[19] The churches in Roman Asia send you their greetings. Aquila and Prisca and the church that meets at their house send you many faithful greetings. [20] All of the Lord's followers send you greetings. Greet one another with a sacred kiss.

[21] I, Paul, add this greeting in my own handwriting. [22] Accursed be anyone who has no love for the Lord. The Lord is coming. [23] May the blessing of the Lord Jesus be with you. [24] My love to all of you who are in union with Christ Jesus.

An Introduction to the Second Letter to the Corinthians

T HE DRAMA OF 2 CORINTHIANS comes from the clear indication that the Christ assemblies of Corinth have rejected much of Paul's advice in 1 Corinthians and how Paul objects strenuously to the way the Corinthians have responded to his first letter. Although we do not have any Corinthian response, Paul's second letter shows that he has received at least one (and probably two) letters from Corinth. This second letter from Paul was probably written around 55 CE.

Paul calls himself an "ambassador" (apostle),* even though in other literature written by someone other than Paul that word is often reserved for followers of Jesus who knew him while he lived, something that Paul does not claim for himself. Contrary to understandings of Paul for much of Christian history, recent scholarship tends to think that Paul always thought of himself as belonging to the traditions of Israel and not as a Christian. Rather, he appears to have thought that the gentiles "in Christ" belong genuinely to the larger constellation of traditions of Israel.

Paul's Corinthian correspondents seem to have been almost entirely gentiles, engaged to one extent or another in associations of Christ. They had men and women in leadership, experienced the power of Christ's resurrection in their present lives, and celebrated a special kind of speaking which Paul calls "speaking in tongues."

In 2 Corinthians we find Paul in distress on several fronts, in addition to his anger about the Corinthians rejecting the advice he gave in his first letter. He has also been attacked physically, often, and so severely that "we were burdened altogether beyond our strength, so much so that we even despaired of life" (1:8). His survival signifies for him an experience of God raising the dead (1:9).

The text of 2 Corinthians is difficult to follow, because there is a definite possibility that this letter actually came to us as a combination of two or three letters, and because Paul's own emotions vary widely within the writing. Most of the writing reveals him to be angry, sulking, or confused. But some of the text shows him

---

* The Greek word *apostolos*, often translated (or better put, transliterated) as "apostle," means "one who is sent" and is used throughout Greek literature to designate a messenger or, in the case of an important messenger, an "ambassador."

to be highly complimentary, fawning over the Corinthians in his expressed love for them.

The great majority of the letter is devoted to Paul talking about his own work in places other than Corinth. He reflects on his experiences of being in prison and in danger. He brags about how much he has accomplished in his work. He complains that the Corinthians have not respected him. He threatens them with harsh treatment when he next sees them. Chapters 8 and 9 interrupt these long reflections on his own struggles with a clear and forceful appeal to the Corinthians to collect money (most probably for the people of Jerusalem).

The Second Letter to the Corinthians is a rich, if not always complimentary, resource for understanding Paul as a person. In his own words, with some cleverness and strategy but with little filter, he pours out his hopes, fears, anger, resentment, and joy. If one wonders why such a letter was ever included in the traditional New Testament, the answer probably lies in its authentic connection to Paul himself, even if he wrote it while he was having a series of bad days.

A primary value of 2 Corinthians for the twenty-first century is the uncensored and wildly emotional character of Paul's expression. This is a very human book, and it helps remind readers of the very human roots of the New Testament, in both its form in this book and its traditional forms.

Recommended Reading

R. P. Martin, *2 Corinthians*
Jerome Murphy-O'Connor, *St. Paul's Corinth: Texts and Archaeology*
Antoinette Clark Wire, *The Corinthian Women Prophets*

The Second Letter to the Corinthians

Introduction

1 ¹ To the church of God in Corinth, and to all Christ's people throughout Greece, from Paul, an apostle of Christ Jesus, by the will of God, and from Timothy, who is also a follower. ² May God, our Father, and the Lord Jesus Christ bless you and give you peace.

³ Blessed is the God and Father of Jesus Christ our Lord, the all-merciful Father, the God ever ready to console, ⁴ who consoles us in all our troubles, so that we may be able to console those who are in any trouble with the consolation that we ourselves receive from him. ⁵ It is true that we have our full share of the sufferings of the Christ, but through the Christ we have also our full share of consolation. ⁶ If we meet with trouble, it is for the sake of your consolation and salvation; and if we find consolation, it is for the sake of the consolation that you will experience when you are called to endure the sufferings that we ourselves are enduring; ⁷ and our hope for you remains unshaken. We know that as you are sharing our sufferings, you will also share our consolation. ⁸ We want you, friends, to know that in the troubles which befell us in Roman Asia, we were burdened altogether beyond our strength, so much so that we even despaired of life. ⁹ Indeed, we had the presentiment that we must die, so that we might rely, not on ourselves, but on God who raises the dead. ¹⁰ And from so imminent a death God delivered us, and will deliver us again; for in him we have placed our hopes of future deliverance, while you, also, help us by your prayers. ¹¹ And then many lips will give thanks on our behalf for the blessing granted us in answer to many prayers.

The Apostle's Relations with His Converts

¹² Indeed, our main ground for satisfaction is this — our conscience tells us that our conduct in the world, and still more in our relations with you, was marked by a purity of motive and a sincerity that were inspired by God, and was based, not on worldly policy, but on the help of God. ¹³ We never write anything to you other than what you will acknowledge to the very end — ¹⁴ and, indeed, you have already partly acknowledged it about us — that you have a right to be proud of us, as we will be proud of you, on the day of our Lord Jesus.

¹⁵ With this conviction in my mind, I planned to come to see you first, so that your pleasure might be doubled — ¹⁶ to visit you both on my way to Macedonia, and to come to you again on my return from Macedonia, and then to get you to send me on my way into Judea. ¹⁷ As this was my plan, where, pray, did I show any fickleness of purpose? Or do you think that my plans are formed on mere impulse, so that in the same breath I say "Yes" and "No"? ¹⁸ As God is true, the message that we brought you does not waver between "Yes" and "No"! ¹⁹ The Child of God, Christ Jesus, whom we — Silas, Timothy, and I — proclaimed among you, never wavered between "Yes" and "'No." With him it has always been "Yes." ²⁰ For, many as were the promises of God, in Christ is the "Yes"' that fulfills them. Therefore, through Christ again, let the "Amen" rise, through us, to the glory of God. ²¹ God who brings us, with you, into close union with the Anointed One, and who consecrated us, ²² also set his seal on us, and

gave us his Spirit in our hearts as a pledge of future blessings.

23 But as my life will answer for it, I call God to witness that it was to spare you that I deferred my visit to Corinth. 24 I do not mean that we are to dictate to you with regard to your faith; on the contrary, we work with you for your true happiness; indeed, it is through your faith that you are standing firm.

2 1 For my own sake, as well, I decided not to pay you another painful visit. 2 If it is I who cause you pain, why, who is there to cheer me, except the person whom I am paining? 3 So I wrote as I did because I was afraid that if I had come, I should have been pained by those who ought to have made me glad; for I felt sure that it was true of you all that my joy was in every case yours also. 4 I wrote to you in sore trouble and distress of heart and with many tears, not to give you pain, but to let you see how intense a love I have for you.

5 Now whoever has caused the pain has not so much pained me, as he has, to some extent — not to be too severe — pained every one of you. 6 The man to whom I refer has been sufficiently punished by the penalty inflicted by the majority of you; 7 so that now you must take the opposite course, and forgive and encourage him, or else he may be overwhelmed by the intensity of his pain. 8 So I entreat you to assure him of your love. 9 I had this further object, also, in what I wrote — to find out whether you might be relied on to be obedient in everything. 10 Anyone you forgive, I forgive them, too. Indeed, for my part, whatever I have forgiven (if I have had to forgive anything), I have forgiven for your sakes, in the presence of Christ, 11 so as to prevent Satan from taking advantage of us; for we are not ignorant of his devices.

12 When I went to the district around Troas to tell the good news of the Christ, even though there was an opening for serving the Master, 13 I could get no peace of mind because I failed to find Titus, my friend; so I took leave of the people there, and went on to Macedonia. 14 All thanks to God, who, through our union with the Anointed One, leads us in one continual triumph, and uses us to spread the sweet perfume of the knowledge of him in every place. 15 For we are the fragrance of Christ ascending to God — both among those who are in the path of salvation and among those who are in the path to ruin. 16 To the latter we are a stench which arises from death and tells of death; to the former a fragrance which arises from life and tells of life. But who is equal to such a task? 17 Unlike many people, we are not in the habit of making profit out of God's message; but in all sincerity, and bearing God's commission, we speak before him in union with Christ.

3 1 Are we beginning to commend ourselves again? Or are we like some who need letters of commendation to you, or from you? 2 You yourselves are our letter — a letter written on our hearts, and one which everybody can read and understand. 3 All can see that you are a letter from Christ delivered by us, a letter written, not with ink, but with the Spirit of the living God, not on "tablets of stone," but on "tablets of human hearts."

The Ministry of the Ambassadors

This, then, is the confidence in regard to God that we have gained through the Christ. 5 I do not mean that we are fit to form any judgment by ourselves, as if on our own authority; 6 our fitness comes from God, who himself made us fit to be ministers of a new covenant, of which the substance is not a written Law, but a Spirit. For the written Law means death, but the Spirit gives life.

[7] If the system of religion which involved death, embodied in a written Law and engraved on stones, began amid such glory, that the Israelites were unable to gaze at the face of Moses because of its glory, though it was but a passing glory, [8] will not the religion that confers the Spirit have still greater glory? [9] For, if there was a glory in the religion that involved condemnation, far greater is the glory of the religion that confers righteousness! [10] Indeed, that which then had glory has lost its glory, because of the glory which surpasses it. [11] And, if that which was to pass away was attended with glory, far more will that which is to endure be surrounded with glory!

[12] With such a hope as this, we speak with all plainness; [13] unlike Moses, who covered his face with a veil to prevent the Israelites from gazing at the disappearance of what was passing away. [14] But their minds were slow to learn. Indeed, to this very day, at the public reading of the old covenant, the same veil remains; only for those who are in union with Christ does it pass away. [15] But even to this day, whenever Moses is read, a veil lies on their hearts. [16] "Yet, whenever someone turns to the Lord, the veil is removed." [17] And the "Lord" is the Spirit, and where the Spirit of the Lord is, there is freedom. [18] And all of us, with faces from which the veil is lifted, seeing, as if reflected in a mirror, the glory of the Lord, are being transformed into his likeness, from glory to glory, as it is given by the Lord, the Spirit.

4 [1] Therefore, since it is by God's mercy that we are engaged in this ministry, we do not lose heart. [2] No, we have renounced the secrecy prompted by shame, refusing to adopt crafty ways, or to tamper with God's message, and commending ourselves to everyone's conscience, in the sight of God, by our exhibition of the truth. [3] And, even if the good news that we bring is veiled, it is veiled only in the case of those who are on the path to ruin — [4] people whose minds have been blinded by the God of this age, unbelievers as they are, so that the light from the good news of the glory of the Christ, who is the incarnation of God, should not shine for them. [5] (For it is not ourselves that we proclaim, but Christ Jesus, as Lord, and ourselves as your servants for Jesus's sake.) [6] Indeed, the same God who said, "Out of darkness light will shine" has shone in our hearts, so that we should bring out into the light the knowledge of the glory of God, seen in the face of Christ.

[7] This treasure we have in these earthen vessels, so that its all-prevailing power may be seen to come from God, and not to be our own. [8] Though hard-pressed on every side, we are never hemmed in; though perplexed, never driven to despair; [9] though pursued, never abandoned; though struck down, never killed! [10] We always bear on our bodies the marks of the death that Jesus died, so that the life also of Jesus may be exhibited in our bodies. [11] Indeed, we who still live are continually being given over to death for Jesus's sake, so that the life also of Jesus may be exhibited in our mortal nature. [12] And so, while death is at work within us, life is at work within you. [13] But in the same spirit of faith as that expressed in the words "I believed, and therefore I spoke," we also believe, and therefore speak. [14] For we know that he who raised the Lord Jesus will raise us also with him, and will bring us, with you, into his presence. [15] For all this is for your sakes, so that the loving kindness of God, spreading from heart to heart, may cause yet more hearts to overflow with thanksgiving, to his glory.

[16] Therefore, as I said, we do not lose heart. No, even though outwardly we are wasting away, yet inwardly we are being renewed day by day. [17] The light burden of our momentary trouble is preparing

for us, in measure transcending thought, a weight of imperishable glory; [18] we, all the while, are gazing not on what is seen, but on what is unseen; for what is seen is transient, but what is unseen is imperishable.

5 [1] For we know that if our tent—that earthly body which is now our home—is taken down, we have a house of God's building, a home not made by hands, imperishable, in heaven. [2] Even while in our present body we sigh, longing to put over it our heavenly house, [3] sure that when we have put it on, we will never be found discarnate. [4] For we who are in this "tent" sigh under our burden, unwilling to take it off, yet wishing to put our heavenly body over it, so that all that is mortal may be absorbed in life. [5] And he who has prepared us for this change is God, who has also given us his Spirit as a pledge.

[6] Therefore we are always confident, knowing that while our home is in the body, we are absent from our home with the Lord. [7] For we guide our lives by faith, and not by what we see. [8] And in this confidence we would gladly leave our home in the body, and make our home with the Lord. [9] Therefore, whether in our home or absent from our home, our one ambition is to please him. [10] For at the court of the Christ we must all appear in our true characters, so that each may reap the results of the life which she has lived in the body, in accordance with her actions—whether good or worthless.

[11] Therefore, because we know the fear inspired by the Lord, it is true that we are trying to win people over, but our motives are plain to God; and I hope that in your inmost hearts they are plain to you also. [12] We are not "commending ourselves" again to you, but rather are giving you cause for pride in us, so that you may have an answer ready for those who pride themselves on appearances and not on character. [13] For, if we were "beside ourselves," it was in God's service! If we are

not in our senses, it is in yours! [14] It is the love of the Christ which compels us, when we reflect that as one died for all, therefore all died; [15] and that he died for all, so that the living should no longer live for themselves, but for him who died and rose for them.

[16] For ourselves, then, from this time forward, we refuse to regard anyone from the world's standpoint. Even if we once thought of Christ from the standpoint of the world, yet now we do so no longer. [17] Therefore, if anyone is in union with Christ, she is a new being! Her old life has passed away; a new life has begun! [18] But all this is the work of God, who reconciled us to himself through the Anointed One, and gave us the Ministry of Reconciliation—[19] to proclaim that God, in Christ, was reconciling the world to himself, not reckoning people's offenses against them, and that he had entrusted us with the message of this reconciliation.

[20] It is, then, on Christ's behalf that we are acting as ambassadors, God, as it were, appealing to you through us. We implore you on Christ's behalf—be reconciled to God. [21] For our sake God made Christ, who was innocent of sin, one with our sinfulness, so that in him we might be made one with the righteousness of God.

6 [1] Therefore, as God's fellow workers, we also appeal to you not to receive his loving kindness in vain. [2] For he says:

"At the time for acceptance I listened
    to you,
and on the day of deliverance I helped
    you."

Now is the time for acceptance! Now is the day of deliverance! [3] Never do we put an obstacle in anyone's way, so that no fault may be found with our ministry. [4] No, we are trying to commend ourselves under all circumstances, as God's ministers should—in many an hour of endurance, in troubles, in hardships, in difficulties, [5] in floggings, in imprisonments, in riots, in toils, in sleepless nights, in fastings; [6] by purity, by knowledge, by patience, by kindliness, by holiness of spirit, by unfeigned love; [7] by the message of truth, and by the power of God; by the weapons of righteousness in the right hand and in the left; [8] amid honor and disrepute, amid slander and praise; regarded as deceivers, yet proved to be true; [9] as unknown, yet well known; as at death's door, yet, see, we are living; as chastised, yet not killed; [10] as saddened, yet always rejoicing; as poor, yet enriching many; as having nothing, and yet possessing all things!

The Ambassador and His Followers

[11] We have been speaking freely to you, dear friends in Corinth; we have opened our heart; [12] there is room there for you, yet there is not room, in your love, for us. [13] Can you not in return — I appeal to you as I should to children — open your hearts to us?

[14] Do not enter into inconsistent relations with those who reject the faith. For what partnership can there be between righteousness and lawlessness? Or what has light to do with darkness? [15] What harmony can there be between Christ and Belial? Or what can those who accept the faith have in common with those who reject it? [16] What agreement can there be between a temple of God and idols? And we are a temple of the living God. That is what God meant when he said:

"I will live among them, and walk
    among them;
and I will be their God, and they will
    be my people.
[17] Therefore 'Come out from among the
    nations, and separate yourselves
    from them,' says the Lord,
'and touch nothing impure;
and I will welcome you;

and I will be a father to you, and you
    will be my sons and daughters,'
says the Lord, the Ruler of all.'"

[7] [1] With these promises, dear friends, let us purify ourselves from everything that pollutes either body or spirit, and, in deepest respect for God, aim at perfect holiness.

[2] Make room for us in your hearts. In no instance have we ever wronged, or harmed, or taken advantage of, anyone. [3] I am not saying this to condemn you. Indeed, I have already said that you are in our heart, to live and die together. [4] I have the utmost confidence in you; I am always boasting about you. I am full of encouragement and, in spite of all our troubles, my heart is overflowing with happiness.

[5] Ever since we reached Macedonia, we have had no rest in body or mind; on every side there have been troubles — conflicts without, anxieties within. [6] But God, who encourages the downcast, has encouraged us by the arrival of Titus. [7] And it is not only by his arrival that we are encouraged, but also by the encouragement which he received from you; for he tells us of your strong affection, your penitence, and your zeal on my behalf — so that I am happier still. [8] For, though I caused you sorrow by my letter, I do not regret it. Even if I were inclined to regret it — for I see that my letter did cause you sorrow though only for a time — [9] I am glad now; not because of the sorrow it caused you, but because your sorrow brought you to repentance. For it was God's will that you should feel sorrow, in order that you should not suffer loss in any way at our hands. [10] For, when sorrow is in accordance with God's will, it results in a repentance leading to salvation, and which will never be regretted. The sure result of the sorrow that the world knows is death. [11] For see what results that other sorrow — sorrow in accordance with God's will — has had in your case. What ear-

nestness it produced! What explanations! What strong feeling! What alarm! What longing! What eagerness! What readiness to punish! You have proved yourselves altogether free from guilt in that matter. [12] So, then, even though I did write to you, it was not for the sake of the wrongdoer, or of the man who was wronged, but to make you conscious, in the sight of God, of your own earnest care for us. And it is this that has encouraged us.

[13] In addition to the encouragement that this gave us, we were made far happier still by the happiness of Titus for his heart has been cheered by you all. [14] Although I have been boasting a little to him about you, you did not put me to shame; but just as everything we had said to you was true, so our boasting to Titus about you has also proved to be the truth. [15] And his affection for you is all the greater, as he remembers the deference that you all showed him, and recalls how you received him with anxious care. [16] I am glad that I can feel perfect confidence in you.

The Palestine Famine Fund

8 [1] We want to remind you, friends, of the love that God has shown to the churches in Macedonia — [2] how, tired though they were by many a trouble, their overflowing happiness, and even their deep poverty, resulted in a flood of generosity. [3] I can bear witness that to the full extent of their power, and even beyond their power, spontaneously, [4] and with many an appeal to us for permission, they showed their love, and contributed their share toward the fund for God's holy people. [5] And that, not only in the way we had expected; but first they gave themselves to the Lord, and to us also, in accordance with God's will. [6] And this led us to beg Titus; since he had started the work for you, he should also see to the completion of this expression of your loving gift. [7] And, remembering how you excel in everything — in faith, in

teaching, in knowledge, in unfailing earnestness, and in the affection that we have awakened in you — I ask you to excel also in this expression of your love.

[8] I am not laying a command on you, but I am making use of the earnestness shown by others to test the genuineness of your affection. [9] For you do not forget the loving kindness of our Lord Jesus Christ — how that for your sakes, although he was rich, he became poor, so that you also might become rich through his poverty. [10] I am only making suggestions on this matter; for this is the best course for you, since you were a year before others, not only in taking action, but also in showing your readiness to do so. [11] And now I want you to complete the work, so that its completion may correspond with your willing readiness — in proportion, of course, to your means. [12] For, where there is willingness, a person's gift is valued by its comparison with what he has, and not with what he does not have. [13] For our object is not to give relief to others and bring distress on you. It is a matter of a fair balance. [14] On this occasion what you can spare will supply what they need, at another time what they can spare may supply your need, and so things will be equal. [15] As scripture says:

> "Those who had much had nothing
> over, and those who had little did
> not lack!"

[16] I thank God for inspiring Titus with the same keen interest in your welfare that I have; [17] for Titus has responded to my appeals and, in his great earnestness, is starting to go to you of his own accord. [18] We are sending with him one of the Lord's followers whose fame in the service of the good news has spread through all the churches; [19] and not only that, but he has been elected by the churches to accompany us on our journey, in connection with this expression of your love, which

we are personally administering to the honor of the Lord, and to show our deep interest. ²⁰ What we are specially guarding against is that any fault should be found with us in regard to our administration of this charitable fund; ²¹ for we are trying to make arrangements which will be right, not only in the eyes of the Lord, but also in the eyes of people. ²² We are also sending with them another of our friends, whose earnestness we have many a time proved in many ways, and whom we now find made even more earnest by his great confidence in you. ²³ If I must say anything about Titus, he is my intimate companion, and he shares my work for you; if it is our friends, they are delegates of the churches, an honor to Christ. ²⁴ Show them, therefore — so that the churches may see it — the proof of your affection, and the ground for our boasting to them about you.

9 ¹ With reference, indeed, to the fund for God's holy people, it is quite superfluous for me to say anything to you. ² I know, of course, your willingness to help, and I am always boasting of it to the Macedonians. I tell them that you in Greece have been ready for a year past; and it was really your zeal that stimulated most of them. ³ So my reason for sending our friends is to prevent what we said about you from proving, in this particular matter, an empty boast, and to enable you to be as well prepared as I have been saying that you are. ⁴ Otherwise, if any Macedonians were to come with me, and find you unprepared, we — to say nothing of you — should feel ashamed of our present confidence. ⁵ Therefore I think it necessary to beg the friends to go to you in advance, and to complete the arrangements for the gift, which you have already promised, so that it may be ready, as a gift, before I come, and not look as if it were being given under pressure.

⁶ Remember the saying, "Scanty sowing, scanty harvest; plentiful sowing, plentiful harvest." ⁷ Let everyone give as she has determined beforehand, not grudgingly or under compulsion; for God loves "a cheerful giver." ⁸ God has power to shower all kinds of blessings on you, so that having, under all circumstances and on all occasions, all that you can need, you may be able to shower all kinds of benefits on others. ⁹ (As scripture says:

> "He scattered broadcast, he gave to the poor; his righteousness continues forever."

¹⁰ And he who supplies "seed to the sower, and bread for eating," will supply you with seed, and cause it to increase, and will multiply "the fruits of your righteousness.") ¹¹ Rich in all things yourselves, you will be able to show liberality to all, which, with our help, will cause thanksgiving to be offered to God. ¹² For the rendering of a public service such as this not only relieves the needs of your fellow Christians, but also results in the offering to God of many a thanksgiving. ¹³ Through the evidence afforded by the service rendered, you cause people to praise God for your fidelity to your profession of faith in the good news of the Christ, as well as for the liberality of your contributions for them and for all others. ¹⁴ And they also, in their prayers for you, express their longing to see you, because of the surpassing love of God displayed toward you. ¹⁵ All thanks to God for his inestimable gift!

The Ambassador's Claims and Authority

10 ¹ Now, I, Paul, make a personal appeal to you by the meekness and gentleness of the Christ — I who, "in your presence, am humble in my bearing toward you, but when absent, am bold in my language to you" — ² I implore you not to drive me to "show my boldness," when I do come, by the confident tone which I expect to have to adopt toward some of you, who are expecting to find us influenced in our conduct by earthly motives. [3] For, though we live an earthly life, we do not wage an earthly war. [4] The weapons for our warfare are not earthly, but, under God, are powerful enough to pull down strongholds. [5] We are engaged in confuting arguments and pulling down every barrier raised against the knowledge of God. We are taking captive every hostile thought, to bring it into submission to the Christ, [6] and are fully prepared to punish every act of rebellion, when once your submission is complete. [7] You look at the outward appearance of things! Let anyone who is confident that he belongs to Christ reflect, for himself, again on the fact that we belong to the Anointed One no less than he does. [8] Even if I boast extravagantly about our authority — which the Lord gave us for building up your faith and not for overthrowing it — still I have no reason to be ashamed. [9] I say this so that it does not seem as if I am trying to overawe you by my letters. [10] For people say, "His letters are impressive and vigorous, but his personal appearance is insignificant and his speaking contemptible." [11] Let such a person be assured of this — that our words in our letters show us to be, when absent, just what our deeds will show us to be, when present. [12] We have not indeed the audacity to class or compare ourselves with some of those who indulge in self-commendation! But when such persons measure themselves by themselves, and compare themselves with themselves, they show a want of wisdom. [13] We, however, will not give way to unlimited boasting, but will confine ourselves to the limits of the sphere to which God limited us, when he permitted us to come as far as Corinth. [14] For it is not the case, as it would be if we were not in the habit of coming to you, that we are exceeding our bounds! Why, we were the very first to reach you with the good news of the Christ! [15] Our boasting, therefore, is not unlimited, nor does it extend to the labors of others; but our hope is that as your faith grows, our influence among you may be very greatly increased — though still confined to our sphere — [16] so that we will be able to tell the good news in the districts beyond you, without trespassing on the sphere assigned to others, or boasting of what has already been done. [17] "Let anyone who boasts make his boast of the Lord." [18] For it is not those who commend themselves that stand the test, but those who are commended by the Lord.

11 [1] I could wish that you would tolerate a little folly in me! But indeed you do tolerate me. [2] I am jealous over you with the jealousy of God. For I engaged you to one husband so that I might present you to the Christ a pure bride. [3] Yet I fear that it may turn out that, just as the snake by his craftiness deceived Eve, so your minds may have lost the loyalty and purity due from you to the Christ. [4] For, if some newcomer is proclaiming a Jesus other than him whom we proclaimed, or if you are receiving a spirit different from the Spirit which you received, or a good news different from that which you welcomed, then you are marvelously tolerant! [5] I do not regard myself as in any way inferior to the most eminent apostles! [6] Though I am no trained orator, yet I am not without knowledge; indeed we made this perfectly clear to you in every way.

[7] Perhaps you say that I did wrong in humbling myself that you might be exalted — I mean because I told you God's good news without payment. [8] I robbed other churches by taking pay from them, so that I might serve you! [9] And, when I was with you in need, I did not become a burden to any of you; for our friends, on coming from Macedonia, supplied my needs. I kept myself, and will keep myself, from being an expense to you in any way. [10] As surely as I know anything of the

truth of Christ, this boast, as far as I am concerned, will not be stopped in any part of Greece. ¹¹ Why? Because I do not love you? God knows that I do!

¹² What I am doing now I will continue to do in order to cut away the ground from under those who are wishing for some ground for attacking me, so that as regards the thing of which they boast they may appear in their true characters, just as we do. ¹³ Such people are false apostles, treacherous workers, disguising themselves as apostles of Christ! ¹⁴ And no wonder; for even Satan disguises himself as an angel of light. ¹⁵ It is not surprising, therefore, if his servants also disguise themselves as servants of righteousness. But their end will be in accordance with their actions.

¹⁶ I say again: Let no one think me a fool! Yet, if you do, at least welcome me as you would a fool, so that I, too, may indulge in a little boasting. ¹⁷ When I speak like this, I am not speaking as the Master would, but as a fool might, in boasting so confidently. ¹⁸ As so many are boasting of earthly things, I, too, will boast. ¹⁹ For all your cleverness, you tolerate fools willingly enough! ²⁰ You tolerate a person even when he enslaves you, when he plunders you, when he gets you into his power, when he puts on airs of superiority, when he strikes you in the face! ²¹ I admit, to my shame, that we have been weak. But whatever the subject on which others are not afraid to boast—though it is foolish to say so—I am not afraid either! ²² Are they Hebrews? So am I! Are they Israelites? So am I! Are they descendants of Abraham? So am I! ²³ Are they "Servants of Christ"? Though it is madness to talk like this, I am more so than they! I have had more of toil, more of imprisonment! I have been flogged times without number. I have been often at death's door. ²⁴ Five times I received at the hands of my own people forty lashes, all but one. ²⁵ Three times I was beaten with rods. Once I was stoned. Three times I was shipwrecked. I have

spent a whole day and night in the deep. ²⁶ My journeys have been many. I have been through dangers from rivers, dangers from robbers, dangers from my own people, dangers from the gentiles, dangers in towns, dangers in the country, dangers on the sea, dangers among people pretending to be followers of the Lord. ²⁷ I have been through toil and hardship. I have passed many a sleepless night; I have endured hunger and thirst; I have often been without food; I have known cold and nakedness. ²⁸ And, not to speak of other things, there is my daily burden of anxiety about all the churches. ²⁹ Who is weak without my being weak? Who is led astray without my burning with indignation? ³⁰ If I must boast, I will boast of things which show my weakness! ³¹ The God and Father of the Lord Jesus—he who is forever blessed—knows that I am speaking the truth. ³² When I was in Damascus, the governor under King Aretas had the gates of that city guarded, so as to arrest me, ³³ but I was let down in a basket through a window in the wall, and so escaped his hands.

12 ¹ I must boast! It is unprofitable; but I will pass to visions and revelations given by the Lord. ² I know a man in union with the Anointed One who, fourteen years ago—whether in the body or out of the body I do not know; God knows—was caught up (this man of whom I am speaking) to the third heaven. ³ And I know that this man—whether in the body or separated from the body I do not know; God knows—⁴ was caught up into Paradise, and heard unspeakable things of which no human being may tell. ⁵ About such a man I will boast, but about myself I will not boast except as regards my weaknesses. ⁶ Yet if I choose to boast, I will not be a fool; for I will be speaking no more than the truth. But I refrain, in case anyone should credit me with more than she can see in me or hear from me, and because of the marvelous character of the revelations. [7] It was for this reason, and to prevent my thinking too highly of myself, that a thorn was sent to pierce my flesh — an instrument of Satan to discipline me — so that I should not think too highly of myself. [8] About this I three times entreated the Lord, praying that it might leave me. [9] But his reply has been, "My help is enough for you; for my strength attains its perfection in the midst of weakness."

Most gladly, then, will I boast all the more of my weaknesses, so that the strength of the Christ may overshadow me. [10] That is why I delight in weakness, ill treatment, hardship, persecution, and difficulties, when borne for Christ. For, when I am weak, then it is that I am strong!

Conclusion

[11] I have been "playing the fool"! It is you who drove me to it. For it is you who ought to have been commending me! Although I am nobody, in no respect did I prove inferior to the most eminent apostles. [12] The marks of the true apostle were exhibited among you in constant endurance, as well as by signs, by marvels, and by miracles. [13] In what respect, I ask, were you treated worse than the other churches, unless it was that, for my part, I refused to become a burden to you? Forgive me the wrong I did to you!

[14] Remember, this is the third time that I have made every preparation to come to see you, and I will refuse to be a burden to you; I want, not your money, but you. It is not the duty of children to put by for their parents, but of parents to put by for their children. [15] For my part, I will most gladly spend, and be spent, for your welfare. Can it be that the more intensely I love you the less I am to be loved? [16] You will admit that I was not a burden to you but you say that I was "crafty" and caught you "by a trick"! [17] Do you assert that I took advantage of you through any of those whom I have sent to you? [18] I urged Titus to go, and I sent another follower with him. Did Titus take any advantage of you? Did we not live in the same Spirit, and tread in the same footsteps?

[19] Have you all this time been fancying that it is to you that we are making our defense? No, it is in the sight of God, and in union with the Anointed One, that we are speaking. And all this, dear friends, is to build up your characters; [20] for I am afraid that perhaps, when I come, I may find that you are not what I want you to be, and, on the other hand, that you may find that I am what you do not want me to be. I am afraid that I may find quarreling, jealousy, ill feeling, rivalry, slandering, backbiting, self-assertion, and disorder. [21] I am afraid that on my next visit, my God may humble me in regard to you, and that I may have to mourn over many who have long been sinning, and have not repented of the impurity, immorality, and sensuality in which they have indulged.

13 [1] For the third time I am coming to see you. "By the word of two or three witnesses each statement will be established." [2] I have said it, and I say it again before I come, just as if I were with you on my second visit, though for the moment absent, I say to those who have been long sinning, as well as to all others — that if I come again, I will spare no one. [3] And that will be the proof which you are looking for, that the Christ speaks through me. There is no weakness in his dealings with you. No, he shows his power among you. [4] For though his crucifixion was due to weakness, his life is due to the power of God. And we, also, are weak in his weakness, but with him we will live for you through the power of God. [5] Put yourselves to the proof, to see whether you are holding to the faith. Test yourselves. Surely you recognize this fact about yourselves — that Jesus Christ is in you! Unless indeed you cannot stand the test! [6] But I hope that you will recognize that we can stand the test. [7] We pray God that you may do nothing wrong, not that we may be seen to stand the test, but that you may do what is right, even though we may seem not to stand the test. [8] We have no power at all against the truth, but we have power in the service of the truth. [9] We are glad when we are weak, if you are strong. And what we pray for is that you may become perfect. [10] This is my reason for writing as I am now doing, while I am away from you, so that when I am with you, I may not act harshly in the exercise of the author-ity which the Lord gave me — and gave me for building up and not for pulling down.

[11] And now, friends, goodbye. Aim at perfection; take courage; agree together; live in peace. And then God, the source of all love and peace, will be with you. [12] Greet one another with a sacred kiss. [13] All Christ's people here send you their greetings.

[14] May the blessing of the Lord Jesus Christ, and the love of God, and the communion with the holy Spirit, be with you all.

An Introduction to the Letter to the Galatians

KNOWN AS ONE OF the most classic writings of Paul, the Letter to the Galatians is full of wildly emotional language and clarion calls to the gentile followers of Christ to reject aligning themselves with either certain traditions of Israel or the abusive dominance of Roman rule.

The letter appears to be directed at some group(s) of Christ followers in central Asia Minor (current-day Turkey). The word *Galatians* refers to what are more generally called "Gauls," a large conglomeration of peoples native to France and central Europe, who immigrated or invaded portions of the Mediterranean. Writing early in the decade of the 50s CE, Paul does not mention specific towns, so it is difficult to tell what parts of central Asia Minor are being addressed. A possible alternate title for this letter might be "To the Barbarians," as a way of mocking the privileges over "barbarians" claimed by both the Roman Empire and the traditions of Israel.

Paul's use of the word *ambassador* (or *apostle*) in this letter contradicts the way the word is used in other texts, where that word is often reserved for followers of Jesus who knew him while he lived. Contrary to most traditional understandings of Paul, recent scholarship tends to think that Paul always thought of himself as belonging to the traditions of Israel and not as a Christian. Instead, he appears to have thought that Christ enabled the gentiles to belong genuinely to the larger constellation of Israel's traditions.

The Letter to the Galatians is concerned primarily with the relationship between these Christ groups of Asia Minor and some traditions of Israel, particularly circumcision. Paul advocates against forced circumcision for gentiles and argues vehemently against other Christ followers who promote circumcision as a way of becoming a part of the traditions of Israel. Paul also opposes what he calls "the Law," which is usually understood as the Law of Israel, but according to recent scholarship perhaps also might refer to the law of the Roman Empire.

For Paul, being "in Christ" entails a new kind of unity of "neither Judean nor Greek, slave nor free, male and female" (3:28). This new unity means a new identity in relationship to God for everyone, and for gentiles especially: "since you belong to Christ, . . . you are Abraham's offspring" (3:29). No matter what status one has, God has sent the spirit of his Son Christ Jesus into the hearts of everyone, making each "no longer a slave, but a son" (4:7).

The Letter to the Galatians is indeed at the heart of Paul's contribution to the traditions of Christianity. Its expressive language is best encountered as an example of his enthusiasm for and experience in the inclusiveness of the early Christ communities.

Recommended Reading

Brigitte Kahl, *Galatians Reimagined: Reading with the Eyes of the Vanquished*
Davina Lopez, *Apostle to the Conquered: Reimagining Paul's Mission*
Louis Martyn, *Galatians: A New Translation with Commentary*

The Letter to the Galatians

Introduction

1 [1] To the churches in Galatia, from Paul, an ambassador whose commission is not from any human authority and is given, not by human beings, but by Jesus Christ and God the Father who raised him from the dead; [2] and from all the followers of the Lord here. [3] May God, our Father, and the Lord Jesus Christ bless you and give you peace. For Christ, to rescue us from this present wicked age, [4] gave himself for our sins, in accordance with the will of God and Father, [5] to whom be ascribed all glory forever and ever. Amen.

[6] I am astonished at your so soon deserting him, who called you through the love of Christ, for a different "good news," [7] which is really no good news at all. But then, I know that there are people who are harassing you, and who want to pervert the good news of the Anointed One. [8] Yet even if we — or if an angel from heaven — were to tell you any other "good news" than that which we told you, may he be accursed! [9] We have said it before, and I repeat it now: If anyone tells you a "good news" other than that which you received, may he be accursed!

[10] Is this, I ask, trying to conciliate people, or God? Am I seeking to please people? If I were still trying to please people, I should not be a slave of Christ.

Paul's Call

[11] I remind you, friends, that the good news which I told is no mere human invention. [12] I, at least, did not receive it from any human being, nor was I taught it, but it came to me through a revelation of Jesus Christ.

[13] You heard, no doubt, of my conduct when I was devoted to the traditions of Israel — how I persecuted the church of God to an extent beyond belief, and made havoc of it, [14] and how, in my devotion to the traditions of Israel, I surpassed many of my contemporaries among my own people in my intense earnestness in upholding the traditions of my ancestors. [15] But when God, who had set me apart even before my birth, and who called me by his grace, [16] saw fit to reveal his Child in me, so that I might tell the good news of him among the gentiles, then at once, instead of consulting any human being, [17] or even going up to Jerusalem to see those who were ambassadors before me, I went to Arabia, and came back again to Damascus. [18] Three years afterward I went up to Jerusalem to make the acquaintance of Peter, and I stayed a fortnight with him. [19] I did not, however, see any other ambassador, except James, the Lord's brother. [20] (As to what I am now writing to you, I call God to witness that I am speaking the truth.) [21] Afterward, I went to the districts of Syria and Cilicia. [22] But I was still unknown even by sight to the churches of Christ in Judea; [23] all that they had heard was: "The man who once persecuted us is now telling the good news of the faith of which he once made havoc." [24] And they praised God for my sake.

2 [1] Fourteen years afterward I went up to Jerusalem again with Barnabas, and I took Titus also with me. [2] It was in obedience to a revelation that I went; and I laid before the ambassadors the good news that I am proclaiming among the gentiles. I did this privately before those who are thought highly of because I was afraid that I might possibly be taking, or might have already taken, a course which would prove fruitless. [3] Yet even my companion, Titus, though a Greek, was not compelled to be circumcised. [4] But because of those who pretended to be followers who had stolen in, the intruders who had crept in to spy on the liberty which we have through union with Christ Jesus, in order to bring us back to slavery — [5] why, we did not for a moment yield submission to them, so that the truth of the good news might be yours always! [6] Of those who are thought somewhat highly of — what they once were makes no difference to me; God does not recognize human distinctions — those, I say, who are thought highly of added nothing to my message. [7] On the contrary, they saw that I had been entrusted with the good news for the gentiles, just as Peter had been for the Judeans. [8] For the one who gave Peter power for his mission to the Judeans gave me, also, power to go to the gentiles. [9] Recognizing the charge entrusted to me, James, Peter, and John, who were regarded as pillars, openly acknowledged Barnabas and me as fellow workers, agreeing that we should go to the gentiles, and they to the Judeans. [10] Only we were to remember the poor — the thing I was myself anxious to do. [11] But when Peter came to Antioch, I opposed him to his face; for he stood self-condemned. [12] Before certain persons came from James, he had been in the habit of eating with the gentile converts; but when they came, he began to withdraw and hold aloof, because he was afraid of offending those who still held to circumcision. [13] The rest of the Judean converts were guilty of the same hypocrisy, so that even Barnabas was led away by it. [14] But when I saw that they were not dealing straightforwardly with the truth of the good news, I said to Peter, before them all, "If you, who were born a Judean, adopt gentile customs, instead of Judean, why are you trying to compel the gentile converts to adopt Judean customs?"

The Law and the Gospel

[15] We, though we are Judeans by birth and not outcasts of gentile origin, know that no one is pronounced righteous as the result of obedience to Law, but only through faith in Christ Jesus. [16] So we placed our faith in Christ Jesus, in order that we might be pronounced righteous, as the result of trust in Christ, and not of obedience to Law; for such obedience will not result in even one person being pronounced righteous. [17] If, while seeking to be pronounced righteous through union with Christ, we were ourselves seen to be sinners, would that make Christ an agent of sin? Heaven forbid! [18] For, if I rebuild the things that I pulled down, I prove myself to have done wrong. [19] I, indeed, through Law became dead to Law, in order to live for God. [20] I have been crucified with Christ, and yet I live. So it is no longer I that live, but it is Christ who lives in me; and, as for my present earthly life, I am living it by faith in the Child of God, who loved me and gave himself for me. [21] I do not reject the love of God. If righteousness comes through Law, then there was no need for Christ to die!

3 [1] Foolish Galatians! Who has been fascinating you — you before whose eyes Jesus Christ was depicted on the cross? [2] Here is the one thing that I want to find out from you: Did you receive the spirit as the result of obedience to Law, or of your having listened with faith? [3] Can you be so foolish? After beginning within the spirit, do you now end with the flesh? [4] Did you go through so much to no purpose? — if indeed it really was to no purpose! [5] The one who supplies you abundantly with his spirit and endows you with such powers — does he do this as the result of obedience to Law? Or as the result of your having listened with faith? ⁶ It is just as it was with Abraham:

"He had faith in God, and his trust was
    regarded by God as righteousness."

⁷ You see, then, that those whose lives are based on faith are the children of Abraham. ⁸ And the writing, foreseeing that God would pronounce the gentiles righteous as the result of faith, foretold the good news to Abraham in the words,

"Through you all the gentiles will be
    blessed."

⁹ And, therefore, those whose lives are based on faith share the blessings bestowed on the faith of Abraham. ¹⁰ All who rely on obedience to Law are under a curse, for it is written:

"Cursed is everyone who does not
    abide by all that is written in the
    book of the Law, and do it."

¹¹ Again, it is evident that no one is pronounced righteous before God through Law, for we read:

"Through faith the righteous will find
    life."

¹² But the Law is not based on faith; no, its words are:

"Those who practice these precepts will
    find life through them."

¹³ Christ redeemed us from the curse pronounced in the Law, by taking the curse on himself for us, for it is written:

"Cursed is anyone who is hanged on a
    tree."

¹⁴ And this he did that the blessing given to Abraham might be extended to the gentiles through their union with Jesus Christ; that so, through our trust, we also might receive the promised gift of the Spirit.

¹⁵ To take an illustration, friends, from daily life: No one sets aside even an agreement between two people, when once it has been confirmed, nor do they add conditions to it. ¹⁶ Now it was to Abraham that the promises were made, "and to his offspring." It was not said "to his offsprings," as if many persons were meant, but the words were "to your offspring," showing that one person was meant — and that was Christ. ¹⁷ My point is this — an agreement already confirmed by God cannot be canceled by the Law, which came four hundred and thirty years later, so as to cause the promise to be set aside. ¹⁸ If our heritage is the result of Law, then it has ceased to be the result of a promise. Yet God conferred it on Abraham by a promise.

¹⁹ What, then, you ask, was the use of the Law? It was a later addition, to make people conscious of their wrongdoings, and intended to last only until the coming of that offspring to whom the promise had been made; and it was delivered through angels by an intermediary. ²⁰ Now mediation implies more than one person, but God is one only. ²¹ Does that set the Law in opposition to God's promises? Heaven forbid! For, if a Law had been given capable of bestowing life, then righteousness would have actually owed its existence to Law. ²² But the writing represents the whole world as being in bondage to sin, so that the promised blessing, dependent, as it is, on the faith of Jesus Christ, may be given to those who trust.

²³ Before the coming of faith, we were kept under the Law, in bondage, awaiting the faith that was destined to be revealed. ²⁴ Thus the Law has proved a guide to lead us to Christ, in order that we may

be pronounced righteous as the result of faith. [25] But now that faith has come we no longer need a guide.

[26] For you are all sons of God, through your faith in Christ Jesus. [27] For all of you who were baptized into union with Christ clothed yourselves with Christ. [28] There is neither Judean nor Greek, slave nor free, male and female; for in Christ Jesus you are all one. [29] And, since you belong to Christ, it follows that you are Abraham's offspring and, under the promise, sharers in the inheritance.

4 [1] My point is this — as long as the heir is under age, there is no difference between him and a slave, though he is master of the whole estate. [2] He is subject to the control of guardians and stewards, during the period for which his father has power to appoint them. [3] And so is it with us; when we were under age, as it were, we were slaves to the elemental principles of this world; [4] but when the full time came, God sent his Child — born a woman's child, born subject to Law — [5] to redeem those who were subject to Law, so that we might receive adoption as children.

[6] And it is because you are children that God sent into our hearts the spirit of his Child, with the cry "Abba, our Father." [7] You, therefore, are no longer a slave, but a son; and, if a son, then an heir also, by God's appointment.

[8] Yet formerly, in your ignorance of God, you became slaves to "gods" which were not gods. [9] But now that you have found God — or, rather, have been found by him — how is it that you are turning back to slavery to those powerless and bankrupt elements whose slaves you now want to be all over again? [10] You are scrupulous in keeping days and months and seasons and years! [11] You make me fear that the labor which I have spent on you may have been wasted.

[12] I entreat you, friends, to become like me, as I became like you. You have never done me any wrong. [13] You remember that it was owing to bodily infirmity that on the first occasion I told you the good news. [14] And as for what must have tried you in my condition, it did not inspire you with scorn or disgust, but you welcomed me as if I had been an angel of God — or Christ Jesus himself! [15] What has become, then, of your contentment? For I can bear witness that had it been possible, you would have torn out your eyes and given them to me! [16] Am I to think, then, that I have become your enemy by telling you the truth? [17] Certain people are seeking your favor, but with no honorable object. No, indeed, they want to isolate you, so that you will have to seek their favor. [18] It is always honorable to have your favor sought in an honorable cause, and not only when I am with you, my dear children — [19] you for whom I am again enduring a mother's pains, until Christ will have been formed in you. [20] But I could wish to be with you now and speak in a different tone, for I am perplexed about you.

[21] Tell me, you who want to be still subject to Law: Why do you not listen to the Law? [22] It is written that Abraham had two sons, one the child of the slave woman and the other the child of the free woman. [23] But the child of the slave woman was born according to the flesh, while the child of the free woman was born through a promise. [24] This story may be taken as an allegory. The women stand for two covenants. One covenant, given from Mount Sinai, produces a race of slaves and is represented by Hagar [25] (the word *Hagar* meaning in Arabia "Mount Sinai") and it ranks with the Jerusalem of today, for she and her children are in slavery. [26] But the Jerusalem above is free, and she it is who is our mother. [27] As it is written:

"Rejoice, you barren one, who does
never bear,

break into shouts, you who are never
in labor,
for many are the children of her who is
desolate —
more than of her who has a husband."

[28] As for you, friends, we, like Isaac, are children born of a promise. [29] Yet at that time the child born of the flesh persecuted the child born according to the spirit; and it is the same now. [30] But what does the writing say?

"Send away the slave woman and her
son; for the slave's son will not be co-
heir with the son of the free woman."

[31] And so, friends, we are not children of a slave, but of her who is free.

The Good News in Daily Life

5 [1] It is for freedom that Christ set us free; stand firm, therefore, and do not again be held under the yoke of slavery. [2] Understand that I, Paul, myself tell you that if you allow yourselves to be circumcised, Christ will avail you nothing. [3] I again declare to everyone who receives circumcision that he binds himself to obey the whole Law. [4] You have severed yourselves from Christ — you who are seeking to be pronounced righteous through Law; you have fallen away from grace. [5] For we, by the help of the Spirit, are eagerly waiting for the fulfillment of our hope — that we may be pronounced saving justice with confidence. [6] If we are in Christ Jesus, neither is circumcision nor the omission of it anything, but faith, working through love, is everything. [7] You were once making good progress! Who has hindered you from obeying the truth? [8] The persuasion brought to bear on you does not come from the one who calls you. [9] A little leaven leavens all the dough. [10] I, through my union with the Lord, am persuaded that you will not be led astray. But the one

who is disturbing your minds will have to bear his punishment, whoever he may be. [11] If I, friends, am still proclaiming circumcision, why am I still persecuted? It seems that the cross has ceased to be an obstacle! [12] I could even wish that the people who are unsettling you would go further still and mutilate themselves.

[13] Remember, friends, to you the call came to give you freedom. Only do not make your freedom an opportunity for self-indulgence, but serve one another in a loving spirit. [14] Indeed, the whole Law has been summed up in this one precept:

"You must love your neighbor as you
love yourself."

[15] But if you are continually wounding and preying on one another, take care that you are not destroyed by one another. [16] This is what I have to say: Let your steps be guided by the spirit, and then you will never gratify the cravings of the flesh. [17] For these cravings of the flesh conflict with the spirit, and the spirit with the flesh — they are two contrary principles — so that you cannot do what you wish. [18] But if you follow the guidance of the spirit, you are not subject to Law. [19] The sins of the flesh are unmistakable. They are sins like these — sexual immorality, impurity, indecency, [20] idolatry, sorcery, quarrels, strife, jealousy, outbursts of passion, rivalries, dissensions, divisions, [21] feelings of envy, drunkenness, revelry, and the like. And I warn you, as I warned you before, that those who indulge in such things will not inherit the realm of God. [22] But the fruit produced by the spirit is love, joy, peace, forbearance, kindliness, generosity, trustfulness, gentleness, self-control. [23] Law is not about these things! [24] And those who belong to Jesus, the Anointed One, have already crucified the flesh, with its passions and its cravings.

[25] Since we are living by the spirit, let us rule our conduct also by the spirit. [26] Do

not let us grow vain, and provoke or envy one another.

6 [1] My friends, even if someone should be caught committing a sin, you who are spiritually minded should, in a gentle spirit, help them to recover themselves, taking care that you yourselves are not put to the test. [2] Bear one another's burdens, and so carry out the Law of the Christ. [3] If a person imagines herself to be somebody, when she is really nobody, she deceives herself. [4] Let everyone test her own work, and then her cause for satisfaction will be in herself and not in a comparison with her neighbor; [5] for everyone must bear her own load. [6] The person, however, who is being instructed in the message ought always to share her possessions with her teacher.

[7] Do not be deceived. God cannot be mocked. What a person sows, that she will reap. [8] For the person who sows the field of the flesh will reap corruption; while the one who sows the field of the spirit will from that spirit reap life through the generations. [9] Let us never tire of doing right, for at the proper season we will reap our harvest, if we do not grow weary. [10] Therefore, I say, as the opportunity occurs, let us treat everyone with kindness, and especially members of the household of the faith.

Postscript

[11] See in what large letters I am writing with my own hand. [12] Those who wish to promote the flesh are the people who are trying to compel you to be circumcised; and they do it only to avoid being persecuted for the cross of Jesus, the Anointed One. [13] Even these men who are circumcised do not themselves keep the Law; yet they want you to be circumcised, so that they may boast of your flesh. [14] But for my part, may I never boast of anything except the cross of Jesus Christ, our Lord, through whom the world has been crucified to me, and I to the world. [15] For neither is circumcision nor the omission of it anything; but a new creation is everything. [16] May all who rule their conduct by this principle find peace and mercy — they who are the Israel of God.

[17] For the future let no one trouble me; for I bear the marks of Jesus branded on my body.

[18] May the blessing of Jesus Christ, our Lord, rest on your souls, friends. Amen.

An Introduction to the Letter to the Philippians

GRIPPING IN BOTH its affection and its embattlement, this authentic letter from Paul lacks, almost completely, the disciplining language and criticism in his other letters. Here is his joy at its most eloquent, even though he is in prison. His usual combativeness against other leaders in the community to whom he is writing disappears in this letter. He is obviously happy with the character of the Philippian community and grateful for the tangible aid they have provided him.

Written sometime between 55 and 58 CE, this letter reflects clear knowledge of and a strong relationship with the addressees. There is some possibility that it is a composite letter, merging parts of three different letters from Paul to Philippi.

The Mutual Support Between Paul and the Philippian Assemblies

Paul and the Philippians are clearly working together. Several times they have sent him physical aid during his imprisonment. He in turn wants to send both Timothy and Epaphroditus to Philippi to help in the Christ movement there. Work of this sort has already been undertaken by others, some of whom Paul does not seem to like, but for whom he is thankful because "either with assumed or with real earnestness, the Anointed One is being made known; and at that I rejoice" (1:18).

Paul senses that he is in fairly immediate danger but is able to frame his connection to the Philippians in terms of how their work and his complement one another within God's holiness: "Even if, when your trust is offered as a sacrifice to God, my lifeblood must be poured out in addition, still I will rejoice and share the joy of you all; and you must also rejoice and share my joy" (2:17–18). This unity with the Philippians also points to a shared goal to "become like him [Christ] in death" (3:11).

The Evolution of Paul's Dedication to the Traditions of Israel and Christ

Paul sees what he and the Philippian assemblies are together as an inimitable part of the traditions of Israel and in some ways as a transformation of those traditions. In speaking of the connection to the traditions of Israel in his own life and the lives of his readers, he says, "We are the true people of the circumcision," going on to allude to the fact that some of the Philippians are not circumcised in that they "exult in Christ Jesus, and . . . do not rely on physical qualifications" (3:2–3).

Paul then goes on to recount his even more extensive credentials in the traditions of Israel: "I was circumcised when eight days old; I am of the race of Israel, and of the tribe of Benjamin; I am a Hebrew, and the child of Hebrews. As to the Law, I was a Pharisee" (3:5). Although these traditions still have meaning for him, he has also grown into "the righteousness which is derived from God and is founded on trust" (3:9).

Philippians offers one of the most endearing portraits of Paul and his work to twenty-first-century readers. There are still moments of combativeness, but this letter puts people of our day in touch with the passionate enthusiasm of Paul for his work in extending his vision and project of a Christ movement for the people of the Mediterranean in the first century.

Recommended Reading

Markus Bockmuehl, *The Epistle to the Philippians*
Gerald F. Hawthorne, *Philippians*
John Reumann, *Philippians*

The Letter to the Philippians

1 ¹ To all God's people at Philippi, with the presiding officers and assistants, from Paul and Timothy, slaves of Christ Jesus. ² Grace and peace to you from God our Father and the Lord Jesus Christ. ³ Every recollection that I have of you is a cause of thankfulness to God, ⁴ always, in every prayer that I offer for you all — my prayers are full of joy — ⁵ because of the share that you have had in spreading the good news, from the first day that you received it until now. ⁶ For of this I am confident, that the one who began a good work in you will complete it in readiness for the day of Jesus Christ. ⁷ And, indeed, I am justified in feeling like this about you all; because you have a warm place in my heart — you who all, both in my imprisonment and in the work of defending and establishing the good news, shared my privilege with me. ⁸ God will bear me witness how I yearn over you all with the tenderness of Christ Jesus. ⁹ And what I pray for is this — that your love may grow yet stronger and stronger, with increasing knowledge and all discernment, ¹⁰ until you are able to appreciate true discernment. And I pray, too, that you may be kept pure and blameless against the day of the Anointed One, ¹¹ bearing a rich harvest of that righteousness which comes through Jesus Christ, to the glory and praise of God.

¹² Friends, I want you to realize that what has happened to me has actually served to forward the good news. ¹³ It has even become evident, not only to all the imperial guard, but to everyone else, that it is for Christ's sake that I am in chains. ¹⁴ And besides this, most of our fellow followers have gained confidence in the Lord through my chains, and now venture with far greater freedom to speak of God's message fearlessly. ¹⁵ It is true that some do proclaim the Anointed One out of jealousy and opposition; but there are others who proclaim him from goodwill. ¹⁶ The latter do it from love for me, knowing that I have been appointed to plead the cause of the good news. ¹⁷ The former spread the news of the Christ in a factious spirit, and not sincerely, thinking to add to the pain of my chains. ¹⁸ But what of that? Only that in some way or other, either with assumed or with real earnestness, the Anointed One is being made known; and at that I rejoice. ¹⁹ Yes, and I will rejoice, for I know that through your prayers and through a rich supply of the spirit of Jesus Christ, all this will make for my salvation. ²⁰ And this will fulfill my earnest expectation and hope that I will have no cause for shame, but that with unfailing courage, now as hitherto, Christ will be glorified in my body, whether by my life or by my death, ²¹ for to me life is Christ, and death is gain. ²² But what if the life here in the body — if this brings me fruit from my labors? Then which to choose I cannot tell! I am sorely perplexed either way! ²³ My own desire is to depart and be with Christ, for this would be far better. ²⁴ But for your sakes, it may be more needful that I should still remain here in the body. ²⁵ Yes, I am confident that this is so, and therefore I am sure that I will stay, and stay near you all, to promote your progress and joy in the faith; ²⁶ so that when you once more have me among you, you, in your union with Christ Jesus, may find in me fresh cause for exultation. ²⁷ Under all circumstances let your lives be worthy of the good news of the Christ, so that whether I come and

see you, or whether I hear of your affairs at a distance, I may know that you are standing firm, animated by one spirit, and joining with one heart in a common struggle for the confidence taught by the good news, [28] without ever shrinking from your opponents. To them this will be a sign of their destruction and of your salvation — a sign from God. [29] For, on behalf of Christ, you have had the privilege granted you, not only of trusting in him, but also of suffering on his behalf. [30] You will be engaged in the same hard struggle as that which you once saw me waging, and which you hear that I am waging still.

2 [1] If, then, in Christ any encouragement comes, if there is any persuasive power in love, if there is any communion with the Spirit, if there is any tenderness or pity, [2] I entreat you to make my happiness complete — live together animated by the same spirit and in mutual love, one in heart, animated by one spirit. [3] Nothing should be done in a factious spirit or from vanity, but each of you should with all humility regard others as better than yourself, [4] and one and all should consider, not only their own interests, but also the interests of others. [5] Let the spirit of Christ Jesus be yours also. [6] Being in the form of God did not count equality with God something to be grasped at, [7] but he emptied himself, taking the form of a slave, becoming as humans are; [8] he was in every way like a human being, and was humbler yet, even to accepting death, death on a cross! [9] And that is why God raised him to the very highest place, and gave him the name which stands above all other names, [10] so that all beings in the heavens, on earth, and under the earth should bend the knee at the name of Jesus, [11] and that every tongue should acknowledge Jesus Christ as Lord — to the glory of God the Father. [12] Therefore, my dear friends, as you have always been obedient in the

past, so now work out your own salvation with anxious care, not only when I am with you, but all the more now that I am absent. [13] Remember it is God who, in his kindness, is at work within you, enabling you both to will and to work. [14] In all that you do, avoid murmuring and dissension, [15] so as to prove yourselves blameless and innocent — faultless children of God, in the midst of an evil-disposed and perverse generation, in which you are seen shining like stars in a dark world, [16] offering to them the message of life; and then I will be able at the day of the Anointed One to boast that I did not run my course for nothing, or toil for nothing. [17] And yet, even if, when your trust is offered as a sacrifice to God, my lifeblood must be poured out in addition, still I will rejoice and share the joy of you all; [18] and you must also rejoice and share my joy. [19] I hope, however, as one who trusts in the Lord Jesus, to send Timothy to you before long, so that I may myself be cheered by receiving news of you. [20] For I have no one but him to send — no one of kindred spirit who would take the same genuine interest in your welfare. [21] They are all pursuing their own aims and not those of Christ Jesus. [22] But you know what Timothy has proved himself to be, and how, like a child working for his father, he worked hard with me in spreading the good news. [23] It is Timothy, then, whom I hope to send, as soon as ever I can foresee how it will go with me. [24] And I am confident, as one who trusts in the Lord Jesus, that before long I myself will follow. [25] Still I think it necessary to send Epaphroditus to you now, for he is my dear friend, fellow worker, and fellow soldier, and he was also your messenger to help me in my need. [26] For he has been longing to see you all, and has been distressed because you heard of his illness. [27] And I can assure you that his illness very nearly proved fatal. But God had pity on him, and not on him only but also on me, so that I might not have sorrow on sorrow. [28] I am all the more ready, therefore, to send him, so that the sight of him may revive your spirits and my own sorrow be lightened. [29] Give him, then, the heartiest of welcomes in the Lord, and hold such people in great honor. [30] For it was owing to his devotion to the Master's work that he was at the point of death, having risked his own life in the effort to supply what was wanting in the help that you sent me.

3 [1] In conclusion, my friends, all joy be yours in the Lord. To repeat what I have already written does not weary me, and is the safe course for you. [2] Beware of those "dogs"! Beware of those mischievous workers! Beware of the men who mutilate themselves! [3] For it is we who are the circumcised — we whose worship is prompted by the spirit of God, who exult in Christ Jesus, and who do not rely on physical qualifications; [4] though I, if anyone, have cause to rely even on them. If anyone thinks he can rely on external privileges, far more can I! [5] I was circumcised when eight days old; I am of the race of Israel, and of the tribe of Benjamin; I am a Hebrew, and the child of Hebrews. As to the Law, I was a Pharisee; [6] as to zeal, I was a persecutor of the church; as to such righteousness as is due to Law, I proved myself blameless. [7] But all the things which I once held to be gains I have now, for the Christ's sake, come to count as loss. [8] More than that, I count everything as loss, for the sake of the exceeding value of the knowledge of Christ Jesus my Lord. And for his sake I have lost everything, and count it as refuse, if I may but gain Christ and be found in him; [9] any righteousness that I have being, not the righteousness that results from Law, but the righteousness which comes through faith in Christ — the righteousness which is derived from God and is founded on trust. [10] Then indeed I

will know Christ, and the power of his resurrection, and all that it means to share his sufferings, [11] in the hope that if I become like him in death, I may possibly attain to the resurrection from the dead. [12] Not that I have already laid hold of it, or that I am already made perfect. But I press on, in the hope of actually laying hold of that for which indeed I was laid hold of by Christ Jesus. [13] For I, friends, do not regard myself as having yet laid hold of it. But this one thing I do — forgetting what lies behind, and straining every nerve for that which lies in front, [14] I press on to the goal, to gain the prize of that heavenward call which God gave me through Christ Jesus. [15] Let all of us, then, whose faith is mature think this way. Then, if on any matter you think otherwise, God will make that also plain to you. [16] Only we are bound to order our lives by what we have already attained.

[17] My friends, unite in following my example, and fix your eyes on those who are living by the pattern which we have set you. [18] For there are many — of whom I have often told you, and now tell you even with tears — who are living in enmity to the cross of the Christ. [19] The end of such people is ruin; for their appetites are their God, and they glory in their shame; their minds are given up to earthly things. [20] But the state of which we are citizens is in heaven; and it is from heaven that we are eagerly looking for a Savior, the Lord Jesus Christ, [21] who, by the exercise of his power to bring everything into subjection to himself, will make this body that we have in our humiliation like to that body which he has in his glory.

4 [1] So then, my dear friends, whom I am longing to see — you who are my joy and my crown, stand fast in union with the Lord, dear friends. [2] I entreat Euodia, and I entreat Syntyche, to live in harmony, in the Lord; [3] yes, and I ask you, Syzgus, my true comrade, to help them, remembering that they toiled by my side in spreading the good news; and so, too, did Clement and my other fellow workers, whose names are in the book of life. ⁴ All joy be yours at all times in the Lord. Again I repeat — all joy be yours. ⁵ Let your forbearing spirit be plain to everyone. The Lord is near. ⁶ Do not be anxious about anything; but under all circumstances, by prayer and entreaty joined with thanksgiving, make your needs known to God. ⁷ Then the peace of God, which is beyond all human understanding, will stand guard over your hearts and thoughts in Christ Jesus.

⁸ In conclusion, friends, whenever you find things that are true or honorable, righteous or pure, lovable or praiseworthy, or if virtue and honor have any meaning, let them fill your thoughts. ⁹ All that you learned and received and heard and saw in me put into practice continually; and then God, the giver of peace, will be with you. ¹⁰ It was a matter of great joy to me, as one in the Lord, that at length your interest in me had revived. The interest indeed you had, but not the opportunity. ¹¹ Do not think that I am saying this under the pressure of want. For I, however I am placed, have learned to be independent of circumstances. ¹² I know how to face humble circumstances, and I know how to face prosperity. Into all and every human experience I have been initiated — into plenty and hunger, into prosperity and want. ¹³ I can do everything in the strength of the one who makes me strong! ¹⁴ Yet you have acted nobly in sharing my troubles. ¹⁵ And you at Philippi know, as well as I, that in the early days of the good news — at the time when I had just left Macedonia — no church, with the one exception of yourselves, had anything to do with me as far as expenditures and receipts are concerned. ¹⁶ Indeed, even while I was still in Thessalonica, you sent more than once to relieve my wants. ¹⁷ It is not that I am anxious for your gifts, but I am anxious to see the abundant return that will be placed to your account. I have enough of everything, and to spare. ¹⁸ My wants are fully satisfied, now that I have received from Epaphroditus the gifts which you sent me — the sweet fragrance of a sacrifice acceptable and pleasing to God. ¹⁹ And my God, out of the greatness of his wealth, will, in glory, fully satisfy your every need, in Christ Jesus. ²⁰ To him, our God and Father, be ascribed all glory forever and ever. Amen. ²¹ Give my greeting to every one of the people of Christ Jesus. The Lord's followers who are with me send you their greetings. ²² All God's people here, and especially those who belong to the emperor's household, send theirs.

²³ May the grace of the Lord Jesus Christ rest on your spirits.

An Introduction to the First Letter
to the Thessalonians

A FRESH AND UNSELFCONSCIOUS picture of Paul's very earliest work in the Christ movement, 1 Thessalonians provides a valuable snapshot of the growing relationship between Paul and one or several Christ assemblies in the Macedonian city of Thessalonica. It shows the enthusiasms and strains of a relatively new relationship and is plainspoken about issues that need to be clarified. As the earliest of Paul's letters, it claimed a place in the traditional New Testament.

Writing in the early 50s CE, Paul does not yet designate himself as "apostle" or, when better translated, "ambassador." He is proud of the Thessalonians and their initial experiences together: "And you yourselves began to follow, not only our example, but the Lord's also; and, in spite of much suffering, you welcomed the message with a joy inspired by the holy Spirit, and so became a pattern to all who believed in Christ throughout Macedonia and Greece. For it was from you that the Lord's message resounded throughout Macedonia and Greece; and, more than that, your faith in God has become known far and wide; so that there is no need for us to say another word. Indeed, in speaking about us, the people themselves tell of the reception you gave us, and how, turning to God from your idols, you came to serve the true and living God" (1:6–9).

Paul has worried about how the relationship is developing, has sent Timothy (an assistant of his in efforts to announce the possibility of gentiles belonging to Israel's God and traditions) to check on the Thessalonians, and is now writing how pleased he is with Timothy's report. Paul gives instruction about what is to happen to Christ followers who have died. He integrates his answer with his early emphasis on the coming of the Lord in the very near future, as he paints a picture of those who have died and those still living meeting in the air. In the meantime, Paul encourages them to "make it your ambition to live quietly, and to attend to your own business, and to work with your hands, as we directed you" (4:11).

For twenty-first-century readers the main value of 1 Thessalonians lies in its portrait of Paul's message at its earliest written stage. It helps us think about Paul's place in the development of the Christ movement by showing what his thought was in a particular early part of his ministry.

Recommended Reading

Beverly Gaventa, *First and Second Thessalonians*
Abraham Malherbe, *The Letters to the Thessalonians*

The First Letter to the Thessalonians

Introduction

1 ¹ To the Thessalonian church in union with God the Father and the Lord Jesus Christ, from Paul, Silas, and Timothy. May God bless you and give you peace.

² We always mention you in our prayers and thank God for you all; ³ recalling continually before our God and Father the efforts that have resulted from your faith, the toil prompted by your love, and the patient endurance sustained by your hope in our Lord Jesus Christ. ⁴ Friends, whom God loves, we know that he has chosen you, ⁵ because the good news that we brought came home to you, not merely as so many words, but with a power and a fullness of conviction due to the holy Spirit. For you know the life that we lived among you for your good. ⁶ And you yourselves began to follow, not only our example, but the Lord's also; and, in spite of much suffering, you welcomed the message with a joy inspired by the holy Spirit, ⁷ and so became a pattern to all who believed in Christ throughout Macedonia and Greece. ⁸ For it was from you that the Lord's message resounded throughout Macedonia and Greece; and, more than that, your faith in God has become known far and wide; so that there is no need for us to say another word. ⁹ Indeed, in speaking about us, the people themselves tell of the reception you gave us, and how, turning to God from your idols, you came to serve the true and living God, ¹⁰ and are now awaiting the return from heaven of his Son whom he raised from the dead — Jesus, our deliverer from the coming wrath.

2 ¹ Yes, friends, you yourselves know that your reception of us was not without result. ² For, although we had experienced suffering and ill treatment, as you know, at Philippi, we had the courage, by the help of our God, to tell you God's good news in spite of great opposition. ³ Our appeal to you was not based on a delusion, nor was it made from unworthy motives, or with any intention of misleading you. ⁴ But having been found worthy by God to be entrusted with the good news, therefore we tell it, with a view to please, not people, but God who proves our hearts. ⁵ Never at any time, as you know, did we use the language of flattery, or make false professions in order to hide selfish aims. God will bear witness to that. ⁶ Nor did we seek to win honor from people, whether from you or from others, although, as ambassadors of Christ, we might have burdened you with our support. ⁷ But we lived among you with the simplicity of a child; we were like a woman nursing her own children. ⁸ In our strong affection for you, that seemed to us the best way of sharing with you, not only God's good news, but our lives as well — so dear had you become to us. ⁹ You will not have forgotten, friends, our labor and toil. Night and day we used to work at our trades, so as not to be a burden to any of you, while we proclaimed to you God's good news. ¹⁰ You will bear witness, and God also, that our relations with you who believed in Christ were pure, and upright, and beyond reproach. ¹¹ Indeed, you know that like a father with his own children, we used to encourage and comfort every one of you, and solemnly plead with you; ¹² so that you should make your daily lives worthy of God who is calling you into the glory of his realm.

¹³ This, too, is a reason why we, on our

part, are continually thanking God — because, in receiving the teaching that you had from us, you accepted it, not as the teaching of humans, but as what it really is — the teaching of God, which is even now doing its work within you who believe. [14] For you, friends, began to follow the example of the churches of God in Judea which are in union with Jesus Christ; you, in your turn, suffering at the hands of your fellow citizens, in the same way as those churches did at the hands of their people — [15] who killed both the Lord Jesus and the prophets, and persecuted us also. They do not try to please God, and they are enemies to all humanity, [16] for they try to prevent us from speaking to the gentiles with a view to their salvation, and so are always filling up the measure of their iniquity. But the wrath has come upon them to the full!

[17] As for ourselves, friends, our having been bereaved of you even for a short time — though in body only, and not in spirit — made us all the more eager to see your faces again; and the longing to do so was strong in us. [18] That was why we made up our minds to go and see you — at least I, Paul, did, more than once — but Satan put difficulties in our way. [19] For what hope or joy will be ours, or what crown will we have to boast of, in the presence of our Lord Jesus, at his coming, if it not be you? [20] You are our pride and our delight!

3 [1] And so, as we could bear it no longer, we made up our minds to remain behind alone at Athens, [2] and sent Timothy, our dear friend and God's minister of the good news of the Christ, to strengthen you, and to encourage you in your faith, [3] so that none of you should be shaken by the troubles through which you are passing. You yourselves know that we are destined to meet with such things. [4] For, even while we were with you, we warned you beforehand that we were certain to encounter trouble. And so it proved, as you know. [5] There-

fore, since I could no longer endure the uncertainty, I sent to make inquiries about your faith, fearing that the Tempter had tempted you, and that our toil might prove to have been in vain. [6] But when Timothy recently returned to us from you with good news of your faith and love, and told us how kindly you think of us — always longing, he said, to see us, just as we are longing to see you — [7] on hearing this, we felt encouraged about you, friends, in the midst of all our difficulties and troubles, by your faith. [8] For it is new life to us to know that you are holding fast to the Lord. [9] How can we thank God enough for all the happiness that you are giving us in the sight of our God? [10] Night and day we pray most earnestly that we may see you face-to-face, and make good any deficiency in your faith.

[11] May our God and Father himself, and Jesus, our Lord, make the way plain for us to come to you. [12] And for you, may the Lord fill you to overflowing with love for one another and for everyone, just as we are filled with love for you; [13] and so make your hearts strong, and your lives pure beyond reproach, in the sight of our God and Father, at the coming of our Lord Jesus, with all his holy ones.

Advice on Daily Life

4 [1] Further, friends, we beg and urge you in the name of our Lord Jesus to carry out more fully than ever — as indeed you are already doing — all that you have heard from us as to what your daily life must be, if it is to please God. [2] For you have not forgotten the directions that we gave you on the authority of our Lord Jesus.

[3] For this is God's purpose — that you should be holy; abstaining from all immorality; [4] each of you learning to gain control over your own body, in a way that is holy and honorable, [5] and not for the mere gratification of your passions, like the gentiles who know nothing of God; [6] none of

you overreaching or taking advantage of your fellow followers of the Lord in such matters. The Lord takes vengeance on all who do such things, as we have already warned you and solemnly declared. [7] For God's call to us does not permit of an impure life, but demands holiness. [8] Therefore the person who disregards this warning disregards, not people, but God who gives you his holy Spirit.

[9] As to love for each other there is no need to write to you; for you have yourselves been taught by God to love one another; [10] and indeed you do act in this spirit toward all his people throughout Macedonia.

Yet, friends, we beg you to do even more. [11] Make it your ambition to live quietly, and to attend to your own business, and to work with your hands, as we directed you; [12] so that your conduct may win respect from those outside the church, and that you may not want for anything.

The Dead in Christ at the Coming of the Lord

[13] We do not want you to be ignorant, friends, about those who have passed to their rest. We do not want you to grieve like other people who have no hope. [14] For, as we believe that Jesus died and rose again, so also we believe that God will bring, with Jesus, those who through him have passed to their rest. [15] This we tell you on the authority of the Lord — that those of us who are still living at the coming of the Lord will not anticipate those who have passed to their rest. [16] For, with a loud summons, with the shout of an archangel, and with the trumpet call of God, the Lord himself will come down from heaven. [17] Then those who died in union with Christ will rise first; and afterward we who are still living will be caught up in the clouds, with them, to meet the Lord in the air; and so we will be forever with the Lord. [18] Therefore, comfort one another with what I have told you.

5 [1] But as to the times and the moments, there is no need, friends, for anyone to write to you. [2] You yourselves know well that the day of the Lord will come just as a thief comes in the night. [3] When people are saying, "All is quiet and safe," it is then that like birth pains on a pregnant woman, ruin comes suddenly upon them, and there will be no escape! [4] You, however, friends, are not in darkness, that the daylight should take you by surprise as if you were thieves. [5] For you all are "children of light" and "children of the day."

We have nothing to do with night, or darkness. [6] Therefore let us not sleep as others do. No, let us be watchful and self-controlled. [7] It is at night that people sleep, and at night that drunkards get drunk. [8] But let us, who belong to the day, control ourselves, and put on faith and love as a breastplate, and the hope of salvation as a helmet. [9] For God destined us, not for wrath, but to win salvation through our Lord Jesus Christ, who died for us, [10] that whether we are still watching or have fallen asleep, we may live with him. [11] Therefore encourage one another, and try to build up one another's characters, as indeed you are doing.

Conclusion

[12] We beg you, friends, to value those who toil among you, and are your leaders in the Lord's service, and give you counsel. [13] Hold them in the very greatest esteem and affection for the sake of their work. Live at peace with one another. [14] We entreat you also, friends — warn the disorderly, comfort the faint-hearted, give a helping hand to the weak, and be patient with everyone. [15] Take care that none of you ever pays back wrong for wrong, but always follow the kindest course with one another and with everyone. [16] Always be

joyful; [17] never cease to pray; [18] under all circumstances give thanks to God. For this is his will for you as made known in Christ Jesus. [19] Do not quench the spirit; [20] do not make light of preaching. [21] Bring everything to the test; cling to what is good; [22] shun every form of evil. [23] May God, the giver of peace, make you altogether holy; and may your spirits, souls, and bodies be kept altogether faultless until the coming of our Lord Jesus Christ. [24] The one who calls you will not fail you; that one will complete the work.

[25] Friends, pray for us.

[26] Greet all the Lord's followers with a sacred kiss. [27] I order you in the Lord's name to have this letter read to all the brothers and sisters.

[28] May the blessing of our Lord Jesus Christ be with you.

An Introduction to the Letter to Philemon

P AUL AND TIMOTHY'S LETTER to Philemon, Apphia, Archippus, and their Christ assembly is a letter about one matter: Paul sending Philemon's slave Onesimus back to him. Paul is in prison while he is writing this letter, and for some reason (Has Onesimus run away from Philemon and been imprisoned for that offense? Is Onesimus an assistant to Paul, even when he is imprisoned?) Onesimus and Paul have been there together. Paul has been associated in Christ with Philemon and asks Philemon in the letter to host him when he visits.

This letter was most likely written in the late 50s CE. Unlike a number of other letters in the traditional New Testament with Paul's name on them, there is no doubt that Paul wrote this one.

This letter provides one of the most direct addresses to a particular social issue in all of Paul's correspondence and as such is extremely helpful in understanding who Paul was and how he understood slavery. Paul's position in the matter of Onesimus is difficult to decipher. On the one hand, he is clearly sending Onesimus back to his owner, Philemon, and as such seems to be participating in the commerce of slavery. On the other hand, Paul requests Philemon to receive Onesimus "no longer as a slave," but as "a dearly beloved brother . . . of the Lord" (1:16). In other words, while observing the technicalities of the system of slavery, Paul seems to be suggesting some kind of change in Onesimus's status. This document's portrait of Paul participating to one extent or another in the Greco-Roman system of slavery remains a puzzle for many in the twenty-first century. On the one hand, it is a valuable picture of Paul in his first-century social environment. On the other hand, it shows him entwined in the oppression of slavery and seemingly in tension with a position he takes elsewhere that there is "neither slave nor free" in Christ (Galatians 3:28; 1 Corinthians 12:13).

Recommended Reading

F. F. Bruce, *The Epistles to the Colossians, to Philemon, and to the Ephesians*
Joseph A. Fitzmyer, *The Letter to Philemon*
N. R. Peterson, *Rediscovering Paul: Philemon and the Sociology of Paul's Narrative*

The Letter to Philemon

Introduction

1 ¹ From Paul, now a prisoner for Christ Jesus, and from Timothy, a fellow follower of the Lord. ² To our dear friend and fellow worker Philemon, to our sister Apphia, to our fellow soldier Archippus; and to the church that meets at Philemon's house; ³ may God, our Father, and the Lord Jesus Christ bless you and give you peace.

Request Regarding a Runaway Slave

I always mention you in my prayers and thank God for you, ⁵ because I hear of the love and the faith which you show, not only to the Lord Jesus, but also to all the holy ones; ⁶ and I pray that your participation in the faith may result in action, as you come to a fuller realization of everything that is good and Christlike in us. ⁷ I have indeed found great joy and encouragement in your love, knowing, as I do, how the hearts of the holy ones have been cheered, friend, by you.

⁸ And so, though my union with Christ enables me, with all confidence, to dictate the course that you should adopt, ⁹ yet the claims of love make me prefer to plead with you — yes, even me, Paul, though I am an ambassador for Christ Jesus and now a prisoner for him as well. ¹⁰ I plead with you for this child of mine, Onesimus, to whom, in my prison, I have become a father. ¹¹ Once he was of little service to you, but now he has become of great service, not only to you, but to me as well; ¹² and I am sending him back to you with this letter — though it is like tearing out my heart. ¹³ For my own sake I should like to keep him with me, so that while I am in prison for the good news, he might attend to my wants on your behalf. ¹⁴ But I do not wish to do anything without your consent, because I want your generosity to be voluntary and not, as it were, compulsory. ¹⁵ It may be that he was separated from you for an hour, for this reason, so that you might have him back forever, ¹⁶ no longer as a slave, but as something better — a dearly loved brother and follower of the Lord, especially dear to me, and how much more so to you, not only as a person, but in the Lord! ¹⁷ If, then, you count me your friend, receive him as you would me. ¹⁸ If he has caused you any loss, or owes you anything, charge it to me. ¹⁹ I, Paul, put my own hand to it — I will repay you myself. I say nothing about your owing me yourself. ²⁰ Yes, friend, let me gain something from you because of your union with the Lord. Cheer my heart in Christ.

²¹ Even as I write, I have such confidence in your compliance with my wishes that I am sure that you will do even more than I am asking. ²² Please also get a lodging ready for me, for I hope that I will be given back to you all in answer to your prayers.

Messages and Blessing

²³ Epaphras, who is my fellow prisoner for Christ Jesus, sends you his greeting; ²⁴ and Marcus, Aristarchus, Demas, and Luke, my fellow workers, send theirs.

²⁵ May the blessing of the Lord Jesus Christ rest on your souls.

LITERATURE IN THE TRADITION
OF PAUL, WITH A SET OF
INTRODUCTORY PRAYERS

Introduction to the Second Book of the Odes of Solomon

THE ODES OF SOLOMON are both one of the most significant discoveries of early Christian literature and perhaps one of the most ignored discoveries of early Christian literature in the past two hundred years. They have been known and published since the early twentieth century and are surely the largest collection of early Christian worship material ever found. The New Orleans Council, which selected the ten new books for this collection, eagerly chose these odes, both for their beautiful and evocative language and in order to make *A New New Testament* a strong witness to actual material from the worship of some early Christ movements.

These forty-one "songs" of early Christianity come most likely from different communities in the first hundred years of Christ movements. However, they also represent for the most part a certain kind of early Christianity in their beliefs, practices, and ways of framing the world. They look and sound very much like the psalms of the Hebrew scriptures, except that they regularly refer to life in what must be various Christ movements; that is, they are definitely "psalms" of a "Christian" character, although they never use the name "Jesus," and rarely even the title "Christ" or "Anointed One." On the other hand, they praise the Word, the Light, the Lord, and the Son of God in ways that make it certain that they belong to traditions about Jesus.

The "Christ" figure often speaks in these odes, making those early Christians who sang them take on the identity of "Christ" as they sang. This identification of the singers with the "Christ" is complemented by the content of the odes in which the "Christ" is a cosmic figure who makes humans one with God.

The title, "The Odes of Solomon," cannot, of course, refer to the author of this collection (since Solomon lived a thousand years before) but serves rather as an affirmation of a strong and intimate connection between this part of early "Christianity" and the traditions of Israel. That this document represents a collection of different odes from different communities makes "Solomon" something like the figure of "David" for the psalms of the Hebrew scriptures. It is difficult also to identify a date of composition for the odes. Most commentators think they are early, with the past thirty years of scholarship pointing more toward the first century than the second. The place of composition is also unclear. The closeness to the psalms of the Hebrew scriptures suggests a "Christ" movement with very strong ties to the traditions of Israel. The odes' language of Syriac points toward

Syria. It is not clear whether the odes were ever in Greek or Aramaic, but the fine poetic style indicates a real possibility that they may originally have been in Syriac.

A New New Testament breaks the odes into four distinct parts, distributed among different sections of the book. Since the odes as a collection do not represent one authorship, the New Orleans Council proposed that they could be broken up into distinct smaller sections. In keeping with the council's and my interest in making the reading of *A New New Testament* as worshipful as possible, I broke the larger document into these parts and used them to provide a spiritual and worshipful dimension to the other documents. The First Book of the Odes of Solomon contains Odes 1 and 3–12. The second book contain Odes 13–22; the third, Odes 23–32; and the fourth, Odes 33–42.*

In Ode 16:1–2 the odist/singer describes what it means to compose and sing these songs:

> Just as the labor of the farmer is the plowshare
> And the labor of the helmsman is the steering of the boat,
> So also is my labor the praise of the Lord through his psalms.
> My trade and my service are in his odes,
> Because his love has fed my heart
> And he has poured forth his fruits upon my lips.

Reflected in the beginning of this ode is the way singing in worship captures the heart of living as well as the seriousness of composing. This picture of living in and with the odes as a regular singer of them and as composer is appropriate for this Second Book of Odes, because with the exception of the first ode (13), the Second Book of Odes forms a unit of songs in the first person.

Nine of the ten odes here feature an "I" who recounts that which has been given to, that which has happened to, and that which is being offered by the "I." In each case, the ode pictures the "I" in direct relationship to a superior who lovingly empowers the speaker/singer in the ode. For instance, in Ode 21,

> And I was raised into the light,
> And I passed before his face.
> And I became near to him . . .

Or in 19:

> A cup of milk was offered to me,
> And I drank it in the sweetness of the joy of the Lord.

---

* This section of general information is found in each introduction to portions of the Odes of Solomon. The second section of each introduction is specific to the odes contained in it.

There is a fundamental ambiguity and double take in the use of the first person within these odes: it is very often unclear whether the "I" speaking is the odist/singer or Christ. Because the singer/composer is addressing a superior being, we do not know in many of these odes whether the pair addressing each other are a human and Christ, a human and God, or Christ and God. For instance, in 15:8–9, whether the speaker is Christ or a human speaking to Christ is not clear:

I put on incorruption through his name
And cast off corruption by his kindness.
Death has been ruined before his face,
And Sheol has been brought to nothing by his word.

In many ways it does not matter who is speaking to whom; the larger project celebrates a cascading sharing of identity between God, Christ, and the one singing the ode.

This larger project recommends itself to readers of the twenty-first century in that this kind of poetic merging of one's own identity with God and/or Christ can provide a larger space in which to claim collective belonging. From such an angle, twenty-first-century readers find their own identity in God and Christ in contrast to the modern quest for one's own true individual self independent of any other identity. The strongly individualist style of much of modern Christianity, which highlights a personal belief in Jesus and God, often has less focus on experiencing oneness with God and/or Christ as these early odes do.

Recommended Reading

James Charlesworth, *The Odes of Solomon: The Syriac Texts edited with Translation and Notes*
M. Franzmann, *The Odes of Solomon: An Analysis of the Poetical Structure and Form*
J. R. Harris and A. Mingana, *The Odes and Psalms of Solomon*

The Second Book of the Odes of Solomon

Ode 13

¹ Look! The Lord is our mirror,
  Open your eyes and see them in him.
² Learn the manner of your faces,
  And announce praises to his Spirit.
Wipe the dirt from your faces.
  Love the Lord's holiness and put it on.
³ Then you will not, at any time, be blemished in front of him.
Halleluiah.

Ode 14

¹ As the eyes of a child upon its father,
  So are my eyes, Lord, toward you at all times,
² Because my breasts and my pleasure are with you.
³ Lord, do not withdraw your mercies from me,
  And do not snatch away your sweetness from me.
⁴ My Lord, extend your Right Hand to me always,
  And be a caretaker for me until the end, according to your desire.
⁵ Let me be beautiful before you, because I have praised you;
  Because of your name, let me be freed from the Evil One.
⁷ And Lord, let your serenity remain with me,
  Along with the fruits of your love.
⁸ Teach me the songs of your truth,
  So that I may produce fruits in you.
And open the lyre of your holy Spirit to me,
  So that I may proclaim you in every note.
⁹ So according to the multitude of your mercies,

Grant such to me, and hurry to grant our requests.
¹⁰ For you are able to do all things that we need.
Halleluiah.

Ode 15

¹ Just as the sun is the joy for those who seek its day
  So also my joy is the Lord.
² Because he is my Sun,
  And his shining rays have raised me
  And his light has removed all darkness from my face.
³ I have obtained eyes through him,
  And I have seen his holy day.
⁴ I have possessed ears
  And heard his truth.
⁵ I have possessed the thought of knowledge
  And have reveled in his hand.
⁶ I abandoned the path of error,
  And I turned toward him, and received redemption from him without grudge.
⁷ He gave to me according to his gift,
  And made me according to his great beauty.
⁸ I put on incorruption through his name
  And cast off corruption by his kindness.
⁹ Death has been ruined before his face,
  And Sheol has been brought to nothing by his word.
¹⁰ Immortal life has ascended in the earth of the Lord.
  It has been made known to his faithful ones
  And it has been given without loss to all of them who relied upon him.
Halleluiah.

Ode 16

Just as the labor of the farmer is the plow-
share
> And the labor of the helmsman is the
steering of the boat,
> So also is my labor the praise of the
Lord through his psalms.

My trade and my service are in his odes,
> Because his love has fed my heart
> And he has poured forth his fruits
upon my lips.

Indeed, my love is the Lord;
> Because of this, I sing to him.

For I am fortified by his hymns,
> And I have faith in him.

I will open my mouth
> And his Spirit will relate through me:
> The glory and beauty of the Lord,

The work of his hands,
> And the plowing of his fingers

To the multitude of his mercies
> And the truth of his word.

For the word of the Lord examines whatever is invisible,
> And which reveals his* thought.

For the eye sees his works,
> And the ear hears his thought.

10 He is the one who expanded the earth,
> Confined the waters in the sea,

11 Extended the heaven,
> And fixed the stars,

12 Established creation and set her up
> And then rested from his labors.

13 He created them to run according to
their courses
> And to perform their deeds,
> And they do not know to cease or to
fail.

14 And the forces are subject to his word.

15 The store of light is the sun,
> And the store of darkness is the night.

16 Therefore he made the sun for the day,
so that there would be light
> And night brings darkness over the
face of the earth.

17 So their reception, one of the other,
> Fulfills the beauty of God.

18 There is nothing outside of the Lord,
> Because the Lord was before anything
else was.

19 Even the generations were already in
his word,
> And the thought of his heart.

20 Splendor and honor to his name.
Halleluiah.

Ode 17

1 Therefore I was crowned by my God,
> And my crown is alive.

2 I was justified by my Lord,
> But my redemption is imperishable.

3 I have been released from useless things,
> I am not culpable.

4 My torments were cut off by his hands,
> I received the face and form of a new
person,
> And I went out in it and I was saved.

5 And the thought of truth guided me,
> I went after her, and did not wander.

[Christ speaks]

6 All who saw me were astonished,
> I seemed to them like a stranger.

7 The one who knew and made me great
> Is the Most High, in all fullness.

8 He glorified me by his kindness
> And raised my understanding to the
height of Truth.

9 And from there he gave me the way of
his paths,†
> And I opened the doors which were
shut.

---

* These masculine pronouns could refer either to the Lord or the Lord's word. The ambiguity is
probably intentional.
† Literally, "walkings."

[10] I destroyed the bars of iron,
   Since my own irons had boiled and
melted away before me.
[11] Nothing appeared closed to me anymore,
   Because I was the opening of everything.
[12] I turned toward all of my captors, in order to dissolve them,
   So that I would not leave anyone bound
or binding.
[13] And I gave my knowledge without envy,
   And my petition in my love.
[14] And I sowed my fruits in hearts,
   Then transformed them through me.
[15] And they received my own gift and they
lived,
   They were gathered to me, and were
freed.
[16] Because they became my members
   And I was their head.
[17] Lord Anointed One, glory to you, our
head.
Halleluiah.

Ode 18

[1] My heart was lifted up and abounded
with the love of the Most High,
   So that I might praise him in the power
of my name.
[2] My members were strengthened
   So that they would not fall from his
power.
[3] Weakness departed from my body,
   And it stood according to the will of
the Lord,
   Because his generation is true.
[4] Lord, because of those who are lacking,
   Do not remove your word from me.
[5] Nor because of their actions
   Refuse your fullness from me.
[6] Do not let light be judged by darkness
   Nor let truth flee from falsehood.
[7] Let your Right Hand set our redemption
to victory
   And let her receive from each place,
and keep it

   On the side of everyone besieged by
sadness.
[8] You are my God; there is neither falsehood nor death in your mouth,
   Only the fullness of your desire.
[9] You do not know emptiness,
   Because it does not know you either.
[10] And you do not know error,
   Because it does not know you either.
[11] And ignorance appeared like dust,
   As foulness of the sea.
[12] And the empty ones considered it great.
   And they became like it in form and
became useless.
[13] But the ones who understood and reflected,
   They were not polluted by their
thoughts
[14] Because they were in the mind of the
Most High,
   And they scorned the ones walking in
error.
[15] Then they spoke truth
   From the breath which the Most High
blew into them.
[16] Glory and great beauty to his name.
Halleluiah.

Ode 19

[1] A cup of milk was offered to me,
   And I drank it in the sweetness of the
joy of the Lord.
[2] The cup is the Son,
   The Father is the one who has been
milked,
   And the holy Spirit milked him.
[3] Because his breasts had become full,
   And it was not desired that his milk
would be released without purpose.
[4] The holy Spirit opened her chest,
   And mixed the milk of the two breasts
of the Father.
[5] She gave the mixture to the generation
when they were ignorant,
   And the ones who received it, they are
in the fullness of the Right Hand.
[6] The womb of the virgin caught it,

And she conceived and gave birth
⁷ So the virgin became a Mother with much love.
⁸ And she brought forth and she bore a child, but without pain for her.

Because she was, it was not without purpose.
⁹ And she did not seek a midwife,

Because he sustained her.
¹⁰ She gave birth like a strong person with will,

She bore according to the manifestation,

And acquired through much majesty.
¹¹ She loved with redemption,

Guarded in kindness

And demonstrated in greatness.
Halleluiah.

Ode 20

¹ I am a minister of the Lord,

And I am consecrated to him.
² And to him I bring the offering of his thought.
³ Truly she* is not like the generation,

Nor is his thought like flesh,

Nor like those who are serving the flesh.
⁴ The offering† of the Lord is justice

And purity of heart and lips.
⁵ Offer your deepest parts without defect,

And do not let your affections confine compassion.

Do not let yourself oppress any other self.
⁶ Do not possess another [person] because every person is like yourself.

Nor strive to cheat your neighbor

Nor deprive her of that which covers her nakedness.
⁷ Rather, put on the kindness of the Lord without suspicion,

Come to his paradise,

And make for yourself a crown from his tree.
⁸ Place it upon your head, rejoice,

And recline upon his serenity.
⁹ And the Lord's splendor will go before you.

You will receive of his lushness and kindness.

And you will be anointed with truth in the glory of his holiness.
¹⁰ Praise and honor to his name.
Halleluiah.

Ode 21

¹ I lifted up my arms to the height,

To the compassion of the Lord.
² Because he cast off my chains from me,

And my helper lifted me up according to his compassion and his redemption.
³ Then I stripped off the darkness

And put on light.
⁴ And there were members for me,

Such that there was no pain in them,

Nor anxiety, nor suffering.
⁵ The thought of the Lord was greatly helpful for me,

And his indestructible fellowship.

And I was raised into the light,

And I passed before his face.

And I became near to him,

While proclaiming and thanking him.
⁶ The Lord caused my heart to flow like a spring,

And it sprang forth upon my lips.
⁷ Then the joy and praise of the Lord multiplied upon my face.
Halleluiah.

Ode 22

[Christ speaks]
¹ The one who brought me down from the height,

---

* The Lord's thought.
† Or "nearness."

And raised me up from the low places.
2 The one who gathers the things in the middle
    And bestows them to me.
3 The one who scatters my accusers,
    And my enemies.
4 The one who gave to me the authority over bonds,
    So that I could obliterate them.
5 The one who, by my hands, demolished the seven-headed sea serpent
    And set me upon its roots so that I could wipe out its offspring.
6 You were there, and you helped me.
    And in every place your name surrounded me.
7 Your Right Hand ravished the evil bile,
    And your hand leveled the way for those who trust in you.
8 And she* collected them from the graves,
    Separated them from the dead.
9 She took dead bones
    And laid flesh over them.
10 But they did not move,
    So she gave them action for life.
11 Your way and presence were without corruption.
    You have brought your generation to ruin,
    So that everything can be destroyed and renewed.
12 Your rock is the foundation for everything,
    And you have built your realm upon her.
    And she became a home of the holy ones.

---

* The conjugations for singular "you" and "she" are the same. This play between the meanings seems intentional.

An Introduction to the Letter to the Ephesians

L USH AND EXPANSIVE, this letter is written in a grand style. Its first two chapters are rich with celebrative proclamation of universal character and origins: God "chose us in Christ before the creation of the universe, so that we might be holy and blameless . . . [H]e made known to us his hidden purpose . . . in view of that divine order which was to mark the completion of the ages, when he should make everything, both in heaven and on earth, center in him" (1:4, 9, 10). The letter keynotes the way gentiles have become a new people because Christ has created "one new humanity" (2:15).

The most ancient manuscripts of this letter do not contain the address to the people "who are at Ephesus" found in the later manuscripts. This confirms that much of the content of the letter was addressed to a general — and not specifically located — audience. Similarly, even though there is much first-person material about Paul in the letter, it is questionable that the letter was written by him. This letter varies from authenticated Paul letters in the views expressed on the traditions of Israel and a commitment to write letters to specific communities rather than the larger "church." This letter can be dated to somewhere between 80 and 120 CE, after Paul died.

This letter's commitment to and eloquence about a great unity in Christ of all kinds of people is often framed both personally and poetically. For instance, in 2:19–22: "you are no longer strangers and aliens, but are fellow citizens with the holy ones and members of God's household. You have been built up on the foundation laid by the ambassadors and prophets, Christ Jesus himself being 'the cornerstone.' United in him, every part of the building, closely joined together, grows into a temple, consecrated by its union with the Lord. And, through union in him, you also are being built up together, to be a place where God lives through the spirit" (2:19–22).

The Legend of Paul Speaks

Contrary to our present-day focus on personal notoriety and plagiarism, the ancient Mediterranean cultures did not necessarily call attention to famous contemporary authors. Rather, a very powerful author would often choose to place his own writing in the mouth of some important figure who had gone before him. This was not seen as either trickery or dishonesty; rather, it was an honor to take someone else's name, and, as many have suggested, this may have been the way

Paul received his own name.* So, the possibility that the Paul of "Ephesians" is not the historical Paul, but perhaps a follower from the ensuing generations, is more typical of the ancient world than sleight of hand.

At any rate, the "Paul" of this letter is more vocal about "himself" than in any other letter. He emphasizes that he is writing from prison, and that he is "the prisoner of Jesus, the Anointed One, for the sake of you gentiles" (3:1). With flair, he then goes on to console them: "I beg you not to be disheartened at the sufferings that I am undergoing for your sakes; for they are your glory" (3:13). Ephesians also includes a relatively long prayer by Paul for the people to whom he is writing (3:15–21), a rarity for a Pauline letter. This prayer does share some themes with the Prayer of the Apostle Paul.

The Household Codes

Like some other letters of the late first and second centuries, both inside and outside this New Testament, Ephesians promotes standards of household order that have their roots in larger Greco-Roman society. These are lists of rules that are not found in the authentic letters of Paul, and that focus on a chain of authority proceeding from the highest male authorities down to the slave.

Ephesians excludes the command to obey the emperor and other government authorities because they are appointed by God, which several other early Christian and many Greco-Roman letters include. But Ephesians 5:22–6:9 also includes: "Wives should submit to their husbands as submitting to the Lord. . . . Husbands, love your wives. . . . Children, obey your parents, as children of the Lord; for that is right. . . . fathers, do not irritate your children, but bring them up with discipline and instruction from the Lord. . . . Slaves, obey your earthly masters . . ."

There is some irony, then, in Ephesians celebrating a new unity of all people created in Christ even as its household codes reinforce social order and make distinctions among men, women, children, and slaves.

Ephesians and A New New Testament

Ephesians' exhilaration about a new belonging to a bigger world in Christ corresponds perhaps most closely to the Gospel of Truth, one of the new documents in A New New Testament. The sensuous and ecstatic vocabulary of these two works breaks out of dogmatic Christian categories and offers some new, less belief-oriented ways of belonging for twenty-first-century readers.

---

* Among others, the fourth- and fifth-century theologian Jerome suggested that Paul was named for Sergius Paulus, possibly Paul's first gentile convert.

Recommended Reading

Lynn H. Cohick, *Ephesians*
Margaret MacDonald, *Colossians and Ephesians*
Pheme Perkins, *Ephesians*

The Letter to the Ephesians

Introduction

1 ¹ To those who are holy, from Paul, an ambassador of Christ Jesus, by the will of God. ² Grace and peace to you from God, our Father, and the Lord Jesus Christ.

³ Blessed is the God and Father of Jesus Christ, our Lord, who has blessed us on high with every spiritual blessing, in the Anointed One. ⁴ For God chose us in Christ before the creation of the universe, so that we might be holy and blameless in his sight, living in the spirit of love. ⁵ From the first God destined us, in his goodwill toward us, to be adopted as sons and daughters through Jesus Christ, ⁶ and so to praise the glory and grace which he gave us in the one he loves; ⁷ for in him, and through the shedding of his blood, we have found release in the pardon of our sinfulness. ⁸ All this accords with the grace which God lavished on us, accompanied by countless gifts of wisdom and discernment, ⁹ when he made known to us his hidden purpose. And it also accords with the goodwill which God purposed to exhibit in the Anointed One, ¹⁰ in view of that divine order which was to mark the completion of the ages, when he should make everything, both in heaven and on earth, center in him. ¹¹ For by our union with him we became God's heritage, having from the first been destined for this in the intention of him who, in all that happens, is carrying out his own fixed purpose; ¹² that we should enhance his glory — we who have been the first to rest our hopes on the Christ. ¹³ And you, too, being in him, after you had heard the message of the truth, the good news of your salvation — you trusted in him and were sealed as his by the holy Spirit, which he had promised. ¹⁴ And the Spirit is a pledge of our future heritage, foreshadowing the full redemption of God's own people — to enhance his glory.

The Power of God Displayed in Christ

¹⁵ And therefore I, ever since I heard of the faith in the Lord Jesus which prevails among you, and of your love in all Christ's people, ¹⁶ have never omitted giving thanks to God on your behalf, whenever I make mention of you in my prayers. ¹⁷ My prayer is that the God of Jesus Christ our Lord, the glorious Father, may inspire you with wisdom and true insight through a fuller knowledge of himself; ¹⁸ that your minds may be so enlightened that you may realize the hope given by God's call, the wealth of the glory of his heritage among his people, ¹⁹ and the extraordinary greatness of the power which he is able to exercise in dealing with us who trust in him. ²⁰ The same mighty power was exerted on the Anointed One, when he raised the Anointed One from the dead and "caused him to sit at his right hand" on high, exalting him above every ruling force, authority, or sovereignty, ²¹ and above every name that can be named, whether in the present age, or in the age to come. ²² And God placed all things under Christ's feet, and made him, as he is above everything, the head of the church, which is his body, the fullness of him, who is filled all in all.

2 ¹ You yourselves were once dead because of your offenses and sinfulness. ² For at one time you lived in sinfulness, following the ways of the world, in subjection to the ruler of the powers of the air — the spirit who is still at work among the disobedient. [3] And it was among them that we all once lived our lives, indulging the cravings of the flesh, and carrying out the desires prompted by that flesh and by our own thoughts. The flesh exposed us to the divine wrath, like the rest of humanity. [4] Yet God, in his abundant compassion, and because of the great love with which he loved us, [5] even though we were "dead" because of our sinfulness, gave life to us in giving life to the Christ. (By God's grace you have been saved.) [6] And, through our union with Christ Jesus, God raised us with him, and caused us to sit with him in heavenly places, [7] in order that by his grace to us in Christ Jesus, he might display in the generations to come the boundless wealth of his grace. [8] For it is by God's grace that you have been saved, through your faith. It is not due to yourselves; the gift is God's. [9] It is not due to anything you have done, so that no one can boast. [10] For we are God's work of art, created by our union with Christ Jesus, for the good works which God had prearranged to make up our lives.

[11] Remember, therefore, that you were once gentiles yourselves, as your bodies showed; you were called the uncircumcised by those who were called the circumcised by reason of a physical operation! [12] Remember that you were at that time far from Christ; you were shut out from the citizenship of Israel; you were strangers to the covenants founded on the promise; you were in the world without hope and without God. [13] But now, through your union with Christ Jesus, you who once were far off have, by the shedding of the blood of the Anointed One, been brought near. [14] He it is who is our peace. He made the two divisions of humanity one, broke down the barrier that separated them, [15] and in his own flesh put an end to the cause of enmity between them — the Law with its injunctions and ordinances — in order to create, through union with himself, one new humanity and so make peace. [16] And when, on the cross, he had destroyed the hostility, he by means of his cross reconciled them both to God, united in one body. [17] He came with the good news of peace for you who were far off, and of peace for those who were near; [18] for it is through him that we both, united in the one Spirit, are now able to approach the Father. [19] It follows, then, that you are no longer strangers and aliens, but are fellow citizens with the holy ones and members of God's household. [20] You have been built up on the foundation laid by the ambassadors and prophets, Christ Jesus himself being "the cornerstone." [21] United in him, every part of the building, closely joined together, grows into a temple, consecrated by its union with the Lord. [22] And, through union in him, you also are being built up together, to be a place where God lives through the spirit.

The Ambassador's Divine Commission to the Gentiles

3 [1] For this reason I, Paul, the prisoner of Jesus, the Anointed One, for the sake of you gentiles — [2] for you have heard, I suppose, of the responsible charge with which God entrusted me for your benefit, [3] and also that it was by direct revelation that the hidden purpose of God was made known to me, as I have already briefly told you. [4] And, by reading what I have written, you will be able to judge how far I understand this hidden purpose of God in Christ. [5] In former generations it was not made known to humanity, as fully as it has now been revealed by the Spirit to the ambassadors and prophets — [6] that in Christ Jesus and through the good news, the gentiles

are co-heirs with us and members of one body, and that they share with us in God's promise. [7] Of this good news I became a servant, in virtue of the charge with which God entrusted me in the exercise of his power — [8] yes, to me, who am less than the least of all God's holy people, was this charge entrusted! — to tell the gentiles the good news of the boundless wealth to be found in the Anointed One, [9] and to make clear to all creation what is God's way of working out that hidden purpose which from the first has been concealed in God; [10] so that now to the authorities and to all the powers on high should be made known, through the church, the all-embracing wisdom of God, [11] in accordance with that purpose which runs through all the generations and which he has now accomplished in Jesus, the Anointed One, our Lord. [12] And in union with him, and through our trust in him, we find courage to approach God with confidence. [13] Therefore, I beg you not to be disheartened at the sufferings that I am undergoing for your sakes; for they are your glory. [14] For this reason, then, I kneel before the Father — [15] from whom all fatherhood in heaven and on earth derives its name — [16] and pray that in proportion to the wealth of his glory, he will strengthen you with his power by breathing his Spirit into your inmost self, [17] so that the Christ, through your faith, may make his home within your hearts in love; and I pray that you, now firmly rooted and established, may, with all God's holy people, [18] have the power to comprehend in all its width and length and height and depth, [19] and to understand — though it surpasses all understanding — the love of the Christ; and so be filled to the full with God himself.

[20] To him who, through his power which is at work within us, is able to do far more than anything that we can ask or conceive — [21] to him be all glory through the church and through Christ Jesus, for all generations, age after age. Amen.

The Gospel and Daily Life

4 [1] I beg you, then — I who am a prisoner in the Lord — to live lives worthy of the call that you have received; [2] always humble and gentle, patient, lovingly bearing one another, [3] and striving to maintain in the bond of peace the unity given by the Spirit. [4] There is but one body and one spirit, just as there was but one hope set before you when you received your call. [5] There is but one Lord, one faith, one baptism. [6] There is but one God and Father of all — the God who is over all, pervades all, and is in all. [7] Every one of us, however, has been entrusted with some charge, each in accordance with the extent of the gift of the Anointed One. [8] That is why it is said:

> "When he went up on high, he led his
>   captives into captivity. And gave gifts
>   to humanity."

[9] Now surely this "going up" must imply that he had already gone down into the world beneath. [10] The one who went down is the same as he who went up — up beyond the highest heaven, so that he might fill all things with his presence. [11] And he it is who gave to the church ambassadors, prophets, bringers of good news, pastors, and teachers, [12] to fit his people for the work of service, for the building up of the body of the Christ. [13] And this will continue, until we all attain to that unity which is given by faith and by a fuller knowledge of the Child of God; until we reach maturity — the full standard of the perfection of the Anointed One. [14] Then we will no longer be like infants, tossed backward and forward, blown about by every breath of human teaching and by people's trickery and craftiness; [15] but holding the truth in a spirit of love, we will grow into complete

union with him who is our head — Christ himself. [16] For from him the whole body, closely joined and knit together by the contact of every part with the source of its life, derives its power to grow, in proportion to the vigor of each individual part; and so is being built up in a spirit of love.

[17] This, then, as one in the Lord, I implore: Do not continue to live such purposeless lives as the gentiles live, [18] with their powers of discernment darkened, cut off from the life of God, owing to the ignorance that prevails among them and to the hardness of their hearts. [19] Lost to all sense of shame, they have abandoned themselves to licentiousness, in order to practice every kind of impurity without restraint. [20] But far different is the lesson you learned from the Anointed One — if, that is, you really listened to him, [21] and through union with him were taught the truth, as it is to be found in Jesus. [22] For you learned with regard to your former way of living that you must cast off your old self, which, yielding to deluding passions, grows corrupt; [23] that the spirit of your minds must be constantly renewed; [24] and that you must clothe yourselves in that new person which was created to resemble God, with the righteousness and holiness springing from the truth.

[25] Since, therefore, you have cast off what is false, you must every one of you speak the truth to your neighbors. For we are united to one another like the parts of a body. [26] Be angry, yet do not sin. Do not let the sun go down on your anger; [27] and give no opportunity to the devil. [28] Let the person who steals steal no longer, but rather let him toil with his hands at honest work, so that he may have something to share with anyone in need. [29] Never let any foul word pass your lips, but only such good words as the occasion demands, so that they may be a help to those who hear them. [30] And do not grieve God's holy Spirit; for it was through that Spirit that God sealed you as his, against the day of redemption. [31] Let all bitterness, passion, anger, brawling, and abusive language be banished from among you, as well as all malice. [32] Be kind to one another, tenderhearted, ready to forgive one another, just as God, in Christ, forgave you.

5 [1] Therefore imitate God, as his dear children, [2] and live a life of love, following the example of the Christ, who loved you and gave himself for you as an offering and a sacrifice to God, that should be fragrant and acceptable.

[3] As for sexual immorality and every kind of impurity, or greed, do not let them even be mentioned among you, as befits God's holy people, [4] nor shameful conduct, nor foolish talk or jesting, for they are wholly out of place among you; but rather thanksgiving. [5] For of this you may be sure — that no one who is unchaste or impure or greedy of gain (for to be greedy of gain is idolatry) can inherit the realm of God.

[6] Do not let anyone deceive you with specious arguments. Those are the sins that bring down the wrath of God on the disobedient. [7] Therefore, have nothing to do with such people. [8] For, although you were once in darkness, now, by your union with the Lord, you are in the light. Live as "children of light" — [9] for the outcome of life in the light may be seen in every form of goodness, righteousness, and sincerity — [10] always trying to find out what is pleasing to the Lord. [11] Take no part in deeds of darkness, from which no good can come; on the contrary, expose them. [12] It is degrading even to speak of the things continually done by them in secret. [13] All such actions, when exposed, have their true character made manifest by the light. [14] For everything that has its true character made manifest is clear as light. And that is why it is said:

"Sleeper, awake!
Arise from the dead,
And the Christ will give you light!"

[15] Take great care, then, how you live —
not unwisely but wisely, [16] making the
most of every opportunity; for these
are evil days. [17] Therefore do not grow
thoughtless, but try to understand what
the Lord's will is. [18] Do not drink wine
to excess, for that leads to profligacy; but
seek to be filled with the spirit of God, and
speak to one another in psalms and hymns
and sacred songs. [19] Sing and make music
in your hearts to the Lord. [20] Always give
thanks for everything to our God and Father, in the name of our Lord Jesus Christ;
[21] and submit to one another because you
honor and respect him.

[22] Wives should submit to their husbands as submitting to the Lord. [23] For a
man is the head of his wife, as the Christ
is the head of the church — being indeed
himself the Savior of his body. [24] But as
the church submits to the Christ, so also
should wives submit to their husbands in
everything. [25] Husbands, love your wives,
just as the Christ loved the church, and
gave himself for her, [26] to make her holy,
after purifying her by the washing with
water, according to his promise; [27] so that
he might himself bring the church, in all
her beauty, into his own presence, with no
spot or wrinkle or blemish of any kind,
but that she might be holy and faultless.
[28] That is how husbands ought to love
their wives — as if they were their own
bodies. A man who loves his wife is really
loving himself; [29] for no one ever yet hated
his own body. But everyone feeds his body
and cares for it, just as the Christ for the
church; [30] for we are members of his body.

[31] "For this cause a man will leave his
father and mother, and be united to his
wife; and the man and his wife will become one."

[32] In this there is a profound truth — I
am speaking of the Anointed One and his
church. [33] However, for you individually,
let each love his wife as if she were himself;
and the wife be careful to respect her husband.

6 [1] Children, obey your parents, as children of the Lord; for that is right. [2] "Honor
your father and mother" — this is the first
commandment with a promise — [3] "so that
you may prosper and have a long life on
earth." [4] And fathers, do not irritate your
children, but bring them up with discipline and instruction from the Lord.

[5] Slaves, obey your earthly masters, with
anxious care, giving them ungrudging service, as if obeying the Anointed One; [6] not
only when their eyes are on you, as if you
had merely to please people, but as slaves
of Christ, who are trying to carry out the
will of God. [7] Give your service heartily
and cheerfully, as working for the Master and not for people; [8] for you know that
everyone will be rewarded by the Master
for any honest work that one has done,
whether slave or free. [9] And masters, treat
your slaves in the same spirit. Give up
threatening them; for you know that he
is both their Master and yours in heaven,
and that before him there is no distinction
of rank.

[10] For the future, find strength in your
union with the Lord, and in the power
which comes from his might. [11] Put on the
full armor of God, so that you may be able
to stand your ground against the strata-
gems of the devil. [12] For ours is no struggle against enemies of flesh and blood,
but against all the various powers of evil
that hold sway in the darkness around
us, against the spirits of wickedness on
high. [13] Therefore, take up the full armor
of God, so that when the evil day comes,
you may be able to withstand the attack,
and, having fought to the end, still to stand
your ground. [14] Stand your ground, then,
"with truth for your belt," and "with right-

eousness for your breastplate," [15] and with the readiness to serve the good news of peace as shoes for your feet. [16] At every onslaught take up faith for your shield; for with it you will be able to extinguish all the flaming darts of the evil one. [17] And receive "the helmet of salvation," and "the sword of the spirit" — which is the message of God — always with prayer and supplication. [18] Pray in spirit at all times. Be intent on this, with unwearying perseverance and supplication for all God's holy people — [19] and on my behalf also, so that when I begin to speak, words may be given me, so that I may fearlessly make known the inmost truth of the good news, [20] on behalf of which I am an ambassador — in chains! Pray that in telling it, I may speak fearlessly as I ought.

Conclusion

[21] To enable you, as well as others, to know all that concerns me and what I am doing, Tychicus, our dear friend and faithful helper in the Master's cause, will tell you everything. [22] I am sending him to you on purpose that you may learn all about us, and that he may cheer your hearts.

[23] May God, the Father, and the Lord Jesus Christ give every follower peace, and love linked with faith. [24] May God's blessing be with all who love our Lord Jesus Christ with an undying love.

An Introduction to the Acts of Paul and Thecla

THIS DOCUMENT DRAMATIZES the saga of Thecla, telling of a young woman's call to an independent life of teaching and healing in the Christ movement. The figure of Paul appears around the edges of the story, primarily as a heroic inspiration for Thecla as she faces overwhelming opposition to her choices. Thecla overcomes the beasts of the arena, various suitors who desire to have her under their control, and city governments.

The authorship of the Acts of Paul and Thecla is unclear, not simply because of the general difficulties of determining actual authors of ancient documents, but also because the document itself gives no hints. Most estimates of the date of this Greek composition are mid-second century, although some scholars place it as early as 70 CE. It is possible that the piece was written in Asia Minor (current-day Turkey) where the saga takes place.

Consisting of nine women and ten men, the New Orleans Council found itself drawn to a number of documents from outside the traditional New Testament that showed women in leadership in the first generations of the Christ movements. Among them were the Gospel of Mary, the Gospel of Philip, The Thunder: Perfect Mind, the Acts of Paul and Thecla, and the Diary of Perpetua, all of which made it through the early rounds of selection. In the final meeting in February 2012, much discussion was pointed toward the Acts of Paul and Thecla and the Diary of Perpetua.

As discussion and debate ensued, it seemed clear that the Gospel of Mary and The Thunder: Perfect Mind would be chosen, and that either the Acts of Paul and Thecla or the Diary of Perpetua would be included as an additional work expressing female authority at the beginning of Christianity. Both of them feature stories of women in leadership threatened with death because of their courage and public presence. Although the Diary of Perpetua may very well also be the first piece composed by a woman in leadership, in the end the council preferred the Acts of Paul and Thecla for two reasons: Paul and Thecla demonstrates more clearly the success of Thecla in standing up to government and cultural authorities, overcoming the negligence of her ally and mentor Paul, and asserting her right to be an independent teacher and healer; and the Diary of Perpetua was clearly composed in the third century, and there were doubts as to whether the council should choose documents not composed in the first or second century.

Unlike many works in *A New New Testament*, the Acts of Paul and Thecla has high drama, clear and consistent characters, and eloquent thematic focus. At each turn, the story moves toward the issue of whether one or another person can prevent Thecla from achieving her chosen goal of following Paul's model of healing and teaching. The story begins after Thecla has already determined her future. The drama lurches from one confrontation with critics of a young woman asserting such independence to another. At each turn, she reaffirms her will and strength to heal and teach independently in the name of Christ, including a scene (34:3) in which she baptizes herself (as Paul seems to be dawdling about baptizing her). Throughout the story, Paul remains the inspiration and perhaps mentor for Thecla, but curiously enough when she is in danger, Paul is not around or is unwilling to advocate for her, and Thecla must draw on her own courage and strength to meet the challenge.

As early as the late second century, the early Christian leader Tertullian condemned this document because of its implications that women were able to lead communities and baptize. This book continued to be a focal point of such protest in the ensuing centuries and actually became very popular in the third through fifth centuries, and indeed the criticism did not diminish its status and popularity in the churches throughout the centuries.

Given its extreme popularity during the time that the traditional New Testament was slowly coming into being, one might ask why the Acts of Paul and Thecla did not become a part of the traditional New Testament. That process was uneven and unclear, without either any final authority or any single decisive moment, but it seems likely that the opposition of some fourth- to sixth-century church authorities to women's leadership may have played a role.

The inclusion of the Acts of Paul and Thecla, joining The Thunder: Perfect Mind and the Gospel of Mary in *A New New Testament,* highlights how important the spiritual and political struggle for mutuality between women and men is for the twenty-first century. In many ways, we hope the presence of these three works changes the commonly held picture of gender and power in the first centuries of Christianity. Given these documents, it is much more difficult to see the New Testament as completely patriarchal. Perhaps even more pivotal, these three books provide much more support for a tradition of gender mutuality and allow twenty-first-century women to see themselves as powerful spiritual leaders. It is also true that four other books added to *A New New Testament* also give new evidence of women's leadership in the first two centuries of the Christ movements: the Odes of Solomon, the Prayer of Thanksgiving, the Secret Revelation of John, and the Gospel of Truth offer aspects of inclusiveness of women.

Still, it is important to note that there is strong advocacy for women's leadership in the traditional New Testament as well. The gospels of Mark, Luke, and John have been recognized as underlining the importance of women's leadership. The image of "neither male nor female in Christ" in the writings of Paul cannot be ignored. And the acclamation of Tabitha as a disciple in the Acts of the Apostles blatantly contradicts claims of churches today that women do not deserve leadership roles.

Recommended Reading

Melissa Aubin, "Reversing Romance: The Acts of Thecla and the Ancient Novel," in *Ancient Fiction and Early Christian Narrative,* edited by Ronald F. Hock, J. Bradley Chance, and Judith Perkins

Jeremy W. Barrier, *The Acts of Paul and Thecla*

Virginia Burrus, *Chastity as Autonomy: Women in the Stories of the Apocryphal Acts*

The Acts of Paul and Thecla

1 [1] As Paul went up from Iconium, after his flight from Antioch, his fellow travelers were Demas and Hermogenes, a bronze worker. They were full of hypocrisy and flattered Paul as if they loved him. [2] But Paul, gazing only at Christ's kindness, did no evil toward them but loved them so much that he made all of the words of the Lord, the teachings and explanations of the good news, the birth and resurrection of the Beloved sweet for them. He described to them, word for word, the great things of Christ and how they had been revealed to him.

2 [1] And a man named Onesiphorus, hearing Paul had come to Iconium, went out with his children, Simmias and Zeno, and his wife Lectra, to meet Paul so that he might welcome him. Titus had described Paul's appearance to him for he had not seen him in the flesh, but only in spirit.

3 [1] And he went down the royal road to Lystra and stood waiting for him, looking at all those walking by, according to Titus's description. [2] And he saw Paul coming—a man small in stature, with a bald head and crooked legs, healthy, with knitted eyebrows, a slightly long nose, and full of kindness—for at times he appeared as a human being and at others he had the face of an angel.

4 [1] And when Paul saw Onesiphorus, he smiled and Onesiphorus said, "Welcome, servant of the blessed God!" And Paul replied, "Grace to you and your household!" [2] But Demas and Hermogenes were jealous and went further into their hypocrisy so that Demos said, "Are we not of the Blessed, too, that you all have not welcomed us just as him?" [3] And Onesiphorus said, "I do not see in you the fruits of justice, but if you are anything, come to my house as well and rest."

5 [1] And when Paul entered into Onesiphorus's house, there was great joy and kneeling and breaking of bread, and the word of God concerning self-control and resurrection. As Paul said, "Blessed are the clear of heart, for they will see God. [2] Blessed are those who observe purity in flesh, for they will become a temple of God. [3] Blessed are the self-possessed, for God will speak to them. [4] Blessed are those who set themselves apart from this world, for they will please God. [5] Blessed are those who have wives as if they do not, for they will be heirs of God. [6] Blessed are those in awe of God, for they will become messengers of God.

6 [1] "Blessed are the ones who tremble at God's words, for they will be called. [2] Blessed are the ones who receive the wisdom of Jesus Christ, for they will be called children of the Highest. [3] Blessed are the ones who keep their baptism, for they will rest with the Father and the Son. [4] Blessed are those on the journey to uniting with Jesus Christ, for they will be in the light. [5] Blessed are the ones who have departed the form of the world through God's love, for they will judge angels and, at the right hand of the Father, they will be praised. [6] Blessed are the compassionate, for they will receive compassion and will not see the day of grievous judgment. [7] Blessed are the bodies of maidens, for they will have favor with God and will not lose the reward for their holiness; for the Father's word will be a work of salvation for them until the day of his Child, and they will have rest forever."

7 [1] And Paul said these things in the middle of the association in Onesiphorus's house. A certain maiden, Thecla — whose mother was Theocleia and was promised in marriage to a man, Thamyris — sat at a window close to the house and listened night and day to the message about holiness spoken by Paul. She did not turn away from the window, but moved forward in faith, rejoicing exceedingly. [2] And yet having seen many women and maidens coming to Paul, she also desired for herself to be deemed worthy, to stand face-to-face with Paul and hear the word of Christ. For she had not yet seen Paul in person, but only heard his word.

8 [1] And since she did not move away from the window, her mother sent for Thamyris, and he came joyfully as if having already received her in marriage. [2] So Thamyris said to Theocleia, "Where is my Thecla?" [3] And Theocleia said, "I have a strange story to tell you. [4] Indeed, for three days and nights Thecla has not risen from the window — either to eat or drink — but gazes as if looking upon some enjoyable sight. In this way she clings to a strange man who teaches deceptive and cunning words, so that I wonder how a maiden of such respect can be so painfully troubled.

9 [1] "Thamyris, this person is threatening the city of the Iconians, and your Thecla as well — for all the women and youth go to him and are taught by him. He says that it is necessary to fear God alone and live purely. [2] And my daughter, like a spider in the window, also is bound to his words, held sway by new desire and fearful emotions. [3] For the maiden fixates on the things he says and is captivated. [4] But go to her and speak to her for she is betrothed to you."

10 [1] And Thamyris went to her, at once loving her and also fearing her passion. He said, "Thecla, my betrothed, why do you sit like this? [2] What is the emotion that binds you in passion? [3] Turn toward your Thamyris and be ashamed." [4] And her mother also said the same things to her, "Child, why do you look down and sit like this, answering nothing but acting like a mad person?" [5] And they cried desperately — Thamyris for the loss of his wife, Theocleia for the loss of her child, and the maidservants for the loss of their mistress. So there was great confusion and mourning in the house. [6] And while these things were happening, Thecla did not turn back, but was fixed to the word of Paul.

11 [1] And Thamyris leaped up and went out into the street, and closely watched those going in to Paul, and those coming out. [2] And he saw two men quarreling with each other and said to them, "Men, who are you? Tell me. And who is this one who is inside with you, misleading the lives of young men and deceiving young women that they should not marry, but remain so, as they are? I promise to give you both much money if you will tell me about him, for I am a most important man of the city."

12 [1] And Demas and Hermogenes said to him, "Who this one is, we do not know, but he deprives young men of wives and young women of husbands, saying, "There is no resurrection for you unless you remain holy and do not sully the flesh, but keep it holy."

13 [1] And Thamyris said to them, "Come, men, into my house and rest with me."

[2] And they departed for an extravagant banquet with much wine and great wealth and a magnificent table. And Thamyris gave them drink, because he loved Thecla and wanted to have her for his wife. [3] And at the banquet Thamyris said, "Men, tell me what his teaching is so that I may know it, for I have more than a little anguish about Thecla because she loves the stranger, and I am deprived of my marriage."

14 [1] And Demas and Hermogenes said, "Bring him to the governor Castellius on the charge of seducing the masses to the new teaching of the Christians. Then he will kill him, and you will have your wife Thecla. [2] And he will teach you that the resurrection, which he says is coming, has already taken place in the children which we have, and that we have risen when we learned to know the true God."

15 [1] But when Thamyris heard these things from them, he was filled with jealousy and wrath. Rising early in the morning, he went to the house of Onesiphorus with the rulers, public officials, and a large crowd with clubs, saying to Paul, "You have corrupted the city of the Iconians and also my betrothed so that she will not want me. Let us go to the governor Castellius." [2] And the whole crowd said, "Arrest the magician! For he has corrupted all of our wives and has seduced the masses!"

16 [1] And Thamyris stood before the court crying out loudly and said, "Proconsul, this person — we do not know where he is from — who does not allow maidens to marry, let him say to you on what account he teaches these things." [2] But Demas and Hermogenes said to Thamyris, "Say he is a Christian and then you will destroy him." [3] And the governor held to his purpose and he called Paul, saying to him, "Who are you and what do you teach? For

it is no small thing they have accused you of."

17 [1] And Paul lifted up his voice, saying, "If I, today, am interrogated for what I teach, then listen, Proconsul. [2] The living God, the God of retribution, the jealous God, the self-sufficient God, desiring the salvation of humanity, has sent me so that I might reclaim them from corruption and impurity, all pleasure and death, that they might no longer sin. For this reason God sent his own child whom I bring good news and teach about. In that one, humans have hope, who alone had compassion for a wandering world so that humanity might no longer be under judgment, but have trust and fear of God, and knowledge of dignity and a love of truth. [3] If, then, I teach the things revealed to me by God, what wrong have I done, Proconsul?" [4] But the governor, hearing these things, ordered Paul to be bound, and he was carried off to prison until the governor might have the leisure for a more careful hearing of him.

18 [1] But in the night Thecla took off her bracelets and gave them to the gatekeeper, and the door was opened for her. She went into the prison and gave the jailer a silver mirror. She went in to Paul and sat at his feet, and she heard the great things of God. [2] And Paul feared nothing having rights in the freedom of God, and Thecla strengthened her trust, kissing his chains.

19 [1] But when Thecla was sought out by her own people and Thamyris, they pursued her through the streets as one who is lost. And one of the fellow slaves of the gatekeeper disclosed that she had left in the night. [2] And they questioned the gatekeeper, and he said to them, "She has gone to the stranger in the prison." [3] And they went as he told them and found her bound in affection. They went out from that place and drew together a crowd, and they declared to the governor what had happened.

20 ¹ And Paul was ordered to be brought to the court. Thecla wallowed in the place where Paul taught as he sat in the prison. ² But the governor ordered that she also be brought to the court. And she went off exulting with joy. ³ When Paul had been brought, the crowd cried out even louder: "He is a magician! Take him away!" ⁴ But the governor heard Paul contentedly as he spoke about the divine works of Christ. And when the governor had considered the counsel he was given, he called Thecla, saying, "Why do you not marry Thamyris according to the law of the Iconians?" ⁵ But she stood looking intently at Paul, and when she did not answer, Theocleia, her mother, cried out, saying, "Burn the lawless one! Burn the one who refuses to be a bride in the middle of the theater so that all the women taught by this man will be afraid!"

21 ¹ And the governor was greatly moved and had Paul whipped and thrown out of the city; but Thecla he condemned to be burned. ² And immediately the governor rose and went off to the theater, and the whole crowd went to the violent spectacle. ³ But Thecla, like a lamb in the wilderness looking around for the shepherd, sought for Paul. ⁴ And when she looked into the face of the crowd, she saw the Lord sitting there in Paul's form and said, "As if I were not able to endure, Paul has come to see me." And she looked intently at him; but he departed into heaven.

22 ¹ And the young men and young women brought firewood and straw so that Thecla might be burned. ² And as she came naked, the governor wept and marveled at the power in her. ³ And the executioners laid out the firewood and ordered her to climb upon the pyre. And when she made the sign of the cross, she climbed upon the firewood. They lit it ⁴ and a great fire blazed, but the fire did not touch her. For God, having compassion, caused a sound under the earth, and a cloud, filled with rain and hail, darkened the sky from above, and the vessel poured forth all that was in it. Many were in danger and died, and the fire was extinguished. And Thecla was saved.

23 ¹ And Paul was fasting with Onesiphorus and his wife and children in an open tomb as they went on the road from Iconium to Daphne. ² And when many days had passed, as they were fasting, the children said to Paul, "We are hungry." ³ And they had nothing with which to buy bread, for Onesiphorus had left behind the things of the world and followed Paul with his entire household. ⁴ And Paul took off his robe and said, "Go, child, and buy more bread and bring it back." ⁵ But when the child was buying bread, he saw his neighbor Thecla and was astounded. And he said, "Thecla, where are you going?" ⁶ And she said, "I am looking for Paul; I was saved from the fire." ⁷ And the child said, "Come, I will lead you to him for he is mourning for you and has been praying and fasting for six days already."

24 ¹ And when she was brought to the tomb, Paul was kneeling and prayed, saying, "Father of Christ, do not let the fire touch Thecla, but stand by her because she is yours." ² But she rose behind him and cried out, "Father who made heaven and earth, Father of your beloved Child, Jesus Christ, I praise you because you quickly granted what I asked for, and you heard me."

25 ¹ And there was much love in the tomb, Paul rejoicing, and Onesiphorus and all of them. ² And they had five loaves and vegetables and water and salt, and rejoiced at the divine works of Christ. ³ And Thecla said to Paul, "I will cut my hair short and follow you wherever you go." [4] But he said, "It is a shameful time and you are fair. May no other trial come upon you worse than the first, and this time you are not able stand firm but are cowardly." [5] And Thecla said, "Only give me the seal of Christ and no trial will touch me." [6] And Paul said to Thecla, "Have patience, and you will receive the water."

26 [1] And Paul sent Onesiphorus and his entire household away to Iconium and, taking Thecla, went to Antioch. [2] But immediately, as they entered, the president of the provincial council of Syria, a certain man named Alexander, saw Thecla and became enamored with her and tried to persuade Paul with money and gifts. [3] But Paul said, "I do not know the woman of whom you speak, nor is she mine." [4] But Alexander, having a lot of power, embraced her on the street. And she would not endure it, but sought after Paul [5] and cried out bitterly, saying, "Do not violate the stranger! Do not violate the slave of God! [6] I am important among the Iconians and because I did not wish to marry Thamyris I have been thrown out of the city." [7] And taking hold of Alexander, she tore off his cloak and took the crown from his head and caused him public shame.

27 [1] But he at once, loving her and also being dishonored by what had happened to him, brought her before the governor. And when she confessed the things she had done, he sentenced her to the wild beasts. [2] And the women were panic-stricken and cried out before the court, "Evil judgment! Unholy judgment!" [3] But Thecla asked the governor that she might remain pure until she was forced to fight the wild animals. [4] And a rich queen, named Tryphaena, whose daughter had died, took Thecla into her care and found solace in her.

28 [1] When the wild animals were led in

procession, they bound her to a ferocious lioness and the queen Tryphaena followed her. [2] But the lioness sat down in front of Thecla and licked her feet, and the entire crowd was astounded. And the charge on her inscription was "Sacrilege." [3] And the women along with the children cried out from above, saying, "God, a godless judgment has been passed in this city!" [4] And after the procession, Tryphaena received her again, for her daughter, Falconilla, who was dead, said to her mother in a dream, "You will have the lonely stranger, Thecla, in place of me so that she might pray for me and I might be transferred to the place of the just."

29 [1] When Tryphaena received her back from the procession, she at once mourned because Thecla was going to fight with the wild animals the next day, but also loved her vehemently like her own daughter, Falconilla, saying, "Thecla, my second child, come here and pray for my child so that she might live forever, for I saw this in a dream." [2] And without hesitation, she lifted her voice and said, "My God, the Child of the Highest, the One in heaven, give her according to her wish so that her daughter, Falconilla, might live forever." [3] After Thecla said these things, Tryphaena mourned that such beauty was to be thrown to the wild animals.

30 [1] And when dawn arrived, Alexander came to take her away, for he was the one who offered the games, saying, "The governor is seated and the crowd is clamoring for us. Take away she who is to fight the wild animals!" [2] But Tryphaena cried out so that he fled, saying, "A second mourning for my Falconilla has come upon my house and there is no one to help — neither my child, for she is dead, nor relatives, for I am a widow. [3] God of my child Thecla, help Thecla!"

31 [1] And the governor sent soldiers to

bring Thecla, [2] but Tryphaena would not stand away from her, but taking her by her hand led her, saying, "I brought my daughter, Falconilla, to the grave, and you, Thecla, I bring to fight the wild animals." [3] And Thecla cried ferociously and wailed to the Lord, saying, "Lord God in whom I trust, with whom I have taken refuge, who rescued me from the fire, render reward to Tryphaena who showed compassion for your slave and guarded my holiness."

32 [1] Then there was an uproar and rumbling of wild animals, and a cry from the people, and the women sitting together, some saying, "Bring in the sacrilegious one!" but others saying, "Let the city be destroyed for this lawlessness! Destroy all of us, Proconsul! Ferocious spectacle! Evil judgment!"

33 [1] And Thecla was taken out of Tryphaena's hands and stripped, and received a girdle and was thrown into the stadium. [2] And lions and bears were thrown in front of her. [3] And a ferocious lioness charged her and then lay down at her feet. [4] And a bear ran up to her, but the lioness charged and met it, and tore the bear apart. [5] And again, a lion that had been trained against humans, which belonged to Alexander, ran up to her, and the lioness engaged the lion, and the two were killed together. [6] And the women mourned even more since the lioness that helped her was dead.

34 [1] And they threw in many wild animals as she stood and stretched out her hands and prayed. [2] But as she finished the prayer, she turned and saw a great pit full of water and said, "Now it is time for me to wash." [3] And she threw herself in, saying, "In the name of Jesus Christ I baptize myself on the last day!" [4] And seeing this, the women and the whole crowd wept, saying, "Do not throw yourself into the water!"; so that even the governor wept because the sea lions* were going to devour such beauty. [5] Then she threw herself into the water in the name of Jesus Christ, but the sea lions, seeing the light of a lightning flash, floated on the surface, dead. [6] And surrounding her was a cloud of fire so that neither the wild animals could touch her nor could she be seen naked.

35 [1] And the women, when other, more frightening, wild animals were being thrown in, cried aloud, and some threw petals, while others nard, and others cinnamon, and yet others cardamom, so that there was an abundance of perfumes. [2] And all the wild animals which were let out were held as if by sleep and did not touch her. So Alexander said to the governor, "I have exceedingly terrorizing bulls. Let us bind them to the one who is to fight the wild animals." [3] And looking sad, the governor turned to him, saying, "Do what you will." [4] And they bound her by the feet between the bulls, and placed burning irons under their genitals in order to agitate them further so they might kill her. [5] Then they leaped up, but a consuming flame burned through the ropes and Thecla was as if she had not been bound.

36 [1] And Tryphaena fainted as she stood by the arena, on the stage,† and the female slaves said, "Queen Tryphaena is dead!" [2] And the governor froze, and the whole city was frightened. And Alexander fell down on the governor's feet and said, "Have mercy on both me and the city and acquit the animal fighter in case the city be destroyed with her. [3] For if Caesar should hear these things he will quickly destroy us

---

* Or "seals."

† Technically, *abaci,* a location on or near the stage.

together with the city, because the queen Tryphaena, a relative of his, died beside the stage.

37 [1] And the governor called out to Thecla from the midst of the wild animals and said to her, "Who are you? [2] And what is it about you that not even one of the wild animals touched you?" [3] And she said, "I indeed am the slave of the living God. And as to what it is about me, I have trusted in the Child of God, in whom he finds pleasure, and through whom not even one of the wild animals touched me. [4] For this one alone is the limit of salvation and the foundation of life through the ages. For he is a refuge for those in a storm; freedom for the oppressed; for the despairing a shelter; and once and for all, whoever does not trust in him will not live but die forever."

38 [1] And when he heard these things, the governor ordered garments to be brought for her and said, "Put on these garments." [2] And she said, "The one who clothed me when I was naked among the wild beasts is this one who will clothe me with salvation in the day of judgment." [3] And having taken the garments, she put them on. [4] And the governor immediately sent forth a decree saying, "God-fearing Thecla, slave of God, I release you." [5] And the women all cried out in a loud voice, as if from one mouth, and gave praise to God, saying, "One is God who has saved Thecla!" so that the whole city shook from their voice.

39 [1] And Tryphaena, receiving the good news, came to meet her with a crowd and embraced Thecla and said, "Now I have confidence that the dead are raised! Now I trust that my child lives! Come inside, and I will assign to you all the things that are mine." [2] Then Thecla went in with her and rested in her house for eight days, instructing her in the word of God so that

even most of the maidservants believed. And there was great joy in the house.

40 [1] But Thecla missed Paul and searched him out, looking around everywhere, and it was reported to her that he was in Myra. [2] And taking young men and young women, she bound herself up and stitched together her garment — a robe in the fashion of a man's — and departed for Myra. And she found Paul speaking the word of God and waited near him. [3] And he was astonished when he saw her and the crowd that was with her, wondering whether another trial was upon her. [4] But observing this, she said to him, "I have received a bath, Paul. For the one who worked together with you for the good news also worked together with me in my baptism."

41 [1] And Paul took her hand and led her to the house of Hermias, and he heard everything from her so that Paul greatly marveled. And those who heard were affirmed and prayed on behalf of Tryphaena. [2] And as Thecla stood up she said to Paul, "I am going to Iconium." [3] And Paul said, "Go and teach the word of God." [4] Then Tryphaena sent her many clothes and gold so she could leave a portion behind for Paul to use in service for the poor.

42 [1] And she left for Iconium, [2] and went to Onesiphorus's house and fell on the floor where Paul had sat and taught the words of God. And she cried, saying, "God of me and of this house where the light shone on me, Christ Jesus the Child of God, my help in prison, my help before governors, my help in the fire, my help with the wild animals — you are God and you are the glory forever. Amen."

43 [1] And she found that Thamyris had died, but that her mother was alive. And she called her mother and said to her,

"Theocleia, Mother, can you believe that the Lord lives in heaven? [2] For if you desire money, the Lord will give it to you through me, or your child. Look, I am standing before you." [3] And bearing witness to these things, she departed for Seleucia, enlightening many with the word of God.

44 [1] But certain ones in the city, Greeks by religion and doctors by profession, sent violent young men to her to ruin her. For they said, "She is a maiden and serves Artemis. Because of this, she has power with healing." [2] And by God's foresight she entered into a rock, alive, and it descended under the earth. [3] And she left for Rome to see Paul and found him sleeping.* [4] And after staying there a little while, she slept with a beautiful sleep. And she is buried about two or three stadia† from the tomb of her teacher Paul.

45 [1] She was cast into the fire when she was seventeen and to the wild animals when she was eighteen. It has been said that she was an ascetic in a cave when she was seventy-two, so all the years of her life were ninety. [2] And after accomplishing many healings, she rests in the place of the holy ones having fallen asleep on the twenty-fourth of September. In Christ Jesus, our Lord, to whom be the glory and strength forever and ever. Amen.

---

* That is, he had died.
† A quarter to three-eighths of a mile.

An Introduction to the Letter to the Colossians

B URSTING WITH VITALITY about the success of a Christ movement among the many different peoples around the Mediterranean, this letter throbs with the wide dimensions of a "worldwide" message. Of course, the "world" (1:6) here means all the different cultures of the Mediterranean unified by the Roman Empire. For the Christ movement, an image of "the assembly" (1:18) portrays all these cultures as more spiritually united than they ever could be through Roman conquest.

The status of this letter, however, has confused many readers, in terms of both whether it was written by Paul and whether it was addressed to the Christ assemblies in Colossae. The letter's date has been part of this confusion. Colossians' portrait of Christ and its interest in a true "assembly" consisting of different groups worldwide differ dramatically from the authentic writings of Paul, such as Galatians and 1 Corinthians. On the other hand, some of this letter's vocabulary is very close to that of Paul's authentic letters. The complete destruction of the city of Colossae by an earthquake in 60 CE presents further complication. Scholars are fairly evenly divided on whether Paul wrote none, part, or all of this letter. Those who think it was written later must obviously also assert that it was not written to Colossae, a proposal that fits with the more general tone of the letter.

Colossians is quite well known for its ancient song praising a cosmic Christ:

He is the image of the unseen God, firstborn of all creation.
In him all things were created, those in the heavens and on the earth,
The visible and the invisible, whether thrones or lordships, rulers or authorities —
All things have been created through him and for him.
He is before all things and all things cohere in him.
He is the head of the body — the assembly;
He is the beginning, the firstborn from the dead,
So that he might have the first place in everything.
In him, the entire fullness of everything was pleased to dwell,
And through him to reconcile all things in him,
Whether those on earth or in the heavens, through the blood of his cross. (1:15–20)

This letter focuses entirely on gentile people and portrays them as "once having been alienated and hateful in your intentions, doing evil works, . . . now reconciled in the body of his flesh, through death, presenting you holy, blameless, and without reproach before" Christ (1:21–22). This focus celebrates a larger body of Christ, "not Greek and Jew, circumcision and uncircumcision, Barbarian, Scythian, slave, free: but Christ . . . [in] all things and all in Christ" (3:11). In this spirit the letter's author instructs, "As the chosen of God, holy and beloved, put on compassion, goodness, humility, gentleness, and patience, bearing up one another and, if there are complaints, forgiving each other: as the Lord forgave, so also should you. Above all, add to these things love, which is a bond of maturity. Let the peace of Christ settle in your hearts, to which indeed you were called in one body, and be thankful" (3:12–15).

In some contrast, Colossians also includes household codes of behavior that originated in Greco-Roman culture but in this case are applied to the members of the Christ assemblies:

> Wives, be obedient to your husbands as is fitting in the Lord. Husbands, love your wives and do not show anger toward them. Children, regard your parents in all things, for this pleases the Lord. Parents, do not provoke your children, or they may be disheartened. Slaves, regard your human masters in all things, not just in front of them or as people pleasers, but openheartedly, fearing the Lord. Whatever your daily work, do it as if for the Lord and not humans, knowing that you will receive the reward of inheritance from the Lord — you all serve the Master, Christ. For the unjust will be repaid for what they did wrong, and there is no partiality. Masters, grant justice and equality to your slaves, knowing that you also have a master in heaven. (3:18–4:1)

Not unlike a number of letters in the traditional New Testament, Colossians mixes these instructions for the subservience of women and slaves with high celebration of a real new world with all people united in a new spirit of "compassion, goodness, humility, gentleness, and patience." One of the strong values of the New Orleans Council lay in choosing documents that did not include such put-downs of women and slaves. This does not mean that all the new documents are without difficulties, or that all early Christian books outside the traditional New Testament are free of such prejudice against oppressed persons. Rather, the council's choices have produced a new New Testament that does have more resources to resist such oppression and less occasion for promoting it.

Recommended Reading

Markus Barth and Helmut Blanke, *Colossians*
Margaret MacDonald, *Colossians and Ephesians*
Jerry L. Sumney, *Colossians*

The Letter to the Colossians

1 ¹ Paul, an ambassador of Christ Jesus by the will of God, and Timothy, our brother, ² to the holy and faithful brothers and sisters in Christ in Colossae — grace to you and peace from God our Father. ³ We give thanks to God, the Father of our Master, Jesus Christ, always praying for you, ⁴ having heard of your faith in Christ Jesus and the love you have for the holy ones, ⁵ because of the hope that is stored for you in the heavens, which you heard before in the word of the truth of the good news that has come to you. ⁶ It is bearing fruit and growing in the whole world, just as it is in you from the day in which you heard it and truly knew the grace of God. ⁷ You learned this from Epaphras, our beloved fellow slave, who is a faithful servant of Christ for you and ⁸ who has shown us your love in the Spirit. ⁹ Because of this, from the day we heard it, we have not stopped praying for you and asking that you be filled with the knowledge of God's will in all wisdom and spiritual insight, ¹⁰ so that you may walk in a way worthy of the Master, a pleasing way, with every good work bearing fruit and growing in the knowledge of God. ¹¹ In God's power, may you be made strong according to the strength of God's glory, enduring and suffering with joy and ¹² giving thanks to the Father who has qualified you for a share of the holy ones' allotment in the light. ¹³ God has rescued us from the authority of the darkness and transferred us into the domain of his beloved Child, ¹⁴ in whom we have deliverance, the release from sin.

¹⁵ He is the image of the unseen God,
  firstborn of all creation.
¹⁶ In him all things were created, those in
  the heavens and on the earth,
The visible and the invisible, whether
  thrones or lordships, rulers or
  authorities —
All things have been created through
  him and for him.
¹⁷ He is before all things and all things
  cohere in him.
¹⁸ He is the head of the body — the
  assembly;
He is the beginning, the firstborn from
  the dead,
So that he might have the first place in
  everything.
¹⁹ In him, the entire fullness of everything
  was pleased to dwell,
²⁰ And through him to reconcile all
  things in him,
Whether those on earth or in the
  heavens, through the blood of his
  cross.

²¹ And you, once having been alienated and hateful in your intentions, doing evil works, ²² he has now reconciled in the body of his flesh, through death, presenting you holy, blameless, and without reproach before him — ²³ as long as you remain in the trust which has been founded and firm, not shifting away from the hope of the good news which you heard proclaimed in all creation under heaven, of which I, Paul, became a manager. ²⁴ Now I take pleasure in suffering on your behalf, and I fill the lack in Christ's oppression in my flesh on behalf of his body, which is the association. ²⁵ I became its servant according to God's directions that were given to me for you to fulfill the will of God. ²⁶ The mystery, hidden through ages and generations, has now been made known to his holy ones. ²⁷ To them God wanted to make known the wealth of the

glory of this mystery among the nations, which is Christ in you, the hope of glory. [28] We proclaim Christ, warning and teaching all people in wisdom so that we may present them mature in Christ. [29] For this I work, struggling according to his works that powerfully work within me.

2 [1] For I want you all to know how much I have struggled for you and the ones in Laodicea, and for all who have not seen my face in person. [2] I have done this so that their hearts might be encouraged and knit together in love, having all the treasures of assured awareness of the knowledge of God's mystery, that is, Christ. [3] In him all the treasures of wisdom and knowledge are hidden. [4] This I say so that none of you will be misled with persuasive words. [5] For though I am far from you in body, I am with you in spirit, rejoicing to see the character and foundation of your trust in Christ. [6] Therefore, as you all have received him, live in Jesus Christ the Lord. [7] Root and build yourselves up in him, confirming your faith as you were taught, in abundant gratitude. [8] See that no one takes you captive through philosophy and empty treachery according to the traditions of humans and the worldly elements rather than according to Christ. [9] For in him dwells the entire fullness of the divine body, and [10] you all are made full in him, the one who is the head of all the rulers and authorities. [11] And also in him you were circumcised with a circumcision not of hands, but by taking off the fleshy body through the circumcision of Christ. [12] You all were buried together with him in baptism and were raised through trust in the workings of God, the one who raised him from the dead. [13] When you were dead in transgressions and the uncircumcision of your flesh, God made you alive together with him, forgiving all our transgressions, [14] wiping out the words in the decree against us by taking it away from our midst and nailing it to the cross. [15] God,

having disarmed the rulers and authorities, exposed them in public, triumphing over them. [16] Therefore, let no one judge you in respect to food and drink, festivals, new moons, or sabbaths. [17] These are but a shadow of the things to come compared to the body of Christ. [18] Let no one judge you, wanting you to lower yourselves and worship the angels, dwelling on visions, puffed up by their fleshy minds, [19] and not holding to the head, out of which the whole body — supported and brought together through its joints and ligaments — grows with the growth of God. [20] If you died with Christ to the worldly elements, why are you living in the world, submitting to its ordinances and opinions like: [21] "Do not hold or taste or touch"? These rules refer to things that will all be destroyed with use according to the orders and teachings of humans. These things appear reasonable, to have wisdom in self-imposed service, humility, and austere treatment of the body, but are of no value against the indulgence of the flesh.

3 [1] Therefore, if you were raised with Christ, seek the things above, where Christ is, seated at the right hand of God. [2] Understand the things above and not the things on earth, [3] for you all died and your life is hidden with Christ in God. [4] When Christ, your life, is made known, you all will also be made known with him in glory. [5] Therefore put to death that which is earthly: unchastity, depravity, passion, desire for evil, and greed, which is idolatry. [6] Because of these things God's anger comes on the disobedient. [7] These are the ways in which you once lived, [8] but now put away these things: anger, rage, depravity, slander, and abusive language from your mouths. [9] Do not lie to one another, having taken off the old self and its practices, [10] and put on the new self, being renewed in knowledge according to the image of its creator. [11] Here, there is not Greek and Jew, circumcision and uncircumcision, Barbarian, Scythian, slave, free: but Christ is all things and all in Christ. [12] As the chosen of God, holy and beloved, put on compassion, goodness, humility, gentleness, and patience, [13] bearing up one another and, if there are complaints, forgiving each other: as the Lord forgave, so also should you. [14] Above all, add to these things love, which is a bond of maturity. [15] Let the peace of Christ settle in your hearts, to which indeed you were called in one body, and be thankful. [16] Let the word of Christ abide in you richly. Teach and counsel each other with psalms, hymns, and spiritual songs, with grace singing in your hearts to God. [17] In everything, whatever you do, in speech or work, do all things in the name of the Lord, Jesus, giving thanks to God, the Father, through him. [18] Wives, be obedient to your husbands as is fitting in the Lord. [19] Husbands, love your wives and do not show anger toward them. [20] Children, regard your parents in all things, for this pleases the Lord. [21] Parents, do not provoke your children, or they may be disheartened. [22] Slaves, regard your human masters in all things, not just in front of them or as people pleasers, but openheartedly, fearing the Lord. Whatever your daily work, do it as if for the Lord and not humans, knowing that you will receive the reward of inheritance from the Lord—you all serve the Master, Christ. For the unjust will be repaid for what they did wrong, and there is no partiality.

4 [1] Masters, grant justice and equality to your slaves, knowing that you also have a master in heaven. [2] Persist in prayer and remain wakeful and thankful in it. [3] Also pray together for us so that God may open for us a door for the word, that we may speak the mystery of Christ, on account of which I am in prison, [4] so that I may reveal it, as is required, in my speech. [5] Walk in wisdom toward outsiders, making use of the opportunity. [6] May you always speak with kindness, seasoned with salt, so you know how to specifically answer each one. [7] Tychicus will tell you all about how I am doing. He is a beloved brother, trusted servant, and fellow slave in the Lord, [8] whom I sent to you all so that you may know the things that concern us and that he might encourage you in your hearts. [9] He is with Onesimus, our trusted and beloved brother, who is one of your own. Together they will tell you what is happening here. [10] Welcome Arstarchus, my fellow prisoner, and Mark, the cousin of Barnabas—concerning whom you have received instructions—as well, if he should come to you. [11] And Jesus, who is called Justus, greets you. These are the only ones of the circumcision who are my coworkers in the realm of God, and are a comfort to me. [12] Epaphras, also one of you and a slave of Christ Jesus, greets you. He is always struggling for you in prayer so that you might be mature and fully assured in all that God wills. [13] I bear witness for him that he has labored much for you and for those in Laodicea and Hierapolis. [14] Luke, the beloved physician, and Demas greet you. [15] Greet the Laodicean brothers and sisters, and Nympha and the association at her house for me. [16] And after you all read this letter, make sure that it is also read in the Laodecean association, and that the one to Laodecea is also read by you. [17] And say to Archippus, "See that you fulfill the service you received in the Lord." [18] I, Paul, write this greeting with my own hand. Remember my bonds. Grace be with you.

An Introduction to the Second Letter to the Thessalonians

T HIS LETTER PORTRAYS APPARENT turmoil and threat from those inside the Christ movement who live an "an ill-ordered life" (3:6), those outside the movement "inflicting suffering on you" (1:6), and those "in the form of all kinds of deceptive miracles, signs, and marvels, as well as of wicked attempts to delude" (2:9). In addition, the letter sees great danger in "that lawless human, that son of loss, who so opposes himself to everyone that he is spoken of as a god or as an object of worship, and so exalts himself above them, that he seats himself in the Temple of God, and displays himself as God" (perhaps the Roman emperor) (2:3–4), and "Satan" (2:9). This letter envisions the appearance of the Lord Jesus with the angels of power as the imminent solution to all these threats.

The voice of this letter, written in Greek and belonging to the traditional New Testament, is very different from Paul's, and it is unlikely that he wrote this letter, even though he has traditionally been credited with it. The range of concerns and the embattled character of the author and addressees place it more likely in the late first or second century. There is an artificial link with the First Letter to the Thessalonians in that both letters show some interest in a second coming of Jesus. But their interests are also quite different, with the first letter being concerned with how those who have died and those who have not will meet, and the second letter explicitly concentrating on the punishment to be exacted on all the opponents of the "Thessalonians."

The historical Paul who wrote letters to the Galatians, the Romans, and the Philippians proclaimed the power of being in "Christ," where there was neither Judean nor Greek, slave nor free, male nor female (Galatians 3:28); and little of that spirit seems visible in 2 Thessalonians. Here the celebrative dimension of the historical Paul seems to have been replaced by completely embattled circumstances that overwhelm both the author and the reader. Perhaps some inspiration can be drawn from this letter's vigilance against the horror of a human being who "so opposes himself to everyone that he is spoken of as a god or as an object of worship, and so exalts himself above them, that he seats himself in the Temple of God, and displays himself as God" (2:4). It points directly to the Roman emperor in the days of the author and invites readers today to think whether there are contemporary leaders who are trying to make themselves into God.

Recommended Reading

Beverly Gaventa, *First and Second Thessalonians*

The Second Letter to the Thessalonians

Introduction

1 ¹ To the Thessalonian church in union with God our Father and the Lord Jesus Christ, from Paul, Silas, and Timothy. ² May God, the Father, and the Lord Jesus Christ bless you and give you peace.

³ Friends, it is our duty always to thank God about you, as is but right, considering the wonderful growth of your trust, and because, without exception, your love for one another is continually increasing. ⁴ So much is this the case that we ourselves speak with pride, before the churches of God, of the patience and faith which you have shown, in spite of all the persecutions and troubles that you are enduring. ⁵ These persecutions will vindicate the justice of God's judgment, and will result in your being reckoned worthy of God's realm, for the sake of which you are now suffering; ⁶ since God deems it just to inflict suffering on those who are now inflicting suffering on you, ⁷ and to give relief to you who are suffering, as well as to us, at the appearing of the Lord Jesus from heaven with his mighty angels, in flaming fire. ⁸ Then he will inflict punishment on those who refuse to know God, and on those who turn a deaf ear to the good news of Jesus, our Lord. ⁹ They will pay the penalty of unutterable ruin — banished from the presence of the Lord and from the glorious manifestation of his might, ¹⁰ when he comes to be honored in his people, and to be revered in all who have learned to believe in him (for you also believed our testimony) — as he will be on that day. ¹¹ With this in view, our constant prayer for you is that our God may count you worthy of the call that you have received, and by his power make perfect your delight in all goodness and the efforts that have resulted from your faith. ¹² Then, in the grace of our God and the Lord Jesus Christ, will the name of Jesus, our Lord, be honored in you, and you in him.

Events That Must Precede the Lord's Coming

2 ¹ As to the coming of our Lord Jesus Christ, and our being gathered to meet him, we beg you, friends, ² not lightly to let your minds become unsettled, nor yet to be disturbed by any revelation, or by any message, or by any letter, purporting to come from us, to the effect that the day of the Lord is come. ³ Do not let anyone deceive you, whatever he may do. For it will not come until after the great rebellion, and the appearing of that lawless human, that son of loss, ⁴ who so opposes himself to everyone that he is spoken of as a god or as an object of worship, and so exalts himself above them, that he seats himself in the Temple of God, and displays himself as God! ⁵ Do you not remember how, when I was with you, I used to speak to you of all this? ⁶ And you know now what the restraining influence is which prevents his appearing before his appointed time. ⁷ Wickedness, indeed, is already at work in secret; but only until he who at present restrains it is removed out of the way. ⁸ Then will the lawless one appear, but the Lord Jesus will destroy him with the breath of his lips, and annihilate him by the splendor of his coming. ⁹ For at the coming of the Lord there will be great activity on the part of Satan, in the form of all kinds of deceptive miracles, signs, and

marvels, as well as of wicked attempts to delude — [10] to the ruin of those who are on the path to destruction, because they have never received and loved the truth to their own salvation. [11] That is why God places them under the influence of a delusion, to cause them to believe a lie; [12] so that sentence may be passed on all those who refuse to believe the truth, but delight in wickedness.

[13] But, friends, whom the Lord loves, it is our duty always to thank God about you, for, from the first, God chose you for salvation through the purifying influence of the spirit, and your belief in the truth. [14] To this you were called by the good news which we brought you, to attain to the glory of our Lord Jesus Christ. [15] Stand firm then, friends, and hold fast to the truths that we taught you, whether by word or by letter. [16] And may our Lord Jesus Christ himself, and God our Father, who loved us and, in his grace, gave us unfailing consolation and good ground for hope, [17] console your hearts, and strengthen you to do and to say all that is right.

Conclusion

3 [1] In conclusion, friends, pray for us — pray that the Lord's message may spread rapidly, and be received everywhere with honor, as it was among you; [2] and that we may be preserved from wrong-headed and wicked people — for trust is not in everyone. [3] But the Lord will not fail you; he will give you strength, and guard you from evil. [4] Yes, and the confidence that our union with the Lord enables us to place in you leads us to believe that you are doing, and will do, what we direct you. [5] May the Lord bring you to the love of God, and to the patience of the Christ.

[6] We beg you, friends, in the name of the Lord Jesus Christ, to avoid any follower who is living an ill-ordered life, which is not in agreement with the teaching that you received from us. [7] For you know well that you ought to follow our example. When we were with you, our life was not ill-ordered, [8] nor did we eat anyone's bread without paying for it. Night and day, laboring and toiling, we used to work at our trades, so as not to be a burden on any of you. [9] This was not because we had not a right to receive support, but our object was to give you a pattern for you to copy. [10] Indeed, when we were with you, the rule we laid down was: "Whoever does not choose to work will not get to eat." [11] We hear that there are among you people who are living ill-ordered lives and who, instead of attending to their own business, are mere busybodies. [12] All such people we beg, and implore, in the name of the Lord Jesus Christ, to attend quietly to their business, and earn their own living. [13] You, friends, must not grow weary of doing what is right. [14] If people disregard what we have said in this letter, take note of them and avoid their company, so that they may feel ashamed. [15] Yet do not think of them as an enemy, but caution them as you would a brother or sister. [16] May the Lord, from whom all peace comes, himself give you his peace at all times and in all ways. May he be with you all.

[17] I, Paul, add this greeting in my own handwriting. It is my signature to every letter. This is how I write. [18] May the blessing of our Lord Jesus Christ be with you all.

An Introduction to the First Letter to Timothy

THERE ARE A NUMBER of indications that this letter is not from Paul himself, but from someone in a later generation writing in his name, a common convention of the Greek literature of the time. This "Paul" has some beliefs and teachings that are quite different from those in the collection of authentic letters of Paul (for example, here the Law is considered good as it keeps misbehavers under control, but in Galatians and Romans it is not good for gentiles at all). In addition, this letter pays strong attention to offices (such as elders and deacons) in the Christ assemblies that did not seem to exist when Paul was writing. If the letter is from substantially later than Paul, it is also probable that the addressee, Timothy, is also a symbolic rather than historical designation. All these discrepancies with the earlier letters of Paul point to a second-century gentile context.

The letter does passionately address a number of important issues in second-century Christ movements. It focuses on two dimensions of the Christ communities' collective life. First, it is very concerned with the proper kinds of leadership and teaching. It sets a number of standards for the roles of elders and deacons. The elders must be married men, gentle, not money-loving, and they must have experience in the Christ community (3:1–7). There can be men and women deacons, and they too must be respectable, honest, and not drink too much (3:8–13). Teachers must be male but can be young as well as old. The letter warns against teachers who promote celibacy and prohibit certain foods.

Second, the letter is very concerned with limiting the role and behavior of women. In addition to the ban on women elders and teachers, women's dress is strictly prescribed. Modesty is the norm, and no braided hair or jewelry is allowed. Women "will be saved by bearing children, if women never abandon faith, love, or holiness, and behave with modesty" (2:15). There is special concern about the activities of "widows," who appear in this case to have special roles not just limited to having had a husband who died. Widows need to repay their debt to their parents (5:4), not gossip (5:13), and take care of family before doing anything else (5:3–7). One cannot be considered a widow unless one is at least sixty years old, because young women who have lost their husbands are unreliable and frivolous, and some of them "follow Satan" (5:10–15).

It is interesting to contrast this letter with other *New New Testament* works. The Gospel of Luke and the Acts of the Apostles identify a woman named Tabitha as a disciple (Acts 9:36) practically in the same breath as a man named Timothy (16:1). Luke-Acts' picture of a woman disciple is in glaring distinction from this document under the same name and character, Timothy, which forbids women any such roles. Similarly, the Gospel of Mary portrays its lead character, Mary Magdalene, not only as a teacher, but as the person whom Jesus loved most (10:10). And the Acts of Paul and Thecla lauds the woman Thecla who baptizes herself after Paul neglects her request to baptize her (34:3–5). These additions to *A New New Testament* as well as traditional books such as the Gospel of John and the Acts of the Apostles oppose many of the stands against women taken in 1 Timothy.

Recommended Reading

Raymond F. Collins, *I & II Timothy and Titus: A Commentary*
Martin Dibelius and Hans Conzelmann, *The Pastoral Epistles*
Luke T. Johnson, *The First and Second Letters to Timothy*

The First Letter to Timothy

Introduction

1 [1] From Paul, an apostle of Christ Jesus by the appointment of God, our Savior, and Christ Jesus, our hope. [2] To Timothy, my true child in the faith: may God, the Father, and Christ Jesus, our Lord, bless you, and be merciful to you, and give you peace.

[3] I beg you, as I did when I was on my way into Macedonia, to remain at Ephesus; that you may instruct certain people there not to teach new and strange doctrines, [4] nor to devote their attention to legends and interminable genealogies, which tend to give rise to argument rather than to further that divine plan which is revealed in the faith. [5] The object of all instruction is to call forth that love which comes from a pure heart, a clear conscience, and a sincere faith. [6] And it is because they have not aimed at these things that the attention of certain people has been diverted to unprofitable subjects. [7] They want to be teachers of the Law, and yet do not understand either the words they use, or the subjects on which they speak so confidently. [8] We know, of course, that the Law is excellent, when used legitimately, [9] by one who recognizes that laws were not made for good people, but for the lawless and disorderly, for irreligious and wicked people, for those who are irreverent and profane, for those who mistreat their fathers or mothers, for murderers, [10] for the immoral, for perverts, for slave dealers, for liars, for perjurers, and for whatever else is opposed to sound teaching — [11] as is taught in the glorious good news of the ever-blessed God, with which I was entrusted.

[12] I am thankful to Christ Jesus, our Lord, who has been my strength, for showing that he thought me worthy of trust by appointing me to his ministry, [13] though I once used to blaspheme, and to persecute, and to insult. Yet mercy was shown me, because I acted in ignorance, while still an unbeliever; [14] and the loving kindness of our Lord was boundless, and filled me with that faith and love which come from union with Christ Jesus. [15] How true the saying is, and worthy of the fullest acceptance, that "Christ Jesus came into the world to save sinners"! And there is no greater sinner than I! [16] Yet mercy was shown me for the express purpose that Christ Jesus might exhibit in my case, beyond all others, his exhaustless patience, as an example for those who were afterward to believe in him and attain life from generation to generation. [17] To the king for all time, ever-living, invisible, the one God, be ascribed honor and glory forever and ever. Amen.

[18] This, then, is the charge that I lay on you, Timothy, my child, in accordance with what was predicted of you: fight the good fight in the spirit of those predictions, [19] with faith, and with a clear conscience; and it is because they have thrust this aside that, as regards the faith, some have wrecked their lives. [20] Hymenaeus and Alexander are instances — the men whom I delivered over to Satan so that they might be taught not to blaspheme.

General Directions on Church Matters

2 [1] First of all, then, I ask that petitions, prayers, intercessions, and thanksgivings should be offered for everyone, [2] especially for kings and all who are in high positions, in order that we may lead a quiet and peaceful life in a deeply religious and reverent spirit. [3] This will be good and acceptable in the eyes of God, our Savior, [4] whose will is that everyone should be saved, and attain to a full knowledge of the truth. [5] There is but one God, and one mediator between God and people — the person, Christ Jesus, [6] who gave himself as a ransom on behalf of all people.

This must be our testimony, as opportunities present themselves; [7] and it was for this that I was myself appointed a herald and an ambassador (I am telling the simple truth and no lie) — a teacher of the gentiles in the trust and truth.

[8] My desire, then, is that it should be the custom everywhere for the men to lead the prayers, with hands reverently uplifted, avoiding heated controversy.

[9] I also desire that women should adorn themselves with appropriate dress, worn quietly and modestly, and not with wreaths or gold ornaments for the hair, or pearls, or costly clothing, [10] but — as is proper for women who profess to be religious — with good actions. [11] A woman must learn, listening in silence with all deference. [12] I do not consent to them becoming teachers, or exercising authority over men; they ought not speak. [13] Adam was formed first, not Eve. [14] And it was not Adam who was deceived; it was the woman who was entirely deceived and fell into sin. [15] Women "will be saved by bearing children, if women never abandon faith, love, or holiness, and behave with modesty."

3 [1] How true is this saying: "To aspire to be a presiding officer in the church is to be ambitious for a noble task." [2] The presiding officer should be of blameless character; married; living a temperate, discreet, and well-ordered life; hospitable, and a skillful teacher, [3] not addicted to drink or

brawling, but of a forbearing and peaceable disposition, and not a lover of money; [4] he should provide for his own household well, and his children should be kept under control and be well behaved. [5] If someone does not know how to provide for his own household, how can he take charge of the church of God? [6] The presiding officer should not be a recent convert, or he might become blinded by pride and fall under the same condemnation as the devil. [7] He should also be well spoken of by outsiders, so that he may not incur censure and so fall into the devil's trap. [8] So, too, assistant officers should be serious and straightforward, not given to taking much drink or to questionable moneymaking, [9] but people who hold the deep truths of the faith and have a clear conscience. [10] They should be tested first, and only appointed to their office if no objection is raised against them. [11] It should be the same with the women in this office. They should be serious, not gossips, sober, and trustworthy in all respects. [12] Assistant officers should be married and manage their children and their households well. [13] Those who have filled that post with honor gain for themselves an honorable position, as well as great confidence through the faith that they place in Christ Jesus.

Special Directions to Timothy

[14] I am writing this to you, though I hope that I will come to see you before long; [15] but in case I should be delayed, I want you to know what your conduct ought to be in the household of God, which is the church of the living God — the pillar and stay of the truth. [16] Yes, and confessedly wonderful are the deep truths of our religion; for:

"He was revealed in our nature,
pronounced righteous in spirit,
seen by angels,

proclaimed among the gentiles,
believed on in the world,
Taken up into glory."

4 [1] But the Spirit distinctly says that in later times there will be some who will fall away from the faith, and devote their attention to misleading spirits, and to the teaching of demons, [2] who will make use of the hypocrisy of lying teachers. These people's consciences are seared, [3] and they forbid marriage and enjoin abstinence from certain kinds of food; though God created these foods to be enjoyed thankfully by those who hold the faith and have attained a full knowledge of the truth. [4] Everything created by God is good, and there is nothing that need be rejected — provided only that it is received thankfully; [5] for it is consecrated by God's blessing and by prayer.

[6] Put all this before the followers, and you will be a good servant of Christ Jesus, sustained by the precepts of the faith and of that good teaching by which you have guided your life. [7] As for profane legends and old wives' tales, leave them alone. Train yourself to lead a religious life; [8] for while the training of the body is of service in some respects, religion is of service in all, carrying with it, as it does, a promise of life both here and hereafter. [9] How true that saying is and worthy of the fullest acceptance! [10] With that aim we toil and struggle, for we have set our hopes on the living God, who is the Savior of all, and especially of those who hold the faith.

[11] Remember these things in your teaching. [12] Do not let anyone look down on you because you are young, but by your conversation, your conduct, your love, your faith, and your purity be an example to those who hold the faith. [13] Until I come, apply yourself to public reading, preaching, and teaching. [14] Do not neglect the divine gift within you, which was given you, amid many a prediction, when the hands of the officers of the church were laid on your head. [15] Practice these things, devote yourself to them, so that your progress may be plain to everyone. [16] Look to yourself as well as to your teaching. Persevere in this, for your doing so will mean salvation for yourself as well as for your hearers.

5 [1] Do not reprimand an older man, but plead with him as if he were your father. Treat the young men as brothers, [2] the older women as mothers, and the younger women as sisters — with all purity. [3] Show consideration for widows — I mean those who are really widowed. [4] But if a widow has children or grandchildren, let them learn to show proper regard for the members of their own family first, and to make some return to their parents; for that is pleasing in God's sight. [5] As for the woman who is really widowed and left quite alone, her hopes are fixed on God, and she devotes herself to prayers and supplications night and day. [6] But the life of a widow who is devoted to pleasure is a living death. [7] Those are the points you should teach, so that there may be no call for your censure. [8] Anyone who fails to provide for his own relations, and especially for those under his own roof, has disowned the faith, and is worse than an unbeliever. [9] A widow, when her name is added to the list, should not be less than sixty years old; she should have been a faithful wife, [10] and be well spoken of for her kind actions. She should have brought up children, have shown hospitality to strangers, have washed the feet of the holy ones, have relieved those who were in distress, and devoted herself to every kind of good action. [11] But you should exclude the younger widows from the list; for when they grow restive under the yoke of the Christ, they want to marry, [12] and so they bring condemnation on themselves for having broken their previous promise. [13] And not only that, but they learn to be idle as they go about from house to house. Nor are they merely idle, but they also become gossips and busybodies, and talk of what they ought not. [14] Therefore I advise young widows to marry, bear children, and attend to their homes, and so avoid giving the enemy an opportunity for scandal. [15] There are some who have already left us, to follow Satan. [16] Any woman in the assembly who has relations who are widows ought to relieve them and not allow them to become a burden to the assembly, so that the assembly may relieve those widows who are really widowed.

[17] Those officers of the assembly who fill their office well should be held deserving of especial consideration, particularly those whose work lies in preaching and teaching. [18] The words of scripture are:

"You should not muzzle the ox while it is treading out the grain."

and again:

"The worker is worth his wages."

[19] Do not receive a charge against an officer of the church, unless it is supported by two or three witnesses; [20] but rebuke offenders publicly, so that others may take warning. [21] I charge you solemnly, before God and Christ Jesus and the chosen angels, to carry out these directions, unswayed by prejudice, never acting with partiality. [22] Never ordain anyone hastily, and take no part in the wrongdoing of others. Keep your life pure. [23] Do not continue to drink water only, but take a little wine because of the weakness of your stomach, and your frequent ailments. [24] There are some people whose sins are conspicuous and lead on to judgment, while there are others whose sins dog their steps. [25] In the same way noble deeds become conspicuous, and those which are otherwise cannot be concealed.

6 [1] All who are in the position of slaves should regard their masters as deserving of the greatest respect, so that the name of God, and our teaching, may not be maligned. [2] Those who have masters should not think less of them because they are also followers of Christ, but on the contrary they should serve them all the better, because those who are to benefit by their good work are dear to them as their brothers and sisters in Christ.

Conclusion

Those are the things to insist on in your teaching. [3] Anyone who teaches otherwise, and refuses his assent to sound instruction—the instruction of our Lord Jesus Christ—and to the teaching of religion, [4] is puffed up with conceit, not really knowing anything, but having a morbid craving for discussions and arguments. Such things only give rise to envy, quarreling, recriminations, base suspicions, [5] and incessant wrangling on the part of these corrupt-minded people who have lost all hold on the truth, and who think of religion only as a source of gain. [6] And a great source of gain religion is, when it brings contentment with it! [7] For we brought nothing into the world, because we cannot even carry anything out of it. [8] So, with food and shelter, we will be content. [9] Those who want to be rich fall into the net of temptation, and become the prey of many foolish and harmful ambitions, which plunge people into destruction and ruin. [10] Love of money is a source of all kinds of evil; and in their eagerness to be rich some have wandered away from the faith, and have been pierced to the heart by many a regret.

[11] But you must, servant of God, avoid all this. Aim at righteousness, piety, faith, love, endurance, gentleness. [12] Run the great race of the faith, and win the eternal life. It was for this that you received

the call, and, in the presence of many witnesses, made the great profession of faith. [13] I beg you, as in the sight of God, the source of all life, and of Christ Jesus who before Pontius Pilate made the great profession of faith — [14] I implore you to keep his command free from stain or reproach, until the appearing of our Lord Jesus Christ. [15] This will be brought about in his own time by the one ever-blessed Potentate, the king of all kings and Lord of all lords, [16] who alone is possessed of immortality and dwells in unapproachable light, whom no one has ever seen or ever can see — to whom be ascribed honor and power forever. Amen.

[17] Teach those who are wealthy in this life not to pride themselves, or fix their hopes, on so uncertain a thing as wealth, but on God, who gives us a wealth of enjoyment on every side. [18] Teach them to show kindness, to exhibit a wealth of good actions, to be openhanded and generous, [19] storing up for themselves what in the future will prove to be a good foundation, so that they may gain the only true life.

[20] Timothy, guard what has been entrusted to you. Avoid the profane prattle and contradictions of what some miscall "theology," [21] for there are those who, while asserting their proficiency in it, have yet, as regards the faith, gone altogether astray.

God bless you all.

An Introduction to the Second Letter to Timothy

L IKE 1 TIMOTHY, 2 Timothy is probably a letter from the legend of Paul, not from the historical Paul. It takes the form of a final message from a teacher to a student. Much of the letter focuses on what to do in the face of persecution, presumably from Roman powers. As this was a primary problem of second- and third-century Christianity, this letter most plausibly fits in the second century, but it is difficult to know whether to place it in the earlier or later part of that century.

This Paul presents himself as having been persecuted throughout his work in the Christ movement, as a model for how to respond to such suffering. Writing in Greek, he presents faithfulness in persecution as a duty to Christ Jesus, who also suffered such attacks. This relationship with Christ, however, is not without nuance and complexity. This Paul quotes an unidentified source about how one's own constancy relates to Jesus: "'If we have shared his death, we will also share his life. If we continue to endure, we will also share his throne. If we should ever disown him, he, too, will disown us. If we lose our trust, he is still to be trusted, for he cannot be false to himself!'" (2:11–13). Here the difficulties of staying true in the midst of persecution are recognized, and it is suggested that reward, punishment, and forgiveness are all available from Christ.

This Paul mixes seamlessly the dangers from outside persecution and from bad teachers within the Christ movements. The presence of false teachers and profiteering, self-serving people around the Christ assemblies is associated with the coming of the last days. As he nears his last days, this Paul charges Timothy to stick to his teaching and refute those who are in error.

In our time many followers of Christ also paint an embattled picture of their lives due to the hostility of many within the larger society and what they regard as false teachers. Second Timothy reinforces this reaction in the twenty-first century, for better or for worse.

Recommended Reading

Raymond F. Collins, *I & II Timothy and Titus: A Commentary*
Martin Dibelius and Hans Conzelmann, *The Pastoral Epistles*
Luke T. Johnson, *The First and Second Letters to Timothy*

The Second Letter to Timothy

Introduction

1 ¹ To Timothy, my dear child, from Paul, who, by the will of God, is an apostle of Christ Jesus, charged to proclaim the life that comes from union with Christ Jesus. ² May God, the Father, and Christ Jesus, our Lord, bless you, and be merciful to you, and give you peace.

³ I am thankful to God, whom I serve, as my ancestors did, with a clear conscience, when I remember you, as I never fail to do, in my prayers — night and day alike — ⁴ as I think of your tears, longing to see you, that my happiness may be completed, ⁵ now that I have been reminded of the sincere faith that you have shown. That faith was seen first in your grandmother Lois and your mother Eunice, and is now, I am convinced, in you also. ⁶ And that is my reason for reminding you to stir into flame that gift of God which is yours through your ordination at my hands. ⁷ For the Spirit which God gave us was not a spirit of cowardice, but a spirit of power, love, and self-control. ⁸ Do not, therefore, be ashamed of the testimony which we have to bear to our Lord, nor yet of me who am a prisoner for him; but join with me in suffering for the good news, as far as God enables you. ⁹ It was God who saved us, and from him we received our solemn call — not as a reward for anything that we had done, but in fulfillment of his own loving purpose. For that love was extended to us, through Christ Jesus, before time began, ¹⁰ and has now been made apparent through the appearing of our Savior, Christ Jesus, who has made an end of death, and has brought life and immortality to light by that good news, ¹¹ of which I was myself appointed a herald and apostle, and teacher. ¹² That is why I am under-going these sufferings; yet I feel no shame, for I know in whom I have put my faith, and am convinced that he is able to guard what I have entrusted to him until "that day." ¹³ Keep before you, as an example of sound teaching, all that you learned from me as you listened with that faith and love which come from union with Christ Jesus. ¹⁴ Guard by the help of the holy Spirit, who is within us, the glorious trust that has been committed to you.

¹⁵ You know, of course, that all our friends in Roman Asia turned their backs on me, and among them Phygellus and Hermogenes. ¹⁶ May the Lord show mercy to the household of Onesiphorus; for he often cheered me and was not ashamed of my chains. ¹⁷ On the contrary, when he arrived in Rome, he sought eagerly for me until he found me. ¹⁸ The Lord grant that he may find mercy at the hands of the Lord on "that day." The many services that he rendered at Ephesus you have the best means of knowing.

Injunctions to Timothy

2 ¹ You must, then, my child, find strength in the help which comes from union with Christ Jesus; ² and what you learned from me, in the presence of many listeners, entrust to reliable people, who will be able in their turn to teach others. ³ Share hardships with me, as a true soldier of Christ Jesus. ⁴ A soldier on active service, to please his superior officer, always avoids entangling himself in the affairs of ordinary life. ⁵ No athlete is ever awarded the wreath of victory unless he has kept the rules. ⁶ The laborer who does the work should be the first to receive a share of the fruits of the earth. ⁷ Reflect on what I say; the Lord will

always help you to understand. [8] Keep before your mind Jesus Christ, raised from
the dead, a descendant of David, as told
in the good news entrusted to me, [9] in the
service of which I am suffering hardships,
even to being put in fetters as a criminal. But the message of God is not fet-
tered; [10] and that is why I submit to anything for the sake of God's people: so that
they also may obtain the salvation which
comes from union with Christ Jesus, and
imperishable glory. [11] How true this saying is: "If we have shared his death, we will
also share his life. [12] If we continue to endure, we will also share his throne. If we
should ever disown him, he, too, will disown us. [13] If we lose our trust, he is still to
be trusted, for he cannot be false to himself!"

[14] Remind people of all this; tell them
solemnly, as in the sight of God, to avoid
controversy, a useless thing and the ruin of
those who listen to it. [15] Do your utmost to
show yourself true to God, a worker with
no reason to be ashamed, accurate in delivering the message of the truth. [16] Avoid
profane prattle. Those who indulge in
it only get deeper into irreligious ways,
[17] and their teaching will spread like a can-
cer. Hymenaeus and Philetus are instances
of this. [18] They have gone completely
astray as regards the truth; they say that a
resurrection has already taken place, and
so upset some people's faith. [19] Yet God's
firm foundation still stands unmoved, and
it bears this inscription:

"The Lord knows those who are his";

and this:

"Let all those who use the name of the
Lord turn away from wickedness."

[20] Now in a large house there are not
only things of gold and silver, but also others of wood and earthenware, some for
better and some for common use. [21] If,
then, a person has escaped from the pollution of such errors as I have mentioned,
he will be like a thing kept for better use,
set apart, serviceable to its owner, ready
for any good purpose. [22] Flee from the
passions of youth, but pursue righteousness, faith, love, and peace, in the company of those who, with a pure heart,
invoke the Lord. [23] Shun foolish and ignorant discussions, for you know that they
only breed quarrels; [24] and a servant of the
Lord should never quarrel. He ought, on
the contrary, to be courteous to everyone,
skillful teachers, and forbearing. [25] He
should instruct his opponents in a gentle
spirit; for, possibly, God may give those
opponents a repentance that will lead to a
fuller knowledge of truth, [26] and they may
yet come to a sober mind, and escape from
the devil's net, when captured by the Lord's
servant to do the will of God.

3 [1] Be sure of this, that in the last days
difficult times will come. [2] People will be
selfish, mercenary, boastful, haughty, and
blasphemous; disobedient to their parents, ungrateful, impure, [3] incapable of
affection, merciless, slanderous, wanting in self-control, brutal, careless of the
right, [4] treacherous, reckless, and puffed
up with pride; they will love pleasure more
than they love God; [5] and while they retain the outward form of religion, they
will not allow it to influence them. Turn
your back on such people as these. [6] For
among them are to be found those who
creep into homes and captivate weak
women — women who, loaded with sins,
and slaves to all kinds of passions, [7] are
always learning, and yet never able to attain to a real knowledge of the truth. [8] Just
as Jannes and Jambres opposed Moses, so
do these people, in their turn, oppose the
truth. Their minds are corrupted, and, as
regards the faith, they are utterly worthless. [9] They will not, however, make further progress; for their wicked folly will be
plain to everyone, just as the folly Jannes

and Jambres was. [10] But you, Timothy, were a close observer of my teaching, my conduct, my purposes, my faith, my forbearance, my love, and my patient endurance, [11] as well as of my persecutions, and of the sufferings which I met with at Antioch, Iconium, and Lystra. You know what persecutions I underwent; and yet the Lord brought me safe out of all! [12] Yes, and all who aim at living a religious life in union with Christ Jesus will have to suffer persecution; [13] but wicked people and impostors will go from bad to worse, deceiving others and deceived themselves. [14] You, however, must stand by what you learned and accepted as true. You know who they were from whom you learned it; [15] and that from your childhood you have known the sacred writings, which can give you the wisdom that, through belief in Christ Jesus, leads to salvation. [16] All scripture is God-breathed: helpful for teaching, for refuting error, for giving guidance, and for training others in righteousness; [17] so that God's people may be capable and equipped for good work of every kind.

4 [1] I solemnly charge you, in the sight of God and of Christ Jesus, who will one day judge the living and the dead — I charge you by his appearing and by his realm: [2] Proclaim the message, be ready in season and out of season, convince, rebuke, encourage, never failing to instruct with forbearance. [3] For a time will come when people will not tolerate sound teaching. They will follow their own wishes, and, in their itching for novelty, procure themselves a crowd of teachers. [4] They will turn a deaf ear to the truth, and give their attention to legends instead. [5] But you, Timothy, must always be temperate. Face hardships; do the work of a missionary; discharge all the duties of your office.

[6] As for me, my lifeblood is already being poured out; the time of my departure is close at hand. [7] I have run the great race; I have finished the course; I have kept the faith. [8] And now the crown of righteousness awaits me, which the Lord, the just judge, will give me on "that day" — and not only to me, but to all who have loved his appearing.

Conclusion

Do your utmost to come to me soon; [10] for Demas, in his love for the world, has deserted me. He has gone to Thessalonica, Crescens to Galatia, and Titus to Dalmatia. [11] There is no one but Luke with me. Pick up Mark on your way, and bring him with you, for he is useful to me in my work. [12] I have sent Tychicus to Ephesus. [13] Bring with you, when you come, the cloak which I left at Troas with Carpus, and the books, especially the parchments. [14] Alexander, the coppersmith, showed much ill feeling toward me. "The Lord will give him what his actions deserve." [15] You must also be on your guard against him, for he is strongly opposed to our teaching. [16] At my first trial no one stood by me. They all deserted me. May it never be counted against them! [17] But the Lord came to my help and strengthened me, in order that through me, the proclamation should be made so widely that all the gentiles should hear it; and I was rescued "out of the Lion's mouth." [18] The Lord will rescue me from all evil, and bring me safe into his heavenly kingdom. All glory to him forever and ever! Amen.

[19] Give my greeting to Prisca and Aquila, and to the household of Onesiphorus. [20] Erastus remained at Corinth, and I left Thophimus ill at Miletus. [21] Do your utmost to come before winter. Eubulus, Pudens, Linus, and Claudia send you their greetings, and so do the rest of the Lord's followers.

[22] May the Lord be with your soul. God bless you all.

An Introduction to the Letter to Titus

THE LETTER TO TITUS is one of a number of documents in *A New New Testament* that outline different kinds of strategies for Christ communities in the second century, as they faced persecution and criticism. This letter differs from some and agrees with others in its strategy for the communities to continue, as much as possible, to do good and kind deeds, while also making clear their allegiance to the Roman rulers as divinely ordained.

In Greek, the letter outlines its strategy in some detail, making note of the required moderation of the elders and the president of the community. But it goes on to require all community members to be moderate and to act within their expected family roles. Young men and women are not to be rash, and slaves are to make sure they are fully obedient to their masters. This strategy also necessitates that the community quickly distance itself from any teachers who are behaving rebelliously. This letter has a tendency to emphasize the stories of the Judeans.

Like a number of others in the existing New Testament and the Prayer of the Apostle Paul in this *New New Testament,* this letter claims to be from Paul but was probably written in his name (a proper convention in the traditions of both Israel and the Greco-Romans) several generations after Paul.

Like Titus, some documents within *A New New Testament* that strategize about being persecuted seem to recommend downplaying the role of the Roman Empire in persecuting Christ people. Although Titus's case for not opposing Rome is perhaps the most thorough, Paul's Letter to the Romans and 1 Peter also refer to Rome as a power ordained by God. On the other hand, books like the Revelation to John declare war on Rome as an idolatrous enemy. The Secret Revelation of John has a similar condemnation of the Roman rulers but refuses to advocate violence to overcome this persecution. The Letter of Peter to Philip is perhaps the most nuanced of them all in calling Christ people to face their persecution, but to concentrate on teaching and healing no matter what.

Recommended Reading

Raymond F. Collins, *I & II Timothy and Titus: A Commentary*
D. R. MacDonald, *The Legend and the Apostle: The Battle for Paul in Story and Canon*

The Letter to Titus

Introduction

1 [1] From Paul, a servant of God, and an ambassador of Jesus Christ, charged to strengthen the faith of God's chosen people, and their knowledge of that truth which makes for godliness [2] and is based on the hope of life through the generations, which God, who never lies, promised before the ages began, [3] and has revealed at his own time in his message, with the proclamation of which I was entrusted by the command of God our Savior. [4] To Titus, my true child in our one faith: may God, the Father, and Christ Jesus, our Savior, bless you and give you peace.

Mission of Titus in Crete

My reason for leaving you in Crete was that you might put in order what had been left unsettled, and appoint officers of the church in the various towns, as I myself directed you. [6] They are to be of irreproachable character, faithful to their partners, whose children believe and have never been charged with dissolute conduct or have been unruly. [7] For a presiding officer, as God's steward, ought to be of irreproachable character; not self-willed or quick-tempered, nor addicted to drink or to brawling or to questionable money-making. [8] On the contrary, he should be hospitable, eager for the right, discreet, upright, someone of holy life and capable of self-restraint, [9] who holds teaching that can be relied on as being in accordance with previous teaching; so that he may be able to encourage others by sound teaching, as well as to refute our opponents.

[10] There are, indeed, many unruly persons—great talkers who deceive themselves, principally converts from Judaism —[11] whose mouths ought to be stopped; for they upset whole households by teaching what they ought not to teach, merely to make questionable gains. [12] It was a Cretan—one of their own teachers—who said: "Cretans are always liars, base brutes, and gluttonous idlers"; and his statement is true. [13] Therefore rebuke them sharply, so that they may be sound in the faith, [14] and may pay no attention to Judean legends, or to the directions of those who turn their backs on the truth. [15] Everything is pure to the pure-minded, but to those whose minds are polluted and who are unbelievers nothing is pure. Their minds and consciences are alike polluted. [16] They profess to know God, but by their actions they disown him. They are degraded and self-willed; and, as far as anything good is concerned, they are utterly worthless.

2 [1] You should, however, speak of such subjects as properly have a place in sound teaching. [2] Teach that the older men should be temperate, serious, and discreet; strong in faith, love, and endurance. [3] So, too, that the older women should be reverent in their demeanor, and that they should avoid scandal, and beware of becoming slaves to drink; [4] that they should teach what is right, so as to train the younger women to love their husbands and children, [5] and to be discreet, pure-minded, domesticated, good women, respecting the authority of their husbands, in order that God's message may not be maligned. [6] And so again with the younger men—impress on them the need of discretion. [7] Above all, set an example of doing good. Show sincerity in your teaching, and a serious spirit; [8] let the instruction that you give be sound and above reproach, so that the enemy may be ashamed when he fails to find anything bad to say about us. [9] Tell slaves to respect their owners' authority in all circumstances, and to try their best to please them. [10] Teach them not to contradict or to pilfer, but to show such praiseworthy fidelity in everything as to recommend the teaching about God our Savior by all that they do.

[11] For the loving kindness of God has been revealed, bringing salvation for all; [12] leading us to renounce irreligious ways and worldly ambitions, and to live discreet, upright, and religious lives here in this present world, [13] while we are awaiting our blessed hope — the appearing in glory of our great God and Savior, Christ Jesus. [14] For he gave himself on our behalf, to deliver us from all wickedness, and to purify for himself a people who should be peculiarly his own and eager to do good. [15] Speak of all this, and encourage and rebuke with all authority. Do not let anyone despise you.

3 [1] Remind your hearers to respect and obey the governing powers that be, to be ready for every kind of good work, to speak ill of no one, to avoid quarreling, [2] to be forbearing, and under all circumstances to show a gentle spirit in dealing with others, whoever they may be. [3] There was, you remember, a time when we ourselves were foolish, disobedient, misled, slaves to all kinds of passions and vices, living in a spirit of malice and envy, detested ourselves and hating one another. [4] But when the kindness of God our Savior and his love for humanity were revealed, he saved us, [5] not as the result of any righteous ac-

tions that we had done, but in fulfillment of his merciful purposes. He saved us by that washing which was a new birth to us, and by the renewing power of the holy Spirit, [6] which he poured out on us abundantly through Jesus Christ our Savior; [7] that having been pronounced righteous through his grace, we might enter on our inheritance with the hope of life from generation to generation. [8] How true that saying is! And it is on these subjects that I desire you to lay especial stress, so that those who have learned to trust in God may be careful to devote themselves to doing good. Such subjects are excellent in themselves, and of real use to humanity. [9] But have nothing to do with foolish discussions, or with genealogies, or with controversy, or disputes about the Law. They are useless and futile. [10] If someone is causing divisions among you, after warning him once or twice, have nothing more to say to him. [11] You may be sure that such a person has forsaken the truth and is in the wrong; he stands self-condemned.

Conclusion

[12] As soon as I send Artemas or Tychicus to you, join me as quickly as possible at Nicopolis, for I have arranged to spend the winter there. [13] Do your best to help Zenas, the teacher of the Law, and Apollos on their way, and see that they want for nothing. [14] Let all our people learn to devote themselves to doing good, so as to meet the most pressing needs, and that their lives may not be unfruitful.

[15] All who are with me here send you their greeting. Give my greeting to our friends in the faith.

God bless you all.

DIVERSE LETTERS, WITH A SET OF
INTRODUCTORY PRAYERS

An Introduction to the Third Book of
the Odes of Solomon

T HE ODES OF SOLOMON are simultaneously one of the most significant discoveries of early Christian literature and one of the most ignored discoveries of early Christian literature in the past two hundred years. Found in piles of research in a well-traveled and expert scholar's office in the early twentieth century,
they have been published since shortly after their "discovery." They are indisputably the largest trove of early Christian worship material ever found in one document, which is almost a third the size of the Bible's book of 150 psalms. The New
Orleans Council eagerly chose to include these odes, both for their beautiful and
evocative language and in order to make *A New New Testament* a strong witness to
actual material from the worship of some early Christ movements.

These forty-one "songs" of early Christianity are most likely a collection from
different communities over a period of time. Nevertheless, they also represent for
the most part a certain kind of early Christianity in their beliefs, practices, and
ways of framing the world. They look and sound very much like the psalms of the
Hebrew scriptures, except that they have regular references to the Word, the Light,
the Lord, and the Son of God in ways that indicate that they belong to a Christ
movement; that is, they are definitely "psalms" of a "Christian" character, although
they never use the name "Jesus," and rarely even the title "Christ" or "Anointed
One."

The "Christ" figure often speaks in these odes, making those early Christians
who sang them take on the identity of "Christ." This identification of the singers
with the "Christ" is complemented by the content of the odes in which the "Christ"
is a cosmic figure who makes humans one with God.

The title, "The Odes of Solomon," cannot, of course, refer to the author of this
collection (King Solomon lived a thousand years before) but serves rather as an affirmation of a strong and intimate connection between this part of early "Christianity" and the traditions of Israel. That this document represents a collection
of different odes from different communities makes "Solomon" something like
the figure of "David" for the psalms of the Hebrew scriptures. Knowing when the
odes were composed presents many challenges. Most commentators think they are
early, with the past thirty years of scholarship pointing more toward the first century than the second. Although perhaps not as inscrutable as the authorship of the
odes, the place of composition is also unclear. The closeness to the psalms of the
Hebrew scriptures suggests a "Christ" movement with very strong ties to the traditions of Israel. The odes' language of Syriac would point toward Syria.

A New New Testament breaks the odes into four distinct parts, distributed among different sections of the book. Since the odes as a collection do not represent one authorship, the New Orleans Council proposed that they could be broken up into distinct smaller sections. In keeping with the council's and my interest in making the reading of *A New New Testament* as worshipful as possible, I broke the larger document into these four distinct parts and used them to provide a spiritual and worshipful dimension to the other documents. The First Book of the Odes of Solomon contains Odes 1 and 3–12. The second book contains Odes 13–22; the third, Odes 23–32; and the fourth, Odes 33–42.*

The Third Book of the Odes of Solomon includes several psalmlike odes of praise, like those found also in the first and second books. But there are also two quite surprising forms found only in the third book. Odes 23 and 24 break most of the conventions of the first twenty-two odes, in that 23 and 24 are stories, where the elements of praise and prayer are muted.

An even more strikingly different form occurs in Odes 25, 27, 28, and 31. These odes are extended pleas and accounts from a persecuted voice. Similar to both Hebrew psalms of distress and images from the death of Jesus, these odes strongly claim the legacy of suffering, oppression, and crucifixion in early Christianity. In this way they represent a fascinating combination of psalms, gospel passion stories, and persecution accounts from early Christianity. Very similarly to many of the odes that mix the identities of the Christ figure and the odist/singer(s), these four "suffering" odes unite Christ's suffering and the pain of those who sing about him. They make clear that those who are in pain and sing the odes are connected to one another, to Christ, and to God.

There are two particularly significant reasons for the Third Book of the Odes of Solomon to be read at this juncture in *A New New Testament*. First — and as is the case for the first and second books — these odes are meant to mark a more emotive and spiritual reading. Because they are specifically prayers, they call forth different kinds of consciousness from the reader. They can be read on several different levels. Their prayerful and often first-person form allows one to think about what it was like to pray in the first and second centuries. Their image-filled and creative prayer style allows one to read them as poetic prayer. Rather than simply pointing to first-century people petitioning for something, these prayers offer an entry into the imagination of first- and second-century Christ followers. As personal and poetic expressions, they invite the twenty-first-century reader to associate these odes with personal and poetic images of their own lives.

The second reason for this Third Book of the Odes of Solomon to be read at this

---

* This section of general information is found in each introduction to a portion of the Odes of Solomon. The second section of each introduction is specific to the odes contained in it.

juncture is its focus on suffering. This is particularly appropriate, as the books in this section, "Diverse Letters with a Set of Introductory Prayers," contain a number of documents focused on the issue of suffering. The Letter to the Hebrews, the First Letter of Peter, and the Letter of Peter to Philip intentionally address the experience of early Christ followers' suffering. These prayers/odes invite the reader to feel the experience of suffering that the subsequent letters about suffering address. The prayerful character of these odes then presents an opportunity for the reading of the letters to be in more direct experiential contact with the subsequent letters' evocation of suffering.

Recommended Reading

James Charlesworth, *The Odes of Solomon: The Syriac Texts edited with Translation and Notes*
M. Franzmann, *The Odes of Solomon: An Analysis of the Poetical Structure and Form*
J. R. Harris and A. Mingana, *The Odes and Psalms of Solomon*

The Third Book of the Odes of Solomon

Ode 23

1 Joy is of the holy ones,
  And who shall put it on except them alone?

2 Kindness is of the chosen ones,
  And who shall receive it except those who relied on it from the beginning?

3 Love is for the chosen ones,
  And who shall put it on except those who possessed it from the beginning?

4 Walk in the knowledge of the Lord,
  And you will know the kindness of the Lord without grudge,
  Both according to his joy and the fullness of his understanding.

5 His thought was like a letter,
  And his will descended from the height.

6 It was sent out as an arrow from a bow,
  Which has been hurled with ferocity.

7 And many hands assailed the letter,
  To seize, to take, and to read her.

8 But she escaped their fingers,
  And they were afraid of her, and the seal upon her,

9 Since they were not permitted to loosen her seal,
  For the power that was upon the seal was higher than theirs.

10 Therefore those who had seen her went after the letter,
  So that they might learn where she stopped,
  Who would read her and who would hear her.

11 Instead a wheel received her,
  And came over her.

12 A sign of the realm and divine plan
  Was with her.

13 And everything that was confounding to the wheel
  Was cut and cleaved for her.

14 She overwhelmed a multitude of opponents,
  And buried rivers with earth.

15 She crossed over and uprooted many forests,
  And she made a broad path.

16 The head went down to the feet,
  Because the wheel ran as far as the feet,
  And whatever had come upon her.

17 The letter was one of injunction,
  And so all of the regions were gathered together.

18 There was seen at her head, the head which had been revealed,
  And the child of Truth, from the Father of the Most High.

19 And the child inherited everything, and possessed it,
  And the calculation of the many was stopped.

20 Then all who were led astray grew hasty and fled,
  And those who had persecuted withered and were wiped out.

21 Then the letter became a great volume,
  Which was written entirely by the finger of God.

22 And upon her were the name of the Father,
  And of the Child,* and of the holy Spirit,

---

* Literally, "Son."

To govern forever and ever.
Halleluiah.

Ode 24

¹ The dove hovered over the head of our
Anointed Lord
  Because he is our head.
² She sang over him,
  And her voice was heard.
³ The inhabitants were afraid,
  And the strangers were shaken.
⁴ The bird left to fly,
  And every creeping thing died in its
cave.
⁵ The depths were opened and concealed,
  And they were seeking the Lord as
those about to give birth.
⁶ But he was not given to them for food,
  Because he was not their own.
⁷ Then the depths were sunk by the plung-
ing of the Lord,
  And they perished by that thought
which they had from the beginning.
⁸ For they corrupted from the beginning,
  And the end of their corruption was
life.
⁹ All who were lacking perished by them,
  Because they did not compare to the
word in order to remain.
¹⁰ The Lord destroyed the devices
  Of all of those who did not have Truth
with them.
¹¹ For those who had exalted themselves
in their own hearts
  Lacked in wisdom.
¹² They were rejected
  Because Truth was not with them,
¹³ Because the Lord indicated his path,
  And spread out his kindness.
¹⁴ So those who recognized it
  Knew his sanctity.
Halleluiah.

Ode 25

¹ I was freed from my bonds,

And I fled toward you, my God.
² Because you are the Right Hand of redemption,
  And my own helper.
³ You have held back those who would
stand against me,
  And they were not seen again.
⁴ Because your presence was with me,
  Which released me through your kindness.
⁵ But I was scorned and rejected in many
eyes,
  And I was, in their eyes, like lead.
⁶ And from you there was resilience
  And help for me.
⁷ You set for me a lamp, on my right and
my left,
  So that there would not be anything
that was not light in me.
⁸ I clothed myself in the garment of your
spirit,
  And I removed my garments of skin.
⁹ Because your Right Hand exalted me
  And caused weakness to pass from
me.
¹⁰ I grew strong in your truth
  And sanctified in your justice.
¹¹ Then all of them who were against me
  Were afraid of me.
¹² And I was confirmed by his sweetness,
  And his rest is forever and ever.
Halleluiah.

Ode 26

¹ I poured forth praise to the Lord,
  Because I was his own.
² I will speak his holy ode,
  Because my heart is with him.
³ For his lyre is in my hands,
  And the odes of his rest will not be silent.
⁴ I will shout to him from all of my heart.
  I will praise and extol him from all of
my members.
⁵ Truly his glory extends from east to west,
⁶ His fame from south to north.

⁷ And his fullness from the top of the summits
    Until their edges.
⁸ Who can write the odes of the Lord,
    Or who can read them?
⁹ Or who can instruct his entire self for life,
    So that his self may be saved?
¹⁰ Or who can press upon the Most High,
    So that she would speak from his mouth?
¹¹ Who can interpret the wonders of the Lord?
    Since the one who interprets will be destroyed,
    And that which was interpreted will remain.
¹² Truly it is sufficient to perceive and be satisfied,
    For the odists stand in serenity,
¹³ Like a river that has an abundant source,
    And leads to the relief of those who seek it.
Halleluiah.

Ode 27

¹ I stretched out my hands
    And sanctified my Lord,
² Because the extension of my hands
    Is his sign
³ And my stretching
    Is the cross that is raised up.
Halleluiah.

Ode 28

¹ Like the wings of doves over their chicks,
    And as the mouths of the chicks toward their mouths,
    So also are the wings of the spirit over my heart.
² My heart delights and jumps
    Like an infant jumps joyously in its mother's womb.

³ I had faith, and because of this I was also at rest,
    Since the one in whom I trusted is faithful.
⁴ He has blessed me continually
    And my head is toward him.
⁵ And sword will not divide me from him,
    Nor dagger.
⁶ Because I have prepared myself, before annihilation comes,
    I have been placed in his incorruptible wings.
⁷ Then immortal lives embraced me,
    And kissed me.
⁸ And the spirit which is in me is from them,
    And she cannot die, because she is life.
[Christ speaks]
⁹ The ones who saw me were amazed,
    Because I was persecuted.
¹⁰ They thought I had been consumed,
    Because I appeared to them as one of the lost.
¹¹ But oppression became salvation for me.
¹² I became their despised one,
    Because there was no jealousy in me.
¹³ Because I did good to everyone, I was hated.
¹⁴ And they surrounded me like rabid dogs,
    Those who in ignorance turn upon their masters,*
¹⁵ Because their minds are ruined,
    And their thinking is altered.
¹⁶ But I was carrying water in my Right Hand,
    And endured their bitterness through my sweetness.
¹⁷ I did not perish, because I was not their brother,
    Neither was my birth like theirs.
¹⁸ So they sought my death, but they did not find it,

---

* This is the same word as "Lord."

Because I was older than their memory,

And they cast lots against me in vain.

19 Those who were after me,

They longed in vain to destroy the memory of the one who existed before them.

20 Because the thought of consciousness of the Most High cannot be preceded,

And his heart exceeds all wisdom. Halleluiah.

Ode 29

1 The Lord is my hope,

I shall not be ashamed of him.

2 For he made me according to his splendor,

And he gave me goodness from his own goodness.

3 By means of his mercies he raised me,

And according to his great beauty he lifted me up.

4 He caused me to ascend from the depths of Sheol,

And he tore me from the mouth of death.

5 And I humiliated my adversaries,

And he justified me in his kindness.

6 For I trusted in the Anointed One of the Lord,

And it appeared to me that he is the Lord.

7 He showed me his sign,

Led me by his light,

8 And gave me the staff of his power,

So that I might subdue the calculations of peoples,

9 In order to wage war with his word,

And to take command with his power.

10 The Lord abolished my enemy by his word

And it became as the dust which the wind carries away.

11 Then I gave praise to the Most High

Because he made great both his servant and the child of his maidservant. Halleluiah.

Ode 30

1 Draw up for yourselves water from the living fountain of the Lord,

Because it has been opened for you.

2 Come all of you thirsty ones, and take a drink

And be soothed by the spring of the Lord

3 Because it is beautiful and clean

And restores the self.

4 Indeed its waters are much sweeter than honey,

And the honeycomb of bees does not compare with it,

5 Because it emerged from the lips of the Lord

And its name comes from the heart of the Lord.

6 It came limitless and invisible,

And until it was given in the middle, they did not recognize it.

7 They are blessed, those who have drunk from it,

And who have been soothed by it.

Halleluiah.

Ode 31

1 The depths dissolved before the Lord,

And darkness was obliterated from his sight.

2 Error stumbled, and perished by him,

And contempt received no path.

3 He opened his mouth and spoke kindness and joy

And spoke new praise to his name.

4 He raised his voice to the Most High,

And offered to him those who had become children through his hand.

5 And his person was justified

Because his holy Father had given him such.

[Christ speaks]

6 Come out, you who have been tormented,

And receive joy.

7 Acquire yourselves through generosity,

And receive immortal life.
⁸ They condemned me when I stood up,
    The one who had not been condemned.
⁹ Then they divided my spoil,
    When nothing was owed to him.
¹⁰ But I endured, and was silent and at peace,
    So that I could not be shaken by them.
¹¹ Instead, I stood unmoving, like a solid rock
    Which is struck by the pounding waves and endures.
¹² I endured their bitterness because of humility,
    So that I might redeem and teach my people.

¹³ And so that I would not empty out the promises to the first fathers,
    To whom I had been promised for the salvation of their offspring.
Halleluiah.

Ode 32

¹ For the blessed ones, laughter is from their hearts
    And light is from the one who dwells in them.
² And the word from the truth exists of itself,
³ Because that one has become strong in the sacred power of the Most High,
    And is unshaken forever.
Halleluiah.

An Introduction to the Letter of James

THE LETTER OF JAMES is famous for its pressing agenda to do good works, especially in relation to poor people. It expresses hardly any interest in belief, spirituality, faith, or doctrine. It focuses on both the social morals and the integrity of people.

This document does identify its author as "James," but it is unlikely that this "James" is either James, the brother of Jesus, or James, the other disciple of Jesus. It is unlikely that either of those first-generation Galilean followers of Jesus knew how to read or write, much less in Greek (the language of this book), as they were both almost certainly peasants who spoke only Aramaic. The letter also describes a level of organization in the communities it addresses that would have taken several generations to develop, and therefore it most likely was written at a significantly later time than when either James was alive. It is difficult to know precisely when this letter was written, but the material leads us to believe it is likely from anytime between 75 and 120 CE.

Not unlike a formal business letter today, the conventional way of writing a letter in the ancient Mediterranean followed a prescribed form. It called for an extended and formal address to its audience, an expression of thanksgiving to the recipients of the letter, a central message, ethical instructions to the recipients, and an elaborate sign-off. The Letter of James does not follow this prescribed form and was therefore probably not ever sent as a letter. Its first sentence designates it as a general "letter" to "the twelve tribes that are living abroad." This designation is difficult to understand, as it would be impossible for it to be sent to hundreds of thousands of those practicing the traditions of Israel outside the boundaries of that territory.

In form, James resembles a letter less than a sayings document, where a number of teachings are gathered. It quotes some teachings from the Hebrew scriptures as well as several from Jesus's own teachings. It might also be a written version of teachings organized for meetings at meals, the primary place where early Christians received lessons in groups. The meeting place for the various groups addressed is called the "synagogue" in James (2:2), and the quotations from both Hebrew scriptures and Jesus traditions fit completely within Israel's traditions. In this regard, James is one of the early documents that most thoroughly show developed Jesus movements lying completely within the traditions of Israel. There is no evidence of gentiles within the groups, and Torah is used as the standard of behavior (4:11–12).

The teachings collected and articulated in James are most concerned about two issues: the hypocrisy of rich Jesus people who ignore the plight of people in poverty, and the danger of talking without discipline. One section reads: "Listen, my dear friends. Has not God chosen those who are poor in the things of this world to be rich through their faith, and to possess the realm promised to those who love him? But you — you insult the poor man! Is it not the rich who oppress you? Is it not they who drag you into law courts? Is it not they who malign that honorable name which has been bestowed on you?" (2:5–7). The other focus of James is a reproach of those who talk too much or without thinking first about what they are saying. This could possibly connect with a concern that some people only talk but do not think about what they can do, especially for those in economic distress.

In readings of the traditional New Testament, James has been pictured mostly as a kind of outlier letter. Martin Luther did not like its attack on the power of faith, called it a "straw epistle," and proposed that it be removed from the New Testament. In our broader collection, its sayings compare with the sayings of Jesus in the Gospel of Thomas and with the Gospel of Truth's instructions to "strengthen the feet of those who stumble and stretch your hands to those who are weak. Feed those who are hungry and give rest to the weary" (17:13–14).

Recommended Reading

S. A. Laws, *A Commentary on the Epistle of James*
Wesley Wachob, editor, *Reading James with New Eyes: Methodological Reassessments of the Letter of James*

The Letter of James

Greeting

1 ¹ James, a slave of God and of the Lord Jesus Christ, greets the twelve tribes that are living abroad.

Advice on Various Subjects

² My friends, whatever may be the temptations that beset you from time to time, always regard them as a reason for rejoicing, ³ knowing, as you do, that the testing of your faith develops endurance. ⁴ And let endurance do its work perfectly, so that you may be altogether perfect, and in no respect deficient.

⁵ If one of you is deficient in wisdom, let her ask wisdom from the God who gives freely to everyone without reproaches, and it will be given to her. ⁶ But let her ask with confidence, never doubting; for the person who doubts is like a wave of the sea driven here and there at the mercy of the wind — ⁷ such a person must not expect that she will receive anything from the Lord, ⁸ vacillating as she is, irresolute at every turn.

⁹ Let a follower in humble circumstances be proud of his exalted position, but a rich follower of his humiliation; ¹⁰ for the rich will pass away "like the flower of the grass." ¹¹ As the sun rises, and the hot wind blows, the grass withers, its flower fades, and all its beauty is gone. So it is with the rich. In the midst of their pursuits they will come to an untimely end.

¹² Blessed is the person who remains firm under temptation, for, when he has stood the test, he will receive the crown of life, which the Lord has promised to those who love him. ¹³ Let no one say, when he is tempted, "It is God who is tempting me!" For God, who cannot be tempted to do wrong, does not himself tempt anyone. ¹⁴ A person is in every case tempted by his own passions — allured and enticed by them. ¹⁵ Then passion conceives and gives birth to sin, and sin, on reaching maturity, brings forth death. ¹⁶ Do not be deceived, my dear friends. ¹⁷ Every good thing given us, and every perfect gift, is from above, and comes down to us from the Father of the lights in the heavens, who is himself never subject to change or to eclipse. ¹⁸ Because he so willed, he gave us life, through the message of the truth, so that we should be, as it were, a down payment on still further creations.

¹⁹ Mark this, my brothers — let everyone be quick to listen, slow to speak, and slow to get angry; ²⁰ for men's anger does not forward the righteous purpose of God. ²¹ Therefore, have done with all filthiness and whatever wickedness still remains, and in a humble spirit receive that message which has been planted in your hearts and is able to save your souls. ²² Put that message into practice, and do not merely listen to it — deceiving yourselves. ²³ For, when anyone listens to it and does not practice it, he is like a person looking at his own face in a mirror. ²⁴ He looks at himself, then goes on his way, ²⁵ but the person who looks carefully into the perfect Law, the Law of freedom, and continues to do so, not listening to it and then forgetting it, but putting it into practice — that person will be blessed in what he does. ²⁶ When a person appears to be observant, yet does not bridle his tongue, but imposes on his own conscience, that person's religious observances are valueless. ²⁷ That religious observance which is pure and spotless in the eyes of God our Father is this — to visit orphans and widows in their trouble, and

to keep oneself uncontaminated by the world.

Warning on Various Subjects

2 [1] My friends, are you really trying to combine faith in Jesus Christ, our glorified Lord, with the attention to rank? [2] Suppose a visitor should enter your synagogue, with gold rings and in grand clothes, and suppose a poor man should come in also, in shabby clothes, [3] and you are deferential to the visitor who is wearing grand clothes, and say, "There is a good seat for you here," but to the poor man, "You must stand; or sit down there by my footstool." [4] Is not that to make distinctions among yourselves, and show yourselves prejudiced judges? [5] Listen, my dear friends. Has not God chosen those who are poor in the things of this world to be rich through their faith, and to possess the realm promised to those who love him? [6] But you — you insult the poor man! Is it not the rich who oppress you? Is it not they who drag you into law courts? [7] Is it not they who malign that honorable name which has been bestowed on you? [8] Yet, if you keep the realm's Law which runs, "You must love your neighbor as you love yourself," you are doing right; [9] but if you pay attention to rank, you commit a sin, and stand convicted by that same Law of being offenders against it. [10] For a person who has laid the Law, as a whole, to heart, but has failed in one particular, is accountable for breaking all its provisions. [11] The one who said, "You must not commit adultery" also said, "You must not murder." If, then, you commit murder but not adultery, you are still an offender against the Law. [12] Therefore, speak and act as people who are to be judged by the "Law of freedom." [13] For there will be justice without mercy for the person who has not acted mercifully. Mercy triumphs over justice.

[14] My friends, what is the good of a person's saying that she has faith, if she does not prove it by actions? Can such faith save her? [15] Suppose some brother or sister should be in need of clothes and of daily bread, [16] and one of you were to say to her, "Go, and peace be with you; find warmth and food for yourself," and yet you were not to give her the necessaries of life, what good would it be to her? [17] In just the same way faith, if not followed by actions, is, by itself, a lifeless thing. [18] Someone, indeed, may say, "You are a person of faith, and I am a person of action."

"Then show me your faith," I reply, "apart from any actions, and I will show you my faith by my actions." [19] It is a part of your faith, is it not, that there is one God? Good; yet even the demons have that faith, and tremble at the thought. [20] Now do you really want to understand, fool, how it is that faith without actions leads to nothing? [21] Look at our ancestor Abraham. Was it not the result of his actions that he was pronounced righteous after he had offered his son, Isaac, on the altar? [22] You see how, in his case, faith and actions went together; that his faith was perfected as the result of his actions; [23] and that in this way the words of the writings came true: "Abraham believed God, and that was regarded by God as righteousness," and "He was called the friend of God." [24] You see, then, that it is as the result of her actions that a person is pronounced righteous, and not of her faith only. [25] Was it not the same with the prostitute Rahab? Was it not as the result of her actions that she was pronounced righteous, after she had welcomed the messengers and helped them escape? [26] Exactly as a body is dead without a spirit, so faith is dead without actions.

3 [1] I do not want many of you, my friends, to become teachers, knowing, as you do, that we who teach will be judged by a more severe standard than others. [2] We often make mistakes, every one of us. Anyone who does not make mistakes when speaking is indeed a perfect person, able to bridle his whole body as well. ³ When we put bits into horses' mouths, to make them obey us, we control the rest of their bodies so. ⁴ Again, think of ships. Large as they are, and even when driven by fierce winds, they are controlled by a very small rudder and steered in whatever direction the man at the helm may determine. ⁵ So it is with the tongue. Small as it is, it is a great boaster. Think how tiny a spark may set the largest forest ablaze! ⁶ And the tongue is like a spark. Among the members of our body it proves itself a world of mischief; it contaminates the whole body; it sets the wheels of life on fire, and is itself set on fire by the flames of Gehenna. ⁷ For while all sorts of beasts and birds, and of reptiles and creatures in the sea, are tamable, and actually have been tamed by man, ⁸ no human being can tame the tongue. It is a restless plague! It is charged with deadly poison! ⁹ With it we bless our Lord and Father, and with it we curse people who are made in God's likeness. ¹⁰ From the very same mouth come blessings and curses! My friends, it is not right that this should be so. ¹¹ Does a spring give both good and bad water from the same source? ¹² Can a fig tree, my friends, bear olives? Or a vine bear figs? No, nor can a brackish well give good water.

¹³ Who among you claims to be wise and intelligent? Let him show that his actions are the outcome of a good life lived in the gentleness of Wisdom-Sophia.* ¹⁴ But while you harbor envy and bitterness and a spirit of rivalry in your hearts, do not boast or lie to the detriment of the truth. ¹⁵ That is not the Wisdom-Sophia which comes from above; no, it is earthly, animal, devilish. ¹⁶ For, where envy and rivalry ex-

ist, there you will also find disorder and all kinds of base actions. ¹⁷ But the Wisdom-Sophia from above is, before every thing else, pure; then peace-loving, gentle, open to conviction, rich in compassion and good deeds, and free from partiality and insincerity. ¹⁸ And righteousness, its fruit, is sown in peace by those who work for peace.

4 ¹ What is the cause of the fighting and quarreling that go on among you? Is it not to be found in the desires which are always at war within you? ² You crave, yet do not obtain. You murder and rage, yet cannot gain your end. You quarrel and fight. You do not obtain, because you do not ask. ³ You ask, yet do not receive, because you ask for a wrong purpose — to spend what you get on your pleasures. ⁴ Unfaithful people! Do you not know that to be friends with the world means to be at enmity with God? Therefore whoever chooses to be friends with the world makes himself an enemy to God. ⁵ Do you suppose there is no meaning in the passage of scripture which asks, "Is envy to result from the longings of the spirit which God has implanted within you?" ⁶ No; the gift that God gives is for a nobler end; and that is why it is said, "God is opposed to the haughty, but gives help to the humble." ⁷ Therefore submit to God; but resist the devil, and he will flee from you. ⁸ Draw near to God, and God will draw near to you. Make your hands clean, you sinners; and your hearts pure, you vacillator! ⁹ Grieve, mourn, and lament! Let your laughter be turned to mourning, and your happiness to gloom! ¹⁰ Humble yourselves before the Lord, and he will exalt you. ¹¹ Do not disparage one another, friends. The person who disparages others, or

---

* This treatment of *wisdom* relies on the divine person of Wisdom portrayed in Proverbs 1–9, Matthew 11, and 1 Corinthians 2. The Greek word for wisdom is *sophia*. In this way the Greek word and its English translation are used together to indicate the personhood of Wisdom in these verses.

passes judgment on them, disparages the Law and passes judgment on the Law. But if you pass judgment on the Law, you are not obeying it, but judging it. [12] There is only one lawgiver and judge — the one who has the power both to save and to destroy. But who are you that pass judgment on your neighbor?

[13] Listen to me, you who say, "Today or tomorrow we will go to such and such a town, spend a year there, and trade, and make money." [14] And yet you do not know what your life will be like tomorrow! For you are but a mist appearing for a little while and then disappearing. [15] You ought, rather, to say, "If the Lord wills, we will live and do this or that." [16] But as it is, you are constantly boasting presumptuously! All such boasting is wicked. [17] The person, then, who knows what is right but fails to do it — that is sin in him.

5 [1] Listen to me, you rich people, weep and wail for the miseries that are coming upon you! [2] Your riches have wasted away, and your clothes have become moth-eaten. [3] Your gold and silver are rusted; and the rust on them will be evidence against you, and will eat into your flesh. It was fire, so to speak, that you stored up for yourselves in these last days. [4] I tell you, the wages of the laborers who mowed your fields, which you have been fraudulently keeping back, are crying out against you, and the outcries of your reapers have reached the ears of the Lord of Hosts! [5] You have lived on earth a life of extravagance and luxury; you have indulged your fancies in a time of bloodshed. [6] You have condemned, you have murdered, the righteous one! Must not God be opposed to you?

Concluding Appeal

Be patient, then, friends, until the coming of the Lord. Even the farmer has to wait for the precious fruit of the earth, watching over it patiently, until it has had the spring and summer rains. [8] And you must be patient also, and not be discouraged; for the Lord's coming is near. [9] Do not make complaints against one another, friends, or judgment will be passed on you. The judge is already standing at the door! [10] Friends, as an example of the patient endurance of suffering, take the prophets who spoke in the name of the Lord. [11] We count those who displayed such endurance blessed! You have heard, too, of Job's endurance, and have seen what the Lord's purpose was, for the Lord is full of pity and compassion.

[12] Above all things, my friends, never take an oath, either by heaven, or by earth, or by anything else. With you let "Yes" suffice for yes, and "No" for no, so that you may escape condemnation.

[13] If any of you is in trouble, let her pray; if anyone is happy, let her sing hymns. [14] If anyone of you is ill, let her send for the officers of the church, and let them pray over her, after anointing her with oil in the name of the Lord. [15] The prayer offered in faith will save the person who is sick, and the Lord will raise her from her bed; and if she has committed sins, they will be forgiven. [16] Therefore, confess your sins to one another and pray for one another, so that you may be cured. Great is the power of a good person's fervent prayer. [17] Elijah was only human like ourselves, but when he prayed fervently that it might not rain, no rain fell on the land for three years and a half. [18] And when he prayed again, the clouds brought rain, and the land bore crops. [19] My friends, should one of you be led astray from the truth, and someone bring you back again, [20] be sure that the person who brings a sinner back from her mistaken ways will save that person's soul from death, and throw a veil over countless sins.

An Introduction to the Letter to the Hebrews

THE CREATIVE METAPHORS for life in Jesus Christ in the Letter to the Hebrews are some of the most imaginative of any book in *A New New Testament*. But Hebrews has been mostly ignored by official Christendom; in a real way, it has been treated as if it were never really discovered, even though it was included in the traditional New Testament. It has been considered an obscure book that does not fit well with conventional Christianity. It extensively reworks Hebrew scripture by combining it often with Greek philosophy, introduces an entirely new concept of Jesus simultaneously as priest and sacrifice, and invents an entirely new lineage for Jesus. For its creativity alone it deserves to share the limelight with those books that have been added to *A New New Testament*.

Perhaps because of its adventuresome approach, the basic data about the Letter to the Hebrews have been contested for most of its existence. It does not really seem to take the consistent form of a letter; many suggest it is more like a teaching or sermon. Grouped very early on with the letters of Paul, it does not have his name attached and expresses thinking quite different from Paul's usual line. The "To the Hebrews" title may very well have been added later, especially as it is not mentioned or acknowledged in the document's contents, and the document is written in Greek. It has been very difficult to determine the time and circumstances of composition; the letter can be dated to anywhere from 65 to 100 CE.

The special attention this document pays to Hebrew scriptures and the Jerusalem Temple suggests deep roots in Israel's traditions. On the other hand, parts of it appear to be influenced by Greek philosophy, especially the neo-Platonist movement. And many have found it to treat the symbols generated by the Roman emperor's family in the last part of the first century. One place where all these elements are especially strong is Egypt, but it is possible to imagine that the letter was written in other locations.

The Earthly and Heavenly Temple and Priest

With the possible exception of the Gospel of John, Hebrews depends on a two-tiered universe most heavily of any document in *A New New Testament*. The earthly sanctuary and the priesthood in Jerusalem are reflections of and are radically inferior to the sanctuary and priesthood in heaven. Jesus is featured in the heavenly tier, and here in this letter we get a rare glimpse of Jesus as priest, a picture of Jesus rooted in Hebrew scriptures through a fairly obscure story, in Genesis 14, of a non-Israelite king and priest of Salem. Jesus gains access for himself and his followers to the higher world by sacrificing himself.

It may not be appropriate to see this new life in Jesus as an afterlife experience, but as a new way of thinking about reality in the lived present. This new realm seems to be in tension with both the Roman emperor's claim of ruling over the whole earth and with Israel's former glory in its now-destroyed Jerusalem Temple. Having spiritually ascended with Jesus, even while they are still living on earth, Jesus's followers now are greater than geographical Israel, which the Romans disgraced by destroying the Temple in Jerusalem. And Jesus's ascended followers are now also rivals to the emperor.

Persistence, Confidence, and Persecution

Like documents such as the Letter of Peter to Philip and the Secret Revelation of John, Hebrews seems to have been written for people who need to persist in the face of great difficulties. The ancient addressees of this book are "in all sincerity of heart and in perfect faith" (10:22) by their having crossed over into Jesus's new higher temple. By his death, Jesus has delivered "all those who, from fear of death, had all their lives been living in slavery" (2:15) and has enabled them no longer to fear but to be confident and to persist.

It is not just Jesus's courageous death but the confidence and persistence of a "throng of witnesses" (12:1 as an end to chapter 11's long list of Abel, Enoch, Noah, Abraham, Sarah, Isaac, Jacob, and Moses) that allow the Christ people to persevere in such difficult times.

Jesus Higher Than the Angels, Moses, and David

Hebrews focuses on the heroes of Israel's traditions but also reworks Hebrew scriptures to demonstrate that these examples are less important than Jesus himself. So there is a link between Jesus and Israel's epic figures, but Jesus is superior to them. For instance, "Now if Joshua had given rest to the people, God would not have spoken of another and later day" (4:8).

In light of the Roman rulers' claims of divine status, Hebrews places strong emphasis on positioning Jesus higher than the angels. "Let all the angels of God bow down before him. . . . As yet, however, we do not see everything placed under him. What our eyes do see is Jesus, who was made for a while lower than angels, now, because of his sufferings and death, crowned with glory and honor . . ." (1:6; 2:8–9). And this higher status of Jesus is a result of him suffering "to help those who are tempted" (2:18).

Hebrews and *A New New Testament*

More study of Hebrews may indeed reveal parallels with its stepchild status within the traditional New Testament and the now-emerging powerful works added to *A New New Testament*. There are, however, not many exact parallels between these new works and Hebrews. In some cases (the Gospel of Truth) one can see these new works as similar to Hebrews in their common devotion to both the Hebrew scriptures and Greek philosophy. But probably the most evocative comparison is not so much their common language or ideas, but their adventuresome efforts to invent new language, their imagination, and their efforts to communicate the powerful meanings arising from the breadth of early Christianity.

Recommended Reading

David L. Allen, *Hebrews*

Harold W. Attridge, *The Epistle to the Hebrews*

D. A. deSilva, *Perseverance in Gratitude: A Socio-Rhetorical Commentary on the Epistle to the Hebrews*

The Letter to the Hebrews

Christ the Mediator

1 ¹ God, who, of old, at many times and in many ways, spoke to our ancestors, by the prophets, ² has in these latter days spoken to us by the Son, whom he appointed the heir of all things, and through whom he made the universe. ³ For he is the radiance of the glory of God and the expression of his being, upholding all creation by the power of his word; and when he had cleansed the sins of humanity, he took his seat at the right hand of God's Majesty on high, ⁴ having shown himself as much greater than the angels as the name that he has inherited surpasses theirs.

⁵ For to which of the angels did God ever say,

> "You are my Son; this day I have
>   become your Father"?

or again:

> "I will be to him a Father, and he will
>   be to me a Son"?

⁶ And again, when God brought the firstborn into the world, he said,

> "Let all the angels of God bow down
>   before him."

⁷ Speaking of the angels, he said,

> "He makes the winds his angels
> and the flames of fire his servants";

⁸ while of the Son he said,

> "God is your throne forever and ever;
> the scepter of his realm is the scepter
>   of justice;

> you love righteousness and hate
>   iniquity;
> therefore God, your God, has anointed
>   you with the festal oil more
>   abundantly than your peers."

¹⁰ Again:

> "You, Lord, in the beginning did lay the
>   foundation of the earth,
> and the heavens are the work of your
>   hands.
> ¹¹ They will perish, but you remain;
> as a garment they will all grow old;
> ¹² as a mantle you will fold them up,
> and as a garment they will be
>   changed,
> but you are the same, and your years
>   will know no end."

¹³ To which of the angels has God ever said,

> "Sit you at my right hand
> until I put your enemies as a stool for
>   your feet"?

¹⁴ Are not all the angels spirits in the service of God, sent out to minister for the sake of those who are destined to obtain salvation?

2 ¹ Therefore, we must give still more heed to what we were taught, so we do not drift away. ² For, if the message which was delivered by angels had its authority confirmed, so that every offense against it, or neglect of it, met with a fitting requital, ³ how can we, of all people, expect to escape, if we disregard so great a salvation? It was the Master who at the outset spoke of this salvation, and its authority was con-

firmed for us by those who heard him, [4] while God himself added his testimony to it by signs, and marvels, and many different miracles, as well as by imparting the holy Spirit as he saw fit.

[5] God has not given to angels the control of that future world of which we are speaking! [6] No; a writer has declared somewhere,

> "What are mere mortals that you
>   should remember them?
> Or human beings that you should care
>   for them?
> You have made them, for a while, lower
>   than angels;
> with glory and honor you have
>   crowned them;
> you have set them over all that your
>   hands have made;
> you have placed all things beneath
>   their feet."

This placing of everything under him means that there was nothing which was not placed under him. As yet, however, we do not see everything placed under him. [9] What our eyes do see is Jesus, who was made for a while lower than angels, now, because of his sufferings and death, crowned with glory and honor; so that his tasting the bitterness of death should, in God's loving kindness, be on behalf of all humanity. [10] It was indeed fitting that God, for whom and through whom all things exist, should, when leading many children to glory, make the author of their salvation perfect through suffering. [11] For the one who purifies, and those whom he purifies, all spring from One; and therefore he is not ashamed to call them his brothers and sisters, when

[12] he says,

> "I will tell of your name to my brothers
>   and sisters,
> in the midst of the congregation I will
>   sing your praise."

[13] And again:

> "As for me, I will put my trust in God."

And yet again:

> "See, here am I and the children whom
>   God gave me."

[14] Therefore, since flesh is the common heritage of the children, Jesus also shared it, in order that by death he might render powerless him whose power lies in death — that is, the devil — [15] and so might deliver all those who, from fear of death, had all their lives been living in slavery. [16] It was not, surely, to the help of the angels that Jesus came, but to the help of the descendants of Abraham. [17] And consequently it was necessary that he should in all points be made like his brothers and sisters, in order that he might prove a merciful as well as a faithful high priest in humanity's relations with God, for the purpose of expiating the sins of the people. [18] The fact that he himself suffered under temptation enables him to help those who are tempted.

3 [1] Therefore, my holy friends, you who, all alike, have received the call from heaven, fix your attention on Jesus, the ambassador and high priest of our belonging. [2] See how faithful he was to the God who appointed him, as Moses was in the whole house of God. [3] He has been deemed worthy of a far higher honor than Moses, just as the founder of the house is held in greater regard than the house itself. [4] For every house has its founder, and the founder of the universe is God. [5] While the faithful service of Moses in the whole house of God was that of a servant, whose duty was to bear testimony to a message still to come, [6] the faithfulness of Christ was that of a son set over the house of God. And we are his house — if only we retain, unshaken to the end, the

courage and confidence inspired by our hope.

⁷ Therefore, as the holy Spirit says,

"If today you hear God's voice,
harden not your hearts, as when Israel
    provoked me
on the day when they tried my patience
    in the desert,
where your ancestors tried my
    forbearance,
and saw my mighty deeds for forty
    years.
¹⁰ Therefore, I was sorely vexed with that
    generation,
And I said, 'Their hearts are always
    straying;
they have never learned my ways';
¹¹ while in my wrath I swore,
'They will never enter upon my rest.'"

¹² Be careful, friends, that there is never found in any one of you a wicked and faithless heart, shown by that person separating herself from the living God. ¹³ Rather, encourage one another daily — while there is a "today" — to prevent anyone among you from being hardened by the deceitfulness of sin. ¹⁴ For we now all share in the Christ, if indeed we retain, unshaken to the end, the confidence that we had at the first. ¹⁵ To use the words of scripture:

"If today you hear God's voice,
harden not your hearts, as when Israel
    provoked me."

¹⁶ Who were they who heard God speak and yet provoked him? Were they not all those who left Egypt under the leadership of Moses? ¹⁷ And with whom was it that God was sorely vexed for forty years? Was it not with those who had sinned, and who fell dead in the desert? ¹⁸ And who were they to whom God swore that they should not enter upon his rest, if not those who had proved faithless? ¹⁹ We see, then, that

they failed to enter upon it because of their want of trust.

4 ¹ We must, therefore, be very careful, though there is a promise still standing that we will enter upon God's rest, that none of you even appear to have missed it. ² For we have had the good news told us just as they had. But the message which they heard did them no good, since they did not share the faith of those who were attentive to it. ³ Upon that rest we who have believed are now entering. As God has said,

"In my wrath I swore,
'They will never enter upon my rest.'"

Although God's work was finished at the creation of the world; ⁴ for, in a passage referring to the seventh day, you will find these words:

"God rested on the seventh day after all
    his work."

⁵ On the other hand, we read in that passage:

"They will never enter upon my rest."

⁶ Since, then, there is still a promise that some will enter upon this rest, and since those who were first told the good news did not enter upon it, because of their disbelief, ⁷ again God fixed a day. "Today," he said, speaking after a long interval through the mouth of David, in the passage already quoted:

"If today you hear God's voice,
    harden not your hearts."

⁸ Now if Joshua had given rest to the people, God would not have spoken of another and later day. ⁹ There is, then, a sabbath rest still awaiting God's people. ¹⁰ For

they who enter upon God's rest do themselves rest after their work, just as God did. [11] Let us, therefore, make every effort to enter upon that rest, so that none of us falls through such disbelief as that of which we have had an example. [12] God's message is a living and active power, sharper than any two-edged sword, piercing its way until it penetrates soul and spirit — not the joints only but the marrow — and detecting the inmost thoughts and purposes of the heart. [13] There is no created thing that can hide itself from the sight of God. Everything is exposed and laid bare before the eyes of him to whom we have to give account.

[14] We have, then, in Jesus, the Son of God, a great high priest who has passed into the highest heaven; let us, therefore, hold fast to the faith which we have professed. [15] Our high priest is not one unable to sympathize with our weaknesses, but one who has in every way been tempted, exactly as we have been, but without sinning. [16] Therefore, let us boldly draw near to the throne of love, to find pity and love for the hour of need.

5 [1] Every high priest, taken from among the people, is appointed as his representative in his relations with God, to offer both gifts and sacrifices in expiation of sins. [2] And he is able to sympathize with the ignorant and deluded, since he is himself subject to weakness, [3] and is therefore bound to offer sacrifices for sins, not only for the people, but equally so for himself. [4] Nor does anyone take that high office on himself, until he has been called to do so by God, as Aaron was. [5] In the same way, even the Christ did not take the honor of the high priesthood on himself, but he was appointed by him who said to him,

"You are my Son; this day I have
    become your Father";

[6] and on another occasion also:

"You are a priest for all time of the
    order of Melchizedek."

[7] Jesus, in the days of his earthly life, offered prayers and supplications, with earnest cries and with tears, to him who was able to save him from death; and he was heard because of his devout submission. [8] Son though he was, he learned obedience from his sufferings; [9] and, being made perfect, he became to all those who obey him the source of eternal salvation, [10] while God himself pronounced him a high priest of the order of Melchizedek.

[11] Now on this subject I have much to say, but it is difficult to explain it to you, because you have shown yourselves so slow to learn. [12] For whereas, considering the time that has elapsed, you ought to be teaching others, you still need someone to teach you the alphabet of the divine revelation, and need again to be fed with "milk" instead of with "solid food." [13] For everyone who still has to take "milk" knows nothing of the teaching of righteousness; she is a mere infant. [14] But "solid food" is for trusting people of mature faith — those whose faculties have been trained by practice to distinguish right from wrong.

6 [1] Therefore, let us leave behind the elementary teaching about the Christ and press on to perfection, not always laying over again a foundation of repentance for dead actions, of faith in God — [2] teaching concerning baptisms and the laying on of hands, the resurrection of the dead and a final judgment. [3] Yes and, with God's help, we will. [4] For if those who were once for all brought into the light, and learned to appreciate the gift from heaven, and came to share in the holy Spirit, [5] and learned to appreciate the beauty of the divine message, and the new powers of the coming

age — [6] if those, I say, fell away, it would be impossible to bring them again to repentance; they would be crucifying the Child of God over again for themselves, and exposing him to public contempt. [7] The ground drinks the showers that fall on it from time to time, and it produces vegetation useful to those who tilled it, and receives a blessing from God; [8] but if it bears thorns and thistles, it is regarded as worthless, it is in danger of being cursed, and its end will be the fire.

[9] But about you, dear friends, even though we speak in this way, we are confident of better things — of things that point to your salvation. [10] For God is not unjust, and will not forget the work that you did, and the love that you showed for God's name, in sending help to your brothers and sisters — as you are still doing. [11] But our great desire is that every one of you should be equally earnest to attain to a full conviction that our hope will be fulfilled, and that you should keep that hope to the end. [12] Then you will not show yourselves slow to learn, but you will copy those who, through faith and perseverance, are now entering upon the enjoyment of God's promises.

[13] When God gave his promise to Abraham, since there was no one greater by whom he could swear, he swore by himself. [14] His words were:

"I will assuredly bless you and increase your numbers."

[15] And so, after persevering, Abraham obtained the fulfillment of God's promise. [16] People, of course, swear by what is greater than themselves, and with them an oath is accepted as putting a matter beyond all dispute. [17] And therefore God, in his desire to show, with unmistakable plainness, to those who were to enter into the enjoyment of what he had promised, the unchangeableness of his purpose, bound himself with an oath. [18] For he intended us to find great encouragement in these two unchangeable things, which make it impossible for God to prove false — we, I mean, who fled for safety where we might lay hold of the hope set before us. [19] This hope is an anchor for our souls, secure and strong, and it reaches into the sanctuary that lies behind the curtain, [20] where Jesus, our forerunner, has entered on our behalf, after being made for all time a high priest of the order of Melchizedek.

Paramount Priesthood of the Anointed One

7 [1] It was this Melchizedek, king of Salem and priest of the Most High God, who met Abraham returning from the slaughter of the kings, and gave him his blessing; [2] and it was to him that Abraham allotted a tithe of all the spoil. The meaning of his name is "king of righteousness," and besides that, he was also king of Salem, which means "king of peace." [3] There is no record of his father, or mother, or lineage, nor again of any beginning of his days, or end of his life. In this he resembles the Child of God, and stands before us as a priest whose priesthood is continuous.

[4] Consider, then, the importance of this Melchizedek, to whom even the patriarch Abraham himself gave a tithe of the choicest spoils. [5] Those descendants of Levi who are from time to time appointed to the priesthood are directed to collect tithes from the people in accordance with the Law — that is, from their own kindred, although they also are descended from Abraham. [6] But Melchizedek, although not of this lineage, received tithes from Abraham, and gave his blessing to the man who had God's promises. [7] Now no one can dispute that it is the superior who blesses the inferior. [8] In the one case the tithes are received by people

who are mortal; in the other case by one about whom there is the statement that his life still continues. [9] Moreover, in a sense, even Levi, who is the receiver of the tithes, has, through Abraham, paid tithes; [10] for Levi was still in the body of his ancestor when Melchizedek met Abraham.

[11] If, then, perfection had been attainable through the Levitical priesthood — and it was under this priesthood that the people received the Law — why was it still necessary that a priest of a different order should appear, a priest of the order of Melchizedek and not of the order of Aaron? [12] With the change of the priesthood a change of the Law became a necessity. [13] And the one of whom all this is said belonged to quite a different tribe, no member of which has ever served at the altar. [14] For it is plain that our Lord had sprung from the tribe of Judah, though of that tribe Moses said nothing about their being priests. [15] All this becomes even yet plainer when we remember that a new priest has appeared, resembling Melchizedek, [16] and that he was appointed, not under a Law regulating only earthly matters, but by virtue of a life beyond the reach of death; [17] for that is the meaning of the declaration:

"You are for all time a priest of the
    order of Melchizedek."

[18] On the one hand, we have the abolition of a previous regulation as being both inefficient and useless [19] (for the Law never brought anything to perfection); and, on the other hand, we have the introduction of a better hope, which enables us to draw near to God. [20] Then again, the appointment of this new priest was ratified by an oath, which is not so with the Levitical priests, [21] but his appointment was ratified by an oath, when God said to him,

"The Lord has sworn, and will not

change, 'You are a priest for all
    time.'"

[22] And the oath shows the corresponding superiority of the covenant of which Jesus is the guarantee. [23] Again, new Levitical priests are continually being appointed, because death prevents their remaining in office; [24] but Jesus remains for all time, and therefore the priesthood that he holds will never pass to another. [25] And that is why he is able to save perfectly those who come to God through him, living forever, as he does, to intercede on their behalf.

[26] This was the high priest that we needed — holy, innocent, spotless, withdrawn from sinners, exalted above the highest heaven, [27] one who has no need to offer sacrifices daily as those high priests have, first for their own sins, and then for those of the people. For this he did once and for all, when he offered himself as the sacrifice. [28] The Law appoints as high priests men who are weak, but the words of God's oath, which was later than the Law, name the Son as, for all time, the perfect priest.

8 [1] To sum up what I have been saying: Such is the high priest that we have, one who has taken his seat at the right hand of the throne of God's majesty in heaven, [2] where he ministers in the sanctuary, in that true tent set up by the Lord and not by humans. [3] Every high priest is appointed for the purpose of offering gifts and sacrifices to God; it follows, therefore, that this high priest must have some offering to make. [4] If he were, however, still on earth, he would not even be a priest, since there are already priests who offer the gifts as the Law directs. [5] (These priests, it is true, are engaged in a service which is only a copy and shadow of the heavenly realities, as is shown by the directions given to Moses when he was about to construct the tent. "Look to it," are the words, "that you make every part in accordance with the pattern shown you on the mountain.") [6] But Jesus, as we see, has obtained a ministry as far excelling theirs, as the covenant of which he is the intermediary, based, as it is, on better promises, excels the former covenant. [7] If that first covenant had been faultless, there would have been no occasion for a second. [8] But finding fault with the people, God says,

"'A time is coming,' says the Lord,
'when I will ratify a new covenant with
the people of Israel and with the
people of Judah —
not such a covenant as I made with
their ancestors
on the day when I took them by the
hand to lead them out of the land of
Egypt.
For they did not abide by their
covenant with me,
and therefore I disregarded them,' says
the Lord.
[10] 'This is the covenant that I will make
with the people of Israel
after those days,' says the Lord.
'I will impress my laws on their
minds,
and will inscribe them on their hearts;
and I will be their God,
and they will be my people.
[11] There will be no need for anyone to
instruct his fellow citizen,
or for a person to say to her relatives,
'Learn to know the Lord';
for everyone will know me,
from the lowest to the highest.
[12] For I will be merciful to their
wrongdoings,
and I will no longer remember their
sins.'"

[13] By speaking of a new covenant, God at once renders the former covenant obsolete; and whatever becomes obsolete and loses its force is virtually annulled.

Another Sanctuary

9 [1] It is true that even the first covenant had its regulations for divine worship, and its sanctuary — though only a material one. [2] For a tent was constructed, with an outer part which contained the stand for the lamps, and the table, and the consecrated bread. This is called the sanctuary. [3] The part of the tent behind the second curtain is called the inner sanctuary. [4] In it is the gold incense altar, and the ark containing the covenant, completely covered with gold. In the ark is a gold casket containing the manna, Aaron's rod that budded, and the tablets on which the covenant was written; [5] while above it, and overshadowing the cover on which atonement was made, are the cherubim of the presence. Now is not the time to discuss these things in detail. [6] Such, then, was the arrangement of the tent. Into the outer part priests are constantly going, in the discharge of their sacred duties; [7] but into the inner only the high priest goes, and that but once a year, and never without taking the blood of a victim, which he offers on his own behalf, and on behalf of the errors of the people. [8] By this the holy Spirit is teaching that the way into the sanctuary was hidden, as long as the outer part of the tent still remained. [9] For that was only a type, to continue down to the present time; and, in keeping with it, both gifts and sacrifices are offered, though incapable of satisfying the conscience of the worshiper; [10] the whole system being concerned only with food and drink and various ablutions — external ceremonials imposed until the coming of the new order.

[11] But when Christ came, he appeared as high priest of that better system which was established; and he entered through that nobler and more perfect "tent," not made by human hands — that is to say, not a part of this present creation. [12] Nor was it with the blood of goats and calves, but with his own blood, that he entered, once and for all, into the sanctuary, and

obtained our eternal deliverance. [13] For, if the blood of goats and bulls, and the sprinkling of the ashes of a heifer, purify those who have been defiled (as far as ceremonial purification goes), [14] how much more will the blood of the Anointed One, who, through his long-lasting Spirit, offered himself up to God, as a victim without blemish, purify our consciences from a lifeless formality, and fit us for the service of the living God! [15] And that is why he is the intermediary of a new covenant; in order that, as a death has taken place to effect a deliverance from the offenses committed under the first covenant, those who have received the call may obtain the eternal inheritance promised to them. [16] Whenever such a covenant as a will is in question, the death of the testator must of necessity be alleged. [17] For such a covenant takes effect only on death; it does not come into force as long as the testator is alive. [18] This explains why even the first covenant was not ratified without the shedding of blood. [19] For, when every command had been announced to all the people by Moses in accordance with the Law, he took the blood of the calves and of the goats, with water, scarlet wool, and a bunch of hyssop, and sprinkled even the book of the Law, as well as all the people, [20] saying, as he did so, "This is the blood that renders valid the covenant which God has commanded to be made with you." [21] And in the same way he also sprinkled with the blood the tent and all the things that were used in public worship. [22] Indeed, under the Law, almost everything is purified with blood; and, unless blood is shed, no forgiveness is to be obtained.

[23] While, then, it was necessary for the copies of the heavenly realities to be purified by such means as these, the heavenly realities themselves required better sacrifices. [24] For it was not into a sanctuary made by human hands, which merely foreshadowed the true one, that Christ entered, but into heaven itself, so that he might now appear in the presence of God on our behalf. [25] Nor yet was it to offer himself many times, as year after year the high priest entered the sanctuary with an offering of blood — but not his own blood; [26] for then Christ would have had to undergo death many times since the creation of the world. But now, once and for all, at the close of the age, he has appeared, in order to abolish sin by the sacrifice of himself. [27] And, as it is ordained for people to die but once (death being followed by judgment), [28] so it is with the Anointed One. He was offered up once and for all, to "bear away the sins of many"; and the second time he will appear — but without any burden of sin — to those who are waiting for him, to bring salvation.

10 [1] The Law, though able to foreshadow the better system which was coming, never had its actual substance. Its priests, with those sacrifices which they offer continuously year after year, can never make those who come to worship perfect. [2] Otherwise, would not the offering of these sacrifices have been abandoned, as the worshipers, having been once purified, would have had their consciences clear from sins? [3] But, on the contrary, these sacrifices recall their sins to mind year after year. [4] For the blood of bulls and goats is powerless to remove sins. [5] That is why, when he was coming into the world, he declared,

"Sacrifice and offering you do not
  desire, but you provide for me a
  body;
you take no pleasure in burnt offerings
  and sacrifices for sin.
So I said, 'See, I have come' (as is
  written of me in the pages of the
  book)
'to do your will, God.'"

[8] First come the words: "You do not desire, nor do you take pleasure in, sacrifices, offerings, burnt offerings, and sac-

rifices for sin" (offerings regularly made under the Law), [9] and then there is added, "See, I have come to do your will." The former sacrifices are set aside to be replaced by the latter. [10] And it is in the fulfillment of the will of God that we have been purified by the sacrifice, once and for all, of the body of Jesus Christ. [11] Every other priest stands day after day at his ministrations, and offers the same sacrifices over and over again — sacrifices that can never take sins away. [12] But this priest, after he had offered one sacrifice for sins, which should serve for all time, took his seat at the right hand of God, [13] and has since then been waiting for his enemies to be put as a stool for his feet. [14] By a single offering he has made perfect for all time those who are being purified. [15] We have also the testimony of the holy Spirit. For, after saying,

[16] "'This is the covenant that I will make
      with them
   after those days,' says the Lord;
   'I will impress my laws on their hearts,
   and will inscribe them on their minds,'"

[17] then we have:

"And their sins and their iniquities I
   will no longer remember."

[18] And, when these are forgiven, there is no further need of an offering for sin.

Encouragement and Warning

[19] Therefore, friends, since we may enter the sanctuary with confidence, in virtue of the blood of Jesus, [20] by the way which he inaugurated for us — a new and living way, a way through the sanctuary curtain (that is, his human nature); [21] and, since we have in him a great priest set over the house of God, [22] let us draw near to God in all sincerity of heart and in perfect faith, with our hearts purified by the sprinkled blood from all consciousness of wrong, and with our bodies washed with pure water. [23] Let us maintain the confession of our hope unshaken, for he who has given us his promise will not fail us. [24] Let us vie with one another in a rivalry of love and noble actions. [25] And let us not, as some do, cease to meet together; but on the contrary, let us encourage one another, and all the more now that you see the day drawing near. [26] Remember, if we sin willfully after we have gained a full knowledge of the truth, there can be no further sacrifice for sin; [27] there is only a fearful anticipation of judgment, and a burning indignation which will destroy all opponents. [28] When someone disregarded the Law of Moses, he was, on the evidence of two or three witnesses, put to death without pity. [29] How much worse, then, think you, will be the punishment deserved by those who have trampled underfoot the Son of God, who have treated the blood that rendered the covenant valid — the blood by which they were purified — as if it were not holy, and who have outraged the spirit of grace? [30] We know who it was that said,

"It is for me to avenge, I will requite";

and again:

"The Lord will judge the people."

[31] It is a fearful thing to fall into the hands of the living God.

[32] Call to mind those early days in which, after you had received the light, you patiently underwent a long and painful conflict. [33] Sometimes, in consequence of the taunts and injuries heaped on you, you became a public spectacle; and sometimes you suffered through having shown yourselves to be the friends of people who were in the same position in which you had been. [34] For you not only sympathized

with those who were in prison, but you even took the confiscation of your possessions joyfully, knowing, as you did, that you had in yourselves a greater possession and a lasting one. ³⁵ Do not, therefore, abandon the confidence that you have gained, for it has a great reward awaiting it. ³⁶ You still have need of patient endurance, in order that when you have done God's will, you may obtain the fulfillment of his promise.

³⁷ "For there is indeed but a very little
  while
  ere he who is coming will have come,
    without delay;
³⁸ and through faith the righteous will
    find life,
  but if anyone draws back, my heart can
    find no pleasure in him."

³⁹ But we do not belong to those who draw back, to their ruin, but to those who have faith, to the saving of their souls.

Examples of Faith

11 ¹ Trust is the realization of things hoped for — the proof of things not seen. ² And it was for trust that the people of old were renowned. ³ Trust enables us to perceive that the universe was created at the bidding of God — so that we know that what we see was not made out of visible things. ⁴ Trust made the sacrifice which Abel offered to God a better sacrifice than Cain's, and won him renown as a righteous man, God himself establishing his renown by accepting his gifts; and it is by the example of his faith that Abel, though dead, still speaks. ⁵ Trust led to Enoch's removal from earth, so that he might not experience death. "He could not be found because God had removed him." For, before his removal, he was renowned as having pleased God; ⁶ but without faith it is impossible to please God, for he who comes to God must have confidence that God exists, and rewards those who seek God.

⁷ It was faith that enabled Noah, after he had received the divine warning about what could not then be foreseen, to build, in reverent obedience, an ark in which to save his family. By his confidence he condemned the world, and became possessed of that righteousness which follows on trust.

⁸ It was faith that enabled Abraham to obey the call that he received, and to set out for the place which he was afterward to obtain as his own; and he set out not knowing where he was going. ⁹ It was trust that made him go to live as an emigrant in the promised land — as in a strange country — living there in tents with Isaac and Jacob, who shared the promise with him. ¹⁰ For he was looking for the city with the sure foundations, whose architect and builder is God.

¹¹ Again, it was confidence that enabled Sarah to conceive (though she was past the age for childbearing), because she felt sure that he who had given her the promise would not fail her. ¹² And so from one man — and that when his powers were dead — there sprang a people as numerous as the stars in the heavens or the countless grains of sand on the shore.

¹³ All these died sustained by trust. They did not obtain the promised blessings, but they saw them from a distance and welcomed the sight, and they acknowledged themselves to be only aliens and strangers on the earth. ¹⁴ Those who speak like this show plainly that they are seeking their homeland. ¹⁵ If they had been thinking of the land that they had left, they could have found opportunities to return. ¹⁶ But no, they were longing for a better, a heavenly, land! And therefore God was not ashamed to be called their God; indeed he had already prepared them a city. ¹⁷ It was faith that enabled Abraham, when put to the test, to offer Isaac as a sacrifice — he who

had received the promises offering up his only son, [18] of whom it had been said,

"It is through Isaac that there will be descendants to bear your name."

[19] For he argued that God was even able to raise a man from the dead — and indeed, figuratively speaking, Abraham did receive Isaac back from the dead. [20] It was faith that enabled Isaac to bless Jacob and Esau, even with regard to the future. [21] Trust enabled Jacob, when dying, to give his blessing to each of the sons of Joseph, and "to bow himself in worship as he leaned on the top of his staff." [22] Confidence caused Joseph, when his end was near, to speak of the future migration of the Israelites, and to give instructions with regard to his bones. [23] Faith caused the parents of Moses to hide the child for three months after his birth, for they saw that he was a beautiful child; and they would not respect the king's order. [24] It was trust that caused Moses, when he was grown up, to refuse the title of "son of a daughter of Pharaoh." [25] He preferred sharing the hardships of God's people to enjoying the short-lived pleasures of sin. [26] For he counted "the reproaches that are heaped on the Christ" of greater value than the treasures of Egypt, looking forward, as he did, to the reward awaiting him. [27] Confidence caused him to leave Egypt, though undaunted by the king's anger, for he was strengthened in his endurance by the vision of the invisible God. [28] Faith led him to institute the Passover and the sprinkling of the blood, so that the Destroyer might not touch the eldest children of the Israelites. [29] Trust enabled the people to cross the Red Sea, as if it had been dry land, while the Egyptians, when they attempted to do so, were drowned. [30] Confidence caused the walls of Jericho to fall after being encircled for seven days. [31] Faith saved Rahab the prostitute from perishing with the unbelievers, after she had entertained the spies with friendliness.

[32] Need I add anything more? Time would fail me if I attempted to relate the stories of Gideon, Barak, Samson, and Jephthah, and those of David, Samuel, and the prophets. [33] By their trust they subdued kingdoms, ruled righteously, gained the fulfillment of God's promises, shut the mouths of lions, [34] quelled the fury of the flames, escaped the edge of the sword, found strength in the hour of weakness, displayed their prowess in war, and routed hostile armies. [35] Women received back their dead raised to life. Some were tortured on the wheel, and refused release in order that they might rise to a better life. [36] Others had to face taunts and blows, and even chains and imprisonment. [37] They were stoned to death, they were tortured, they were sawn asunder, they were put to the sword; they wandered about clothed in the skins of sheep or goats, destitute, persecuted, ill used — [38] people of whom the world was not worthy — roaming in lonely places, and on the mountains, and in caves and holes in the ground. [39] Yet, though they all won renown by their trust, they did not obtain the final fulfillment of God's promise; [40] since God had in view some better thing for us, so that they would only reach perfection together with us.

12 [1] Seeing, therefore, that there is on every side of us such a throng of witnesses, let us also lay aside everything that hinders us, and the sin that clings about us, and run with patient endurance the race that lies before us, [2] our eyes fixed on Jesus, the leader and perfect example of our trust, who, for the joy that lay before him, endured the cross, heedless of its shame, and now "has taken his seat at the right hand" of the throne of God. [3] Weigh well the example of him who had to endure such opposition from "people who were sinning against themselves," so that you should not grow weary or faint-hearted. [4] You have not yet, in your struggle with sin, resisted to the death; [5] and you have forgotten the encouraging words which are addressed to you as God's children:

"My child, think not lightly of the
  Lord's discipline,
do not despond when he rebukes you;
  for it is the one God loves that is
  disciplined,
and God chastises every child whom he
  acknowledges."

[7] It is for your discipline that you have to persevere through all this. God is dealing with you as his children. For where is there a child whom his father does not discipline? [8] If you are left without that discipline, in which all children share, it shows that you are illegitimate, and not true children. [9] Further, when our earthly fathers disciplined us, we respected them. Should we not, then, much rather yield submission to the Father of souls, and live? [10] Our fathers disciplined us for only a short time and as seemed best to them; but God disciplines us for our true good, to enable us to share his holiness. [11] No discipline is pleasant at the time; on the contrary, it is painful. But afterward its fruit is seen in the peacefulness of a righteous life which is the lot of those who have been trained under it. [12] Therefore, lift again the down-dropped hands and straighten the weakened knees; [13] make straight paths for your feet, so that the lame limb may not be put out of joint, but rather be cured.

Conclusion

[14] Try earnestly to live at peace with everyone, and to attain to that purity without which no one will see the Lord. [15] Take care that no one fails to use the loving help of God, that no bitterness is allowed to take root and spring up, and cause trouble, and so poison the whole community. [16] Take care that no one becomes immoral, or irreligious like Esau, who sold his birthright for a single meal. [17] For you know that even afterward, when he wished to claim his father's blessing, he was rejected — for he never found an opportunity to repair his error — though he begged for the blessing with tears.

[18] It is not to tangible flaming fire that you have drawn near, nor to gloom, and darkness, and storm, [19] and the blast of a trumpet, and an audible voice. Those who heard that voice entreated that they might hear no more, [20] for they could not bear to think of the command — if even an animal touches the mountain, it is to be stoned to death; [21] and so fearful was the sight that Moses said, "I tremble with fear." [22] No, but it is to Mount Zion that you have drawn near, the city of the living God, the heavenly Jerusalem, to countless hosts of angels, [23] to the festal gathering and assemblage of God's firstborn whose names are enrolled in heaven, to God the judge of all people, to the spirits of the righteous who have attained perfection, [24] to Jesus, the intermediary of a new covenant, and to the sprinkled blood that tells of better things than the blood of Abel. [25] Beware how you refuse to hear him who is speaking. For, if the people on earth did not escape punishment, when they refused to listen to the one who taught them on earth the divine will, far worse will it be for us if we turn away from him who is teaching us from heaven. [26] Then his voice shook the earth, but now his declaration is:

"Still once more I will cause not only
  the earth to tremble, but also the
  heavens."

[27] And those words "still once more" indicate the passing away of all that is shaken — that is, of all created things — in

order that only what is unshaken may remain. ²⁸ Therefore, let us, who have received a realm that cannot be shaken, be thankful, and so offer acceptable worship to God, with awe and the deepest respect. ²⁹ For our God is a consuming fire.

13 ¹ Let your love for the Lord's followers continue. ² Do not neglect to show hospitality; for, through being hospitable, people have all unawares entertained angels. ³ Remember the prisoners, as if you were their fellow prisoners, and the tortured, not forgetting that you also are still in the body. ⁴ Let marriage be honored by all and the married life be pure; for God will judge those who are immoral and those who commit adultery. ⁵ Do not let your conduct be ruled by the love of money. Be content with what you have, for God himself has said,

"I will never forsake you, nor will I ever abandon you."

⁶ Therefore we may say with confidence,

"The Lord is my helper, I will not be afraid.
What can mere people do to me?"

⁷ Do not forget your leaders, who told you God's message. Recall the outcome of their lives, and imitate their faith.

⁸ Jesus Christ is the same yesterday and today — yes, and forever. ⁹ Do not let yourselves be carried away by the various novel forms of teaching. It is better to rely for spiritual strength on the divine help than on regulations regarding food; for those whose lives are guided by such regulations have not found them of service. ¹⁰ We are not without an altar; but it is one at which those who still worship in the tent have no right to eat. ¹¹ The bodies of those animals whose blood is brought by the high priest into the sanctuary, as an offering for sin, are burned outside the camp. ¹² And so Jesus, also, to purify the people by his own blood, suffered outside the gate. ¹³ Therefore let us go out to him outside the camp, bearing the same reproaches as he; ¹⁴ for here we have no permanent city, but are looking for the city that is to be. ¹⁵ Through him let us offer, as our sacrifice, continual praise to God — an offering from lips that glorify his name. ¹⁶ Never forget to do kindly acts and to share what you have with others, for such sacrifices are acceptable to God. ¹⁷ Obey your leaders, and submit to their control, for they are watching over your souls, since they will have to render an account, so that they may do it with joy, and not in sorrow. That would not be to your advantage.

¹⁸ Pray for us, for we are sure that our consciences are clear, since our wish is to be occupied with what is good. ¹⁹ And I the more earnestly ask for your prayers, so that I may be restored to you the sooner.

²⁰ May God, the source of all peace, who brought back from the dead the one who, by virtue of the blood that rendered valid the unchangeable covenant, is the great shepherd of God's sheep, Jesus, our Lord — ²¹ may God make you perfect in everything that is good, so that you may be able to do his will. May God bring out in us all that is pleasing in his sight, through Jesus Christ, to whom be all glory forever and ever. Amen.

²² I beg you, friends, to bear with these words of advice. For I have written only very briefly to you.

²³ You will be glad to hear that our friend Timothy has been set free. If he comes here soon, we will visit you together.

²⁴ Give our greeting to all your leaders, and to all Christ's people. Our friends from Italy send their greetings to you.

²⁵ May God bless you all.

An Introduction to the First Letter of Peter

WRITTEN EXPLICITLY TO many different Christ groups at the eastern end of the Mediterranean, this letter gives clear evidence of both an increased influence of the movement and an increased persecution of it. Although it includes a number of quotations from the Hebrew scriptures, it seems to address a mainly gentile population. It speaks of the disparate populations it addresses as a bold new people: "But you are a chosen race, a royal priesthood, a consecrated nation, God's own people, entrusted with the proclamation of the goodness of the one who called you out of darkness into his wonderful light. Once you were not a people, but now you are God's people; once you had not found mercy, but now you have found mercy" (2:9–10).

The Greek of this document is quite polished and seems not to fit with what a Galilean peasant like Peter could write. This sophisticated language, its assertion that the many different churches to which it was written were already "a royal priesthood and a consecrated nation," and references within the letter to a system of formal congregational offices not evident in the first two generations of the Christ movement lead many to think that Peter was not the author. It also seems most probably written in the late first or early second century.

The letter explicitly refers to persecutions of those in the Christ movement. But its instructions to those suffering are cautious and aim to keep people from such pain and loss. Blessing those who are persecuted (perhaps with reference to the Jesus sayings), the author tries to thread the needle between hiding and open resistance:

> Who, indeed, is there to harm you, if you prove yourselves to be eager for what is good? Even if you should suffer for righteousness, count yourselves blessed! Do not let people terrify you, or allow yourselves to be dismayed. Revere the Anointed One as Lord in your hearts; always ready to give an answer to anyone who asks your reason for the hope that you cherish, but giving it with courtesy and respect, and keeping your consciences clear, so that whenever you are maligned, those who vilify your good conduct in Christ may be put to shame. (3:13–16)

This combination of caution and honesty also applies to how one should relate to the forces of the Roman emperor: "Submit to all human institutions for the Lord's sake, alike to the emperor as the supreme authority. . . . Act as free people, yet not using your freedom as those do who make it a cloak for wickedness, but as slaves of God" (2:13, 16).

In other parts of the letter, the author follows the conventions of the Greco-

Roman household codes that undergird masters' authority over slaves and husbands over wives. The letter also instructs women not to braid their hair or wear fine jewelry and clothes.

The First Letter of Peter contains the most direct mention in *A New New Testament* of Christ descending into the "prison" of those who have died. This may be related to other early Christian creeds about Christ preaching to those in the underworld after his death, but before his resurrection.

This letter's delicate combination of asserting the power of the early Christ movement and delicately attempting to avoid additional conflict with Roman authorities, all while experiencing persecution, paints a delicate picture of the movement after several generations. It reflects some of the tensions described in some of the books newly added to *A New New Testament* such as the Acts of Paul and Thecla and the Letter of Peter to Philip, in which persecution from Rome is also dealt with as both a major threat and an occasion to be careful.

Recommended Reading

Paul J. Achtemeier, *1 Peter*
John Elliott, *I Peter: A New Translation with Introduction and Commentary*
J. Ramsey Michaels, *1 Peter*

The First Letter of Peter

Introduction

1 ¹ To the people of God who are living abroad, dispersed throughout Pontus, Galatia, Cappadocia, Roman Asia, and Bithynia, ² and who were chosen in accordance with the foreknowledge of God the Father, through the consecration of the Spirit, to learn obedience, and to be purified by the sprinkling of the blood of Jesus Christ, from Peter, an ambassador of Jesus Christ. May grace and peace be yours in ever-increasing measure.

Hope of Salvation

Blessed is the God and Father of our Lord Jesus Christ, who has, in his great mercy, through the resurrection of Jesus Christ from the dead, ⁴ given us the new life of undying hope, that promises an inheritance, imperishable, stainless, unfading, which has been reserved for you in heaven — ⁵ for you who, through trust, are being guarded by the power of God, awaiting a salvation that is ready to be revealed in the last days. ⁶ At the thought of this you are full of exultation, though (if it has been necessary) you have suffered for the moment somewhat from various trials; ⁷ that the genuineness of your faith — a thing far more precious than gold, which is perishable, yet has to be tested by fire — may win praise and glory and honor at the appearing of Jesus Christ. ⁸ Though you have never seen him, yet you love him; though you do not even now see him, yet you believe in him, and exalt with a triumphant happiness too great for words, ⁹ as you receive the reward of your faith in the salvation of your souls! ¹⁰ It was this salvation that the prophets, who spoke long ago of the blessing intended for you, sought, and strove to comprehend; ¹¹ as they strove to discern what that time could be, to which the spirit of Christ within them was pointing, when foretelling the sufferings that Christ would have to endure, and the glories that would follow. ¹² And it was revealed to them that it was not for themselves, but for you, that they were acting as servants of the truths which have now been told to you, by those who, with the help of the holy Spirit sent from heaven, have brought you the good news — truths into which even angels long to look.

Character

¹³ Therefore concentrate your minds, with the strictest self-control, and fix your hopes on the grace that is coming for you at the appearing of Jesus Christ. ¹⁴ Be like obedient children; do not let your lives be shaped by the passions which once swayed you in the days of your ignorance, ¹⁵ but in your whole life show yourselves to be holy, after the pattern of the Holy One from whom you received your call. ¹⁶ For it is written,

"You will be holy, because I am holy."

¹⁷ And since you call on him as Father, who judges everyone impartially by what he has done, let respectful awe be the spirit of your lives during the time of your stay on earth. ¹⁸ For you know that it was not by perishable things, such as silver and gold, that you were ransomed from the aimless way of living which was handed down to you from your ancestors, ¹⁹ but by precious blood, as it were of a lamb,

unblemished and spotless, the blood of Christ. [20] Destined for this before the beginning of the world, he has been revealed in these last days for your sakes, [21] who, through him, are trusting in God who raised him from the dead and gave him glory, so that your faith and hope are now in God.

[22] Now that, by your obedience to the truth, you have purified your lives, so that there is growing up among you a genuine affection, love one another earnestly with all your hearts; [23] since your new life has come, not from perishable, but imperishable, seed, through the message of the ever-living God. [24] For:

"All earthly life is but as grass,
and all its splendor as the flower of
    grass.
The grass fades,
its flower falls,
[25] but the teaching of the Lord remains
    forever."

And that is the teaching of the good news which has been told to you.

2 [1] Now that you have done with all malice, all deceitfulness, insincerity, jealous feelings, and all backbiting, [2] like newly born infants, crave pure spiritual milk, so that you may be enabled by it to grow until you attain salvation — [3] since you have found by experience that the Lord is kind. [4] Come to him, then, as to a living stone, rejected, indeed, by humans, but in God's eyes choice and precious; [5] and, as living stones, form yourselves into a spiritual house, to be a consecrated priesthood, for the offering of spiritual sacrifices that will be acceptable to God through Jesus Christ. [6] For there is a passage of writing that runs,

"See, I am placing in Zion a choice and
    precious cornerstone;

and those who believe in him will have
    no cause for shame.'"

[7] It is to you, then, who believe in him that he is precious, but to those who do not believe he is a stone which, though rejected by the builders, has now itself become the cornerstone, [8] and a stumbling block, and a rock which will prove a hindrance. They stumble because they do not accept the message. This was the fate destined for them. [9] But you are a chosen race, a royal priesthood, a consecrated nation, God's own people, entrusted with the proclamation of the goodness of the one who called you out of darkness into his wonderful light. [10] Once you were not a people, but now you are God's people; once you had not found mercy, but now you have found mercy.

Practical Appeals

[11] Dear friends, I beg you, as pilgrims and strangers on earth, to refrain from indulging the cravings of flesh, for they make war on the soul. [12] Let your daily life among the gentiles be so upright that whenever they malign you as evildoers, they may learn, as they watch, from the uprightness of your conduct, to praise God at the time when he will visit them.

[13] Submit to all human institutions for the Lord's sake, alike to the emperor as the supreme authority, [14] and to governors as sent by him to punish evildoers and to commend those who do right. [15] For God's will is this — that you should silence the ignorance of foolish people by doing what is right. [16] Act as free people, yet not using your freedom as those do who make it a cloak for wickedness, but as slaves of God. [17] Show honor to everyone, love the Lord's followers, revere God, honor the emperor.

[18] Those of you who are domestic servants should always be submissive and respectful to your masters, not only to those

who are good and considerate, but also to those who are arbitrary. ¹⁹ For this wins God's approval when, because conscious of God's presence, a person who is suffering unjustly bears her troubles patiently. ²⁰ What credit can you claim when, after doing wrong, you take your punishment for it patiently? But, on the other hand, if, after doing right, you take your sufferings patiently, that does win the approval of God. ²¹ For it was to this that you were called! For Christ, too, suffered — on your behalf — and left you an example, that you should follow in his steps. ²² He never sinned, nor was anything deceitful ever heard from his lips. ²³ He was abused, but he did not answer with abuse; he suffered, but he did not threaten; he entrusted himself to him whose judgments are just. ²⁴ And he himself carried our sins in his own body to the cross, so that we might die to our sins, and live for righteousness. His bruising was your healing. ²⁵ Once you were straying like sheep, but now you have returned to the shepherd and guardian of your souls.

3 ¹ Again, you married women should submit to your husbands, so that if any of them reject the message, they may, apart from the message, be won over by the conduct of their wives, ² as they watch your submissive and blameless conduct. ³ Yours should be, not the external adornment of the arrangement of the hair, the wearing of jewelry, or the putting on of dresses, ⁴ but the inner life with the imperishable beauty of a quiet and gentle spirit; for this is very precious in God's sight. ⁵ It was by this that the holy women of old, who rested their hopes on God, adorned themselves; submitting to their husbands, ⁶ as Sarah did, who obeyed Abraham, and called him master. And you are her true children, as long as you live good lives, and let nothing terrify you.

⁷ Again, those of you who are married men should live considerately with your wives, showing due regard to their sex, as physically weaker than your own, and not forgetting that they share with you in the gift of life. Then you will be able to pray without hindrance.

⁸ Lastly, you should all be united, sympathetic, full of love for each other, kindhearted, humble-minded; ⁹ never returning evil for evil, or abuse for abuse, but, on the contrary, blessing. It was to this that you were called — to obtain a blessing!

¹⁰ "The person who wants to enjoy life
and see happy days —
let him keep his tongue from evil
and his lips from deceitful words,
¹¹ let him turn from evil and do good,
let him seek for peace and follow after
it;
¹² for the eyes of the Lord are on the
righteous,
and his ears are attentive to their
prayers,
but the face of the Lord is set against
those who do wrong."

¹³ Who, indeed, is there to harm you, if you prove yourselves to be eager for what is good? ¹⁴ Even if you should suffer for righteousness, count yourselves blessed! Do not let people terrify you, or allow yourselves to be dismayed. ¹⁵ Revere the Anointed One as Lord in your hearts; always ready to give an answer to anyone who asks your reason for the hope that you cherish, but giving it with courtesy and respect, ¹⁶ and keeping your consciences clear, so that whenever you are maligned, those who vilify your good conduct in Christ may be put to shame. ¹⁷ It is better that you should suffer, if that should be God's will, for doing right, than for doing wrong. ¹⁸ For Christ himself died to atone for sins once for all — the good on behalf of the bad — that he might bring you to God; his body being put to death,

but his spirit entering on new life. [19] And it was then that he went and preached to the imprisoned spirits, [20] who once were disobedient, at the time when God patiently waited, in the days of Noah, while the ark was being prepared; in which some few lives, eight in all, were saved by means of water. [21] And baptism, which this foreshadowed, now saves you — not the mere cleansing of the body, but the search of a clear conscience after God — through the resurrection of Jesus Christ, [22] who has gone into heaven, and is at God's right hand, where angels and archangels and the powers of heaven now yield submission to him.

4 [1] Since, then, Christ suffered in body, arm yourselves with the same resolve as he; for the one who has suffered in body has ceased to sin, [2] and so will live the rest of his earthly life guided, not by human passions, but by the will of God. [3] Surely in the past you have spent time enough living as the gentiles delight to live. For your path has lain among scenes of debauchery, licentiousness, drunkenness, revelry, hard drinking, and profane idolatry. [4] And because you do not run to the same extremes of profligacy as others, they are astonished, and malign you. [5] But they will have to answer for their conduct to him who is ready to judge both the living and the dead. [6] For that was why the good news was told to the dead also — that after they have been judged in the body, as people are judged, they might live in the spirit, as God lives.

[7] But the end of all things is near. Therefore exercise self-restraint and be calm, so that you may be able to pray. [8] Above all things, let your love for one another be earnest, for love throws a veil over countless sins. [9] Never grudge hospitality to one another. [10] Whatever the gift that each has received, use it in the service of others, as good stewards of the varied bounty of God. [11] When anyone speaks, let her speak as one who is delivering the oracles of God. When anyone is endeavoring to serve others, let her do so in reliance on the strength which God supplies; so that in everything God may be honored through Jesus Christ — to whom be ascribed all honor and might forever and ever. Amen.

[12] Dear friends, do not be astonished at the trial of fire that you are passing through, to test you, as though something strange were happening to you. [13] No, the more you share the sufferings of the Christ, the more may you rejoice, that when the time comes for the manifestation of his glory, you may rejoice and exult. [14] If you are insulted for bearing the name of Christ, count yourselves blessed; because the divine glory and the spirit of God are resting on you. [15] I need hardly say that no one among you must suffer as a murderer, or a thief, or a criminal, or as an informer. [16] But if someone suffers as a Christian, do not let her be ashamed of it; let her bring honor to God even though she bears that name. [17] For the time has come for judgment to begin with the house of God; and if it begins with us, what will be the end of those who reject God's good news? [18] If a good person is saved only with difficulty, what will become of the godless and the sinful?' [19] Therefore, I say, let those who suffer, because God wills it so, commit their lives into the hands of a faithful Creator, and persevere in doing right.

Conclusion

5 [1] As for the older ones among you, who bear office in the church, I, their fellow officer, and a witness to the sufferings of the Christ, who will also share in the glory that is to be revealed — [2] I beg you to be true shepherds of the flock of God among you, not because you are compelled, but of your own free will; not from a base love of gain, but with a ready spirit; [3] not as lords of your charges, but as examples to your flock. [4] Then, when the chief shepherd appears, you will win the crown of glory that never fades. [5] Again, you younger ones should show deference to the older. And all of you should put on the badge of humility in mutual service, for God is opposed to the proud, but gives his help to the humble.

[6] Humble yourselves, therefore, under the mighty hand of God, so that he may exalt you in his good time, [7] laying all your anxieties on him, for he is concerned about you. [8] Exercise self-control, be watchful. Your adversary, the devil, like a roaring lion, is prowling about, eager to devour you. [9] Stand firm against him, strong in your confidence; knowing, as you do, that the sufferings which you are undergoing are being endured to the full by the Lord's followers throughout the world. [10] God, from whom all help comes, and who called you in Christ into his never-ending glory, will, when you have suffered for a little while, himself perfect, establish, strengthen you. [11] To that one be ascribed dominion forever. Amen.

[12] I have been writing to you briefly by the hand of Silas, our true-hearted brother (for so I regard him), to encourage you, and to bear my testimony that in what I have written is to be found the true love of God. On that take your stand. [13] Your sister church in "Babylon" sends you greeting, and so does Mark, who is as a son to me. [14] Greet one another with the kiss of love.

May God give his peace to you all in Christ.

An Introduction to the Letter of Peter to Philip

I N DISTINCTION TO A NUMBER of documents that greet the danger of persecution with either an injunction to suffer like Christ or to appear as moderate and harmless as possible, the Letter of Peter to Philip emphasizes the primacy and necessity of announcing Christ's message and healing despite any threat.

Although this document begins as a letter from the apostle Peter to the apostle Philip, it quickly becomes more of a story about them. So the title of the document — as is the case for many first- and second-century documents — was probably attached later. Like most documents that address the danger of persecution, the story was most likely written sometime in the second century. This means that the author and addressee are not really Peter and Philip, nor is the story historically reliable but was likely written by some Christ-related author in the second century to help the Christ people of the time think about how to face Rome's powerful and violent threats. Regardless, it is a story with a remarkable combination of insight, courage, and collective deliberation.

The New Orleans Council considered at least ten other documents that deal with oppression of the Christ movement by the Roman Empire and added several of these, such as the Acts of Paul and Thecla and the Secret Revelation of John, to this new collection. It found itself especially drawn to the clear thinking under fire of this Letter of Peter to Philip. The commitment in this letter — to be willing to face persecution without providing a blanket endorsement of martyrdom — was at the heart of the council's choice. In this way, leaders at the New Orleans Council in 2012 claimed this letter as a message for Christ followers today to avoid a martyrdom complex, even while being courageous in the face of powers that harm people in our world.

The story opens with Peter and Philip estranged, but this is quickly overcome when they agree to meet in response to Peter's invitation. They go to Mount Olivet where they used to pray with Jesus. This time they pray not with him, but to him; he appears to them in a great light. He reprimands them for looking for him, as he is "with you forever." They seek him out primarily because they are being threatened with death and need to know why this is happening and what to do. Jesus first considers their question about why they are being threatened so violently (presumably by the Roman Empire) and then goes on to recommend a unique strategy and posit another kind of integrity.

Jesus's basic answer to the first question is that there has been a cosmic mistake in the relationship between the Mother and Father God of everyone. This divine mistake has resulted in arrogant powers taking over humanity. These arrogant powers have blinded humanity to its origins in God, and they want to destroy the apostles because the apostles know of humanity's origins in God. Here again, Jesus's answer is surprisingly different from many early (and modern) Christian answers about why arrogant powers triumph over the hope and healing of Christ. Most Christian stories blame the leaders or the people themselves for such suffering. In this answer from Jesus, he acknowledges that it has been a problem with the (generally loving and life-giving) divine powers, not the fault of the humans. This answer was a bold new thought for early Christ people under persecution and another reason that the New Orleans Council felt strongly that this letter needed to be added to *A New New Testament*.

Jesus then tells the apostles to go out and proclaim salvation. This salvation announces the divine goodness and power of God, and the falseness of the arrogant and violent powers. The apostles and Peter then go out, perform healings, and preach salvation. Jesus blesses them on their way.

In the face of violent threats, the Letter of Peter to Philip does not proclaim the inevitability of a death like Jesus's crucifixion. Nor does it, as documents such as Titus and 1 Peter do, urge Christ people to look tame and unthreatening. It blesses Christ's instructions to proclaim openly the goodness of God and the perversion of the arrogant powers; and it suggests that the result of this action will be healing. The healing happens because of the Christ people's courage and Jesus's ongoing presence with them, even after he has died.

A Note on Chapter and Verse Numbering

Since this text is so "new," no version of the otherwise standard chapter and verse format exists. So we have had to add our own chapter and versification to this edition. The Letter of Peter to Philip has been made available in several formats and translations to the public without chapter and verse over the past thirty years. We do think it also very important that there be a chapter and verse system, since it breaks up the text into units that belong together. We do, however, want to alert readers that availability of this text in non–chapter and verse form or in the ancient manuscript form of simply noting the column and line numbers of the original document does not match our new chapter and verse format.

Recommended Reading

Karen King, "Toward a Discussion of the Category 'Gnosis/Gnosticism': The Case of the Epistle of Peter to Philip," pp. 445–65 in *Jesus in apokryphen Evangelienüberlieferungen: Beiträge zu außerkanonischen Jesusüberlieferungen aus verschiedenen Sprach- und Kulturtraditionen*, edited by Jörg Frey and Jens Schröter

The Letter of Peter to Philip

1 [1] The letter of Peter which he sent to Philip.

Peter's Letter to Philip

[2] Peter, the ambassador of Jesus Christ, to Philip, our beloved brother and fellow ambassador, and the brothers and sisters who are with you all: greetings. [3] I want you to understand, our brother, that we received orders from our Lord and the Savior of the whole world that we should come together to teach and proclaim about the salvation which was promised to us by our Lord, Jesus Christ. [4] But you were divided from us and did not want us to come together and understand how we should organize ourselves that we might tell the good news. So, would it be acceptable to you, our brother, to come according to the commands of our God, Jesus?

The Followers Come Together and Pray

2 [1] When Philip received and read it, he went to Peter and rejoiced with gladness. Then Peter gathered the others and went to the mountain called Olives where they had gathered with the blessed Christ when he was in the body. When the ambassadors came together and lay upon their knees, they prayed in this way, saying:

[2] "Father, Father, Father of the light, who has immortality, hear us, just as you have delighted in your holy Child, Jesus Christ. For he became for us a light-giver in the darkness. Please hear us."

[3] And they prayed again, saying:

"Child of life, Child of deathlessness, who dwells in the light; the Child, Christ of deathlessness, our rescuer, give us your power for they seek to kill us."

Jesus Christ Comes to His Followers

3 [1] Then a great light appeared so that the mountain gleamed from the sight of the one who appeared. And a voice called out to them, saying, "Listen to my words that I might speak to you. Why are you seeking me? I am Jesus Christ who is with you forever."

[2] Then the ambassadors answered and said to him, "Lord, we wish to understand the lack of the generations and their fullness; how are we restrained in this dwelling place, how have we come here, and in what way shall we leave? How do we have the authority of freedom? Why do the powers fight against us?"

The Creation of the Generations

4 [1] A voice came to them from the light, saying, "You yourselves are witness that I said all these things to you, but because of your distrust I shall speak again. The need of the generations — this is the lack. [2] The disobedience and ill consideration of the Mother appeared without the command of the greatness of the Father. She wanted to set up generations, and when she spoke, the Self-willed one came forth. But when she left a part of herself behind, the Self-willed one grabbed it and he became deficient. This is the lack of the generations. [3] When the Self-willed one took her part, he planted it and placed powers and authorities over it, then contained it in the mortal generations. All the powers of the world rejoiced because they had been generated. But they do not know the preexistent Father since they are strangers to him. It is the Self-willed one to whom they gave power and they served and praised him. [4] The Self-willed one became arrogant because of the power's praise. He was envious and wanted to make an image in place of an image and a form in place of a form. He appointed the powers within his authority to form mortal bodies, and they came into being from a misrepresentation of the form which came forth.

Jesus's Teaching on Fullness

5 [1] "Concerning the fullness, I was the one sent down into the body because of the seed which had fallen away. I came down in their mortal form, but they did not recognize me. They thought that I was a mortal man. [2] I spoke with the one who is mine, and he listened to me, just as you, too, have listened today. And I gave him authority that he might enter into the inheritance of his fatherhood. I took the one who is mine and the generations were filled in his salvation. And since he was lacking, he became fullness.

[3] "Because you all are being restrained, you are mine. When you strip off from yourselves what is corrupt, then you will become light-givers in the midst of mortal humans. This is because you are going to fight against the powers. They do not have your peace since they do not want you to be saved."

Jesus's Teaching on the Rulers

6 [1] The ambassadors worshiped again, saying, "Lord, tell us how shall we fight against the rulers since they are over us?"

[2] Then a voice called out from the appearance, saying, "You all will fight against them in this way: the rulers fight against the inner part of humans, but you will fight against them in this way — come together and teach salvation in the world with a promise. [3] Strengthen yourselves with the power of my father and offer your prayers. The Father will help you as he helped you by sending me. Do not be afraid, I am with you forever — as I said to you before when I was in the body."

[4] Then lightning and thunder came from the heavens, and what appeared to them was carried off up to the heavens. The ambassadors gave thanks to the Lord with every blessing and returned to Jerusalem. [5] While they were going there, they spoke with each other on the road about the light which came. A conversation occurred concerning the Lord. [6] They said, "If he, our Lord, suffered, how much then will we suffer?" Peter responded and said, "He suffered for our sake and it is necessary that we must also suffer because of our smallness."

[7] Then a voice came to them, saying, "I have told you all many times that it is necessary for you to suffer. It is necessary that you be brought to synagogues and governors so that you will suffer. But those who will not suffer will not save their lives."*

The Ambassadors Return to Jerusalem to Heal and Teach

7 [1] And the ambassadors rejoiced much and went up to Jerusalem. They went up to the Temple and taught salvation in the name of the Lord, Jesus Christ, and they healed the crowd.

[2] Peter opened his mouth and said to his followers, "When our Lord, Jesus, was in the body, he showed us everything, for

---

* The text is broken here for two to three lines. See Mark 8:35 and parallels.

he came down. My brothers and sisters, listen to my voice."

3 And Peter was filled with holy spirit and said to them this: "Our light-giver, Jesus, came down and was crucified. He wore a crown of thorns and put on a purple garment. "He was crucified on a cross, buried in a tomb, and rose from the dead. 4 My brothers and sisters, Jesus was a stranger to this suffering, but we are the ones who suffer because of the transgression of the Mother. Because of this, he did everything like us. 5 For the Lord Jesus, the child of the Father's immeasurable glory, is the author of our lives. My brothers and sisters, therefore, let us not listen to these lawless ones and walk in fear before them." 6 Then Peter gathered the others together and said

to them, "Our Lord, Jesus Christ, author of our peace, give us a spirit of understanding so that we may also do great deeds." 7 Then Peter and the other ambassadors saw and were filled with holy spirit, and each one performed healings. They separated to proclaim about the Lord, Jesus. And they gathered, greeted each other, and said, "Amen."

8 Then Jesus appeared and said to them, "Peace to you all and everyone who trusts in my name. And when you depart, joy, grace, and power to you all. And do not be afraid; know I am with you forever."

9 And the ambassadors parted from each other to proclaim with four words. And they went in the power of Jesus, in peace.

An Introduction to the Second Letter of Peter

QUOTING A WIDER SPECTRUM of earlier Christian books than perhaps any other book in *A New New Testament*, this letter may well be the last book written in this collection. Its citing of Paul, some gospels, Jude, and 1 Peter could project it easily into the second half of the second century. Even though it is in the traditional New Testament—often thought of as the earliest group of works from early Christianity—it was almost certainly written substantially later than documents like the Gospel of Thomas (now added to *A New New Testament*), the Letter to the Romans (from the traditional New Testament), and the Odes of Solomon (now added).

There are many reasons to think that Peter did not author this letter. The thinking and instruction in the letter do not match up well with the more general picture of Peter as a leader in the early church and the things he represented (Judean practice, inclusion of only those born and circumcised within the traditions of Israel). Most of the issues addressed in the letter are more typical of mid- to late second-century Christian interests, therefore making the letter most likely several eras later than Peter could have lived.

The Greek used in the letter is better than what Peter, as a Galilean peasant, would have known. The citation of other early Christian literature means that this letter was created after the end of Peter's life. So it is more likely that this letter was written in the name of Peter by a second-century author.

Second Peter concentrates on the danger of false prophets and teachers, the need to respect apostolic authority, and the coming punishment for many people when "all these things are in the process of dissolution" (3:11). The readers of the letter are exhorted to exhibit model behavior, especially of self-control, endurance, and mutual affection (1:4–10).

This letter's inclusion in the traditional New Testament indicates that the traditional New Testament did not just represent the earliest Christian documents. Instead, this letter is an important sample of literature that addressed mid- to late second-century issues in the name of the authoritative and first-generation Peter. Its defensiveness and authoritarian bent make it pale in comparison to the joyous mood of the Gospel of Truth and the Odes of Solomon, the courageous address of trauma and loss in the Gospel of Mark, and the cosmic drama of the Revelation to John. The contrast among these documents highlights how the ways of following Jesus in the twenty-first century also are dramatically different from one another.

Recommended Reading

Richard Bauckham, *Jude, 2 Peter*
R. Lewis Donelson, *I & II Peter and Jude*
Jerome H. Neyrey, *2 Peter, Jude*

The Second Letter of Peter

Introduction

1 ¹ To those to whom, through the justice of our God and Savior Jesus Christ, there has been granted faith equally privileged with our own, from Simon Peter, a slave and an ambassador of Jesus Christ.

² May grace and peace be yours in ever-increasing measure, as you advance in the knowledge of God and of Jesus, our Lord. ³ For his divine power has given us everything that is needful for a life of devotion, as we advance in the knowledge of the one who called us by a glorious manifestation of his goodness. ⁴ For it was through this that he gave us what we prize as the greatest of his promises, that through them you might participate in the divine nature, now that you have fled from the corruption in the world resulting from human passions. ⁵ Yes, and for this reason do your best to supplement your faith by goodness, goodness by knowledge, ⁶ knowledge by self-control, self-control by endurance, endurance by piety, ⁷ devotion by mutual affection, and mutual affection by love. ⁸ For, when these virtues are yours, in increasing measure, they prevent your being indifferent to, or destitute of, a fuller knowledge of our Lord Jesus Christ. ⁹ Surely the person who has not these virtues is shortsighted even to blindness, and has chosen to forget that he has been purified from his sins of the past! ¹⁰ Therefore, friends, do your best to put your call and selection beyond all doubt; for, if you do this, you will never fall. ¹¹ For in this way you will be given a triumphant admission into the never-ending domain of our Lord and Savior, Jesus Christ.

The Transfiguration and the "Second Coming" of the Anointed One

¹² I will, therefore, always be ready to remind you of all this, even though you know it and are firmly established in the truth that you now hold. ¹³ But I think it my duty, as long as I live in this tent, to rouse you by awakening memories of the past; ¹⁴ for I know that the time for this tent of mine to be put away is soon coming, as our Lord Jesus Christ himself assured me. ¹⁵ So I will do my best to enable you, at any time after my departure, to call these truths to mind. ¹⁶ For we were not following cleverly devised stories when we told you of the coming in power of our Lord Jesus Christ, but we had been eyewitnesses of his majesty. ¹⁷ For he received honor and glory from God the Father, when from the glory of the divine majesty there were borne to his ears words such as these: "This is my dearly loved Son, who brings me great joy." ¹⁸ These were the words that we heard, borne to our ears from heaven, when we were with him on that holy mountain. ¹⁹ And still stronger is the assurance that we have in the teaching of the prophets; to which you will do well to pay attention (as if it were a lamp shining in a gloomy place), until the day dawns and the morning star rises in your hearts. ²⁰ But first be assured of this: there is no prophetic teaching found in writing that can be interpreted by a person's unaided reason; ²¹ for no prophetic teaching ever came in the old days at the mere wish of people, but people, moved by the holy Spirit, being carried from God.

Warnings

2 ¹ But there were false prophets also in the nation, just as there will be false teachers among you, people who will secretly introduce ruinous divisions, disowning even the Lord who bought them, and bringing speedy ruin on themselves. ² There will be many, too, who will follow their licentious courses, and cause the way of the truth to be maligned. ³ In their covetousness they will try to make you a source of profit by their fabrications; but for a long time past their sentence has not been standing idle, nor their ruin slumbering. ⁴ Remember, God did not spare angels when they sinned, but sent them down to the underworld, and committed them to caverns of darkness, to be kept under guard for judgment. ⁵ Nor did he spare the world of old; though he preserved Noah, the proclaimer of righteousness, and seven others, when he brought a flood on the godless world. ⁶ He condemned the cities of Sodom and Gomorrah and reduced them to ashes, holding them up as a warning to the godless of what was in store for them; ⁷ but he rescued righteous Lot, whose heart was vexed by the wanton licentiousness of his neighbors; ⁸ for, seeing and hearing what he did, as he lived his righteous life among them, day after day, Lot's righteous soul was tortured by their wicked doings. ⁹ The Lord, therefore, knows how to deliver the devoted from temptation, and to keep the wicked, who are even now suffering punishment, in readiness for the day of judgment — ¹⁰ especially those who, following the promptings of flesh, indulge their polluting passions and despise all control. Audacious and self-willed, they feel no awe of the celestial beings, maligning them, ¹¹ even where angels, though excelling them in strength and power, do not bring against them a malignant charge before the Lord. ¹² These people, however, like animals without reason, intended by nature to be caught and killed — these people, I say, malign those of whom they know nothing, and will assuredly perish through their own corruption, ¹³ suffering themselves as the penalty for the suffering that they have inflicted. They think that pleasure consists in the self-indulgence of the moment. They are a stain and a disgrace, indulging, as they do, in their wanton revelry, even while joining you at your feasts. ¹⁴ They have eyes only for adultery, eyes never tired of sin; they entice weak souls; their minds are trained to covet; they live under a curse. ¹⁵ Leaving the straight road, they have gone astray and followed in the steps of Balaam, the son of Beor, who set his heart on the reward for wrongdoing, ¹⁶ but was rebuked for his offense. A dumb animal spoke with a human voice, and checked the prophet's madness. ¹⁷ These people are like springs without water, or mists driven before a gale; and for them the blackest darkness has been reserved. ¹⁸ With boastful and foolish talk, they appeal to the passions of the flesh, and, by their profligacy, entice those who are just escaping from the people who live such misguided lives. ¹⁹ They promise them freedom, while they themselves are slaves to corrupt habits; for a person is the slave of anything to which he gives way. ²⁰ If, after having escaped the polluting influences of the world, through knowing our Lord and Savior, Jesus Christ, people are again entangled in them, and give way to them, their last state has become worse than their first. ²¹ It would, indeed, have been better for them not to have known the way of righteousness than, after knowing it, to turn away from the holy command delivered to them. ²² In their case is seen the truth of the proverb, "A dog returns to what it has vomited" and "a sow after washing to her wallowing place in the mud."

A Reassertion of the Coming of the Christ

3 [1] This, dear friends, is my second letter to you. In both of them I have tried, by appealing to your remembrance, to arouse your better feelings. [2] I want you to recall what was foretold by the holy prophets, as well as the command of our Lord and Savior given to you through your ambassadors. [3] First be assured of this, that as the age draws to an end, scoffers, led by their own passions, [4] will come and ask scoffingly, "Where is his promised coming? Ever since our ancestors passed to their rest, everything remains just as it was when the world was first created!" [5] For they willfully shut their eyes to the fact that long ago the heavens existed; and the earth, also — formed out of water and by the action of water, by the fiat of God; [6] and that by the same means the world which then existed was destroyed in a deluge of water. [7] But the present heavens and earth, by the same fiat, have been reserved for fire, and are being kept for the day of the judgment and destruction of the godless.

[8] But you, dear friends, must never shut your eyes to the fact that to the Lord, one day is the same as a thousand years, and a thousand years as one day. [9] The Lord is not slow to fulfill his promise, as some count slowness; but is forbearing with you, as it is not his will that any of you should perish, but that all should be brought to repentance. [10] The day of the Lord will come like a thief; and on that day the heavens will pass away with a crash, the elements will be burned up and dissolved, and the earth and all that is in it will be disclosed. [11] Now, since all these things are in the process of dissolution, think what you yourselves ought to be — what holy and devoted lives you ought to lead, [12] while you wait for the coming of the day of God and strive to make it come soon. At its coming the heavens will be dissolved in fire, and the elements melted by heat, [13] but we look for new heavens and a new earth, where righteousness will have its home, in fulfillment of the promise of God.

[14] Therefore, dear friends, in expectation of these things, make every effort to be found by him spotless, blameless, and at peace. [15] Regard our Lord's forbearance as your one hope of salvation. This is what our dear brother Paul wrote to you, with the wisdom that God gave him. [16] It is the same in all his letters, when he speaks in them about these subjects. Some things in them are difficult to understand, which untaught and weak people distort, just as they do all other writings, to their own ruin. [17] You must, therefore, dear friends, now that you know this beforehand, be on your guard against being led away by the errors of reckless people, and so lapsing from your present steadfastness; [18] and advance in the love and knowledge of our Lord and Savior, Jesus Christ. All glory be to him now and forever.

An Introduction to the Letter of Jude

T HE LETTER OF JUDE has much to teach about the struggles of early Christian communities among themselves, but many of those lessons have yet to be identified because few people have paid attention to this document. Scholars have determined that this is an authentic letter, written in Greek by someone named Jude (probably not the disciple of Jesus), but it does not have a specific addressee. The content of the letter opposes what seems to be a relatively particular set of beliefs, practices, and situations.

The letter does quote sources from the traditions of Israel written after the books of the Torah and the prophets, so it seems likely that the author belonged to spiritual Israel. Because of the wide distribution of the people of Israel around the Mediterranean, it is not possible to determine where the author lived. This letter was probably written sometime in the second century, as it appeals to the authority of apostles, and this custom belongs primarily in that period. Jude shares a great deal of content, almost word-for-word, with 2 Peter. Most scholars believe that the author of 2 Peter (not the apostle Peter) took material from Jude, rather than vice versa, because of the focus on a specific rather than a general situation and an earlier set of references in Jude.

The letter forcefully confronts a series of Jude's opponents from within circles of Christ followers. There are false teachers to be opposed. Jude contests unspecified sexual practices and violence and instructs the reader to hate even the clothes of these people. Even with quite a few specific charges within the letter, no one has yet connected those criticized to any known Christian group.

This letter, then, stands as hauntingly unexplored territory in the traditional New Testament. Its passionate and very specific address to a situation unknown and mostly unexamined for more than 1,500 years begs for attention and careful analysis. In an ironic way, Jude resembles many of the newly discovered documents from early Christianity, both those now included in *A New New Testament* and those so far from common or scholarly knowledge that they remain at the very margins of recognition. Insight awaits within the traditional New Testament, in the fascinating new documents of *A New New Testament,* and in those more shadowy documents of early Christianity not yet examined carefully.

Recommended Reading

Richard Bauckham, *Jude, 2 Peter*
R. Lewis Donelson, *I & II Peter and Jude*
Jerome H. Neyrey, *2 Peter, Jude*

The Letter of Jude

Introduction

1 ¹ To those who, having received the call, have been loved by God the Father and protected by Jesus Christ, from Jude, a slave of Jesus Christ, and the brother of James. ² May mercy, peace, and love be yours in ever-increasing measure.

Warnings Against Moral Corruption

Dear friends, while I was making every effort to write to you about our common salvation, I felt that I must write to you at once to encourage you to fight in defense of the faith that has once and for all been entrusted to the keeping of the holy ones. ⁴ For there have crept in among you certain godless people, whose sentence has long since been pronounced, and who make the mercy of God an excuse for profligacy, and disown our only Lord and Master, Jesus Christ.

⁵ Now I want to remind you — but you already know it all — that though the Lord delivered the people from Egypt, yet he afterward destroyed those who refused to believe in him; ⁶ and that even those angels who did not keep to their appointed spheres, but left their proper homes, have been kept by him for the judgment of the great day in everlasting chains and black darkness. ⁷ Like Sodom and Gomorrah and the towns near them, which gave themselves up to fornication, and fell into unnatural vice, these angels now stand out as a warning, undergoing, as they are, punishment in never-ending fire.

⁸ Yet in the same way these people, too, cherishing vain dreams, pollute our human nature, reject control, and malign the celestial beings. ⁹ Yet even Michael the archangel, when, in his dispute with the devil, he was arguing about the body of Moses, did not venture to charge him with maligning, but said merely, "The Lord rebuke you!" ¹⁰ But these people malign whatever they do not understand, while they use such things as they know by instinct (like the animals that have no reason) for their own corruption. ¹¹ Alas for them! They walk in the steps of Cain; led astray by Balaam's love of gain, they plunge into sin, and meet their ruin through rebellion like Korah. ¹² These are the people who are blots on your love feasts, when they feast together and provide without scruple for themselves alone. They are clouds without rain, driven before the winds; they are leafless trees without a vestige of fruit, dead through and through, torn up by the roots; ¹³ they are wild sea waves, foaming with their own shame; they are wandering stars, for which the blackest darkness has been reserved forever.

¹⁴ To these people, as to others, Enoch, the seventh in descent from Adam, declared, "See! The Lord has come with his hosts of holy ones around him, ¹⁵ to execute judgment on all people, and to convict all godless people of all their godless acts, which in their ungodliness they have committed, and of all the harsh words which they have spoken against him, godless sinners that they are!"

¹⁶ These people are always murmuring, and complaining of their lot; they follow where their passions lead them; they have arrogant words on their lips; and they flatter others for the sake of what they can get from them.

¹⁷ But you should, dear friends, recall what was foretold by the ambassadors of

our Lord Jesus Christ; [18] how they used to say to you, "As time draws to an end, there will be scoffers who will be led by their godless passions." [19] These are the people —animal and unspiritual—who cause divisions. [20] But you must, dear friends, build up your characters on the foundation of your most holy faith, pray under the guidance of the holy Spirit, [21] and keep within the love of God, while waiting for the mercy of our Lord Jesus Christ, to bring you to life through the generations. [22] To some show pity, because they are in doubt. Drag them out of the fire, and save them. [23] To others show pity, but with caution, hating the clothing polluted by their touch.

Ascription

[24] To the one who is able to guard you from falling, and to bring you into his glorious presence, blameless and rejoicing— [25] to the one God, our Savior, be ascribed, through Jesus Christ, our Lord, glory, majesty, power, and dominion, as it was before time began, is now, and will be for all time to come. Amen.

LITERATURE IN THE TRADITION
OF JOHN, WITH AN
INTRODUCTORY SET OF PRAYERS

This section is mostly composed of literature in the tradition of one or another John. The three letters and the Secret Revelation of John are all associated with the follower of Jesus. The Revelation to John can fall in this group, even though since the second century CE many have thought it to be in the name of a different John. One other major piece of Johannine literature, the Gospel of John, deserves to be associated with this final section, but for other reasons it is found in the earlier section, "Gospels, Poems, and Songs Between Heaven and Earth."

An Introduction to the Fourth Book
of the Odes of Solomon

T HE ODES OF SOLOMON are simultaneously one of the most significant discoveries of early Christian literature and one of the most ignored discoveries of early Christian literature in the past two hundred years. Found in piles of research in a well-traveled and expert scholar's office in the early twentieth century, they have been published since shortly after their "discovery." They are indisputably the largest trove of early Christian worship material ever found in one document, which is almost a third the size of the Bible's book of 150 psalms. The New Orleans Council eagerly chose to include these odes, both for their beautiful and evocative language and in order to make *A New New Testament* a strong witness to actual material from the worship of some early Christ movements.

These forty-one "songs" of early Christianity are most likely a collection from different communities over parts of the first and second centuries. However, they also represent for the most part a particular kind of early Christianity in their beliefs, practices, and ways of framing the world. They look and sound very much like the psalms of the Hebrew scriptures, except that they have regular references to the Word, the Light, the Lord, and the Son of God in ways that indicate their belonging to a Christ movement; that is, they are definitely "psalms" of a "Christian" character, although they never use the name "Jesus," and rarely even the title "Christ" or "Anointed One."

The "Christ" figure often speaks in these odes, making those early Christians who sang them take on the identity of "Christ." This identification of the singers with the "Christ" matches the content of the odes in which the "Christ" is a cosmic figure who makes humans one with God.

The title, "The Odes of Solomon," cannot, of course, refer to the author of this collection (since Solomon lived a thousand years before) but serves rather as an affirmation of a strong and intimate connection between this part of early "Christianity" and the traditions of Israel. That this document represents a collection of different odes from different communities makes "Solomon" something like the figure of "David" in the psalms of the Hebrew scriptures. It is difficult also to identify a date of composition for the odes. Most commentators think they are early, with the past thirty years of scholarship pointing more toward the first century than the second. The place of composition is also unclear. The closeness to the psalms of the Hebrew scriptures suggests a "Christ" movement with very strong ties to the traditions of Israel. The odes' language of Syriac would point toward

Syria. It is not clear whether the odes were ever in Greek or Aramaic, but the fine poetic style indicates a real possibility that they may originally have been in Syriac.

A New New Testament breaks the odes into four distinct parts, distributed among different sections of the book. Since the odes as a collection do not represent one authorship, the New Orleans Council proposed that they could be broken up into distinct smaller collections. In keeping with the council's and my interest in making the reading of *A New New Testament* as worshipful as possible, I broke the larger document into these four distinct parts and used them to provide a spiritual and worshipful dimension to the other documents. The First Book of the Odes of Solomon contains Odes 1 and 3–12. The second book contains Odes 13–22; the third, Odes 23–32; and the fourth, Odes 33–42.*

The Fourth Book of the Odes of Solomon contains the most embattled songs of the whole collection. Although still sprinkled with psalms of praise, there is a distinct turn in these odes toward ongoing conflicts and difficulties in life. These conflicts and challenges seem at least in part to belong to what is known about the early Christ movements in general; that is, it seems likely that the difficulties alluded to in these odes had to do with the violence the Roman Empire imposed arbitrarily and over a broad spectrum of territories, the disintegrating sense of belonging among the conquered tribes and nations, and new rounds of ethnic and sexual conflict. In Ode 33:1 a "Corruptor" "caused constant destruction." In 35:3, "Everyone was shaken and frightened." In 38:1–2, "the light of Truth . . . led me, and brought me, then caused me to pass over chasms and fissures"; and in 38:10, the "Liar and the Error" appear to challenge the light of Truth.

In each conflict "the Lord" comes to the aid of the odist/singer and goodness is reclaimed. The last ode (42) seems almost to summarize these conflicts and difficulties, but the character of resolution and triumph is proclaimed more clearly and with some surprises. Here the triumph is not represented as a battle so much as the emergence of persistent love in the person of Christ: "For they have rejected those who persecute them and laid over themselves the yoke of my love. As the arm of the bridegroom over the bride, so also is my yoke upon those who understand me. . . . I was not rejected, nor was I believed to be, and I did not perish, though they wished it upon me" (42:7–8, 10).

There are two other odes that share a major similarity. Odes 33 and 36 portray a divine feminine character as a pivotal figure of goodness. In Ode 33 there is a cosmic conflict between the Corrupter and the perfect Virgin. After the Corrupter has both caused great destruction and attracted many people, the perfect Virgin calls to humanity:

---

* This section of general information is found in each introduction to a portion of the Odes of Solomon. The second section of each introduction is specific to the odes contained in it.

"Sons and daughters of humanity
Return yourselves and come.
Abandon the ways of that Corrupter,
And come near to me.
He led you into wrong, but I will bring you out from ruin,
And make you wise in the ways of Truth.
Do not be corrupted, nor perish.
Hear me and be saved,
For I have spoken the generosity of the Lord among you.
And you will be redeemed and blessed by my hand." (33:6–11)

Somewhat similarly, in Ode 36 the odist/singer

. . . rested on the Spirit of the Lord,
And she raised me up to the high place
And she caused me to stand on my feet in the high place of the Lord . . .
While I was proclaiming in the preparation of his odes.
She gave birth to me before the face of the Lord.
And while I was the Child of Humanity
I was called the Light, the Child of God . . .
For she made me according to the greatness of the Most High
And he renewed me according to his renewal,
And anointed me from his fullness. (36:1–3, 4–5)

It is surprising to twenty-first-century readers to see these divine feminine characters integrated so seamlessly into the vocabulary of more familiar characters such as Son of God, the Most High, and the Spirit. The ancient world — both in general and within the early Christ movements — was much more comfortable with and interested in transgender identities than our twenty-first-century Western world. This ancient and early Christ movement blurring of what many modern sensitivities think of as firm sexual boundaries can be a major spiritual resource for twenty-first-century readers. Here the Son of God and the divine feminine Spirit of God are one, beckoning to the modern world with intimacy and an identity that is itself inherently cross-gendered. The fragile defensiveness of sexed identities in the twentieth and twenty-first centuries is offered a chance to relax and know a multisexual intimacy in God.

Perhaps at least as valuable are the pictures in Ode 33 of the perfect Virgin confronting the Corrupter on behalf of humanity and in Ode 36 of the child-bearing Spirit first giving birth to the Son of God and then subsequently working with the Most High to make the Son of God great, new, and perfect. In each of these cases the power of goodness over corruption resides primarily in a feminine figure. Both the perfect Virgin and the child-bearing Spirit save humanity and develop the Son of God into a more powerful figure of goodness. For the twenty-first-century reader, this is a powerful deconstruction of divine power and goodness as typically masculine. It offers a new kind of Son of God and humanity that are rooted in a divine feminine and presents new and complex models of what it means to be men and women.

Perhaps most evocative in these and most of the other odes is the fairly typical self-presentation of the Christ figure in the voice of the "I," the odist/singer. Here the humans who are singing and worshiping identify with the Son of the divine wedding of Spirit and Most High. The singing of these odes makes the human singer into a divine person. As these words are sung and read, not only do they make the singers a part of God, but that divinity in whom they find themselves is part child-bearing Spirit and part the (masculine) Most High. Twenty-first-century readers rarely encounter a scripture that offers them integration of their humanity with divinity and participation in a God that is both feminine and masculine.

Recommended Reading

James Charlesworth, *The Odes of Solomon: The Syriac Texts Edited with Translation and Notes*
M. Franzmann, *The Odes of Solomon: An Analysis of the Poetical Structure and Form*
J. R. Harris and A. Mingana, *The Odes and Psalms of Solomon*

The Fourth Book of the Odes of Solomon

Ode 33

[1] Then Generosity hastened again, and divorced the Corruptor,

And she descended into him in order to renounce him.

[2] But he caused constant destruction before him,

And corrupted all that he had cultivated.

[3] He stood on the head of a summit, and let out his voice

From one edge of the earth to the other.

[4] Then he drew to him all of those who had heard him,

Since he did not appear like the Evil One.

[5] However, the unblemished virgin stood,

Who was preaching and inviting, and said,

[6] "Sons and daughters of humanity,

Return yourselves and come.

[7] Abandon the ways of that Corruptor,

And come near to me.

[8] He led you into wrong, but I will bring you out from ruin,

And make you wise in the ways of Truth.

[9] Do not be corrupted, nor perish.

[10] Hear me and be saved,

For I have spoken the generosity of the Lord among you.

[11] And you will be redeemed and blessed by my hand.

I am your judge.

[12] Those who put me on will not be refused,

Instead they will acquire incorruption in the new generation.

[13] My chosen ones walked in me,

I will make my paths known to those who seek me.

And I will entrust my name in them. Halleluiah.

Ode 34

[1] There is no difficult path where the heart is simple

Nor a burden in honest thoughts

[2] Nor a storm in the depth of enlightened thought.

[3] Where one is fortified by beauty

There is nothing at odds in them.

[4] The image of that which is below

Is that which is above.

[5] Indeed everything is from above,

And from below there is nothing.

However, it is supposed by those in whom there is no understanding.

[6] Comfort has been revealed for your salvation,

Trust and live and be saved. Halleluiah.

Ode 35

[1] The sprinkling of the Lord shaded me with serenity,

And caused a cloud of peace to rise over my head.

[2] So that she might watch me at all times,

And she became a salvation for me.

[3] Everyone was shaken and frightened,

Smoke and judgment rose from them.

[4] But I was calm in the order of the Lord,

More than shade he was for me, more than foundation.

[5] I was like a young one who is carried by its mother.

And he gave me milk, the dew of the Lord.

[6] I was brought up in his favor,

And I remained in his fullness.
[7] Then I stretched out my hands in the elevation of my entire self,

I directed myself toward the Most High,

And I was redeemed toward him.
Halleluiah.

Ode 36

[1] I rested on the Spirit of the Lord,

And she raised me up to the high place
[2] And she caused me to stand on my feet in the high place of the Lord

Before his fullness and splendor,

While I was proclaiming in the preparation of his odes.
[3] She gave birth to me before the face of the Lord.

And while I was the Child of Humanity*

I was called the Light, the Child of God,

Because I was glorified among the glorious,

And first among the great ones.
[4] For she made me according to the greatness of the Most High

And he renewed me according to his renewal,
[5] And anointed me from his fullness.

I became one of those who are near him
[6] And my mouth was opened like a cloud of dew

And my heart gushed forth a fountain of justice.
[7] And my access was through peace,

And I was set up in the Spirit of Instruction.
Halleluiah.

Ode 37

[1] I extended my hands toward the Lord,

And toward the Most High I raised my voice.
[2] Then I spoke with the lips of my heart

And he heard me when my voice found him.
[3] And his word came toward me,

Who gave me the fruits of my labors;
[4] Even gave me a resting place in the comfort of the Lord.
Halleluiah.

Ode 38

[1] I went up to the light of Truth as to a chariot,

And Truth led me, and brought me,
[2] Then caused me to pass over chasms and fissures,

And I was removed from cliffs and valleys.
[3] Truth became a haven of salvation for me,

And set me upon the place of immortal life.
[4] He went with me, gave me rest, and did not permit that I should stray

Because he was and is Truth.
[5] And there was no danger for me, since I was walking with him,

And I did not err in anything since I obeyed him.
[6] For Error fled from him,

And did not ever encounter him.
[7] But Truth proceeded in the honest path,

And showed me everything that I did not recognize.
[8] All of the drugs of Error, and those trappings of death that seem to be of true joy,
[9] And the corrupting of the Corruptor,

I saw when the bride who corrupts was adorned,

And the bridegroom who destroys is destroyed.
[10] So I asked Truth, "Who are they?"

---

* Literally, "Son of Man."

And he said to me, "This is the Liar and the Error,

[11] They imitate the Beloved and his Bride,

And cause the generation to stray, and they ruin it.

[12] And they invite many to the wedding feast,

They give them the wine of their intoxication to drink.

[13] Then their wisdom and understanding are vomited up,

making them foolish.

[14] And they abandon them,

Then they linger while raving and ruined.

[15] Since there is no heart in them,

Neither are they seeking it."

[16] But I have been made wise so that I will not fall into the hands of the Liars.

And I rejoiced for myself because Truth had gone with me.

[17] I was established, lived, and was redeemed,

And my foundations were set upon the hand of the Lord,

Because he planted me.

[18] For he set the root

and irrigated it, supported it

And blessed it, so its fruits will be forever.

[19] Then it dug deep, and it grew up and spread out

And it was full and it was enlarged.

[20] The Lord alone was glorified,

In his planting and his cultivation,

[21] In his care and the blessing of his lips,

In the beautiful planting of his Right Hand,

[22] And in the discovery of his planting

And the understanding of his mind. Halleluiah.

Ode 39

[1] The power of the Lord is like raging rivers,

Those who rebuke him are sent tumbling headfirst.

[2] But they* hinder their paths,

And spoil their passages,

[3] And plunder their bodies,

And disfigure their natures.

[4] For they are sharper than lightning bolts,

And even faster.

[5] But those who cross over them in faith

Will not be terrified.

[6] And those who walk in them without defect

Shall not be bewildered.

[7] Because the sign in them is the Lord,

And the sign is the way for those who cross over in the name of the Lord.

[8] Therefore put on the name of the Most High, and know him,

And you will cross over without danger,

Then the rivers will be under you.

[9] The Lord has bridged them with his Word,

And he walked and passed over them on foot.

[10] And his footsteps stood firm upon the waters, and they were not wiped away.

Rather they are like a cross† that was fixed in Truth.

[11] Here and there the waves rose up,

But the footsteps of our Lord Messiah stand.

[12] And they are not wiped out, nor are they altered.

[13] So the way has been set for those who cross over after him,

And for those who follow the path of his faith,

Who lean upon his name. Halleluiah.

---

* This refers back to the rivers, acting upon those who rebuke the Lord.

† This can just mean a beam of wood.

Ode 40

¹ As drops of honey from the honeycomb of bees,

And the flow of milk from the one who loves her children,

So also is my hope upon you, my God.

² As a fountain gushes forth its waters,

So also my heart pours forth the splendor of the Lord,

And my lips send out praise to him.

³ Then my tongue becomes sweet in his anthems,

And my members become fat in his odes.

⁴ Also my face beams with his exultation,

And my spirit rejoices in his love,

And my entire self shines.

⁵ And all who are afraid can rely on him,

And salvation will be confirmed in them.

⁶ His abundance is immortal life,

And the ones who receive it are without devastation.

Halleluiah.

Ode 41

¹ Let all to whom the Lord has given birth proclaim him,

And let us receive the Truth of his faith.

² And let his children be known to him,

So that we may sing with his love.

³ We live in the Lord through his generosity

And we receive life through his Anointed One.

⁴ Indeed a momentous day has dawned for us,

And the one who gave to us from his glory is astonishing.

⁵ Therefore let us agree together, on account of the name of the Lord,

And let us honor him and his goodness.

⁶ And let our faces shine with his light,

And let our hearts meditate in his love night and day.

⁷ Let us rejoice in the Lord's exultation.

[Christ speaks]

⁸ All who see me will be amazed

Because I am of a different sort.

⁹ For the Father of Truth remembered me,

The one who possessed me from the beginning.

¹⁰ Indeed his riches bore me,

Along with the contemplation of his heart.

[Odist speaks]

¹¹ And his word is in each path of ours,

The redeemer who sustains life, and does not reject ourselves,

¹² The person who was humiliated

And was raised by his own righteousness.

¹³ The child of the Most High appeared

In the fullness of the Father.

¹⁴ And light shone from the word

That was in him before he existed.

¹⁵ The Anointed One is one with* Truth,

And he was known before the foundations of the generation,

So that he might give life to people forever in the Truth of his name.

¹⁶ A new hymn to the Lord from those who love him.

Halleluiah.

Ode 42

¹ I stretched out my hands and approached my Lord,

Because the extension of my hands is a sign.

² And my extension is the upright cross

That was suspended over the path of the honest one.

[Christ speaks]

---

* Also "in," "by," or "through."

³ And I became useless to those who [did not] know me,

Because I hide myself from those who embrace me.

⁴ And I will be with those who love me.

⁵ All of those who pursued me have died,

But those who hoped in me sought me, because I am living.

⁶ Then I rose and I was with them,

And I will speak through their mouths.

⁷ For they have rejected those who persecute them

And laid over themselves the yoke of my love.

⁸ As the arm of the bridegroom over the bride,

So also is my yoke upon those who understand me.

⁹ As the bridal feast is laid out by the house of the couple,

So also is my love upon those who believe in me.

¹⁰ I was not rejected, nor was I believed to be,

And I did not perish, though they wished it upon me.

¹¹ Sheol saw me and was shattered,

And Death vomited me up, and many with me.

¹² I was vinegar and bitterness to it,

And I descended in it as far as its depths went.

¹³ And he released both feet and head

Because it was not able to endure my presence.

¹⁴ And I made an assembly of the living among his dead

And I spoke to them with living lips,

So that my word might not be empty.

¹⁵ Those who had died ran toward me,

And they cried out, and said, "Child of God, spare us.

¹⁶ And do with us in keeping with your kindness,

And bring us away from the chains of darkness.

¹⁷ Then open the door for us,

Through which we may go out to you,

For we perceive that our death does not approach you.

¹⁸ Let us also be saved through you,

Because you are our redeemer."

¹⁹ Then I heard their voice,

And I placed their faith in my heart.

²⁰ Then I set my name upon their head,

So that they are the children of the free,

And they are my own.
Halleluiah.

An Introduction to the First Letter of John

ALTHOUGH ENTITLED "The First Letter of John," this book does not have the form of a letter as found elsewhere in early Christian or, more broadly, Greco-Roman correspondence. For instance, in its body it names neither an addressee nor a sender/author. The name "John" occurs only in the title, and titles in much ancient literature are by another hand than the author's. Nevertheless, the style and vocabulary of 1 John are very similar to those of the Gospel of John, leading many to think that they are from the same author (also unnamed in the gospel) or one of the gospel author's close associates. Traditionally many believe that this "letter" was written by Jesus's disciple John, but this idea is very difficult to prove from the letter and is challenged by many close readers of the text.

The date of 1 John's composition tends to be aligned with that of the Gospel of John, but there is no agreement on whether 1 John was written slightly before or slightly after the gospel. This would date 1 John to sometime in the 80s or 90s CE. Similarly, there is little agreement on where 1 John was composed, with the possibilities ranging from Israel through Asia Minor. Unlike the Gospel of John, the "letter" demonstrates little direct knowledge of the traditions and practices of Israel.

Love is a significant theme in 1 John. This is the only document in *A New New Testament* (and also the traditional New Testament) that contains the idea that "God is love." Like the Gospel of John, 1 John contains the command to "love one another" and does not include the commands to love one's neighbor or enemies. Unlike the Gospel of John, this "letter" does not use the relationship between the Son and the Father as the model for love. Rather, in 1 John love is used for both the love between God and humans and the love among humans, and this connection is made explicit in the command to "love one another, because love comes from God" (4:7).

The First Letter of John also occupies itself with intense conflict among its initial ancient readers and with targeted opponents in "the world." It is one of two documents in *A New New Testament* (the other is 2 John) that use the term *antichrist,* apparently to refer to a group formerly within the 1 John movement who have split with the author of the "letter" (2:19). There is more than one antichrist, according to 2:18. In addition, the "letter" expresses antagonism toward those "in the world," liars, and those who do not believe certain things about Jesus.

In many ways the almost ecstatic vocabulary of 1 John concerning the intimate, loving relationship between God and humans is most reminiscent of the Gospel of Truth, where this same intimacy is expressed as a uniting fragrance between humans and God. And the rhythmic contemplation in 1 John has strong similarities to the Odes of Solomon. It is then quite reasonable to think of a family of early Christ movement texts as including the Gospel of John, the Gospel of Truth, 1 John, and the Odes of Solomon. Such a family of early texts would, of course, look quite similar to *A New New Testament*.

Reading 1 John in the twenty-first century is probably most deeply enhanced by reading it as a companion to the Odes of Solomon and the Gospel of Truth. The steady ecstatic dimension of the Gospel of Truth can connect with 1 John's meditations on love and soften its harsh attack on the competitors of its Christ movement. In this collection 1 John directly follows the Fourth Book of the Odes of Solomon. This is especially appropriate as both 1 John and the Fourth Book of the Odes are concerned with conflict and suffering. Indeed the Fourth Book of the Odes makes 1 John's bitter attack on the "antichrist" less violent and gives it a more gracious context.

Recommended Reading

Judith M. Lieu, *I, II, & III John*
Georg Strecker, *The Johannine Letters*

The First Letter of John

1 ¹ That which was from the beginning, that which we have heard, that which we have seen with our eyes, that which we watched reverently and touched with our hands, concerning the word of life ² and the life was made visible, and we have seen it, and now bear witness to it, and tell you of the life of the generations, which was with the Father and was made visible to us. ³ It is of what we have seen and heard that we now tell you, so that you may have communion with us. And our communion is with the Father and with his Son, Jesus Christ. ⁴ And we are writing all this to you that our joy may be complete.

⁵ This, then, is the message that we have heard from him and now tell you: "God is light, and there is no darkness in him at all." ⁶ If we say that we have communion with God, and yet continue to walk in the darkness, we lie, and are not doing what is true. ⁷ But if we walk in the light, as God is in the light, we have communion with one another, and the blood of his Son Jesus purifies us from all sin. ⁸ If we say that there is no sin in us, we deceive ourselves, and the truth is not in us. ⁹ If we confess our sins, God may be trusted, in his righteousness, to forgive us our sins and purify us from all wickedness. ¹⁰ If we say that we have not sinned, we are making God a liar, and God's word has no place in us.

2 ¹ Children, I am writing these things to you so that you may not sin; but if anyone should sin, we have one who can advocate for us with the Father — Jesus Christ, the righteous — ² and he is the offering for our sins, and not for ours only, but for those of the whole world besides. ³ And by this we have learned to know him if we obey his commandments. ⁴ The person who says, "I know Jesus," but does not keep his commandments, is a liar, and the truth has no place in him; ⁵ but whenever a person obeys his word, in that person the love of God has indeed reached its perfection. By this we know that we are in union with God — ⁶ "whoever says I abide in God" is bound to walk as Christ walked.

⁷ Beloved, it is no new commandment that I am writing to you, but an old commandment, which you have had from the first. That old commandment is the word that you have heard. ⁸ Yet, in a way, it is a new commandment that I am writing to you, that is true in Christ and in you, for the darkness is passing away and the true light is already shining. ⁹ The person who says that he is in the light, and yet hates others, is in the darkness even now. ¹⁰ The person who loves others is always in the light, and there is nothing within him to cause him to stumble; ¹¹ while the person who hates others is in the darkness, and is living in the darkness, and does not know where he is going, because the darkness prevents him from seeing.

¹² I am writing, children, to you, because your sins have been forgiven you for Christ's sake. ¹³ I am writing, adults in the faith, to you, because you have learned to know him who has been from the beginning. I am writing, young ones in the faith, to you, because you have conquered the evil one. I write, children, to you, because you have learned to know the Father. ¹⁴ I write, adults, to you, because you have learned to know him who has been from the beginning. I write, young ones, to you, because you are strong, and God's message is always in your hearts, and you have conquered the evil one. ¹⁵ Do not love the world or what the world can offer. When

anyone loves the world, there is no love for the Father in him; [16] for all that the world can offer — the gratification of the earthly nature, the gratification of the eye, the pretentious life — belongs, not to the Father, but to the world. [17] And the world, and all that it gratifies, is passing away, but they who do God's will remain forever.

[18] Children, these are the last days. You were told that an antichrist was coming; and many antichrists have already arisen. By that we know that these are the last days. [19] From us, it is true, they went out, but they had never belonged to us; for, if they had belonged to us, they would have remained among us. They left us that it might be made clear that they do not, any of them, belong to us. [20] You, however, have received anointing from the Holy One. [21] You all know — but I am not writing to you because you do not know the truth, but because you do know it, and because nothing false can come from the truth.

[22] Who is a liar, if not the person who rejects the truth that Jesus is the Christ? That person is the antichrist, the person who rejects the Father and the Son. [23] No one who rejects the Son has found the Father; the person who acknowledges the Son has found the Father also. [24] As for you, let what you were told at the first be always in your thoughts. If, then, what you were told at the first is always in your thoughts, you yourselves will maintain your union both with the Son and with the Father. [25] And this is what he himself promised us, life through generations!

[26] In writing this to you, I have in mind those who are trying to mislead you. [27] But for you the anointing that you received from the Christ abides in you, and you are not in need of anyone to teach you; but since his anointing teaches you about everything, and since it is a real anointing, and no lie, then, as it has taught you, maintain your union with him. [28] Yes, children, maintain your union with Christ, so that

whenever he appears, our confidence may not fail us, and we may not be ashamed before him at his coming. [29] Knowing him to be righteous, you realize that everyone who lives righteously has received the new life from him.

3 [1] See what love the Father has given us, that we should be called children of God, as indeed we are. The reason why the world does not know us is that it has not learned to know him. [2] Beloved, we are God's children now; what we will be has not yet been revealed. What we do know is that when it is revealed, we will be like the Anointed One; because we will see him as he is. [3] And all who have this hope in the Anointed One purify themselves, as the Anointed One is pure.

[4] Everyone who commits sin is living in lawlessness. Sin is lawlessness. [5] And you know that the Anointed One appeared to take away our sins; and in him sin has no place. [6] No one who maintains union with him lives in sin; no one who lives in sin has ever really seen him or learned to know him. [7] Children, do not let anyone mislead you. The person who lives righteously is righteous, as the Anointed One is righteous. [8] The person who lives sinfully belongs to the devil, for the devil has sinned from the first. It was for this that the Son of God appeared, that he might undo the devil's work.

[9] No one who has received the new life from God lives sinfully, because the nature of God dwells within her; and she cannot live in sin, because she has received the new life from God. [10] By this the children of God are distinguished from the children of the devil — no one who lives unrighteously comes from God, and especially the person who does not love others. [11] For these are the tidings that we heard from the first — that we are to love one another. [12] We must not be like Cain, who belonged to the evil one and killed his brother. And why did he kill him? It was

because his life was bad while his brother's was good.

[13] Do not wonder, friends, if the world hates you. [14] We know that we have passed out of death into life, because we love each other. The person who does not love remains in a state of death. [15] The person who hates another is a murderer; and you know that no murderer has the life of the ages within her.

[16] We have learned to know what love is from this — that Christ laid down his life on our behalf. Therefore we also ought to lay down our lives for each other. [17] But if anyone has worldly possessions, and yet looks on while one of our own is in need, and steels her heart against that person, how can it be said that the love of God is within her? [18] Children, do not let our love be mere words, or end in talk; let it be true and show itself in acts.

[19] By that we will know that we are on the side of the truth; and we will satisfy ourselves in God's sight, [20] that if our conscience condemns us, yet God is greater than our conscience and knows everything. [21] Beloved, if our conscience does not condemn us, then we approach God with confidence, [22] and we receive from him whatever we ask, because we are laying his commandments to heart, and are doing what is pleasing in his sight. [23] His commandment is this — that we should put our trust in the name of his Son, Jesus Christ, and love one another, in accordance with the commandment that he gave us. [24] And the person who obeys his commandments maintains union with Christ, and Christ with her. And by this we know that Christ maintains union with us — by the Spirit he has given us.

4 [1] Beloved, do not trust every spirit, but test each spirit, to see whether it proceeds from God; because many false prophets have gone out into the world.

[2] This is the way by which to know the spirit of God — all inspiration that acknowledges Jesus Christ as having come in our human nature is from God; [3] while every spirit that does not acknowledge Jesus is not from God. It is the spirit of the antichrist; you have heard that it was to come, and it is now already in the world.

[4] Children, you have come from God, and you have successfully resisted such people as these, because he who is in you is greater than the one who is in the world. [5] Those people belong to the world; and therefore they speak as the world speaks, and the world listens to them. [6] We come from God. He who knows God listens to us; the person who does not come from God does not listen to us. By that we may know the true spirit from the false.

[7] Beloved, let us love one another, because love comes from God; and everyone who loves has received the new life from God and knows God. [8] The person who does not love has not learned to know God; for God is love. [9] The love of God was revealed to us by his sending his only Son into the world, so that we might find life through him. [10] His love is seen in this — not in our having loved God, but in his loving us and sending his Son to be an atoning sacrifice for our sins.

[11] Beloved, since God loved us in this way, we, surely, ought to love one another. [12] No human eyes have ever seen God, yet if we love one another, God remains in union with us, and his love attains its perfection in us. [13] We know that we remain in union with him, and he with us, by this — by his having given us some measure of his Spirit. [14] Moreover, our eyes have seen — and we are testifying to the fact — that the Father has sent the Son to be the Savior of the world. [15] Whoever acknowledges that Jesus Christ is the Son of God — God remains in union with him, and he with God. [16] And, moreover, we have learned to know, and have accepted as a fact, the love which God has for us.

God is love; and whoever lives in love lives in God, and God in him. [17] It is through this that love has attained its perfection in us, so that we may have confidence on the day of judgment, because what Christ is, that we also are in this world. [18] There is no fear in love, but love, when perfect, drives out fear, because fear implies punishment, and the person who feels fear has not attained to perfect love. [19] We love, because God first loved us. [20] If someone says, "I love God," and yet hates a brother or sister, he is a liar; for those who do not love their brother or sister, whom they have seen, cannot love God, whom they have not seen. [21] Indeed, we have this commandment from God: Those who love God must also love each other.

5 [1] Everyone who believes that Jesus is the Anointed One is born of God; and everyone who loves him who gave that life loves him who has received it. [2] By this we know that we love God's children — when we love God and carry out his commandments. [3] For to love God is to obey the commandments; and these commandments are not burdensome, [4] because whatever has been born of God conquers the world. And this is the power that has conquered the world, our trust. [5] Who is the person that conquers the world but the person who trusts that Jesus is the Son of God? [6] This is the one who came through water and blood — Jesus Christ himself; not through water only, but through water and blood. And there is the spirit also to bear testimony, and the spirit is truth itself. [7] It is a threefold testimony — [8] that of the spirit, the water, and the blood — and these three are at one. [9] We accept the testimony of people, but God's testimony is still stronger; and there is the testimony of God — the fact that he has already borne

testimony about his Son. [10] The person who believes in the Son of God has that testimony within her. The person who does not believe God has made God a liar, by refusing to believe in that testimony which he has borne about his Son. [11] And that testimony is that God gave us never-ending life, and that this life is in his Son. [12] The person who finds the Son finds life; the person who does not find the Son of God does not find life.

[13] I write this to you so that you may realize that you have found life through the ages — you who believe in the name of the Son of God. [14] And this is the confidence with which we approach him, that whenever we ask anything that is in accordance with his will, he listens to us. [15] And if we realize that he listens to us — whatever we ask — we realize that we have what we have asked from him. [16] If anyone sees a brother or a sister committing some sin that is not a deadly sin, he will ask, and so be the means of giving life to him — to any whose sin is not deadly. There is such a thing as deadly sin; I do not say that a person should pray about that. [17] Every wrong action is sin, and there is sin that is not deadly.

[18] We know that those born of God do not sin, but the one who has received the new life from God keeps that new life, and then the evil one does not touch her. [19] We realize that we come from God, while all the world is under the influence of the evil one. [20] We realize, too, that the Son of God has come among us, and has given us the understanding so that we may know the true God; and we are in union with the true God, his Son, Jesus Christ. He is the true God and he is never-ending life. [21] Children, keep yourselves from idols.

An Introduction to the Second Letter of John

I N CONTRAST TO 1 JOHN, 2 John has most of the earmarks of a real letter in the ancient world. It is from someone calling himself "the elder" and is addressed to someone called "the lady" and her children. The letter also contains greetings by the elder "from the children of your eminent sister" (13). And it contains direct address to specific relationships and occasions. The document is so short that it has been difficult to understand who and where "the elder" and "the lady" were. There is little reference to anyone called "lady" in other early Christ movement documents but, on the other hand, many references to various people carrying the title "elder." The letter itself gives no details about who these people might be.

The vocabulary of this letter is very similar to that in both the Gospel of John and 1 John, and the content shares with both of these a central tenet to love one another. It has in common with 1 John its anxiety about the antichrist(s) (7). But as neither John's gospel nor 1 John claims to be written by "the elder," the exact authorial relationship with these other two books remains unclear. The similarities have led scholars to surmise that 2 John was written in the 80s or 90s, either slightly before or after 1 John and the Gospel of John. This has led a number of scholars to think that the authorship of these three documents is the same or at least within the same school of teachers.

This brief letter has charm for the twenty-first century. Just the idea of "the elder" writing a letter to "the lady" is enough to tease one's imagination about what situation occasioned such an address in the early Christ movements. One might meditate on their relationship outside of and within their respective participation in a Christ movement of the first century, taking into account the letter's atmosphere of mutual respect. And one might notice how the furtive power of "the lady" is reminiscent of the ways feminine power emerges in the new documents of the Odes of Solomon, The Thunder: Perfect Mind, the Gospel of Truth, and the Acts of Paul and Thecla.

Recommended Reading

Judith M. Lieu, *I, II, & III John*
Georg Strecker, *The Johannine Letters*

The Second Letter of John

1 ¹ The elder to an elect lady and her children, whom I love in truth, and not I only, but also all those who know the truth. ² We love you for the sake of that truth which is always in our hearts; yes, and it will be ours forever. ³ Grace, mercy, and peace will be ours, from God, the Father, and of Jesus Christ, the Father's Child — in truth and love. ⁴ It was a great joy to me to find some of your children walking in the truth, in obedience to the commandment that we received from the Father. ⁵ And now, dear lady — not as though I were writing a new commandment for you; no, it is the commandment which we had from the first — let us love one another. ⁶ And this is love — that we walk according to the Father's commandments. This is the commandment you heard from the beginning — you must walk in it. ⁷ I say this because many impostors have gone out into the world — people who do not acknowledge that Jesus as Christ is the one coming in the flesh. It is that rejection which marks someone as an impostor and an antichrist. ⁸ Take care that you do not lose the fruit of all our work; rather, reap the benefit of it in full. ⁹ Everyone who does not abide in the teaching of the Christ, but goes beyond it, has failed to find God; the person who keeps to that teaching has found both the Father and the Son. ¹⁰ If anyone comes to you and does not bring this teaching, do not receive him into your house or welcome him; ¹¹ for the person who welcomes him is sharing with him in his wicked deeds. ¹² Though I have a great deal to say to you, I would rather not trust it to paper and ink, but I am hoping to come and see you, and to speak with you face-to-face, so that our joy may be complete. ¹³ The children of your eminent sister send you their greetings.

An Introduction to the Third Letter of John

L IKE 2 JOHN, 3 John seems to be a real letter. It, like 2 John, is from someone calling himself "the elder" but has a different addressee; 3 John is written
to the elder's "dear friend Gaius." This letter also makes reference to several other
people in the "church" by name, accusing one of being a bad leader and approving of another one. It shares with 1 John, 2 John, and the Gospel of John a sense
of coming from an embattled community and strongly criticizes other, perhaps
neighboring and formerly allied, Christ groups. But none of the names or references overlap in any of these documents (except for the clear overlapping authorship with 2 John). Because of its brevity and the lack of similar name references in
other early Christian literature, it is very difficult to know who any of these people were. Scholars surmise that this Greek letter may have been written in similar
times (80s or 90s) and circumstances to the Gospel of John and 1 John.

The brevity of this letter, the obscurity of its references, and its strong defensive
and attacking attitude make it difficult to access for a twenty-first-century reader.
It lacks the eloquence of the brief Prayer of the Apostle Paul or the short Prayer
of Thanksgiving (both added to *A New New Testament*) or the affection of 1 and
2 John. Perhaps it could inspire an embattled community of today to keep up its
fight, but such counsel in itself is not always wise. On the other hand, one might
think also about the damage that such embattled mentalities can create within
people.

Recommended Reading

Judith M. Lieu, *I, II, & III John*
Georg Strecker, *The Johannine Letters*

The Third Letter of John

1 ¹ The elder to the beloved Gaius, whom I love in truth. ² Beloved, I pray that all may be well with you and that you may have good health, just as it is well with your soul. ³ For it was a great joy to me when some brothers and sisters came and testified to your fidelity to the truth — namely, that you walk in the truth. ⁴ Nothing gives me greater pleasure than to hear that my children are walking in the truth. ⁵ Beloved, you do faithfully whatever you do for other brothers and sisters, even when they are strangers to you; ⁶ they have testified before the church to your love; and you will do well to help them on their way in a manner worthy of God. ⁷ For it was on behalf of the name that they left their homes, and refused to take anything from the gentiles. ⁸ We, therefore, ought to give such people a hearty welcome, and so take our share in their work for the truth. ⁹ I wrote something to the church; but Diotrephes, who loves to be first among them, declines to recognize us. ¹⁰ Therefore, when I come, I will not forget his conduct in ridiculing us with his wicked tongue. Not content with that, he not only declines to recognize our friends who are followers himself, but actually prevents those who would, and expels them from the church. ¹¹ Beloved, take what is good for your example, not what is bad. The person who does what is good is from God; the person who does what is bad has never seen God. ¹² Everyone has always had a good word for Demetrius, and the truth itself speaks for him. Yes, and we also add our good word, and you know that what we say about him is true. ¹³ I have a great deal to say to you, but I do not care to trust it to pen and ink in a letter. ¹⁴ I hope, however, it will not be long before I see you, and then we will speak face-to-face. Peace to you. Our friends here send you their greetings. Greet each one of our friends.

An Introduction to the Revelation to John

D IFFERING IN SHAPE and tone from anything else in *A New New Testament*, the Revelation to John pictures a cataclysmic battle on earth and in the skies. Featuring a wide array of visions, it includes first-person accounts of violent clashes and scourges that consume much of the earth. Although deeply connected to many early Christian beliefs, the book almost never uses the word *Jesus*, preferring to give him other titles like "the living one," "the first and the last," a "lamb," and a "warrior."

Most scholars place the writing of the book in the 90s CE, at a time when some outside sources refer to persecutions of Christ people by the Roman Empire. The location for the composition of the Revelation to John seems to be western Asia Minor (current-day Turkey). The text itself says that the author saw the visions in the book on the island of Patmos off the coast of western Asia Minor, but frequent references to a series of cities in Asia Minor suggest that some of the book's composition happened in multiple locations.

The author names himself "John" in the text. Since the second century, church leaders and scholars have debated whether this is the same John associated with the gospel of that name. The style and content of the two books are quite different, although the time of composition for the gospel and Revelation are relatively close. Ancient Christian writings make a distinction between John, the Apostle or the Beloved (of the gospel), and John, the Divine or the Revelator (of the Revelation). To ancient and modern readers, then, it seems unlikely that these two Johns are the same person.

The document's first three chapters are only vaguely related to the main body of visions of cosmic conflict and resolution. The first chapter contains an address and greeting similar to that of other early Christian and Greco-Roman letters, but after chapter 3 there are no other letterlike aspects of the book. The letterlike greeting is followed by a first-person recounting of a vision of what can only be Christ but is never identified as such. Then the vision of one with eyes like a flame and a sword for a tongue prompts two chapters of mini-letters to seven different groups.

The cosmic visions begin in chapter 4 and proceed through the end in chapter 22. These visions begin in God's heavenly court and end with the descent of the holy city Jerusalem to earth. The sixteen chapters between these serene scenes of resolution in chapters 4 and 21–22 are filled with curses on the earth, battles in the heavens and on earth, and war, sometimes led by a figure that seems to be Jesus.

Christ People Resisting the Roman Empire

Perhaps with the exception of the Secret Revelation of John, the Revelation to John expresses the most explicit condemnation of Roman imperial domination of any book in *A New New Testament*. The most obvious opposition to Rome by the Revelation to John comes in chapters 17 and 18. Here an angel reveals to the author a vision of the punishment of "the great harlot . . . with whom all the kings of the earth have had licentious intercourse" (17:1–2). She is "drunk with the blood of the holy ones" (17:6) and is riding on a beast with seven heads. The angel explains, "The seven heads are seven hills on which the woman is seated. They are also seven emperors" (17:9–10). This almost explicit reference to the seven hills of Rome is paired with naming the great prostitute "Babylon the Great" (17:5; 18:2, 10). In the first century CE, Babylon was no longer an empire or city of significance. Revelation's code of Babylon for Rome would have been obvious to first-century readers, as the sixth-century BCE Babylonian Empire destroyed the Jerusalem Temple just as Rome had done again only decades before the Revelation to John was written. As the angel says, "As for the woman whom you saw, she is the great city that holds sway over all the kings of the earth" (17:18).

In chapter 18, the angel shows the author a vision of the great city being destroyed: "Alas! Alas! Great city! City clothed in fine linen, and purple and scarlet cloth! City adorned with gold ornaments, and precious stones, and pearls! In a single hour your vast wealth vanished" (18:16). The contents of this vision are in fact a straightforward description of the kinds of wealth Rome acquired from conquering all the nations of the Mediterranean basin. The book features a prediction by the author that "all the kings of the earth who had licentious intercourse with her and shared her luxury will weep and lament over her" (18:9).

It is possible to see the teachings of Jesus and the writings of Paul as also opposed to the Roman Empire, but the Revelation to John makes this opposition the heart of its message.

The New Jerusalem

Dante and Milton describe God's triumph at the end of time as happening in heaven. The Revelation to John finishes differently. Its triumph comes with the descent of the heavenly city Jerusalem to earth (chapters 21 and 22). Contrary to almost all twenty-first-century Christian imaginings of God's triumph, this is an earthly victory in which God comes to live on earth. As the angel in chapter 21 has it: "See! The tent of God is set up among people. God will live among them, and they will be God's peoples, and God will be among them, and will wipe away all tears from their eyes" (21:3–4).

Similarly, the description of the New Jerusalem on earth features God's permanent presence there: "The throne of God and of the Lamb will be within it, and his slaves will worship God; they will see God's face" (22:3–4).

In contrast to what the television evangelists of the twenty-first century say, the Revelation to John's promising meaning for today has to do with its vision of a happy and just ending on earth for humanity which has been brutalized by a vicious empire. It is true that the punitive violence of most of its visions gives pause. But its vehement resistance to that oppressive empire has some exemplary aspects.

The New Orleans Council decided that in contrast to the traditional New Testament, the last book in this collection would not be this Revelation to John but the newly added Secret Revelation of John. In many ways these two books have much in common. Both envision the final power and goodness of God for all people. Both do so against the backdrop of the violence of the Roman Empire toward millions of people and its emperor's claim to be the Son of God. But the Secret Revelation of John does not envision the final power and goodness of God for all people as attained violently. Rather, such a resolution for all humanity arrives as a result of Christ's teaching about God's goodness and Rome's fraud.

Recommended Reading

Adella Yarbro Collins, *Crisis and Catharsis: The Power of the Apocalypse*
Elisabeth Schuessler Fiorenza, *Revelation: Vision of a Just World*
Eugene H. Peterson, *Reversed Thunder: The Revelation of John and the Praying Imagination*

The Revelation to John

1 [1] The revelation of Jesus Christ, which God gave to him to make known to his slaves, concerning what must shortly take place, and which he sent and revealed by his angel to his servant John, [2] who testified to the message of God and to the testimony to Jesus Christ, omitting nothing of what he had seen. [3] Blessed is the one who reads, and blessed are they who listen to, the words of this prophecy, and lay to heart what is here written; for the time is near.

Messages to the Seven Churches

From John, to the seven churches which are in Roman Asia. Blessing and peace be yours from the one who is, and who was, and who will be, and from the seven spirits that are before his throne, [5] and from Jesus Christ, the faithful witness, the firstborn from the dead, and the ruler of all the kings of the earth. To the one who loves us and freed us from our sins by his own blood — [6] and he made us a kingdom of priests in the service of God, his Father! — to that one be ascribed glory and dominion forever. Amen. [7] "He is coming among the clouds!" Every eye will see him, even those who pierced him; "and all the nations of the earth will mourn over him." So will it be. Amen.

[8] "I am the Alpha and the Omega," says the Lord, the God who is, and who was, and who will be, the Almighty.

[9] I, John, who am your brother, and who share with you in the suffering and kingship and endurance of Jesus, found myself on the island called Patmos, for the sake of the message of God and the testimony to Jesus. [10] I was in the spirit on the Lord's day, and I heard behind me a loud voice, like the blast of a trumpet. [11] It said, "Write what you see in a book and send it to the seven churches, to Ephesus, Smyrna, Pergamus, Thyatira, Sardis, Philadelphia, and Laodicea." [12] I turned to see what voice it was that spoke to me; and when I turned, I saw seven golden lamps, [13] and in the midst of the lamps one like a Child of Humanity, in a robe reaching to his feet, and with a golden band across his breast. [14] The hair of his head was as white as wool, as white as snow; his eyes were like flaming fire; [15] and his feet were like brass as when molten in a furnace; his voice was like the sound of many streams, [16] in his right hand he held seven stars, from his mouth came a sharp two-edged sword, and his face was like "the sun in the fullness of its power." [17] And when I saw him, I fell at his feet like one dead. He laid his hand on me and said, "Do not be afraid. I am the first and the last, [18] the ever-living. I died, and I am alive forever and ever. And I hold the keys of the grave and of the place of the dead. [19] Therefore write of what you have seen and of what is happening now and of what is about to take place — [20] the secret meaning of the seven stars which you saw in my right hand, and the seven golden lamps. The seven stars are the angels of the seven churches, and the seven lamps are the seven churches.

2 [1] "To the angel of the church in Ephesus write:

These are the words of him who holds the seven stars in his right hand, and walks among the seven golden lamps: [2] I know your life, your toil and endurance, and I know that you cannot tolerate evildoers. I know, too, how you tested those who declare that they are apostles, though they are not, and how you proved them false. ³ You possess endurance, and have borne much for my name, and have never grown weary. ⁴ But this I have against you: you have abandoned your first love. ⁵ Therefore remember from what you have fallen, and repent, and live the life that you lived before; or else I will come and remove your lamp from its place, unless you repent. ⁶ But this is in your favor—you hate the life lived by the Nikolaitans, and I also hate it. ⁷ Let the one who has ears hear what the Spirit is saying to the churches. To the one who conquers—to that one I will give the right to eat the fruit of the tree of life, which stands in the Paradise of God.

"To the angel of the church in Smyrna write:

These are the words of him who is the first and the last, who died, but is restored to life: ⁹ I know your persecution and your poverty—yet you are rich! I know, too, the slander that comes from those who declare that they are Judeans, though they are not, but are a congregation of Satan. ¹⁰ Do not be afraid of what you are about to suffer. The devil is about to throw some of you into prison so that you may be tempted, and may undergo persecution for ten days. Be faithful even to death, and I will give you the crown of life. ¹¹ Let those who have ears hear what the Spirit is saying to the churches. Those who conquer will suffer no hurt from the second death.

¹² "To the angel of the church in Pergamum write:

These are the words of him who holds the sharp two-edged sword: ¹³ I know

where you live, where the throne of Satan stands. And yet you hold to my name, and you did not disown my faith even in the days of Antipas, my faithful witness, who was put to death among you where Satan dwells. ¹⁴ Yet I have a few things against you: You have among you those who hold to the teaching of Balaam, who taught Balak to put temptations in the way of the Israelites, so that they should eat idol offerings and commit licentious acts. ¹⁵ Again you have among you those who hold in the same way to the teaching of the Nikolaitans. ¹⁶ Therefore repent, or else I will come quickly and contend with such people with words that will cut like a sword. ¹⁷ Let those who have ears hear what the Spirit is saying to the churches. To those who conquer—to them I will give a share of the mystic manna, and I will give them a white stone; and on the stone will be inscribed a new name, which no one knows except the person who receives it.

¹⁸ "To the angel of the church in Thyatira write:

These are the words of the Son of God, "whose eyes are like flaming fire, and whose feet are like brass": ¹⁹ I know your life, your love, faith, service, and endurance; and I know that your life of late has been better than it was at first. ²⁰ Yet I have this against you: you tolerate the woman Jezebel, who declares that she is a prophetess and misleads my servants by her teaching, until they commit licentious acts and eat idol offerings. ²¹ I gave her time to repent, but she is determined not to turn from her licentiousness. ²² Therefore I am laying her on a bed of sickness, and bringing great suffering on those who are unfaithful with her, unless they repent and turn from a life like hers. ²³ I will also put her children to death; and all the churches will learn that I am he who "looks into people's hearts and souls"; and I will give to each one of you what your life deserves. ²⁴ But I say to the rest of you at Thyatira — all who do not accept such teaching, who did not learn the secrets of Satan, as people call them — I am not laying on you any further burden; ²⁵ only hold fast to what you have received, until I come. ²⁶ To those who conquer and are careful to live my life to the end — to them I will give authority over the nations, ²⁷ and "they will rule them with an iron rod, as when earthen vessels are broken in pieces" (as I myself have received from my Father), ²⁸ and I will give them the morning star. ²⁹ Let those who have ears hear what the Spirit is saying to the churches.

3 ¹ "To the angel of the church in Sardis write:

These are the words of him who has the seven spirits of God and the seven stars: I know your life, and that people say of you that you are living, though you are dead. ² Be on the watch, and strengthen what still survives, though once it was all but dead; for I have not found your life perfect in the eyes of my God. ³ Therefore remember what you have received and heard, and lay it to heart and repent. Unless you are on the watch, I will come like a thief, and you will not know at what hour I am coming to you. ⁴ Yet there are some few among you at Sardis who did not soil their robes; they will walk with me, robed in white, for they are worthy. ⁵ Those who conquer will be clothed in these white robes, and I will not strike their names out of the book of life; but I will own them before my Father, and before his angels. ⁶ Let those who have ears hear what the Spirit is saying to the churches.

⁷ "To the angel of the church in Philadelphia write:

These are the words of him who is holy and true, who holds the key of David, who opens and no one will shut, and shuts and no one opens: ⁸ I know your life (see, I have set a door open before you which no one is able to shut), I know that though you have but little strength, you kept my teaching in mind, and did not disown my name. ⁹ Listen, I give some of the congregation of Satan, the people who declare that they are Judeans, though they are not, but are lying — I will make them come and bow down at your feet, and they will learn that I loved you. ¹⁰ Because you kept in mind the story of my endurance, I will keep you in the hour of trial that is about to come on the whole world, the hour that will test all who are living on earth. ¹¹ I will come quickly. Hold to what you have received so that no one may take your crown. ¹² Those who conquer — I will make them a pillar in the Temple of my God; and never more will they leave it; and I will write on them the name of my God and the name of the city of my God, the New Jerusalem, which is coming down out of heaven from my God, and I will write on them my new name. ¹³ Let those who have ears hear what the Spirit is saying to the churches.

¹⁴ "To the angel of the church in Laodicea write:

These are the words of the Unchanging One, "the witness faithful and true, the beginning of the creation of God": ¹⁵ I know your life; I know that you are neither cold nor hot. If only you were either cold or hot! ¹⁶ But now, because you are lukewarm, neither hot nor cold, I am about to spit you out of my mouth. ¹⁷ You say, "I am rich and have grown rich, and I want for nothing," and you do not know that you are wretched, miserable, poor, blind, naked! [18] Therefore I counsel you to buy from me gold which has been refined by fire so that you may grow rich; and white robes, so that you may be clothed and your shameful nakedness be hidden; and ointment to anoint your eyes, so that you may see. [19] All whom I love I rebuke and discipline. Therefore be in earnest and repent. [20] I am standing at the door and knocking! If anyone hears my voice and opens the door, I will go in, and will feast with him, and he will feast with me. [21] To those who conquer — to them I will give the right to sit beside me on my throne, as I, when I conquered, took my seat beside my Father on his throne. [22] Let those who have ears hear what the Spirit is saying to the churches."

The Vision of the Seven Seals

4 [1] After this, in my vision, I saw an open door in the heavens, and the first voice that I heard was like the blast of a trumpet speaking to me. It said, "Come up here and I will show you what must take place." [2] Immediately after this I was in the spirit. There stood a throne in heaven, and on the throne was One seated. [3] That One who was seated on it was in appearance like a jasper and a sardius; and "around the throne there was a rainbow" of the color of an emerald. [4] And around the throne were twenty-four other thrones, and on these I saw twenty-four elders sitting clothed in white robes; and on their heads they had crowns of gold. [5] Out from the throne come flashes of lightning, cries, and peals of thunder! There are seven torches burning in front of the throne, which are the seven spirits of God; [6] and in front of the throne is what seemed to be a sea of glass, resembling crystal, while within the space before the throne and around the throne

are four creatures full of eyes in front and behind. [7] The first creature is like a lion, the second creature like a calf, the third creature has a face like a human's, and the fourth creature is like an eagle on the wing. [8] These four creatures have each of them six wings, and all around, and within, they are full of eyes; and day and night they never cease to say:

"Holy, holy, holy is the Lord, our God,
the Almighty, who was, and who is,
and who will be."

[9] And whenever these creatures give praise and honor and thanks to the one who is seated on the throne, to him who lives forever and ever, [10] the twenty-four elders prostrate themselves before him who is seated on the throne, and worship him who lives forever and ever, and throw down their crowns before the throne, saying,

[11] "Worthy are you, our Lord and God, to receive all praise, and honor, and power, for you did create all things, and at your bidding they came into being and were created."

5 [1] Then I saw at the right hand of the One who was "seated on the throne a book, with writing inside and out, and sealed" with seven seals; [2] and I saw a mighty angel who was proclaiming in a loud voice, "Who is worthy to open the book and break its seals?" [3] But no one either in heaven or on earth or under the earth was able to open the book or look within it. [4] At this I wept long, because no one could be found who was worthy to open the book or look within it. [5] But one of the elders said to me, "Do not weep. The lion conquered — the lion of the tribe of Judah, the scion of David — and can therefore open the book with its seven seals."

[6] Then, within the space between the throne and the four creatures, and in the midst of the elders, I saw, standing, a

Lamb, which seemed to have been sacrificed. It had seven horns and seven eyes. (These eyes are the seven spirits of God, and they are sent into all the world.) [7] The Lamb came forward; and he has taken the book from the right hand of the one who was seated on the throne. [8] And, when he had taken the book, the four creatures and the twenty-four councilors prostrated themselves before the Lamb, each of them holding a harp and golden bowls full of incense. (These are the prayers of Christ's people.) [9] And they are singing a new song:

"You are worthy to take the book
    and break its seals, for you were
    sacrificed, and with your blood you
    did buy for God people of every
    tribe, and language, and people, and
    nation,
[10] and did make them a kingdom of
    priests in the service of our God,
    and they are reigning on the earth."

[11] Then, in my vision, I heard the voices of many angels around the throne, and of the creatures, and of the elders. In number they were ten thousand times ten thousand and thousands of thousands, [12] and they cried in a loud voice:

"Worthy is the Lamb that was slaughtered to receive all power, and
    wealth, and wisdom, and might, and
    honor, and praise, and blessing."

[13] And I heard every created thing in the air, and on the earth, and under the earth, and on the sea, and all that is in them crying,

"To the One who is seated on the
    throne and to the Lamb be ascribed
    all blessing, and honor, and praise,
    and dominion forever and ever."

[14] And the four creatures said, "Amen," and the elders prostrated themselves and worshiped.

6 [1] Then I saw the Lamb break one of the seven seals, and I heard one of the four creatures crying with a voice like thunder, "Come." [2] And in my vision I saw a white horse. Its rider held a bow, and he was given a crown, and he went out conquering and to conquer.

[3] When the Lamb broke the second seal, I heard the second creature crying, "Come." [4] Then there went out another horse, a red horse, and to its rider was given the power to deprive the earth of peace, so that people should kill one another; and he was given a great sword.

[5] When the Lamb broke the third seal, I heard the third creature crying, "Come." And in my vision I saw a black horse. Its rider held scales in his hand. [6] And I heard what seemed to be a voice, coming from among the four creatures, crying, "A quart of wheat for a silver coin, and three quarts of barley for a silver coin! But do not harm the oil and the wine."

[7] When the Lamb broke the fourth seal, I heard the voice of the fourth creature crying, "Come." [8] And in my vision I saw a gray horse. His rider's name was death, and the master of the place of death rode behind him; and power was given them over the fourth part of the earth, so that they might destroy with sword and famine and death, and by means of the wild beasts of the earth.

[9] When the Lamb opened the fifth seal, I saw under the altar the souls of those who had been killed for the sake of God's message and for the testimony which they had borne. [10] They cried in a loud voice, "How long, sovereign Lord, holy and true, before you will give judgment and avenge our blood on all who are living on the earth?" [11] Then to each of them was given a white robe, and they were told to rest yet a little longer, until the number of their fellow servants and of their friends

in Christ's service who were about to be put to death, as they had been, should be complete. ¹² And I saw the Lamb break the sixth seal, and then there was a great earthquake. The sun became black, like sackcloth, and the moon, which was at its full, like blood. ¹³ The stars of the heavens fell to the earth, as when a fig tree, shaken by a strong wind, drops its unripe fruit. ¹⁴ The heavens disappeared like a scroll when it is rolled up, and every mountain and island was moved from its place. ¹⁵ Then all the kings of the earth, and the princes, and the generals, and the rich, and the powerful, and every slave and free person, hid themselves in the caves and under the rocks of the mountains; ¹⁶ and they are crying to the mountains and the rocks, "Fall on us, and hide us from the eyes of him who is seated on the throne, and from the wrath of the Lamb, ¹⁷ for the great day of their wrath is come, and who can stand to meet it?"

7 ¹ After this, I saw four angels standing on the four corners of the earth, restraining the four winds of the earth, so that no wind should blow over the earth, or over the sea, or against any tree. ² And, in the east, I saw another angel ascending, holding the seal of the living God; and he cried in a loud voice to the four angels, to whom there had been given power to harm the earth and the sea: ³ "Do not harm the earth, or the sea, or the trees, until we have sealed the slaves of our God on their foreheads." ⁴ I heard, too, the number of those who had been sealed. It was one hundred and forty-four thousand; and they were from every tribe of Israel.

From the tribe of Judah twelve
    thousand were sealed,
from the tribe of Reuben twelve
    thousand,
from the tribe of Gad twelve thousand,
⁶ from the tribe of Asher twelve
    thousand,

from the tribe of Napthali twelve
    thousand,
from the tribe of Manasseh twelve
    thousand,
from the tribe of Simeon twelve
    thousand,
from the tribe of Levi twelve thousand,
from the tribe of Issachar twelve
    thousand,
from the tribe of Zebulon twelve
    thousand,
from the tribe of Joseph twelve
    thousand,
from the tribe of Benjamin twelve
    thousand were sealed.

⁹ After this, in my vision, I saw a vast throng which no one could number, of people from every nation and of all tribes, and peoples, and languages. They stood in front of the throne and in front of the Lamb, robed in white, holding palm branches in their hands. ¹⁰ And they are crying in a loud voice,

"Salvation be ascribed to our God who
    is seated on his throne and to the
    Lamb."

¹¹ And all the angels were standing around the throne and the elders and the four creatures, and they prostrated themselves on their faces in front of the throne and worshiped God, ¹² saying,

"Amen. Blessing and praise, and
    wisdom, and thanksgiving, and
    honor, and power, and might be
    ascribed to our God forever and
    ever. Amen."

¹³ Then one of the elders turned to me and said, "Who are these who are robed in white? And where did they come from?"
¹⁴ "My Lord," I answered, "it is you who know."
"These," he said, "are they who come through the great persecution; they

washed their robes white in the blood of the Lamb. [15] And therefore it is that they are before the throne of God, and are serving him day and night in his Temple; and the One who is seated on the throne will shelter them. [16] Never again will they be hungry, never again will they be thirsty, nor will the sun smite them, nor any scorching heat; [17] for the Lamb that stands in the space before the throne will be their shepherd, and will lead them to life-giving springs of water; and God will wipe away all tears from their eyes."

8 [1] As soon as the Lamb had broken the seventh seal, there was silence in heaven for, it might be, half an hour.

Vision of Seven Trumpet Blasts

Then I saw the seven angels who stand before God, and seven trumpets were given to them.

[3] Next, another angel came and stood at the altar with a golden censer in his hand; and a great quantity of incense was given to him, to mingle with the prayers of the holy ones on the golden altar before the throne. [4] The smoke of the incense ascended, with the prayers of the holy ones, from the hand of the angel before God. [5] Then the angel took the censer, and filled it with fire from the altar, and threw it down on the earth; and there followed peals of thunder, cries, flashes of lightning, and an earthquake. [6] Then the seven angels holding the seven trumpets prepared to blow their blasts.

[7] The first blew; and there came hail and fire mixed with blood, and it fell on the earth. A third part of the earth was burned up, and a third of the trees, and every blade of grass.

[8] Then the second angel blew; and what appeared to be a great mountain, burning, was hurled into the sea. A third of the sea became blood, [9] and a third part of all created things that are in the sea — that is, of all living things — died, and a third of the ships were destroyed.

[10] Then the third angel blew; and there fell from the heavens a great star, burning like a torch. It fell on a third of the rivers and on the springs. [11] (The star is called "Wormwood.") A third of the water became bitter as wormwood, and so bitter was the water that many died from drinking it.

[12] Then the fourth angel blew; and a third of the sun and a third of the moon and a third of the stars were blasted, so that a third of them were eclipsed, and for a third part of the day there was no light, and at night it was the same.

[13] And, in my vision, I heard an eagle flying in mid-heaven and crying in a loud voice, "Woe, woe, woe for all who live on the earth, at the other trumpet blasts of the three angels who have yet to blow."

9 [1] Then the fifth angel blew; and I saw a star that had fallen on the earth from the heavens, and to him was given the key of the bottomless pit. [2] He opened the bottomless pit, and from the pit rose a smoke like the smoke of a great furnace. The sun and the air grew dark because of the smoke from the pit. [3] Out of the smoke locusts descended on the earth, and they received the same power as that possessed by scorpions. [4] They were told not to harm the grass, or any plant, or any tree, but only those who have not "the seal of God on their foreheads." [5] Yet they were not allowed to kill them, but it was ordered that they should be tortured for five months. Their torture was like the torture caused by a scorpion when it stings a person. [6] In those days people "will seek death and will not find it"; they will long to die, but death flees from them. [7] In appearance the locusts were like horses equipped for battle. On their heads there were what appeared to be crowns that shone like gold, their faces resembled human faces, [8] and they had hair like the hair of a woman, their teeth were like lions' teeth, [9] and they had what seemed to be iron breastplates, while the noise of their wings was like the noise of chariots drawn by many horses, galloping into battle. [10] They have tails like scorpions, and stings, and in their tails lies their power to harm people for five months. [11] They have as their king the angel of the bottomless pit, whose name, in Hebrew, is "Abaddon," while in Greek his name is "Apollyon" (the destroyer).

[12] The first woe has passed; and still there are two woes to follow!

[13] Then the sixth angel blew; and I heard a voice proceeding from the corners of the golden altar that stood before God. [14] It spoke to the sixth angel — the angel with the trumpet — and said, "Let loose the four angels that are in chains at the great river Euphrates." [15] Then the four angels that were held in readiness for that hour and day and month and year were let loose, to destroy a third of humankind. [16] The number of the hosts of cavalry was ten thousand times ten thousand, twice told; I heard their number. [17] And this is what the horses and their riders appeared to be like in my vision: they had breastplates of fire, blood-red and sulfurous, and the heads of the horses were like lions' heads, while out of their mouths issued fire, and smoke, and sulfur. [18] Through these three curses a third of humanity perished — because of the fire, and the smoke, and the sulfur that issued from their mouths; [19] for the power of the horses lies in their mouths and in their tails. For their tails are like snakes, with heads, and it is with them that they do harm. [20] But those who were left of humanity, who had not perished through these curses, did not repent and turn away from what their own hands had made; they would not abandon the worship of demons, and of idols made of gold or silver or brass or stone or wood, which can neither see, nor hear, nor walk; [21] and they did not repent of their murders, or their sorceries, or their licentiousness, or their thefts.

10 [1] Then I saw another mighty angel descending from heaven. His robe was a cloud; over his head was the rainbow; his face was like the sun, and his feet like pillars of fire; [2] in his hand he held a little book open. He set his right foot on the sea, and his left on the land; [3] and he cried in a loud voice like the roaring of a lion. At his cry the seven peals of thunder spoke, each with its own voice. [4] And when they spoke, I was about to write; but I heard a voice from heaven say, "Keep secret what the seven peals of thunder said, and do not write it down." [5] Then the angel whom I had seen standing on the sea and on the land "raised his right hand to the heavens, [6] and swore by him who lives forever and ever, who created the heavens and all that is in them, and the earth and all that is in it, and the sea and all that is in it," that time should cease to be. [7] Moreover at the time when the seventh angel will speak, when he is ready to blow his blast, then the hidden purposes of God, of which he told the good news to his servants, the prophets, are at once fulfilled. [8] Then came the voice which I had heard from heaven. It spoke to me again, and said, "Go and take the book that is open in the hand of the angel who stands on the sea and on the land." [9] So I went to the angel and asked him to give me the little book. And he said, "Take it, and eat it. It will be bitter to your stomach, but in your mouth it will be as sweet as honey." [10] I took the little book out of the angel's hand and ate it, and, while in my mouth, it was like the sweetest honey; but when I had eaten it, it was bitter to my stomach. [11] And I was told, "You must prophesy again about men of many peoples, and nations, and languages, and about many kings."

11 [1] Then I was given a measure like

a rod, and a voice said to me, "Go and measure the Temple of God and the altar, and count the worshipers there. ² But omit the court outside the Temple, and do not measure that, for it has been given up to the nations; and the holy city will be under their heel for forty-two months. ³ Then I will give permission to my two witnesses, and for those twelve hundred and sixty days they will continue teaching, clothed in sackcloth. ⁴ These two are represented by the two olive trees and the two lamps that stand before the Lord of the earth. ⁵ When anyone wishes to harm them, fire comes from their mouths and consumes their enemies; and whoever wishes to harm them will, in this way, inevitably perish. ⁶ These two have the power to close the heavens, so that no rain may fall during the time that they are teaching; and they have power "to turn the streams into blood, and to smite the land with any curse," whenever they will. ⁷ As soon as they have completed their testimony, the wild beast that ascends from the bottomless pit will make war on them and conquer and kill them. ⁸ Their dead bodies will lie in the streets of the great city, which is mystically spoken of as Sodom and Egypt, where their Master was crucified. ⁹ People of all nations, and tribes, and languages, and races look at their dead bodies for three days and a half, and do not allow them to be laid in a grave. ¹⁰ Those who live on the earth rejoice over them and are merry, and they will send presents to one another, because these two prophets brought torments on those who live on the earth. ¹¹ After three days and a half the life-giving breath of God entered these two, and they stood up on their feet, and a great terror took possession of those who were watching them. ¹² The two heard a loud voice from heaven which said to them, "Come up here," and they went up to heaven in the cloud, while their enemies

watched them. ¹³ At that very time a great earthquake occurred. A tenth part of the city fell, and seven thousand people perished in the earthquake. Those who escaped were much terrified, and praised the God of heaven.

¹⁴ The second woe has passed; and there is a third woe soon to follow!

¹⁵ Then the seventh angel blew; and loud voices were heard in heaven, saying,

"The realm of the world has become
    the realm of our Lord and of his
    Anointed One, and he will reign
    forever and ever."

¹⁶ At this the twenty-four elders, who were seated on their thrones before God, prostrated themselves on their faces and worshiped, ¹⁷ saying,

"We thank you, Lord, our God, the
    Almighty, who is and who was, that
    you have assumed your great power
    and reigned.
¹⁸ The nations were enraged, and your
    wrath fell on them; the time came
    for the dead to be judged, and for
    you to give the reward to your slaves
    the prophets, and to the people of
    Christ, and to those who honor
    your name — the high and the low
    alike — and to destroy those who are
    destroying the earth."

¹⁹ Then the Temple of God in heaven was opened, and the ark containing his covenant was seen in his Temple; and there followed flashes of lightning, cries, peals of thunder, an earthquake, and a great storm of hail.

Vision of Seven Figures

12 ¹ Then a great portent was seen in the heavens — a woman whose robe was the sun, and who had the moon under her

feet, and on her head a crown of twelve stars. ² She was pregnant; and she is crying out in the pain and agony of childbirth. ³ Another portent also was seen in the heavens. There was a great red dragon, with seven heads and ten horns, and on his heads were seven diadems. ⁴ His tail draws after it a third of the stars in the heavens, and it hurled them down on the earth. The dragon is standing in front of the woman who is about to give birth to the child, so that he may devour it as soon as it is born. ⁵ The woman gave birth to a son, a male child, who is destined to rule all the nations with an iron rod; and her child was at once caught up to God on the throne. ⁶ But the woman fled into the wilderness, where there is a place prepared for her by God, to be tended there for twelve hundred and sixty days.

⁷ Then a battle took place in the heavens. Michael and his angels fought with the dragon. But though the dragon, with his angels, fought, ⁸ he did not prevail; and there was no place left for them any longer in the heavens. ⁹ Then the great dragon, the primeval snake, known as the "devil" and "Satan," who deceives all the world, was hurled down to the earth, and his angels were hurled down with him. ¹⁰ And I heard a loud voice in heaven which said:

"Now has begun the day of the
    salvation, and power, and dominion
    of our God, and the rule of his
    Anointed One; for the accuser of
    our people has been hurled down,
    the one who has been accusing them
    before our God day and night.
¹¹ Their victory was due to the blood of
    the Lamb, and to the message to
    which they bore their testimony.
    In their love of life they shrank not
    from death.
¹² Therefore, be glad, heaven, and all who
    live in heaven! Alas for the earth and
    for the sea, for the devil has gone

down to you in great fury, knowing that he has but little time."

¹³ When the dragon saw that he was hurled down to the earth, he pursued the woman who had given birth to the male child. ¹⁴ But to the woman were given the two wings of the great eagle, so that she might fly to her place in the wilderness, where she is being tended for "one year, and for two years, and for half a year" in safety from the snake. ¹⁵ Then the snake poured water from its mouth after the woman, like a river, so that it might sweep her away. ¹⁶ But earth came to her help, and opened her mouth and drank up the river which the dragon had poured out of its mouth. ¹⁷ The dragon was enraged at the woman, and went to fight with the rest of her offspring — those who lay to heart the commands of God and bear their testimony to Jesus; and he took his stand on the seashore.

13 ¹ Then I saw, "rising out of the sea, a wild beast with ten horns" and seven heads. On its horns were ten diadems, and on its heads were blasphemous names. ² The beast that I saw was like a leopard; but its feet were like a bear's, and its mouth like the mouth of a lion. The dragon gave it his power and his throne, and wide dominion. ³ One of its heads seemed to me to have been mortally wounded, but its deadly wound had been healed. The whole earth followed the beast, wondering; ⁴ and men worshiped the dragon, because he had given his dominion to the beast; while, as they worshiped the beast, they said, "Who can compare with the beast? And who can fight with it?" ⁵ The beast was given a mouth that spoke proudly and blasphemously, and it was empowered to work its will for forty-two months. ⁶ It opened its mouth only to blaspheme God, to blaspheme his name and his tent — those who live in his tent in heaven. ⁷ It had been permitted to fight with the holy ones and to conquer them, and it had received power over every tribe, and people, and language, and nation. [8] All who are living on earth will worship it — all whose names have not been written in the Lamb's book of life, the Lamb that has been sacrificed from the foundation of the world. [9] Let those who have ears hear. [10] "Whoever is destined for captivity goes into captivity." Whoever will kill with the sword must inevitably be killed with the sword. (Here there is need for endurance and faith on the part of the holy ones.)

[11] Then I saw, rising out of the earth, another wild beast. It had two horns like those of a lamb, and its voice was like a dragon's. [12] It exercises all the authority of the first beast under its eyes; and it makes the earth and all who are living on it worship that first beast, whose mortal wound was healed. [13] It performs great marvels, even causing fire to fall from the heavens to the earth, before people's eyes; [14] and in consequence of the marvels which it was allowed to perform under the eyes of the beast, it is able to deceive all who are living on the earth. It tells those who live on the earth to make a statue in honor of the beast, who, despite the wound from the sword, yet lived. [15] It was permitted to breathe life into the image of the beast, so that the image of the beast might speak; and it was also permitted to cause all who refused to worship the image of the beast to be put to death. [16] High and low, rich and poor, free and enslaved — it causes a brand to be put on the right hand or on the forehead of every one of them, [17] so that no one is able to buy or sell, except those that bear this brand — either the name of the beast or the number indicated by the letters of his name. [18] (Here there is need for discernment.) Let the one who has the ability compute the number of the beast; for the number indicates a person's name. Its number is six hundred and sixty-six.

14 [1] Then, in my vision, I saw the Lamb standing on Mount Zion. With him were a hundred and forty-four thousand, with his name and the name of his Father written on their foreheads. [2] And I heard a sound from heaven, like the sound of many waters, and like the sound of a loud peal of thunder; the sound that I heard was like the music of harpists playing on their harps. [3] They are singing what seems to be a new song, before the throne, and before the four creatures and the councilors; and no one was able to learn that song except the hundred and forty-four thousand who had been redeemed from earth. [4] These are the men who never defiled themselves in their intercourse with women; they are as pure as virgins. These are the men who follow the Lamb wherever he goes. They were redeemed as the first fruits of mankind for God and for the Lamb. [5] "No lie was ever heard on their lips." They are beyond reach of blame.

[6] Then I saw another angel, flying in mid-heaven. He had the good news, decreed through the generations, to announce to those who live on the earth — to those of every nation, and tribe, and language, and people; [7] and he cried in a loud voice, "Reverence God, and give God praise (for the hour of judgment has come), and worship the One who made the heaven and the earth and the sea and all springs of water."

[8] Then a second angel followed, crying, "She has fallen! She has fallen — Babylon the Great, who has made all the nations drink the maddening wine of her licentiousness!"

[9] Then a third angel followed them, crying in a loud voice, "Whoever worships the beast and its image, and receives its brand on his forehead or on his hand, [10] that person will drink the maddening wine of God that has been poured unmixed into the cup of his wrath, and they will be tortured with fire and sulfur before the eyes of the holy angels and before the eyes of the Lamb. [11] The smoke from their tor-

ture rises forever and ever, and they have no rest day nor night — those who worship the beast and its image, and all who are branded with its name." ¹² (Here there is need for endurance on the part of the holy ones — those who lay to heart the commands of God and the faith of Jesus.) ¹³ Then I heard a voice from heaven saying, "Write: 'Blessed are the dead who from this hour die in union with the Lord.'"

"Yes," answers the Spirit, "that they may rest from their toil. Their good deeds go with them."

¹⁴ Then, in my vision, I saw a white cloud, and on the cloud there was sitting one like a Child of Humanity. On his head he had a crown of gold, and in his hand a sharp sickle.

¹⁵ Then another angel came out from the Temple, crying in a loud voice to him who was sitting on the cloud, "Take your sickle and reap, for the time to reap has come; the harvest of earth is ready." ¹⁶ He who was sitting on the cloud brought his sickle down on the earth, and the harvest of earth was reaped.

¹⁷ Then another angel came out of the Temple in heaven; he, also, had a sharp sickle.

¹⁸ Then another angel came out of the altar; he had power over fire, and he called in a loud voice to the angel that had the sharp sickle, "Take your sharp sickle, and gather the bunches from the vine of earth, for its grapes are ripe." ¹⁹ The angel brought his sickle down on the earth and gathered the fruit of the vine of earth, and threw it into the great winepress of the wrath of God. ²⁰ The "grapes were trodden in the press" outside the city; and blood came out of the press, rising as high as the bridles of the horses for a distance of two hundred miles.

Vision of Seven Curses

15 ¹ Then I saw another portent in the heavens — a great and marvelous portent — seven angels with the seven last curses; because with them the wrath of God is ended.

² Then I saw what appeared to be a sea of glass mixed with fire; and, standing by this sea of glass, holding the harps of God, I saw those who had come victorious out of the conflict with the beast and its image and the number that formed its name. ³ They are singing the song of Moses, the slave of God, and the song of the Lamb:

"Great and marvelous are your deeds,
  Lord, our God, the Almighty.
Righteous and true are your ways,
  king of ages.
⁴ Who will not honor and praise your
  name, Lord? You alone are holy!
All nations will come and worship
  before you, for your judgments have
  become manifest."

⁵ After this I saw that the inmost shrine of the tent of testimony in heaven was opened, ⁶ and out of it came the seven angels with the seven curses. They were adorned with precious stones, pure and bright, and had golden girdles around their breasts. ⁷ One of the four creatures gave the seven angels seven golden bowls, filled with the wrath of God who lives forever and ever. ⁸ "The Temple was filled with smoke from the glory" and majesty of God; and no one could enter the Temple, until the seven curses inflicted by the seven angels were at an end.

16 ¹ Then I heard a loud voice, which came from the Temple, saying to the seven angels, "Go and empty the seven bowls of the wrath of God on the earth."

² The first angel went and emptied his bowl on the earth; and it turned to loathsome and painful sores on all who bore the brand of the beast and who worshiped its image.

³ Then the second angel emptied his bowl on the sea; and it turned to blood

like the blood of a corpse, and every living thing died — everything in the sea.

4 Then the third angel emptied his bowl on the rivers and springs of water; and it turned to blood. 5 And I heard the angel of the waters saying, "Righteous are you, you who is and who was, the Holy One, in inflicting this judgment; 6 for they shed the blood of the holy ones and of the prophets, and you have given them blood to drink. It is what they deserve." 7 And I heard the response from the altar: "Yes, Lord, our God, the Almighty, true and righteous are your judgments."

8 Then the fourth angel emptied his bowl on the sun; and he was permitted to scorch people with fire; 9 and people were scorched by the intense heat. They blasphemed the name of God who controlled these curses, yet they did not repent and give him praise.

10 Then the fifth angel emptied his bowl on the throne of the beast; and darkness fell on its empire. People gnawed their tongues for pain, 11 and blasphemed the God of heaven, because of their pains and because of their sores; yet they did not repent of what they had done.

12 Then the sixth angel emptied his bowl on the great river Euphrates; and the water in the river was dried up, so that the road for the kings of the East might be made ready. 13 And I saw three foul spirits, like frogs, come from the mouth of the dragon and from the mouth of the beast and from the mouth of the false prophet. 14 They are the spirits of demons, and perform marvels; they go to kings all over the world, to collect them for the battle on the great day of Almighty God. 15 ("I am coming like a thief! Happy will he be who is on the watch, and keeps his clothing at hand, so that he will not have to walk about unclothed and let people see his nakedness.") 16 And the spirits collected the kings at the place called in Hebrew "Har-Magedon."

17 Then the seventh angel emptied his bowl on the air. (A loud voice came from the throne in the Temple; it said, "All is over.") 18 There followed "flashes of lightning, cries, and peals of thunder"; and there was a great earthquake, such as had not occurred since people began to be on the earth — none so great; 19 and the great city was torn in three, and the cities of the nation fell, and God remembered Babylon the Great, and gave her the maddening wine cup of his wrath; 20 and every island vanished, and the mountains disappeared. 21 Great hailstones, a pound in weight, are falling on people from the heavens. And people blasphemed God because of the curse of the hail, for it was a very terrible curse.

Doom of the Enemies

17 1 Then one of the seven angels who held the seven bowls came and spoke to me. "Come here," he said, "and I will show you the sentence passed on that great harlot who is seated at the meeting of many waters, 2 and with whom all the kings of the earth have had licentious intercourse; while all who live on the earth have been made drunk by the wine of her licentiousness." 3 And he bore me away in a trance to a lonely place, and I saw a woman seated on a scarlet beast, which was covered with blasphemous names; it had seven heads and ten horns. 4 The woman was clothed in purple and scarlet, and glittering with gold ornaments, precious stones, and pearls. In her hand she held a gold cup, full of idolatrous abominations, and the unclean fruits of her licentiousness; 5 while on her forehead there was written this secret name — Babylon the Great, the mother of harlots and of all idolatrous abominations on earth. 6 And I saw the woman drunk with the blood of the holy ones and with the blood of the witnesses for Jesus. When I saw her, I was amazed beyond measure; 7 but the angel said to me, "Why were you amazed? I will tell you the secret meaning of the vision of this woman, and of the

beast, with the seven heads and ten horns, that carries her. [8] The beast that you saw was, but is not, and is about to rise out of the bottomless pit, and is on its way to destruction. Those who are living on earth will be amazed — those whose names have not been written in the book of life from the foundation of the world — when they see that the beast was, but is not, and yet will come." [9] (Here there is need for the discerning mind.) The seven heads are seven hills on which the woman is seated. [10] They are also seven emperors; of whom five have fallen and one remains, while one is not yet come. When he comes, he must stay for a little while. [11] So must the beast that was, but is not. He counts as an eighth king, although he is one of the seven, and is on his way to destruction. [12] The ten horns that you saw are ten kings, who have not yet received their kingdoms, but for an hour they receive the authority of kings, together with the beast. [13] These kings are of one mind in surrendering their power and authority to the beast. [14] They will fight with the Lamb, but the Lamb will conquer them, for he is Lord of lords and king of kings; so, too, will those with him who have received the call and are chosen and faithful. [15] And the angel said to me, "The waters that you saw, where the harlot is seated, are throngs and tribes of all nations and languages. [16] The ten horns that you saw, and the beast — they will hate the harlot, and cause her to become deserted and strip her bare; they will eat her flesh and utterly consume her with fire. [17] For God has put it into their minds to carry out his purpose, in carrying out their common purpose and surrendering their kingdoms to the beast, until God's decrees will be executed. [18] As for the woman whom you saw, she is the great city that holds sway over all the kings of the earth."

18 [1] After this I saw another angel descending from heaven, invested with great authority; and the earth was illuminated by his splendor. [2] With a mighty voice he cried, "She has fallen! She has fallen — Babylon the Great! She has become an abode of demons, a stronghold of every wicked spirit, a stronghold of every foul and hateful bird. [3] For, after drinking the maddening wine of her licentiousness, all the nations have fallen; while all the kings of the earth have had licentious intercourse with her, and the merchants of the earth have grown rich through the excess of her luxury." [4] Then I heard another voice from heaven saying, "Come out of her, my people, so that you may not participate in her sins, and that you may not suffer from the curses inflicted on her. [5] For her sins are heaped up to the heavens, and God has not forgotten her misdeeds. [6] Pay her back the treatment with which she has treated you; yes, repay twice over what her actions deserve; in the cup which she mixed for you, mix for her as much again; [7] for her self-glorification and her luxury, give her now an equal measure of torture and misery. In her heart she says, 'I sit here a queen; no widow am I; I will never know misery.' [8] Therefore in one day will these curses strike her — death, misery, and famine — and she will be utterly consumed by fire; for mighty is the Lord God who condemned her. [9] All the kings of the earth who had licentious intercourse with her and shared her luxury will weep and lament over her, when they see the smoke from the burning city, [10] while they stand at a distance, horrified at her torture, and cry, 'Alas! Alas! Great city! Mighty city of Babylon! In a single hour your judgment fell.' [11] And the merchants of the earth weep and wail over her, because no longer does anyone buy their cargoes — [12] their cargoes of gold, or silver, or precious stones, or pearls, or fine linen, or purple robes, or silk, or scarlet cloth; nor their many scented woods; nor their many articles of ivory; nor their many articles of choicest wood, or brass, or iron, or marble; [13] nor their cinnamon, or spice, or incense, or perfumes, or frankincense, or wine, or oil, or fine flour, or wheat, or cattle, or sheep; nor their horses, or chariots, or slaves; nor the bodies and souls of people. [14] The fruit that your soul craved is no longer within your reach, and all dainties and luxuries are lost to you, never to be found again.' [15] The merchants who sold these things, and grew rich by her, will stand at a distance weeping and wailing, horrified at her torture, and crying, [16] 'Alas! Alas! Great city! City clothed in fine linen, and purple and scarlet cloth! City adorned with gold ornaments, and precious stones, and pearls! [17] In a single hour your vast wealth vanished.' Every ship's captain and all who sail to any port, and sailors, and all who get their living from the sea, stood at a distance, [18] and seeing the smoke from the burning city, cried, 'What city can compare with the great city?' [19] They threw dust on their heads, and, as they wept and wailed, they cried, 'Alas! Alas! Great city! All who have ships on the sea grew rich through her magnificence. In a single hour it has vanished.' [20] Rejoice over her, heaven, and all you holy ones, and ambassadors, and prophets, for God has avenged you on her!" [21] Then a mighty angel took up a stone like a great millstone, and threw it into the sea, crying, "So will Babylon, the great city, be violently overthrown, never more to be seen. [22] No more will the music of harpists, or minstrels, or flute players, or trumpeters be heard in you, no more will any worker, skilled in any art, be found in you; no more will the sound of a mill be heard in you; [23] no more will the light of a lamp shine in you; no more will the voices of groom and bride be heard in you. Your merchants were the great ones of the earth, for all the nations were deceived by your magical charms. [24] Yes, and in her was to be found the blood of the prophets and of the holy ones, and of all who have been put to death on the earth."

19 [1] After this, I heard what seemed to be a great shout from a vast throng in heaven, crying,

> "Hallelujah! To our God belong
>   salvation, and glory, and power,
> for true and righteous are his
>   judgments. For he has passed
>   judgment on the great harlot who
>   was corrupting the earth by her
>   licentiousness, and he has taken
>   vengeance on her for the blood of
>   his slaves."

[3] Again they cried, "Hallelujah!" And the smoke from her ruins rises forever and ever. [4] Then the twenty-four elders and the four creatures prostrated themselves and worshiped God who was seated on the throne, crying, "Amen, hallelujah!"; [5] and from the throne there came a voice which said,

> "Praise our God, all you who serve and
>   worship God, both high and low."

[6] Then I heard "what seemed to be the shout of a vast throng, like the sound of many waters," and like the sound of loud peals of thunder, crying,

> "Hallelujah! For the Lord is king, our
>   God, the Almighty.
> Let us rejoice and exalt; and we will
>   pay him honor, for the hour for the
>   marriage of the Lamb has come, and
>   his bride has made herself ready.
> And to her it has been granted to robe
>   herself in fine linen, white and pure,
>   for that linen is the good deeds of
>   the people of the Anointed One."

[9] Then a voice said to me, "Write: 'Blessed are those who have been summoned to the marriage feast of the Lamb.'" And the voice said, "These words of God are true." [10] I prostrated myself at the feet of him who spoke to worship him, but

he said to me, "Forbear; I am your fellow slave, and the fellow slave of your brothers and sisters who bear their testimony to Jesus. Worship God. For to bear testimony to Jesus needs the inspiration of the prophets." [11] Then I saw that heaven lay open. There appears a white horse; its rider is called "faithful" and "true"; righteously does he judge and make war. [12] His eyes are flaming fires; on his head there are many diadems, and he bears a name, written, which no one knows but himself; [13] he has been clothed in a garment sprinkled with blood; and the name by which he is called is "The Word of God." [14] The armies of heaven followed him, mounted on white horses and clothed in fine linen, white and pure. [15] From his mouth comes a sharp sword, with which to smite the nations; and he will rule them with an iron rod. He treads the grapes in the press of the maddening wine of the wrath of Almighty God; [16] and on his robe and on his thigh he has this name written — king of kings and Lord of lords.

[17] Then I saw an angel standing on the sun. He cried in a loud voice to all the birds that fly in mid-heaven, "Gather and come to the great feast of God, [18] to eat the flesh of kings, and the flesh of commanders, and the flesh of mighty people, and the flesh of horses and their riders, and the flesh of all free and enslaved, and of high and low." [19] Then I saw the beast and the kings of the earth and their armies, gathered together to fight with him who sat on the horse and with his army. [20] The beast was captured, and with him was taken the false prophet who performed the marvels before the eyes of the beast, with which he deceived those who had received the brand of the beast and those who worshiped his image. Alive, they were thrown, both of them, into the lake of fire — of burning sulfur. [21] The rest were killed by the sword which came out of the mouth of him who rode on the horse; and all the birds fed on their flesh.

20 [1] Then I saw an angel coming down from heaven, with the key of the bottomless pit and a great chain in his hand. [2] He seized the dragon, the primeval snake (who is the "devil" or "Satan"), and bound him in chains for a thousand years. [3] He flung him into the bottomless pit and locked it, and set his seal on it; that he should not deceive the nations anymore, until the thousand years were ended. After that he must be let loose for a while.

[4] Then I saw thrones, and to those who took their seats on them authority was given to act as judges. And I saw the souls of those who had been beheaded because of the testimony to Jesus and because of the message of God, for they had refused to worship the beast or its image, and had not received the brand on their foreheads and on their hands. They were restored to life, and they reigned with the Anointed One for a thousand years. [5] (The rest of the dead were not restored to life until the thousand years were ended.) This is the first resurrection. [6] Blessed and holy will be the ones who share in that first resurrection. The second death has no power over them; but they will be priests of God, and the Anointed One, and they will reign with him for the thousand years.

[7] When the thousand years are ended, Satan will be let loose from his prison, [8] and he will come out to deceive the nations that live in the four corners of the earth — Gog and Magog. He will come to gather them together for battle; and their number will be as great as the sand on the seashore. [9] They went up over the breadth of the whole earth, and surrounded the camp of the holy ones and the city that he loves. Then fire fell from the heavens and consumed them; [10] and the devil, their deceiver, was hurled into the lake of fire and sulfur, where the beast and the false prophet already were, and they will be tortured day and night forever and ever.

[11] Then I saw a great white throne, and him who was seated on it. "The earth and

the heavens fled from his presence; no place was left for them." [12] And I saw the dead, high and low, standing before the throne; and books were opened. Then another book was opened, the book of life; and the dead were judged, according to their actions, by what was written in the books. [13] The sea gave up its dead, and earth and the lord of the place of death gave up their dead; and they were judged, one by one, each according to his actions. [14] Then death and the lord of the place of death were hurled into the lake of fire. This is the second death — the lake of fire; [15] and all whose names were not found written in the book of life were hurled into the lake of fire.

The New Creation

21 [1] Then I saw new heavens and a new earth. The former heavens and the former earth had passed away; and the sea has ceased to be. [2] And I saw the holy city, Jerusalem, descending new out of heaven from God, like a bride adorned in readiness for her husband. [3] And I heard a loud voice from the throne, which said, "See! The tent of God is set up among people. God will live among them, and they will be God's peoples, and God will be among them, and will wipe away all tears from their eyes. There will be no more death, nor will there be any more grief or crying or pain. The old order has passed away." [5] And the One who was seated on the throne said, "See, I make all things new!" And he said, "Write this, for these words may be trusted and are true." [6] And he said to me, "They are fulfilled. I am the Alpha and the Omega, the beginning and the end. To those who thirst I will give of the spring of the water of life, freely. [7] Those who conquer will enter into possession of these things, and I will be their God, and they will be my children. [8] But as for cowards, unbelievers, the degraded, murderers, the impure, sorcerers, idolaters, and all liars — their place will be in the burning lake of fire and sulfur. That is the second death."

[9] Then one of the seven angels who had the seven bowls, and were laden with the seven last curses, came and spoke to me. "Come here," he said, "and I will show you the bride, the one the Lamb has married." [10] He carried me away in a trance to a great high mountain, and showed me Jerusalem, the holy city, descending out of heaven from God, filled with the glory of God. [11] Its brilliance was like a precious stone, like a jasper, transparent as crystal. [12] It had a great high wall, in which were twelve gates; and at these gates there were twelve angels, and there were names inscribed on the gates, the names of the twelve tribes of the Israelites. [13] There were three gates on the east, three gates on the north, three gates on the south, and three gates on the west. [14] The wall of the city had twelve foundation stones, on which were the twelve names of the twelve ambassadors of the Lamb. [15] And the angel who was speaking to me had as a measure a gold rod, with which to measure the city and its gates and its wall. [16] The city is square; the length and the breadth are the same. The angel measured with his rod; it was twelve hundred miles; its length, and breadth, and height are equal. [17] Then he measured the wall; it was two hundred and eighty-eight feet, as people measure, that is, as the angel measured. [18] The material of the wall of the city was jasper, and the city was built of pure gold, which shone like clear glass. [19] The foundations of the wall of the city were ornamented with every kind of precious stone. The first foundation stone was a jasper; the second a sapphire; the third a chalcedony; the fourth an emerald; [20] the fifth a sardonyx; the sixth a carnelian; the seventh a chrysolite; the eighth a beryl; the ninth a topaz; the tenth a chrysoprase; the eleventh a hyacinth; and the twelfth an amethyst. [21] The twelve gates were made of twelve pearls,

each gate of one pearl. The street of the city was of pure gold, transparent as glass. [22] And I saw no temple there, for the Lord, our God, the Almighty, and the Lamb are its temple. [23] The city has no need of "the sun or the moon to shine on it, for the glory of God illuminated it," and its lamp was the Lamb. [24] "The nations walk by the light of it; and the kings of the earth bring their glory into it. [25] Its gates will never be shut by day," and there will be no night there. [26] And people will bring the glory and honor of the nations into it. [27] "Never will any unhallowed thing enter it," nor they whose life is shameful and false, but only "those whose names have been written in the Lamb's book of life."

22 [1] And the angel showed me a river of the water of life, as clear as crystal, issuing from the throne of God and of the Lamb, [2] in the middle of the street of the city. On each side of the river was a tree of life which bore twelve kinds of fruit, yielding its fruit each month; and the leaves of the tree were for the healing of the nations. [3] Everything that is accursed will cease to be. The throne of God and of the Lamb will be within it, and his slaves will worship God; [4] they will see God's face, and God's name will be on their foreheads. [5] Night will cease to be. They have no need of the light of a lamp, nor have they the light of the sun; for the "Lord God will be their light, and they will reign forever and ever."

Conclusion

Then the angel said to me, "These words may be trusted and are true. The Lord, the God that inspires the prophets, sent his angel to show his servants what must quickly take place; [7] and they said, 'I will come quickly.' Blessed will the one be who lays to heart the words of the prophecy contained in this book."

[8] It was I, John, who heard and saw these things; and, when I heard and saw them, I prostrated myself in worship at the feet of the angel that showed them to me. [9] But he said to me, "Forbear; I am your fellow slave, and the fellow slave of your fellow prophets, and of all who lay to heart the words in this book. Worship God."

[10] Then the angel said to me, "Do not keep secret the words of the prophecy contained in this book; for the time is near. [11] Let the wrongdoer continue to do wrong; the filthy-minded continue to be filthy; the righteous continue to act righteously; and the holy-minded continue to be holy." [12] ("I will come quickly. I bring my rewards with me, to give to each what her actions deserve. [13] I am the Alpha and the Omega, the first and the last, the beginning and the end.") [14] Blessed will they be who wash their robes, that they may have the right to approach the tree of life, and may enter the city by the gates. [15] Outside will be the filthy, the sorcerers, the impure, the murderers, the idolaters, and all who love the false and live it.

[16] "I, Jesus, sent my angel to bear testimony to you about these things before the churches. I am the scion and the offspring of David, the bright star of the morning."

[17] "Come," say the Spirit and the Bride; and let the one who hears say, "Come." Let the one who thirsts come; let the one who will take the water of life freely.

[18] I declare to all who hear the words of the prophecy contained in this book: If anyone adds to it, God will add to his troubles the curses described in this book; [19] and if anyone takes away any of the words in the book containing this prophecy, God will take away his share in the tree of life, and in the holy city—as described in this book."

[20] The one whose testimony this is says, "Assuredly I will come quickly." "Amen, come, Lord Jesus."

[21] May the grace of the Lord Jesus be with his people. Amen.

An Introduction to the Secret Revelation of John

ACCORDING TO THE Secret Revelation of John, soon after his resurrection Christ gave his disciple John a vision. The actual author of this document is unknown, but it was most likely a Christian teacher who probably wrote in Greek around 150 CE, possibly in Alexandria, Egypt. Although part of the Secret Revelation of John was known to the second-century church father Irenaeus, it was lost until the discovery of four copies that were translated into the Egyptian (Coptic) language. The first copy (the Berlin Codex) appeared on the antiquities market in Cairo in 1896, and three more manuscripts were unearthed among a cache of papyrus books near the village of Nag Hammadi in 1945. All were at least partially damaged — as we might expect of books over 1,500 years old. The translation in this collection is largely from the Berlin Codex (BG), but it sometimes draws upon Nag Hammadi Codex II (NHC II) to fill in damaged spaces or to offer additional material found only there.

The First Christian Story

Before the Secret Revelation of John no Christian writing had told the whole story of creation and salvation from beginning to end. When the disciple John is grieving after the Savior's departure, the heavens open and the Savior appears to him. He reveals to John the entire nature of the universe, beginning with a description of God as the transcendent Invisible Spirit and Father. From him came first the Mother (Pronoia-Barbelo) and then the Son (Autogenes-Christ), followed by a multitude of luminous powers. Together they constitute the divine spiritual world above.

The lower world originated when the youngest of the powerful figures called "eternal generations," Wisdom-Sophia, boldly gave birth without the consent of her male partner and fellow aeon, God, the Father. Her child, called Yaldabaoth or the Chief Ruler, is the creator God (known from Genesis) who forms the lower world with its astral rulers. When he boasts to these minions, "I am a jealous God and there is none except me," he shows himself to be both ignorant and arrogant. To instruct him in the truth, the Savior reveals his luminous image in the form of a human being on the waters below. The Chief Ruler and his minions create the first human according to the divine image of the Savior above, but also in their own flawed likeness. When Adam is unable to move, the Chief Ruler breathes the spirit of the Mother into him, and Adam becomes superior to the lower powers who formed him. Jealous, Yaldabaoth encases him in flesh so that he becomes subject to ignorance, suffering, and death. In this way, all people come to have a double heritage; they are in truth the spiritual children of God, filled with the inner light and divine goodness; but at the same time humanity has become polluted with sin and ignorance, shackled by the fetters of the mortal body and its deceptive passions, and subject to the violence and torment of malicious pretender gods.

History is the story of repeated but ineffective attempts by the inferior world rulers to dominate the superior humans; each attempt has been countered by saviors sent by the true Mother into the lower world to teach humanity about their spiritual nature and to strengthen them with the gift of her Spirit so that they are able to overcome the violence, deception, injustice, and humiliations and suffering of mortal existence. In the end, all humanity will return to the divine world above, except a few who turn back from the truth.

This wide-scoped story creatively combines material from the first chapters of Genesis and second-century Greek philosophy. The main characters came from Genesis, astrology, Jewish Wisdom literature, or the Gospel of John and then were molded and adapted to express the dramatic hope in the dangerous circumstances of the early Christ people. Elements found in this story appear in a number of other early Christ movement documents, including the Gospel of John, the Letter to the Ephesians, "On the Origin of the World," and "The Reality of the Rulers" (two documents found at Nag Hammadi but not included in *A New New Testament*). Since the manuscripts of the Secret Revelation of John were found only within the past century, it is difficult to know what Christians of earlier eras would think of this elaborate story. Twentieth-century scholarship and church leadership have responded very hesitantly to it, mostly putting it aside as irrelevant gnostic* speculation. As is obvious from the enthusiasm of the New Orleans Council in selecting this book to be in *A New New Testament* and in this introduction, it seems probable that those twentieth-century reactions may have been too defensive.

Utopia, Justice, and Social Critique

The prevalent Christian worldview, which is drawn most notably from the Revelation to John, presents good and evil in terms of the opposing forces of God and Satan, locked in violent struggle. So, too, the Secret Revelation of John paints a dualistic portrait of the universe, but one in which all the violence is on the side of false gods. They alone bring suffering and death to human beings, keeping them ignorant and grieving through deception, toil, and the distracting pleasures of wealth, food, and sexual desire. The true God works through the illuminating light of

---

* See a treatment of this nineteenth- and twentieth-century inaccurate scholarly notion of gnosticism in chapter 5 of the "Companion to *A New New Testament*" in the latter section of this book.

truth, compassion, and moral goodness, bringing true teaching, the inner power of the Spirit, and protection from evil through baptism and anointing.

Much of the Savior's revelation is shaped by contrasting the world above with the world below, and in doing so he offers potent possibilities for exposing and criticizing structures of evil and domination. In portraying the world above as a monarchy ruled by powers of light and life, of reason and goodness, the Secret Revelation of John offers a utopian image against which the dark and death-dealing evils of this world are starkly exposed. It describes human suffering not only in relation to human sin and impotence, but as a result of the violence and deceptions wrought by unjust, ignorant, and malicious forces. At the same time, the Savior also tells John that it is difficult to distinguish what is truly good from what only appears to be good. Because the lower gods created the world as a kind of parody of the divine world, and because they actively try to keep people ignorant through lies and violence, human beings need to learn the truth through Christ's revelation. They need to learn, too, that the tree of *their* deceptive knowledge offers only the bitter fruit of ignorance and the knowledge of sin.

Much as the Revelation to John continues to produce readers who look at current events for signs of the end time and the second coming, the Secret Revelation of John may have aimed to produce wise and resistant readers during times of persecution and oppression under the Roman Empire. Through Christ's teaching, such readers were to have been able to expose the arrogance, the ignorance, and the lies of worldly powers, and to discern the true Spirit from the counterfeit. These readers were to recognize that suffering and violence are never the will of the true God and to seek and cultivate their true spiritual natures, created in the image of God and filled with the Spirit of the Mother.

Sex and Salvation

For Christians accustomed to predominantly masculine images of the biblical God, the Secret Revelation of John might bring surprise. It is filled with imagery of God as the divine Mother, as well as the Father and Son. Along with Christ, powerful saviors include the female wisdom figures of Providence-Pronoia, the luminous Reflection-Epinoia, and Eve. These figures in the Secret Revelation of John seem sometimes to be the same divine person and sometime a similar, but slightly different, divine person. The alliance among and overlapping identities of these figures do not occur just in this text, but also in other texts from Nag Hammadi and even in other unrelated ancient literature and statuary. The presence of these figures illustrates how the Secret Revelation of John is deeply indebted to Jewish literature, which also celebrates the figure of Wisdom-Sophia as a central divine "persona" who was sent to teach and save humanity, to protect and strengthen Adam, Noah, and all humanity (Wisdom 9:13–21; 10:1–2).

Still another female figure, Wisdom-Sophia, the youngest of the heavenly aeons, is responsible for breaking the harmony of the divine sphere through her bold and independent action. The result is a portrait of the universe that contrasts the proper patriarchal household of God above with a fatherless world below, headed by a sexually violent and deviant bastard.

Wisdom-Sophia's action makes her into a kind of Eve figure, but in this story the real Eve is not the cause of humankind's fall, but of its redemption. Here she is Adam's teacher, and the sexual intercourse of Adam and Eve marks not original sin, but a step toward salvation through Christ. When Adam recognizes his own spiritual essence in Eve, their union then leads to the birth of Seth, a child in the true likeness of the Child of Humanity. There is no condemnation of sex as such, but only of the world rulers' lustful desire, sexual deceit, and rape. And indeed, Christ tells John that the curse of Yaldabaoth, the lower god, proclaiming that the male should rule over the female, was done in ignorance — that the subordination of women to men is against God's holy design. In the Secret Revelation of John, then, we have a complex story that affirms the values of household order and sexual life, while strongly critiquing unjust domination, violence, and rape.

At first reading, the story of the Secret Revelation of John will often seem strange to many readers who know the Revelation to John's story, where God's rescue of humanity comes at great cost in the destruction of much of the earth and the death of thousands. But on further acquaintance, many will recognize the powerful and well-known Christian themes that Christ's teaching reveals God's love for humanity, and spiritual truth often stands in opposition to worldly "wisdom." In the Secret Revelation of John, injustice and cruel domination are overcome by the power of the Spirit, by knowledge, and by goodness without violence and destruction, offering a tradition from within the early Christian movement that is both an alternative to stories of divine wrath and judgment and an affirmation of hope and trust.

Recommended Reading

Karen L. King, *The Secret Revelation of John*

The Secret Revelation of John

(NHC II) **1** [1] The teaching [of the Savi]or and the re[vel]ation of the mysteries [2] [together with the things] hidden in silence a[nd those (things) w]hich he taught to Joh[n, his dis]ciple.*

The Savior Appears to John

(BG) **2** [1] Now it happened one day when John the brother of James, the sons of Zebedee, was going up to the Temple, a Pharisee named Arimanios approached him. [2] And he said to him, "Where is your teacher, the one whom you used to follow?"

[3] He said to him, "He returned to the place from which he came."

[4] The Pharisee said to me, "This Nazorene deceived you (pl.) with error. He filled [your (pl.) ears with lies], and he shut [your hearts]. [5] He turned you (pl.) [from] the traditions of your fathers."

[6] When I heard these things, I turned from the Temple to the mountain which was a place of desert. [7] And I grieved greatly in my heart, saying, [8] "How was the Savior appointed? [9] Why was he sent into the world by his father who sent him? [10] Who is his father? [11] And of what sort is that eternal generation to which we will go? [12] He told us that the eternal generation is modeled on that indestructible generation, [13] but he did not teach us about what sort the latter is."

3 [1] Just then, while I was thinking these things, the heavens opened, [2] and the whole creation below the heaven was illuminated with light [below] heaven. [3] And the [whole] world [quak]ed.

[4] I was afraid an[d I watch]ed. [5] And behold a child [appeared to] me. [6] Then [he changed himself] into the form of an old man [who had l]ight existing within him. [8] [Although I was watch]ing him, I did not [understand th]is wonder, whether it is a [woman] having numerous forms [in the l]ight — for its forms [appea]red through each oth[er — or] if it is one [likeness th]at has three aspects.

[9] [He sa]id [to me], "John, wh[y] are you doubting and [fearful]? [10] For you are not a stranger [to this like]ness. Do not be faint-[hearted]! [11] I am the one who dwells with [you (pl.) al]ways. [12] I am the [Father.] I am the Mother. [I] am [the S]on. [13] I am the one who exists forever, undefil[ed and un]mixed. [14] N[ow I have come] to instruct you [about what] exists and what [has come] into being and what mu[st] come into being, [15] so that you will [understand] the things which are invisible a[nd those which] are visible, [16] and to t[each you] about the perfe[ct Human].

[17] "Now then lift up your [face to] me and listen. [Receive the things that I] will tell you toda[y [18] so that] you yourself will tell the[m to your fel]low spirits who are [from] the im[mov]able generation [of the] perfect Human."

The Father

4 [1] And [I asked] to know.

---

* Readers will note that at some points verses are missing in this translation. That is because additional verses present only in NHC II/IV are not in BG. For an English translation of all versions, see King, *The Secret Revelation of John.* In the translation here, letters and words in brackets are surmised where the particular manuscript is damaged.

[2] He said to me, "[The Unit]y is a monarchy [with nothing] ruling over it. [3] [It is] the Go[d and] Father of the All, the [h]oly, the invisible, [who ex]ists over the All, the one who [. . .] incorruption, [4] [existing as] pure light, into which it is not possible for any light of the eye to gaze.

[5] "It is the Spirit. It is not appropriate to think about It as god or that It is something similar. [6] For It surpasses divinity. It is a dominion having nothing to rule over It. [7] For there is nothing existing before It nor does It have need of them. [8] It does not need life. [10] For It is eternal. It does not need anything. [11] For It cannot be made perfect as though were deficient and only required perfecting. Rather It is always totally perfect. [12] It is light. [13] It cannot be limited because there is nothing before It to limit It. [14] It is inscrutable for there is no one before It to scrutinize It. [15] It is immeasurable because there is no other to measure It as though (anything) exists before It. [16] It is invisible because there is no one to see It. [17] (It is) an eternity existing forever. [18] (It is) ineffable because no one has comprehended It in order to speak about It. [19] (It is) the one whose name cannot be spoken because no one exists before It to name It. [20] It is the immeasurable light, the pure one who is holy and unpolluted, [21] the ineffable one who is incorruptibly perfect. [22] It is neither perfection nor blessedness nor divinity, but It is a thing far superior to these. [23] It is not boundless nor is It limited, but It is a thing far superior to these.

[24] "For It is neither corporeal nor incorporeal. [25] It is neither large nor small. [26] It is not a quantity. [27] It is not a creature. [28] Neither is it possible for anyone to know It. [29] It is not something pertaining to the All which exists, rather It is a thing which is better than these — not as being superior (to others as though It is comparable to them) but as that which belongs to Itself. [30] It does not participate in an eternal generation (as a constitutive part of it).

Time does not exist with regard to It. For whoever participates in an eternal generation would have to have had it prepared for It by others. [31] And time was not delimited for It since It does not receive from another who sets limits. [33] And It does not need (anything). Nothing from the All exists before It.

[34] "All It asks for is Itself alone within the perfect light. [35] It will contemplate the unmixed light, the immeasurable vastness. [37] (It is) the eternity who gives eternalness, the light who gives light, the life who gives life, the blessed one who gives blessedness, the understanding which gives understanding, the ever good one who gives good, the one who does good — [38] not such that It possesses but such that It gives — the mercy which gives mercy, the grace which gives grace.

5 [1] "What shall I say to you about the immeasurable light? What is incomprehensible (can only be expressed as) the likeness of the light. [2] In this manner, I will speak to you as far as I will be able to know It — for who could know It infinitely?

[3] "His eternal generation is indestructible, being in a state of tranquility, at rest in silence. [4] (It is) the one that exists before the All, for It is the head of all the eternal generations — [5] if another thing does exist with It.

[6] "For none of those among us understood the things which belong to the immeasurable one except the one who appeared in It. [7] It is he who told these things to us.

The Mother

"(It is) the one who knows Itself alone in the light-water that surrounds It, which is the spring of living water, the light which is full of purity. [9] The spring of the Spirit flowed from the living water of the light [10] and It abundantly supplied all the eternal generations and the worlds.

[11] "In every way It perceived Its own image, seeing it in the pure light-water which surrounds It. [13] And Its thinking became a thing. [14] She appeared. She stood in Its presence in the brilliance of the light; [15] she is the power which is before the All. [16] It is she who appeared, [17] she who is the perfect Providence-Pronoia* of the All, [18] the light, the likeness of the light, [19] the image of the Invisible, [20] she who is the perfect power, Barbelo, the perfect eternal generation of the glory.

[21] "She glorifies It because she appeared through It [22] and she perceived It. [23] She is the primal Thought (Protennoia), Its image. [25] She became a primal Human, which is the virginal Spirit, [26] the triple male, the one belonging to the triple power, the triple na[med], the triple begotten one, the androgynous eternal generation which does not grow old, who came from Its Providence-Pronoia.

6 [1] "And Barbelo requested It to give to him Foreknowledge. [2] It assented. [3] When It had assented, Foreknowledge appeared. [4] He stood with Thought, who is Providence-Pronoia. [6] She glorified the Invisible one and the perfect power, Barbelo, for they came into being through her.

[7] "Again, this power requested (It) to give her Incorruption. [8] And It assented. [9] When It had assented, Incorruption appeared [10] and she stood with Thought and Foreknowledge, [11] glorifying the Invisible one and Barbelo since she had come into being because of her.

[12] "She requested (It) to give her Eternal Life. [13] It assented. [14] When It had assented, Eternal Life appeared. [15] And they stood, [16] glorifying It and Barbelo, for they had come into being because of her [17] from the revelation of the invisible Spirit.

[23] "This is the pentad of the Eternal Generations of the Father, [24] who is the primal Human, the image of the Invisible one, [25] namely: Barbelo, Thought, Foreknowledge, Incorruptibility, and Eternal Life. [26] This is the androgynous pentad which is the decad of the Eternal Generations, the Father from the unbegotten Father.

The Son

7 [1] "Barbelo gazed intently into It, the pure light. [2] She turned herself toward It. [3] She gave birth to a spark of blessed light, [4] but it was not equal to her in greatness. [5] This is the Only-begotten who appeared from the Father, [6] the divine Autogenes, the firstborn son of the All of the Spirit of pure light.

[7] "The invisible Spirit rejoiced over the light which had come into being, the one who was the first to appear from the primal power, which is Its Providence-Pronoia, Barbelo. [8] And It anointed him with Its goodness/Christhood [9] so that he became perfect. There was no lack of good/Christ within him [10] because he was anointed in the invisible Spirit's goodness/Christhood which It poured out for him. [11] And he received the anointing through the virgi[nal Sp]irit. [12] He stood in [Its pre]sence, glorying the invisible Spirit and the perfect Pronoi[a], [13] from whom he had appeared.

[14] "And he asked to be given one single thing, Mind. [15] The invisible Spirit assented. [16] Mind appeared. [17] He stood with Christ, glorifying him and Barbelo, [18] for all these had come into being in silence and thought.

[19] "The invisible Spirit willed to perform a work. [20] Its will became a work. [21] He appeared. He stood with Mind and

---

* This translation gives the English meaning of the Greco-Coptic word *Pronoia* but also keeps the Greco-Coptic word since it also acts as a name in this text.

Light, glorifying It. [22] The Word followed the Will. [23] For through the Word, Christ created everything. [24] The divine Autogenes, Eternal Life and Will, Mind and Foreknowledge stood, [25] glorifying the invisible Spirit and Barbelo since they had come into being through her.

[26] "Through the Spirit, he perfected the divine eternal Autogenes, the son of Barbelo, so that he stood before the eternal virginal invisible Spirit. [27] It was the divine Autogenes Christ that It honored with great honor, [28] namely, he who had come into being from Its primal Ennoia. [29] That one is the one whom the invisible Spirit appointed as god over the All, the true god. [30] It gave to him all authority and It caused the truth which is in It to be subject to him in order that he might know the All. (NHC II) [31] (He is) that one whose name they call by a name which is more exalted than any name. (BG) [32] (He is) that one whose name they will speak among those who are worthy of it.

The Luminous Beings and Eternal Generations of the Divine Realm

8 [1] "For from the light, which is the Christ, and Immortality, through the divine [Spirit], [2] the four great Lights appeared from the divine Autogenes so that they might stand before him.

[3] "The three (are): Will [and] Thought and Life. [4] And the four are: Grace, Understanding, Perception, and Prudence. [5] Grace (belongs to) the primal Light Harmozel, who is the angel of light in the primal Eternal Generation; [6] with him are three Eternal Generations: Grace, Truth, Form. [7] The second Light Oroiael is the one he placed over the second Eternal Generation; [8] with him are three Eternal Generations: Providence-Pronoia, Perception, Memory. [9] The third Light Daveithe is the one he placed over the third Eternal

Generation; [10] with him are three Eternal Generations: Understanding, Lov[e, Likeness]. [11] The fourth Light Eleleth is the one he placed over the fourth Eternal Generation; [12] with him are three Eternal Generations: Perfection, Peace, Wisdom. [13] These are the four Lights which stand before the divine Autogenetor, [14] the twelve Eternal Generations which are placed beside the Child, the great Autogenetor Christ, through the approval of the divine invisible Spirit. [15] The twelve Eternal Generations belong to the Son of Autogenetos.

9 [1] "All things were firmly founded through the will of the holy Spirit, through Autogenes. [2] And from the first Understanding and the perfect Mind, through God, through the approval of the great invisible Spirit and the approval of Autogenes, It named the true perfect Human, the primal revelation, Adam. [3] It set him over the primal Eternal Generation beside the great divine Autogenetor Christ, being the primal Eternal Generation of Harmozel and Its powers with him. [4] And the invisible Spirit gave him an unconquerable intellectual power. [5] He said, 'I glorify and I praise the invisible Spirit [6] for it is because of you that all things came into being and all things (are) in you. [7] And I praise you and Autogenes and the three Eternal Generations: the Father and the Mother and the Child, the perfect power.'

[8] "And It placed his Child Seth over the second Light Oroiael.

[9] "And in the third Eternal Generation was placed the seed of Seth, the souls of the saints who dwell forever in the third Light Daveithe.

[10] "And in the fourth Eternal Generation were placed the souls who did understand their perfection, [11] yet they did not repent immediately but they persisted a while. [12] In the end, however, they repented. [13] They will remain in the fourth

Light Eleleth, [14] the one who yoked them to himself, glorifying the invisible Spirit.

Wisdom-Sophia's* Bold Action and the Birth of Yaldabaoth

10 [1] "Our fellow sister, Wisdom-Sophia, being an Eternal Generation, thought a thought from within herself and in the thought of the Spirit and the Foreknowledge. [2] She freely willed the likeness to appear from within herself [3] although the Spirit had not agreed with her nor had It consented nor had her partner approved, the male virginal Spirit. [4] But she did not find her concord. [5] As she was about to acquiesce without the approval of the Spirit or the understanding of her own concord, [6] she swelled out.

[7] "Because of the audacity within her, her thought was not able to be idle [8] and her product came forth, being imperfect, ugly in his appearance, because she had made it without her partner. [9] And he did not resemble the likeness of the Mother, for he had another form. [10] As she deliberated, she saw that he had become modeled after a different likeness, [11] having the face of a serpent and the face of a lion. [12] His eyes were shining with fire. [13] She cast him away from her outside of those places so that none of the immortals might see him, [14] because she had given birth to him in ignorance.

[15] "She united a luminous cloud with him. [16] She placed a throne in the midst of the cloud so that no one might see him [17] except the holy Spirit who is called Life, the mother of everyone. [18] And she named him Yaldabaoth. [19] He is the Chief Ruler, the one who attained a great power from the Mother.

The Creation of the Lower Heavens and Their Ruling Authorities

11 [1] "He removed himself from her. [2] He abandoned the place in which he had been born. [3] He seized another place. [4] He created for himself an eternal generation, which blazes with a shining fire, in which he now dwells.

[5] "And he copulated with Madness, who is in him. [6] He begat authorities who are under him, [7] the twelve angels, each one of them to his own eternal generation following the model of the immortal Eternal Generations. [8] And he created for each one of them seven angels each and for the angels three powers — [9] these are all under him, three hundred and sixty angelic beings with his third power, [10] following the likeness of the primal model which is prior to him.

[11] "Now when the authorities appeared from the chief begetter, the chief ruler of the darkness, these were their names from the ignorance of he who had begotten them: [12] The first is Yaoth. [13] The second is Hermas, who is the eye of the fire. [14] The third is Galila. [15] The fourth is Yobel. [16] The fifth is Adonaios. [17] The sixth is Sabaoth. [18] The seventh is Kainan and Kae, who is named Cain, who is the sun. [19] The eighth is Abiressine. [20] The ninth is Yobel. [21] The tenth is Harmoupiael. [22] The eleventh is Adonin. [23] The twelfth is Belias.

[24] They all have double names: one set of names from desire and wrath, but yet other names which are given to them by the glory of heaven. [25] The (latter) are the ones which reveal their nature in truth. [26] Saklas called them by the names which are from illusion and their power. [27] On the one hand, through (the names

---

* This translation gives the English meaning of the Greco-Coptic word *Sophia* but also keeps the Greco-Coptic word since it also acts as a name in this text.

given by the glory of heaven), they are reproved and weakened, like the seasons, [28] while on the other hand, through those (of Saklas) they grow strengthened and increase.

[29] "And he commanded that seven kings should rule over the heavens and five over the chaos of Hades.

12 [16] The names of the glories who are over the seven heavens are these: [17] The first is Iaoth, the lion-faced. [18] The second is Eloaios, the donkey-faced. [19] The third is Astaphaios, the hyena-faced. [20] The fourth is Iao, the snake-faced with seven heads. [21] The fifth is Adonaios, the serpent-faced. [22] The sixth is Adoni the monkey-faced. [23] The seventh is Sabbataios, whose face is a flame of fire that shines. [24] This is the hebdomad of the week. [25] These are those who rule the world.

[26] "Yaldabaoth-Saklas (is) the one whose forms are without number [27] such that he can appear with any face at will.

13 [1] "He allotted them (portions) out of his own fire, [2] but he did not give them any of his power from the pure light of the power which he had drawn from the Mother. [3] Because of the glory which is in him from the power of the light of the Mother, he became Christ to them. [4] Because of that, he made them call him God, [5] thus being disobedient to the reality from which he had come into being.

[6] "And he joined with the authorities. [7] When he spoke, the seven powers came into being, [8] and he named them. Beginning with the highest, he placed authorities (as follows): [9] The first, then, is Pronoia with the first (authority) Yaoth. [10] The second is Divinity with the second one Eloaios. [11] The third is Goodness/Christhood with the third one Astaphoios. [12] The fourth is Fire with the fourth one Yao. [13] The fifth is Kingship with the fifth one Sabaoth. [14] The sixth is Understanding with the sixth one Ad[oni. [15] The]

seven[th] is Wisdom-Sophia [wi]th the seventh one Sabbataios. [16] These are the ones who have a firmament corresponding to each heaven and eternal generation [21] according to the likeness of the Eternal Generation which exists from the beginning, [22] in the model of the indestructible ones.

The Arrogant Claim of the Lower God and the Repentance of Wisdom-Sophia

14 [1] "He saw the creation below him and the multitude of angels which are below him who came into being from him. [2] And he said to them, 'I am a jealous God; without me there is nothing' — [3] already indicating to the angels who are below him that another God does exist. [4] For if there were no other (god) over him, of whom would he be jealous?

[5] "Then the Mother began to move to and fro as she understood her deficiency. [6] It was her own perfection that had caused her to be blamed, [7] because her partner had not been in concord with her."

[8] But I said, "Christ, what does it mean 'to move to and fro'?"

[9] He smiled and said, "You think it happened like Moses said 'upon the water.' [10] But in fact, she saw the evil and rebellion which would happen through her offspring. [11] She repented, and as she was coming and going in the ignorant darkness, [12] she began to be ashamed and she did not dare to return [13] but she continued coming and going. [14] Now her coming and going is 'to move to and fro.'

[15] "Now when the Arrogant one got a power from the Mother, [16] he was ignorant of many beings who were superior to his Mother, [17] for he said about his Mother that she alone existed. [18] He saw the great multitude of angels that he had created. [19] He was mighty over them.

[20] "And when the Mother understood

that the untimely birth of the darkness was not perfect [21] because her partner had not been in concord with her, [22] she repented. She wept great tears.

[23] "And It heard the entreaty of her repentance and the brothers prayed for her. [24] The holy invisible Spirit assented. When the invisible Spirit had assented, It poured upon her a Spirit from the perfection. [25] When her partner came down to her to put right her deficiencies, [26] it was through Pronoia that he willed to put right her deficiencies. [27] She was not, however, conveyed to her own Eternal Generation, [28] but because of the great ignorance which had appeared in her, she dwelled in the Ninth until she puts right her deficiency.

The Creation of the First Human

15 [1] "A voice came to her: [2] 'The Human exists and the Child of the Human.' [3] The chief ruler Yaldabaoth heard, [4] but he did not think that the voice had come [from the exalted height above].

[6] "The holy, perfect Father, the first Human of human form, taught them about himself. [7] The Blessed one revealed his likeness to them.

[8] "And the whole dominion of the seven authorities bent down. [11] They saw the pattern of the image in the water. [12] They said to each other, 'Let us create a human in the image of God and with the likeness.' [14] They created out of each other and all their powers.

[16] "They molded a form out of themselves and each one of (their) powers created from its power a soul. [17] They created by imitating the image which they had seen, [18] the image of the one who exists from the beginning, the perfect Human.

[19] They said, 'Let us give him the name Adam so that that name and its power might illumine us.'

[20] "And the powers began (creating their respective souls) from (the image) below: [21] The first is Divinity; it is a soul of bone. [22] The second is Christhood/Goodness; it is a soul of sinew. [23] The third is Fire; it is a soul of flesh. [24] The fourth is Pronoia; it is a soul of marrow which is the whole foundation of the body. [25] The fifth is Kingdom; it is a soul [of blood]. [26] The sixth is Understanding; it is a soul of skin. [27] The seventh is Wisdom; it is a soul of hair.

[28] "And they set the whole body in order. [29] And their angels stood before them. [30] They created a substantial soul out of the things which had first been prepared by the authorities, [31] the harmony of the joined parts.

17 [64] "And they created the whole body, which was joined together by the multitude of angels.*

Adam Receives the Spirit of the Mother

18 [1] "And it remained inactive a long time [2] because neither the seven authorities nor the three hundred and sixty angels who had forged [the links of the chain] were able to awaken it.

[3] "And (the Mother) wanted to retrieve the power which she had given to the ruler from (her) audacity. [4] She went in innocence and entreated the Father of the All, whose mercy is great, and the luminous God. [5] Following a holy design, he sent Autogenes and his four lights in the shape of angels of the Chief Ruler. [6] They advised

---

* Chapters 16 and 17 are found only in NHC II. They contain an extensive list of parts of the human body and the names of demons associated with each. The purpose of the list is apparently for healing the body from demonic influences that cause illness. With the exception of 17:64, chapters 16 and 17 are omitted here.

him with the goal of extracting the power of the Mother from within him.

[7] "They said to him, 'Blow into his face from the spirit which is in you and the object will arise.' [8] And he blew into it from his spirit, which is the power from the Mother, [10] into the body. [11] And [at that moment] he moved.

[12] "Immediately [the rest of the] authorities became jealous [13] because he had come into being through them all [14] and they had given the powers that existed within them to the human [15] and he possessed the souls of the seven authorities and their powers. [16] His wisdom was greater than them all and greater even than the Chief Ruler. [17] And they knew that he was naked of evil because he was wiser than they and he had entered into the light. [18] They lifted him and brought him down into the lowest region of all matter.

The Luminous Reflection-Epinoia* of Life

[19] "But the blessed Father is a merciful benefactor. [20] He had mercy on the [Mother's] power that had been taken [from] the [Chief] Ruler [21] lest they might have power over the body. [22] He and his mercy sent the good Spirit as a helper to the primal one who had gone down, who was named Adam. [23] (His helper is) the Reflection-Epinoia of the light, the one whom he named Life. [24] It is she who labors for the whole creation [25] by toiling with him, [26] by setting him right in his own perfect temple, [27] and by teaching him about the descent of his deficiency and instructing him about his ascent. [28] And the Epinoia of the light was hidden within him so that the rulers might not know [29] but our sister Wisdom-Sophia, who is like us, would set

right her deficiencies through the Epinoia of the light.

Adam Becomes Mortal

19 [1] "And the human shone because of the shadow of the light which is in him. [2] And his thinking was superior to those who had made him. [3] And they bent down. [4] They saw that the human was superior to them. [5] They took counsel with the whole angelic host of the rulers and the rest of their powers. [6] Then they mixed fire and earth with water and flame. [7] They seized them and the four winds, blowing with fire, [8] joining them with each other, [making a] great disturbance; [9] they brought him down into the shadow of death. [10] Yet again they made another form from earth, water, fire, and spirit [11] which is from matter, darkness, desire, and the adversarial spirit. [12] This is the chain. This is the tomb of the molded body with which they clothed the human, the fetter of the flesh.

[14] "He is the primal one who came down and the primal partition. [15] But it is the Reflection-Epinoia of the primal light who dwells in him who awakens his thinking.

The Trees of Paradise and the Serpent

20 [1] "The Chief Ruler took him and placed him in paradise, [2] of which he said, 'It is [a] delight for him' but really so that he might deceive him. [3] For their delight is bitter and their beauty is licentious. [4] Their delight is a deception and their tree is iniquity. [5] Their fruit is an incurable poison and their promise is death to him. [6] Their tree which they planted is the tree of life.

[7] "For my part, I will teach you about the mystery of their life. [8] It is their coun-

---

* This translation gives the English meaning of the Greco-Coptic word *Epinoia* but also keeps the Greco-Coptic word since it also acts as a name in this text.

terfeit spirit which dwells in them, [9] whose purpose is to make him wander so that he does not know his perfection.

[10] "That tree is of this sort: Its root is bitter. [11] Its branches are shadows of death. [12] Its leaves are hate and deception. [13] Its fragrance is an ointment of evil. [14] And its fruit is the desire for death. [15] Its seed drinks from darkness. [16] The dwelling place of those who taste it is Hades.

[18] "But the tree which they call 'knowledge of good and evil' is the Reflection-Epinoia of the light. [19] Concerning her they commanded, 'Do not taste (of it),' which means 'Do not listen to her.' [20] They issued this commandment against him so that he might not look up to his perfection [21] and realize that he was naked of his perfection.

[22] "But as for me, I set them right so that they would eat."

[23] I said to him, "Christ, was it not the serpent who instructed her?"

[24] He laughed [25] and said, "The serpent is the one who instructed her about the sowing of desire, pollution, and destruction because they are useful to it. [26] Yet it knew that she would not obey it [27] because she is wiser than it.

Eve

21 [1] "And he wanted to bring out the power which had been given to him. [2] And he cast a trance upon Adam."

[3] I said to him, "Christ, what is the trance?"

[4] He said, "It is not like Moses said [5] that he caused him to sleep but it was his sensibility that he covered with a shroud. [6] He weighed him down with insensibility. [7] For indeed it is said by the prophet, 'I will make the ears of their hearts heavy so that they might not understand and might not see.'

[8] "Then the Reflection-Epinoia of the light hid herself in him.

[9] "And according to his will, he wanted to bring her from the rib. [10] But the Epinoia of the light is ungraspable. [11] The darkness pursued her, but it was not able to lay hold of her. [12] He wanted to bring the power from him (Adam) [13] to make another kind of molded form in a woman's shape. [15] And he stood her up before him — [16] not 'He took a rib' as Moses said. [17] He created the woman beside him.

[18] "Immediately he became sober from the drunkenness of the darkness. The Reflection Epinoia of the light uncovered the shroud from his understanding. [19] Immediately when he recognized his essence, [20] he said, 'Now this is bone from my bone and flesh from my flesh. Because of this man will leave his father and his mother and he will cling to his wife, and from two they will become a single flesh.' [21] For the Mother's partner will be sent forth [23] and she will be set right. [24] Because of this, Adam named her the mother of all the living by the authority of the exalted height and the revelation.

[25] "Reflection-Epinoia taught him about knowledge. [26] From the tree in the form of an eagle, [29] she taught him to eat of knowledge [30] so that he might remember his perfection [31] for both were in a fallen state of ignorance.

Yaldabaoth's Curse, Rape, and Sexual Desire

22 [1] "Yaldabaoth knew that they had withdrawn from him. [2] He cursed them. [4] Moreover, he adds concerning the female that the male should rule over her [5] for he does not understand the mystery which came to pass from the design of the holy height. [6] But they were afraid to curse him, [7] thereby revealing his ignorance. [8] All his angels cast them out of paradise. [9] He clothed him with a dark gloom.

[10] "Then Yaldabaoth saw the virgin who stood beside Adam. [12] He was full of

senseless folly, [13] desiring to sow a seed in her. [15] He defiled her. [17] He begat the first son, Yawe the bear face, and similarly the second, Eloeim the cat face. [18] The one is righteous, while the other is unrighteous. [19] Eloeim is righteous; Yawe is unrighteous. [20] He set the righteous one over fire and spirit, while (he set) the unrighteous one over water and earth. [21] Among the generations of all humanity, these are called Cain and Abel.

[22] "Up to the present day, marital intercourse came about from the Chief Ruler. [23] He planted a desire for seed in Adam [24] so that from this essence (of desire) a likeness from their counterfeit spirit might be begotten. [25] He set two rulers over the principalities so that they might rule over the tomb.

The Birth of Seth and the Sending of the Spirit

[26] "He recognized his essence which is like him. [27] Adam begot Seth [28] just as it is in the generation which is above in the eternal generations.

[29] "Likewise the Mother sent what belongs to her; the Spirit came down to it (the generation) [30] to awaken the essence that is like it (the Spirit) following the model of the perfection, [31] to awaken them from forgetfulness and the wickedness of the tomb. [34] And it (the Spirit) remained like this for a while: [35] it labored on behalf of her seed so that when the Spirit from the holy eternal generation should come, [36] it will set right the deficiency by (establishing) the uprightness of the eternal generation [37] so that it might become a holy perfection; thus it would come to pass that there would be no deficiency in it."

The Salvation of All Souls

23 [1] I said, "Christ, will the souls of everyone live in the pure light?"

[2] He said to me, "You have arrived at an insight of great things [3] such as are difficult to disclose to any others except those who are from that immovable generation. [4] Those upon whom the Spirit of the Life descends, having been yoked with the power, they will be saved and become perfect. [5] And they will be worthy to enter these realms of the great Lights. [6] For they will be worthy to be purified there from all evil and the enticements of wickedness. [7] For they do not give themselves to anything else except this incorruptible congregation [8] and they attend to it without anger or envy or fear or desire or overindulgence. [9] They are not restrained by any of these nor by anything else in them except only the flesh [10] to which they are subject while they are waiting fervently for (the time) when they will be brought forth and those who receive (them) will admit them [11] into the honor of the imperishable eternal life and the calling, [12] enduring all things, bearing all things so that they might complete the contest and inherit eternal life."

[13] I said, "Christ, what will the souls do, upon whom the power and the Spirit of Life descended but who did not do these things, in order that they might also be saved?"

[14] He said to me, "Those upon whom that Spirit comes will live in any case and come out from evil. [15] For the power enters into every human being — for without it, it is not possible for them to stand upright. [16] After it (the soul) is born, then the Spirit of Life is brought to it. [17] If the powerful Spirit of Life comes, it strengthens the power, which is the soul, and it is not led astray into wickedness. [18] But those into whom the counterfeit spirit enters are drawn by it and they are led astray."

[19] I said, "Christ, when the souls [of those] leave the flesh, where will they go?"

[20] He laughed and said to me, "To a place of the soul, which is the power greater than the counterfeit spirit.

[21] "This (soul) is powerful. [22] It flees

from the works of wickedness [23] and it is saved by the incorruptible oversight [24] and brought up to the repose of the eternal generations." [25] I said, "Christ, what about those who do not know the All — what are their souls or where will they go?"

[26] He said to me, "In those, a counterfeit spirit proliferated by causing them to stumble. [27] And in that way he burdens their soul and draws it into works of wickedness, and he leads it into forgetfulness. [28] After it has become naked in this way, he hands it over to the authorities who came into being from the Ruler. [29] And again they cast them into fetters. [30] And they consort with them until they are saved from forgetfulness and it receives some knowledge. [31] And in this way, it becomes perfect and is saved."

[32] I said, "Christ, how does the soul become smaller and enter again into the nature of the mother or the human?"

[33] He rejoiced when I asked this, and he said, "Blessed are you for paying close attention! [34] Because of this they submit themselves to another who has the Spirit of Life in it. [35] By following and obeying him, it is saved, [36] and of course it does not enter another flesh."

[37] I said to him, "Christ, where are the souls of those who understood but turned away?"

[38] He said to me, "Those to whom repentance did not come will go to the place to which the angels of poverty will withdraw. [39] And they will be guarded for the day when all those who blasphemed against the holy Spirit will be punished. [40] They will be tortured in eternal punishment."

The Counterfeit Spirit

24 [1] I said, "Christ, where did the counterfeit spirit come from?"

[2] He said to me, "(It all began) when the Mother whose mercy is great and the holy Spirit, the compassionate, who troubles herself with us — the seed — [3] that is, the Reflection-Epinoia of the light awakened the thinking of human beings of the generation of the eternal, luminous, perfect Human. [4] Then the Chief Ruler knew that they surpassed him in the excellence of their wisdom. [5] He wanted to restrict their plan [6] for he was ignorant. He did not understand [that] they were wiser than he.

[7] "He made a plan with his powers. [9] They begot Fate (NHC II) [10] which is the last of the counterfeit chains. [11] And it is such that (it makes) each one different from every other. [12] And it is painful and it oppresses that (soul) since the gods and angels and demons and all the generations have intermingled with it up to the present day. [13] For from that Fate appeared every iniquity and injustice and blasphemy and the fetter of forgetfulness and ignorance and every harsh command and severe sins and great fears. [14] And this is how they made the whole creation blind so that they might not know the God who is above them all. [15] And because of the fetter of forgetfulness, their sins were hidden. (BG) [16] And they bound the gods of heaven and angels and demons and human beings with measures and seasons and times in order to keep them all in its fetter — for it was lord over them all.

The Flood

[17] "He had a wicked and perverted thought, [18] and he had regrets about all the things which had come into being through him. [19] He planned to bring a flood over the whole establishment of humanity.

[20] "And the greatness of Providence-Pronoia, who is the Reflection-Epinoia of light, instructed Noah. [21] He preached to people, [22] but they did not believe him. [23] It is not like Moses said, that he hid himself in an ark, but she sheltered him somewhere — [24] not Noah more (than others) but also some people from the immovable generation. [25] They entered

a place. [26] They were sheltered by a luminous cloud. [27] And he recognized his sovereignty [28] along with those who were with him in the light which illumined them, [29] for darkness flowed out over everything upon the earth.

25 [1] "He made a plan with his angels. [2] Their angels were sent to the daughters of men [4] so that they might raise offspring from them, to be a respite for them. [5] But at first they did not succeed. [6] They all came together to make a plan [7] to create the counterfeit spirit — for they remembered the Spirit which had descended.

[9] "And the angels altered their appearance into the likeness of their husbands [10] and their 'husbands' sated them with the spirit, which molested them in the darkness out of wickedness.

[11] "They brought them gold, silver, gifts, and metals of copper, iron, and every sort. [12] They beguiled them into temptation [13] so that they would not remember their immovable Providence-Pronoia. [17] They took them [18] and begot children out of darkness through their counterfeit spirit. [19] It closed their hearts. [20] They became hard by the hardening of the counterfeit spirit until now.

The Providence-Pronoia Hymn (NHC II)

26 [1] "Therefore I, the perfect Providence-Pronoia of the All, changed into my seed. [2] For I existed from the first, traveling on every road. [3] For I am the wealth of the light. [4] I am the remembrance of the fullness. [5] I traveled into the vastness of the dark, [6] and I persevered until I entered the midst of the prison. [7] And the foundations of chaos quaked. [8] And I hid myself from them because of their evil, [9] and they did not recognize me.

[10] "Again I returned for the second time and I traveled. [11] I came forth into those who belong to the light, [12] which is

I, the remembrance of the Pronoia. [13] I entered the midst of the dark and the inside of Hades, [14] seeking to put my household in order. [15] And the foundations of chaos quaked such that (it seemed) they would fall down upon those who dwell in the chaos and destroy them. [16] And again I fled up to my luminous root [17] so that they would not be destroyed before the time was right.

[18] "Still for a third time, I who am the light that exists in the light and the remembrance of the Pronoia, [19] I traveled in order to enter into the midst of the darkness and the inside of Hades. [20] I filled my countenance with the light of the consummation of their eternal generation. [21] And I entered the midst of their prison, which is the prison of the body.

[22] "And I said, 'Whoever hears, arise from lethargic sleep!'

[23] "And he wept, shedding tears; heavy tears he wiped from himself. [24] And he said, 'Who is it who calls my name [25] and from where does this hope come to me who am dwelling in the fetters of the prison?'

[26] "And I said, 'I am the Providence-Pronoia of the pure light; [27] I am the thought of the virginal Spirit, the one who raises you to the place of honor. [28] Arise and remember that you are the one who has heard, [29] and follow your root, which is I, the compassionate. [30] Fortify yourself against the angels of poverty and the demons of chaos and all those who ensnare you, [31] and be watchful of the lethargic sleep and the garment of the inside of Hades.'

[32] "And I raised him up and sealed him with the light of the water with five seals [33] so that death would not have power over him from this day on.

The Farewell of the Savior (NHC II)

27 [1] "Behold, now I will go up to the perfect eternal generation. [2] I have completed everything for you in your ears. [3] I have told you (John) all things [4] so that you might write them down and give them in secret to your fellow spirits. [5] For this is the mystery of the immoveable generation."

[10] And the Savior gave these things to him so that he might write them down and keep them secure.

[11] And he said to him, "Cursed be anyone who should exchange these things for a gift, whether for food or drink or clothing or anything else of this kind."

[12] And these things were given to him in a mystery. [13] And immediately he disappeared before him.

[14] And he (John) went to his fellow disciples. [15] He related to them the things which the Savior had said to him.

[16] Jesus Christ Amen.

The Secret Revelation according to John

A Companion to
A New New Testament

A Preamble

THE GENIE IS OUT of the bottle. Sampling the powerful and provocative texts of *A New New Testament* almost inevitably prompts a torrent of thoughts, questions, inspirations, and emotions. Where did these new books come from? Why weren't they included in the traditional New Testament? How do the new books differ from the traditional ones? When they are read together, what happens? Tell me more about what was happening in the first centuries after Jesus lived.

This new stage of discovery can be enhanced by some additional information that is known to the scholarly community but is not widely available to the public. The chapters of this "Companion" explain the power of reading all these documents together and provide the kind of detailed context that can transform our understanding of a particular book or character in both the new and traditional documents.

More, however, is needed than just historical information to honor the interest and longings of the reader of *A New New Testament*. In the past twenty years I have encountered a jumble of questions, thoughts, and feelings in response to the books in this selected and expanded New Testament; these responses have shown me that we must also address what these texts mean today, not just what scholars know about what they meant long ago. What twenty-first-century meanings become apparent when the traditional and added documents are read alongside one another? How does this new mix affect one's attitudes and practices in relationship to conventional Christianity? Where can one turn for reorientation, reaffirmation, and regrouping? This "Companion" provides both information and strategies for growing spiritually and intellectually when reading this reimagined early Christian collection, for pondering more clearly the questions and issues that emerge, and for taking stock of the implications of this book for one's own life and the larger world.

This "Companion" is an aid to reading the actual books of this *New New Testament*. Reading all of the chapters of the "Companion" at one time gives a bigger picture of how these books belong together, both in their ancient settings and today. But it is also important to use the "Companion" while flipping back and forth between it and the ancient books of *A New New Testament* as questions and issues arise. It acts, then, as a partner to the texts, the more in-depth introductions to each of the ancient books, and the reader's own questions.

1

The Discoveries of New Documents
from Old Worlds

WHERE DO THE NEW BOOKS in *A New New Testament* come from? One answer has to do with the string of recent discoveries of fascinating ancient manuscripts. Where were the manuscripts of these new books found? What are they? And what are they not? Knowing about the circumstances of the manuscript discoveries does not explain everything about them, but it helps situate the ways in which the books have come into our lives. Seeing these documents as actual manuscripts grounds them in the specific customs and technologies of the ancient world. It gives some material context to their powerful ideas, and it places the new ones and the traditional ones in the same picture, that of having been written in the ancient world with many contingencies almost unimaginable for most readers.

Religious Manuscripts in the Greco-Roman Mediterranean and Near East

Manuscripts have rarely survived from the time of Christian beginnings (1–500 CE). Humidity, sun, and insects by and large have destroyed most parchment and papyrus documents from that time. Those not destroyed come, for the most part, from Egypt and other North African locations, where the desert dryness occasionally prevented their decay and deterioration, or from very special efforts even in ancient times to preserve them.

From both carbon dating and analysis of handwriting styles, it is apparent that almost all the manuscripts from the first two hundred years of Christian writings were copies of copies of copies; that is, almost all the extant manuscripts of these texts came from many years later than the centuries in which they were written, perhaps as early as the third century and as late as the nineteenth century. We have only two scraps of manuscripts of early writings dating from the first hundred years after Jesus died. Both — from the Gospel of John and the Gospel of Thomas — are less than eight inches square in size; they are simply tiny morsels of the full gospels.

In addition to these difficulties in narrowing down dates, the manuscripts are almost all damaged. Some have gaping holes in the papyrus; on others the ink has detached or has been accidentally rubbed off. These holes and loss of ink substantially inhibit the reading of the documents.

Finally, some manuscripts of the same text do not agree with one another. Quite

Rylands Library Papyrus P52 in the Rylands Library. This papyrus fragment of the Gospel of John 18:31–33 is perhaps the earliest manuscript evidence of any early Christian writing. It dates to the latter part of the first century CE. Rylands Library, Papyrus P52

REPRODUCED BY COURTESY OF THE UNIVERSITY LIBRARIAN AND DIRECTOR, JOHN RYLANDS LIBRARY, UNIVERSITY OF MANCHESTER

frequently, different manuscripts of Plutarch, Augustine, or the Gospel of Matthew, for instance, do not have the same words in each copy. One of the tasks of scholarly manuscript work is resolving and reconciling the different wordings in various manuscripts; but this still does not result in a single true version, simply a highly studied and carefully reconstructed version.

All of these factors regarding ancient manuscripts in general also hold for the manuscripts of the traditional New Testament. There are no original manuscripts of them. The manuscripts of the New Testament gospels and letters are copies of copies of copies. As is the case for other ancient manuscripts — bills for payment of grain or lists of town officials — behind twenty-first-century New Testaments lie partial manuscripts, manuscripts with holes in them, with words obscured, and with wording that disagrees with companion manuscripts.

Manuscripts have been "discovered" in many different places. Perhaps the most romantic and exciting discoveries are of manuscripts unearthed in some archaeological dig or accidentally uncovered in storage spaces or other ruins. But many manuscripts have been discovered in libraries of the Near East or the Mediterranean region in infrequently examined collections of ancient documents. Others have been discovered in the markets and bazaars of cities and towns to which they were brought by merchants or farmers who came upon them in the countryside. Still others, as is the case for some of the new documents in *A New New Testament,* have been discovered after being cast aside by Western researchers.

The Discoveries of the Books Added to *A New New Testament*

The ten books added to *A New New Testament* come from four quite different sources, each with a story attached. Seven of the ten were discovered together, and the other three came to light in three other rather distinct ways.

The majority of these new documents were part of perhaps the most dramatic discovery ever of early Christ movement literature. The impact of the 1945 finding of a jar of fifty-two documents from early Christianity in the Egyptian desert near the town of Nag Hammadi cannot be underestimated. Despite a relatively luke-warm reception by scholars, churches, and the public during its first fifty years in the light of day, with every passing year in the past two decades, the monumental significance of the Nag Hammadi find has become more evident.

After the discovery of the jar by Egyptian farmers in the hills around the Nile River, the contents only slowly came to light, even to scholars. Left for more than a year in or near the farmers' dwellings, the documents — bound in twelve codices (the scholarly word for primitively bound books) and one parcel — were distrib-uted to several parties and made their way through intermediaries and salespeople to some scholarly groups. Gradually, under joint sponsorship by the United Na-tions and the Egyptian government, a body of scholars took on the arduous tasks of examining the manuscripts, deciphering the texts in their original Coptic, and translating them. This process took over thirty years. Although some of the indi-vidual books were published during the initial decades, the first complete Eng-lish edition (*The Nag Hammadi Library in English,* edited by James M. Robinson) of the books discovered at Nag Hammadi was not published until 1978. That first edition contained a laboriously reconstructed story of the details of the discovery in Egypt; a proposal that the jar had come from an ancient Pachomian monastery whose ruins were less than five miles away from the discovery; and the wrangling of scholars, Egyptian officials, and international agencies concerning the docu-ments.

The following books in *A New New Testament* were in the Nag Hammadi jar: the Prayer of Thanksgiving, the Gospel of Thomas, the Gospel of Truth, The Thunder: Perfect Mind, the Prayer of the Apostle Paul, the Letter of Peter to Philip, and the Secret Revelation of John.

The Odes of Solomon, which were not discovered at Nag Hammadi and are di-vided into four books for publication here, have the most curious story. Several fragments of odes had appeared in various references over a number of centu-ries. Another relatively early Christian document, *Pistis Sophia,* quotes extensively from a document it calls the Odes of Solomon. But these fragments, quotations, and individual finds did not necessarily guarantee that anyone would find an in-tact collection of odes.

The real discoverer of the first intact collection of all the odes may never be known. The act of documented discovery was astonishingly ordinary. One day in 1909 Professor J. Rendel Harris, an extraordinarily accomplished scholar of early Christianity, was rummaging through papers in his (apparently messy) office and found there a more or less complete ancient Syriac document of forty-one odes. For the rest of his life he was unable to remember exactly how this document had come into his collection of materials, although he had some vague memories of its

Books from the Nag Hammadi Discovery

The books according to codex (a primitively bound book). The seven books included in *A New New Testament* are in bold.

CODEX 1   **The Prayer of the Apostle Paul**
The Secret Revelation of James
The Gospel of Truth (also in Codex 12)
The Treatise on the Resurrection
The Tripartite Tractate

CODEX 2   The Secret Revelation of John (also in Codices 3 and 4)
The Gospel of Thomas
The Gospel of Philip
The Reality of the Rulers
On the Origin of the World (also in "Codex" 13)
The Exegesis of the Soul
The Book of Thomas the Contender

CODEX 3   The Gospel of the Egyptians (also in Codex 4)
Eugnostos the Blessed (also in Codex 4) and
    The Wisdom-Sophia of Jesus Christ
The Dialogue of the Savior

CODEX 5   The Revelation of Paul
The First Revelation of James
The Second Revelation of James
The Revelation of Adam

CODEX 6   The Acts of Peter and the Twelve Apostles
The Thunder: Perfect Mind
Authoritative Teacher
The Concept of Our Great Power
Plato, *The Republic*
The Discourse on the Eighth and the Ninth
The Prayer of Thanksgiving
Asclepius

CODEX 7	The Paraphrase of Shem
	The Second Treatise of the Great Seth
	Revelation of Peter
	The Teaching of Silvanus
	The Three Steles of Seth
CODEX 8	Zostrianos
	The Letter of Peter to Philip
CODEX 9	Melchizedek
	The Thought of Norea
	The Testimony of Truth
CODEX 10	Marsanes
CODEX 11	The Interpretation of Knowledge
	A Valentinian Exposition, On Anointing, On Baptism
	A and B, On the Eucharist A and B
	Allogenes
	Hypsiphrone
CODEX 12	The Sentences of Sextus
	Fragments
"CODEX" 13	The Three Forms of Forethought

being brought to him from somewhere in "the region of the Tigris." In the meantime, close examination of this document in terms of its material, its writing style, and its relationship to the extensive quotes in *Pistis Sophia* have verified it as authentic.

The Gospel of Mary also has a somewhat tortured story of discovery, and here too the complications happened mainly within the turbulent and disordered life of a professor. The closest verifiable Near Eastern location for the Gospel of Mary comes from its purchase in a Cairo antiquities market in 1896 by a German scholar, Carl Reinhardt. There are stories about where it had been before it arrived at the Cairo market (it was allegedly found by a peasant in a niche of a wall in central

Egypt), but closer investigation has indicated that this story was an attempt more to conceal the place where it was found than to throw light on the discovery.

The Gospel of Mary was taken from Cairo to Germany for the purposes of translation and study. Unfortunately, due to two world wars, a plumbing disaster in a print shop, and the eventual sickness and death of the first translator and commentator, it took almost sixty years and the work of yet another researcher before the Gospel of Mary was translated and published (in German) in 1955.

The Acts of Paul and Thecla was never lost and therefore never "discovered." Written in the late first or early second century, this book became both popular and controversial almost immediately from the time of its composition. Its portrait of an astounding woman protagonist and its deft, subtle critique of Paul caught the attention of Christ movements quite quickly. By the end of the second century Tertullian was criticizing its popularity and warning against its story of Thecla, who baptized herself after Paul could not find the time or the will to do it. Over the centuries, Christians cited it as a source of strength for the persecuted, those sent out in mission, and women. In the eighteenth and nineteenth centuries it became key reading material in a vibrant Syriac movement of women religious.

With its long-standing popularity even in the earliest centuries, why was it not included in the early pre–New Testament lists of recommended reading for early Christians? Why did it not eventually become a part of the traditional New Testament? Tertullian's opposition could have been a factor in its exclusion. But its cherished status throughout the entire period in which the traditional New Testament slowly took shape does tell us something else about the making of the traditional New Testament: a book's inclusion may not necessarily have been a result of its strong meaning for or popularity with the general Christian population.

Ancient Document Discoveries and Twenty-first-Century Spiritual Seeking

These books from the earliest Christ movements, discovered in the sands or markets of Egypt, or — more hilariously — in the piles of paper in an absent-minded professor's office, can make a real difference in the spiritual lives of ordinary people in the twenty-first century. Lives have changed in the past two decades since the Gospel of Mary was made widely available and inspired women to think of themselves as real leaders in conventionally male-dominated situations. The Gospel of Thomas proclaims the radical availability of God inside people, and The Thunder: Perfect Mind reframes what it means to be women and men. These kinds of significant meanings in the lives of real people are at the heart of what the New Orleans Council of twenty-first-century bishops, denominational leaders, authors, and prestigious scholars wanted for the public in its embrace of new books for *A New New Testament.*

The curious case of the Acts of Paul and Thecla also has lessons for spiritual journeys in the twenty-first century. Paul and Thecla was never lost and was always popular. Nevertheless, it never made it into the traditional New Testament and therefore its moving message did not reach millions of people for over 1,500 years. Will the recent insight and courage of the New Orleans Council allow the imminent spiritual discovery of Paul and Thecla to reach the public in an expanded way? Was it the flood of new discoveries of documents under the sand and piles of scholarly papers that allowed the council to see the Paul and Thecla treasure under their noses? Will the emerging spiritual thirst of the public in the midst of the decline of churches and the rise of secularism now make people more interested in Paul and Thecla? No matter what Paul and Thecla's future may turn out to be, this document serves as a reminder of the ancient spiritual traditions lying dormant not just in Egyptian sands, but in the recesses of our memories and practices.

The material discovery of valuable ancient resources, the spiritual discovery of literature right under our noses, and the lingering spiritual longing of this twenty-first-century moment are by themselves not sufficient to rouse people to claim a sense of belonging to each other or the wider world we inhabit. Perhaps some combination of these resources might provide connective tissue for such a sense of belonging, courage, and nurture. It may be that the discovery of these documents — covered up in one way or another, lost in someone's office for years, suppressed by church self-satisfaction, and pummeled by world wars on another continent — allows them to be connected to a new sense of spiritual desire.

2

The Books of A New New Testament:
An Overview

I F YOU ASK MOST members of the public today what books are in the traditional New Testament, they just laugh; they don't know these books. Perhaps 50 percent of the overall public knows the four gospels of the traditional New Testament: Matthew, Mark, Luke, and John. Fewer than 10 percent knows even the names of a majority of the books. Even regular churchgoing people who take the New Testament seriously quickly admit that they cannot rattle off the names of the books, much less tell you what the various Christian scriptures are about. Even though a majority of Americans identify as "Christian" and say they "believe" the New Testament at one level or another, only a tiny percentage can talk about what most of the books contain.

So a basic overview of all the books — both those added to the traditional New Testament and those already in it — is in order.

A New New Testament is not like some other collections of early Christ movement literature; this book is not a collation of a wide variety of the recent discoveries from that early period. Such collections do exist and are readily available to the public. Rather, this book is a smaller, curated grouping of those early documents, selected by a prestigious and experienced council of twenty-first-century spiritual leaders who did so as a response to my request to select the writings that provided the most spiritual insight and nurture. Nor is *A New New Testament* yet another version of the traditional New Testament with some other ancient pieces of early Christian or Jewish literature called the "apocrypha" added to the back part of the book. Instead, this book integrates important recently discovered ancient books from the Christ movements into the heart of traditional gospels, letters, and the like.

One can count ten additions to the traditional New Testament in this *New New Testament.* They are (in order of appearance) the Prayer of Thanksgiving, the Gospel of Thomas, the Odes of Solomon, The Thunder: Perfect Mind, the Gospel of Mary, the Gospel of Truth, the Prayer of the Apostle Paul, the Acts of Paul and Thecla, the Letter of Peter to Philip, and the Secret Revelation of John.

These new books represent a similar variety to those already in the traditional New Testament. New gospels — Thomas, Mary, and Truth — are added to the four traditional ones. There is one new letter: the Letter of Peter to Philip. There is a new Revelation in the tradition of John: the Secret Revelation of John. There is a

Books of A New New Testament

The books in their Table of Contents order and within their respective categories, with the new books in bold type.

AN ANCIENT PRAYER FROM THE EARLY
CHRIST MOVEMENTS
   The Prayer of Thanksgiving

GOSPELS FEATURING JESUS'S TEACHINGS
   The Gospel of Thomas
   The Gospel of Matthew
   The Gospel of Mark
   The Gospel of Luke and The Acts of the Apostles

GOSPELS, POEMS, AND SONGS
BETWEEN HEAVEN AND EARTH
   The First Book of the Odes of Solomon
   The Thunder: Perfect Mind
   The Gospel of John
   The Gospel of Mary
   The Gospel of Truth

THE WRITINGS OF PAUL AND AN
INTRODUCTORY PRAYER
   The Prayer of the Apostle Paul
   The Letter to the Romans
   The First Letter to the Corinthians
   The Second Letter to the Corinthians
   The Letter to the Galatians
   The Letter to the Philippians
   The First Letter to the Thessalonians
   The Letter to Philemon

LITERATURE IN THE TRADITION OF PAUL,
WITH A SET OF INTRODUCTORY PRAYERS
   The Second Book of the Odes of Solomon
   The Letter to the Ephesians
   The Acts of Paul and Thecla

The Letter to the Colossians
The Second Letter to the Thessalonians
The First Letter to Timothy
The Second Letter to Timothy
The Letter to Titus

*DIVERSE LETTERS, WITH A SET OF
INTRODUCTORY PRAYERS*
The Third Book of the Odes of Solomon
The Letter of James
The Letter to the Hebrews
The First Letter of Peter
The Letter of Peter to Philip
The Second Letter of Peter
The Letter of Jude

*LITERATURE IN THE TRADITION OF JOHN,
WITH AN INTRODUCTORY SET OF PRAYERS*
The Fourth Book of the Odes of Solomon
The First Letter of John
The Second Letter of John
The Third Letter of John
The Revelation to John
The Secret Revelation of John

new book of "Acts"; the Acts of Paul and Thecla, similar in style to the traditional Acts of the Apostles, is strikingly different in its content, especially considering that its primary character is a woman, Thecla.

There are also new elements brought from these texts to the New Testament. Several prayers have been added to the collection, prayers that can claim some similarity to the traditional Lord's Prayer. These two documents, the Prayer of Thanksgiving and the Prayer of the Apostle Paul, are short enough that a twenty-first-century reader can use them as prayers, but long enough to contribute substantial new thoughts and feelings to our approach to the New Testament as a whole.

Although not explicitly referred to as prayers, the four books of the Odes of Solomon contain mostly prayers. These four books provide some of the most surprising content of *A New New Testament.* The odes sound very much like the psalms of the Hebrew scriptures, but most of them incorporate the person of Christ. Rich in creative imagery and expression, they single-handedly have made a major addition to the prayer vocabulary of Christianity, not just in the ancient world but also in the twenty-first century. These new prayers from the earliest times of the Christ movements accompany each section of *A New New Testament* in order to prompt the possibility of reading each set of books with a spiritual mood and perspective.

The first two groupings of books in the complete *New New Testament* consist primarily of gospels. In the first, "Gospels Featuring Jesus's Teachings," all four gospels stand in close connection. They represent a strong interest in short, pithy sayings attributed to Jesus. In some ways, this kind of teaching of Jesus is most strikingly evident in the Gospel of Thomas, which stands in this collection as the first gospel and as the only new work in this group. There are 114 such Jesus teachings in Thomas, with more or less half completely new and the other half similar to those found in the other three gospels of this grouping: Matthew, Mark, and Luke. Thomas's version of these sayings is most notable because there is no story between the teachings, whereas Matthew, Mark, and Luke lodge their teachings within a larger story of Jesus's life.

The second group of books, "Gospels, Poems, and Songs Between Heaven and Earth," is also primarily made up of gospels, but they are quite different gospels from those featuring Jesus's teachings. This group of gospels includes the traditional John and two new gospels: Mary (Magdalene) and Truth. These three gospels share a similar emphasis and style with one another and with the other two documents in this section: The Thunder: Perfect Mind and the First Book of the Odes of Solomon. All five of these books speak from a broader stage that includes heaven and earth and the beginning and end of the universe than the pithy sayings of the first gospel grouping. For instance, both Jesus in the Gospel of John and the unidentified (mostly) feminine voice that speaks throughout The Thunder: Perfect Mind speak in the voice of a strong divine character, even while both divine characters are undergoing humiliation and attack. Both John and Thunder portray a powerful and vulnerable divine person in the middle of trauma, delight, and connection with the universe. This is not unlike Mary Magdalene's message to the sorrowful disciples after Jesus has left them, where Mary hails a teaching of Jesus, which only she knows, concerning the ascent of the soul toward God in the middle of the pains and challenges of daily life. This ascent to God in Mary parallels the joyous voice of the Gospel of Truth, which soars ecstatically in unity with God, even while embracing people in painful circumstances.

It would be a mistake not to emphasize the New Orleans Council's intense appreciation of and enthusiasm for one particular poem. The Thunder: Perfect Mind, already known quite well by some of the international artistic community and featured in the works of artists as diverse as novelists Toni Morrison and Umberto Eco and filmmakers Ridley Scott and Julie Dash, drew deep and sustained praise as the New Orleans Council worked in 2011 and 2012 on selecting which books to add to *A New New Testament.* Indeed, at least a plurality of the council proposed in its final session that The Thunder: Perfect Mind was so important spiritually for twenty-first-century readers that it should be the lead document in the book. With great hesitation and mixed feelings, I chose not to follow this advice, in order for this book's overall approach to look more like an integration of the new and the old books, as well as to maintain a more conventional ordering of the books.

The group of "The Writings of Paul" is introduced by the Prayer of the Apostle Paul, not at all known until it was discovered in the mid-twentieth century and even now hardly known. All the writings in this group are quite certainly actual letters from Paul to specific Christ communities of the first century. They all belong to the traditional New Testament. They are, however, separated from some of the traditional New Testament letters of Paul, which may well not actually have been written by Paul and for this reason are grouped separately.

The "Literature in the Tradition of Paul" grouping combines pseudonymous letters of "Paul" with the ancient Acts of Paul and Thecla (known since the second century but never added until now to the New Testament traditions of Paul) and prayers from the Second Book of the Odes of Solomon, which shares many of the themes of the Pauline traditions.

The "Diverse Letters" group forms a quirky assemblage of various documents, some of which are real letters and some of which are probably not letters but documents posing as letters. The idea of a letter that was not meant to be sent to anyone was fairly common in the ancient world, so the existence of such "letters" is neither odd nor fraudulent. Not unlike the traditional New Testament, which groups many of these works under titles like "the Pastoral Letters," "the Catholic Letters," or "the Post-Pauline Letters," this group of documents is at least as much a demonstration of the wide diversity of literature from the early Christ movements as anything else.

Other than the introductory prayer material from the Third Book of the Odes of Solomon, there is only one new book in this "Diverse Letters" group. The Letter of Peter to Philip falls into this group, both because it is called a letter but is not one, and because it represents the very diverse set of Christ movement writings not easily categorized as a gospel or in the Pauline tradition. The remarkable dimension of the Letter of Peter to Philip is the nuanced position it takes relative to the second-century attacks by government officials on Christ followers. Instead of insisting that all Christ followers must submit as martyrs, as much other second-century literature not in *A New New Testament* proposes, or recommending that the Roman emperor should be obeyed as a representative of God's order like other literature from the traditional New Testament, the Letter of Peter to Philip breaks open another possibility. It acknowledges the necessity of facing one's persecutors but demands that the most important thing is to continue teaching and healing. If

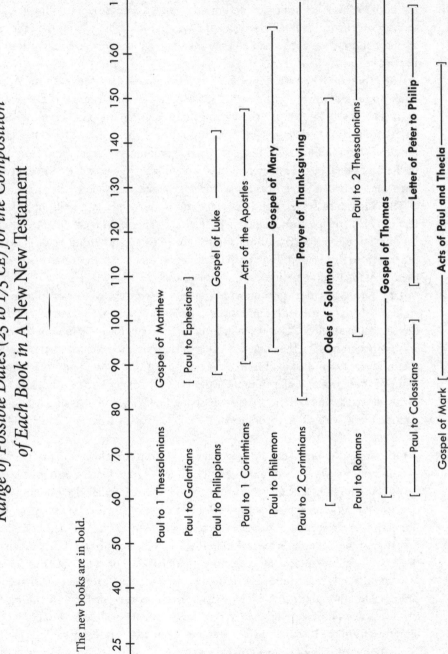

Range of Possible Dates (25 to 175 CE) for the Composition of Each Book in A New New Testament

The new books are in bold.

Letter of James

Gospel of Truth

Secret Revelation of John

Letter to the Hebrews

1 Peter

Prayer of the Apostle Paul

The Thunder: Perfect Mind

Gospel of John

1 John

Revelation to John

2 John

3 John

Letter of Jude

Paul to 1 Timothy

2 Peter

Paul to 2 Timothy

Paul to Titus

in one's teaching and healing one must die, then that should not be avoided, says this addition to the traditional New Testament. But it quickly adds that it is not the dying that is important in itself, but rather the imperative to heal and teach.

The "Literature in the Tradition of John" grouping at the end of *A New New Testament* brings together the longest new book in this collection with a variety of literature associated with the name John. The Gospel of John, found in the second group of more cosmic documents in this *New New Testament*, could also have been placed in this last grouping of books related to John. A recent discovery, the Secret Revelation of John, is the last document in the whole book and stands in brilliant and distinctive summary with the three traditional letters of John and the traditional Revelation to John. The Secret Revelation of John closes *A New New Testament*, a variation on the traditional New Testament closing with the Revelation to John. Both of these books are visions of the final victory of God in conflict with the cruel and violent Roman Empire. But the new ending with the Secret Revelation of John strikes a very different tone for God's final victory. Unlike the world in flames found in the traditional Revelation to John's vision of God's final triumph, the Secret Revelation portrays a consummate ending by virtue of Christ's successful teaching about God's compassion and goodness. Instead of the traditional Revelation's final verses cursing anyone who would change any words, the Secret Revelation finishes with John proclaiming Christ's vision and teaching.

Although estimating when an ancient document was written is a difficult and risky task, all the documents — traditional and added — in *A New New Testament* were probably composed between 25 and 175 CE. Many of the proposed dates of the writing of these works need to be understood as being within a certain range, and scholars still hotly debate when the best date of authorship is. There is little direct evidence for any proposed date, and the proposals — even those in this book — are open to challenge.

The manuscripts of the "original" author are all almost certainly lost, and the existing manuscripts of both the new and traditional books are distant copies of any original composition, which makes it incredibly difficult to home in on an exact date of composition. Another problem comes from the fact that many manuscripts have no title (titles as such were not important to ancient readers). So titles were regularly added to later copies of the manuscripts, as a kind of afterthought and without verification of who may actually have been the author. In addition, the titles that are extant mostly act as simple designations of the authors of the books. However, ancient custom by both the authors themselves and the copiers of the manuscripts tended to designate the author as a prestigious ancient figure rather than the actual composer of a given manuscript. Perhaps the most illustrious example of this practice was Plato's practice to designate Socrates as the author of the philosophy in his books, even when it is obvious that many of these thoughts came from Plato himself, not Socrates. So, if an ancient document carries the title of a famous person (such as Socrates or Paul), it cannot be assumed that this designates the time of the writing of that document or the real author.

More detailed information about each book is found in the introduction immediately preceding it.

3

Two Surprising Stories:
How the Traditional New Testament Came to Be;
How A New New Testament Came to Be

WHEN PEOPLE FIRST ENCOUNTER *A New New Testament,* they are bound to ask some basic questions. Who chose to add these new books to this New Testament? Whose idea was it to start this project? Why add books to the traditional New Testament? What was the basis for the process of selecting the new books? How long did it take? What books were not chosen and why?

Less obvious, but no less shocking and interwoven into this book's mission, is to ask and answer this question: How did the traditional New Testament come into being? The answer to this question ends up being at least as provocative and surprising as the ones about this new New Testament.

Let's take these two sets of questions and answers in historical order, first laying out the way the traditional New Testament came to be and then describing the process of this new edition's appearance.

How the New Testament Came into Being

Hardly anyone ever asks how the New Testament, as a book, came to be. In *Alice in Wonderland*–like scenarios, our society celebrates and grounds itself in the New Testament but never asks about the process of its creation. Why? Perhaps the larger belief that the New Testament comes from God prompts people to assume that its existence is either self-evident or too mysterious to investigate. But its production is neither self-evident nor too mysterious. There is quite clear — if somewhat complicated — information about its origins, which hardly anyone knows.

The Lists of Recommended Books

The theologian Marcion seems to have been the first person to make a list of what early "Christian" books to read. Around the middle of the second century, Marcion declared that everything written for followers of Christ was in error except for the works of Paul and certain parts of the Gospel of Luke. These errors were bound up in what he perceived as an overdependence on the traditions of Israel in books like the Gospel of Matthew, the Gospel of John, and the Gospel and letters of John. Curiously, at least for twenty-first-century readers, the opponents of Marcion, who burned his writings, did not produce recommended reading lists of their own.

Perhaps the most assertive opponent of Marcion was Irenaeus, the bishop of Lyons, France, who as a regional supervisor of Christ communities also became quite well known as a writer throughout western Europe. Most of Irenaeus's critique of Marcion focused on Marcion's beliefs and had little to do with Marcion's list of authoritative books. Without making his own list of books, Irenaeus seems to have been the first thinker to use *new testament* as a kind of inexact term for "Christian" documents in distinction from the Hebrew scriptures, which were authoritative for the early Christ movements. Irenaeus also seems to have been aware that there were a number of gospels and expressed his preference. In response either to Marcion's insistence on the one Gospel of Luke or to the existence of multiple gospels, Irenaeus was the first to designate Matthew, Mark, Luke, and John as the most authoritative gospels. His reason for choosing just four may appear strange to twenty-first-century minds: Irenaeus's main point in defense of these gospels was that one must have four gospels since there are four corners to the earth and the wind blows from four directions.

Another implicit endorsement of these four gospels also occurred in the late second century. The Syrian theologian Tatian did not so much designate them as authoritative as use them as sources for a cut-and-paste story combining all four gospels. This new amalgamation of Matthew, Mark, Luke, and John (called the *Diatessaron*) seems to have been a response to rising concern among the Christ people about differences among the many gospels. Tatian saw these four gospels as very valuable sources and brought them together in a way that tried to harmonize their somewhat different stories.

The other "list" of gospels from the late second century was from Clement of Alexandria. He rejected the full authority of Mark and Luke and accepted only Matthew and John, because only Matthew and John were at that time thought to have been written by apostles. In contrast to the response to Marcion's limiting of authoritative gospels to portions of Luke, no one accused Clement of Alexandria of being a heretic for his rejection of Mark and Luke, and no one destroyed his writings.

Over the next hundred years or so (190–310 CE), there seems to have been little interest in establishing an authoritative list of books. If there was such interest, we have no evidence of it. In fact, in the late second and early third centuries the Montanist communities' experience of Christ came through new visions and messages. So in contrast to those early "Christians" who wanted to narrow the list of authoritative documents, the Montanists presented a new set of inspired writings, underscoring the lack of strong third-century interest in limiting the books to be read to a certain list.

Nor did the famous Council of Nicea in the early fourth century produce any such list. Even though Nicea did issue its famous creed as a response to the request of the newly converted Christian emperor, Constantine, for some clarity on Christian standards, there is no evidence that the council made any decisions designating authoritative literature.

However, Constantine's commissioned historian Eusebius — from whom we have most of our information about the council — did produce a list, most likely in response to a similar question from the emperor. Eusebius created three categories of early Christian literature:

1. "Recognized" (Matthew, Mark, Luke, John, Acts of the Apostles, fourteen letters of Paul, 1 Peter, 1 John)
2. "Disputed" (James, Jude, 2 Peter, 2 John, 3 John)
3. "Spurious" (the Acts of Paul, the Apocalypse of Peter, the Teaching of the Twelve Apostles)

The Revelation to John seems to be both "recognized" and "spurious" in Eusebius's somewhat confusing discussion, a fact that highlights the character of his lists. In using the categories of "recognized, disputed, or spurious," it is not clear that Eusebius was making judgments about the value of the different books so much as reporting on which books were indeed recognized, which ones were actually disputed, and which ones were generally rejected. Some writers in our day cite Eusebius's lists as authoritative. On closer look it seems rather that he was simply reporting on the state of conversation in the early fourth century.

The fourth century was eventful, if uneven, in regard to the eventual New Testament. Many historians place the Muratorian fragment in the fourth century, although it can be dated to anywhere from 180 to 800 CE. This document, without a known author, recommended to an unspecified group of churches Matthew, Mark, Luke, John, the Acts of the Apostles, thirteen letters of Paul, Jude, "two [letters] with the title John," and the Wisdom of Solomon (a book without any mention of Jesus and now thought to have probably been written by a Jewish author in the city of Alexandria, Egypt). It does not list either of the letters of Peter, 3 John, or the Letter to the Hebrews.

The regional church council of Laodicea in Asia Minor met in 363 and 364. There are no written records of this council, but later reports contain two different lists from the council, one recommending the same twenty-seven books as are in the New Testament, the other recommending twenty-six books and leaving out the Revelation to John. Another regional gathering in the latter part of the fourth century came together in Hippo, North Africa, but here, too, there were no records of what was decided or even what the agenda was. A later council in Carthage, also in North Africa, reported in 397 that the Hippo "synod" had produced a list of the same twenty-seven books that are in the New Testament today.

Lists and Collections of Writings in Early Christianity and the Implicit Emergence of the New Testament

50–75 CE   Sayings of Jesus are collected (early versions of Gospel of Thomas and the "Q" sayings collection reconstructed by modern scholars).

Teachings of Jesus are cited as authoritative outside collections.

Gospel of Mark composed.

"Q" collection of sayings of Jesus completed.

75–100 CE   Possible collections of Paul's writings.

Gospel and letters of John composed, but no evidence of them being collected together.

100–125 CE   Gospel of Thomas edited and amplified.

Gospel of Truth composed.

Gospel of Mary composed.

Gospel of Luke composed.

125–150 CE   Idea of authoritative "writings" (scriptures) develops, without indication of which writings are authoritative and which are not.

Letter to Titus (from a legendary Paul) composed.

150–175 CE   Marcion collects one version of Gospel of Luke and letters of Paul as authoritative (and rejects Hebrew scriptures). Tatian composes the *Diatessaron*, a cut-and-paste combination of Matthew, Mark, Luke, and John. 2 Peter composed.

175–200 CE   Irenaeus of Lyon collects four gospels as authoritative (Matthew, Mark, Luke, and John), defends Hebrew scriptures as authoritative, and coins the term *New Testament* as a companion notion to the Hebrew scriptures but does not seem to think of the New Testament as a designated set of writings.

Clement of Alexandria rejects the full authority of Mark

and Luke and asserts that Matthew and John have superior value, because they were written by "apostles."

200–250 CE   Montanist movement proclaims and writes a set of new revelations through vision and prophecy, sparking reaction by other elements of early Christianity that begin to seek to establish more ancient authority.

250–300 CE   No documented activity of proposing or making collections of writings from the earlier periods.

300–350 CE   Eusebius responds to Emperor Constantine's request for more clarity on authority of "writings" by dividing them into "recognized" (Matthew, Mark, Luke, John, Acts of Apostles, fourteen letters of Paul, 1 Peter, 1 John), "disputed" (James, Jude, 2 Peter, 2 John, 3 John), and "spurious" (the Acts of Paul, the Apocalypse of Peter, the Teaching of the Twelve Apostles). The Revelation to John seems to be either "recognized" or "spurious" in Eusebius.

The Council of Nicea, convened by Emperor Constantine for clarification of what was authoritative for Christianity, proposes a creed of beliefs but does not consider which books are authoritative and which are not.

350–400 CE   The Muratorian fragment (dated with difficulty anywhere from 180 to 800 CE) lists Matthew, Mark, Luke, John, thirteen letters of Paul, Jude, "two [letters] with the title John," and the Wisdom of Solomon (no Petrine letters, no 3 John, no Hebrews).

Athanasius of Alexandria's festal letter is the first list of writings that includes the twenty-seven writings of the twenty-first-century New Testament, and none other. Athanasius calls this list the "New Testament" and uses *canon* to refer to his list. As far as is known, there was no actual collection or book of this "New Testament."

After Athanasius, Cyril of Jerusalem lists twenty-six writings in the festal letter and excludes Revelation.

400–425 CE   *The Apostolic Constitutions* cites all of Athanasius of Alexandria's list except Revelation and adds 1 Clement, 2 Clement, and eight books of the *Constitutions* to the list.

For most scholars of New Testament canon, the decisive moment for the formation of the New Testament came in the spring of 367 CE when Athanasius, a leading Christian theologian of the time and a bishop in North Africa, wrote a "festal letter" at Easter instructing the Christians of North Africa to read a certain twenty-seven books as their authoritative literature. As in Hippo and possibly Laodicea, these twenty-seven books were the same books that eventually came to be the New Testament. Athanasius called this list the "New Testament" and used *canon* (a term whose basic meaning was "measuring rod") to refer to it. Although not explicit, it is probable that Athanasius used the term *new testament* in order to distinguish it from the books of the *old testament*, a term coined earlier by Irenaeus for the Hebrew scriptures. The letter was not meant for all of Christianity at the time, but just the Christians of North Africa. Nor did Athanasius, or the leaders in Laodicea or Hippo, do anything to make sure that the churches of North Africa were provided with copies of these twenty-seven books, even though they were not widely available to the churches he led.

The Apostolic Constitutions, a church manual most likely written in the late fourth or early fifth century by an unknown author, listed everything on Athanasius's list except the Revelation to John, but it added 1 Clement, 2 Clement, and eight books of the *Constitutions.* This list demonstrates some increasing agreement at the beginning of the fifth century on the authoritative status of the four gospels, the Acts of the Apostles, thirteen letters of Paul, Hebrews, the two letters of Peter, the three letters of John, and Jude; but it destabilizes Athanasius's list of twenty-seven with its own list of thirty-six books.

One complex issue related to this discussion of ancient lists is its exclusion of a major non-Western part of ancient Christianity. While Western Christianity grew toward its Catholic and Protestant conceptions of the New Testament, the churches of Syriac and Ethiopian origin treated all of these issues quite differently. These churches developed separate and more expansive lists, and even today they differ from Western Christianity as to what scriptures are authoritative.

The Collections of Christian Literature

During the first five centuries of Christ communities, there were a number of collections of Christian literature. In contrast to the lists that various early "Christian" leaders made, these collections bear little relationship to the eventual New Testament.

Most scholars think that by the end of the first century there were at least several collections of the letters of Paul. It is quite certain that in the second century a number of "Christian" schools emerged, modeled mostly on philosophical schools of the time. These schools had at their disposal a number of written works, both from the "Christian" writers of the first and second centuries and from important philosophical writers as well. These school collections contained works from the eventual New Testament and works outside it. By the fourth century, such school collections could have been relatively large. But there seems to have been little interest in these collections forming the basis of the various lists of recommended instructions for "Christians" at large.

At some point in the third century monasteries also became centers of considerable study and began to have libraries within their building complexes. One of the largest and earliest collections of this sort is the Nag Hammadi "library" found in a jar several miles from a fourth-century Pachomian monastery in central Egypt. These monasteries also became places that produced copies of early Christian literature. One interesting aspect of the Nag Hammadi collection is that it is in the form of actual books. From other non-Christian libraries of that time, we know that by the fourth century such a monastic library would probably have contained both books and scrolls.

It is probable that some of these collections included all twenty-seven little books of the eventual New Testament, but it seems unlikely that any of these collections contained only these twenty-seven or even grouped them together as a "New Testament." Indeed, it is highly improbable that there were any separate collections of the twenty-seven books of the New Testament in the first four hundred years of Christian tradition.

The Actual Production of New Testaments

Although we have very few actual examples, it is almost certain that some of the collections of "Christian" literature of the fourth century were gathered into multiple books in leather-bound editions. For instance, the collections found at Nag Hammadi do consist of leather-bound books, each of which contains two to ten separate small books.

There are two reasons to doubt that the first five hundred years of "Christianity" witnessed the production of one book called the New Testament. First, the technology of book production was such that combining all twenty-seven texts into one was more or less impossible. And, of course, as seen in our study of the lists of books for "Christians" to read at that time, there was no consensus on what the "mandatory" New Testament content was until at least the fifth century.

Around the year 400, it seems likely that the theologian and translator Jerome had finished translating a collection of the twenty-seven books of the eventual New Testament. In 383 Pope Damasus requested that Jerome, who had already been hard at work translating both the Hebrew scriptures and early Christian literature, do a Latin translation of the four gospels that would serve the churches at large as a standard and readable document. This request seems to have been followed by other such requests, so that by 405 CE Jerome had produced a unified translation of all twenty-seven documents of the New Testament, which came to be called the "Vulgate." Later versions of the Vulgate contain an introduction to the translation most likely written by Jerome himself. This introduction both assumes and declares that the Vulgate translation of the twenty-seven, and only twenty-seven, books has special authority for Latin Christians. So, although it was not actually one physical book, both its unified translation and its introduction bring it quite close to being an actual book called the New Testament.

The first actual New Testaments — physical books under that title — were probably produced within two or three centuries of Jerome, as Jerome's translation gained authority in the churches. This production of a single physical book of the New Testament somewhere between the seventh and ninth centuries signaled the end of at least a six-hundred-year process. But even here there were a number of limits. Perhaps most important is that this "New Testament" was only for those who read Latin. In the seventh through ninth centuries of flourishing Syrian and Ethiopian Christianity, scrolls and codices did not follow the consensus of Latin-speaking North Africa and western Europe. In those regions authoritative collections of Christian books continued to be different. Even today, the fifth-century decisions of a major part of Syrian Christianity to have a New Testament contain just twenty-two books (excluding 2 Peter, 2 John, 3 John, Jude, and the Revelation of John) are still held to be authoritative.

In the ensuing thousand or so years (450–1500 CE) in both the East and West, many different versions of the New Testament were produced. Although the majority of these versions contained just the twenty-seven books of the New Testament we know today, often a few books were added or subtracted. The vast majority of these New Testaments were in Greek and Latin, languages that no one spoke in most of the areas where Christianity existed, and that limited their reading to an elite class and scholars. This stood in some contrast to the earliest manuscripts of the individual writings of the Christ movements, which were written in Greek, Coptic, and Syriac, the languages spoken by most people in the eastern Mediterranean.

The invention of the printing press in the early fifteenth century precipitated two major shifts in the physical form of the New Testament. The New Testament became available to the broader population beyond those who read it in the ancient Latin and Greek when it was translated into the common tongues and produced for mass distribution. Rather suddenly the New Testament was of direct interest to common folk, who now had much better access to these scriptures.

This change in public consciousness produced several responses from church leaders. Martin Luther tried unsuccessfully to have four books — Hebrews, James, Jude, and Revelation — removed from the New Testament as it would be read by the new Protestant public. And, in the sixteenth century, several church-wide bodies, including the Roman Catholic Council of Trent, declared for the first time that these twenty-seven specific books officially constituted the New Testament.

Making Sense of the Creation of the New Testament

The production of the first actual New Testament occurred at the earliest some seven hundred years after Jesus. Less than six hundred years ago, the Roman Catholic Council of Trent and its Protestant competitors officially declared what the contents of the New Testament should be. These facts are not debated, even by the most conservative Christian scholars.

From a certain angle, the New Testament is a much later and more fragile reality than is assumed in our day. Yet its strength in American culture is undeniable. It serves a wide range of people with much of their spiritual sustenance. The New Testament does contain many very ancient perspectives on the early moments of Christianity. In spite of the scholarly projects recently made public that question some of its historical accuracy, the New Testament does hold a number of images, events, and sayings from the historical Jesus, Paul, and even Mary Magdalene. Perhaps even more significant and despite its obvious flaws in its socially outdated positions on slavery, women, and other issues, it makes good on many of its promises for insight and renewal in the lives of its readers today.

This place of honor for the New Testament in American culture, its strong if ragged witness to the earliest generations of the Jesus movements, and its decent track record for spiritual inspiration hide the fact that the New Testament has been at least as much of a process as a product. But recognizing that the New Testament has been in process for its entire existence, and intensely so for its first five hundred years, does not deny its great value. Indeed, it shows the living character of both the New Testament itself and the larger Christian practice of meditating on and immersing oneself in scripture. To be sure, the uneven and ongoing way that Christians have identified what was or was not authoritative reading material undermines some claims about the New Testament as directly attached to the generation of Jesus.

But the ways Christians have read and do read the New Testament show that their avid and inspired engagement does not depend solely on these claims, but on a larger intimacy created over the centuries in reading different parts of the New Testament on a variety of terms. The understanding that the woman reading the New Testament on the subway on her way to work and the man reading in the evening before he beds the cows down gain from their time with the New Testament rarely depends on when it was established historically. Indeed, the many different translations and accompanying devotional aids to the New Testament belie any claim that the text has to be completely uniform and stable.

In the past two hundred years some kinds of Christianity have tried to make the New Testament an unchanging text for all times. The longer history of the

New Testament as a text in process challenges these brittle claims and encourages a more flexible relationship to the texts. It could very well be that the panic some Christians in the modern world have about the New Testament's stability has more to do with how overwhelming changes in life and society threaten their identities than whether the New Testament needs to be seen as something permanent and fixed. And it could be that the flexibility both the New Testament and its longer-term Christian readership have shown is a resource for the crisis-filled times in which we live.

How *A New New Testament* Came into Being

Neither the existing New Testament nor this *New New Testament* dropped from heaven into the waiting arms of humanity. Both were a part of a larger and halting process. *A New New Testament* came into being through a fledgling process, one I conceived of and engineered, so I know its origins better than anyone. However, readers should bring a critical perspective to my description of how this edition came into being; as one of its primary promoters I am not an objective party. Nevertheless, I lay out here the story of *A New New Testament*'s birth in the hope that as honest a description as possible will help readers see the merits and problems with this book.

Precedents to *A New New Testament*

It might be said that this is the first revision of Christian scriptures in the 1,500 years that the New Testament has been in existence. It certainly is the case that — to the best of my knowledge — no one has bound and published an explicitly alternative version of the New Testament.

Closer examination reveals, however, that in the past thousand years there are some near likenesses. Perhaps most blatant — although almost entirely unknown in Europe and the Americas — is the reality that official Syrian and Ethiopian Christianity has never had the same New Testament as the West. Nor do many people know that Martin Luther, the father of the Protestant Reformation, tried to change the contents of the New Testament as a part of his leadership in Protestant beginnings in the sixteenth century. Luther tried unsuccessfully to remove books from the New Testament, and he succeeded in removing a number of books from the existing Protestant "Old Testament," opening a still-existent rift with Catholicism, Episcopalianism, and Eastern Orthodoxy.

To the best of my knowledge, the idea for something like this volume was first proposed by the late Robert Funk, one of the leading New Testament scholars of the second half of the twentieth century, the founder of the Jesus Seminar, and the executive director of the Westar Institute. Several times in the late 1990s Funk proposed to groups of scholars meeting regularly at the Westar Institute that, subsequent to the institute's work with the Jesus Seminar, Westar should proceed to form and produce a new New Testament.

According to Funk, such a plan would involve removing some books from the existing New Testament that in his eyes were objectionable and adding a number of recently discovered documents. In November 1996, Funk hosted a Westar meeting in New Orleans simultaneous to a meeting of the Society of Biblical Literature, the guild of biblical scholars in North America, where he reiterated his proposal for a new New Testament. At that meeting Harvard biblical scholar Karen King gave a presentation called "Christianity Without Canon." Funk invited King to chair such an effort to form and publish a new New Testament but she declined.* As one of some one hundred "fellows" of Westar, I attended that New Orleans gathering and at least two semiannual meetings of the Westar, where the new New Testament proposal was discussed. For reasons still unclear to me, the Canon Seminar ceased to meet or exist.†

So, this book is somewhat related to Funk's initial idea. It is also substantially different. Funk not only proposed adding new documents to the New Testament but also — with ambitions perhaps not unlike those of Martin Luther — wanted to remove some books; this book keeps all of the traditional New Testament in place. Funk's criteria for inclusion were completely based on the authority of late twentieth-century liberal biblical scholarship. He explicitly denied any church authority in establishing what the contents of his new New Testament would be and at least advertised that he was not interested in its religious use. Funk wanted the new New Testament to debunk conventional Christian authority, to be a vehicle for the truth of scholarship. Hence for him, the project would create *the*‡ new New Testament, in contrast to this book, which is called *A New New Testament* and encourages others to actively consider and produce yet further new New Testaments. *A New New Testament* was formed by the decisions of a group made up of a majority of church authorities and a minority of scholars and non-Christian spiritual leaders. This relates to the central difference between the project Funk envisioned and this one in your hands: this *New New Testament* is primarily a collection that is meant to act as a resource for the spiritual curiosity and development of a wide public. Those of us who put *A New New Testament* together acknowledge that it will have scholarly value but have placed the central emphasis on the spiritual value of reading the existing New Testament alongside some of the powerful recently discovered documents.

---

* The Westar Institute did form a "Canon Seminar," which lasted for a bit over a year, and King participated in at least two of the meetings.

† Although the Westar Institute continues to meet semiannually even now, its Canon Seminar and the new New Testament idea were not pursued after 1999. Funk died in 2005.

‡ Occasionally Funk used the title *A New New Testament* but tended to prefer *The New New Testament*.

The Initial Steps Toward *A New New Testament*

Since the early 1990s I have been leading groups in churches, colleges, and semi-naries around the country in studying books in the existing New Testament to-gether with recently discovered documents. My main resources for these studies have been my training as a professor and pastor in teaching ancient Christian texts and my deep appreciation for the scholarship of Karen King.

My motivation in presenting this material over these two decades has mostly been a response to the massive spiritual discontent and seeking I have witnessed among a broad spectrum of the North American public. This is not a particular in-sight of mine; it is commonplace to note that in our time huge sections of the pop-ulation are disillusioned with conventional religious life and thirsting for new spir-itual vitality. As a religious leader, I have taken this discontent and spiritual search seriously, trying to listen carefully to people and to notice where I myself also ex-hibit similar discontent and desire for something different.

As I have listened, it has become clear to me that this spiritual crisis is so exten-sive that there is no one simple solution for it. I am still and always in the middle of discerning ways to respond to what I experience as a spiritual search of real in-tegrity among a great many people in North America. Yet, it is clear that the many groups I have encountered have regularly been reassured and inspired by reading the new and old documents from the first 175 years of Christianity together; that is, one way of breaking new ground for those in spiritual crisis or search is by adding material to their discussion through offering these new and old documents along-side one another.

The results of these groups have been quite consistent. Most people are sur-prised that the new documents exist. Occasionally a few people in these groups are afraid of them. Because I present the new documents as near relatives of those in the existing New Testament, participants are engaged by both the similarities and the differences between the old and the new. In hundreds of such sessions, a near consensus has emerged. People delight in the ways that reading the recently discovered and already canonized documents together make for new spiritual in-sights. Generally these groups find themselves deeply relieved to have met what seem like long-lost relatives of their inner search without needing to reject much of the New Testament they respect. The experience of leading these studies has pushed me to conceive of *A New New Testament* in the way it has now come to exist.

Refining the Vision

As I imagined more details about this project, four values and strategies became clear:

1. This *New New Testament* would not romanticize all the new documents and condemn the existing New Testament. In keeping with experience, the book

would create an extended and multilateral dialogue among the new and the old documents by putting them all in the same Testament, therefore allowing them, in this format, to have similar and shared authority.

2. Both the spiritual and intellectual aspects of putting all these documents together would be honored. The goals of the book would not be reduced to just educating the public about how these books belong together. Equally important would be ways that the book could elicit spiritual growth and attachment to this new combination of texts from the beginnings of Christianity.

3. This book would not claim to be *The* New New Testament. While it would emphasize the need for new kinds of twenty-first-century spirituality, it would not propose that this collection was a final authority, the perfect Word of God, or the scholarly solution to everybody's petty religious fixations.

4. The selection of which books would be added to *A New New Testament* could not be made by me alone. Whatever my wisdom is on this subject, it could not be sufficient for such a monumental task.

The contents of *A New New Testament* needed to be selected in a manner similar to the way historical Christianity made many of its crucial choices: by a collective decision-making process. Selecting which books would belong to *A New New Testament* ultimately lay with a council of spiritual leaders of national rank. These council members — but not the books added — were to be selected according to criteria I determined, but those criteria were meant to honor how such large decisions have been made by Christians and other religious movements in the past.

The primary criterion was that the majority of the "council" be spiritual leaders of national rank from within Christianity. The second criterion, less central than the first, was that a minority of scholars of early Christian literature and the New Testament be invited. Each of these scholars was a person invested in the spiritual development and search of the public at large. Finally, as I knew from my own pastoral experience that many spiritual seekers of our day find great comfort in spiritual leaders from outside Christianity, several nationally known non-Christian spiritual leaders were also invited.

Sifting the Many Recently Discovered Documents

Between April and August 2011, I recruited twenty spiritual leaders for the council.* Naming the selecting body a "council" was meant to echo playfully the his-

---

* In the early fall of 2011, one of the twenty, a Roman Catholic bishop, rescinded his willingness to serve on the council because of poor health.

torical decision-making process of various church bodies over many centuries, in which various leaders came together to address crucial issues. In many ways, this name proved very appropriate in that its members were indeed important national spiritual leaders from a variety of backgrounds and experience. The term *council* was perhaps a slight misnomer in that although many of its members were functioning authorities in various denominations and institutions, they were not official delegates from those organizations, and, to a certain extent, the final number of nineteen members made it considerably smaller than many of the historical church councils.

While I was recruiting the council, I also began my own sifting process, so that the council would not have to work through a burdensome number of those hundred documents. By early July I had decided on approximately forty documents, which eventually became forty-three (several were eliminated due to a lack of good manuscripts, and several were added by council members). My criteria for deciding which of these documents to recommend to the council were mostly technical. Documents for which there are only one or two extant copies that were too fragmentary or full of holes would not be considered. Although dating when these documents were written is a very difficult, controversial, and inexact process, I decided not to include any documents for which no scholar had made a case that they were composed between 25 and 175 CE. I chose 175 CE because this was the latest date any scholars have thought the documents of the existing New Testament had been written; 25 CE is the earliest possible date for similar reasons.

While the council was being recruited, Karen King — who was one of the first to be invited and to accept a position — urged me to think about having a smaller group of six to ten people sift the documents down from forty-three to twenty or so in a first stage, before a larger group made the final cut. This seemed wise and a good use of people's time. So as the council came together, I formed a kind of subcommittee that would narrow down the group of texts to be considered. As the summer progressed, we set up a ten-person sub-council meeting in central New Jersey for October 2011, and a full council meeting in New Orleans for February 2012.

Recruiting the council was a very surprising process. My goal was to recruit as wide a spectrum of mostly Christian religious leaders as possible. As I began to formulate a list of potential candidates, the two main requirements were that each person have substantial experience in leading significant portions of the American public and that each of them be able to work collegially without needing to call too much attention to himself or herself in the process. To my surprise, almost everyone I approached was not simply willing but enthusiastic about participating. Some people were not available on the necessary dates, and a very few did not like the idea at all. Of the four who did not accept my invitation for reasons other than scheduling problems, three were evangelical Christian leaders who opposed

Final Three Stages of the 2011–12 Council's Selection of Additions to A New New Testament

A sub-council met in October 2011 to consider forty-three different documents for inclusion in *A New New Testament*. The sub-council was asked to reduce this group to somewhere between fifteen and twenty documents. Here are the initial forty-three:

The Acts of Paul and Thecla
1 Clement
2 Clement
The Demonstration of Apostolic Preaching from Irenaeus
The Dialogue of the Savior
The Diary of Perpetua
The Discourse on the Eighth and the Ninth
The First Revelation (Apocalypse) of James
The Gospel of Judas
The Gospel of Mary (Magdalene)
The Gospel of Nicodemus I
The Gospel of Peter
The Gospel of Philip
The Gospel of Thomas
The Gospel of Truth
Ignatius to the Ephesians
Ignatius to the Romans
Ignatius to the Smyrneans
The Infancy Gospel of James
The Letter of the Apostles
The Letter of the Martyrs of Lyons
The Letter of Peter to Philip

The Martyrdom of Polycarp
The Odes of Solomon
On Baptism from Tertullian
On the Origin of the World
On Prayer from Tertullian
The Prayer of the Apostle Paul
The Prayer of Thanksgiving
The Reality of the Rulers (The Hypostatis of the Archons)
The Revelation (Apocalypse) of Adam
The Revelation (Apocalypse) of Paul
The Second Revelation (Apocalypse) of James
The Secret Revelation of James
The Secret Revelation of John
The Sentences of Sextus
The Teaching of the Twelve Apostles (Didache)
The Testimony of Truth
The Three Forms of First Thought
The Thought of Norea
The Thunder: Perfect Mind
The Treatise on the Resurrection
The Wisdom of Solomon

The nineteen documents that were chosen by the sub-council in October from the thirty-nine given them were:

The Acts of Paul and Thecla
1 Clement
The Diary of Perpetua
The First Revelation of James
The Gospel of Mary

The Gospel of Philip
The Gospel of Thomas
The Gospel of Truth
The Infancy Gospel of James
The Letter of the Martyrs of Lyon

The Letter of Peter to Philip
The Odes of Solomon
The Prayer of the Apostle Paul
The Prayer of Thanksgiving
The Secret Revelation of James

The Secret Revelation of John
The Teaching of the Twelve
  Apostles
The Thunder: Perfect Mind
The Treatise on the Resurrection

The ten documents chosen by the full New Orleans Council as additions to *A New New Testament* were:

The Acts of Paul and Thecla
The Gospel of Mary
The Gospel of Thomas
The Gospel of Truth
The Letter of Peter to Philip

The Odes of Solomon
The Prayer of the Apostle Paul
The Prayer of Thanksgiving
The Secret Revelation of John
The Thunder: Perfect Mind

the idea of adding material to the New Testament, and one was a liberal Christian church leader who thought that any such book should include documents from all of Christian history rather than just documents from the first two centuries.

I wanted the council to include leaders from a wide range of Christian perspectives. It eventually included Presbyterians (two), Roman Catholics (three), Episcopalians (three), United Methodists (four), United Church of Christ members (two), a Lutheran, two rabbis, and one representative of yogic traditions. Eleven members are ordained clergy and two are women religious. Nine are women and ten are men. Six are people of color. Two are bishops. Two are or were the head of their national denomination, and one is the national executive for a primary office of his denomination. Six are scholars and graduate teachers of New Testament.* Perhaps the greatest thrill and ensuing disappointment in this recruiting process was when both a Roman Catholic bishop and a Muslim professor agreed to be the twentieth member of the council, and both had to resign for health reasons.

The Sub-council Meeting

Nine of the ten sub-council members convened in New Jersey in October as a subcommittee and succeeded in winnowing the field of documents to nineteen. This meeting also expanded several dimensions of the process. In order to make sure that my initial reduction of the number of documents from about one hundred to forty-three did not do any of the documents an injustice, all members of the coun-

---

* See pages 555–558 for the names and brief biographical sketches of the members of the New Orleans Council.

cil — whether they served on the subcommittee or not — were invited to nominate additional documents, with the following rules: any document not in my list could be added if three council members supported the change, and if the document dated from the time period established of 25 to 175 CE.

As the sub-council deliberated on which of the proposed forty-three books to eliminate from consideration for the next round of full council consideration, it indeed did pay close attention to my request that a primary reason for something to be in *A New New Testament* be its spiritual value for twenty-first-century readers; each of them had different ideas about what was spiritually important for the twenty-first century. One other criterion, which was not supplied or suggested by me, emerged as the sub-council meetings proceeded. The sub-council preferred books with more intact manuscripts. This criterion applied especially to a number of manuscripts from Nag Hammadi, which were the only existing manuscripts of particular writings and as manuscripts were damaged enough not to have very complete texts. This sub-council found itself disagreeing on two other issues regarding criteria. Some were drawn to choose texts that focused on the figure of Jesus, while others were not bothered by texts that had less mention of him. Similarly, there was no consensus on whether it mattered that a text was earlier and closer to the time of Jesus or not.

The sub-council heard a strong argument from Karen King that the Diary of Perpetua be considered for inclusion, but the text violated our date boundaries; it was clearly written sometime between 200 and 210 CE. King argued that the real possibility that the Diary of Perpetua was the first early Christian document to be written by a woman and was a gripping firsthand account of a Christian martyr were important enough factors for *A New New Testament* to be opened to it. In our discussion I opposed its inclusion on the basis that it was too late (beyond 175 CE) to be considered a contemporary writing of the traditional New Testament. King's argument was persuasive to a number of the sub-council, and the document easily received the three votes needed.

But the sub-council also agreed that this addition of Perpetua obliged us to consider a number of other well-known documents in the period 175 to 210 CE. The sub-council subsequently considered Tertullian's "On Prayer" and "On Baptism" and Irenaeus's "The Demonstration of the Apostolic Teaching" from the period 176 to 210 CE. None of these documents received the necessary three votes from the sub-council to be considered candidates for inclusion in *A New New Testament*. This made for more integrity in the council's process in that there was no special privilege given to the Diary of Perpetua. One other document was added at the New Jersey meeting by three supporting votes, and it was well within the earlier time frame of composition. This document, the Infancy Gospel of James, was proposed by council members because of its unique and early stories of Jesus's birth and childhood.

This sub-council meeting, the first stage of spiritual leaders from around the country creating *A New New Testament,* effectively cut the potential number of documents down to nineteen choices for the New Orleans gathering in February 2012. At the start of the October meeting, I was happy that such important religious leaders and scholars were coming together for this purpose but was curious to see what levels of interest, intimidation, and lack of ease this group would bring with it. The biggest surprise was not just the way the group demanded to have its own say about the results, but the unmitigated passion for the task held by all.

The Full Council Meeting — New Orleans, February 2012

The full council met in New Orleans and decided to add ten more books to *A New New Testament.* These books are (in order, from highest number of votes received to lowest): the Gospel of Mary, The Thunder: Perfect Mind, the Gospel of Thomas, the Odes of Solomon, the Prayer of Thanksgiving, the Acts of Paul and Thecla, the Gospel of Truth, the Prayer of the Apostle Paul, the Letter of Peter to Philip, and the Secret Revelation of John.[*][†]

The council deliberations were amiable, intense, and peppered with considerable disagreement. Even in their relatively short time together, these leaders developed strong bonds to each other and to their common task. I commissioned the council to give primary attention to the spiritual value of documents for twenty-first-century North America when weighing their decisions; they had been selected because they were all people with extensive leadership experience in deciding on or recommending reading to a large public for its spiritual welfare. I refused to set special values or criteria for the group, implicitly acknowledging that such a range of spiritual leaders would have different criteria.

The council conversations placed a high value on spiritual inspiration and formation for twenty-first-century readers, and — as at the October sub-council meeting — there were quite different ideas among the council members as to what is important for spiritual growth in the twenty-first century. But the entire council found itself agreeing strongly that the need for twenty-first-century spiritual nurture would be helped by the addition of the prayer-filled documents of the Prayer of the Apostle Paul, the Prayer of Thanksgiving, and the Odes of Solomon.

The New Orleans Council focused a great deal of attention on what the various

---

[*] Three other documents were nearly added: the Treatise on the Resurrection, the Teaching of the Twelve Apostles, and the Secret Revelation of James.

[†] In July of 2011 — before the council was formed or met — I had made a list for myself of the books I personally would wish to have included in *A New New Testament.* That list was as follows: the Teaching of the Twelve Apostles, the Gospel of Mary, the Gospel of Thomas, The Thunder: Perfect Mind, the Odes of Solomon, the Gospel of Peter, the Sentences of Sextus, the Prayer of Thanksgiving, the Prayer of the Apostle Paul, the Treatise on the Resurrection, 1 Clement, and the Reality of the Rulers. Six of my list were eventually chosen by the council, and six were not.

early Christ documents could say to the culture wars of twenty-first-century North America relative to sexual orientation, women's rights, and abortion. In these discussions there were very strong differences. The differences were not drawn along the lines of the culture wars; everyone had agreed to be a part of a project whose purpose was to expand notions of the Christian canon, which made for a generally liberal consensus in terms of our time. Nevertheless, there was stark disagreement on what documents would help twenty-first-century readers in the debates. Documents such as the Gospel of Mary, The Thunder: Perfect Mind, and the Acts of Paul and Thecla, all of which feature strong feminine voices, were often promoted in discussion as part of a commitment to advocacy for women. On the other hand, the debate was strongest among like-minded members in terms of whether the fascinating pictures of how very early Christ followers lived together according to the Teaching of the Twelve Apostles was important enough to choose it despite its ban on abortion. This document was — in two close votes — kept out of *A New New Testament* on these grounds.

Despite some harrowing debates and not having known each other prior to that October, by the end of the council meeting in New Orleans in February, this group of national leaders found themselves very attached to one another. They left New Orleans deeply committed to a book that almost none of them had heard of a scant ten months beforehand.

4

What's New in A New New Testament: *Claiming a New Vision of the Early Christ Movements*

There is newness around every corner in this book. Some of it is obvious, but some of it flows powerfully below the surface. There is much genuinely new content in *A New New Testament*. There is an astonishing marriage of traditional and fresh ideas. There are startling challenges to rethink how the New Testament and Christianity itself came into being. There are beautiful prayers, stories, and proposals to nourish today's thirst for spirituality that are both grounded in tradition and new to almost everyone's experience.

While engaging all this obvious freshness, it is important to notice the channels below the surface. Going deeper into the implications and integrative potential of *A New New Testament* promises additional resources and growth. Most powerful in this regard is the possibility of claiming for the twenty-first century new meanings inherent in the first- and second-century Christ movements.

A New New Testament *Puts More Pieces of Early Christianity Together for the Twenty-first-Century Public's Spiritual Growth*

A New New Testament is an ambitious attempt to enrich the spiritual experience of reading the New Testament. By giving some of the new books equal status alongside the traditional New Testament contents, it provides a wider spectrum of beliefs, practices, teachings, and stories and focuses new attention on them by placing them alongside the traditional gospels and letters.

The first additional dimension of spiritual renewal in reading *A New New Testament* is that its more expansive collection reduces the tendency to think that there is one right way to believe, grow, and practice. This allows readers to engage the spiritual dimensions of early Christianity with somewhat less pressure to rule out all but one way of Christian practice and belief. It allows multiple points of view to coexist at the very heart of Christianity.

This appreciation must be qualified in two ways. The traditional New Testament has a reputation — from the ways some people and churches have used it — of being a book that promotes just one way to believe and practice, but in fact it has much more flexibility and breadth of practice and belief than are usually credited. On the other side, we also need to recognize that some of the "new" documents included in *A New New Testament* sometimes participate in tendencies to judge others and accuse them of false belief and practice.

A second additional element of spiritual renewal inherent in this book consists of the way its various pictures of early Christianity end up being too wide and complicated to support the idea that orthodox Christianity was foreordained to become the dominant force of Christianity. This new and even more diverse collection contradicts the "master narrative" — the assumed story of Christian beginnings. In the way it is told, this "master narrative" suggests strongly that how traditional Christianity turned out was inevitable, ordained by God. But *A New New Testament*'s more diverse picture of Christian beginnings supports the possibility that Christian practice and belief in our day might birth new and different ways of seeing God, morality, worship, human sexuality, and work. Again, in actuality the traditional New Testament also has rather impressive diversity, but through the lens of the "master narrative" it became an unfortunate and inaccurate symbol of inevitable Christian unanimity. The tension between *A New New Testament* and the "master narrative" clears a spiritual space in our day for authentic new developments in Christianity.

Some Brief Examples of What Happens When New and Traditional Documents Are Read Together

When one reads *A New New Testament,* the combination of documents sparks a wide range of fresh perspectives. In some cases these new views are eye-popping in what they bring to one's imagination about what happened in the first two centuries. In other cases, the additional information simply tweaks the older picture a bit. At least as important as how this combination of documents changes one's understanding of early Christian history is how it prompts new meanings for life in the twenty-first century. A few examples demonstrate these possibilities.

How Early Christians Worshiped

There are some brief glimpses in the existing New Testament of what the worship of early Christians looked like. It seems fairly clear that many early Christian worship gatherings happened around an extended and festive meal. And in the traditional New Testament books of Ephesians and Colossians there are instructions to "sing psalms and hymns and inspired songs" at such gatherings. But it is not nearly as clear what those "songs" were, or what happened at the meal.

The four books of the Odes of Solomon, the massive collection of new psalmlike Christ-centered songs now included in *A New New Testament,* render this picture much more vivid and interesting. The Odes of Solomon put real and lively imagery into the vague phrase about early Christians singing together. Forty-one different odes provide great detail about what some early Christians sang together:

I poured forth praise to the Lord,
Because I was his own.
I will speak his holy ode,
Because my heart is with him.
For his lyre is in my hands,
And the odes of his rest will not be silent. (26:1–3)

My love is the Lord; because of this, I sing to him. (16:3)

Look! The Lord is our mirror, open your eyes and see them in him. (13:1)

Sometimes those singing sing as if they are Christ. In this section, Christ is singing of his having been freed from prison:

I opened the doors which were shut.
I destroyed the bars of iron,
Since my own irons had boiled and melted away before me.
Nothing appeared closed to me anymore,
Because I was the opening of everything. (17:9–11)

The imagery in some cases at the same time sounds traditional and wildly different:

The cup is the Son,
The Father is the one who has been milked,
And the holy Spirit milked him,
Because his breasts had become full. . . . (19:2–3)

Not only does reading the Odes of Solomon alongside Ephesians and Colossians conjure more clearly the scene of early Christ people singing together, it also expands imagery for twenty-first-century prayers. Here there are definitely echoes of traditional ideas of the Father, Son, and holy Spirit, even while sounding very new notes of the Father feeding the Christ people with milk from his breast. The odes expand both understanding of the early Christians and the spiritual possibilities for today.

Most straightforwardly, their psalmlike quality combined with their original poetry enables them to serve as prayer in our time, as illustrated by the following excerpts:

Like the wings of doves over their chicks,
And as the mouths of the chicks toward their mouths,

So also are the wings of the spirit over my heart.
My heart delights and jumps
Like an infant jumps joyously in its mother's womb. (28:1–2)

Or

Come all of you thirsty ones, and take a drink
And be soothed by the spring of the Lord
Because it is beautiful and clean
And restores the self.
Indeed its waters are much sweeter than honey,
And the honeycomb of bees does not compare with it,
Because it emerged from the lips of the Lord
And the name comes from the heart of the Lord. (30:2–5)

As these odes were almost certainly sung in the worship of the early Christ people, it is also quite easy to imagine twenty-first-century composers putting the words to music.

As spiritual practice, the odes, whose words often sound similar to biblical psalms, nonetheless also introduce a new tone in that very often it is Christ who is singing the song or prayer. For instance, in Ode 8, Christ sings (or says):

Hear the word of truth, and
Receive the knowledge of the Most High.
Your flesh may not understand what I say to you,
Nor your clothing what I show you.
Keep my mystery, you who are kept by it.
Keep my faith, you who are kept by it. (8:8–10)

In other words, the odes that the early Christians sang were words that they understood Christ to be singing with them.

In many ways, this is a contribution to spiritual practice for the twenty-first century. To understand one's own spiritual expression as a joining with Christ in song adds a number of layers of meaning. In the particular case of Ode 8, the sense of early Christians having some truth and faith to impart is complemented and reinforced in their joining Christ in song. So not only do the Odes of Solomon provide new "Christian" psalms from the first or second century, they furnish an additional way of relating to Christ by singing along with him.

Similarly, other "new" literature in this *New New Testament* expands the brief descriptions of prayers and proclamations about the early Christian meal. In the traditional New Testament picture of the early Christians eating together, often — but not always — the "body" and "blood" of Christ are mentioned. The Prayer of Thanksgiving in this book provides these powerful words of prayer during the meal, completely fresh to Christians of our day:

O light of life,
we have known you.
O womb of all that grows,
we have known you.
O womb pregnant with the nature of the Father,
we have known you.
O never-ending endurance of the Father who gives birth,
so we worship your goodness.
One wish we ask:
we wish to be protected in knowledge.
One protection we desire:
that we not stumble in this life. (7–12)

Here neither Jesus's last supper nor the imagery of body and blood are evoked as prayers around the early Christian bread and cup. Instead, in this meal prayer, the sharing of the bread and cup is experienced as a birth from the womb of God. Without necessarily eliminating the imagery of body and blood, this prayer opens up both a more diverse image of early Christian worship and evocative language for Christian communion today. Or, more expansively, the existence of first- and second-century communion prayers that do not tell the story of the last supper or use "body" and "blood" vocabulary could inspire twenty-first-century people to compose additional and different prayers for their sharing of bread and cup.

The Great "I Am" of Early Christianity

In the Hebrew scriptures, God is revealed to Moses in the burning bush as "I am," "I am who I am," or "I am the one who is" (depending on how one translates the Hebrew in Exodus 3). Here God as the great "I am" can be understood as the one in whose being all other being exists or the one who is being itself.

Some very early Christian traditions seem to have borrowed this vocabulary about the divine one who reveals "himself" and applied it to Jesus. The Gospel of John has Jesus speaking as a great "I am." Throughout this gospel, Jesus says things like

I am the bread of life. (6:35)

I am the way, and the truth, and the life. (14:6)

I am the good shepherd. (10:11)

I am the true vine. (15:1)

I am the light of the world. (8:12)

Even while he is portrayed as a human being who weeps, is betrayed and crucified, Jesus is the great "I am" in the Gospel of John. Instead of making Jesus an inaccessible figure, he embodies all that is — a vine growing, a piece of bread, even experiences of loss and pain.

In a similar way, in the Gospel of Thomas, Jesus says: "I am the light which is above them all, I am the all. The all has come forth from me, and all has split open before me. Lift the stone, you will find me there. Split the piece of wood, I am there" (77:1–2).

These parts of early Christianity saw in Jesus the great "I am" in which bread, light, shepherd, a rock, the suffering human, a piece of wood, and God's own self were found. In some ways, Jesus's very vulnerable self was the occasion to find God luminescent in the ordinary dimensions of life.

The work in *A New New Testament* that seems to celebrate this intersection of the divine, the human, and the rest of the universe perhaps even more than the gospels of John and Thomas is The Thunder: Perfect Mind. Here the "I am" voice persists throughout almost the entire poem. Some excerpts illustrate how Thunder identifies the self-revealing God with suffering and especially dimensions of women's experience:

> I was sent out from power . . . (1:1)
>
> I am the first and the last
> I am she who is honored and she who is mocked
> I am the whore and the holy woman . . . (1:5)
>
> I am the mother and the daughter . . . (1:6)
>
> I am humiliation and pride . . . (2:7)
>
> I am security and I am fear . . . (2:9)
>
> I am she who is disgraced and she who is important . . . (2:10)
>
> Do not be arrogant to me when I am thrown to the ground . . . (2:12)
>
> Do not stare at me when I am thrown out among the condemned . . . (2:14)
>
> I am he whose image is multiple in Egypt
> And she who is without an image among the barbarians . . . (3:5)

This great "I am" never gives herself/himself a name, but the closeness of this "I am" to the crucified "I am" in the Gospel of John and the piece of wood in the Gospel of Thomas is striking, even suggesting a primarily feminine Jesus. The fascination of early Christians seeing the powerful and great "I am" in the crucified

Jesus or those thrown to the ground and condemned makes possible a new way of thinking about Jesus and life.

Some early followers of Jesus, then, seem to have been attracted and committed to Jesus as an "I am" in which what it means to be human and what it means to be divine come together. This is quite different from some kinds of later Christianity which emphasize the huge gulf between the almighty God and sinful humanity. There seems to have been in the first two centuries a sense that stories and teachings of Jesus helped people feel a part of the larger universe and a belonging in the great "I am" of God. It was a sense found in both the canonical Gospel of John and the noncanonical Gospel of Thomas and The Thunder: Perfect Mind. Reading Thomas and Thunder alongside of John both helps reclaim the canonical gospel and identifies the additional resources in the new documents.

There are many in our day who also celebrate the connectivity of all things and the ways everything and everyone belong in God. In addition to these early Christian documents, some medieval Christian mystics like Hildegard of Bingen and Meister Eckhart made this divine connectivity a part of their prayers and writings. Reading Thunder, Thomas, and John together opens up a vista of new kinds of meaning for twenty-first-century churches and the public at large.

Putting more pieces of early Christianity together allows for a more supple social body, a larger and even more creative set of traditions, and a richer and more complex view of the Christian history that gives birth to the dynamics of spiritual practice and faith today.

Some Perspective on Christian Identity Today and the History of Early Christianity

Not unlike some other groups in our time, Christians today often find a substantial part of who they are in who they are not; those of us who are Christians with some consistency find our identity in contrasting ourselves with others. Curiously, however, Christians' discovering themselves through their opposition to others rarely ends in all Christians being against the same thing. For instance, evangelical and liberal Christians seem to benefit mutually more from being against each other than from any core idea on which they agree or even by being against the same thing. Similarly, Catholics and Protestants often — although perhaps less now than in other ages — know who they are by saying they are not the "other."

This defining of what it means to be Christian by some others who are not the "right" kind of Christians is deeply entangled in the way Christians have told the story of how Christianity began. No matter how the story is told, it regularly includes as a central aspect how the "real" Christians distinguished themselves from the "not-so-real" Christians. The story is framed in different ways. The authentic early Christians believed one way and the phony ones another; the good early

Christians followed what Jesus really said while the false ones followed teachings that he really didn't say; the best early Christians said that the bread was the real body of Jesus, while the false ones said they just ate in memory of him (or vice versa).

One can find endless such distinctions about which early Christians were the real ones in the stories of Christian beginnings told by different people. It seems that telling a story of contested identities in early Christianity has been a help to contemporary Christians in sorting out who they are today relative to the many differences of the twenty-first century. The discrepancies among storytellers about which differences in early Christianity matter make it easy to see the inconsistencies of this approach. Ironically, however, when one looks at the way scholarly historians have told the "history" of early Christianity, it is equally inconsistent and unconsciously framed around the principle of some true early Christians and some false ones. Almost all these historians differ on what exactly made some early Christians authentic and others fraudulent. For some historians the crucial issue is who believed the "right" thing; for others it is which early Christians remained too Jewish or — on the other hand — which were not attached enough to Jewish ideas. For still others the difference that mattered was which Christians collaborated with the cruel Roman Empire and which resisted this empire.

It was these two persistent occurrences — the tendency of ancient and modern Christians to know who they are by virtue of who they are not and the ways historians of ancient Christianity kept repeating this same pattern in their scholarship — that prompted one leading scholar of early Christianity to a different way of thinking about the history of Christian beginnings which now serves as an important backdrop for the open-ended diversity visible in A New New Testament.

Rewriting the History of Early Christianity Without Canonical or Creedal Blinders

Many scholars of the past four generations have explored the impression that early Christ movements were far more diverse than the "master narrative" lets on. Indeed, it is much more common for historians of the first two centuries to characterize both these early Christ movements and the traditional New Testament as diverse.

The one scholar who has brought these ideas together with the massive new discoveries of early Christ movement literature in the past 150 years, especially Nag Hammadi, is Professor Karen King at Harvard Divinity School. Particularly in the past decade, King has published a series of books and articles that directly challenge the "master narrative" and invite a complete rethinking of Christianity's beginnings through the lens of the new literature.

Giving up on the task of differentiating the true early Christians from the false ones, King opts rather to "construct a more complete narrative that will reflect the particular interests and perspectives of diverse Christians engaged in experimentation, compromise, collaboration, and synthesis."* Key to such a task is that "when historians set aside the anachronistic classification of early Christian literature into orthodox and heretical forms, analyzing both the similarities and differences among the extant remains, then a much more complex picture emerges."†

For King, "Here is where the recent discovery of early Christian writings from Egypt is so utterly crucial. These writings are of inestimable importance in drawing aside the curtain of later perspectives behind which Christian beginnings lie, and exposing the vitality and diversity of early Christian life and reflection. They demonstrate that reading the story of Christian origins backwards through the lenses of canon and creed has given an account of formation of only one kind of Christianity, and even that one only partially."‡

King's approach does not assume that the New Testament is the privileged source of early Christian history and includes the many recently discovered early Christian documents, primarily — although not exclusively — from Nag Hammadi. Her books on *The Secret Revelation of John*, *The Gospel of Mary*, and *The Gospel of Judas* portray literature as providing important dimensions to early Christianity and are self-conscious projects in writing an overall history of early Christianity from a new perspective. It needs to be quickly added that in contrast to some other scholars of noncanonical literature and other popular romanticizations of this literature, King does not see noncanonical literature as exhibiting Christianities that are more valuable or authentic than the works in the New Testament. Rather, the point for her is that "[t]he multiformity of early Christianity becomes even more evident when we remove our canonical spectacles."§

King understands this to be a very large project. But it is one in which in addition to painstakingly technical linguistic and historical analyses of specific ancient texts are accomplished, she has already rendered some broad strokes of an emerging picture:

> We are only beginning to construct the pieces of a fuller and more accurate narrative of Christian beginnings. At this point I can only say that it will be a story of diverse groups of people engaged in the difficult business of working out what it means to be a Christian in a world of rapid change, increased intercultural contact, and dominated overall by Roman imperial power. The story will talk about the issues that concerned the first Christians, their differences of opinion, the debates they had, and the solutions they devised, both successes and failures. It will portray some of them as pretty

---

* *The Gospel of Mary Magdala: Jesus and the First Woman Apostle*, p. 168.
† Ibid., p. 156.
‡ Ibid., p. 157.
§ Ibid., p. 163.

radical social experimenters, and others as more willing to compromise with the values of the dominant culture. It will talk about the kind of communities they formed, about the utopian ideals of a loving God they nourished, and the burning desire for justice and for revenge that moved their imaginations.*

She does not pretend to chart all that happened. She sees the early way the Christ people governed as an experimentation "with a variety of formal arrangements, from relatively unstructured charismatic organizations to more fixed hierarchical orders." From the diversity in this book, we can see why she asserts that in some places "leadership was shared among men and women according to the movement of the Spirit in inspiring gifts of prophecy, teaching, healing, administration, and service, while in others it was much more patriarchal."†

It would be a mistake to think that King's rewriting of the history of early Christianity is simply an intellectual project intended to bring more diverse evidence to light. King herself is also concerned about how scholarly historical writings undergird Christians who claim their own identities through opposition to someone else's alleged heresy. So she rejects any pretense that she is objective, clearly stating that her purpose includes providing more contemporary ethical perspectives on the reading of early Christian texts than the conventional presentation of early Christian history has. In her readings of Christian beginnings, "[c]ontemporary Christians may gain new insights and resources for reflecting on what it means to be a Christian in a pluralistic world, and for addressing the pressing need to rethink the relationship of Christianity to Judaism, Islam, and other religious traditions in order to meet the demands for social well-being and justice."‡ Her new picture of Christian beginnings in relationship to the discovery of additional documents from the nascent Christ movements undergirds the twenty-first-century public's efforts to reclaim Christian beginnings for their own growth and development.

---

* *The Gospel of Mary Magdala,* p. 169.
† Ibid., p. 188.
‡ Ibid., p. 156.

5

Giving Birth to A New New Testament *and Retiring*[*] *the Idea of Gnosticism*

O NE OF THE STANDARD twenty-first-century responses to the additional books in *A New New Testament* is something like this: "Aren't these books gnostic?" and "Isn't gnosticism an early Christian heresy?" Such responses are serious ones that reflect interest in these discoveries and a level of awareness about early Christianity not held by everyone.

Unfortunately, at the same time it is becoming clearer that the notion of "gnosticism" is so flawed that it is of little or no use in understanding either the recent discoveries or Christian beginnings. Indeed, close examination of how the idea of "gnosticism" came to be shows that it is not an accurate way to characterize anything in early Christianity. Rather, according to an increasing range of scholars, it is a modern scholarly invention without sufficient basis in the documents of Christian beginnings. As it pertains so directly to books such as the Gospel of Thomas, the Gospel of Mary, The Thunder: Perfect Mind, the Secret Revelation of John, and the Letter of Peter to Philip, the new analysis of how the idea of "gnosticism" came to be and why it should be retired deserves some additional attention.

The process of labeling the documents as gnosticism and deciding what that means is complicated and subtle and has recently been untangled by two scholars of early Christianity. Both Karen King and Michael Williams, professor at the University of Washington, have independently authored detailed studies of what Williams calls the "dubious category" of gnosticism.

Their analysis goes like this:

Although the word *gnostic* was used throughout the ancient world, it did not connote a problematic belief. It had several different meanings. The late second-century Christian leader Clement of Alexandria, for instance, used *gnostic* to designate a Christian whose spiritual development had deepened significantly. Other ancient leaders often used *gnostic* to designate an opponent or "know-it-all." There is no use of the word *gnostic* to designate a certain kind of religious movement within or without Christianity. The word *gnosis* (the normal and main Greek word

---

[*] The notion of "retiring" the idea of "gnosticism" derives from the work of Karen King, most specifically in her book *What Is Gnosticism?*, pp. 218–36.

for "knowledge") meant a range of things, from practical knowledge to academic knowledge, but it hardly ever connoted something negative. Finally, the word *gnosticism,* supposedly the term for a harmful/heretical early Christian movement, did not exist at all in the world of early Christianity. It is only in significant hindsight that people have imagined such a movement or associated many of the newly discovered first- and second-century documents with it. So for King and Williams, it would be best, as King gently suggests, to "retire" the term *gnosticism,* as it was not a term any groups of early Christianity used for themselves or their opponents. And, although more than half of contemporary scholars of Christian beginnings still use the term, the various scholarly proposals of what "gnosticism" was do not come close to agreeing with one another.

Although Christians of various stripes have accused many rival groups of heresy from the second century until now, it was not until the seventeenth century that the word *gnosticism* was invented to describe a heretical early Christian movement. Henry More, an English Puritan author, university lecturer, and clergyperson in the mid- to late 1600s, was probably the first person to coin the term *gnosticism.* He did so not because he was particularly interested in ancient Christianity, but because he needed something heretical from early Christianity to compare with his seventeenth-century Catholic rivals. Although More wrote extensively on a range of spiritual, philosophical, and theological issues (but rarely on early Christianity), he may have written the term *gnosticism* only once. The idea that Catholicism was like an ancient Christian heresy was a small part of his broader anti-Catholic theme.

It is not clear how this passing remark from More became a later technical term for Western biblical scholars to use, but there is no trace of anyone responding to More's coinage in the seventeenth century. The term *gnosticism* first came into strong usage in the late 1800s; liberal biblical scholarship of that time began to make "gnosticism" into something significant for understanding early Christianity. A leading German theologian, church person, and biblical scholar, Adolf von Harnack, was one of the first to use the term as a central part of his explanation for how Christianity began. For Harnack, "gnosticism" was the strong effort, beginning in the early stages of the first century, to make the meaning of Jesus acceptable in terms of Greek civilization. As such, it was for him both an inevitable component of Christianity's success and a perversion of its original message.

In quick succession other theologians and biblical scholars — mostly liberal in their orientation — started using the term *gnosticism,* primarily to describe one of the main ways a harmful and perverting dimension of early Christianity took root. None of these scholars agreed with the others on the nature of the perversion, but they all did seem to like the term *gnosticism* as a label for this major unhealthy impulse within early Christianity. This trend has continued until the present day.

In the middle of the twentieth century this relatively technical proposal about gnosticism suddenly became much more important. In 1945 the Nag Hammadi collection of fifty-two early Christian documents was discovered; almost all of them were previously unknown. Some of the Nag Hammadi texts sounded a great deal like documents already in the New Testament. Some of these documents had similar messages but different forms. Others seemed to be quite like some things that Harnack and his successors had imagined. Still others were so new in their content or form that they simply confounded their readers.

Although it is not clear why, the Nag Hammadi documents were quite quickly and almost completely categorized by their translators as products of "gnosticism." Although now — nearly seventy years after the discovery — some scholars are beginning to rethink this thorough designation of all fifty-two documents as "gnostic," by and large Nag Hammadi and "gnosticism" have become practically synonyms for any of the public who know about them.

In part, of course, this quick generalization was due to the fact that "gnosticism" had always needed some evidence, and now — with Nag Hammadi — there were suddenly documents that sounded very different from what the "master narrative" termed "normative Christianity." And it is the case that some of the Nag Hammadi documents do resemble — in parts or as wholes — one or another of the descriptions of "gnosticism" produced over the past century.

Perhaps most telling about this rush to judge Nag Hammadi as equal to gnosticism is Christianity's persistent need to declare groups within its circle, but with different ideas, as heretics. The pervasiveness of this heresy-condemning characteristic in Christianity is especially evident when we notice that mostly liberal Christian biblical scholars, who ostensibly do not picture themselves as dogmatic, nevertheless produced the idea of "gnosticism" in early Christianity. For better or worse, those of us who are Christians seem often to be our most articulate selves when we are defending ourselves against the beliefs or practices of other Christians.

The real loss to the public lies in not being able to access additional resources during the past 120 years of spiritual crises and lack of resources. It is vital to remember how traumatized Christianity is in our day, and how much new perspectives and new resources might help those attached to it. Christian vitality is undercut from a variety of perspectives. Christian self-understanding has been deeply wounded by the prevalence of materialist lifestyles that reduce what matters so often to what one possesses. Church corruption has caused many people — Christian and non-Christian alike — to question the integrity of the faith. Many Christians live in constant worry that scientific discovery may somehow discredit Christian tradition. The social crises of our day continue to destabilize what people can claim in Christianity. So the bogus production of the idea that all these new documents are "gnostic" and therefore irrelevant or evil has dealt a serious blow to how Christians can make sense of and celebrate their heritage and the resources of early Christianity. In doing so, those continuing to speak of gnosticism have limited the possibility of twenty-first-century seekers using the newly discovered documents as resources with which to think about the many crises of our day.

Gnosticism Becomes Fashionable

Despite the flawed thinking about the existence of "gnosticism" and the way it has become attached to Christian ideas of heresy, something quite unexpected has happened. Even as many Christians have settled into a vague worry about the dangers of "gnosticism," "gnosticism" itself has actually become popular in portions of the public and even around the edges of Christianity itself.

More than fifty national and international religious organizations now exist for the promotion and coordination of gnostic religion. Nearly one thousand local gnostic organizations are easily counted. Many of these organizations call themselves "churches" or "religious orders," but very few, if any, seem to be interested in identifying themselves as "Christian." One might say that "gnosticism" has become a budding new religion,* mostly in the United States but to some extent in Europe and Australia. The popularity of these groups has increased substantially since the discovery and translation of the Nag Hammadi documents. Ironically, many of these groups make very similar — but dubious — claims to the Christian opponents of so-called gnosticism that the fifty-two Nag Hammadi documents represent a unified set of beliefs that are alternatives to Christianity. The difference is that these gnostic churches find solace in the idea that there was a unified ancient religious movement called "gnosticism."

There are at least two main historical sources of this new "gnostic religion." The first is a set of spiritual movements from the late nineteenth and early twentieth centuries. Ironically, the second source is a preeminent scholar of early Christianity, Professor Elaine Pagels of Princeton University, whose popular publications have focused on introducing the Nag Hammadi documents to the public, but who has no ambition to found or support a new religion.

---

* A small list of groups adhering to some kind of religious affiliation with gnosticism includes Gnostic Druid Fellowship, Gnostic Essene Fellowship, Gnostic Peace Fellowship, Gnostic Shaman Fellowship, Gnostic Society of Initiates, Gnostic Yoga Fellowship, Golden Temple of Gnostic Wisdom, Ecclesia Gnostica, Ecclesia Gnostica Catholica, Ageac-Gnosis and Esotericism, Ecclesia Gnostica Aeterna, Christian Gnostic Fellowship, Ecclesia Gnostica Mysteriorum, Gnostic Institute of Anthropology, North American College of Gnostic Bishops, the Apostolic Johannite Church, the Gnosis Archive, and l'Eglise Gnostique.

Modern Spiritual Movements and "Gnosticism"

In late nineteenth- and early twentieth-century Europe and North America, dissatisfaction with Christianity and the discovery of Buddhism and Hinduism prompted a range of spiritual and intellectual movements. By and large these movements were critical of Christian churches in their time but generally leaned favorably toward the teachings of Jesus and his early followers. These new movements then began to appeal to Eastern religious teachings and practice as a new way of becoming less dependent on Christian churches and more open to spiritual and intellectual integrity.

Two of the more successful and influential of these phenomena were the theosophical organizations and the anthroposophical movement. Both enjoyed significant success in the United States and elsewhere. And both movements explicitly styled themselves as successors to the ancient tradition of "gnosticism." They were the first to find public success by associating with what they claimed to be "ancient gnosticism."

Although not the only one, Madame Helena Blavatsky was perhaps the most prominent founder of theosophical organizations around the world. In 1875 in New York City, after having become an American citizen, she cofounded with Henry Olcott the Theosophical Society in America. Blavatsky herself used the terms *gnosis, gnostic,* and perhaps *gnosticism* in entirely positive references. She understood gnostics/gnosticism to be an early mystical expression of the first several centuries of Jesus traditions that actually corresponded to Hindu teachings.

A parallel, and related, movement began in the same period. Born in Austria in 1861, Rudolf Steiner became an editor, joined the theosophical movement for a while, in the early twentieth century broke with theosophy, and founded his own movement called the Anthroposophical Society. Anthroposophy was birthed out of the spiritual impulses of the German poet and philosopher Johann Wolfgang von Goethe. Although somewhat critical of conventional Christianity, unlike theosophy, anthroposophy has developed strong connections to Christ traditions and churches.

Steiner himself was an avid student of what he called "gnosis." He had a central mystical experience of Christ, and until his death in 1925 he studied the Christian theologians and church historians concerning early Christianity. He lectured about "gnosis," the "gnostic" perspective, and "gnosticism"; and he related gnosticism more closely to early Christianity than Blavatsky did in her concentration on Eastern religion.

The Late-Twentieth-Century Books of Elaine Pagels

Almost certainly the biggest cause of the religious popularity of "gnosticism" in our day comes from a contemporary scholar of early Christianity, Elaine Pagels.

It is probably not an overstatement to say that Pagels has influenced religion in America more directly than any New Testament scholar in the past fifty years. Her book *The Gnostic Gospels,* written in 1979 and still selling briskly, transformed much public consciousness about the discovery of the Nag Hammadi collection in Egypt.

Much of this powerful shift had to do with her subtle, but thorough, challenge to the strong negative impression of Nag Hammadi and other noncanonical early Christian literature. Outside of the anthroposophical and theosophical movements, it was mostly Pagels who opened an avenue to the Nag Hammadi documents as serious spiritual literature of our day, all without ever really indicating what her own spiritual relationship to them was. In crafting this portrait of Nag Hammadi as "a new perspective,"* she provided mainstream credentials for the twentieth-century version of spiritual seekers beyond conventional Christian norms.

Pagels's success had to do with her framing Nag Hammadi as a unified "gnostic" point of view sympathetic with liberal religious sentiments of the late twentieth century enhanced by her straightforward and well-written information about the discoveries and the first generation of study of them. She portrayed Nag Hammadi in tension with church authority but in sympathy with twentieth-century liberal religious sentiments.

She portrays these "Gnostic Gospels" (her general term for Nag Hammadi and a few other documents) as being close in message to Eastern religion.† Although Pagels was not as speculative as Madame Blavatsky one hundred years before, her portrait of a unified "gnosticism" as resembling Eastern traditions that was so attractive to twentieth-century spiritual seekers had the advantage of both her scholarly status and the more grounded information she provided.

Pagels offers contrasts between orthodox Christians "unanimous both in proclaiming Christ's passion and death and in affirming martyrdom"‡ and "Gnostic sources. . . [that] are more complex."§ Such a juxtaposition offered great consolation from the "Gnostic Gospels" to liberal twentieth-century readers tired of a soulless church structure. This framing of the content of Nag Hammadi both as "Gnostic Gospels" and as in opposition to "orthodox leaders" who suppress "gnos-

---

* *The Gnostic Gospels,* p. 150.
† "Does not such teaching—the identity of the divine and human, the concern with illusion and enlightenment, the founder who presented not as Lord, but as spiritual guide—sound more Eastern than Western? Some scholars have suggested that if the names were changed, the 'living Buddha' appropriately could say what the *Gospel of Thomas* attributes to the living Jesus." Ibid., pp. xx–xxi.
‡ Ibid., p. 89.
§ Ibid., p. 94.

ticism" appealed strongly and appropriately to alienated liberal people of the late twentieth century.

This subtle and strategic shaping of her argument for liberals in the modern age is clearly expressed in Pagels's concluding remarks. Although it certainly has a strategy similar to those of Blavatsky and Steiner, it is far more informed, less esoteric, more refined and subtle, and supplied with much more evidence: "Now that the Nag Hammadi discoveries give us a new perspective on this process, we can understand why certain creative persons throughout the ages, from Valentinus and Haracleon to Blake, Rembrandt, Dostoyevsky, Tolstoy, and Nietzsche, found themselves at the edges of orthodoxy. All were fascinated with the figure of Christ — his birth, life, teachings, death, and resurrection; all returned constantly to Christian symbols to express their own experience. And yet they found themselves in revolt against orthodox institutions. An increasing number of people today share their experience."*

The project of *A New New Testament* would not have been in any way possible without the courageous and brilliant work of Elaine Pagels. Her strong gifts of insight, scholarship, strategy, clear writing, and determination have paved the way out of heresy-baiting for the Nag Hammadi texts and other literature. Her advocacy for the strongly positive values in Nag Hammadi literature and the ways she made these values clear to a broader audience have been especially crucial in claiming this literature. Yet her strategy and framing of the Nag Hammadi documents now — after the work of other scholars — appear somewhat problematic in terms of what the next steps might be toward building strong spiritual relationships with these new texts.

Perhaps the biggest problem is her acceptance of the terms *gnosticism, gnostic,* and *gnosis* as crucial for understanding this literature. There are two significant problems here. First, such acceptance implies that all the Nag Hammadi documents belong together and are consistent expressions of one belief system, religion, or school of thought. This is a major overstatement. Pagels herself regularly refers to the "diversity" of Nag Hammadi. And many scholars are now pressing against thinking of these documents as any kind of system of thought or belief, much less gnosticism.

Second, this idea that all Nag Hammadi documents belong to a "gnostic" system leaves in place the assumption that there was such a thing as "gnosticism" in the ancient Christian world. Ironically, Pagels's proposal that each document belongs to a larger coherence of "Gnostic Gospels" supports the questionable scholarship of the past two centuries which invented the idea of "gnosticism" and made it seem nearly heretical. So the current public's understanding of these documents is to

---

* Ibid., p. 150.

some extent confused by Pagels's endorsement of the idea of a contest between the orthodox and the "gnostics." Furthermore, her proposal that "gnostic" truth can help people today in their spiritual search now functions to blunt the clear debunking of that idea by King and Williams. The popularity of Pagels's work has made it difficult for the later proposals of the likes of King and Williams to gain footholds in the public's understanding.

Strangely, then, the very important scholarship that helped rescue Nag Hammadi from condemnation as heresy and gave it a sense of real spiritual value for our day now also has the effect of skewing the understanding of the documents themselves. As the public makes additional efforts to test the strength of these new documents and to build spiritual and intellectual relationships with them, it is important not to overdraw the case for them any more than to slot them into the category of heresy. (This, of course, is also the case with the existing New Testament. It too has often been portrayed as the perfect and authoritative "Word" straight from God without acknowledging some of its problems.) The hypothesis that there was such a thing as "gnosticism" has made thinking about new discoveries and the traditional New Testament together difficult. Given the way the documents of Nag Hammadi belong to the rich diversity of the early Christ movements, they do not need to be seen in obligatory opposition to the works in the traditional New Testament. The stark boundaries the idea of "gnosticism" places between the books of the traditional New Testament and the many recent discoveries of writings of early Christ movements make it very difficult to take seriously the deep connections between these two groupings of literature.

A New New Testament is not a project to promote a final selection of holy books that can be deemed pure and holy in every respect. It sees itself neither outside the bounds of Christianity nor in some privileged Christian status to guarantee truth. Those who formulated the contents of *A New New Testament* along with me wanted to avoid too many claims for any new or old documents. Rather, the possibilities for this book have to do with reading some of these valuable new books alongside the valuable old ones. Pagels's masterful efforts in almost single-handedly rescuing many of these new books so that they have real value in people's lives today cannot be underestimated. Nor can they be the last steps in the process she has helped unleash.

The advent of *A New New Testament* offers the twenty-first-century public a hands-on way of claiming the depth of diversity within Christian beginnings. Karen King's foundational historical work now has a partner in twenty-first-century spiritual quests in which the rainbow of practice, spirituality, and belief of early Christianity is deeply engaged through the reading of new and traditional texts together.

6

A Rich Explosion of Meaning

THE PREVIOUS CHAPTERS of this "Companion to *A New New Testament*" frame a tableau full of meaning for twenty-first-century readers. The first two centuries of early Christianity were rich with diverse and inspired literature. As they came into being, these many books — certainly hundreds of them, of which only one hundred or so survived — were not cordoned off into the New Testament and second-tier books. Rather, they fell over one another in a rush of articulation of a variety of hopes, insights, agonies, celebrations, and proclamations. It took an additional two to three hundred years for an unevenly paced and diffuse process to come up with even a basic division of the New Testament and its runners-up, which then took an additional several hundred years to codify, after which Martin Luther tried to undo some of the results. It was in response to Luther's critiques that the first official church proclamations of what belonged to the New Testament happened in the 1500s and 1600s.

In other words, for many centuries a very wide range of literature nurtured and inspired Christians. The fencing off of the New Testament as the sole authority has been provisional and inexact for all but a few centuries, in which even then disputes, the writings of saints and theologians, and denominational divisions provided curious and inspired subtexts. Upon closer examination, as the previous chapters noted, the New Testament itself is not doctrinally unified and contains a stunning diversity of viewpoints on who Jesus was and early Christian practice.

In the modern era, the discovery of many diverse ancient Christian texts has reopened a door to this richness, allowing many questions and a surplus of meanings to spill out into public consciousness. The curious mix of naïve enthusiasm, church defensiveness, scholarship's invention of gnosticism, and the subsequent romanticization of gnostics in response to these new documents has not helped make things clearer to the larger public.

Nevertheless, the past twenty years have begun to witness an appetite for the unstable mix of new and old documents from the first two centuries of Christianity. Enigmatic combinations of scholarly research, wide-ranging spiritual searches for combinations of the new and the old, and public curiosity have produced sustained attraction to an original mix of many early Christian documents. From this surge of interest has come not so much one new truth, but an explosion of different meanings from early Christianity for twenty-first-century readers.

Both the heady enthusiasm for any new discoveries — whether the Gospel of Thomas or the Gospel of Judas — and the obvious defensiveness of Christian institutions have proven inadequate for this moment of sustained interest in the explosive diversity of inspired documents from the first two centuries of Christianity. It has turned out that neither some loyal return to the existing New Testament nor a full-blown embrace of every new discovery works for very long in today's spiritual and intellectual climate.

As this turbulent and inspiring mix continues to bubble, *A New New Testament* emerges as a way of being in the middle of this explosion of new meanings. Obviously it does not exhaust the meanings coming from the expanding early Christian mix, but it allows for a steady relationship with a mix of these old and new documents. The keen deliberations of the 2012 New Orleans Council help focus attention on some of the more important insights, promises, and practices in those first 150 years. There are a number of ways this explosion of meaning appears in the diverse collection of *A New New Testament.** Some of the meanings come from the fresh new ideas in the added documents. Other meanings come from the forms of the new literature that are different from those in the existing New Testament. Yet other meanings occur when the new and traditional documents complement one another.

New Meanings from New Material

Although most often the new documents share meanings with the traditional ones, there are some very surprising new ideas in some of these documents. Here is a not-at-all-comprehensive sampling:

- The Letter of Peter to Philip catches early Christians in the middle of dangerous persecution in ways not portrayed in any of the existing New Testament. The way this letter portrays the early Christians' response to Roman state violence that killed some of them and threatened to kill more is tender and thoughtful and does not smack of a wholesale call to martyrdom.

  Courageous resistance, patient contemplation, and clever strategizing in the face of murderous power provide striking new meanings for readers about how to maintain integrity in the face of violent power. No existing New Testament document comes close to this experience of direct confrontation and wise deliberation in the face of systemic persecution.

---

* This survey of the different ways meanings explode onto the scene when the variety of early Christ movement writings are read together is similar to the dynamics addressed in chapter 5's investigation of the diversity of these texts in their ancient settings and ways to appropriate such diversity today.

- The Gospel of Truth encourages its readers with an almost incomparable assurance of the power and goodness of human beings: "Say then from the heart that you are the perfect day and within you dwells the light that never ends. Speak of the truth with those who seek it and of knowledge with those who have sinned through their transgressions. Strengthen the feet of those who stumble and stretch your hands to those who are weak" (17:11–13).

  This saying exudes meaning from the encounter of the reader with a whole range of life experiences. Full of light that will never fail, truth, sincerity, recovery, steadiness after a fall, and rest for the weary is at hand for both the reader and those to whom the reader relates.

- In the Gospel of Mary Magdalene, Peter says that Jesus loved her more than any woman. Later, Levi says that Jesus loved her more than the disciples. This new meaning contrasts with other portraits both in and outside the existing New Testament of Jesus loving everyone the same or having a special attachment to the disciples above others.

New Meanings from New Forms

New meanings do not just come from ideas, but also from the form of the text. There are gospels, letters, "acts," and revelations both inside the existing New Testament and outside it. But there are other textual forms from the early Christ movements that do not correspond to the traditional New Testament forms. Here are a few sample ways this happens in *A New New Testament*:

- Compared to the traditional New Testament, one of the most striking new forms in *A New New Testament* is the prayer. Two of the ten new documents are prayers — not a collection of prayers, but stand-alone prayers. Neither the Prayer of Thanksgiving nor the Prayer of the Apostle Paul has the context of a story about Jesus; they are prayers on their own.

  This emphasis on the form and content of prayer as a major dimension of early Christianity is different. Here prayer itself has central meaning, both as a practice and as a document.

- The Gospel of Thomas contains only sayings of Jesus. There is no story, and no events are presented. It is simply 114 teachings of Jesus.

  This form of a "sayings gospel" does exist elsewhere, but not in the traditional New Testament. Although at first scholars thought that this was simply a crude compilation of sayings, study now confirms that this exclusive concentration on Jesus's teachings is meant to convey a different meaning from a gospel of stories. Here the good news is the content of the sayings themselves.

The meaning conveyed is that Jesus's words matter more than anything, and that to know Jesus best, one needs to know him as a teacher.

- Another new form is on full exhibition in *A New New Testament*. The four books of the Odes of Solomon are unique to New Testament literature. Very similar to the psalms of the Hebrew scriptures, these odes are songs, in this case of early Christians rather than the people of Israel. In many places in the forty-one different songs Christ plays a major role, sometimes as the object of praise, but often as the one in whose voice the ode is sung.

Here too the odes are actual ancient Christian songs, which gives a whole new meaning to twenty-first-century readings of them. The form invites the reader to receive them and participate in them with actual music, either by singing the words or by listening to music while reading them.

New Meanings from Comparisons of the Existing New Testament with New Books

- In the Gospel of Luke, Jesus proclaims that some people say that the realm of God is over there, and other say that it is somewhere else, but the realm of God is really within you. In the Gospel of Mary, Jesus teaches the same thought about the Child of Humanity who lives inside you, and in the Gospel of Thomas Jesus says that realm of God is inside you and outside you.

  These teachings in many ways overlap, and in many ways they are different. Reading them together to a certain extent allows them to explain and expand one another. Luke and Mary agree that there is a presence inside of us, which can be considered the presence of a divine person (Mary) or of God's realm (Luke). Thomas celebrates this inner presence but insists that there is also an outer presence.

- In both the Revelation to John (from the traditional New Testament) and the (new) Secret Revelation of John, the world is at the mercy of destructive powers that imperil humanity. In both books, God finally triumphs over these powers and saves humanity from them.

  In this way both books affirm safety and purpose for humanity. And — to the surprise of many readers — both books' happy endings occur on earth without recourse to an afterlife. Yet there are profound differences as well. In the Revelation to John the triumph of God comes through God's military victory over the forces of evil with Jesus as a warrior leading the way to final victory. Also in this book, God punishes much of the earth for evil, destroying much of it and killing many people. God's defeat of the evil powers in the Secret Revelation of John does not come through destruction, and Jesus is not portrayed as a military leader. Rather, in the Secret Revelation, the evil powers are defeated by Christ coming to teach humanity about the true God. This wipes the ignorance from them, and they are no longer subject to the evil powers.

• In the Gospel of Mary, the Savior teaches that "[t]here is no sin, but it is you who make sin when you do the things that are like the nature of adultery, which is called 'sin'" (3:3–4). Paul's Letter to the Romans makes a very similar point to "regard yourselves as dead to sin, but as living for God" (6:11).

  In both documents, sin disappears as a reality through the way people regard themselves. But this idea can be missed more easily in Romans; as Mary says much more directly, there is no such thing as sin.

• In the Gospel of John after Jesus's death the disciples are shut up in a room, and Jesus suddenly appears to them as reassurance. In the Gospel of Mary, the disciples are crying and afraid because Jesus is no longer with them, and Mary comes to comfort them and to tell them some of Jesus's teachings.

  In both gospels someone reassures the disciples that they are not alone. But in Mary this reassurance comes from Mary Magdalene's message of Jesus's teachings, while in John it is Jesus who gives them confidence, not so much with his teachings as with his instructions. In both cases, the disciples end up going out with renewed courage. They share the sense that in despair, comfort is available. The difference in meaning lies in the fact that not only Jesus can give this comfort.

• In 2 Corinthians, Paul recounts how someone (probably himself) ascended to the third heaven and then came back to live a regular life (12:2). In the Gospel of Mary, she recounts a teaching from Jesus of how the soul traverses the spheres in a journey toward God. Here too the journey to the heavens is not after death, but during one's life.

  Both of these texts envision an ascent to the heavens as a part of life, not as an after-death experience. Paul recounts his own experience. In the Gospel of Mary, it is a teaching about what everyone might experience. A shared meaning is that people within their lifetimes can ascend into the heavens. A difference in meaning is that in the Gospel of Mary, Jesus (through Mary Magdalene) taught how everyone could make such an ascent to God while still alive.

• In the Gospel of John, Jesus often speaks with the formula "I am. . . ." He says: "I am the good shepherd . . . I am the bread of life . . . I am the way, and the truth, and the life . . . I am the light of the world." The "I am" formula was known both in the Bible and in the broader Mediterranean cultures as indicative of a divine being speaking. So, Jesus's "I am" serves to reveal him as a divine person. This is also true of the voice in The Thunder: Perfect Mind, which speaks even more consistently with the divine "I am." The "I am" of both Thunder and John are, however, quite different from other divine "I am"s of the ancient world, in that Thunder's and John's divine voices also identify themselves as humiliated. Jesus in John's story is abused and crucified. Thunder's "I am" reveals herself as both "she who is disgraced and she who is important . . . she whom you chased and she whom you captured . . . [and] she who exists in all fears and in trembling boldness. . . ." (2:10; 7:9; 2:18)

These two "I am"s paint a powerful and vulnerable picture of divinity. They give new meaning to the character of God as a source of strength, even while being intimately connected to suffering and humiliation. They share this extremely Christian picture of the vulnerable divine being, while coming to it with different genders. Humiliation and triumph as well as male and female are revelatory of God.

- Also in the Gospel of John is the assertion of a unity between God and humans. Jesus says, "I am in the Father, and you in me, and I in you" (14:20). The Gospel of Truth has very similar teachings, which seem to have been in dialogue with the writers of the Gospel of John. The Gospel of Truth reads: "This is the way of those who hold something of the immeasurable greatness from above. They stretch toward the full one alone, who is a Mother for them. . . . they rest in the one who rests. They are not troubled or twisted around the truth, but they are truth. And the Father is within them and they are in the Father" (27:1–2, 4–6).

Both the gospels of John and Truth teach that humans are in God and God in humans. The two gospels share this conviction eloquently. There are, however, differences, mainly around the third divine figure in each gospel. The third figure in the saying of John's gospel is Jesus as he teaches about this divine-human connection that comes to realization in him. Although Jesus figures importantly in the Gospel of Truth, its third figure is the Mother, the unique and perfect one. As these two gospels agree about the unity of humanity and divinity, one wonders how the Mother and Jesus overlap. Is Jesus the Mother, as is the case in some of the Odes of Solomon? Or is the Gospel of Truth pointing more toward a unity of the Mother and the Father?

An Unimaginable Richness of Meaning

One could easily write another book just outlining the many new ideas, new forms, and fascinating comparisons among the books of A New New Testament. This brief chapter has identified fourteen different new meanings coming from this new collection, some of which have broad implications.

These new meanings do not easily cohere into one simple system of belief or one clear practice of one religion. Rather, they spin and tumble forth explosively, pointing to many different kinds of spiritual, personal, and social renewal and insight. As noted throughout this book, this is also the case with the existing New Testament, which is not easily tamed by systems of belief and practice. In adding ten new works from the first 150 years of Christ and Jesus movements, *A New New Testament* has simply added to the intensity of the many levels of meaning generated.

Claiming particular promise, guidance, challenge, and inspiration from the explosion of so many meanings can happen quickly in some respects and in other ways may take more processing and adjustments. For instance, reading seven gospels together rather than four makes ideas and impressions spill forth at a rate we are not used to when reading the Bible. Some of the new meanings in this mix of gospels are so gripping that they quickly become pivotal for a larger sense of how to live life. Other meanings need to sink in slowly and end up being acknowledged only indirectly or subconsciously.

Reading odes or psalms to the Christ or in Christ's voice provokes new thoughts and feelings that can both root someone more deeply in Christ and shake the same person or others up. Having a woman as the central figure in two of the books of *A New New Testament* rivets some with unthinkable joy and others with shock. Even a first round of claiming some of the powerful new meanings requires time and changes lives. Sometimes reading these documents alongside the traditional New Testament helps make them clearer or feel more comfortable. The emphasis on God's presence in human beings and vice versa in all three of the new gospels allows the same message in the traditional New Testament to be more easily recognized. Sometimes reading all these books together frees the old works up or gives them new contexts for us to live new lives in our imagination and spiritual practice. The occasional fragments of prayers and songs in the existing New Testament texts have stronger resonance when put in the context of the three new works that consist completely of prayers and songs.

It is nearly certain that all the ways this new combination of books provide insight will continue to provide sparks of meaning in directions that are not yet discernible. And, as is often the case, series of new sparks can eventually result in bigger explosions. It is my sense that it will take a good decade to begin to know all the implications of this new kind of reading of early Christian works for spiritual nurture and inspiration. In the meantime, the explosions of meaning light up the sky with wisdom, challenge, and possibility.

Epilogue:
What's Next for A New New Testament?

AFTER HER THIRD COURSE with me focusing on all this literature, a seminary student decided to write a novel about a first-century love affair and how several books from the Nag Hammadi discovery fueled its passion. After having read the Gospel of Thomas over and over again for a year, a young pastor started composing music for it to be sung. Reading The Thunder: Perfect Mind a number of times propelled Pulitzer Prize–winning novelist Toni Morrison to use Thunder for the dedication page in two of her books. A friend of mine hides the Gospel of Mary under her bed so that no one will find out that she reads it every night. When a pastor from Harlem discovered the Acts of Paul and Thecla, she rushed to the library to find out more about it and could find only one book and a few articles. When the executives of Prada read Thunder, they commissioned a five-minute commercial, using its text to sell perfume.

There is a steady stream of graduate students coming my way who want to build careers around the new texts. My experience over the past twenty years with thousands of people who have read these new books alongside the traditional New Testament shows that in the majority of cases, things change when these texts are read. On the other hand, in North America, where these books are known best, the vast majority of people do not know anything about them and — for the most part — seem to be doing fine without them.

Obviously I am too involved in this book to be able to judge clearly what its future will bring. But I do have a great deal of experience in seeing what reading this literature does to people, churches, classrooms, and society, and so I might be able to venture some thoughts on what the future holds for this book.

Personal Responses

Individual reader experiences of this book vary a great deal. Reading energy and interest sometimes come from those who think of themselves as exiled from church because of its narrowness, those who have not ever been related formally to church, and those deeply involved in church. Curiously enough, with a few exceptions, the personal responses from this varied population are quite similar to one another.

One of the first things that happens to many people reading the material in *A New New Testament* is that they return to read the material a number of times over a period of months. For instance, there is the drama of Thecla in the Acts of Paul and Thecla as she is attacked and bullied by people and — because of her passion to teach and heal like Paul (who ignores her) — ends up with her seizing her own future, baptizing herself, and going out on her own. This is a story of an early Christ follower like none other, and people find themselves taking time to read it often to make sense of it.

One of the primary ways my seminary and graduate students have responded is through the arts. There is something in the personal discovery of these texts that beckons toward artistic expression. One student who had never danced with a text before or choreographed anything produced a dance about the Gospel of Thomas. Another made a film for the first time in her life after her first encounter with the Gospel of Mary. Others paint, write poetry, sing songs, and compose plays.

These artistic responses fit best, I think, with the larger question about how the texts in this book relate to one's spiritual practice or help one find a spiritual practice. To a certain extent such practice can be dancing with the texts, simply reading them regularly, writing a journal in response to them, praying the texts themselves (especially the Prayer of Thanksgiving, the Prayer of the Apostle Paul, and the four books of the Odes of Solomon), or reading them together with others. For those not so artistically inclined, reading background material on the texts is another way of deepening one's relationship to them and clarifying the possibilities for larger meaning to emerge from the texts or not. The appendices in this book and the available study guides are meant to be companions to such further reading. The individual introductions to each ancient text as well as the chapters in this "Companion" also provide more information for study. In any case, the future almost certainly will include repeated reading of these new and old texts, searches for how to connect them with spiritual practice, and strong reliance on artistic expression.

Church Responses

Hundreds of churches are already deeply involved in the reading of the more well-known texts like the Gospel of Mary and the Gospel of Thomas. These usually take the form of study groups, which are based within recent books on these gospels by the likes of Richard Valantasis, Karen King, John Dominic Crossan, or Elaine Pagels. It seems likely to me that *A New New Testament* will spawn many such study groups both inside and outside churches. The appendices in this book and the study guides — on the publisher's website, www.hmhbooks.com/anewnewtesta ment — are meant to facilitate such study groups.

One of the major challenges of this book to churches is the incorporation of the additional documents in worship. For pastors to begin preaching on these texts on Sunday morning seems an obvious possibility. Reading these texts in worship as additional readings or psalms are regularly read can easily be done. The many Odes of Solomon are obvious candidates for psalmlike worship, but every kind of text can be read as a second reading. Given the emphasis in this book on reading the new books alongside the traditional books, churches could have one traditional text read and then a new one.

In terms of the longer future, it seems that the destabilization of the established New Testament and the creativity of adding deeply meaningful texts from the early Christ movements could open up a larger reimagination of Christian self-understanding in our day. In this era in which church institutions, loyalty, and attractiveness are in such clear decline, large-scale rethinking seems to be called for. The desperate clinging to past structures and tradition in the past century has not helped churches thrive, so bigger reimagined frames of what it means to be church are necessary. I have already written in these pages that in our day and location it will take more than a shift in scriptures to revitalize churches. On the other hand, this reframing of what scriptures Christians might claim can act as a wedge into the tight and unhealthy structures of twenty-first-century church in order to prompt additional rethinking and action.

A new vision for these texts in church has also come forward from one of the council members, Rev. Chebon Kernell. Kernell, a chief national program officer for Native American ministries for the United Methodist denomination and a United Methodist pastor in Oklahoma, has noticed how the action of introducing the recently discovered ancient Mediterranean texts into the New Testament has precipitated for him the possibility of adding Native American texts to the New Testament. He points out that the "master narrative" of Christianity leaves out the story of his people. He envisions the possibility that the texts added to *A New New Testament* might interrupt the exclusiveness of the traditional New Testament enough to allow Native Americans to loosen their current narrow Christian scriptural perspectives in order to make space for Native stories, songs, and traditional expression. Key, of course, to Kernell's hopes is his insistence that adding these Native American traditions would not be for non-Native Christians, but simply for his people.

Rev. Kernell's vision poses larger questions about the terms on which one might make other additions to the New Testament. If we can add new documents from the sands of Egypt and new stories from Native peoples, what else could we add? My current strategy for the near future of the next decade or so is based on three principles: (1) There is a need for more new New Testaments; (2) it is important to allow time to see what real contributions this current *New New Testament* chosen by the New Orleans Council can make in our time before moving too quickly to another version of a new New Testament; (3) the decision-making process of what to add to future new New Testaments should observe a democratic, participatory "council-like" structure and be clear on whom the council represents in its decisions. As an example, decisions to add in Kernell's vision would be made by a representative group in relationship to all or some particular Native Americans.

Educational Responses

A New New Testament offers value as a centerpiece for college courses. Its span of texts, reader-friendly introductions, and wider background information make for a natural survey course of early Christian literature, as an introduction to the New Testament, an introduction to noncanonical literature, or an alternative to either. The great advantage of such college settings lies very much in their library resources and easy access to the broader range of secondary literature on this material. The ways this book promotes the use of both traditional New Testament texts and newly discovered ones also lends itself to use of the book in courses about religious practice and belief, and the study of religion itself.

The bubble of secrecy has burst on some of the new discoveries from Christian beginnings, and over the past fifteen years a number of new books on this material have appeared. Some of these books are written for lay readers without much background and some are not. In the introduction to each ancient document and after the introduction to each new book in *A New New Testament,* I have listed readings for further learning on each document.

It is clear, however, that the newness of some of this literature has combined with the reticence of scholarly and church response to limit the resources available on both these recently discovered documents and the suggestion of reading them alongside the traditional New Testament. There is a pulsing need for more published and online resources. It is my sincerest hope that *A New New Testament* will prompt such new resources.

The immediately needed resources include at least one book written on the historical and literary background of each of the new texts in this book, guides to meditating and praying on these texts, and books and essays on the meaning of each of these new texts. Such books, essays, and online resources need to be written for a general audience, as it is a general audience that is reading *A New New Testament*. This does not mean that more research and scholarly writing do not also need to be accomplished in the near future to fuel the general-audience books. As of now, too many scholarly works on these books are fixated on the questions of whether the particular document is "gnostic" or not. This kind of perspective is both out of date in terms of scholarship and part of a larger effort suggesting that these texts are somehow inferior, so better scholarly publishing is needed as soon as possible.

For churches, more resources are needed to help integrate these new texts into worship and to fit them into artistic and expressive frames. Composers for the Odes of Solomon, dramatic readers for the stories of Paul and Thecla or the self-proclaiming divinity of The Thunder: Perfect Mind, and painters and musicians for meditations on the Gospel of Truth can provide powerfully participatory experiences in worship.

The future of *A New New Testament* also includes going beyond the texts that the 2012 New Orleans Council chose. Although I am confident that the council's choices are powerful and valuable, it is also clear that it would be a mistake to think this was a final choice. As I have said several times in these pages, I hope that the future includes other groups that will examine all the new documents and choose different ones to act as companions to the traditional books. It is also important to see that new resources on recently discovered documents from the early Christ movements need to go beyond the texts considered here. New books and online resources about other recently discovered texts for both a general readership and scholars are needed. On this level, better translations are needed for these texts. The translations of the works included in this book were so poor that we had to commission new translations for almost all of the new pieces. This also signals the need for new students and scholars to work on this material and for the guild of New Testament studies to signal an openness to such study and scholarship. And, on an even more demanding level, there are certainly more documents to be discovered by scholars and archaeologists.

Public Artists and Audiences

In this age when spiritual search is growing and religious institutions are declining, there is a substantial future for public expressive and reflective activity outside of traditional churches, synagogues, and cathedrals. Theater, film, Internet, dance, and music often now provide for the public the occasion for display of loyalty, belonging, and ritual that formal religion used to do. As noted previously, already in our day the drama of discovery of ancient texts from the Christ movement has expressed itself most eloquently in this artistic realm. The novel and movie *The Da Vinci Code* has shown how much hope people can place in such texts. And, in terms of the documents in *A New New Testament*, The Thunder: Perfect Mind has made a much bigger splash in film, novels, and music than it has in churches. Filmmakers Ridley Scott and Julie Dash, novelists Umberto Eco and Toni Morrison, and a host of musicians have displayed and performed Thunder to a very broad audience.

It could very well be, then, that these texts have a strong future in film, painting, theater, music, and poetic performance. A Broadway play about Paul and Thecla, more film about Thunder, the Gospel of Mary, or paintings or solos about the womb of God in the Prayer of Thanksgiving all beckon.

Key Future Issues Addressed by *A New New Testament*

It is difficult to know all of the different resources that may come from *A New New Testament*. Although one can tell at some level what issues exercised the New Orleans Council most in making the choices it did, it is not at all clear what other kinds of resources the combination of old and new texts can provide for our time. To me there are at least two current issues for which *A New New Testament* frames a new future. These two issues are Jesus and gender relations/identity.

Jesus

This book offers very clear resources for the foreseeable future in giving additional meaning to who Jesus is for our time. This is because the picture of who Jesus is in *A New New Testament* is simply bigger, broader, and deeper than the picture of Jesus in the traditional New Testament. Although the Jesus in the Gospel of Thomas has many similarities with the Jesus in Matthew, Mark, and Luke, Thomas's Jesus is also stunningly different. In Thomas, Jesus climbs up on a dining couch with Salome, is challenged by her at that point, and then proceeds in a conversation with her that confirms that she is his disciple. Thomas's Jesus says that all his followers come "from the light" and are children of the light. This Jesus never teaches about his crucifixion or resurrection, in contrast to the way that Jesus in Matthew, Mark, and Luke concentrates on this aspect of his identity.

Similarly different from Matthew, Mark, and Luke, but not at all the same as Thomas, Jesus on the cross is pictured in the Gospel of Truth as fruit on a tree, and Jesus's crucifixion is likened to a book that upon its being nailed to a tree becomes published. The eighth Ode of Solomon portrays Jesus as offering his breasts to his followers so that "they could drink my own consecrated milk, that through it they might live."

In *A New New Testament* there is simply more Jesus. In this book he is all that he is in the traditional New Testament, but he also bursts the boundaries of the traditional collection so that he is understood in many additional ways. These new portraits of Jesus alongside of the traditional ones offer both a wider spectrum of ways to relate to him and more perspectives with which to think about what the traditional images of him mean. So, as of *A New New Testament*'s advent, Jesus's future is simply bigger.

Gender and Identity

Gender identity from a Christian perspective has a broader future in *A New New Testament*. This book shows that the early Christ movements' vocabulary for thinking about who women and men are was far broader and deeper than that which the traditional New Testament reflects. To be sure, the traditional New Testament's breaking of gender boundaries still shines in Paul's proclamation that there is no longer "male and female," but that all are one in Christ. But the complexities and richness of new gender identity are multiplied in *A New New Testament*.

The powerful identity, self-understanding, and eloquence of Thecla in the Acts of Paul and Thecla and Mary Magdalene in the Gospel of Mary far outstrip the qualities of any woman in the traditional New Testament. These two books with an insulted yet powerful woman as the primary character expand the ways of thinking about who women are both in early Christianity and in the twenty-first century.

Similarly, the new gender identities of Jesus in the Secret Revelation of John, the Odes of Solomon, and the Gospel of Truth (described briefly in the preceding section on Jesus) radically expand the future ways of thinking about gender identity for both Jesus and those who follow him. It is true that Paul's First Letter to the Corinthians in the traditional New Testament expands Jesus's sexual identity by portraying him as the same person as the feminine divine figure of Wisdom-Sophia in the book of Proverbs in the Hebrew scriptures. But this picture of a bigendered Jesus is far more developed in the Secret Revelation of John that has been added to this book. Similarly, Jesus and the Father are pictured with breasts that nurture followers with milk in the Gospel of Truth and the Odes of Solomon. Who men and women are from the perspective of *A New New Testament* is richer and more complicated.

Conflict

In our time of culture wars in which religion is a particularly volatile flashpoint, it seems likely that *A New New Testament* will cause significant conflict. In North America where about one-third of the people describe the New Testament as the perfect and unchangeable Word of God, there is a good chance that some of them will be upset by adding ten books to that same New Testament. In this religious climate where many truths of former times are crumbling or being threatened from a variety of angles, it is quite possible that for a considerable portion of the population, defensiveness will outmaneuver open-mindedness and prompt hostility.

I know why I have produced *A New New Testament*. For my entire pastoral and professorial career I have seen people in search of spiritual renewal find rewarding, nurturing, and empowering spirit from a wide variety of sources. In particular I have seen those who open themselves up to present challenges, shifts, and resources become bigger and more vibrant persons of integrity. Even more specifically, among the many resources for spiritual growth one of the more available has been the combination of the traditional New Testament and recent discoveries of ancient Christ movement documents.

A New New Testament springs from the thirty-plus years of my ministry within the local church and higher education. From listening to the spiritual thirst of people, preaching thousands of sermons, baptizing hundreds of people, teaching hundreds of professionals, marrying hundreds of couples, and teaching thousands of lay people, I have a solid impression of the needs of churched and non-churched individuals and what is at stake for them when they search for what to read for their own spiritual health. I know that there is no single answer for them, and that this spiritual journey has integrity in and of itself. I know that the material in *A New New Testament* is trustworthy and look forward to continuing to be present to it in a variety of conversations. I will continue to love the complicated mix of traditional and new New Testament texts and will forget neither its strengths and promise nor its occasional shortcomings.

On the other hand, I know that I make mistakes, sometimes overstate or understate something I know, and do not always listen as carefully as I should to my conversation partners. I hope to learn from moments of conflict and my mistakes around this book. I am determined to be a steady and gracious conversation partner with a public that needs more honest, informed, and courageous dialogue about religion and the Bible.

Although my personality does not thrive on conflict, I have learned how to be in conflict with some integrity and have been on conflicted national stages over the past twenty-five years. I know that conflict about religion in our day can be both productive and destructive. It is my hope that the parts of my ongoing work with *A New New Testament* that involve conflict can produce more on the constructive than the destructive side of the ledger.

It is difficult to predict what kinds of behavior will result from American religious conflict. For me, the broad spectrum of the American public will be best served when this conflict is experienced most prominently as debate and while looking directly at and considering the lessons of the traditional and newly discovered texts from the early Christ movements.

Renewal

There is great possibility for renewal on many levels in the public reading and discussion of this book over the next generation of readers. Although I have emphasized most strongly the spiritual development possible in my framing of this future, I am equally sanguine and hopeful about how it may help renew thoughtful reflection on meaning for the twenty-first century, the place of religion in our world, and the future of Christianity. The renewal of responsible and informed discussion across classes, cultures, and age groups also can happen when such a mix of traditional and experimental material comes into public view.

On one level this book is a bold venture. Although it does not dispute the authority of the traditional New Testament and invites others to produce alternative versions of new New Testaments, it is also true that it could be considered the first revision of Christian scripture in at least four hundred, and possibly fourteen hundred, years. In the same vein, my invitation to a range of national spiritual leaders to make the decisions about what books were added and my naming that group a "council" — even when it was not sanctioned by any official church — are bold steps. I consciously took these actions because my pastoral and professorial experience had taught me that timid steps by religious leaders do not do justice to the crisis and potential of this moment in history.

On the other hand, this book is modest. Despite the obvious flaws in the traditional New Testament (as one small example, its endorsement of slavery at least seven times and its exhortation to slaves to remain obedient to their masters as if their masters were God), this project has resisted many recommendations that we remove the objectionable books from the traditional New Testament. Nor have we accepted the more radical recommendations that the books added include works from beyond the era of the traditional New Testament. The modesty of my decision to decline such urgings stands in the face of the obvious profound truths of much that has been written since 175 CE. Finally, the restraint of *A New New Testament* has been exhibited in its unwillingness to make the books added more attractive than they really are. These recent discoveries have flaws, flaws not dissimilar from those of the traditional New Testament, and I and my translation team have refused to alter — or improve — them beyond what the ancient texts themselves reveal.

Renewal as a social and religious experience honors both boldness and modesty. It does not seek to rip all the roots out or to start with a blank slate. Rather, renewal takes seriously the contingencies of all efforts and the mixed results of all experience, calculating that a mix of boldness and modesty produces incremental growth and learning. May the future of *A New New Testament* be so.

The Council for *A New New Testament*

Modeled on early church councils of the first six centuries CE that made important decisions for larger groups of Christians, this council worked from August 2011 through its final meeting over three days in February 2012 to determine which works from the first two centuries should be added to the traditional New Testament to form *A New New Testament*. It was chaired by Hal Taussig. Every member of the council had an equal vote and voice in the decision-making process. For additional information about the council process, see the "Companion to *A New New Testament*."

Margaret Aymer is Associate Professor of New Testament and Area Chair of Biblical Studies at the Interdenominational Theological Center in Atlanta, Georgia. Her publications include *First Pure, Then Peaceable: Frederick Douglass, Darkness and the Epistle of James* (T&T Clark, 2008) and *Confessing the Beatitudes*, a Bible study of the *Horizons* magazine.

Geoffrey Black is the Chief Minister and President of United Church of Christ. Prior to his election as the head of his denomination, he served in a number of regional and national offices of the UCC. He has served for many years as a local pastor. Ecumenical commitment, concern for equal justice, and African American empowerment have been key elements of his ministry.

Margaret Brennan is an Immaculate Heart of Mary Sister from Monroe, Michigan. In her long ministry of over sixty years, she taught briefly in high school, obtained a doctorate in theology, held leadership positions in her community and in the Leadership Conference of Women Religious (LCWR), and afterward taught pastoral theology at the Toronto School of Theology for twenty-five years.

Lisa Bridge holds an M.Div. from Union Theological Seminary, an M.S. from Bank Street College, and a B.A. from Purdue University. She ran one of New York's largest classical yoga schools for several years and has expertise in Yogic and Buddhist traditions. Lisa is the Program Manager for Children and Youth Ministries at Trinity Wall Street Church in New York. She also served on *A New New Testament*'s New Jersey Sub-council.

John Dominic Crossan received a Doctorate of Divinity from Maynooth College, Ireland, in 1959 and did postdoctoral research at the Pontifical Biblical Institute,

Rome, 1959 to 1961, and at the École Biblique, Jerusalem, 1965 to 1967. He joined DePaul University, Chicago, in 1969 and remained there until 1995. He is now a professor emeritus in its Department of Religious Studies. He also served on *A New New Testament*'s New Jersey Sub-council.

Nancy Fuchs Kreimer was ordained a rabbi in 1982. She holds a Ph.D. in Jewish-Christian Relations from Temple University and is Director of the Department of Multifaith Studies at the Reconstructionist Rabbinical College. She is currently coediting a volume of personal spiritual essays by Jewish women scholars, *Chapters of the Heart*. She also served on *A New New Testament*'s New Jersey Sub-council.

Bishop Susan Wolfe Hassinger was elected in 1996 as a bishop in the United Methodist Church. Now retired from that ministry, she is currently Bishop-in-Residence and Lecturer in Practical Theology at Boston University School of Theology and engages in spiritual direction with individuals and groups. She also served on *A New New Testament*'s New Jersey Sub-council.

Bishop Alfred Johnson was elected in 1996 as a bishop in the United Methodist Church. Now retired from the active episcopate, he is currently Pastor of the Church of the Village, United Methodist, in New York City. He served as bishop of the annual conferences of New Jersey and directed the unification of those conferences.

Chebon Kernell has served as pastor of First American United Methodist Church of the Oklahoma Indian Missionary Conference for the past seven years. Rev. Kernell is a member of the Seminole Nation of Oklahoma and is currently the Executive Secretary of Native American/Indigenous Ministries of the General Board of Global Ministries of the United Methodist Church. He also served on *A New New Testament*'s New Jersey Sub-council.

Karen L. King is the Hollis Professor of Divinity, Harvard University's oldest endowed professorship (1721). She is the author of numerous books and articles on the diversity of ancient Christianity, women and gender studies, and religion and violence, including *What Is Gnosticism?*, *The Secret Revelation of John,* and *The Gospel of Mary of Magdala: Jesus and the First Woman Apostle*. She also served on *A New New Testament*'s New Jersey Sub-council.

Celene Lillie is a Ph.D. candidate in New Testament Studies at Union Theological Seminary in New York, where she also completed her M.Div. and M.Phil., and holds a B.A. in Contemplative Psychology from Naropa University. She is a coauthor of *The Thunder: Perfect Mind: A New Translation and Introduction*. She is the Director of Translation for *A New New Testament*. She also served on *A New New Testament*'s New Jersey Sub-council.

Stephen D. Moore is Professor of New Testament at Drew Theological School. He has authored or edited twenty scholarly books and published more than seventy scholarly articles and essays. He serves on the editorial boards of several journals, including the *Journal of Biblical Literature,* and is a former executive editor of the *Journal for the Study of the New Testament*. He also served on *A New New Testament*'s New Jersey Sub-council.

J. Paul Rajashekar is Luther D. Reed Professor of Systematic Theology and former Dean of the Lutheran Theological Seminary at Philadelphia. Prior to joining the faculty of the Lutheran Seminary, he served as an Executive Secretary for Interreligious Dialogue in the Lutheran World Federation, Geneva, Switzerland, and as a Professor of Theology and Ethics at the United Theological College, Bangalore.

Bruce Reyes-Chow is a Presbyterian minister, blogger, and social media consultant based in San Francisco, California. Bruce was the founding pastor of the young adult faith community Mission Bay Community Church; he was elected as the youngest-ever Moderator of the Presbyterian Church (USA) in 2008 and recently published the e-book *The Definitive-ish Guide for Using Social Media in the Church*.

Mark Singleton gained his Ph.D. in Divinity from the University of Cambridge. His research interests include contemporary South Asian religion, the intersection of religion and politics, and new religious movements, particularly those inspired by Asian practices. His books include *Yoga Body: The Origins of Modern Posture Practice*. He teaches at St. John's College, Santa Fe, New Mexico.

Nancy Sylvester, IHM, is founder of the Institute for Communal Contemplation and Dialogue. She has served in the presidency of the Leadership Conference of Women Religious and as National Coordinator of NETWORK, a national Catholic social justice lobby.

Hal Taussig is Visiting Professor of New Testament, Union Theological Seminary in New York, and Professor of Early Christianity, Reconstructionist Rabbinical College. He is a co-pastor at Chestnut Hill United Church in Philadelphia. He is the author or coauthor of thirteen books and was a member of *A New New Testament*'s New Jersey Sub-council.

Barbara Brown Taylor teaches religion at Piedmont College in rural northeast Georgia. She is the author of twelve books, including the *New York Times* bestseller *An Altar in the World,* and coeditor of *Feasting on the Word,* a twelve-volume commentary series on the Revised Common Lectionary.

Rabbi Arthur Waskow, since writing the unprecedented multicultural *Freedom Seder* in 1969, has been among the leaders of movements for Jewish renewal and Abrahamic cooperation. He directs the Shalom Center (http://www.theshalom center.org). His interfaith work includes writing (including *The Tent of Abraham*), speaking at major interfaith and international conferences, and joining in public multireligious services and nonviolent demonstrations.

Acknowledgments

I am grateful to a wide range of persons for their participation in the production of this book. My partner, Susan Cole, has been present to me in subtle and profound ways at every stage of this work. With actual interest in the work, keen counsel and strategy, intriguing and enjoyable distractions, patience and impatience in appropriate measure and timing, and wonderfully strong opinions, she was at the very heart of making sense of it all. Karen King, my longtime friend and scholarly colleague, whose work forms much of the basis for this book and who first introduced me to this literature substantively some thirty years ago, has brought measures of enthusiasm, wisdom, and loyalty to this project that added much substance and spirit. This book would not have happened at all without my dear friends Howard Bilofsky and Margaret Shapiro, who cared about each phase, talked me through every crisis, celebrated each milestone, and cooked me and Susan countless delicious dinners. My congregation at Chestnut Hill United Church unselfconsciously gave me its intense intellectual devotion and its courage and compassion in being church. For the completion of the manuscript and council process I am indebted to the members of my production team, Celene Lillie (as director of translation), Lisa Bridge (as project manager), Alexis Waller, Jennifer Warner, Barbara Rice, Emily Otto, Judi Fahnestock, Ron Fahnestock, and Tim Thomson-Hohl. The graduate student bodies at Union Theological Seminary in New York and Chestnut Hill College's program in spirituality provided platforms of intelligence and attentiveness that were crucial in my developing and refining the ideas at the core of this book. At the heart of this process was the intellectual companionship of Maia Kotrosits and Celene Lillie. Candice and Peter Olson, Chris Parris-Lamb, and David Gernert provided insight and leadership in getting the book to the right publisher. At Houghton Mifflin Harcourt, the incisive brilliance of senior editor Jenna Johnson was vital to the quality of writing in the book, and the courageous and supportive leadership of publisher Bruce Nichols made crucial differences in the imagination of the project.

Sixty-seven Major Writings of the Early Christ Movements

The following sixty-seven documents are the primary documents that were considered at one stage or another in the process of adding ten books to *A New New Testament*. Those that finally became a part of this book are in bold. For a broader picture of the process of culling these sixty-seven — with perhaps ten others very briefly considered — see the "Companion to *A New New Testament*."

The Acts of Paul and Thecla — a story from the first or second century of a woman leader in an early Christ movement as she claims her leadership in the face of many threats. See the additional information in the text itself and its introduction in this book.

The Acts of Peter and the Twelve Apostles — an address in the Nag Hammadi collection to the cosmic plot of rulers to corrupt the world.

Allogenes — the story and meaning of the figure of "the Stranger" and his obtaining of freedom from the powers of darkness. Found in the Nag Hammadi collection.

Asclepius — a set of teachings attributed to the renowned ancient teacher, with no explicit connection to the traditions of the Christ movement, but found in the Nag Hammadi collection.

Authoritative Teacher — a set of sayings from an unidentified teacher to correct the errors of humanity and show the true shape of God's creation. Found in the Nag Hammadi collection.

The Book of Thomas the Contender — an assertion of the dangers of false teachers and women leaders in the early Christ movements. From the Nag Hammadi collection.

1 Clement — a very early letter from early Christ people in Rome to those in

Corinth from the first century, emphasizing the deep meaning in many Hebrew scripture passages.

2 Clement — a collation of meditations or "sermons" by a person named Clement of unknown origins.

The Concept of Our Great Power — a litany and teaching of praise for the light and love of the divine Father. Found in the Nag Hammadi collection.

The Demonstration of Apostolic Preaching from Irenaeus — an authentic writing from the late second- and early third-century leader Irenaeus, setting criteria for how Christ movement leaders should proclaim their message.

The Dialogue of the Savior — a distinct mix of the sayings of Jesus and early "Christian" interest in the origins of the world, humanity, and the saving teaching of the Savior. Found in the Nag Hammadi collection.

The Diary of Perpetua — the only document considered that is certainly not earlier than the third century, perhaps the first early Christian writing authored by a woman, telling the story of her arrest and imprisonment prior to her execution by Roman authorities.

The Discourse on the Eighth and the Ninth — a book of instructions for spiritual practice and enlightenment, found in the Nag Hammadi collection.

Eugnostos the Blessed — an elaborate discussion and recommendation of the spheres of spiritual beings related to the Christ and the Father of Light. Found in the Nag Hammadi collection.

The Exegesis of the Soul — a reflection from the Nag Hammadi collection on the imprisonment of the soul and the positive and negative roles of a set of feminine spirits.

The First Revelation of James — an extensive discussion between James and Jesus of how to face persecution and suffering. Found in the Nag Hammadi collection.

Fragments from Nag Hammadi — a collection of sayings and instructions from several damaged papyri.

The Gospel of the Egyptians — seemingly distinguished from a document of the same name quoted in later Christian writings, this Nag Hammadi document contemplates a series of cosmic conflicts and the path to God despite it.

The Gospel of Judas — a very recently discovered story about Jesus selecting Judas as his primary confidant and discussing with him his death.

The Gospel of Mary (Magdalene) — an account from a damaged manuscript of Mary as Jesus's closest confidante, and her teaching to and comfort of the other disciples, some of whom reject her teaching. See the additional information in the text itself and its introduction in this book.

The Gospel of Nicodemus — perhaps the earliest document of a complete story about Jesus descending into hell between his death and resurrection, rejected by the 2012 council because of unreliable manuscript attestation.

The Gospel of Peter — a partial gospel found in the nineteenth century but perhaps hailing from the mid-first century, telling the story of Jesus's arrest, death, and resurrection in ways similar to and different from such stories in the traditional New Testament.

The Gospel of Philip — a complex combination of teachings by Jesus, reflections on what it means to be a Christ follower under persecution, and instructions about spiritual practice for Christ people. Found in the Nag Hammadi collection.

The Gospel of Thomas — a complete book of 114 sayings from the Nag Hammadi collection and attributed to Jesus, many of which are formerly unknown and others of which are in the traditional New Testament. See the additional information in the text itself and its introduction in this book.

The Gospel of Truth — a joyous celebration of connection to Christ found among the Nag Hammadi collection. See the additional information in the text itself and its introduction in this book.

Ignatius to the Ephesians — an authentic letter from the ousted bishop of Antioch, fervently expressing his desire that the Christ movements unify their practices and beliefs.

Ignatius to the Romans — an authentic letter from the ousted bishop of Antioch in the early to mid-second century, declaring the author's desire to die at the hands of the authorities in Rome.

Ignatius to the Smyrneans — an authentic letter from the ousted bishop of Antioch, making a strong case for Christ followers to die as a sign of their faith in their confrontation with Roman authorities.

The Infancy Gospel of James — a well-attested manuscript tradition of an extended story of Jesus's birth beginning with Mary's pregnancy.

The Infancy Gospel of Thomas — a set of stories of Jesus's life as a child, including numerous miracles he did while interacting with his playmates.

The Interpretation of Knowledge — a proposal for ways that wise actions and teachings can overcome the corruption of the world. Found in the Nag Hammadi collection.

The Letter of the Apostles — a second-century proposal of a set of beliefs and stories that could unify the diverse Christ movements.

The Letter of the Martyrs of Lyons — a section of the writings of the fourth-century secretary to the Roman emperor Constantine, allegedly recounting the deaths of a number of Christ followers at the hands of Roman authorities in the late second century.

The Letter of Peter to Philip — a tender consideration in the Nag Hammadi collection of how to proclaim the message of healing from Christ in the face of persecution by the rulers. See the additional information in the text itself and its introduction in this book.

The Martyrdom of Polycarp — a early to mid-second-century story of the death of an aging leader of a Christ movement at the hands of Roman authorities.

Melchizedek — a declaration by the ancient king from Genesis on the virtues of unification with the Father of light through the message of the Savior.

The Odes of Solomon — a very ancient collection of songs, psalms, and poems, some of which refer to or are in the voice of Christ. See the additional information in the text itself and the various introductions in this book.

On Anointing — instructions and reflections on rituals of anointing from the Nag Hammadi collection.

On Baptism A and B — instructions and reflections on baptism for the Christ people from the Nag Hammadi collection.

On Baptism from Tertullian — a late second-century edict from the prolific writer on how Christ people should baptize and what they should believe about baptism.

On the Eucharist A and B — a somewhat broken document with portions of teachings about the meal the Christ movements celebrated. Found in the Nag Hammadi collection.

On the Origin of the World — a reflection from the Nag Hammadi collection on the meaning of the story of the corruption of God's original creation by rulers claiming to be God and God's resolve to free humanity. From the Nag Hammadi collection.

On Prayer from Tertullian — a late second-century edict from the prolific writer on how Christ people should pray and what they should believe about prayer.

The Paraphrase of Shem — an elaboration of the truths of Hebrew scriptures and tradition in the face of rulers enslaving the people of the world. Found in the Nag Hammadi collection.

The Prayer of the Apostle Paul — a complete prayer attributed to the apostle Paul and found among the Nag Hammadi collection. See the additional information in the text itself and its introduction in this book.

The Prayer of Thanksgiving — an eloquent and early prayer for use of those gathered at a meal as a spiritual community, found in the Nag Hammadi collection. See the additional information in the text itself and its introduction in this book.

The Reality of the Rulers — a story from the Nag Hammadi collection of how the original creation had been perverted and humanity enslaved by rulers claiming to be God and how the real God will free humanity.

The Revelation of Adam — a conversation and story with Adam telling his son Seth how the world has been enslaved and how Seth can rescue it.

The Revelation of Paul — the story of the ascent of Paul to God while in the present life. Found in the Nag Hammadi collection.

The Second Revelation of James — an emphasis on the virtues of James's leadership of the early Christ movement, especially by virtue of his having been murdered by government authorities. Found in the Nag Hammadi collection.

The Second Treatise of the Great Seth — another address to the enslavement of the world by cruel rulers, this time addressed successfully by Seth and Christ. Found in the Nag Hammadi collection.

The Secret Revelation of James — an early collection of stories, sayings, and reflections about Jesus found in the Nag Hammadi collection.

The Secret Revelation of John — the story told by Christ to John about how the original creation had been perverted and humanity had been enslaved by rulers claiming to be God and how Christ's teachings will free humanity and unify it with God. See the additional information in the text itself and its introduction in this book.

The Sentences of Sextus — an extensive collection of nuanced wisdom sayings and proverbs from the unknown teacher of Sextus. The teachings are often close in content and spirit to those attributed to Jesus. Found in the Nag Hammadi collection.

The Teaching of Silvanus — instructions on the dangers of the world and on how to respond with belief and wisdom. Found in the Nag Hammadi collection.

The Teaching of the Twelve Apostles (Didache) — a very ancient handbook for Christ movements addressing debated issues about behavior and belief. Almost selected by the 2012 council to be a part of *A New New Testament*.

The Testimony of Truth — a persistent program of teachings for the Christ people to resist the ruling powers without violence or preaching of the end of the world. Found in the Nag Hammadi collection.

The Thought of Norea — a short appeal for the powerful feminine figure of Norea to be joined to the Father of All. Found in the Nag Hammadi collection.

The Three Forms of Forethought — the self-revelation of a divine feminine savior who celebrates her own power, her connection to the great God, and her connection to Jesus. Found in the Nag Hammadi collection.

The Three Steles of Seth — an action plan for how to claim God's primacy in the face of the horrors of the rulers of the world. Found in the Nag Hammadi collection.

The Thunder: Perfect Mind — a poetic self-description of a mostly feminine divine figure who identifies not only with the powerful but with the disenfranchised. See the additional information in the text itself and its introduction in this book.

The Treatise on the Resurrection — a discussion of the importance of the resurrection and its present, not just future, reality, found among the Nag Hammadi collection. Almost selected by the 2012 council to be a part of *A New New Testament*.

The Tripartite Tractate — an extensive proposal of the place of Christ in a larger cosmic order, found in the Nag Hammadi collection.

A Valentinian Exposition — a treatise of devotion in the Nag Hammadi collection to the Father of light and love. Found in the Nag Hammadi collection.

The Wisdom of Solomon — a very early set of poems and stories about Wisdom-Sophia, the divine feminine figure from the Hebrew scriptures. This document belongs to the "Old Testament" of the Roman Catholic and Episcopal churches but was also formally considered as being about Christ by the writer of the list of recommended books for Christ people in the "Muratorian Canon."

The Wisdom-Sophia of Jesus Christ — a situating of Christ in relationship to a range of spiritual beings, including the figure of Wisdom-Sophia from the Hebrew scriptures. Found in the Nag Hammadi collection.

Zostrianos — the teachings of the great Near Eastern sage and his instructions for living without succumbing to the rulers of the world.

The Books of the Nag Hammadi Library

The discovery of fifty-two books from early Christianity near the Egyptian village of Nag Hammadi in 1945 is almost certainly the most important discovery ever of writings from the Christ movements of the first two centuries. The list of books from the Nag Hammadi discovery is presented here, according to codex (primitively bound book). The seven books from Nag Hammadi that are now in *A New New Testament* are in bold. For further information on Nag Hammadi, see the "Companion to *A New New Testament*."

CODEX 1
The Prayer of the Apostle Paul
The Secret Revelation of James
The Gospel of Truth (also in Codex 12)
The Treatise on the Resurrection
The Tripartite Tractate

CODEX 2
The Secret Revelation of John (also in Codices 3 and 4)
The Gospel of Thomas
The Gospel of Philip
The Reality of the Rulers
On the Origin of the World (also in "Codex" 13)
The Exegesis of the Soul
The Book of Thomas the Contender

CODEX 3
The Gospel of the Egyptians (also in Codex 4)
Eugnostos the Blessed (also in Codex 4) and The Wisdom-Sophia of Jesus Christ
The Dialogue of the Savior

CODEX 5
The Revelation of Paul
The First Revelation of James
The Second Revelation of James
The Revelation of Adam

CODEX 6
The Acts of Peter and the Twelve Apostles
The Thunder: Perfect Mind
Authoritative Teacher
The Concept of Our Great Power
Plato, *The Republic*
The Discourse on the Eighth and the Ninth
The Prayer of Thanksgiving
Asclepius

CODEX 7
The Paraphrase of Shem
The Second Treatise of the Great Seth
The Revelation of Peter
The Teaching of Silvanus
The Three Steles of Seth

Study Guide

There is so much in *A New New Testament* that it bears some further reflection in order to learn on deeper levels and to identify next steps in thinking about this literature. This study guide is structured to facilitate three different stages of reading: first impressions, getting to know specific documents better through comparing traditional and new documents, and bringing it home. This guide assumes that it is helpful to study beginning with stage one and proceeding, but it is possible to skip any particular stage. The guide can be used by single readers and by groups. It is designed for multiple sessions, but any session can be used independently of the others.

This study guide has been produced with several quite different settings in mind: a regular classroom, an individual, an informal group of readers, and a church setting. These perspectives, of course, do not necessarily exclude one another, but in some cases they are quite different. It is fine if your own setting requires that some aspects of the study guide be dropped or changed.

As a study guide it makes use of the actual texts in this book, the individual introductions to each of those ancient texts, the six-chapter "Companion" in the latter part of the book, and the "How to Read *A New New Testament*" section. In this way it allows an individual or group to do further thinking about the historical context and how the individual books came into being, how the traditional New Testament material and the new books added to *A New New Testament* complement and contrast with each other, and what twenty-first-century meanings are offered by each of these old and new texts.

This study guide is not meant to act as an introduction to *A New New Testament*. It assumes that the individuals and groups using it have already done some reading in *A New New Testament* and have decided that it is worth pursuing with some intentionality, additional resources, and/or company. On the other hand, because this book is imposing in both its adventurous newness and its size, the study guide does not assume that the people using it already know most of what is in it.

Although this study guide is structured in three major units, it can be divided into up to thirteen sessions. A dashed line indicates where the units might be divided into separate study sessions.

FIRST STAGE OF STUDY
Confirming, Cross-Examining, and Claiming First Impressions
--

This unit of the study guide can be worked through in one or two sessions and is meant to help consolidate, challenge, and organize one's first impressions.

I. Turn to the Table of Contents of the book. Review all the ancient books of *A New New Testament*.

- Make a list of the books you have read and remember something about them. This list should be drawn from all of the books, both traditional and new.

- From this list make two additional and smaller lists:

  1. A list of the five books that you most liked and/or were engaged by
  2. A list of three books that you most disliked

  Examine these last two lists and write down a sentence or two beside each book about why you liked or disliked it.

II. If you are doing this in a group, discuss with one another your final two lists and why you liked or disliked the different books. If you are doing this study alone, think more about why you liked or disliked each particular book.

III. For those in a group study, now collate among the group which books were most liked and least liked. Once there is a group list of preferences and rejects, discuss the following questions (these questions can also be asked by individuals following the study guide):

- Are there similarities among the five to ten preferred books? How many of them are from the traditional New Testament? How many of them are new additions to *A New New Testament*?

- What does the group's list of preferred books say about what the group thinks is valuable about the literature of the early Christ movements?

- What does the group's list of preferred books say about the group itself, its intellectual and spiritual commitments, and its values?

- Do the group's most disliked books have any significance? What is it?

IV. Read the introductions to the group's (or individual's) top three books. (This will not take more than fifteen minutes.)

- Discuss what the introduction says to you about your group's most preferred book; your group's second most preferred book; your group's third most preferred book.

- What questions do you still have about these three books?

- Examine the list of recommended books at the back of this book and see if any of the titles might help with your next level of thinking about these books. Individuals in the group or doing this study guide by themselves might also take note of the possibility of reading the introductions to some of the books you most liked or disliked. Similarly, individuals might consult the list of recommended reading at the back of this book.

V. Have each individual pause for five minutes and write down one to three next steps for studying *A New New Testament*. Some options may be:

- Pursue the next three to five preferred books on your own list in terms of additional reading of the introductions and other works.

- Read for the first time or reread some of the books in *A New New Testament* that you noticed at the beginning that you had not read or could not remember.

- Read over the six chapters of "A Companion to *A New New Testament*."

- Think about what your top preferred books mean to you, what they seem to promise for you, and what your further questions of them are.

VI. In the group, invite each person to say in just two sentences one of the next steps that person wrote down.

STAGE TWO
Studying the Specific Characteristics of Individual Documents Through Comparing Traditional and New Documents

This second unit helps the study of specific documents and aims particularly at learning to identify certain characteristics, messages, and meanings of one or another book by comparing one aspect of four books. This unit can be worked through in two to five sessions, depending on the level of interest and the pace of the group. Groups can concentrate on one gospel per session or two gospels per session. It would not be wise to attempt to do all four gospels in one session.

This unit examines how Jesus is presented in specific documents. Such a study can be done on any number of issues in different books of this collection. Other specific issues for such study could be: How do the respective four (four being an arbitrary number) documents view women? What are the most important moral convictions of the respective four documents? What does community consist of and what are the community values in the respective documents?

I. In preparation for study, read the Gospel of Thomas and the introduction to the Gospel of Thomas found immediately prior to it in this book. (This gospel is too long to be read in a study session. Although the introduction is not so long, it will help not to have to read it during the guided study.)

II. Convene as a group (or proceed as an individual). Ask who Jesus is in the Gospel of Thomas. Before people respond, have them notice that this question assumes that Jesus may be different in different books of both *A New New Testament* and the traditional New Testament. Often, this question is met with some confusion, mostly because conventional assumptions are that all gospels — indeed all of the writings of the traditional New Testament — agree on who Jesus is. But even within the traditional New Testament there are substantial differences in what Jesus teaches, what he does, and what he means. So in asking who Jesus is in a particular book, it is important to make sure that the answer comes from within the book, not from another book, one's own beliefs, or conventional assumptions. In order to assist with the question "Who is Jesus in the Gospel of Thomas?" the following other questions may be asked:

- What kind of person does Jesus seem to be in the Gospel of Thomas? Is he kind? How judgmental and angry is he? What seems to be important to him? How powerful is he in this gospel? What kind of power does he have?

- What seem to be some central themes and subjects of Jesus's teaching in the Gospel of Thomas?

- What does Jesus do in the Gospel of Thomas?

- What kinds of relationships does Jesus have in the Gospel of Thomas? With whom?

- What did you learn from the introduction to the Gospel of Thomas in this book?

III. Ask the question again in summary form about who Jesus is in the Gospel of Thomas. At this more integrative stage, ask how Jesus in the Gospel of Thomas differs from your assumptions about Jesus. What possibilities for who Jesus is have you learned from the Gospel of Thomas?

If this is a group study, ask different individuals to answer for themselves. Check several times during the discussion as to how much agreement there is about Jesus in the group.

IV. Ask these questions: What would it mean to give authority to Jesus as he is portrayed in the Gospel of Thomas? What would it be like to consider this Jesus in Thomas to be the authoritative Jesus? What would change from how you have thought about Jesus before? What is added to Jesus by the Gospel of Thomas? What is missing for you in Jesus according to the Gospel of Thomas?

V. In preparation for study, read the Gospel of John and the introduction to the Gospel of John found immediately prior to it in this book. (This gospel is too long to be read in a study session. Although the introduction is not so long, it will help not to have to read it during the guided study.)

VI. Convene as a group (or proceed as an individual). Ask who Jesus is in the Gospel of John. Here, too, remind people before they respond that this question assumes that Jesus may be different in different books. Often, this question is met with some confusion, mostly because conventional assumptions are that all gospels — indeed, all of the writings of the traditional New Testament — agree on who Jesus is. But even within the traditional New Testament there are substantial differences in what Jesus teaches, what he does, and what he means. So in asking who Jesus is in a particular book, it is important to make sure that the answer comes from within the book, not from another book, one's own beliefs, or conventional assumptions. In order to assist with the question "Who is Jesus in the Gospel of John?" the following other questions may be asked:

- What kind of person does Jesus seem to be in the Gospel of John? Is he kind? How judgmental and angry is he? What seems to be important to him? How powerful is he in this gospel? What kind of power does he have?

- What seem to be some central themes and subjects of Jesus's teaching in the Gospel of John? How different are they from Jesus's teachings in the Gospel of Thomas? How different are they from Jesus's teachings in the Gospel of Matthew? (The answer to this question will depend on some people knowing something about the Gospel of Matthew, so if there are no such people, skip the question.)

- What does Jesus do in the Gospel of John?

- What kinds of relationships does Jesus have in the Gospel of John? With whom?

- What did you learn from the introduction to the Gospel of John in this book?

VII. Ask the question again in summary form about who Jesus is in the Gospel of John. At this more integrative stage, ask how Jesus in the Gospel of John differs from your assumptions about Jesus. What possibilities for who Jesus is have you learned from the Gospel of John?

If this is a group study, ask different individuals to answer for themselves. Check several times during the discussion as to how much agreement there is about Jesus in the group.

VIII. Ask these questions: What would it mean to give authority to Jesus as he is portrayed in the Gospel of John? What would it be like to consider this Jesus in John to be the authoritative Jesus? What would change from how you have thought about Jesus before? What is added to Jesus by the Gospel of John? What is missing for you in Jesus according to the Gospel of John?

IX. Ask these questions: How do you compare Jesus in the Gospel of John and in the Gospel of Thomas? What attracts you to the Jesus of one or the other? What do you have questions about in terms of Jesus in one gospel or the other?

X. In preparation for study, read the Gospel of Matthew and the introduction to the Gospel of Matthew found immediately prior to it in this book. (This gospel is too long to be read in a study session. Although the introduction is not so long, it will help not to have to read it during the guided study.)

XI. Convene as a group (or proceed as an individual). Ask who Jesus is in the Gospel of Matthew. Here, too, remind people before they respond that this question assumes that Jesus may be different in different books. So in asking who Jesus is in a particular book, it is important to make sure that the answer comes from within the book, not from another book, one's own beliefs, or conventional assumptions. In order to assist with the question "Who is Jesus in the Gospel of Matthew?" the following other questions may be asked:

- What kind of person does Jesus seem to be in the Gospel of Matthew? Is he kind? How judgmental and angry is he? What seems to be important to him? How powerful is he in this gospel? Is he more or less powerful than Jesus in the Gospel of John? What kind of power does he have?

- What seem to be some central themes and subjects of Jesus's teaching in the Gospel of Matthew? How different are they from Jesus's teachings in the Gospel of Thomas? How different are they from Jesus's teachings in the Gospel of John?

- What does Jesus do in the Gospel of Matthew?

- What kind of relationships does Jesus have in the Gospel of Matthew? With whom?

- What did you learn from the introduction to the Gospel of Matthew in this book?

XII. Ask the question again in summary form about who Jesus is in the Gospel of Matthew. At this more integrative stage, ask how Jesus in the Gospel of Matthew differs from your assumptions about Jesus. What possibilities for who Jesus is have you learned from the Gospel of Matthew?

If this is a group study, ask different individuals to answer for themselves. Check several times during the discussion as to how much agreement there is about Jesus in the group.

XIII. Ask these questions: What would it mean to give authority to Jesus as he is portrayed in the Gospel of Matthew? What would it be like to consider this Jesus in Matthew to be the authoritative Jesus? What would change from how you have thought about Jesus before? What is added to Jesus by the Gospel of Matthew? What is missing for you in Jesus according to the Gospel of Matthew?

XIV. Ask these questions: How do you compare Jesus in the Gospel of Matthew and in the Gospel of Thomas? How do you compare Jesus in the Gospel of Matthew and in the Gospel of John? What attracts you to the Jesus of one or the other? What do you have questions about in terms of Jesus in one gospel or the other?

XV. In preparation for study, read the Gospel of Mary and the introduction to the Gospel of Mary found immediately prior to it in this book. (This gospel is too long to be read in a study session. Although the introduction is not so long, it will help not to have to read it during the guided study.)

XVI. Convene as a group (or proceed as an individual). Ask who Jesus is in the Gospel of Mary. Here, too, remind people before they respond that this question assumes that Jesus may be different in different books. So in asking who Jesus is in a particular book, it is important to make sure that the answer comes from within the book, not from another book, one's own beliefs, or conventional assumptions.

In order to assist with the question "Who is Jesus in the Gospel of Mary?" the following other questions may be asked:

- What kind of person does Jesus seem to be in the Gospel of Mary? Is he kind? How judgmental and angry is he? What seems to be important to him? How powerful is he in this gospel? Is he more or less powerful than Jesus in the Gospel of John? What kind of power does he have?

- What seem to be some central themes and subjects of Jesus's teaching in the Gospel of Mary? How different are they from Jesus's teachings in the Gospel of Thomas? How different are they from Jesus's teachings in the Gospel of John?

- What does Jesus do in the Gospel of Mary?

- What kinds of relationships does Jesus have in the Gospel of Mary? With whom?

- What did you learn from the introduction to the Gospel of Mary in this book?

XVII. Ask the question again in summary form about who Jesus is in the Gospel of Mary. At this more integrative stage, ask how Jesus in the Gospel of Mary differs from your assumptions about Jesus. What possibilities for who Jesus is have you learned from the Gospel of Mary?

If this is a group study, ask different individuals to answer for themselves. Check several times during the discussion as to how much agreement there is about Jesus in the group.

XVIII. Ask these questions: What would it mean to give authority to Jesus as he is portrayed in the Gospel of Mary? What would it be like to consider this Jesus in Mary to be the authoritative Jesus? What would change from how you have thought about Jesus before? What is added to Jesus by the Gospel of Mary? What is missing for you in Jesus according to the Gospel of Mary?

XIX. Ask these questions: How do you compare Jesus in the Gospel of Mary and in the Gospel of Thomas? How do you compare Jesus in the Gospel of Mary and in the Gospel of John? What attracts you to the Jesus of one or the other? What do you have questions about in terms of Jesus in one gospel or the other?

XX. In a final session or as the final element of the last session, ask the overarching question of who Jesus is for you.

XXI. Review the previous four studies of Jesus in the gospels of Thomas, John, Matthew, and Mary. Ask which gospels brought the group the most meaning in their respective portraits of Jesus during this study. What did the group learn about the new possibilities for who Jesus was in the early Christ movements? What did the group learn about the new possibilities for who Jesus is today?

XXII. Ask then who Jesus is for you. If this a group study, first have everyone write in silence about this question. Then ask those who are willing to share their thinking on who Jesus is for them.

- -

STAGE THREE
Bringing It Home
--

I. This third unit of the study guide uses the six chapters of "A Companion to *A New New Testament*" to help integrate the learning from the first two units and from additional reading in *A New New Testament*. It can be worked through in three to six sessions. In the "Companion to *A New New Testament*" read the Preamble, chapter 1, and chapter 2. These chapters cover a general introduction to the documents newly added to the book and to the ways they were discovered.

II. Answer the following questions:

- What do you notice about the ten documents that have been added to *A New New Testament*? In general, what do these ten have in common? (Notice that the Odes of Solomon are broken up into four different books so that on one level there are thirteen new books.) Is there anything that sets these ten apart from the books of the traditional New Testament? As a group of ten, in what ways are they similar to the books of the traditional New Testament?

- Are there books or kinds of books you wish had also been added? In these ten are there books that you wish had not been added?

- As a group, what do these ten added books mean to you?

- Chapter 2 of the "Companion" outlines the ways these ten books have come to *A New New Testament*. What is your reaction to these accounts of discovery, accident, neglect, and serendipity? What else would you like to know about the origins of these ten books?

- -

III. In the "Companion to *A New New Testament*" read the first half of chapter 3 subtitled "How the New Testament Came into Being."

IV. Answer the following questions:

- Before you read the material in chapter 3, how did you think the traditional New Testament came into being?

- What were the two biggest surprises to you about how the New Testament emerged?

- How does this information about how the New Testament came into being affect you?

- What additional information would you like about this process? If you are willing to read an additional book about this, *The Biblical Canon: Its Origin, Transmission, and Authority* by Lee McDonald is an excellent source. It covers the origins of both the Hebrew scriptures and the New Testament. If you are primarily interested in the questions posed by *A New New Testament,* you may want to go directly to part 3 of that book.

V. In the "Companion to *A New New Testament,*" read the second half of chapter 3 entitled "How *A New New Testament* Came into Being" and the brief descriptions of the members of the council that selected the ten books to be added to *A New New Testament.*

VI. Answer the following questions:

- Compare the ways this book came into being with the way the traditional New Testament came into being.

- Examine the members of the council that chose the additional books. What do you think of them as a group? In this book, Hal Taussig asserts that the council members were not given any criteria that they all needed to agree on in their selection process. Nevertheless, as you examine who they are, what values do you think they may have had in common?

- What do you think of the idea of such a religiously and ethnically diverse group choosing the new books? Would you have preferred that they all be Christians?

- Hal Taussig states in the book that he was unable to find evangelical Christians to join the council, because they objected to the idea of adding books to the New Testament. What do you think of the (failed) idea of trying to get evangelical Christians on the council?

- As the author states in the book, a Muslim professor and a Roman Catholic bishop had agreed to be on the council but had to resign because of health considerations. What difference do you think they would have made in the selection process?

- The author states that his major selection principle for the council was that its members be nationally known and experienced spiritual leaders. He also states that he intentionally limited the number of scholars of the New Testament and early Christianity, preferring to have a less academically and more spiritually focused group. What is your opinion of this decision?

VII. In the "Companion to *A New New Testament*," read chapter 4, "What's New in *A New New Testament*: Claiming a New Vision of the Early Christ Movements."

VIII. Answer the following questions:

- The leading claim of this chapter is that "*A New New Testament* puts more pieces of early Christianity together for the twenty-first-century public's spiritual growth." Assess this claim. How much does it apply to you? How much might it apply to other people you know?

- The book proposes: "The first additional dimension of spiritual renewal in reading *A New New Testament* is that its more expansive collection reduces the tendency to think that there is one right way to believe, grow, and practice." Assess this claim for yourself and others. Do you think that spiritual renewal results from reducing the tendency to think that there is one right way?

- What do you think of this chapter's claim that this book deepens the general understanding of how early Christians worshiped?

- This chapter outlines Professor Karen King's larger project of rewriting the history of early Christianity without creedal or canonical boundaries. According to this brief description, what is your response to King's academic project?

IX. In the "Companion to *A New New Testament*," read chapter 5, "Giving Birth to *A New New Testament* and Retiring the Idea of Gnosticism."

X. Answer the following questions:

- This chapter follows a number of recent scholars in proposing that the standard academic idea of gnosticism be "retired," because of its flawed picture of the early centuries of Christianity. Assess this argument against the idea of gnosticism as a way of framing some of the early Christian beliefs and practices.

- This book hails Professor Elaine Pagels as a pioneer in the study of many of these newly discovered documents, credits her with being the most influential scholar of our day relative to public understanding, states that *A New New Testament* is very indebted to her work and could not have been formulated without it, *and* critiques her ongoing use of the term *gnostic* to describe many recently discovered books from the early Christ movement. How do you assess Professor Pagels's work for yourself? (If those following this study guide wish to pursue this question in depth, Pagels's classic book *The Gnostic Gospels* is recommended.)

XI. In the "Companion to *A New New Testament*," read chapter 6, "A Rich Explosion of Meaning."

XII. Answer the following questions:

- Chapter 6 presents the Letter of Peter to Philip, the Gospel of Mary, the Gospel of Truth, and the Acts of Paul and Thecla as examples of new meaning for our day created by the newly discovered or published material. Which of these new documents is most significant for you personally?

- This chapter proposes that new meanings also come from new forms of literature in the early Christ movements, particularly the Gospel of Thomas, the Prayer of Thanksgiving, the Prayer of the Apostle Paul, and the Odes of Solomon. Which of these forms is most meaningful to you?

- The nonexistence of sin is a point made by both Paul in his Letter to the Romans and by the Gospel of Mary Magdalene. What do you think of this assertion? What meaning comes to you from these books on this point? Since each book makes a somewhat different argument, do you prefer one assertion over the other?

- This chapter compares the divine self-revelation of Jesus in the Gospel of John and the divine self-revelation of a primarily unidentified feminine voice in The Thunder: Perfect Mind. Compare each of these voices, and think about what you hear from each of them. How similar are these voices?

XIII. In the "Companion to *A New New Testament*," read the Epilogue, "What's Next for *A New New Testament*?"

XIV. Answer the following questions:

- The epilogue explores possible ways churches in the near future might receive *A New New Testament*. Do you care about the future of churches in general? What do you see in *A New New Testament* that might help churches frame their future for the better?

- The epilogue presents the thoughts of council member, general secretary in the national United Methodist Church, and Seminole nation member Chebon Kernell, who contemplates adding more books of Native tradition and practice to form *A Native American New Testament*. What do you think of this idea? What differences and similarities do you see between Kernell's vision and this current *New New Testament*?

- At the end of the epilogue the author vacillates between thinking of *A New New Testament* as bold or modest. Does it strike you as one or the other? Or would you characterize it some other way?

Recommended Reading

This list of recommended reading is meant for the general reader and is not meant to be a comprehensive list of all literature that is relevant to the scholar. These recommended readings are intended to facilitate next steps in thinking about this literature, in exploration of the meanings of the books and the character of the literature of the early Christ movements.

In almost all cases, the works recommended are book-length and separately published. In a few cases I have listed an article or essay because it provides important information on a book or topic that has not been studied sufficiently at the book level. I have not listed publishers and dates of publication but have verified that each of these books and articles is available for purchase or at libraries.

There are individual recommended readings for each book of *A New New Testament* located at the end of the separate introductions. Those readings focus on books about the particular document.

Literature on Overarching Topics Related to *A New New Testament*

Historical Background to the Writings of the Early Christ Movements

Crossan, John Dominic. *The Birth of Christianity: Discovering What Happened in the Years Immediately After the Execution of Jesus.*
———. *Four Other Gospels: Shadows on the Contours of Canon.*
———. *The Historical Jesus: The Life of a Mediterranean Jewish Peasant.*
Fiorenza, Elisabeth Schussler. *In Memory of Her: A Feminist Theological Reconstruction of Christian Origins.*
———. *Searching the Scriptures, Volumes I and II.*
Mack, Burton. *Who Wrote the New Testament?*
Mays, James L., editor, with the Society of Biblical Literature. *Harper's Bible Commentary.*

The Nag Hammadi Library

Layton, Bentley. *The Gnostic Bible.*
Meyer, Marvin. *The Coptic Gnostic Library.*
Robinson, James M., editor. *The Nag Hammadi Library in English.*

The Formation of the Traditional New Testament

Carr, David. *Writing on the Tablet of the Heart.*
McDonald, Lee. *The Biblical Canon: Its Origin, Transmission, and Authority.*

Smith, Jonathan Z. "Canons, Catalogues, and Classics." In *Canonization and Decanonization*, edited by Arie van der Kooij et al.
———. "Sacred Persistence: Toward a Redescription of Canon." In *Imagining Religion* by Jonathan Z. Smith.

Noncanonical Literature

Keefer, Kyle. "A Postscript to the Book: Authenticating the Pseudopigrapha." In *Reading Bibles, Writing Bodies*, edited by Timothy Beale and David Gunn.
King, Karen L. *What Is Gnosticism?*
Pagels, Elaine. *The Gnostic Gospels.*

What Is Scripture?

Gunn, David. "What Does the Bible Say? A Question of Text and Canon." In *Reading Bibles, Writing Bodies*, edited by Timothy Beale and David Gunn.
Wimbush, Vincent L. "Reading Darkly." In *African Americans and the Bible*, edited by Vincent L. Wimbush.
———. *Theorizing Scriptures: New Critical Orientations to a Cultural Phenomenon.*

Artistic Writings Related to *A New New Testament*

Eco, Umberto. *Foucault's Pendulum* (its use of The Thunder: Perfect Mind).
Morrison, Toni. *Jazz* (its use of The Thunder: Perfect Mind).
———. *Parade* (its use of The Thunder: Perfect Mind).

Subject Index

Scripture Index